THEY WENT THATAWAY

THEY WENT THATAWAY

Compiled By

CHARLES HUGHES HAMLIN

Professional Genealogist

Member of

Virginia Genealogical Society
Sons of American Revolution
Society of Colonial Wars
The Huguenot Society
The Jamestowne Society
National Genealogical Society
American Legion
Veterans of Foreign Wars

Three Volumes in One

GENEALOGICAL PUBLISHING CO., INC.
BALTIMORE   1975

Originally Published
Richmond, Virginia

Volume 1—1964
Volume 2—1965
Volume 3—1966

Reprinted
Three Volumes in One
Genealogical Publishing Co., Inc.
Baltimore, 1974

Baltimore, 1975

Library of Congress Catalogue Card Number 64-4203
International Standard Book Number 0-8063-0588-6

Made in the United States of America

THEY WENT THATAWAY

Volume 1

Dedicated to my daughter,

Vicki

And to my sisters,

Mary and Daisy

PREFACE

        I do not think it possible for a genealogical
tome to have a better preface than the one used by that
ancient churchman, Master Wace, in his "Chronicle of the
Norman Conquest."

        I salute you, over the centuries, Master Wace,
in the name of any who may perchance read this manuscript
of mine and in it your priceless words of philosophy and
wisdom.

              (Taylor's translation)

   "All things hasten to decay; all fall; all perish;
all come to an end. Man dieth, iron consumeth,
wood decayeth, towers crumble, strong walls fall
down, the rose withereth away, the war-horse
waxeth feeble, gay trappings grow old, all the
works of man's hands perish.

Thus we are taught that all die, both clerk and
lay; and short would be the fame of any after
death, if their history did not endure by being
written in the book of the clerk."

                --Charles Hughes Hamlin

FOREWORD

Before, during and after the Revolutionary War, the younger sons of Virginia families as well as hundreds of Virginia families, their friends, neighbors, and kinsmen transported themselves bodily and migrated into the rich, lush, and fertile lands to the south and west.

They set forth by horseback, on foot, or by wagon train. Many carried their slaves, horses, cattle, other stock, household furniture, and prized possessions of every sort. Many more carried only their long rifle, powder horn, and bullet pouch. Most all of them carried a tradition of English, Scotch-Irish, French or German ancestry. Of these, the English predominated.

These men were not weaklings or cowards. They went forth into a vast, unknown wilderness frequented by savages, wild beasts and dangers of every description. They were empire builders as truly as their ancestors who first set out across the vast, uncharted seas.

They also carried with them their love of freedom, independence, fair play, their love of justice and equality within the law. They carried with them their love and belief in God.

They fought and they built and they died by the thousands but they left their children and descendants one of the mightest nations the world has ever seen. They left as a heritage, a nation that is the hope of the world of the future.

Their descendants can then be justifiably proud of their ancestors and it is to be hoped that if these ancestors could return that they would be as proud of their descendants.

What then of the individual who lives today? It has been truly said that he is the connecting link between the past and the future. It has also been truly said that a knowledge of one's forebears is a birth-right.

We therefore would like to know something of the trials, tribulations, deeds and efforts of our own individual ancestors. Therefore, we need first and primarily a true, authentic, and correct pedigree. A pedigree that is fully proven in each and every generation. A pedigree that consists of proof or evidence that is indisputable and unquestionable as far as the facts or the records

will permit or will allow us to proceed in the ascendant. I
daresay that there is not one person in a thousand who would
knowingly create a false or spurious pedigree. To do so would
not only be very obnoxious but as a forgery, would be fooling
only themselves. However, we are also just fooling ourselves
when we proceed with the construction of a pedigree without the
necessary proof or with insufficient evidence.

The type of records contained within this volume are all
prima facie proof and/or evidence and are all abstracted from
public records. They all have the cited authority to the original
source. They all contain the proof of origin of one or more
Virginians or individuals who formerly resided in Virginia and
who later moved to other States, Territories, or Countries.

In most cases, they also prove the County of origin in
Virginia and the County and State to which the individual migrated.
In many cases, they also name the parents of the individual and/or
his brothers, sisters, nieces, nephews, or other related kinsman.

These records have been accumulated by me in my capacity
as both an amateur and a professional genealogist. These are the
type of records desired by family historians, hereditary societies,
historians, and librarians, as well as genealogists. In some cases
some of these records have taken much time, money, and effort to
find. In some cases these are the only records in existance which
prove the "link" between Virginia and the new country of the
individual in the record and are therefore the only record which
will positively prove his identity. Some of my friends have sug-
gested that I title this book, "Genealogical Gems'" - "Nuggets of
Gold" - "'The Lost Sons of Virginia'" etc., but they are much more
than these. They are truly and actually "links" in a vast migration
chain of Virginians who went forth to seek their fortune and the
future of their descendants in lands far from home.

It is greatly to be hoped and desired that other
genealogists or historians will be influenced to search deep
within their files and to be instrumental in making them available in seeking out more of our "Lost Sons of Virginia."

--Charles Hughes Hamlin

Richmond, Virginia
September 10, 1963

THEY WENT THATAWAY

Norfolk County, Virginia - Deed Book 12, page 86-

ISLAND OF BARBADOS - PARISH OF ST. MICHAEL'S - Power of Attorney dated
20th August 1734 in which Elizabeth Tucker of the Parish and Island
aforesaid "do appoint my esteemed friend, Mr. John Tucker of the County
of Norfolk, Colony of Virginia, Merchant and in his absence or death,
my good friend, Mr. William Pearson, Merchant" - my true and lawful
attorney to secure, receive, etc., - due me from my late husband, George
Tucker, dec'd., estate - etc. - Witnesses: Edward Pugh, Hancock
Ellegood, Recorded: 20 June 1735.

Norfolk County, Virginia - Deed Book 13, page 1 -

ISLE OF BARBADOS - PARISH OF ST. THOMAS - Deed of Gift dated 18th
November 1741 by Elizabeth Abyvon, formerly Elizabeth Emperor, (spins-
ter) (now widow) of land in Norfolk County, Va. to her son, George
Abyvon, etc.

York County, Virginia - Orders, Wills #3, (Trans) page 29 -

11th September 1657 - Power of Attorney by William Allen, OF YE CITTY OF
LONDON, Merchant to Gilbert Metcalfe, OF LONDON, Merchant and to Thomas
Bushrod of Essex Lodge, neare Yorke River in Virginia, Merchant - empower-
ing them to receive in his name and stead, goods, money, tobacco, etc., in
Yorke River Mock Jack Bay or places thereunto adjacent, etc., - Witnesses:
John Prise, Richard Hallman, Witten Boner. Recorded: 21st December 1657.

Ibid - Page 62 -

16th July 1659 - Indenture in which John Woods, of LONDON, Merchant -
for a valuable consideration and sum of tobacco - sells to Robert Jones,
"taylor" in Virginia - one heiffer about three years old - etc. Teste:
John Wook, John Furnine. Recorded: 24 August 1659.

Ibid - page 102 -

23rd August 1660 - Henry Andrew, OF LONDON, Merchant appeared before
Frederick Ixem, Notary and Tabellion Publique of LONDON and gave a Letter
of Attorney to George Light of Virginia, Planter, to ask, demand, recover, etc., from Elizabeth Jones, Widow and executrix of Richard Jones,
late of Virginia, dec'd., Witnesses (evidently in London): Robert
Spencer, William Scorey, Symon Bulstrode.

2

LONDON the 2nd of May 1660 - "Brother, I doe hereby desire you to deliver unto Mr. Robert Whitehaire or Richard Merrest and in their absence then unto Mr. Christopher Harris in Queen's Creek in York River - five hhds mault - ten barrels of salt and one young mare named John Symonds - all aboard the John Lymbrey, Commander of the John and Sarah - The danger of ye seas and mortality and escapes excepted, being upon the proper account of my friend, George Lee"- (signed) - William Nevitt. Recorded: 21st June 1661.

Ibid - page 119 -

3rd June 1661 - IN VIRGINIA - Shipped by the Grace of God in good order and well conditioned by mee, Robert Whithaire in and upon ye good shipp called ye Recovery, whereof is Master under God for this present voyage, Captain Thomas Stanton and now riding at anker (sic) in James River and by ye Grace of God, bound for the Port of London - to say - 3 hhds of Virginia leafe - etc., to be delivered to Mr. Robert Vaulx, etc. - Soe God send ye shipp to her desired port in safety. Recorded 24 June 1661.

Ibid - page 137 -

20th December 1661 - In the difference between Mrs. Elizabeth Jones, Relict of Mr. Richard Jones, dec'd., and Mr. Richard Longman, Senior, Defendant - etc. - It is ordered that Mr. Richard Longman Junior be not any wayes hindered in his intended voyage FOR ENGLAND, he leaving an Attorney in ye country to defend ye said suit.

Ibid - page 137 -

21st December 1661 - Whereas a chest of goods shipped aboard ye "Waterhouse", Captain John Fox, Commander, by Joane, wife of Thomas Wardley, was to remain by condition as security to Jonathan Newell for performance of several things by Thomas Wardley and Joane, his wife and the said conditions being performed by ye said Thomas Wardley signing, sealing, and delivering a conveyance indented for an annuity of five pds to his sisters, Anne and Elleinor Wardley in ENGLAND, etc.

Ibid - page 147 -

10th February 1660 - Letter of Attorney from Thomas Andrews, Attorney of Escamues Hickes and Katherine, his wife, OF MIDDLESEX, ENGLAND - to his true and loving friend, Charles Dunne of Virginia to be his lawful deputy to recover all debts, etc., due ye said Escamues Hickes or ye said Katherine (his wife) etc. Witnesses: Edward Lockey, Thomas Ballard.

Ibid - page 163 -

1 April 1662 - Indenture in which Lawrence Smith, Attorney of John Cheseman OF THE PARISH OF ST. MARY MAGDALENE, IN BURMUNDSEY, IN THE COUNTY OF SURRY, ENGLAND, Merchant - by Letter of Attorney from the said John Cheesman (?) - etc. - confirms the bargain and sale dated 20 August

1661 to Edmund Cheesman, Gent., of the Poquoson Parish in the County of
Yorke in the CONTINENT OF VIRGINIA - for the yearly rent of 50 lbs of good
and lawful money of England - all the Estate, both real and personal of
John Cheseman and Margaret, his wife now, etc. in York County in Virginia,
etc. for twenty years - and if the said John Cheseman and Margaret, his
now wife, do not live for twenty years, then for natural love and affection he doth have for (his brother) Edmond Cheseman, as by will and
testament bearing date 6th August 1658, gives and grants all his lands,
etc., to the said Edmond Cheseman for his natural life and then to be
returned to his sonne, Edmond and his sonne, Thomas and their heyres
male, etc. Witnesses: John Lilly, Thomas Ashley, Richard Roberts
Senior. Recorded: 14th April 1662.

Ibid - Book #6, page 25 -

CITY OF LONDON - 22nd March 1677 - William Fellowes of London, Wood-
monger, and Margaret, his wife, the relict and executrix of the Last
Will and Testament of Phillip Chesley, late of Queen's Creek in York
River, in Virginia, dec'd., appeared before William Scasey (?) Notary
and Tabellion Publique of the said City of London, Merchant - to give
a Power of Attorney to Samuell Timpson, of London, Merchant - to manage
the two plantations on Yorke River in Virginia - etc. - and to receive
of and from Alexander Walker and Mastin Gordener, both of Virginia
aforesaid, etc. (signed) Will Fellows and Margaret Chesley als Fellows.
Witnesses: Zach Tayler, Thomas Grantham, Cald (?) Phillips, Micajah
Perry. Recorded 9 April 1677.

Virginia Gazette, January 1, 1767 -

(York County, December 30, 1766) - The subscriber, being desirous to
return to ENGLAND, would be willing to sell off his stock in trade, his
storehouse, with all its Appurtenances. (signed) George Wilson.

York County, Virginia - Orders, Wills, #14, page 12 -

24 May 1710 - Power of Attorney from Daniel Westall OF THE CITY OF
LONDON to Mr. John Clayton of Virginia was proved in Court by the oaths
of Captain Joshua Cook and William Baylor, witnesses thereto and admitted to record, etc. (Daniel Westall, Citizen and Hosier of London)

Ibid - #13, page 54 -

24th May 1707 - Mary Whaley, Widow, now in her Majestie's Colony of
Virginia, but by God's Grace bound on a voyage to England - gives a
letter of attorney to Henry Cary and Edward Jackling, Gents. - etc. -
Witnesses: Michael Archer, Christopher Jackson. Recorded: 24 May 1707.

Ibid - page 68 -

20th February 1706 - CITY OF LONDON - Personally appeared Robert Cary
of LONDON, Merchant, executor of the last Will and Testament of William
Ayleward, late of Virginia, Merchant, but since deceased IN THE KINGDOM
OF FRANCE - doth appoint Joseph Walker, Merchant, in Virginia, my true

and lawful Attorney, etc. Witnesses: Thomas Bagwell, Thomas Bagwell Junior, Thomas Jones, John Marshall, Daniel Sullivan. Recorded: 24 June 1707.

Surry County, Virginia - Orders, Wills, Deeds (1684-1686) -

(Transcript page No. 81) - 22nd March 1685 - These may certify to all whom it may concern that I, John Hewlitt, intend with God's permission FOR ENGLAND this present shipping. If any person have any debts, dews (sic) or demands, lett them repaire to me where they shall receive all just satisfaction that may be required.

Northumberland County, Va. Record Book (1652-1658) page 106 -

29th October 1656 - Know all men by these presents that I, WILLIAM BARKER, OF RATCLIFT, IN THE COUNTY OF MIDDLESEX (ENGLAND), MARRINER, for divers good and valuable causes and considerations thereunto me moving, have made, constituted, ordained, affirmed, deputed, and putt by these presents my very loving friend, Thomas Smith, OF LIMEHOUSE, IN THE AFORESAID COUNTY OF MIDDLESEX, MARRINER, NOW BOUND OUTWARDS ON A VOYAGE TO VIRGINIA, IN THE PARTS BEYOND THE SEAS, my true and lawful deputy and attorney, for me and in my name, etc. - to receive, etc. all and every, of any person or persons whatsoever in Virginia aforesaid, etc. Witnesses: Robert Carter (?), John Parker, John Carter. Recorded: 4th May 1657.

2nd May 1657 - These presents witnesseth that I, Thomas Smith, by and being the lawful attorney of Captain William Barker, doe acquit and discharge Francis Clay, his executors or assigns, of and from all Bonds, Bills, Accounts, and all demands from the beginning of the world until this present day, etc. Recorded: 4th May 1657. Witnesses: Walter Brodhurst, Richard Wright.

Spotsylvania County, Virginia - Deed Book A (1722-1729) -

5th March 1727 - Indenture in which Thomas Tyler of St. George's Parish and County of Spotsylvania, Colony of Virginia sells to Charles Tyler of GREAT BRITAIN, IN SALLOPS COUNTY AND HOPTON WAFTER PARISH - for 80 pds sterling - 500 acres of land patented by the said Thomas Tyler 30th June 1726 in said County of Spotsylvania, etc. Witnesses: William Johnson, Thomas Chew, Recorded: March 5th 1727/8

Ibid - Deed Book F (1761-1766) -

2nd April 1764 - Indenture in which Thomas Ward of LANCASTER COUNTY, LIVERPOOL, (ENGLAND), Merchant gives power of attorney to James Hunter of Fredericksburg, Colony of Virginia, Merchant and to William Quincey OF LIVERPOOL AFORESAID, Mariner, etc. Witnesses: John Breakhill, Samuel Davis, Henry Silvester, John Brew, James Richardson, James Benn Rowe. Recorded: 2nd July 1764.

Goochland County, Virginia - Deed Book 16, page 397 -

April 20, 1795 - Jane Payne of Virginia, one of the United States of

America - widow of John Payne the elder, deceased, of Goochland County,
Virginia - formerly Jane Chichester, widow and relict of John Chichester,
deceased, late of Lancaster County, Virginia - gives a Power of Attorney
to Armistead Long, now of Virginia - now bound on a voyage to Great
Britain - giving him full power and authority to ask, recover, demand,
receive, etc. all such sums of money due her in the Kingdom of Great
Britain and all such sums of money, lands, etc., due her as a legatee
under the Will of Richard Chichester, dated 16 May 1743 and of John
Chichester, dated 24 September 1753, of the Kingdom of Great Britain, etc.
Witnesses: George W. Payne, Robert Payne, Shad (?) Alvice. Recorded:
20 April 1795.

York County, Virginia - Deeds, Orders, Wills #4, page 184 -

17th September 1667 - Power of Attorney given by Richard Walton, Citizen
and Merchant taylor OF LONDON and my wife, True, the daughter of Elizabeth Freind alias Lockey, the naturall sister of Edward Lockey, LATE OF
YORKE RIVER IN VIRGINIA in the parts beyond the seas, Merchant, who
lately deceased HERE IN LONDON - do constitute and appoint John Baskervwyle, Gent., Clerk to the Yorke Court in Virginia aforesaid, and Richard
Bushrod, Yorke aforesaid, Gent., our true and lawful attornies, etc.
signed by Richard and True Walton. Witnesses: Richard Robinson, Will
Hall, Henry Bradshaw, servant to Henry Lewes Senior.

Ibid - page 276 -

18th May 1734 - Indenture in which Lawrence Smith of the Parish of
Abingdon, County of Gloucester sells to Henry Sharkey, of THE PARISH OF
ST. MARGARETS, WESTMINISTER, Gent., - ten houses near Brewhouse Yard in
the PARISH OF ST. MARGARETS, WESTMINISTER IN THE COUNTY OF MIDDLESEX,
ENGLAND, etc. - Witnesses: John Ballard, Edward Moss, John Sharkey.
Recorded: 20th May 1734.

Westmoreland County, Virginia - Deeds and Wills #3, page 93 -

October 8, 1702 - Record of the Naturalization papers of Jacob Ramey,
A NATURAL BORN SUBJECT OF THE FRENCH KING by virtue of the Oath of
Allegiance which he took September 29th, 1680 before Sir Henry Chicheley,
Knt., His Majesty's Deputy Governor of the Colony of Virginia.

Mecklenburg County, Virginia - Deed Book 10, page 13 -

September 1, 1798 - Power of Attorney given by James Kidd OF THE COUNTY
OF OGLETHORP, STATE OF GEORGIA, empowering his son, William Kidd of
Mecklenburg County, State of Virginia, to collect debts and sell land
belonging to him in the said county of Mecklenburg, Virginia.

Charlotte County, Virginia - Deed Book 15, page 43 -

Indenture dated 6th January 1819 in which John Roberts and Susanna,
his wife - William Hatchett and Jane, his wife - James McCargo and
Prudence, his wife - Bartholomew Roberts and Rebecca, his wife - all
representatives and legatees of Francis Roberts, deceased sell to

Thomas Roberts their certain lots or parcels of land that fell to them by the death of Martha Roberts, widow of Francis Roberts, dec'd., being her dower of the tract of land of which the said Francis died seized of - containing 140 acres, etc.

NOTE BY C.H.H. - In recording the above record the Magistrate states that William Hatchett and his wife are now of CLARK COUNTY, GEORGIA; Bartholomew Roberts and his wife are now of MORGAN COUNTY, GEORGIA; John Roberts and James McCargo and their wives are still of Charlotte County, Virginia. To further identify the above cited individuals reference is made to Charlotte County, Va. marriages by Knorr, revealing that:-

> December 3, 1787 - William Hatchett = Jane Roberts
> May 8, 1798 - James McCargo = Prudence Roberts
> December 26, 1800 - Bartholomew Roberts = Rebecca M. Fears
> March 7, 1803 - Thomas Roberts = Sallie Herndon, daughter of
> Joseph Herndon.

Halifax County, Virginia - Deed Book 26, page 402 -

Indenture dated 24 April 1817 in which Septimus Taylor OF JACKSON COUNTY IN THE STATE OF GEORGIA sells to Francis Taylor Junior of Halifax County, Virginia - for $406.00 - a tract of land in Halifax County, Va. on the southside of the Dan River - containing 100½ acres, etc. Witnesses: William Brandon Junior, Alexander Brandon, Thomas Brandon Junior.

NOTE BY C.H.H. - The above cited Septimus Taylor (Jr.) and Francis Taylor were brothers and both were designated as sons of Septimus Taylor Senior of Halifax County, Virginia in his Will probated 22nd June 1801 (WB 6, p. 265) Septimus Senior also names wife, Elizabeth (Brandon) and daughters, Margaret and Nancy.

Wilkes County, Georgia - Deed Book (1784-1785) -

Indenture dated January 26, 1785 in which Joseph Williams and Frankey, his wife, OF WILKES COUNTY, GEORGIA sell 400 acres of land on Upton's Creek to WILLIAMSON BIRD OF PRINCE EDWARD COUNTY, VIRGINIA, etc. Witnesses: Ganaway Martin, George Gresham.

Norfolk County, Virginia - W. & D. "I" (1736-1753) page 50 -

Know all men by these presents that I, Caleb Davis OF THE COLONY OF GEORGIA, MERCHANT - for the great love and respect I have and bear unto Sophia Kenner, eldest daughter of Matthew Kenner of the County of Norfolk, Colony of Virginia, etc. doe give and bequeath unto the said Sophia Kenner and to her heirs forever, a negro woman named Phyllis, about the age of seventeen years, which I bought of her father, Mr. Matthew Kenner and case of her death (Sophia's) then I give the said negro to Sarah Kenner, daughter of the said Matthew and Mary Kenner, etc. (balance of deed torn) - dated ninth_____Anno Domine MDIIXXXXI Witnesses: John Portlock, John Wallis, Thomas Watkins. Recorded: 25th May 1741.

Charles City County, Virginia - Will Book 4, page 16 -

Will of Wyatt Walker - dated 2nd September 1832 - Probated 22nd March

1833. Legatees: To my sons: William Walker, Robert C. Walker, George Minge Walker NOW LIVING IN THE STATE OF GEORGIA, Thomas W. Walker and his son, Mondingo Walker, my grandson, Stephen D. Walker, my dear wife (not named). Executors: my sons, William, Thomas W: and Robert C. Walker. Witnesses: J. S. Stubblefield, George W. Chancy, Jordan C. Christian.

Russell County, Virginia - Will Book 2, page 64 -

STATE OF GEORGIA, TATTNALL COUNTY - Power of Attorney dated 30th April 1803 in which William Williams and Rachel, his wife, empower their "trusty friend" George McCoy to act and receive any and all due them from the Estate of Robert McCoy, dec'd., etc. Witnesses: David Foreman, Isaac Foreman, Ribart MacKey.

Ibid - page 66 -

STATE OF GEORGIA, TATTNALL COUNTY - 12th December 1803 - Rachel Williams gives a separate Power of Attorney, in her own name for herself and her husband, William Williams, renouncing all her right, title, claim, and interest, as legatee of the Estate of Robert McCoy, dec'd., Witnesses: Robert Scott, Thomas McCudon (?), Robert McKoy. Recorded: Russell County, Virginia 27th March 1804.

Botetourt County, Virginia - Will Book E, page 343 -

Will of William Little of Botetourt County, Virginia dated 23rd (?) 1819 - Recorded January 16, 1830 by Richard Talbot, Clerk of Court at JEFFERSON COUNTY, INDIANA and further recorded in Botetourt County, Virginia at November Court 1832 -
    Legatees:
    Brothers, David and John Little
    Sister, Rebecca Little
    My other brothers and sisters - (not named)
    Brother, John, my executor for property in Virginia
    and Alexander McNutt and John Robinson, executors for my property
    in Indiana
Witnesses: John Amoz (?) - Thomas Hughes

Augusta County, Virginia - Deed Book 40, page 362 -

27 January 1816 - Whereas I, Edward Askins OF THE COUNTY OF PERRY IN THE INDIANA TERRITORY (Note: became a State this same year) - have sold to John Buchanan of Augusta County, State of Virginia, a tract of land containing by survey 127 acres, he is to have it - which land is situated in Augusta County, Virginia on the Waters of Christians Creek and was devised to me by Will of John Askins, dec'd. I authorize William Wilson Senior of said County to be my attorney in fact to convey said land - (There then follows an affidavit by the Clerk of the County Court of BRECKENRIDGE COUNTY, KENTUCKY that the above Edward Askins acknowledged the Power of Attorney to be his act, etc. Recorded: Augusta County, Va. March 25, 1816.

Russell County, Virginia - Deed Book 9, page 142 -

Indenture dated 26th September 1830 in which John Williams and Judith,
his wife, OF THE COUNTY OF WASHINGTON, STATE OF ILLINOIS - Pouncey
Smith and Lodemia, his wife, OF THE COUNTY OF BARREN, STATE OF KENTUCKY,
Marcus Faulkner and Elizabeth, his wife, OF THE COUNTY OF WASHINGTON,
STATE OF ILLINOIS and Jacob Waggoner and Harriet, his wife - heirs and
distributees of John Williams, dec'd., sell to James Williams OF THE
COUNTY OF BARREN, STATE OF KENTUCKY - for $1000.00 - all their right,
title, and interest in a certain tract of land IN RUSSELL COUNTY, VIR-
GINIA containing 200 acres on both sides of Mockasin Creek, etc.

Hopkins County, Kentucky - Deed Book 2, page 357 -

9th March 1819 - John Lewis of the County of Logan and State of
Kentucky - sells to Robert Patton of the COUNTY OF SPOTSYLVANIA AND
STATE OF VIRGINIA - for $1556.00 - land lying in the County of Hopkins
on the Waters of Deer Creek, it being part of a military survey of
1500 acres, surveyed and patented in the name of William Grayson and
conveyed by Seth Barton to Warner W. Lewis and deeded by Warner Lewis to
the said John Lewis, etc. Witnesses: Warner Washington Lewis, James B.
Bigger, Gabriel Lewis, Spencer Curd - (Clerk, Logan County).

Ibid - page 360 -

January 13, 1819 - Lazarus Pine OF FREDERICK COUNTY, VIRGINIA sells to
Nimrod Bishop and Stephen Glasscock (BOTH OF FAUQUIER COUNTY, VIRGINIA) -
for $800.00 - Two tracts of land which he holds in a joint deed with the
said Nimrod Bishop, which was conveyed to them by John Hopkins of
FREDERICK COUNTY, VIRGINIA -(and) one lot containing 227 acres in
HOPKINS COUNTY, KENTUCKY and the other lot or grant containing 657 acres,
also in Hopkins County, Kentucky and partly in Henderson County, Kentucky.

NOTE BY CHH - (Ibid, page 361) - 26th January 1819 - Nimrod Bishop of
FAUQUIER COUNTY, VIRGINIA sells 227 acres - for $850.00 to Miles Baker of
Hopkins County, Kentucky.

Fauquier County, Virginia - Deed Book 17, page 360 -

14th November 1818 - Nathaniel Pettit OF THE STATE OF KENTUCKY (no County
stated) - sells for $820.00 - to John Kemper - all his right, title, in-
terest, claims, and demands of and to that part of the real property of
"My father, Obadiah Pettit, dec'd.," lying and being in the County of
Fauquier, Virginia and also my right, title, etc., in the Estate of
Nathaniel Owens, dec'd., - Witnesses: Daniel Withers, George H. Payne,
John A. W.(?) Smith. NOTE BY CHH: Fauquier County Marriage Bonds, p.110 -
19 October 1781 - Nathaniel Pettit to Rebecca Owens - Nathaniel Owens,
Security.

Albemarle County, Virginia - Will Book 4, page 31 h

Will of Thomas Jones - dated 13 March - probated September Court 1799 -
To my son, Thomas Jones, one bay mare and saddle which he wrode (sic) to

KENTUCKY - To my son, Edmund Jones, one bay mare colt which he calls his - Balance of my estate to my beloved wife for her natural life and then to be divided equally among all my children, namely - Ann Mallory, Thomas Jones, Edmond Jones, Jane Jones, Elizabeth Jones, Henry Jones, Sarah Jones, Joseph Jones and Phillemon (or Phillmore ?) Jones - Executors: Major Henry Burk, my wife, Agnes Jones and my sons, Thomas and Edmond Jones.

Land Grants of Virginia - Book Z, page 547 -

23 May 1786 - 400 acres to John Dicken - Treasury Warrant no. 601 (issued 15th October 1779) - surveyed 15th May 1784 in the COUNTY OF LINCOLN (Now Kentucky) - on Doctor's Fork of Chaplains Fork about one and one-half miles above Potses' including an improvement made by James Wady.

Ibid - Book 25, page 463 -

20 January 1792 - 500 acres to John Dicken, assignee of John Campbell - Treasury Warrant No. 4285, issued 23 March 1780 - Surveyed 20 April 1790 IN THE COUNTY OF NELSON (NOW KENTUCKY) - on Coperas Lick Run and Caney Run, being the Waters of Rolling Fork of Salt River.

Hopkins County, Kentucky - Deed Book 2, page 204 -

March 12, 1818 - Jesse Woodson of POWHATAN COUNTY, VIRGINIA - sells to Alfred Townes of Hopkins County, Kentucky (by Asa Wier, his attorney in fact) - for $39.00 - a lot in the Town of Bellville, in Hopkins County, Kentucky (Lot #13) - etc. Witnesses: James Thompson, Stephen Ashley, Sam Woodson, Clerk.

Loudoun County, Virginia Deed Book X, page 251 -

Power of Attorney given by Jacob Ramey of Loudoun County, Virginia to Nathaniel Grigsby of the same County and State to collect any and all sums of money due him and to sell, alien, release and deliver lands, etc. belonging to him in NELSON COUNTY, KENTUCKY or to let out, rent, or lease the same (on a yearly basis), etc. Recorded in NELSON COUNTY, DISTRICT OF KENTUCKY on the 10th December 1788 - Recorded in Loudoun County, Virginia October 18, 1796. Witnesses: George Mason, James Revell, Jacob Grigsby - (Note by CHH: Nelson County, Kentucky was formed 1784 from Jefferson County, at that time, Virginia.)

Henry County, Virginia, Deed Book 6, page 649 -

October 28, 1805 - Sanford Ramey of the County of Henry, State of Virginia gives his Power of Attorney to Sanford Connelly of the County of Fluvanna, State of Virginia - to act in his behalf in connection with a certain tract of land that he (Sanford Ramey) owns in MASON COUNTY, KENTUCKY "whereon now lives the Widow Ramey", etc.

Mason County, Kentucky Will Book C, page 226 -

July Term 1811 - Division of the Estate of Jacob Ramey's Heirs - The Commissioners met at the house of Mrs. Deborah Ramey, Widow of Jacob

Ramey, dec'd. - Heirs: Catherine Ramey, John Preston and wife, Jane, James
Dimmitt and wife, Elizabeth, Sanford Ramey, Nancy Ramey. (Note by CHH:
Deborah Ramey, wife of Jacob Ramey, is stated by descendants to have been
nee Deborah Lea (Lee) daughter of Stephen Lea of Loudoun County, Virginia
but I have done no research to confirm this)

Mason County, Kentucky, Deed Book N, page 362 -

May 13, 1814 - Indenture made by Sanford Ramey Senior of Henry County,
Virginia by Sanford Ramey Junior, his Attorney-in-fact, of the one part
to Alexander K. Marshall of MASON COUNTY, KENTUCKY of the other part, etc.
Witnesses: George B. Morton, Andrew Wood, Isham Key, William Fleming.

Frederick County, Virginia, Superior Court Will Book 1, page 313 -

Will of Lewis Wolfe, dated September 5, 1791 - Probated 20th April 1792 -
leaves a legacy of 500 acres of land "IN KENTUCKY" to his son, George
Wolfe - other legatees were his sons, Lewis, Thomas, and John Wolfe and
daughters, Elizabeth, Polly, and Catherine Wolfe - wife, Catherine Wolfe.

Lunenburg County, Virginia Deed Book 24, page 452 -

STATE OF KENTUCKY - COUNTY OF HENRY - Personally appeared before me,
Samuel Nelson and Henry Young, Justices of the Peace of the County and
State aforesaid - Judith Sibley, the wife of Leonard Sibley, and acknowledged her right of dower in a tract of land lying and being in the
County of Lunenburg, State of Virginia - containing 100 acres - which land
the said Sibley sold to Hugh Willard - the said Judith Sibley relinquishes
her right of dower. (Note by CHH - I do not have the date of this indenture but Leonard Sibley purchased the above 100 acres of land in Lunenburg
County, Virginia on 18th August 1812 from Thomas Chandler and Rachel, his
wife, in which record is revealed that as of that date, Leonard Sibley was
"of Prince Edward County, Virginia". The estate of Leonard Sibley was in-
ventoried and appraised June 1824 in OLDHAM COUNTY, KENTUCKY)

Frederick County, Virginia, Will Book 8, page 505 -

Will of James LaRue, dated July 1804 - Probated 5 December 1809 - Legatees:
wife, Mary - sons, Samuel and John Larue - daughters, Phebe and Clarissy
LaRue - mentions lands he owns "IN THE STATE OF KENTUCKY" and directs that
his slaves be freed as they each reach the age of 30 years.

Franklin County, Virginia - Deed Book 3, page 250 -

August 4, 1795 - We, John Richardson - Daniel Richardson and Aaron
Richardson - OF THE COUNTY OF MADISON, STATE OF KENTUCKY - appoint our
friend, Joshua Brook, of the County of Franklin, State of Virginia, our
lawful attorney, etc. to dispose of, in our absence, a tract of land in
said County of Franklin, Virginia - containing 125 acres, etc. Recorded
on above date at MADISON COUNTY, KENTUCKY and recorded in Franklin County,
Virginia at December Court 1795. (Note by CHH: In Madison County, Kentucky,
Book A, (1785 - 1806) is recorded the Will of Aaron Richardson, dated
December 19, 1803 - probated 2nd April 1804, naming his wife, Sarah and

brother, Daniel Richardson, his executors - he also names seven children, Laviney, Thomas, William, Patty, Caley, Benjamin and John Richardson. Witnesses: Peter Bennett and Thomas Parsell.

Washington County, Virginia Will Book 2, page 204 -

October 9, 1798 - Joseph Colvill of the COUNTY OF MONTGOMERY, COMMONWEALTH (SIC) OF KENTUCKY appoints Joseph Hays of Washington County, State of Virginia his full, true, and lawful attorney to transact business in his name concerning the Estate of his father, Andrew Collvill Senior, dec'd. (Note by CHH: ibid ref. page 140 - record of the inventory and appraisal of the Estate of Andrew Colvill, dec'd., dated 29 June 1797, recorded 17th October 1797, the Administrators being Mary Colvill and Joseph Hays.)

Harrison County, Kentucky Deed Book A, page 150 -

December (?) 1795 - Indenture in which Joseph Craig Senior of FAYETTE COUNTY, KENTUCKY sells to William Wiatt and John Anderson of FREDERICKS-BURG, VIRGINIA - land located in Harrison County, Kentucky - (Note by CHH: Harrison County, Kentucky was formed 1793 from Bourbon and Scott Counties, Kentucky.)

Washington County, Virginia Deed Book B, page 172 -

May 11, 1805 - Power of Attorney from Alexander Montgomery of the COUNTY OF FAYETTE, STATE OF KENTUCKY appointing William Pemberton of the County of Washington, State of Virginia his lawful Attorney, em-powering him to sell 200 acres of land in the said County of Washington, Virginia, etc. Witnesses: Joseph Canady, Michael Montgomery, John M. ___ , John McCormick, Andrew Russell. Recorded 2nd May 1808.

Land Bounty Warrant - (Original in Virginia State Library) -

STATE OF KENTUCKY - COUNTY OF WASHINGTON - dated 14 October 1811 - Power of Attorney by Lewis Thomas of the above County and State, lately a Captain in the 7th Virginia Regiment on Continental Establishment - em-powering Samuel McGraw of the City of Richmond, Virginia to apply for and to receive from the proper authorities any land warrant to which he is entitled for his services in the Revolutionary War, etc. (Note by CHH: In this same folder are affidavits (originals) concerning Captain Lewis Thomas, written by General Peter Muhlenburg, General James Wood, General Joseph Winlock (Justice of Washington County, Kentucky), and Mark Hardin of Washington Co., Kentucky. There is also a Power of Attorney by Lewis Thomas, Captain 7th Regiment, to David Gray, dated 25th February 1784.

Prince William County, Virginia, Will Book G, page 474 -

Will of Burr Harrison, dated 5 February 1789 - Probated 7th February 1791, among other legatees is a bequest to his son, Cuthbert Harrison, of a military claim of 2000 acres of land, "IN THE COUNTRY OF KENTUCKY".

Charlotte County, Virginia, Deed Book 17, page 149 -

Indenture dated 2nd September 1823 in which John McQuie and Elizabeth, his
wife, who was formerly Elizabeth Rice of the COUNTY OF GARRARD, IN THE STATE
OF KENTUCKY, sell to Thomas Roberts of the County of Charlotte, Virginia -
a tract of land containing 209 acres on Horsepen Creek in the said County
(of Charlotte).

Early Records of Hampshire County (now West Virginia) by Sage & Jones, page 43 -

October 19, 1796 - Thomas Noble of Frederick County, Virginia makes a Bill
of Sale of 157-3/4 acres of land on New Creek - as Attorney for Ignatius
Wheeler of KENTUCKY to William James of Hampshire County, Virginia. Recorded
December 19, 1796. (Note by CHH: Ignatius Wheeler had evidently migrated
to FAYETTE COUNTY, KENTUCKY as on August 8, 1804 he gives his consent to
the marriage of Mariann Wheeler to Thomas Tudor in that County.)

Washington County, Virginia, Deed Book 8, page 54 -

27th May 1822 - Indenture in which John Montgomery and Elizabeth, his wife-
Robert Craig and Sally, his wife - OF THE COUNTY OF ROCKCASTLE IN THE STATE
OF KENTUCKY - sell to Andrew Russell in the County of Washington, State of
Virginia - for $1200.00 - all the right, title, and interest they have in a
certain tract of land, estimated to contain 347 acres in an original survey
to David Carson, deceased, as conveyed to David Craig, deceased, the ancestor
of the said Elizabeth, wife of the said John (Montgomery) - and the said
Robert Craig - the right of the said Elizabeth and of the said Robert being
one undivided fourth part thereof which descended to them from the said
David Craig, dec'd., their father, etc.

Powhatan County, Virginia, Deed Book 9, page 62 -

13th August 1824 - Indenture in which James B. Boatwright and Mary P., his
wife - heirs and legatees of Benjamin Boatwright, deceased, of the COUNTY
OF MADISON, STATE OF KENTUCKY, of the one part - sell Elizabeth Boatwright,
of the COUNTY OF GARRARD, STATE OF KENTUCKY, of the other part - for $100.00 -
their right, title, and interest (being the eighth part) in a tract of land
containing 190-3/4 acres in the COUNTY OF POWHATAN, STATE OF VIRGINIA - on
both sides of the main Buckingham Road, it being the land on which Benjamin
Boatwright, dec'd., lived at his death, etc. Sworn to and recorded by David
Frame, Clerk of Court of Madison County, Kentucky and recorded in Powhatan
County, Virginia by William Dance, Clerk on 18th of November 1824. (Note
by CHH: Benjamin Boatright (born 1769 died Powhatan County, Virginia, June 13,
1816) married April 19, 1797 Elizabeth Blackburn (born 1779), daughter of
James Blackburn and his wife, Rhoda Baugh.)

Fauquier County, Virginia, Deed Book 17, page 377 -

23rd September 1808 - We, Samuel Pettit and William Pettit, OF THE COUNTY
OF SCOTT AND STATE OF KENTUCKY constitute and appoint Thomas Pettit, of the
County of Fauquier, State of Virginia and John H. Pettit, of the County of
Culpeper, Virginia our true and lawful attorney in fact to transact all
business relative to the Estate of Obadiah Pettit, dec'd., wherein we are
interested and to which Estate we are legatees, etc. (Sworn to before

Fielding Bradford and Peter Mason, Justices of the Peace for Scott County, Kentucky and certified to by Cary L. Clarke, Clerk of Scott County, Kentucky). Note by CHH: Keturah Pettit of Fauquier County, Virginia also gives her Power of Attorney to John H. Pettit of Culpeper County, Virginia.

Augusta County, Virginia, Deed Book 2A, page 398 -

25th May 1803 - Indenture in which Robert McChesney and Elizabeth, his wife, sell to John Johnston for the sum of $1.00 - a certain tract of land which was conveyed by the said John and Zachariah Johnston unto the said McChesney sometime in the month of July 1802 - containing by estimate 1000 acres of land situated and being on Red River, where the State line crosses said West Fork of Red River AND THE COUNTY OF CHRISTIAN, STATE OF KENTUCKY, etc. AND WHERE THE CAROLINA LINE crosses it, etc. Witnesses: John Purvis, Joseph White, M. Garber (?) Junior - "Acknowledged and Certified Staunton District Court, September 7, 1803" - "For lands lying in CHRISTIAN COUNTY, KENTUCKY."

Norfolk County, Virginia - Deed Book 10, page 74a -

7th June 1718 - Indenture in which James Holmes, LATE OF THE KINGDOM OF IRELAND, brother and next heire of to Gabr___(?) Holmes, dec'd., OF THE SAME DOMINION sells to Moses Prescott of Norfolk County in Virginia - James Holmes in consideration of ye sum of ten pds which was due and owing from ye said Gabrele Holmes to ye said Moses Prescott - for which he hath discharged the Administration of ye decedent's Estate - (sells) 100 acres of land in Norfolk County, etc. Witnesses: (_?_) Wilson, Katherine Wilson. Recorded: June 19, 1718.

Chesterfield County, Virginia - Register of Marriages, page 481 -

12th September 1853 - William Walsh, Widower, age 25, BORN DUBLIN, IRELAND - son of Cornelius and Catherine Walsh married to Mary Ann Whitworth, age 23 - BORN IN LANCASTER, ENGLAND, daughter of John and Sallie Whitworth - W. G. Williams, Minister - who states that License was issued in Henrico County.

Records of Augusta County, Vol. 2, By Chalkley - page 25 -

Executions: April 1799 - (D to I) - Donaghe vs John Kyle of Rockingham, heir at law of William Kyle, dec'd., - Writ to Rockingham 31 July 1797 Plea in abatement shows that William Kyle left two elder brothers, THEN LIVING IN IRELAND, the eldest named Charles, and the second named James, who were both alive when the defendant CAME FROM IRELAND, which was served years after the death of William, brother of the defendant (John) - William died about 1781 - bond by William Kyle, James Blair, and James Donango, all of Augusta County to James Todd of Macklenburg (sic) County of North Carolina - 2nd August 1778. Note by CHH: The Bond is headed "STATE OF NORTH CAROLINA."

Essex County, Virginia, Will Book 13, page 336 -

Will of John Livingston, dated 2nd March 1781 - probated 20th August 1781 - To my beloved wife, Susannah Livingston, each and every (one) of the

slaves that of wright (sic) I should have received with her in marriage
and which may have been and now are in the possession of her brother, Mr.
Thomas Walker, and likewise the one-half of all the personal estate which
she is entitled to by the death of her father, Samuel Walker, Gent., late
of the Town of Hampton, dec'd., who died intestate, etc. - all my silver
spoons and tea spoons that my brother, Captain Muscoe Livingston is to have
moulded (sic) at Philadelphia, (silver for which he now has in his possession)
after my estate is settled, I give the other half to my nephew, John
Livingston (OF THE ISLAND) OF JAMAICA, son of my brother, Muscoe - My executors my worthy friends, Robert Beverley, Esq., Dr. John Brokenbough, and
my brother, Muscoe. Witnesses: Ro. Brooke, John Maghews, William Andrews,
John Walker.

CODICIL: dated 13th April 1781 - disposes of half of his water grist mill,
that he holds jointly with Captain Henry Garnett, to be sold and also a
rigged schooner called the "Pringle" now running in the trade of the
Rappahannock River.

Fauquier County, Virginia, Deed Book 2, page 280 -

Indenture dated 7th March 1765 in which James Campbell and Judith, his wife,
OF CHARLES COUNTY, PROVINCE OF MARYLAND, MERCHANT, sells to Judson Coolige
of PRINCE GEORGES COUNTY, IN THE PROVINCE OF MARYLAND AFORESAID, Gent., (for
five shillings lease 300 pds sterling of Great Britain release) - a tract of
land in the County of Fauquier, Colony of Virginia, granted by the Lord
Proprietors of the Northern Neck in Virginia unto John Clark of SALEM, IN
THE COUNTY OF ESSEX IN THE PROVINCE OF THE MASSACHUSETTS BAY IN NEW ENGLAND
on the 15th November 1740 and by the said John Clerk (sic) sold and conveyed to the said John Campbell - containing 1748 acres - etc. Witnesses:
Duff Green, W. Ellzey, H. Brooke, Henry Peyton, Jr. Recorded: 23 April 1765.

Fairfax County, Virginia, Will Book "C-1", page 62 -

Will of Venus Lamphier OF PRINCE GEORGES COUNTY, MARYLAND - dated 14 February
1769 - probated (?) November 1769 - To my niece, Betty Patterson, 100 pds
Irish currency out of the sum of 400 pds due me IN IRELAND - To my nephews,
William and Thomas Patterson, one equal third share - To my sister, Susannah
Patterson - to my brother, Going Lamphire - My sister, Susanna Patterson,
excutrix. Witnesses: James Kirk, John Rister, Mary Rister, Richard Neele.
(signed) by Venus Lamphier (HER SEAL).

Cumberland County, Va. Wills & Marriages (1749-99), page 17 -

Will of John Carlyle - dated 16 December 1760 - probated 25 January 1762 -
legatees: wife, Frances - godchildren, Charles Fleming Bates, Robert
Bernard, Tabitha Harris and Samuel Easley. Executors: wife, Frances,
Wade Netherland Sr., John Park, Littleberry Mosby, and my cousin, John
Carlyle TO SELL MY LANDS IN MARYLAND.

Grayson County, Virginia, Deed Book 5, page 380 -

Indenture dated 6th August 1827 in which Fanny (Uphame) Robinson, wife of
John Robinson OF THE COUNTY OF LAFAYETTE, IN THE STATE OF MISSOURI - for the
sum of $400.00 paid to her husband by Minitree Jones (Junior) of the County

of Grayson, State of Virginia - relinquishes her right of dower, as the
wife of the said John Robinson, which she might in anywise claim in and
to the land in Grayson County which came to her by inheritance from her
father, Minitree Jones (Senior) deceased, etc. On page 381 follows a
document from the Justices of Lafayette County, Missouri attesting to
her signature, etc.

Grayson County, Virginia, Deed Book 7, page 118 -

Indenture dated 27 April 1835 in which Churchill Jones, formerly OF THE
COUNTY OF GRAYSON, STATE OF VIRGINIA BUT NOW OF THE STATE OF MISSOURI -
by his attorney in fact, Ezra Nuckolls, sells to John Vaughan a tract
of land in Grayson County, Va. containing by estimate 800 acres, etc.

Grayson County, Virginia, Deed Book 4, page 473 -

Indenture dated 10th September 1823 in which John Robinson and Phanney,
his wife, OF LILLARD COUNTY, STATE OF MISSOURI sell to Minitree Jones
(Junior) of Grayson County, Virginia all their right and interest in the
lands which Minitree Jones Senior, father of the said Phanney, died seized
of - to wit - one lot or equal share of all the undivided lands of the
said Minitree Jones (Sr) dec'd. Witnesses: A(bner) Jones, Joseph
Robinson. Recorded: September 10, 1823.

Fauquier County, Virginia, Will Book 25, page 427 -

Will of Benjamin James dated (_____) 1850 - (no date of probate). Recorded
Fauquier County, April 26, 1855:

"I, BENJAMIN JAMES OF THE CHOCTAW NATION" - legatees: wife, Mary Ann,
$500.00 in specie - sons, Robert, William, John, George, Joseph, Henry,
Asa - slaves to each, all named - daughters, Elizabeth, Susannah, Roda,
Elgira, Abigail, Harriet, Nancy, Keziah - slave to each, all named - To
my grandchildren, heirs of my daughter, Alsey, a note of hand I hold on
Israil Folson for $200.00 on interest at ten percent - To my younger set
of children I have by my present wife, Mary Ann - Executors: George W.
Harkins, John Car, Leroy P. Griggs. Witnesses: William Cobb, Matthew
Glothlymin (?).

page 429: Washington City, D. C., April 25, 1855 - Douglas H. Cooper,
U. S. Agent for the Choctaw Tribe of Indians makes an affidavit that the
foregoing Will is a correct copy of the last Will and Testament of the late
Benjamin James of the said tribe, on file in his office and that the said
Will is according to the customary law of the Choctaws and is to all intents
and purposes valid.

COMMENT BY CHH: I have done no research on the Choctaw Tribe of Indians
but I believe that they had a reservation in the State of Missouri. There
must be a very fine tale or story connected with the above Benjamin James.
I have noticed in Fauquier County Will Book 7, page 392, a Division of the
Real Estate of one Thomas James, dec'd., as per Order of the Court dated
the 23rd of April 1805 in which 285 acres of land were divided into twelve
lots of 23-3/4 acres each and among the twelve heirs is a Benjamin James -
recorded 27 March 1820. Among the names are William James, Elizabeth Green,

Joseph James, George James, John James and as stated, Benjamin James, all
of which names are repeated in the names of the children of Benjamin.

Surry County, Virginia, Orders, Wills, Deeds (1684-1686) - (Trans.) page 88 -

28 November 1685 - Power of Attorney by William Vaughan OF PORTSMOUTH, IN
THE PROVINCE OF NEW HAMPSHIRE IN NEW ENGLAND, Merchant to his trusty friend,
Mr. George Jaffery, OF PORTSMOUTH AFORESAID, Merchant, to recover, receive,
and collect all debts due him IN VIRGINIA OR MARYLAND, etc. Witnesses:
Thomas Wills, Nicholas Miller, John Wakcome (?). Recorded: 3 June 1686,
SURRY COUNTY, VIRGINIA.

Augusta County, Virginia, Deed Book 21, page 145 -

Indenture dated 15th May 1775 in which Archibald Alexander, executor, and
Magdaline Bowyer, relict and executrix of Benjamin Borden the younger, late
of Augusta County, Gent., dec'd., who was the eldest son and heir at law of
his father, Benjamin Borden, the elder, late of Orange County, Gent., dec'd.,
sell to Walter McChesney of the County of Augusta, Colony of Virginia -
Whereas the said Benjamin Borden, the father, at his death was seized of
several tracts of land in Virginia AND IN THE PROVINCE OF NEW JERSEY and did
make his Will in writing 3rd April 1742 and therein did order and direct that
all his Estate in land which he had in Virginia and those IN NEW JERSEY excepting 5000 acres on the waters of the James River and the land he lived on
should be sold and did constitute and appoint Zeruiah, his wife, executrix
and his son, Benjamin Borden, the younger, and William Fernly (?) executors
and which the said Zeruiah and William Fernly hath failed and refused to
prove so the whole burthen fell on Benjamin Borden, the younger, who proved
said will in the County Court of Frederick, etc., doth sell to the said Walter
McChesney for 10 pds - 100 acres in the County of Augusta and is part of a
large tract of 92,100 acres granted to said Borden by patent dated November 6,
1739, etc. and the said Benjamin Borden, the younger, departed this life but
made his Will dated 30 March 1753 and did order his executors, John Lyle and
Archibald Alexander, and with Magdaline, then his wife, to sell all the lands
of his late father remaining unsold, etc. Witnesses: Samuel McChesney,
Samuel McDowell, James Wallace, Andrew Reid. Recorded: November 21, 1775.

Ibid, page 432 (Deed Book 27) -

Indenture dated 9th March 1793 in which Robert Harvey and Martha, his wife,
late Martha Hawkins, relict of Benjamin Hawkins, dec'd., heir-at-law of
Benjamin Borden, the younger, dec'd. and father of the said Martha, of the
County of Botetourt, State of Virginia, etc. - sell to Robert McChesney of
the County of Augusta (Va.) - 129 acres of land, etc. Witnesses: James
Mitchell, Samuel McChesney, James McChesney. Recorded 13 June 1793.

Mecklenburg County, Virginia, Deed Book 3, page 48 -

November 12, 1770 - Indenture in which Mary Graves, of Mecklenburg County,
Colony of Virginia, for natural love and affection, makes a Deed of Gift of
175 acres of land in Mecklenburg County to her son, Elijah Graves OF BUTE
COUNTY IN THE PROVINCE OF NORTH CAROLINA, being the same land on which she
now lives, etc.

A Register of Baptisms and Funerals for Cumberland Parish by John Cameron, Rector, page 79 -

Elizabeth Turner, an adult, daughter of James Turner of WARREN COUNTY, NORTH CAROLINA was baptized May 20th, 1815. Note by CHH: Cumberland Parish at one time consisted of parts of Prince Edward, Nottoway, Lunenburg, and Amelia Counties.

Abstracts of Cumberland County, Virginia, Wills and Marriages (1749-1799) (Photostats in Virginia State Library), page 263 -

Will of John Hancock, dated 12 March 1763 - probated 27 June 1763. Legatees: To my brother, Samuel (Hancock) one-half of tract of land on Tar River, NORTH CAROLINA (the half my father lives on). The other half to my wife, Martha; sons, Samuel, John, and William, and daughter Ann - Executors: my wife, brother Samuel Hancock and John Morton.

Caroline County, Virginia, Deeds 1758-1845, page 11 -

Indenture dated 3rd January 1769 in which Joseph Long OF THE PROVINCE OF NORTH CAROLINA sells John Miller of the County of Caroline, Colony of Virginia - a tract of land in the Parish of St. Mary, County of Caroline - containing 133½ acres being one third part of a tract formerly the property of Elizabeth Rennolds and then of her son, John Rennolds and willed by the said John Rennolds to his three sisters, Elizabeth, Mary and Frances - the said Elizabeth being the mother to the said Joseph Long, etc. Witnesses: Robert Gilchrist, William Dickson, William Bogle, James Miller. Recorded: 9 February 1769.

Norfolk County, Virginia, Deed Book 20, page 107 -

10th December 1761 - Indenture in which Daniel Highsmith and Anne Highsmith, OF THE COUNTY OF HALIFAX, PROVINCE OF NORTH CAROLINA - sell to Richard Granger of the County of Norfolk, Colony of Virginia - for (lease 5 shillings release 10 pds) - 33 acres of land situated, lying and being in the Parish of St. Brides and County of Norfolk - the same being the (one) third part of 98 acres which formerly belonged to Benjamin Beck and at his and his wife's decease fell to their three daughters, Ann Becks, Margaret (sic) Becks, and Margaret (sic) Mercer, etc. Witnesses: James Cleever, Robert Tucker, Jr., William Smith, Abram Wormington, Seth Portlock, Charles Mayle, John Richardson. Recorded: 15th July 1762. (NOTE BY CHH: The Will of Daniel Highsmith was probated in Halifax County, North Carolina in 1772)

Ibid - Deed Book 9, page 102 -

18th September - Indenture in which John Bennett OF CURROTUCK, IN THE COUNTY OF ALBEMARLE IN THE PROVINCE OF NORTH CAROLINA - sells to Benjamin Becks of the Southern Branch precincts of Elizabeth River Parish, in the County of Norfolk, Collony of Virginia - with the consent of his wife, Mary (Bennett) - for 6 pds - 34 acres in said County and Parish (of Norfolk Co.) being part of a tract of land containing 100 acres given by Deed of Gift by Thomas Etheridge Senior unto his son, John Etheride "the elder" as by records of Norfolk County will more fully reveal, etc. - and the said 34 acres given and sett over from the said John Etheridge unto his son, Andrew Etheridge, and by the said Andrew Etheridge sold and sett over to the said Bennett and Mary, his wife, and now by them to the said Benjamin Becks, etc. Witnesses: George Sugg, William Mound. Acknowledged in Court by Joseph Portlock, Attorney for John and Mary Bennett. Recorded 19 December 1711.

Norfolk County, Virginia, Deed Book 8, page 44a -

NORTH CAROLINA - 2nd November 1708 - Know all men by these presents that I, George Becks, OF THE COUNTY OF BATH, cooper, have made, ordained, constituted, appointed, etc., my trusty and well beloved friend, John Murray of Princess Anne County and Collony of Virginia, my true and lawful attorney to ack (sic) in my name and acknowledge the lease of a tract of land in Norfolke Town which formerly belonged to Mrs. Jane Sarveer (?) unto Mr. Samuel Smith, Merchant of Norfolk, etc. Witnesses: Levi Truewhitt, Peter Green. Recorded: 15 February 1708/9.

Southampton County, Virginia, Deed Book 3, page 392 -

26th February 1765 - Indenture in which Hartwell Phillips, OF THE PROVINCE OF NORTH CAROLINA (no county stated) sells to Edmund Branch of the County of Southampton, in the Colony of Virginia - for 50 pds - a certain tract of land in the said County of Southampton, which said tract of land was granted to John Phillips of Surry County (Virginia) by Patent dated 28th August 1746 and by the last Will and Testament of the said John Phillips, devised to his son, Hartwell Phillips, containing 300 acres, be it more or less, etc. Witnesses: Joshua Wood, David Hatfield, Joseph Gray. Recorded: 12th September 1765.

Edgecombe County, North Carolina, Deed Book (1772-75) page 198 -

20th January 1777 - Indenture in which Jacob Underwood of Edgecombe County, North Carolina sells to Thomas Atkinson of Southampton County, Virginia - for 40 pds - a tract of land in Edgecombe County, North Carolina, on the north side of Compass Creek - containing 150 acres, more or less. Recorded: October __, 1777. NOTE BY CHH: Southampton County, Virginia Will Book 2, page 378 - Will of Thomas Atkinson, Senior, probated April 11,1771, proves the above cited Thomas Atkinson (Junior) as his son.

Lunenburg County, Virginia, Deed Book 11, page 124 -

7th March 1768 - Drury Allen of THE COUNTY OF GRANVILLE, PROVINCE OF NORTH CAROLINA - by indenture, sells to Isaac Brizendine of the County of Lunenburg, Colony of Virginia - for 70 pds - a tract of land on the head branches of Couches and Tucking Creeks - containing 300 acres - adjoining lands of Briggs, Stevenson, Carter Cates, Murrell, etc. Witnesses: Lyddal Bacon, Anthony Street, Allen Stokes. Recorded: 11th March 1768 and Elizabeth Allen, wife of Drury, relinquished her dowry rights.

Spotsylvania County, Virginia, Deed Book D, (1742-1751) -

Nathaniel Sanders of NORTHAMPTON COUNTY, PROVINCE OF NORTH CAROLINA gives Bond to Robert Coleman of Spotsylvania County, Colony of Virginia - dated

26th January 1742 - said Nathaniel Sanders had left him by his deceased
father, Nathaniel Sanders (Senior) 400 acres in Spotsylvania County,
Virginia - and for now payment due his Majesty, petitioned by Said Coleman
and was granted same, etc. Witnesses: John Wynell Sanders, George Chapman.
Recorded: 7th June 1743.

Southampton County, Virginia, Deed Book 6, page 11 -

14th September 1781 - We, Bromfield Ridley OF THE COUNTY OF GRANVILLE,
STATE OF NORTH CAROLINA and William Ridley of the County of Southampton,
State of Virginia, Executors and residuary legatees of the last Will and
Testament of James Ridley, late of Southampton County, dec'd., doe forever
quit claim our title to a certain negro woman, Silvia and her two children,
Moses and Frank, and doe by virtue of these presents make over all right,
title, interest, etc., to John Blunt of Southampton County, etc. Witnesses:
Hardy Harris, Timothy Thorpe. Recorded: 9th May 1782.

Amherst County, Virginia, Deed Book E, page 434 -

6th October 1783 - Indenture in which John Jopling of the COUNTY OF BURKE,
STATE OF NORTH CAROLINA sells to John Edmonds Junior of the County of
Amherst, State of Virginia - for 1250 pds current money - "and a likely
black mare" - a tract of land containing 500 acres on the south side of
Berry Mountain, on the south side of Rucker's Run, it being part of a
patent of 2000 acres granted to Samuel Spencer Senior 10th September 1755,
etc. Witnesses: James Pamplin, William Horsley, John Penn, Matthew Tucker,
William Coffey.

Sussex County, Virginia, Deed Book 1, page 201 -

4th October 1797 - Indenture in which John Henry Barker of the COUNTY OF
WARREN, STATE OF NORTH CAROLINA, and Honour (Cutts?) Barker, his wife, sell
to James Jones of the County of Sussex, State of Virginia, for 89 pds - 178
acres in said County of Sussex, etc. Witnesses: Jesse Barker, Charles
Barker. Recorded: December Court 1797.

Albemarle County, Virginia, Deed Book 10, page 296 -

5th November 1793 - Indenture in which Eli Melton, Daniel Melton, William
Jones and Mary, his wife, of RUTHERFORD COUNTY, STATE OF NORTH CAROLINA,
of one part and William Melton and Samuel Hensley of the County of
Albemarle, Virginia, of the other part - Whereas, William Melton, deceased,
being in his lifetime possessed of considerable estate, devised unto his
children by his last Will and Testament, etc. and of whom the above Eli,
Daniel and Mary are three (of his children) etc.

Brunswick County, Virginia, Deed Book 9, page 230 -e

29th April 1768 - Indenture in which John Massey of the COUNTY OF JOHNSON,
PROVINCE OF NORTH CAROLINA sells to John Doby of the County of Brunswick,
Colony of Virginia - for 50 pds - all that tract of land on which he lately
lived in the County of Brunswick, containing 100 acres - bounded on a line
agreed upon by the said John Massey and William Massey, both sons of Joseph

Massey, dec'd., and the said 100 acres having been bequeathed to the said John
Massey by the last Will of the said Joseph Massey, dec'd., and also another
150 acres of land, etc. Witnesses: William Robertson Jr., William Short,
Peter Lee, John Brewer.

Lunenburg County, Virginia, Deed Book 10, page 74 -

15th September 1764 - Indenture in which Rease Brewer of the COUNTY OF HALIFAX,
in THE PROVINCE OF NORTH CAROLINA - sells to Thomas Twitty of the County of
Brunswick, Colony of Virginia - for 175 pds - 400 acres of land in the said
County of Lunenburg, Colony of Virginia, etc. Recorded: 14th February 1765.

Spotsylvania County, Virginia, Deed Book K, page 372 -

November 22, 1782 - John Graves of (Note by CHH: CASWELL COUNTY) STATE OF
NORTH CAROLINA, eldest son and heir-at-law of Thomas Graves (note by CHH:
Will Probated 1768) of Spotsylvania County, Virginia - sells to William
Pettus (Senior) (Note by CHH: who married Susannah, daughter of Thomas
Graves (d. 1768) of Spotsylvania County, Virginia) - for 451 pds, gold or
silver, - 399 acres of land in Spotsylvania County, Virginia. Witnesses:
Joseph Graves, John Graves, William Graves Jr., John Arnold, John W. Pettus,
Recorded: April 17, 1783.

Grayson County, Virginia, Deed Book 2, page 28 -

24th September 1803 - Indenture in which Nelson Powell Jones of ANSON COUNTY,
STATE OF NORTH CAROLINA, sells to Charles Jones - 42 acres of land in the
County of Grayson, State of Virginia, on the west side of New River. Wit-
nesses: M(initree) Jones, Martel Leseur, Edward Pool. Recorded: October
Court 1803. (NOTE by CHH: ibid page 29, same date, same parties, 100 acres
sold - note further by CHH: Nelson Powell Jones was a son of Minitree Jones,
Senior (1752-1821) and his wife, Elizabeth Powell)

Anson County, North Carolina, Deed Book B2, page 342 -

13th November 1790 - William Dabbs of CHARLOTTE COUNTY, VIRGINIA being the
eldest son of Joseph Dabbs, formerly of said State of Virginia, makes a Deed
of Gift "for the love and affection he has and bears unto his only sister,
Mary, the wife of Patrick Boggan, OF THE COUNTY OF ANSON, NORTH CAROLINA - of
two negro women slaves, which said slaves are removed from the State of Virginia by James Webb, who intermarried with Nany, the widow and relict of the
said Joseph Dabbs, dec'd., etc. Teste: Thomas Reed, Josiah Dabbs, Elizabeth
Dabbs, Margaret Boggan. Proved: January Court 1791 by Margaret Boggan.
(Note by CHH: Joseph Dabbs died in Lunenburg County, Virginia 1749 and had
married Nany Hoggett July 1, 1733, daughter of Nathaniel Hoggett.)

Spotsylvania County, Virginia, Deed Book K, page 117 -

December 9, 1779 - Deed of Gift in which William Arnold and Mary, his wife
of RANDOLPH COUNTY, NORTH CAROLINA - "for love and goodwill" convey to John
Arnold of the County of Louisa, State of Virginia - 230 acres of land lying
and being in the County of Spotsylvania, Virginia, etc. Witnesses: William
Graves, William Pettus, William Pettus, Jr., John Z. Lewis, Robert Lewis.
Recorded: 17th April 1783.

Isle of Wight County, Virginia, Deed Book 9, page 304 -

August 14, 1754 - Deed of Gift in which Samuèl Thomas of the COUNTY OF NORTHAMPTON, PROVINCE OF NORTH CAROLINA - "for natural love and affection which he has and bears unto Thomas Whitney Gale and Mary, his wife," "My well beloved niece" - of Isle of Wight County, Virginia - gives, grants, and conveys them a certain tract of land which my father, John Thomas, gave me by Deed of Gift - containing 100 acres - (in Isle of Wight) - Witnesses: William Crocker, John Thomas, Joseph Crocker. Recorded 5th December 1754. (Note by CHH: Mary, the wife of Thomas Whitney Gale, Senior, was a daughter of Richard Thomas, who was a brother of the above "donor" Samuel Thomas, and both were sons of John Thomas, who died in 1726. Samuel Thomas married Elizabeth Sherrer (Sherrod ?) and removed to North Carolina. Richard Thomas had married her sister, Eleanor Sherrer (Sherrod ?).

Mecklenburg County, Virginia, Will Book 3, page 176 -

Will of Daniel Gold -dated 27 May 1793 - Probated 9 September 1793 - "My tract of land containing 300 acres in the COUNTY OF CASWELL, STATE OF NORTH CAROLINA to be equally divided between my two eldest sons, Daniel Gold, Junior and Ephraim Gold. Daniel to have his choice, etc. Other legatees of property in Virginia were: wife, Elizabeth Gold; children, Moore Gold, Pleasant Gold, Mealy (Milly ?) Gold, John Gold, Josiah Gold, Elizabeth Gold, Sarah Griffin, and Mary Griffin. Executors: David Epperson, William Sargent of PERSON COUNTY, NORTH CAROLINA, and Daniel Gold, Junior. Witnesses: Peter Griffin, Mary Sarratt, Charles Hamblin.

Henry County, Virginia, Deed Book 5, page 310 -

30th January 1797 - Indenture in which John Haley of Henry County, State of Virginia sells to Peter Garland of the COUNTY OF ROCKINGHAM, STATE OF NORTH CAROLINA - for 5 pds specie - a certain tract of land in Henry County, on the branches of Leatherwood Creek, being the land that was intended by lines marked off for my son, Barney Haley, and bounded by lands of John King, William Brown, John Nance, etc. containing 100 acres, etc. Recorded same date.

Mecklenburg County, Virginia, Marriage Bonds (Microfilm) - page 20 -

27 June 1794 - Joseph Gooch of GRANVILLE COUNTY, NORTH CAROLINA to Anne Lockett.

Southampton County, Virginia, Deed Book 6, page 10 -

14th March 1780 - Indenture in which James Haisly and Elizabeth, his wife of the COUNTY OF WAYNE, STATE OF NORTH CAROLINA - sell John Stephenson of the County of Southampton, Virginia and Parish of Nottoway - for 40 pds specie - 100 acres of land, which said plantation was left to the said James Haisly by the last Will and Testament of his father, James Haisly, deceased, on which he lived, etc. Recorded 14 March 1782.

Goochland County, Virginia, Deed Book 4, page 208 -

19th September 1743 - Indenture in which William Walker of the COUNTY OF NORTHAMPTON, PROVINCE OF NORTH CAROLINA sells to John Bibby of the Parish of St. James, County of Goochland, Colony of Virginia - for 20 pds - a tract of land in Goochland County, Virginia on the North side of the James River - containing 200 acres - adjoining lands of John Wright, James Christian, John Sim(s), deceased, Charles Allen, Phillip Walker, etc. Witnesses: John McBride, Stephen Hughes, David Patteson. Recorded: 20th September 1743 and Elizabeth, wife of William Walker, relinquished her dower rights.

Henry County, Virginia, Deed Book 1, page 253 -

18th January 1779 - Indenture in which George Hamilton of the County of Henry (Virginia) sells to Alexander Moore, son of William Moore of GUILFORD COUNTY, NORTH CAROLINA - for 120 pds - 250 acres in Henry County. Recorded: 24 June 1779 and Mary, wife of George Hamilton relinquished her dower rights.

Norfolk County, Virginia, Deed Book 18, page 75 -

23rd September 1757 - Indenture in which Aquila Sugg of the COUNTY OF EDGECOMBE, PROVINCE OF NORTH CAROLINA - sells to John Shipwash of the County of Norfolk, in Virginia - for 5 shillings lease 40 pds release - 70 acres of land in the County of Norfolk - said land having been bequeathed said Aquila by his father, George Sugg, deceased by his will dated September 2, 1734 - probated 21 February 1736 - Witnesses: John Coats, Richard Coats, Thomas Wright, Aquila Wallis.

Augusta County, Virginia, Deed Book 10, page 52 -

24th September 1761 - Indenture in which Henry Fuller of the COUNTY OF ORANGE, PROVINCE OF NORTH CAROLINA sells to John Paxton of the County of Augusta, Colony of Virginia for ÷ (lease 5 shillings release 125 pds) 190 acres in County of Augusta, Virginia, on the East side of the North Branch of the James River (being that plantation where Henry Fuller formerly did live). Witnesses: James Campbell, John Thompson, James Hanna, James Trimble. Recorded: November 18, 1761.

Brunswick County, Virginia, Order Book 2, page 229 -

15th January 1782 - Deed in which Samuel Marshall and Jane, his wife, of the COUNTY OF HALIFAX, STATE OF NORTH CAROLINA - sells to Samuel Marshall, Junior OF THE SAME COUNTY AND STATE - for five shillings - 100 acres of land in the County of Brunswick, State of Virginia, being part of a tract of land belonging to the said Samuel Marshall granted by patent dated 20th June 1748.

Brunswick County, Virginia, Deed Book 14, page 127 -

29th January 1785 - Indenture in which Samuel Marshall (Junior) of the COUNTY OF WARREN, STATE OF NORTH CAROLINA - sells to William Marshall of the County of Brunswick, Virginia - for 50 pds - 100 acres of land in the County of Brunswick, etc. Witnesses: Jesse Marshall, Spain Marshall, Becky Marshall, Jack Pennington. Recorded: 22nd August 1785.

Brunswick County, Virginia, Will Book 8, page 447 -

Will of William Marshall, dated 12 April 1815 - probated 27th July 1818 -
legatees: wife, Rebecca - orphans of Spain Marshall - daughter, Rebecca
Fins (?) - "120 acres of land in CASWELL AND PERSON COUNTIES, NORTH
CAROLINA to my son, Jack Marshall, it being part of a tract on which he
now resides" - Executors: my son, Jack and friend, James Malone. Witnesses: A. Malone, John Gee, Robert Mitchell, John Pennington, Buckner
Overby.   Note by CHH: Brunswick County, Virginia Marriages, page 91,
reveals that a Spain Marshall married Unity Johnson on October 10, 1796.

Brunswick County, Virginia, Deed Book 5, page 724 -

22nd April 1755 - Indenture in which William Berry of the COUNTY OF
GRANVILLE, PROVINCE OF NORTH CAROLINA sells for 30 pds - to George Berry
of Brunswick County, Colony of Virginia - 100 acres of land in Brunswick
County. Signed by William and Grace Berry. Witnesses: Edward Fielding,
John Ingram. Recorded: same date.

Brunswick County, Virginia, Deed Book 6, page 473 -

31st January 1760 - Indenture in which William Berry and Grace, his wife,
of the COUNTY OF ORANGE, PROVINCE OF NORTH CAROLINA, sell to John Ingram
of the County of Brunswick, Virginia - for 60 pds - 306 acres of land in
said County of Brunswick. Witnesses: George Berry, Richard Birch,
Richard Harding, Henry Maclin, Giles Kelly. Recorded: 24 June 1760.

Brunswick County, Virginia, Deed Book 6, page 531 -

22nd June 1760 - Indenture in which Grace Berry of the COUNTY OF GRANVILLE,
PROVINCE OF NORTH CAROLINA sells to George Berry - for 30 pds - 100 acres
of land in Brunswick County, Virginia. Recorded 24th June 1760.

Brunswick County, Virginia, Deed Book 6, page 564 -

25th August 1760 - Indenture in which Mary Eaton and Robert Jones, Junior,
OF THE PROVINCE OF NORTH CAROLINA, executrix and executor of the last Will
and Testament of William Eaton, Gent., and late OF SAID PROVINCE (OF NORTH
CAROLINA) deceased - sells to George Berry of the County of Brunswick,
Virginia, etc.

Brunswick County, Virginia, Deed Book 5, page 400 -

6th March 1753 - Indenture in which Richard Wise of THE PROVINCE OF NORTH
CAROLINA sells to Thomas Wise of Brunswick County, Colony of Virginia - for
18 pds - 130 acres of land in Brunswick County, Virginia, etc. Witnesses:
James Wise, John Wise.

Brunswick County, Virginia, Deed Book 6, page 199 -

23rd August 1757 - Indenture in which Thomas Wise, and Mary, his wife, of
JOHNSON COUNTY, PROVINCE OF NORTH CAROLINA sell to Sam(uel) Harrie of
Southampton County, Virginia - for 25 pds - 150 acres of land in

Brunswick County, Virginia, adjoining lands of James Wise, etc.

Brunswick County, Virginia, Deed Book 6, page 566 -

19th August 1760 - Indenture in which Thomas Wise of DOBBS COUNTY, PROVINCE
OF NORTH CAROLINA and his wife, Mary sell to William Robinson, Junior, of
Brunswick County, Virginia - for 20 pds - 130 acres of land, etc. (Note by
CHH: a Mary Wise is named as "daughter" in the Will of Joseph Massie, father
in law of James Wise and also names another daughter, Rebecca Wise, wife of
James Wise - see Will Book 3, page 368 dated 19 August 1760 - Probated 26th
May 1761).

Norfolk County, Virginia, Deed Book 12, page 84 -

Will of Adam Etheridge, dated 18th April 1735 - Probated 17th May 1735 -
"To my loving wife, Elizabeth Etheridge, the Manner plantation and land I
lately lived on, it being the land I bought of William Taylor, lying and be-
ing in the PRECINCT OF PASQUOTANK IN THE COUNTY OF ALBEMARLE, PROVINCE OF
NORTH CAROLINA"- other legatees were: son, Levy Etheridge - daughters,
Lydia Etheridge and Elizabeth Etheridge. Executors: wife, Elizabeth and
son, Levy. Witnesses: Robert Williams, Prudence Williams, Elizabeth
Williams.

Fauquier County, Virginia, Will Book 12, page 21 -

Will of John H. Pettit, dated 24 July 1830 - probated 28th February 1831.
Legatees: To my wife, Catey Pettit, land, slaves, stock, etc. for her
natural life, etc. names five slaves to be set free at death of his wife.
To my nephew, John Walden, son of my sister, Nancy Walden, who now lives
near the VILLAGE OF BLOOMFIELD, JEFFERSON COUNTY, STATE OF OHIO - $100.00.
Executors: friends, John C. Cummins, Elijah Hansbrough, Joseph Thompson,
Witnesses: Reason H. Oliver, John L. Conway, Jonathan Cooper, John Oliver.

Comment by CHH: Will Book 6, page 55 - John H. Pettit and Thomas Pettit,
as administrators of the Estate of Obadiah Pettit, dec'd., from July 9, 1808
to 23 January 1812, records the debits and credits against the Estate and
makes a Settlement of the Estate to the following heirs and distributees:
Keturah Pettit, Nathaniel Pettit, William Pettit, Samuel Pettit, Joseph
McDowell, Francis Walden, Richard Roberts, John H. Pettit, Thomas Pettit.
Recorded: 26 September 1814.

Augusta County, Virginia, Deed Book 40, page 363 -

2nd December 1815 - I, Robert Alexander, OF HIGHLAND COUNTY, STATE OF OHIO,
do make, constitute, appoint, etc., William Alexander of Rockbridge County,
State of Virginia, who is joint executor with me of the Estate of Hugh
Alexander, dec'd., my true and lawful Attorney, in all matters respecting
the Estate of the said Hugh Alexander, dec'd., wherein by his last Will
and Testament dated March 15, 1805 in Augusta County, Virginia, etc. Witnesses: George Shimm (or Shinn), J. D. Scott. Recorded: 25 March 1816.

Washington County, Virginia, Deed Book 6, page 479 -

Indenture dated 24 June 1817 in which Sarah Steele of THE COUNTY OF HIGHLAND,
STATE OF OHIO sells to Robert McChesney of the County of Rockbridge, State

of Virginia - for $500.00 - "All my right, title, and interest claim in my
dower and property claim in a tract of land in Washington County, Virginia"
which tract of land my husband, Samuel Steele sold to the said Robert
McChesney, etc. Witnesses: George Shinn, Hugh Rogers (both Justices of
Highland County, Ohio) - Recorded: Washington County, Virginia 22nd April
1818.

Washington County, Virginia, Deed Book 5, page 450 -

Indenture dated 31 March 1814 in which Samuel Steele, LATE OF THE COUNTY
OF ROCKBRIDGE, STATE OF VIRGINIA BUT NOW OF THE COUNTY OF MONTGOMERY IN
THE STATE OF OHIO sells to Robert McChesney of the County of Rockbridge,
Virginia - for the sum of $100.00 - a certain tract of land lying and
situated in the County of Washington, Virginia - containing 360 acres of
land left by the Will of Samuel Steele, dec'd., to his three sons, Robert,
Samuel, and William Steele to be divided equally between them and the said
Samuel Steele (Junior) doth confirm to the said Robert McChesney all his
right, title, and interest in his said third part, etc. Witnesses: John
B. Whiteside, James McChesney, Zachariah McChesney. Acknowledged at
Rockbridge County Courthouse April 4, 1814. Recorded: Washington County
Courthouse 18th August 1814.

Orange County, Virginia, Deed Book 1, page 422 -

Indenture dated 23 February 1736/7 in which Ludwick Stone (or Stoud) of
the County of Orange, Colony of Virginia, sells to Michael Cryter OF THE
PROVINCE OF PENNSYLVANIA for five shillings lease 100 pds release current
money of Virginia - three parcels or tracts of land - the first tract of
217 acres on the south side of Gerundo River between Mathias Selser and
Michail Coffman - another tract containing 200 acres and another tract lies
near Elk Lick on the north side of Gerundo adjoining to Martin Coffman and
John Prupecker, etc. Witnesses: Gideon Marr, John Newport. Recorded:
24 February 1736/7.

Records of Augusta County (Virginia) Vol. 1, by Chalkley, page 304 -

Augusta County Court Judgments (November 1750) - (B) - Peter Wallace, now
in Virginia, vs John Kyle - Petition on Account dated 1738 - FROM LAN-
CASTER, PENNSYLVANIA - Writ dated 5th September 1750.

Order Book #10, page 457 (Augusta County) -

November 25, 1766 - Alexander Kyle, not an inhabitant of this Colony.

Ibid - Order Book 7, page 211 -

18 May 1762 - Among others who received Certificates of Naturalization
were Garbiel Kyle and George Hammer.

Charlotte County, Virginia, Deed Book 3, page 167 -

Indenture dated 19th October 1772 in which John Caldwell, eldest son of
William Caldwell of the DISTRICT OF NINETY-SIX, PROVINCE OF SOUTH
CAROLINA sells to Edward Brewer of the COUNTY OF CHARLOTTE, COLONY OF

VIRGINIA - Whereas by the last Will and Testament of the said William
Carlwell, dec'd., etc. - all that tract of land containing 250 acres and
being situated IN THE COUNTY OF LUNENBURG, VIRGINIA and which land descended
to the said John Carlwell by the will of his father, the said William
Caldwell - being recorded in the Clerk's Office of the said County of
Lunenburg, etc. for the sum of 270 pds - etc. Witnesses: James Cunningham,
Robert Cardwell, John Caldwell, Beverly Mann, John Rogers. Recorded:
December 7, 1772.

Charlotte County, Virginia, Deed Book 2, page 370 -

Power of Attorney dated 17th December 1770 in which David George of the
County of Charlotte, Colony of Virginia - "INTENDING TO REMOVE TO SOUTH
CAROLINA" - empowers John Brent and Edmond Brewer, etc. Witnesses: James
Daughtery, Richard Dudgeon, Samuel Leason. Recorded: 7th January 1771.

Lunenburg County, Virginia, Deed Book 29, page 68 -

January __, 1826 - Indenture in which Alexander B. Moon of the County of
Lunenburg, State of Virginia and John Moon of GREENVILLE DISTRICT, STATE
of SOUTH CAROLINA - for the sum of $155.00 paid to our father in his life-
time by William Parrott, as is proved to us by his receipt shown us, etc.
do bargain and sell 70 acres of land, etc. (Note by CHH: This record also
appears in the Tennessee section of this MSS - see comments there)

Laurens County, South Carolina, Deed Book "F" page 37 -

Deed dated 20th July 1791 in which Moses Sullivant of Greenville County,
South Carolina sells to Jeremiah Glen(n) OF THE STATE OF VIRGINIA (LUNEN-
BURG COUNTY) - for 150 pds - 150 acres situated in Laurens County, South
Carolina on the waters of Beaver Dam Creek - bounded (in part) on Joseph
Babb's land - land of David Craddock, William Dew, etc. Signed by Moses
and Milly Sullivant. Witnesses: Tyree Glenn, Hewlet Sullivant, Charles
Sullivant.

Spotsylvania County, Virginia, Deed Book "O", page 343 -

May 23, 1793 - Thomas Livingston and James Livingston of EDGEFIELD COUNTY
AND STATE OF SOUTH CAROLINA give a Power of Attorney to their true and
trusty friend, Benjamin Wharton of Spotsylvania County in Virginia to receive all sums of money that may be due them by bonds, legacies, debts, or
other whatsoever in the State of Virginia or any other State -also power
to prosecute in our behalf, etc. Recorded: Spotsylvania County, 5th
July 1796. Note by CHH: Ibid page 342 - another power of attorney reveals that the above cited Benjamin Wharton is the son of Valentine Long
Wharton, generally called "Long" Wharton in Virginia records.

Augusta County, Virginia - Deed Book 37, page 321 -

28th July 1812 - Indenture in which Andrew Steele and Elizabeth, his wife
OF THE COUNTY OF WASHINGTON, STATE OF TENNESSEE, by Andrew Fulton and
Samuel Steele, his attorneys in fact - sell to Peter Whiteman of the County
of Augusta, State of Virginia - by Power of Attorney dated June 9th 1809

of record in Augusta County, Virginia Court - for 1500 pds Virginia currency by Peter Whitemore (sic) - two tracts of land on the Waters of South
River in the said County of Augusta - one containing 216 acres, being the
same tract of land devised to the said Andrew Steele by the last Will of
his father, James Steele, Dec'd., dated 5 June 1802 (Augusta County) -
the other tract containing 160 acres, being the same land conveyed by Deed
to the said Andrew Steele from William Ross and wife (1808) (Augusta
County), etc. Witnesses: Joseph Fawber, James Guthrie, Edward Fulton.
Recorded: 28 September 1812.

Fauquier County, Virginia, Deed Book 13, page 349 -

6th March 1797 - Indenture in which Isaac Cowper and Susanna, his wife,
OF THE TENNESSEE STATE, sell to James Adams of the County of Fauquier,
State of Virginia - for 100 pds - all that tract of land which was de-
vised to the said Susanna Cowper and Mary Campbell before their marriages
by Doctor John Harmans, their father - lying in the County of Fauquier,
Virginia, on the Waters of Goose Creek, etc. Witnesses: James Carter,
Oliver Dodson. (Note by CHH: There follows affidavits by Richard Mitchell,
Clerk of Court OF HAWKINS COUNTY, TENNESSEE and by Thomas Jackson and
John Long, Esquires, Justices of the Peace of HAWKINS COUNTY, TENNESSEE.
Recorded: Fauquier County, Virginia, 24 April 1797.)

Further Note by CHH: (Ibid, page 352) - William and Mary Carter sell
land in Fauquier County which was devised by Doctor John Harmans to Mary
Harmans, his widow, who has since intermarried with William Carter 6th
March 1797 - This deed was also supported by affidavits from the Clerk of
Court of HAWKINS COUNTY, TENNESSEE.)

Rockingham County, North Carolina, Deed Book "2nd O", page 14 -

Power of Attorney dated 6th January 1845 in which Doctor Adolphus D(orsett)
Jones of THE COUNTY OF PERRY, STATE OF TENNESSEE, empowers Jones W. Burton
of the County of Rockingham, North Carolina to sell about (sic) 300 acres
of land with a grist mill, saw mill, and cotton machine, situated on
Matrimony Creek (commonly called Lindsay's Tract) and also another tract
of land called Scuffle Town and a lot in Leakesville, N. C. which fell to
him in the Division of the property of his father, George Washington Jones,
OF HENRY COUNTY, VIRGINIA.

Ibid - Deed Book R, page 40 -

George Washington Jones, OF HENRY COUNTY, VIRGINIA, on 2nd October 1817
purchased for $50.00 a certain lot (#9) in the Town of Leakesville, N. C.
containing 1/2 acre from Alexander Sneed.

Note by CHH: The Marriage Bonds of Rockingham County, N. C., page 131
reveal that Dr. Adolphus D. Jones, on 18 February 1843 married Caroline
L. Reamey (b. 1820) with James C. Walker his surety. Caroline L. Reamey
was the daughter of James Sanford Reamey and his wife, Letitia Hughes, BOTH
OF HENRY COUNTY, VIRGINIA. George Washington Jones married in Henry County,
Virginia Salina Dunlap and was the son of Dr. Benjamin Jones (d. 1843) and
his wife, Elizabeth Reamey (Ramey) both of whom died in Henry County, Va.

Lunenburg County, Virginia - Deed Book 30, page 511 -

22nd December 1836 - Know all men by these presents that I, Alexander B. Moon OF THE COUNTY OF BEDFORD, STATE OF TENNESSEE, Guardian of Ann B. Brown and Mary I. Brown, two of the minor heirs of John and Ermine Brown, both deceased - do nominate and appoint Robert R. Wilson of the County of Lunenburg, Virginia, my true and lawful attorney to receive certain land and slaves from the Estate of John Brown, dec'd.-

Lunenburg County, Virginia - Deed Book 29, page 68 -

January (?) 1826 - Indenture in which Alexander B. Moon of the County of Lunenburg, State of Virginia and John Moon OF GREENVILLE DISTRICT, STATE OF SOUTH CAROLINA - sell for the sum of $155.00 "paid to our father in his lifetime by William Parrott as is proved to us by his receipt shown us" - etc. - 70 acres of land, etc.

Comment: These two records prove that Alexander B. Moon moved from Lunenburg County, Virginia to Tennessee between the years 1826 and 1836 and that his brother, John Moon, had moved to South Carolina before 1826.

Washington County, Virginia - Deed Book 6, page 53 -

10 March 1815 - Indenture in which William King of SULLIVAN COUNTY, TENNESSEE and Elizabeth, his wife - sell to Samuel McChesney of Washington County, Virginia - for $1100.00 - two tracts of land in Washington County, Virginia, containing in all 321 acres, bounded on Hugh McChesney's land - William Rhea - Henderson's State Line - one tract containing 265 acres and the other tract 56 acres, etc. Witnesses: Thomas McChesney, Robert Craig, Jr., (Both Justices of the Peace). Recorded: 21 March 1818.

Ibid - Deed Book 12, page 510 -

16th January 1837 - Indenture in which John Laughton of RIPLEY COUNTY, MISSOURIA (sic) - Andrew Galbrath of HAWKINS COUNTY, TENNESSEE - David Dryden, Wallace Willoughby and William Willoughby OF SULLIVAN COUNTY, TENNESSEE - heirs and distributees of Alexander Laughton, dec'd., sell to Hugh McChesney of Washington County, Virginia, for $30.00, a tract of land in Washington County, Virginia containing 189 acres, etc. Recorded: 27 April 1837.

Washington County, Virginia - Deed Book 13, page 164 -

8th February 1815 (sic) Indenture in which Thomas McChesney of Washington County, Virginia sells to John Sharp of SULLIVAN COUNTY, TENNESSEE - for $833.34 - a tract of land in Washington County, Virginia containing 100 acres, and in addition, 25 acres to be laid off from a tract of 82 acres, etc. Witnesses: William King, Jonathan King.

Washington County, Virginia - Deed Book 13, page 164 -

(continued from above) - At a Court held for Washington County 26 February 1838 (sic) the above deed was proved by the oath of Jonathan King but

William King, NOW A RESIDENT OF THE STATE OF TENNESSEE, was in such a
feeble state of health that his attendance cannot be procured - then
Andrew Russell and Jacob Lynch, being well acquainted with the handwriting of the said Thomas McChesney, "who is now dead", etc.

Ibid - Deed Book 11, page 159 -

5th October 1832 - Indenture in which Isabella McChesney OF THE COUNTY OF
GREEN, IN THE STATE OF TENNESSEE, sells to Francis Preston of the County
of Washington, Virginia - for $500.00 current money of Virginia - all the
right, title, and interest, she, the said Isabella, has in and to a
certain tract of land in the County of Washington, on both sides of
fifteen mile creek - containing 360 acres of land - being the same land
sold by Francis Preston and Sarah B. his wife, to John McChesney, now
deceased by deed dated 16th May 1826 and which said tract of land, the
said John McChesney, by his last Will and Testament, bearing date 24th
March 1828 directed to be sold by his executors and when sold, one-third
of the amount thereof to be paid to the said Isabella McChesney or her
heirs, etc. Recorded: 5th October 1832.

Washington County, Virginia - Deed Book 4, page 274 -

Indenture dated 1st January 1810 in which Abraham Duval, NOW OF THE
COUNTY OF CLAYBORNE (SIC) AND STATE OF TENNESSEE, sells to Solomon
Potter of the County of Washington, State of Virginia, for $200.00 -
a tract of land in Washington County containing 323 acres, being the same
land formerly granted the said Abraham Duval by patent dated 18 October
1796, etc. Witnesses: David Winegar, Frederick Winegar, Peter Winegar.
Recorded: 16th January 1810.

Ibid - page 276 -

Indenture dated 23rd November 1809 in which John Wilcox of the County of
Washington, State of Virginia sells to Peter Winegar OF THE COUNTY OF
HAWKINS, STATE OF TENNESSEE, for $560.00, 100 acres of land in the County
of Washington, Virginia - formerly granted to John Stout by patent dated
9th September 1785 - adjoining lands of Jacob Duval, etc. Signed by John
Wilcox and Pheby Wilcox (his wife). Witnesses: Jacob Devauld, David
Winegar, Frederick Winegar. Recorded: 16th January 1810.

Ibid - page 226 -

Indenture dated June 5, 1809 in which Henry Widener, one of the executors
of the last will and testament of Lewis Whitnor, (sic), dec'd., OF THE
STATE OF TENNESSEE, with the other legatees of the said estate, of the one
part - sell to Jacob Cox OF THE SAME STATE, of the other part - Witnesseth
that the said Henry Whitenor (Widener), Jacob Devault, John Miller, Peter
Cleek and Martin Rowlen (Rowland ?), for the sum of $200.00 sell a tract
of land in Washington County, Virginia, on Possum Creek, a north branch of
the North Fork of Holston River and in Stanley Valley, containing 250
acres, etc. Witnesses: James Gaines, Mathias Cleek, Jacob Wills, George
Mornson, Charles Epperson, John Wills, Frederick Ekerd. Recorded 17th
October 1809. (NOTE BY CHH - the 1810 Tennessee Federal Census of

GRAINGER COUNTY, TENNESSEE, pages 42 and 43, reveals that Jacob Devault, Henry Widener, and Lewis Widener were living in that County in that year on "F" Creek.

Russell County, Virginia - Deed Book 10, page 310 -

Indenture dated 16th February 1836 in which James Little, Harrington Little and John Bays of one part, sell Andrew R. Martin of the other part - for $120.00 - 50 acres of land in the County of Russell, Virginia and the said James Little will forever warrant and defend 2/5 part of said tract - Harrington Little 2/5 part - and John Bays 1/5 part, etc. John Stokely and John Ball, Justices of the Peace OF HAWKINS COUNTY, TENNESSEE certify that Harrington Little PERSONALLY appeared before them and acknowledged the above to be his act and deed and desired them to certify said acknowledgment to the Clerk of Court of Russell County, Virginia, etc. dated 5th September 1836. Evans Perry and Brittain Poteet, Justices for Lee County, Virginia certify to the signature of James Little to the above deed of sale, etc. dated 30th June 1838 - Russell County, Virginia - 7th August 1838 - John Bays acknowledged the above deed of sale to be his act and deed, etc. ordered to be recorded, etc.

Grayson County, Virginia - Deed Book 5, page 6 -

Indenture dated 29th October 1824 in which Arthur Fulton and Naomi, his wife, OF RAY (RHEA) COUNTY, STATE OF TENNESSEE sell to Minitree Jones Junior, all and every part of their interest in the land of which their father (Minitree Jones Senior) died seized - which lot descended to the said Arthur Fulton and Naomi, his wife, by the death of HER FATHER, etc. Witnesses: A. Jones, Willia Vaughan, James Fulton.

Marriage Register, Washington County, Virginia (microfilm) 1785-1902 - page 302

October 29, 1874 - Leander M. McChesney married to Mary Gray - He, age 21, born SULLIVAN COUNTY, TENNESSEE - she, born Washington County, Virginia. He, son of J. C. and Elizabeth McChesney. She, daughter of Frederick G. and Margaret Gray.

Ibid, page 303 -

December 21, 1881 - L. M. McChesney, age 28, widower, married to Nannie K. Cox, age 24, single. He born SULLIVAN COUNTY, TENNESSEE. She born Washington County, Virginia. He, son of J. Craig and Elizabeth McChesney. She, daughter of Isabella Cox. His occupation, farmer.

Ibid, page 504 -

March 31, 1864 - John David Wright, age 25 years 7 months, 7 days married to Elizabeth McChesney, age 30, widow - he born in Louisville, Kentucky. She born SULLIVAN COUNTY, TENNESSEE. He, son of Daniel and Elizabeth Wright. She, daughter of Hugh A. and Julia McChesney.

Brunswick County, Virginia - Deed Book 24, page 153 -

Power of Attorney dated 17th August 1818 in which George Malone OF GILES
COUNTY, STATE OF TENNESSEE empowers Robert Mitchell to receive of James
Malone of Brunswick County, Virginia the sum of $400.00 - for which he is
to convey all his right, title, and interest in the property his father
willed him and now in the hands of his step-mother, Lucy Malone, etc.
(NOTE BY CHH - On page 155, ibid reference, 14th September 1818 Robert
Mitchell, as attorney for George Malone, acknowledges receipt of $400.00
and quits claim to the portion of the estate of George Malone, Sr.,
dec'd., left his son, George Malone, Jr. of GILES COUNTY, TENNESSEE. In
Deed Book 12, page 148, Brunswick Co., Virginia is a marriage contract
dated and recorded 25 January 1777 between George Malone (Sr.) of Brunswick County, Virginia and Lucy Carter, widow and relict of George Carter,
dec'd. In Deed Book 9, page 586 on 24th February 1770 is recorded a Deed
of Gift from John Marshall of Brunswick County, Virginia, to his daughter,
Lucy Carter, etc.

Mecklenburg County, Virginia - Deed Book 20, page 379 -

Indenture dated 11th September 1823 in which Josiah Gold OF WILSON COUNTY,
STATE OF TENNESSEE appoints Elijah Puryear his attorney to secure for him
any part of an estate or legacy due to him IN THE STATE OF VIRGINIA from
his father-in-law's estate by the death "of my wife's mother, Wilmouth
(Averet ?) - Recorded: Mecklenburg County, Virginia 18th December 1823.

Washington County, Virginia - Will Book 5, page 179 et seq -

IN THE NAME OF GOD, AMEN, I, JOHN SHARP OF SULLIVAN COUNTY AND STATE OF
TENNESSEE, etc.   To my wife, Elizabeth, my negro girl Dill - bed and
furniture - $75.00 annually for life, etc.
    To my daughter, Jane McConkey's children - her son, John and her
daughter, Maria Teressa excepted - all that tract of land on which the said
Jane McConkey now resides with this proviso that the said John McConkey and
Harriet, his wife, shall have one equal portion with the children of the
said Jane McConkey (her son, John and her daughter, Maria Teressa, still
excepted, etc.)
    To my daughter, Anne Longacre's children - land - mentions her husband,
Iveson Longacre, etc.
    To my daughter, Sally McChesney's children - two tracts of land lying
in SULLIVAN COUNTY, TENNESSEE and which was transferred to me by Thomas
McChesney by indenture dated 8th February 1815 and also three other tracts
lying in Washington County, Virginia conveyed to me by the said (Thomas)
McChesney by indenture bearing date 8th February 1815, subject to this
condition, that the said Thomas McChesney shall have and hold full possession of the said land during his natural life and after his decease
the said land to be equally divided among the said children and to them
and their heirs forever, etc.
    To my daughter, Peggy Craig's children - a tract of land on Yellow
Creek IN THE STATE OF KENTUCKY on which George W. Craig now lives, subject to this condition, that the said George W. Craig shall have and hold
possession of said land for his natural life and the life of his wife, the
said Peggy Craig, etc.

To the children of my daughter, Marianna, deceased, the tract of land on which Benjamin Pemberton now lives, which is divided from the land on which James Cowan now lives and hereinafter devised to Clarissa Cowan's children,etc

To my daughter, Clarissa Cowan's children, her husband, James Cowan - land, etc. - being part of the tract on which I now reside.

To James Gray, married to my granddaughter, Maria Teressa McConkey, the plantation on the river - called Christley Grubb's place, etc.

To Samuel McConkey, Salina McConkey, James Gray married to Maria Teressa McConkey, Peggy McConkey, Betsey McConkey, Merissa McConkey, Jane McConkey, Clarissa McConkey, and to the children of my grandson, John McConkey, etc.- for the natural life of my daughter, Jane McConkey or until the return of her husband, John McConkey Senior.

To David King a negro girl named Bett and her son, George, etc.

To the children of my daughter, Sally McChesney, deceased, my negro girl Susan and negro boy, Nathan, etc.

To George W. Craig, negro girl and boy, etc.

Other slaves are also given to all the other legatees already named above. Mentions again "MY SONS IN LAW" - David King, Iveson Longacre, George W. Craig Benjamin Pemberton, James Cowan and my daughter, Jane McConkey, $100.00 each.

Leaves legacies of varying amounts of money to the following:

Thomas McChesney, Thomas McConner, children of my daughter, Sally McChesney dec'd., John Sharp McConnell, Sally Merissa McConnell - son-in-law,.John McConkey, Joseph Early, John Sarp Early, Mary Anna Craig, Merrissa Pemberton, John Sharp Longacre, Samuel McConkey, etc.

Executors: son-in-law, Iveson Longacre and grandson, Jonathan King. Dated 2nd June 1823. Probated February Session 1824. Witnesses: Andrew Cowan, John Thomas, John Cowan.

NOTE BY CHH - The executors were required to post bond in the amount of $50,000.00. The Will was probated and recorded in SULLIVAN COUNTY, TENNESSEE 12 October 1824 by Richard Netherland, Clerk and a certified copy was recorded in Washington County, Virginia 21 December 1824 and Jonathan King, one of the executors named therein posted Bond in the amount of $8,000.00 with Thomas McChesney, Hugh Berry, and David King, his securities. Teste: Jacob Lynch, Deputy Clerk, Washington County, Virginia

Northumberland County, Virginia, Record Book 1726-1729, page 8 -

February 16, 1725/6 - Ordered by the court on the motion of John Bashford, son of Simon Bashford, dec'd. that George Ball and Samuel Heath, Justices that affidavits relating to the said John Bashford by the son and heir of Simon Bashford, formerly of WOOLWICH IN THE COUNTY OF KENT IN GREAT BRITAIN.

Ibid -

17 March 1725/6 - Deposition of Elizabeth Dameron, aged 75 years, that she knew Simon Bashford and Grace his wife very well and heard her husband Bartholomew Dameron, etc. said Simon Bashford had several letters from his home in England and sometime afterwards went home for England, etc. when he came back he said his father was dead before he got home. Also knows John Bashford, reputed son of Simon Bashford, was born in our neighborhood at my brother George Dameron's house. I heard John Bashford say he was legally married and when he brought his wife home I was at the wedding feast and the said Bashford had issue, two daughters, which I have seen, etc.

Northumberland County, Virginia, Record Book 1726-1729 -

Deposition of Bartholomew Dameron, aged 48, son of Bartholomew Dameron - much to the same effect as the preceeding paragraph, but also states he heard Simon Bashford say his father was in Woolwich and the sign of one of his houses was the three Daws - has also heard Simon Bashford say his father was a rope maker.

Ibid - page 9 -

Deposition of Dorothy Mahain, aged 70 years, - she knew Simon Bashford and Grace, his wife, and when he returned from England he brought goods and gowns for his wife and apparel for his two sons and that the eldest son was dead before he came home and she heard Simon say that when he was in England he lived in his own house with his mother-in-law.

Ibid -

Deposition of Samuel Mahain, aged 63 years, to same effect.

Ibid -

Deposition of Thomas Dameron, Jr., aged 43 years, remembers birth of John Bashford, son of Simon, in his (Dameron's) father's house - that he is now alive, married and hath two daughters now alive, named Judith and Elizabeth and that he hath heard Simon Bashford own the said John as his son, etc.

City of Richmond, Hustings Deeds #29, page 7 -

23 April 1830 - Indenture in which William Wirt and Elizabeth, his wife, OF CITY OF BALTIMORE AND STATE OF MARYLAND, sell to James Gray of City of Richmond, State of Virginia, for $5250.00, all that lot lying on Shockoe Hill in City of Richmond, between the tenement belonging to the Estate of William Price, dec'd and 6th Street which lot is designated in Young's Plan of the City as Lot #551 - which lot is the same conveyed to said William Wirt 4 April 1809 by deed from Alexander Stuart and wife of record in Superior Court of law for Henrico County, etc.

Culpeper County, Deed Book SS, page 268 -

30 December 1825 - Power of Attorney from John Carter of COUNTY OF MONTGOMERY, STATE OF TENNESSEE, formerly of Culpeper County, Virginia to Richard H. Field of said County of Culpeper to recover for him in his name any legacy or interest in the estate of my late father-in-law, Michael Klugh, dec'd and in the estate of Reuben Klugh, dec'd, in both of which estates I claim an interest having intermarried with Rachel, the daughter of said Michael and sister of said Reuben Klugh, etc. Recorded: 30 December 1825.

Ibid - page 276 -

19 December 1825 - Thomas S. Sims of THE CITY AND COUNTY OF NEW YORK,

Carpenter, gives Power of Attorney to Richard H. Field of Culpeper County, Virginia; Esquire, to recover all such sums of money, debts, rents, etc. as shall be due and payable to him. Acknowledged before William P. Hablett, A.N.P. in NEW YORK CITY the same date. Recorded in Culpeper County, Virginia 10 January 1826.

Culpeper County, Virginia, Will Book C, page 270 -

Will of Henry Field, Junior, dated 7 November 1785, probated 15 October 1787 - To my son, Daniel Field - 530 acres - and a negro and 550 acres of LAND IN KENTUCKY being 1/2 of Ambrose Coffins Tract of 1100 acres. To my son, Henry William S. Field, 1000 acres also 400 acres on Otter Creek in LINCOLN COUNTY (KENTUCKY) - 2 negroes. To my six daughters, Diana Field, Suze Field, Nancy Field, Elizabeth Field, Mary Field and Sarah Field, 1000 acres a piece, out of a tract of 19,015 acres of land located by Benjamin Field. To my daughter Elizabeth Field 300 pds Specie. To my daughter Nancy Delany - negroes. To daughter Molly Field - negroes. To my son George Field - negro. To my loving wife, Mary, for her natural life 300 acres in Culpeper County and then to my son, George Field. Sell 1000 acres out of my tract of 3400 acres in KENTUCKY on HUSTON'S FORK. Balance of my land IN KENTUCKY to my sons, Joseph, John, Thomas and George Field. (Note by CHH: By other records (page 314) some of the estate was in Fayette County, Kentucky). Executors: Daniel Field and Henry William S. Field.

Culpeper County, Virginia, Deed Book R, page 365 -

16 September 1793 - Power of Attorney from Daniel Field, Executor of Benjamin Roberts, dec'd to John Field, son of William Field to divide the land left by the said Benjamin Roberts IN THE DISTRICT OF KENTUCKY among the several legatees under the Will of said Benjamin, etc. Witness: R. B. Voss. Recorded the same day.

Pittsylvania County, Virginia, Deed Book 32, page 348 -

Frances Still of COUNTY OF MADISON, STATE OF ALABAMA by her attorney-in-fact, George Petty, gives a refunding Bond to James Still and George May, administrator of John Still, dec'd of late of Pittsylvania County, Virginia and receives as her legacy one negro woman, Kitty, valued at $350.00 and $316.49 cash as her proportionable share. Recorded: 18 April 1831.

Ibid -

STATE OF TENNESSEE, WILLIAMSON COUNTY, Anna Still of aforesaid county and state, relict and widow of Josiah Still, dec'd late of said county and state, now administratrix of said Josiah, dec'd and daughter of John Still, dec'd of Pittsylvania County, Virginia, appoint as her true and lawful attorney Joel H. Still of said county and state to receive her share of her father's estate in Pittsylvania County, Virginia. Recorded 18 April 1831.

Amelia County, Virginia, Deed Book 13, page 73 -

28 March 1774 - Indenture in which Richard Featherstone and Susanna, his wife, of GRANVILLE COUNTY (NORTH CAROLINA) sell to George Still of Amelia

County, Virginia - for 50 pds - all his parcel of land in Amelia County
on both sides of Seller Creek, containing 42 acres of land adjoining land
of Lew Clark, George Stell, Burrell Featherstone, Charles Hoel Featherstone, etc. Witnesses: Lewis Featherstone, William Featherstone, Lew
Clark. Recorded: 27 October 1774.

Amelia County, Virginia, Deed Book 20, page 106 -

24 March 1788 - Indenture in which Jesse Featherstone OF STATE OF NORTH
CAROLINA, COUNTY OF LINCOLN, and Richard Featherstone, Burrell Featherstone, Charles Featherstone, John Vaughn and Lucy, his wife, Lew Clark
and Elizabeth, his wife, and Jeremiah Stell of County of Amelia, State
of Virginia, of the one part sell to Peter Bland of the latter state and
county of the other part - for 124 pds 10 shillings - a tract of land in
County of Amelia containing 166 acres adjoining land of said Bland, Robert
Jones, Henry Clay (now William Featherstone's) on Leath's Creek, etc.
Witnesses: Edward Bland, Jr., Richard Dennis, Richard Pincham, William
Cabaness. Proved 25 September 1788. Recorded 27 August 1793. (NOTE BY
CHH: Ibid, page 109 - Same date, same parties of 1st part sell Richard
Dennis of Amelia County, Virginia for 70 pds 50 acres of land in Amelia
County, approximately same bounds)

Pittsylvania County, Virginia, Deed Book 32, page 318 -

(Not dated) - George Petty Senior of COUNTY OF MADISON AND STATE OF
ALABAMA, Attorney-in-fact for Frances Stell of the aforesaid County and
State - for natural love and affection which the said Frances Stell bears
towards her daughter Angeline Stell - gives and grants all the right,
title and interest the said Frances Stell in the dower of her mother in
the personal estate of John Stell, dec'd, late of Pittsylvania County,
Virginia. Witnesses: W. M. Ginn, James D.Patton, George Towne. Recorded:
21 March 1831.

Ibid - page 346 -

2 February 1831 - Power of Attorney from Frances Stell, late of County of
Pittsylvania, State of Virginia, but now residing in COUNTY OF MADISON IN
STATE OF ALABAMA - to her trusty friend, George Petty of said County of
MADISON, STATE OF ALABAMA, appointing him her true and lawful attorney to
act for her as one of the children and heirs at law of John Stell, late of
Pittsylvania County, dec'd - and to receive her portion of her father's
estate, etc. Recorded: 18 April 1831.

Bedford County, Virginia, Deed Book 21, page 452 -

13 August 1829 - Indenture in which Andrew Kerr and Susannah, his wife,
late Susanna Houck of GALUR COUNTY, STATE OF OHIO of one part sell to Simon
Sharpe of Bedford County, Virginia, of the other part - for $120.00 a tract
of land in Bedford County on Roaring Run containing 66 acres, being the
same land allotted to the said Susan by the name of Susan Houcke as part
of her portion of the real estate of the late George Kerns, dec'd, and
designated in the division of said Kerns land as lot #8, etc. Recorded:
August 14,1829. (NOTE BY CHH: 11 August 1829 - same parties of 1st part

sell Parham Arrington of Bedford County, Virginia another portion of
Susanna's land (Lot #3) bequeathed to her by George Kerns, dec'd (ibid
page 451) - containing 33 acres, etc.

Brunswick County, Virginia, Deed Book 18, page 149 -

20 October 1795 - Allen Jones of COUNTY OF NORTHAMPTON, STATE OF NORTH
CAROLINA sells to Daniel Huff of Brunswick County, Virginia for 412 pds
4 shillings a tract of land in Brunswick County, adjoining land of
William Gunn, Samuel Moseley, containing 677 acres, etc. Witnesses:
Benjamin Moody, William Huff, William Moody. Recorded: July 27, 1801.

Ibid - page 203 -

24 August 1801 - The Commonwealth of Virginia writes to Jonathan Adams
and John Coulter, Gentlemen Justices of the County Court of HANCOCK, STATE
OF _____ to secure the relinquishing of dower rights by Mary Huff,
wife of James Huff, of the COUNTY OF HANCOCK, STATE OF _____ who sold
land in Brunswick County, Virginia, 2 January 1800 to Thomas Bracy. Herbert
Hill, Clerk Brunswick County, Virginia. Recorded: January 25, 1802. (NOTE
BY CHH: There is a Hancock County in Georgia, Kentucky, Tennessee and West
Virginia, but the only Hancock County formed at this time (1801) was in
Georgia.)

Brunswick County, Virginia, Deed Book 22, page 63 -

November 12, 1811 - STATE OF SOUTH CAROLINA, GREENSVILLE DISTRICT - Power of
Attorney from Julius Huff of District and State aforesaid to Lewis Huff of
County of Brunswick, State of Virginia - to receive for him his part left to
him of the Estate of Samuel Moseley, dec'd, etc. Witnesses: James Tarrant,
Mackenzie Collins (both of S.C.) - Certified by Leonard Tarrant, Esq., Justice
of Peace, SOUTH CAROLINA, GREENSVILLE DISTRICT. Recorded: November 23, 1812.
(NOTE BY CHH: Brunswick County, Virginia Marriage Register, page 77 -
9 November 1793 - James Huff married to Rebecca Moseley, daughter of Samuel
Moseley, who is security.)

Russell County, Virginia, Deed Book 1, page 62 -

12 March 1787 - William Harrelson of Russell County, Commonwealth of Virginia,
in behalf of Elisha Nelson of THE STATE OF NORTH CAROLINA, who acts by a Power
of Attorney from the said Elisha Nelson, sells to Anjer (?) Price of said
County of Russell - for 105 pds - a tract of land containing 294 acres in
Russell County (formerly Washington County) on both sides of Sword's Mill
Creek, a branch of Cedar Creek on waters of Clinch River, which land was
granted said Nelson by patent dated 12 June 1785, etc. Signed by William
Harrelson. Witnesses: Richard Price, Frances Price, Joel Perrin. Recorded:
18 May 1789.

Ibid - page 64 -

2 September 1788 in which William Harrelson of _____COUNTY IN STATE
OF NORTH CAROLINA and Anne, his wife, sell Benjamin Johnson of Russell County,
Virginia - for 100 pds - a tract of land containing 296 acres in Russell
County on the north side of Clinch River on both sides of Dumps Creek - which

said land was granted to the said William Harrelson by patent dated
5 July 1785, etc. Signed and sealed by William Harrelson and Nanna (sic)
Harrelson. Witnesses: Richard Price, Frances Price, Joel Perrin.
Recorded: 19 May 1789.

Comment: I have reason to believe this is Caswell County, North Carolina
but more proof is needed.

Ibid, page 60 -

2 September 1788, in which William Harrelson of COUNTY OF _____ and
STATE OF NORTH CAROLINA and Anne, his wife, sell to Samuel Ewing of
Russell County, Commonwealth of Virginia - for 200 pds current money - a
tract of land known as Ewing's Choice containing 380 acres lying and be-
ing in Russell County, Virginia on both sides of the south fork of Cedar
Creek on the waters of Clinch River, adjoining Alexander McClanahan's
patent land - Thomas Hendrix (?) - which said land was granted to the said
William Harrelson from this Commonwealth of Virginia by patent dated
5 July 1785, etc. Signed and sealed by William Harrelson and "Nanna" (sic)
Harrelson. Witnesses: Richard Price, Frances Price, Joel Perrin.
Recorded: 19 May 1789.

Augusta County, Virginia, Deed book 7, page 203 -

28 August 1755 - Power of Attorney by John Carmichael of COUNTY OF ROWAN,
PROVINCE OF NORTH CAROLINA to his trusty and well beloved friend, William
Buchanan of Augusta County, Colony of Virginia, planter. To sell for him
a certain tract of land on north side of James River on the south fork,
between the surveys of Mr. Thomas Lewis and Mr. Richard Burton's tracts,
containing 100 acres of land which the said Carmichael had of James Patton,
Gent. in November 1751. Witnesses: James Goodfellow, Samuel Norwood.
Recorded: November 19, 1755.

(Note: Ibid, page 291-2 - William Buchanan, Attorney, sold above land
March 18, 1756, to William Burks of Augusta County.)

Augusta County, Virginia, Deed Book 1, page 440 -

17 November 1747 - John Moore of County of Augusta sells to Samuel Anderson
OF COUNTY OF CHESTER, PROVINCE OF PENNSYLVANIA, for five shillings lease,
thirty pds release, 304 acres, 3 roods and 15 perches of land in Augusta
County, adjoining land of George Anderson, etc. Witnesses: James Fulton,
James Glasgow, Robert Alexander. Recorded: 18 November 1747.

Augusta County, Virginia, Will Book 23, page 63 -

Will of Henry Miller of County of Rockingham, State of Virginia and now
AT LITTLE ROCK, TERRITORY OF ARKANSAS - dated 15 February 1836 and pro-
bated January Term 1840. My wife, Hannah Miller,(died in State of
Arkansas) - daughters Eliza Miller, Nancy McCullough, Martha Miller.
Son, Samuel Miller $200.00 as he is now in CITY OF PHILADELPHIA attending
medical lectures; sons, George C. Miller, Robert Grattan Miller, James
Henry Miller, William Miller and Henry Miller, $1000.00 each. Mentions

land he bought in HOT SPRINGS COUNTY IN TERRITORY OF ARKANSAS upon the
Washata River - my lands in SALINE COUNTY, MISSOURI - my house and lot in
TOWN OF FRANKLIN IN HOWARD COUNTY, MISSOURI. Mentions estate of my father,
Samuel Miller, dec'd - my brother William Miller of MISSOURI.

Augusta County, Virginia, Deed Book 37, page 101 -

27 March 1812 - George Moffett and Rebecca, his wife, of COUNTY OF FAYETTE
AND COMMONWEALTH OF KENTUCKY sell to Frances Gilkeson of County of Augusta,
Virginia - for $115.00 - one half of that tract of land in County of
Augusta, near the North Mountains which the said Rebecca Moffett, wife of
George Moffett, claims as heir at law of her deceased brother, Hugh
Gilkinson, etc. 27 March 1812 - Affidavit before Notary Public in TOWN
OF LEXINGTON, COUNTY OF FAYETTE, KENTUCKY. Recorded in Augusta County,
Virginia, April 28, 1812. (Note: Ibid, page 245 - 29 March 1812 - George
and Rebecca sell 270 acres of land in County of Augusta, Virginia which
formerly belonged to George Moffett, Sr., dec'd.)

Rockbridge County, Virginia, Deed Book 80, page 134 -

26 April 1893 - James Z. McChesney and L. J. his wife of KANAWHA COUNTY,
WEST VIRGINIA - Edward Lewis and Mary M. Lewis, his wife, and William C.
Campbell and Prudentia W., his wife, of ROANE COUNTY, WEST VIRGINIA, of one
part sell William Lee of Rockbridge County, Virginia for $3,000.00, a
certain tract of land in Rockbridge County which was conveyed to parties
of first part by J. K. Edmondson by deed dated March 16, 1889 being designated as No. 2, etc. containing 420-47/160 acres, etc. - affidavits by
notary publics of Kanawha County, West Virginia and Roane County, West Virginia. Recorded: May 15, 1893.

Virginia State Library Accession #22956 - (Photostat of original from the
    Collection in the Huntington Library)-

Will of John Markham of Stafford County, Virginia dated January 11, 1804,
Probated 13 February 1804 - To loving wife Jane Markham (for life or widowhood) Slaves, stock, furniture, etc. Sons, Allen Waller and James (underage)
my land, one-half to each, slaves, etc. My three children, Allen Waller,
James and Peggy (Margaret) Markham. To son, John Markham, slave. Another
legacy to my daughter Peggy Markham, slaves named Nat, Violet, Marrah, and
Fanny, when she is age 20 or marries. To daughter Elizabeth Boswell Kennedy
land and slaves - her husband (my son-in-law) Benjamin Kennedy. To son
Lewis Markham the use of my negro girl Esther now in his possession, the use
of my negro woman Judah and her children NOW IN THE STATE OF KENTUCKY in
possession of my son William Markham. To my son William Markham and to his
heirs I give and devise my negro woman named Silvia and nothing more, having
already given him an ample share of my estate. To my daughter Elizabeth
Oden, slaves. To my daughter Mary Markham, negroes. To my daughter Anne
Withers, negro. To my granddaughter Harriet Oden, slave. To my granddaughter
Mary Markham Oden, slave. Certain slaves and their increase to descend to
my first wife's children and their representatives. Executors: My friends
William Mountjoy and Charles Marshall and wife Jane Markham. Witnesses:
J. M. Daniel, Moses Pilcher, J. T. Ford.

Pittsylvania County, Virginia, Deed Book 48, page 311 -

20 April 1843 - Indenture in which James Snead and Frances, his wife, of
the County of CHARLES, STATE OF MISSOURI, give their power of attorney to
their friend John S. Duncan of LINCOLN COUNTY, STATE OF MISSOURI, to act,
receive, receipt for, etc. any property, real, personal or mixed which
may have been willed or devised to us as heirs, legatees or devisees of
our deceased father, Jacob Anderson, dec'd late of Pittsylvania County,
Virginia - and also to act for him as his attorney as heir legatee or
devisee of his deceased father, Evan or Evin Snead, late of Halifax
County, Virginia or willed to him by his mother, if dead, of Halifax
County, etc. Recorded: 18 May 1844. (Follows several affidavits from
County of Lincoln, Missouri.)

Pittsylvania County, Virginia, Deed Book 48, page 349 -

29 May 1844 - John S. Duncan, Attorney for James Snead and Frances, his
wife, formerly Frances Anderson, of the COUNTY OF LINCOLN AND STATE OF
MISSOURI, of one part, for $400.00, grants, conveys, etc. all the right,
title, claim, etc. of the said James Snead and Frances his wife in the
estate, both real and personal, of the late Jacob Anderson, dec'd who
was the father of the said Frances, and also all their interest, claims,
etc. in and to the dower estate of Frances Anderson, the widow of the
said Jacob Anderson, dec'd, etc. Recorded: 31 May 1844.

Marriage Bonds, Pittsylvania County (Microfilm) 1767-1862 page 52 -
January 22, 1812 - Jacob Anderson to Fanny (Frances) Green - Security,
Will Anderson.

Pittsylvania County, Virginia, Will Book 1 (1814-1845), page 13 -

Will of Thomas R. Edwards of COUNTY OF LINCOLN, STATE OF WEST TENNESSEE,
dated 23 April 1820. To my brother (in-law) Joshua Dodson, a negro boy
named Charles - and to my sisters Leathy Susannah and Jaine Dodson, a
negro girl named Ally - to be equally divided among the three last named
children. To my sister Leathy Dodson the feather bed I left with my
mother when I left Virginia. To my brother James Dodson all my right
and title to a tract of land in GRANVILLE COUNTY, NORTH CAROLINA claimed
by my father, Thomas Edwards, Dec'd. My executors to be my step-father
Martin Dodson and Stokley Slayden, both of Halifax County, Virginia.
Witnesses: Samuel Davis, John Rosan, M.D., James Garrett. Proved in
Lincoln County, Tennessee January Term 1821. Recorded: Pittsylvania
County, Virginia 17 September 1821. Executors Bond in amount of $2500.

Accession #22018 - original -

Gloucester County - Indenture dated 10 July 1702 in which William Black-
burn of the Parish of Abingdon and County of Gloucester in Virginia, Gent.
sells to William Smith of said Parish and County, Gent. - whereas Edward
Phelps of the BOROUGH EVESHAM IN THE COUNTY OF _____ IN THE KINGDOM OF
ENGLAND, Yeoman, dec'd and heir of Edward Phelps late of Yorke River in
York County in Virginia, Merchant, dec'd - by his deed of sale by date

4 October 1700 did sell to Mathew Grim (or Trim) of London, Mariner,
and to the said William Blackburn, party of these presents all that
tract of land situated in Yorke County - 250 acres - which was bought
and purchased by the said Edward Phelps dec'd, of Charles Allen of
New Poquosin in York County, planter, on or about the date 4 July 1672 -
(recites further that land should fall to the survivor William Blackburn or Mathew Trim (or Grim). Recorded York County July 24, 1702.
Sealed with red wax in which part of a coat of arms seal in the im-
pression can be made out. Witnesses: Daniel Smith, Thomas Chisman,Jr.,
Jon Baylor.

Washington County, Virginia, Deed Book 104, page 117 -

31 March 1923 - Ida W. McCesney (sic) (McChesney) is included in a list
of the heirs of Ida E. Keller, dec'd - her age is given as 45 and last
known address as ARCADIA, FLORIDA. Recorded 31 March 1923.

Washington County, Virginia, Deed Book 68, page 299 -

March 30, 1906 - Mary J. Gray, widow of R. E. Gray, dec'd, David S. Gray
and Emma J. Gray, his wife, Susan Katherine McChesney and D. W.
McChesney her husband, Bessie A. McChesney and C. H. McChesney her
husband, Julia Grace Anderson and L. M. Anderson her husband and Nelly
G. Hogshead and John S. Hogshead, her husband, parties of first part -
William F. Gray and Allie Gray his wife of second part - and R. M.
Gray and Lula C. Gray, his wife, of third part - whereas R. E. Gray
died seized and possessed of a tract of land containing about 265
acres in Hall's Bottom, Washington County, - leaving surviving him his
widow Mary J. Gray and the following heirs at law to whom said land
descended, the said R. E. Gray having died intestate, viz, David S.
Gray, Susan Katherine McChesney, Bessie A. McChesney, Julia Grace
Anderson, Nelly G. Hogshead, William F. Gray and R. M. Gray - and
whereas said parties have agreed said William F. Gray and R. M. Gray
shall have for their part of said farm a tract of 80 acres, etc. and
in consideration of said division of said farm parties of second part
convey to parties of first part all their right title and claim in and
to the residue of said farm, etc. - affidavits before notary public
follow which proves that Mary J. Gray, David S. Gray and Emma J. his
wife - Susan Katherine McChesney and D. W. McChesney her husband, Bessie
A. McChesney and C. H. McChesney her husband are living in SULLIVAN
COUNTY, TENNESSEE and that R. M. Gray and Lula C. Gray his wife are in
WASHINGTON COUNTY, VIRGINIA - William F. Gray and Allie Gray his wife
are in ANSON COUNTY, SOUTH CAROLINA, Julia Grace Anderson and L. M.
Anderson her husband in the COUNTY OF HAMILTON, STATE OF FLORIDA -
Nellie G. Hogshead and John S. Hogshead her husband are in the COUNTY
OF MENDOCINO, STATE OF CALIFORNIA. Recorded: 11 September 1906.
Comment: Refer to Marriage Register, 1st report, page 173, March 17,
1863 - Mary J. McChesney to Robert Emmett Gray (she daughter of Hugh
A. and Julia A. McChesney.)

Washington County, Virginia, Deed Book, page 243 -

June 5, 1908 - Deed of Release by Mrs. Susan E. Hobbs, widow to
D. W. McChesney, C. H. McChesney and Paul S. McChesney - for $1.00
of all her right, title, claim, etc. in a tract of land in Washington County containing 150 acres known as the "Well Place" which
descended and was inherited by said S. J. McChesney, W. L. Mc-
Chesney, Mary J. Gray and Susan E. Hobbs, from Hugh A. McChesney
and in settlement of said estate the property became the property
of said S. J. McChesney and his heirs - affidavit acknowledges her
signature signed by Susan E. Hobbs in DALLAS COUNTY, TEXAS. Recorded
16 June 1908.

Washington County, Virginia, Deed Book 33, page 82 -

December 2, 1875 - William A. Duckworth and Permelia H., his wife,
of COUNTY OF LIVINGSTON, STATE OF MISSOURI and sell to Thomas J.
McChesney of County of Washington, Virginia - for $100.00 - one-
third interest in a tract of land containing 109 acres which W.M.
Hickey, Jr. died seized, being the interest that descended to said
William A. Duckworth and Permelia, his wife, as the heirs of William
Hickey, Jr., dec'd and being one-third of one-third of said tract
containg 109 acres. Recorded: 26 February 1877.

Washington County, Virginia, Deed Book 31, page 302 -

Mary Jane Hickey of the STATE OF MISSOURI sells to Thomas J. McChesney
of Washington County, Virginia, for $100.00, her interest in land
of which William Hickey, the grandfather of the said Mary Jane died
seized being the interest that descended to said Mary Jane Hickey
as one of the heirs of the said William Hickey, Jr., dec'd, and
being one-third interest in 109 acres, etc. (Note: acknowledged by
Mary Jane Hickey before a Notary Public in COUNTY OF LIVINGSTON,
STATE OF MISSOURI.) Recorded: Washington County, 18 Nov. 1874.

King George County, Virginia, Wills Book #2, page 317 -

21 February 1794 - John, Archbishop of Canterbury, Premate of all
England, etc. sends greetings - We have found on 9th March 1803 at
LONDON the last Will and Testament and two codicils of Duncan
Campbell, Esq. formerly of the Adelphi in Parish of St. Martin in
the Fields in the County of Middlesex, but later of Wilmington in
County of Kent, dec'd - administration granted to John Campbell,Esq.
son of said deceased and to David Pitcairn, doctor of Physick, two
of the surviving executors named in said will, etc. Dugald Campbell,
Esq., the son also of said deceased and also William Mumford, Esq.
to be administrators also when they apply, etc.
    Will of Duncan Campbell of the Adelphia in Parish of St.Martin
in the Fields, in the liberty of Westminister in County of Middlesex,
Esquire - desires to be buried in his own vault in Hackney Churchyard where my late wife is interred.
    To my wife, Mary Campbell, yearly sum of 300 pounds to be paid

her in London in lieu of all dower and thirds, etc. to be paid out of his estate called Salt Spring situated and being in PARISH OF HANOVER IN COUNTY OF CORNWALL IN ISLAND OF JAMAICA - to my said wife for use of my eldest son Dugald Campbell - reversion to my son John Campbell, further reversion to son Duncan Campbell - to son Mumford Campbell - to son William Newell Campbell. My land called Brandshatch in Parish of Kingsdowne in County of Kent. (All sons under age of 21.)

My sons Dugald, John and Duncan are by my former wife and my sons Mumford and William Newell are by my present wife.

To my daughter, Henrietta, late the wife of Colin Campbell, for her natural life (means daughter-in-law) and to children of my said daughter, Henrietta by the said Colin Campbell her late husband.

To my daughter Mary, now wife of William Willox. To my daughter, Ann Campbell - to my daughter, Lannce Campbell - to my daughter, Elizabeth Campbell, - to my daughter, Mary Ann Campbell - to my daughter, Louisa Campbell.

Widow of my brother, Neil Campbell, deceased. My brother-in-law William Mumford, Esq. in County of Kent - settlement of my affairs in America.

Codicil. 3 February 1796 - Henrietta Campbell hath since departed this life - to children of my said daughter Henrietta by her late husband, Colin.

Codicil. 6 March 1797 - To my servant Ann Mills, widow, 15 pounds annually for life.

Probated 4 March 1803. Deceased died on 24th February 1803. Recorded in KING GEORGE COUNTY, VIRGINIA 1st December 1803 and produced in court by Lawrence Berry, one of the executors of John Rose, dec'd, late attorney in fact for said Campbell.

King George County marriages, page 3 - December 2, 1788 - Alexander Campbell to Lucy Fitzhugh.

Prince William County, Virginia, Deed Book R, page 154 -

3 March 1770 - Indenture in which Alexander Campbell and Daniel Campbell sometime merchants in Falmouth in King George County, Colony of Virginia, now merchants IN GLASGOW IN SCOTLAND OF GREAT BRITAIN, sell to William Champe, Gent., of said county and colony of Virginia (son and heir of Col. John Champe, dec'd) - for 12 pounds 18 shillings one lot or ½ acre of land in the Town of Dumfries in County of Prince William (#15), etc. Recorded: 6 August 1770.

Ibid, page 158 -

6 October 1768 in CITY OF GLASGOW - Power of Attorney from Alexander and Daniel Campbell, now of Glasgow, Scotland to Mr. William Carr, merchant in Dumfries, Prince William County, to handle the produce and profits of their several plantations, negroes, cattle, etc.

Prince William County, Virginia, Will Book C, page 107 -

5 November 1736 - Will of John Walker - leaves legacies to NEAREST OF KIN IN SCOTLAND - sets at liberty John Campbell, he not demanding freedom dues, 30 or 40 shillings of small goods out of my store to be delivered by my executors, etc.

Fauquier County, Virginia, Deed Book 13, page 351 -

6 March 1797 - Know ye that we Isaac and Susanna Cowper and James and
Mary Campbell OF THE TENNESSEE STATE - for 10 pds sell to James Adams
of County of Fauquier and State of Virginia all our right and title to
a certain tract of land in County of Fauquier now in possession of a
certain Phillip Thomas which was devised by Dr. John Harman to Susanna
Harman and Mary Harman before their marriage to Isaac Cowper and James
Campbell by their father. Witnesses: Oliver Dodson, James Carter
(signed in Hawkins County, Tennessee. Recorded in Fauquier County,
24 April 1797.)

Ibid, page 352 -

March 1797 - Mary Harmans, widow of Dr. John Harmans, since then inter-
marriage with William Carter, for ten pounds - right and title to land
to James Adams. Also certified to in HAWKINS COUNTY, TENNESSEE and
Recorded 24 April 1797.

Charlotte County, Virginia, Deed Book 13, page 161 -

25 October 1815 - Obediah Brumfield of COUNTY OF MONTGOMERY, STATE OF
TENNESSEE, sells to Carolus Featherston of Charlotte County, Virginia,
a tract of land in said County of Charlotte, containing 53 acres on
waters of Horsepen Creek - for $100.00 - bounded on lands of James
Arnold, William Mays, John Green, etc. Witnesses: Thomas Cox, William
Feathestone, Burwell Feathestone, Moses Eudailey. Recorded: 4 December
1815.

Frederick County, Virginia, Deed Book 11, page 357 -

30 March 1767 - For 5 shillings lease, 21 pounds release, Nicholas
Handsher of County of Frederick, Colony of Virginia - to Hugh Sidwell of
COUNTY OF CHESTER IN PROVINCE OF PENNSYLVANIA, a certain tract of land in
County of Frederick on drains of Opeckon Creek adjoining land of Giles
Chapman, containing 350 acres being part of a greater tract of land con-
taining 500 acres granted to Robert Brooke 9 Feb. 1737 recorded in
County Court of Orange, Va. and conveyed to said Nicholas Handsher 1739.
Witnesses: Thomas Wood, Richard Struman, Michael Lauberger, Richard
Boyce. Recorded: April 7, 1767.

Amelia County, Virginia, Deed Book 20, page 106 -

24 March 1788 - Jesse Featherston of COUNTY OF LINCOLN, STATE OF NORTH
CAROLINA - Richard Featherston, Burrell Featherston - Charles Featherston -
John Vaughn and Lucy his wife - Lew Clark and Elizabeth his wife and
Jeremiah Still of County of Amelia, Virginia - sell to Peter Bland of
latter County and State - for 124 pounds, 10 shillings, 166 acres, etc.
Recorded: 25 September 1788. (Note: Ibid, page 109 - same parties on
same day sell 50 acres to Richard Dennis.)

Chesterfield County, Virginia, Will Book 4, page 244 -

Will of Edward Archer dated 30 December 1789: Wife Mary, son William,
son Field Archer, tract of land whereon my father lived; son Edward
Archer, my lands in NELSON COUNTY, KENTUCKY on Beaverdam Creek a Branch
of Green River, 7 miles above the Long Falls and Town of Greensville,
equally divided among my three sons - William, Field and Edward. My lands
in Dinwiddie County, Lunenburg County, Halifax County to be sold. Executors: friends, Jesse Cogbill, George Markham, and George Robertson and my
three sons. Witnesses: C. Manlove, William Downman, John Archer.

Ibid, page 255 -

Will of Mary Archer (wife of Edward Archer) of Parish of Dale, dated
27 July 1790 - My three sons, William, Field and Edward Archer, daughter
Mary Archer, son William, Executor. Witnesses: Nathaniel Friends,
Benjamin Osborne, John Moseley.

Essex County, Virginia, Will Book #8, page 296 -

Will of Patrick Barclay of Virginia, merchant, NOW IN LONDON, dated in
London 16 May 1746, probated 19 July 1749. One-third of my estate to my
beloved wife, Elizabeth, and the remainder to my son, George Barclay.
Executors: Mr. William Bowden of London, Merchant, Benjamin Hubbard,
John Mitchelson and Andrew Barclay of Virginia, merchants. Witnesses:
George Riddell, Charles Dick, John Gusthart.

Prince George Deeds, etc. (part 2, page 322) -

Will of Randle Platt of Westover Parish, County of Prince George, dated
16 May 1718, 9 June 1719. To Nathaniel Corbett, son of Jone Corbett of
New Kent County, one negro girl. My plantation and seat of land upon
James River in Prince George County (being my now dwelling plantation)
to the said Nathaniel Corbett in fee simple if he attains to lawful age,
if not, all to be sold and given to my loving father, William Platt (if
then living.) To my loving friend Henry Holdercrost of New Kent County
20 pounds - he appointed my executor - all the balance of my estate to
my loving father William Platt of the Parish of Prescott IN THE TOWN OF
WHISTON IN COUNTY OF LANCASTER, KINGDOM OF GREAT BRITAIN - if he is
living - reversion to my loving brother James Platt, deceased - oldest
son (I think called William Platt) - Codicil, 23 April 1719 - also to
Nathaniel Corbett, son of Jone Corbett of New Kent County, my tract of
land in Surry County. Witnesses to will: William Troughton, James
Loften, Peter Finney, William More. Witness to Codicil: Fra. Hardyman,
Benjamin Foster, Thomas Eldridge.

Charles City County, Virginia, Court Orders 1672-1674, page 79 -

3 April 1673 - Judgment is granted Sampson Ellis, one of the legatees of Thomas Bridges, dec'd, Pltf. against John Pleasant, attorney

of Jane Janney and William Beauchamp OF LONDON, Executors of the last Will
of John Beauchamp, late of Virginia, dec'd, who was one of the executors
of the aforesaid Bridges, dec'd. The judgment was 333 lb. tobacco, a
third of a legacy of 1000 lb. tobacco bequeathed to the plantiff by
Bridges.

Nelson County, Virginia, Will Book E, page 21 -

Will of Rowland Edmunds of County of Nelson, State of Virginia, dated 14
January 1834, probated 26 September 1836. Legatees: son, Jefferson
Lewis Edmunds - slaves; son, James Nevil Edmunds, slaves. To the chil-
dren of my deceased daughter, Mary Ann Shelton, formerly the wife of
Samuel Shelton OF SOUTH CAROLINA - two negroes, Rose and Sarah, which
have already been delivered to their father. To daughter Elizabeth Lewis
Mays, wife of George S. Mays, slaves. To son-in-law George Vaughan, Jr.
and his wife, my daughter Polly Clough Vaughan - slaves. Executors:
friend Col. Alexander Brown and sons Jefferson L. Edmunds and James N.
Edmunds. Witnesses: William Jordan, Edmund W. Hill, Richard Phillips,
James W. Kieth. Executors Bond in amount of $14,000.

Old Rappahannock County Records (1656-64), page 231 -

Mr. Thomas James of PARISH OF STEPNEY, COUNTY OF MIDDLESEX ENGLAND,
Marriner, appeared before me, John Daniel, at my public dwelling in
LONDON - admitted and sworn in the presence of witnesses hereafter named
(and) personally appeared John Withey, citizen of London, Pa(inter-?) of
this City of London, etc. testified that the attestant did send over to
Virginia about the month of September 1659 by the said Thomas James in the
good ship called the Anthony of London, of which he is master - one servant
called Henry Martin to Augt Withey, the said attestant's son IN VIRGINIA
which said Augt Withey deceased there before the arrival of the said Thomas
James in Virginia. Therefore, he, the said Thomas James, did sell and dispose of the said servant called Henry Martyn and the said attestant upon
the arrival of the said Thomas James here in London did recover of him
full payment and satisfaction for the said servant and doth therefore
renounce all claim, right, title, etc. which he or Colonel Fauntleroy in
Virginia can, shall, or may have, etc. Signed: John Withey. Witnesses:
John Whithy, Wi_?_ Hopkins. (signed) James Daniel, notary Public.

Ibid, page 232 - 24 September 1659 -

John Withey, citizen and painter OF LONDON, etc. whereas Henry Martin, son
of Henry Martin of Parish of St. Andrew's, Holborne in the County of
Middlesex, coachman, hath by indenture being dated the 20th of this instant
month of September put himself apprentice unto me the said John Withey and
thereby hath consented to serve me or my assigns in Virginia for eight years
from his first arrival at Rappahannock River, etc. doth hereby assign unto
my son, Augt Withey of MANGORETTS (?) IN VIRGINIA, Gent., etc. - all the
service of the said Henry Martin, the younger, etc. for eight years.
(signed) John Withey. Witnesses: John Brundett, James Winders,
Recorded: 10 July 1662, Rappahannock County.

46

Old Rappahannock County, Virginia, page 377 -

(Power of Attorney - shattered and torn) dated _____1662 by V. Arnold of
BARBADOS - to Cuthbert Potter, etc. Witnesses: William ___?___ , Anthony
___?___. An instrument of writing signed by Cuthbert Potter dated July__
and recorded 26 August ____ witnessed by John Apleton cannot be deciphered.

Mecklenburg County, Virginia, Deed Book 5, page 484 -

1 September 1779 in which Mark Skelton of DISTRICT OF NINETY SIX IN SOUTH
CAROLINA, sells to Edward Walton of County of Mecklenburg, Virginia, for
450 pounds, a tract of land in the County of Mecklenburg containing 122
acres, on Butcher's Creek, etc. Witnesses: Richard Swepson, Jr., John
Swepson, Joseph Butler, Samuel Young, A. Robison. Recorded 13 September 1779.

Charlotte County, Deed Book 9, page 181a -

7 May 1802 in which Mary Hamlett, formerly Mary Brooke, of the County of
Charlotte - Isaac Skelton and Elizabeth his wife, formerly Elizabeth Brook,
of the County of Chesterfield, all of Virginia, and William MacQuay and
Sarah his wife, formerly Sarah Brook, OF THE STATE OF KENTUCKY, of one part
to Zachariah Brooke of the County of Charlotte, Virginia of the other part -
whereas a certain William Stokes by deed dated 1 March 1775 did convey to
Thomas Cobbs a tract of land on Williams Fork of Horsepen Creek in Charlotte
County, containing 704 acres, in trust for the use and behalf of Dudley
Brook for the term of his natural life and after his death to (revert) to
the said Elizabeth, Mary and Sarah and Zachariah, then infant children of
the said Dudley Brook, etc. Witnesses: William Clay, Reps Osborne, Henry
Overby, George Brook, Sarah Hutcherson, John McQuie, James Cheaney, Collier
Hutcherson, Thomas Cheaney, Thomas Read, Robert Morton for Isaac Skelton.

Mecklenburg County, Virginia, Deed Book 25, page 189 -

16 April 1830 - Whereas Powell Skelton, deceased, did by his last Will and
Testament, duly proven and recorded in the SHELBY COURT (KENTUCKY) CLERK'S
OFFICE - did devise his wife Elizabeth Skelton and his son William Skelton
the sum of $510.00, etc. - it being a legacy due to him, the said Powell
Skelton, from the estate of his grand(father) Samuel Wooten of Mecklenburg
County, Virginia. Therefore, we Elizabeth Skelton and William Skelton, etc.
appoint our friend Joseph Harrington of SHELBY COUNTY, KENTUCKY, our true
and lawful attorney in fact to demand and receive of Peter Bailey and Samuel
Wooten, Executors of the said estate of Samuel Wooten, deceased, the sum of
$512.00 so devised to us, etc. - There follows an affidavit to the above by
James Whitaker, clerk of court, for Shelby County, Kentucky to the clerk of
court of Mecklenburg County, Virginia to be by him recorded.

Granville County, North Carolina, Deed Book E, page 58-

1761 - William Moore of GRANVILLE COUNTY, NORTH CAROLINA wells to John
Williams Graves of HANOVER COUNTY IN COLONY OF VIRGINIA, 210 Acres on both
sides of Island Creek, etc. Witnesses: Henry Graves, William Graves, Benjamin Hendrick. In the same year (id, page 12) Zachariah Baker of Granville

County, North Carolina, sold William Graves 592 acres on both sides of
Grassy Creek called Spenmarrow. Witnesses: John Christmas, Henry Fagan.

Mecklenburg County, Virginia, Deed Book 3, page 48 -

November 12, 1770 - Mary Graves of Mecklenburg County, Virginia for love
and affection conveys to son, Elijah Graves of BUTE COUNTY, NORTH CAROLINA,
all that tract of land in which now lives, containing 175 acres, etc.
Witnesses: Jacob and John Royster, William Colbreath.

Louisa County, Virginia, Deed Book C, page 76 -

William Graves of GRANVILLE COUNTY, NORTH CAROLINA, Parish of St. John's
for 20 pounds - sells John Forsie, Jr. 431 acres on Beaverdam Creek on
the Albemarle County lines. Witnesses: Bartlett Ford, William Timberlake,
Samuel McGehee.

Grimes, North Carolina Wills and Administrations, page 273 -

Will of Frederick Jones written 9 April 1722, probated 26 March 1723,
PROVINCE OF NORTH CAROLINA - Eldest daughter, Jane, daughters Martha,
Rebecca - eldest son William Harding Jones - sons Frederick and Thomas -
brother Thomas Jones OF VIRGINIA, Gent. to make sale of and dispose of
all my lands lying in KING WILLIAM COUNTY IN VIRGINIA, commonly called
"Horns Quarter" - Brother Thomas Jones of Virginia, Gent. and my two
sons, Executors.

York County, Virginia, Deeds #4 (1729-40), page 451 -

14 November 1736 - Power of Attorney by Joseph Younger OF LONDON, Merchant
to Mr. John Thurston (Thruston) of Virginia, merchant, as his true and
lawful attorney. Witnesses: William Taylor, David Meriwether. Recorded:
20 June 1737.

Albemarle County, Virginia, Deed Book 7, page 526 -

4 September 1781 - Mosias Jones and Elizabeth, his wife, of the COUNTY OF
GREENBRIER (Now WEST VIRGINIA) sell John Moore of County of Albemarle,
Virginia, for 6000 pounds current money of Virginia, a tract of land con-
taining 188 acres in said County of Albemarle on both sides of Mooseman's
River, etc. Witnesses: Benjamin Stratton, Shelly Garrison, Mosias Jones,
Junior. Recorded: 8 November 1781.

Northern Neck Grants by Lord Fairfax, Book Q, page 343 -

14 September 1778 - Grant of 386 acres to Richard Johns and William
Deakens, Junior - both of MONTGOMERY COUNTY, MARYLAND, assignees of
Thomas Campbell, assignee of Achilles Foster - a tract of waste and un-
granted land on the drains of the Mason Spring Run and of Sleepy Creek in
Berkeley County.

Ibid, page 44 -

Grant of 279 acres to Casper Rinker of Frederick County - a tract of waste and ungranted land in HAMPSHIRE COUNTY (Now WEST VIRGINIA) on west side of Crooked Run near Reynolds Road - adjoining land of John Manzey, John Grunty. 18 September 1778.

Northern Neck Grants by Lord Fairfax, Book Q, page 345 -

Grant of 338 acres to Casper Rinker of Frederick County - tract of waste and ungranted land in HAMPSHIRE COUNTY - on Crooked Run adjoining lands of John Manzey, John Grunty. 19 September 1778.

Ibid, page 346 -

Grant of 275 acres to Mr. Cuthbert Bullitt of Prince William County - a tract of waste and ungranted land on Mill Creek on Drains of the South Branch in HAMPSHIRE COUNTY - adjoining Joseph Combs. 19 September 1778.

Ibid, page 347 -

Grant of 424 acres to Captain William Vause of HAMPSHIRE COUNTY (now WEST VIRGINIA) - assignee of Solomon Hedges - tract of waste and ungranted land on South Side of Pattersons Creek and the Manour in said County - adjoining land of Charles Linch - 25 September 1778.

Ibid, page 348 -

Grant of 213 acres to Mr. Humphrey Keyes of BERKELEY COUNTY - assignee of Samuel Pritchard, deceased - tract of waste and ungranted land on both sides of Tenecoat (?), a Branch of the North River of Great Creapehon in HAMPSHIRE COUNTY, survey by John Manzey. 1 October 1778. (Note: page 349, another grant to Humphrey Keyes of 1245 acres in Hampshire County. Page 350, 123 acres grant to Humphrey Keyes in Hampshire County.)

Ibid, Book S, page 78 -

Grant of 222 acres to Thomas Daubins of HAMPSHIRE COUNTY (now WEST VIRGINIA), assignee of Jacob Burkett - survey by Elias Poston - on waters of Cabbin Run, a branch of Petterson's Creek in County of Hampshire - adjoining Jos. Watson, Andrew Gregory. 16 August 1780.

Augusta County, Virginia, Will Book 39, page 244 -

21 September 1863 - We, the undersigned citizens of CHICKASAW COUNTY, STATE OF MISSISSIPPI - power of Attorney to Oliver Williams of same County and State and authority to proceed to VIRGINIA and to demand and take into his possession the following named negroes, to wit - one boy named Haywood who was in possession of Lt. T. W. Hale (or Hite) of Co. H, 11th Miss. - also one boy named Nathan, who was in possession of Thomas U. Gordon of same County and Regiment. These two boys were left at Staunton by one George Steele - also two other boys, to wit - one named Ben who was servant for Capt. J. H. Moore of Co. H, 11th Miss. and the other named Dick who was left there by William Moon of the same County and Regiment, etc. Signed Littleton Hill, Eli Gordon, Lewis Moore. Notarized by J. A. Longbride, Clerk of Probate Court of CHICKASAW COUNTY, STATE OF MISSISSIPPI. Recorded in Augusta County Clerk's Office October 7, 1863 by John A. Imboden, Clerk. Comment: This

record does not necessarily present a "migration link" but is of such interest it is included here, and before it becomes hidden among hundreds of other records again.

Augusta County, Virginia, Deed Book 59, page 177 -

10 November 1837 - In which Joshua Johnson and Jane his wife, and Moses Baker and Mary his wife, of COUNTY OF MONTGOMERY, STATE OF OHIO, of one part - and John McChesney of County of Augusta, State of Virginia. Witnesseth: whereas Samuel Kilpatrick, late of County of Augusta, by his last Will did devise to Peggy Cunningham and her children, which were six in number, all the residue of his estate, etc. (Will aforesaid being dated 25 January 1818) - and whereby the said Peggy Cunningham and her six children, of whom the above named Jane Johnson and Mark Baker are two of them, each became entitled to an undivided one seventh part of a tract of land containing 116 acres - etc. - and whereas the said Peggy Cunningham has departed this life intestate - sell said John McChesney for $65.00 the two undivided sixth(parts, also the undivided one seventh part, etc. Witnesses: J. W. Harker, Erasmus Harker. Notarized before J. W. Harker and John Anderson, Justices of the Peace of Montgomery County, Ohio. Recorded: Augusta County, January 15, 1838 by Jeff Kinney, Clerk.

Ibid, Deed Book 62, page 253 -

16 March 1841 - Susan Cunningham and Jackson Cunningham of COUNTY OF MONTGOMERY, STATE OF OHIO, of one part sell John McChesney of County of Augusta, State of Virginia for $60.00 - Whereas Samuel Kilpatrick, late of County of Augusta, State of Virginia, did by his last Will devise to Peggy Cunningham and her six children - all the residue of his estate (Will dated 25 January 1818) and said Susan and Jackson Cunningham are two of the children and entitled to an undivided one seventh part of a tract of land containing 116 acres - etc. - Witnesses: Hervey Copeland, J.P., George Swanke (both of Montgomery County, Ohio) - Certified by Edwin Smith, Clerk of Court of Montgomery County, Ohio. Recorded: Augusta County, October Term 1841 by Jefferson Kinney, Clerk.

Ibid, Deed Book 65, page 191 -

6 August 1842 - John Cunningham of MONTGOMERY COUNTY, STATE OF OHIO, sells to John McChesney of County of Augusta, State of Virginia for $25.00 a certain tract of land in County of Augusta on waters of Walker Creek, containing 10 acres - adjoining land of James Cunningham, etc. Certified before Isaac P. Foster, J.P. of Montgomery County, Ohio and Jacob Harry, J.P. Recorded: Augusta County February 26, 1845 by Jefferson Kinney, Clerk.

Virginia State Library Bible Records of the Ellis-Mahood Family, Petersburg, Virginia (1763-1870), Accession #24668a -

George Mahood (eldest son of Alexander and Jane Mahood) was born in LOUGHBRICKLAND COUNTY DOWN, IRELAND, on the 21 November 1798. George Mahood was married to Elizabeth Ellis (born January 16, 1801), fourth daughter of Ephraim (born August 2, 1765) and Jane (Heath) Ellis, (born December 15, 1763) on Thursday evening, July 12, 1821.

50

Essex County, Virginia, Deed Book 25 -

Deed of Mortgage 15 March 1750/1 John Livingston, Junior of St. Ann's Parish
in Essex County, to William Beverley of Beverley in COUNTY OF YORKSHIRE IN
KINGDOM OF GREAT BRITTAIN, Esq. - for 246-0-0 land in Essex, which said John
purchased of Phillip Edward Jones and Sarah his wife, and Edward Rowzee, Jr. -
also all land in Essex County excepting 300 acres he holds by his wife
Frances - Witnesses: Thomas Tunstall, Jr., John Tunstall, John Howell.
(Note by CHH: Sarah Jones was daughter of Salvatore Muscoe and Frances,
wife of John,Jr. was another daughter of Salvatore Muscoe and Frances.

Montgomery County, Virginia, Deed Book B, page 218 -

20 May 1790 - Whereas Thomas Ingles of COUNTY OF HAWKINS, STATE OF NORTH
CAROLINA (NOW TENNESSEE) - has heretofore sold John Taylor of County of
Montgomery, Virginia, a tract of land (part of Old Valley) containing 380
acres which lies in County of Wythe,appoints his trusty friend Adam Trigg
of County of Montgomery his lawful attorney to deliver in his name a good
and sufficient title in fee simple to said John Taylor - etc. Test: John
Grills, Charles Taylor. Recorded: Montgomery County, December Court 1795.

Montgomery County, Virginia, Deeds and Wills B, page 127 -

2 June 1788 - State of SOUTH CAROLINA, DISTRICT OF 96 - I, Patrick Calhoun
of the Long Canes in District and State aforesaid appoint John Montgomery,
Esq. of Montgomery County, State of Virginia (my true and trusty friend),
my lawful attorney and in my name to sell and dispose of one or two tracts
of land in County of Montgomery on a Branch of Reed Creek that heads in a
place called the Cove - one tract containing 322 acres, the other tract 159
acres - etc. Witnesses: Thomas Bride, Charles Deveraux, Joseph Montgomery.
Recorded: Montgomery County, 7 November 1787 (sic).

Ibid, page 207 -

5 May 1794 - John Grills, Senior, of the COUNTY OF KNOX AND TERRITORY SOUTH-
WEST OF OHIO appoints his loving son, John Grills, Jr. of County of Montgo-
mery, Virginia, his true and lawful attorney to make unto Adam Helvie or his
assigns a good and lawful right of a tract of land containing 444 acres in
County of Montgomery on both sides of the Falling Spring - into New River -
etc. Witnesses: Thomas Ingles, Lewis Tiner (?). Certified before Charles
McClung, Clerk of County of Knox, etc. Recorded: Montgomery County July
Court 1794.

Rockbridge County, Virginia, Will Book 2, page 303 -

26 May 1786 - SOUTH CAROLINA, CHARLESTON DISTRICT - By Charles Laning, Esq.-
Ordinary - Letter of Administration of George Neely, late of CHARLESTON,
Gentleman, deceased, to John Neely, Administrator, in which Henry Geddes,
John Gamble and James McBridge were ordered to appraise said estate.

Ibid, page 303 -

26 May 1786 - SOUTH CAROLINA, CHARLESTON DISTRICT - John Neely of CHARLESTON,

Shopkeeper, gives bond in amount of 2000 pounds sterling, with Henry
Geddes, Storekeeper and John Cunningham, Storekeeper (both of same place)
as his Securities to Administer estate of George Neely.

Greensville County, Virginia, Will Book 2, page 368 -

Will of Hezekiah Jordan of County of Greensville and State of Virginia,
dated 2 September 1811, probated 9 January 1815. My beloved wife, Mary
Jordan - loan of land and slaves for natural life or widowhood - "but if
my said wife shall prefer going to GEORGIA, then she to have 1/3 part."
My tract of land in GEORGIA to be equally divided between my two sons,
Benjamin S. and Abner Jordan after my wife takes her 1/3 part. (Both
Benjamin S. and Abner are under 18) - in event of wife and sons going to
GEORGIA, executor is to sell his lands in Greensville County, Virginia,
and his lands in NORTHAMPTON COUNTY, NORTH CAROLINA. $1000.00 to each
of my daughters to buy land in GEORGIA (under age of 18) - To my daughter
Jane Smith Jordan - To my daughter Mary Jordan - To daughter Hannah Dawson
Jordan - Executors, my wife Mary Jordan and Henry Smith, Jr. of Southampton
County, Virginia, and Henry Smith, Jr. of Northampton County, North
Carolina - and my son Benjamin S. Jordan (when he arrives to age 18) and
Daniel Mason of COUNTY OF HALIFAX, NORTH CAROLINA. Witnesses: John
Prichard, Samuel Johnson, Richard Crump, Solomon Smith, William Fennie.

Brunswick County, Virginia, Deed Book 13, page 57 -

25 November 1775 - In which James Dupree of PITT COUNTY, NORTH CAROLINA,
sells to Burwell Bass of Brunswick County, Virginia - for 60 pounds - a
tract of land in said County of Brunswick containing 50 acres - etc.
Witnesses: Aaron Atkinson, Anne Atkinson, Mary Atkinson. Recorded:
24 June 1776.

Surry County, Virginia, Deeds and Wills #11, page 242 -

Indenture dated 5 February 1782 - William Hargrave of HALIFAX COUNTY,
NORTH CAROLINA, sells Joshia Bailey of Sussex County in Virginia - for 50
pounds - a tract of land in Surry County, Virginia - adjoining land of
Hartwell Hargraves, Austin Hargraves and others being the piece of land
whereon the late William Hargrave deceased lived and died, containing 125
acres and one other tract of land adjoining, being the land the late
William Hargraves left of Joseph Hargraves, the Elder, containing 75 acres,
both parcels bequeath by Will of said late William Hargraves to his son
William Hargrave, first above mentioned - etc. Witnesses: John White,
John Hancock, William Lanier, Thomas Pretlow. Recorded: 23 April 1782.

Caroline County, Virginia, Deeds (1758-1845), page 11 -

3 January 1769 - In which Joseph Long of PROVINCE OF NORTH CAROLINA, sells
to John Miller of County of Caroline and Colony of Virginia - for 5 shillings - a certain tract of land in Parish of St. Mary's and County of
Caroline, Virginia, 133½ acres, being 1/3 part of a tract of land formerly
the property of Elizabeth Rennolds and then of her son, John Rennolds, and
willed by the said John Rennolds to his three sisters, Elizabeth, Mary and

Frances. The said Elizabeth being mother to the said Joseph Long, etc.
Witnesses: Robert Gilchrist, William Dickson, William Bogle, James Miller.
Recorded: 9 February 1769.

Caroline County, Virginia, Deeds (1758-1845), page 238 -

28 February 1842 - William S. Buckner and Caroline M. Buckner, wife of said
William of the COUNTY OF MONTGOMERY AND STATE OF KENTUCKY - for $800.00 -
in hand paid by Thomas Woodford of County and State aforesaid - sell all our
right, claim, title and interest which we have and each of us has in and to
about 65 or 70 slaves now in the possession of John Thornton of the County
of Caroline, State of Virginia - our interest being the one undivided eighth
part upon the death of the said John Thornton, he being entitled to a life
estate in the said slaves and which the one eighth part was devised to the
said Caroline M. Buckner by Jane Thornton, deceased, late of County of Carolin
Virginia - Acknowledged in Montgomery County, Kentucky Court at Mt. Sterling,
28 February 1842 before James Howard, Clerk.

Surry County, Virginia, Deeds, Orders, Wills (1671-1684), page 184 -

12 May 1678 - I, Mary Clutterbuck of the ISLAND OF BARBADOS in AMERICA, widow,
gives Power of Attorney to "my well beloved friend, Thomas Jordan of Virginia,
Gent." to receive of or from John Whiden, otherwise John Whitney of Virginia,
all debts, goods, etc. he is already or hereafter shall be due and owing, etc.
Witnesses: Ni: Meriwether, John Parrecke, John Watkins. Recorded 21 February
1678 (seal Red Wax.)

Henry County, Virginia, Deed Book 7, page 66 -

24 November 1806 - James Larimore and Caty his wife of STOKES COUNTY, STATE
OF NORTH CAROLINA, sell to Terry Hughes of Henry County, Virginia for 200
pounds - three tracts or parcels of land in County of Henry on the Mayo and
Marrowbone waters, containing 641 acres - first tract containing 210 acres
by patent being dated 1 October 1789. Second tract containing 220 acres by
patent dated 29 June 1793. Third tract containing 211 acres, etc. Recorded:
24 November 1806.

Halifax County, Virginia, Deed Book 12, page 205 -

27 April 1781 - Gideon Harrelson of CASWELL COUNTY, STATE OF NORTH CAROLINA,
sells to Drury Malone of County of Lunenburg, State of Virginia, for 6000
pounds current money of Virginia a certain tract of land in Halifax County,
Virginia on the North side of main Coleman's Creek - adjoining land of Col.
Peter Rogers', Col. Joseph Jones, Reuben Pickett, Alexander Harrelson - con-
taining 260 acres, etc. - Witnesses: Alexander Harrelson, Thomas Estes,
Peter Rogers. Certified 21 February 1782. Recorded: 21 June 1782.
Note by CHH - Caswell County was formed 1777 from Orange County, North
Carolina. Gideon Harrelson, son of John (D. 1765 Halifax Co., Va.) son of
Peter (D. 1733 Hanover County, Va.)

Halifax County, Virginia, Deed Book 16, page 344 -

20 February 1795 - Drury Malone, County of Halifax, Virginia, and Alexander
Harrelson of the COUNTY OF EDGEFIELD AND STATE OF SOUTH CAROLINA sell

William Collins of County of Halifax in Virginia - for 75 pounds, 11 shillings, 3 pence - a certain tract of land in Halifax County on the North
side of Coleman's Creek containing 100 acres - etc. Witnesses: William
Sams, Thomas Collins, George Collins. Recorded: 27 April 1795.

Halifax County, Virginia, Deed Book 18, page 179 -

30 November 1798 - Benjamin Stanfield of Halifax County, State of Virginia
sells to Lea Harrellson of PERSON COUNTY, STATE OF NORTH CAROLINA - for
100 pounds - a certain tract of land in County of Halifax on West side of
Lawson's Creek, etc. (No acreage given) - Witnesses: Alexander Cunningham, Robert Stanfield, Whit Holloway, William Murray, L. Ragland.
Recorded: 24 June 1799.

Orange County, Virginia, Deed Book 17, page 283 -

22 April 1784 - Thomas Walker, Jr. of Albemarle County, State of Virginia,
appoints Reuben Lindsay of said County and State, his true and lawful
attorney to collect all debts, legacies, etc. due to me IN THE STATE OF
PENNSYLVANIA. Also to receive all property that I may have a right to in
said state - and to pay all debts that are properly authenticated which
may be produced against me. Witnesses: William Moore, Joseph Hawkins,
George Nichols. Recorded: Same date.

Washington County, Virginia, Deed Book 1, page 332 -

15 January 1794 - John Sharp, Senior of COUNTY OF SULLIVAN and Territory
of U.S. SOUTH OF THE RIVER OHIO (TENNESSEE) - sells to Benjamin Sharp of
County of Lee, State of Virginia - for $2000.00 - 367 acres in County of
Washington, State of Virginia on Beaver Creek, a branch of Holstern River,
conveyed to said John Sharp from Edmund Pendleton by deed dated 6th January
1773, etc. Witnesses: William King, David King, John Sharp. Recorded:
18 March 1794. (Note: Same parties, same date - for $200.00 - 100 acres
same bounds, land granted said John Sharp by patent dated 6 June 1793.)

Washington County, Virginia Deed Book 5, page 157 -

17 November 1812 - Adam Ely of COUNTY OF FRANKLIN, IN INDIANA TERRITORY,
who acts by virtue of a Power of Attorney from Simon Ely recorded in
courts of FRANKLIN IN INDIANA TERRITORY and Washington County, State of
Virginia sells to George Lindemood of County of Washington, Virginia,
for $85.00 - two tracts of land in said County of Washington on waters of
Beaver Creek, one tract containing 61 acres, the other tract containing
17 acres. The said two tracts being part of 200 acres granted to Simon
Ely by patent dated 1 October 1800, etc. Recorded: Washington County
Court 17 November 1812.

Washington County, Virginia, Deed Book 7, page 286 -

15 November 1820 - James Reamy of COUNTY OF FLOYD, STATE OF KENTUCKY,
sells to George Hayton and Margaret Hayton, widow of John Hayton,
deceased - for $300.00 - a certain tract of land containing 90 acres in
County of Washington, Virginia, on North side of Middle Fork of Holstern

River - adjoining John Byars land, Nathaniel Harris, Jacob Wolf, Jacob Roman, etc. Recorded: Washington County, Virginia 19 December 1820.

Washington County, Deed Book 7, page 287 -

30 October 1820 - Benjamin Gray of COUNTY OF LIMESTONE, STATE OF ALABAMA, sells to John Goodson of County of Washington, State of Virginia - for $450.00 - a certain tract of land in Washington County on Beaver Creek, South of the Great Road, adjoining land on which said Goodson now lives - containing 50 acres - which land was devised by my deceased father, Joseph Gray, to me, etc. Witnesses: Joseph Gray, Matthias Grimes, Thomas Gray, Samuel E. Goodson. Recorded 19 December 1820.

Washington County, Virginia, Deed Book 3, page 86 -

29 September 1803 - Samuel McReynolds of BLOUNT COUNTY, STATE OF TENNESSEE, sells to William Remy of Washington County, State of Virginia for !"$12-1/3 dollars" - a certain tract of land in Washington County, Virginia on both sides of Anderson's Creek, a branch of Walker's Creek adjoining land of Halbert McClure, said Remy's line - containing 15 acres, etc. Witnesses: William Remy, Junior, John Remy, Daniel Remy. Recorded 18 October 1803.

Augusta County, Virginia, Executors and Administrators Bonds 1827-1837, (Micro-film - not indexed and not paged)

28 March 1832 - Lewis Wayland with Abraham Wayland, his Security, gives Bond in the sum of $1500.00 as Administrator of the Estate of Frederick Hammer, deceased. Recorded: March Term 1832, Augusta County, Virginia. David M. Perine, Register of Wills of BALTIMORE COUNTY, MARYLAND, certifies that by the records of his office, letters of administration of the Estate of Frederick Hammer, deceased, was granted unto Augustus Hammer and Laurence Thomson on 24th March 1818. Subscribed 24 February 1832. James Harwood, Presiding Justice of the Orphan's Court, CITY OF BALTIMORE, MARYLAND, certifies that the attestation by David M. Perine is in due form.

Ibid-

31 May 1832 - Lewis Wayland, with William Kinney, Jr., his Security, gives Bond in amount of $500.00 as administrator of Estate of Samuel McKean, deceased. Recorded: May Term 1832, Augusta County, Virginia.
David M. Perine, Registrar of Wills for BALTIMORE COUNTY, MARYLAND, on the 12 April 1832, certifies that by the records of his office, Letters of Administration of the Estate of Samuel McKean, deceased, granted to James Campbell. James Harwood, Presiding Justice of Orphan's Court of BALTIMORE COUNTY, MARYLAND, certifies to due form.

Augusta County, Virginia, Deed Book 129, page 190 -

10 October 1898 - Whereas R. A. McChesney, deceased, departed this life leaving to survive him his widow Amanda J. McChesney - Cara Mc(Chesney) Berry and R. A. Berry, her husband - and J. B. McChesney and Jennie, his wife, heirs-at-law - etc. - sell property for $790.00 in Village of

Middlebrook, lots 35 and 37, and parts of lots 61 and 62, etc. (Note:
J. B. McChesney and Jennie, his wife, acknowledge their act and deed in
COUNTY OF ADAIR, STATE OF MISSOURI 25 October 1898 and R. A. Berry and
Cara, his wife, in the COUNTY OF JEFFERSON, STATE OF ALABAMA 4 November
1898. Recorded: November 17, 1898.

Augusta County, Virginia, Deed Book 129, page 19 -

10 October 1882 - Jane A. Brown, Walter B. Clark and Eliza Pinking, his
wife, Benjamin C. Ivey and Adelia, his wife, of first part - ALL OF THE
PARISH OF RED RIVER IN THE STATE OF LOUISIANA - sell to R. A. McChesney
of Augusta County, State of Virginia - for $1.00 - all their right, title,
and interest in and to a certain lot of land lying east of the Village
of Middlebrook, County of Augusta, Virginia, containing 1/2 acre, it
being the same lot conveyed by deed from Jacob C. Hess and G. W. Hess and
wife to W. S. McChesney, R. A. McChesney and the heirs of John A. Brown,
deceased (D.B. 87, page 225) - said grantors interest in said lot being
the undivided 1/3 part. Acknowledged and certified before D. H. Hayes,
N.P. of Red River Parish, Louisiana 14 April 1883. In recording by
Clerk mentions they are the heirs of John A. Brown, deceased - to Dr.
R. A. McChesney. Recorded August 29, 1898.

Princess Anne County, Virginia, Deed Book #12, page 106 -

Indenture dated 24 December 1770 - In which James Gamewell of PASQUOTANK
COUNTY AND PROVINCE OF NORTH CAROLINA, sells to James King, Senior of
Princess Anne County, Colony of Virginia - for 25 pounds - a tract of land
containing 25 acres in County of Princess Anne on Pungo Ridge, adjoining
the said James King's other land and is the same land the said King sold
to the said James Gamewell sometime ago, etc. Witnesses: John Ackiss,
William Ackiss, Jonathan Whitehead, Phillip Fisher, William Mackie.
Recorded: January 1771.

Fluvanna County, Virginia, Deed Book 1, page 220 -

13 December 1785 - Indenture in which Joseph Fitzpatrick of Fluvanna
County as Attorney in full for William Fitzpatrick of STATE OF GEORGIA
of one part and Duncan McLaughlan of Fluvanna of the other part - for
28 pounds - sells a tract of land containing 150 acres patent land on
Middle Fork of Cunningham Creek in County of Fluvanna, it being the
tract of land which Joseph Fitzpatrick, deceased, deeded to his son
William Fitzpatrick, etc. Witnesses: Silvanus Bryant, Robert Wright,
Robert Allen. Recorded: December 7, 1786.

Ibid, page 125 -

17 April 1786 - In which Benjamin Fitzpatrick, Attorney for William
Fitzpatrick OF STATE OF GEORGIA, sells to John Depp of Powhatan County,
Virginia for 40 pounds, a tract of land in said County of Fluvanna, con-
taining 400 acres by patent, etc. Witnesses: William Barnett, Robert
Wright, Ezekiel Perkins, P. Napier. (Note by CHH - Other records reveal
"Greene County, Georgia".)

Albemarle County, Virginia, Deed Book 3, page 141 -

1762 - William Burns of PROVINCE OF NORTH CAROLINA sells to Joseph Fitzpatrick
of County of Albemarle, Parish of St. Anne, for 40 pounds, 180 acres of land
in County of Albemarle on head of Ivy Creek, etc. Witnesses: John Gillum,
Thomas Fitzpatrick, John Gay, Benjamin Fitzpatrick.

Register of Overwharton Parish, Stafford County, Virginia, by King, page 218 -

In 1790, Major John Lee was joined by Elizabeth, his wife, in conveying the
800 acre plantation of Captain John Lee in Stafford County to Susannah
(Crump) Hewitt (1723-1797), widow of James Hewitt of King George County.
In 1792 they (Major John Lee and Elizabeth, his wife) disposed of their real
estate in Orange County and moved to WOODFORD COUNTY, KENTUCKY. He was the
son of Hancock Lee, Jr. (1709-1762) and Mary Willis, his wife, who was the
eldest child of Colonel Henry Willis (ca 1690-1740) of Fredericksburg, Va.

Goochland County, Deed Book 17, page 209 -

12 April 1798 - Hubbard Furlong of the STATE OF SOUTH CAROLINA, COUNTY OF
ABBEVILLE (sic) sells to Martin Thacker of County of Goochland, Virginia -
for 36 pounds - 100 acres of land in County of Goochland, adjoining land of
Benjamin Thacker, Thomas Mitchell, John Hunter and Thomas Hodges, etc.
Witnesses: Francis Drake, Benjamin Hackney, John Williams. Recorded:
16 April 1798.

Madison County, Virginia, Deed Book 3, page 87 -

16 February 1801 - Tinsley Vernon of ROCKINGHAM COUNTY, STATE OF NORTH
CAROLINA, gives Power of Attorney to Richard Vernon of Madison County, Virginia, as his true and lawful attorney to sell his land in Madison County
to Joseph Field of said county. Recorded: 27 August 1801.

Madison County, Virginia, Deed Book 3, page 173 -

Anthony Vernon and Fanny, his wife, of the STATE OF KENTUCKY sell to Robert
Beale of County of Madison, State of Virginia for 442 pounds - all that tract
of land in Parish of Brumfield, County of Madison, Virginia, containing 221
acres, etc. Witnesses: Churchill Gibbs, Joseph Brock, Asa Graves, Richard
Cave. Recorded 22 April 1802.

Madison County, Virginia, Deed Book 6, page 340 -

10 December 1818 - Anthony Vernon and Frances, his wife, of HARDIN COUNTY,
STATE OF KENTUCKY, sell to Thomas Jackson of County of Madison, State of Virginia for $1100.00 - a tract of land in Madison County, Virginia, containing
95 acres - with exception of one acre of land laid off to Arnold for his mill
dam. Affidavits from Justices of Hardin County, Kentucky certifying signature
Recorded: Madison County, Virginia, 11 February 1819.

Madison County, Virginia, Deed Book 1, page 14 -

26 September 1793 - Power of Attorney from Richard Vernon of County of Madison

State of Virginia - being old and infirm and cannot of course go and see
to the surveying of land in the COUNTY OF STOKES, STATE OF NORTH CAROLINA -
appoints his friends John Vawter and Anthony Dearry his lawful attorney.
Recorded same date.

Madison County, Virginia, Deed Book 1, page 14 -

26 September 1793 - Power of Attorney from Richard Vernon of Madison
County, Virginia, appointing his trusty friend and nephew, Richard Vernon
of GUILFORD COUNTY, NORTH CAROLINA, his lawful attorney to sell two small
tracts of land in said county and state containing 400 acres. Recorded
same date.

Madison County, Deed Book 1, page 152 -

7 October 1794 - Richard Vernon of County of Madison, State of Virginia,
appoints his trusty friends - Benjamin Quinn, Weeden Sleet (?) and William
Quinn of SCOTT COUNTY, STATE OF KENTUCKY, his lawful attorney to settle
all his business of whatever kind it may be in the western country.
Recorded 23 December 1794.

Madison County, Virginia, Deed Book 2, page 34 -

(Not dated) - Order by Commonwealth of Virginia to Justices of COUNTY OF
SCOTT, STATE OF KENTUCKY, to obtain a relinquishment of dower rights from
Frances Vernon, wife of Anthony Vernon of this county and state to property sold by said Anthony Vernon in Madison County, State of Virginia, to
Samuel Smith, being 1/3 part of a tract of land which Thomas Quinn devised
to his three children in County of Culpeper, now Madison, Virginia, etc.
(Returned by Justices 22 August 1796, with the indenture of sale as
annexed) Viz:
_____1796 - Anthony Vernon and Frances, his wife, of STATE OF KENTUCKY,
sell to Samuel Smith of County of Madison, State of Virginia, etc. -
and whereas Thomas Quinn in his life time was possessed of a tract of land
in County of Culpeper, now called Madison County, being given to him by his
father and bounded by the Rapidan River on one side, and by his brother John
Quinn on the upper side and Captain Benjamin Cave on the lower side and
which land the said Thomas Quinn devised to his three children - and the
land never having been divided and the said Anthony having intermarried with
Frances, one of the children, etc. - for 185 pounds their 1/3 part of
above mentioned land, formerly the property of Thomas Quinn, etc., certified
before Justices of SCOTT COUNTY, KENTUCKY, 23 August 1796. Recorded:
Madison County, Virginia, 26 January 1797.

Madison County, Virginia, Deed Book 2, page 252 -

31 October 1798 - Anthony Vernon and Fanny, his wife, of COUNTY OF HARDIN,
STATE OF KENTUCKY, sell to Henry Rennolds of County of Madison, State of
Virginia, for 90 pounds - a tract of land in said county of Madison - con-
taining 55 acres, etc. Witnesses: Tinsley Vernon, Taylor Lindsay, Joshua
Lindsay, John Rennolds. Recorded: 27 December 1798.

Spotsylvania County, Virginia, Records by Crozier - Deed Book A, page 93 -

May 6, 1724 - John Hannis and Catherine, his wife, late of THE ISLAND OF
BARBADOES, and now of Essex County, Virginia, sell to Robert Beverley of
Essex County - for 60 pounds sterling - 1000 acres of land in Spotsylvania
County, etc. Witnesses: Benjamin Robinson, Archibald McPherson, Nicholas
Davis. Recorded: October 6, 1724.

Ibid - Deed Book A, page 96 -

11 July 1722 - A proclamation by Governor Alexander Spotswood naturalizing
Jacob Haltxclow, a native of NASSAAC SIEGEN in GERMANY - having settled and
inhabited for several years in the County of Stafford. Dated at Williamsburg, Virginia.

Ibid - Deed Book A, page 97 -

December 21, 1725 - Alexander Spotswood of the County of Spotsylvania, but
now residing in LONDON, Esquire, and John Grame OF THE PARISH OF ST. JAMES,
CLERKENWELL, IN THE COUNTY OF MIDDLESEX (ENGLAND), Gent., and John Mackmath
of the PARISH OF ST. MARY'S AT ROTHERHETH IN THE COUNTY OF SURRY (ENGLAND),
Gent.- The said Spotswood for and in consideration of the said John Grame's
removing with his family to VIRGINIA to take the care and management of the
said Spotswood's estate and effects in the colony - two plantations called
Bear Quarter and Wild Cat Quarter, near Germanna on the Wild Cat Run, otherwise the Flatt Run in Spotsylvania County. These estates to John Grame
during his natural life and then to his wife, Katherine Grame; at her decease
to go to John Macmath, etc. Witnesses: Benjamin Graves, John Macmath, John
Dunlop. Recorded: May 11, 1726.

Ibid - Deed Book A, page 102 -

March 5, 1727 - Thomas Tyler of St. George Parish, Spotsylvania County, sells
to Charles Tyler OF GREAT BRITAIN, IN SALLOP COUNTY AND HOPTON WAFTER PARISH
for 80 pounds sterling - 500 acres of land in St. George Parish, Spotsylvania
County, patented by the said Thomas Tyler, June 30, 1726, etc. Witnesses:
William Johnson, Thomas Chew. Recorded: March 5, 1727/8.

Ibid - Deed Book A, page 106 -

April 12, 1729 - John Mulkey, cooper, of St. George Parish, Spotsylvania
County, sells to Joseph Cottman of SOMERSET COUNTY, MARYLAND, for 30 pounds
current money - 1000 acres of land in St. George Parish, Spotsylvania County.
Witnesses: William Johnson, John Robinson, Joseph Parker. Recorded:
April 2, 1729 and Sarah, wife of John Mulkey, relinquished her right of dower
by her attorney, John Waller.

Ibid - Deed Book A, page 109 -

August 18, 1729 - Sylvanua Pumphary, late of THE PROVENCE OF MARYLAND, now
in the Colony of Virginia, sells to William Russell, one negro slave named
Ceaser (sic) for value received. Witnesses: Nathan Pumphary, Edward Teals.
Recorded: September 15, 1729.

Spotsylvania County, Virginia, Records by Crozier - Deed Book A, page 109 -

December 2, 1729 - John Thompson of St. Peter's Parish, New Kent County, Virginia, planter, sells to Benjamin Cottman of STEPENEY PARISH, SOMERSET COUNTY, PROVINCE OF MARYLAND - for 9 pounds 10 shillings - 100 acres of land in St. George Parish, Spotsylvania County, patented by one James Cannon and conveyed to said Thomson. Witnesses: Lewis Davis Yancey, G. Home. Recorded: December 2, 1729.

Ibid - Deed Book B, page 115 -

October 7, 1730 - Henry Willis and John Waller, Gent., Feoffees and Trustees for the Town of Fredericksburg, sell to John Williams of THE CITY OF BRISTOL (ENGLAND), mariner - for 2 pounds 15 shillings, Lots #49 and 52. Witnesses: J. Mercer, John Waller, Jr. Recorded: same date.

Ibid - Deed B, page 126 -

August 8, 1733 - Thomas Jackson and Margaret, his wife, of St. Marks Parish, Spotsylvania County, sell to William Crosthwait late OF THE PROVINCE OF PENNSYLVANIA, but now of the Parish and County aforesaid for 50 pounds - 100 acres of land whereon said Crosthwait now lives, etc. Witnesses: John Red, Henry Downs, John Scelton (sic). Recorded: same date. (Note by CHH: Deed Book C, a deed dated April 25, 1738 proves that William Crosthwait had removed to Orange County, Virginia.)

Ibid - Deed Book C, page 146 -

January 27, 1737 - Thomas Grayson of DEAL, IN KENT (ENGLAND) eldest son of John Grayson of Spotsylvania County, Colony of Virginia, lately deceased, sells to Thomas Turner of King George County, Gent., for 250 pounds sterling, 500 acres of land in Spotsylvania County, etc. Witnesses: James Hume, John Graham, John Moncure, Ignats (sic) Semmes, Peter Simms, Henry Donaldson, John Bean. Recorded: July 4, 1738.

Ibid - Deed Book C, page 147 -

March 19, 1738 - John Hobson OF CHARLES COUNTY, PROVINCE OF MARYLAND, sells to Griffin Fautleroy of St. Stephens Parish, Northumberland County, Virginia, Gent., for 20 pounds, 400 acres of land at head of River Ta in Spotsylvania County, formerly granted Daniel Brown of Spotsylvania County by patent dated February 24, 1730. Witnesses: William Johnston, John Waller, A. Foster, Edmund Waller, Benjamin Waller. Recorded: April 3, 1739.

Ibid - Deed Book D, page 162 -

January 26, 1742 - Nathaniel Sanders of NORTHAMPTON COUNTY IN NORTH CAROLINA, gives Bond to Robert Coleman of Spotsylvania County, Virginia - the said Nathaniel Sanders had 400 acres of land in Spotsylvania County left him by his deceased father, Nathaniel Sanders, etc. Witnesses: John Wynell Sanders, George Chapman. Recorded: June 7, 1743.

Spotsylvania County, Virginia, Records by Crozier, Deed Book D, page 178 -

November 6, 1748 - Henry Chew, late of CALVERT COUNTY, MARYLAND, makes a Deed
of Gift to his daughter, Jane Chew "for and in consideration of her going TO
NORTH CAROLINA with me" - of 3 negroes and 2,000 pounds sterling. Witnesses:
Larkin Chew, Joseph Brock, John Spooner, Patrick Cary. Recorded: Dec. 6,1748

Ibid, Deed Book D, page 185 -

January 31, 1750 - Samuel Kennerly of OVER, IN THE COUNTY OF CHESTER, joiner,
eldest son and heir of Samuel Kennerly, late of St. Marks Parish, Orange
County, Virginia, joiner, deceased, gives his power of attorney to Frances
Thornton of Caroline County, Rappahannock River in Virginia, Gent. Witnesses:
Thomas Word, William Quinney. Recorded: May 7, 1751. (Comment by CHH:
Parties interested in the above individuals will have to research to determine
the location of the County of Chester.)

Ibid, Deed Book D, page 186 -

March 3, 1750 - Jean Morison, IN THE SHIRE OF ABERDEEN, NORTH BRITAIN, lawful
daughter to the deceased John Morison, merchant in Stone haven. Procreate(sic
betwixt him and Patience Wallace, his spouse, who was the only surviving siste
of the deceased David Wallace, planter, on James River, Virginia. Power of
Attorney to Captain John Thomson, Commander of the ship Anne, OF ABERDEEN.
This Power of Attorney mentions Colonel Thomas Turner of King George County,
etc. Witnesses: George Trail, Alexander Morison, Andrew Thomson. Acknowledg
before Alexander Robertson, Esq. Provost OF THE CITY OF ABERDEEN, March 14,
1750. Recorded: Spotsylvania County, Virginia, September 3, 1751.

Ibid, Deed Book D, page 186 -

March 1, 1750/1 - Margaret Black, alias Allan, widow of the deceased James
Allan, merchant, in and late Baillie of HAMILTON, and mother of John Allan,
merchant, in HAMILTON, eldest lawful son of the deceased James Allan, thereafter of Spotsylvania County, Virginia, deceased - Whereas said John Allan
of Spotsylvania County, Virginia, merchant, deceased, did by his Will devise
to his mother, the said Margaret Black alias Allan, 400 pounds sterling, etc.
The said Margaret Black alias Allan, gives her Power of Attorney to Samuel
Ritchie, Archibald Ritchie and John Miller of Essex County, Virginia, merchants. Witnesses: James Allan, Gaven Roger, William Williamson. Recorded:
September 3, 1751.

Ibid, Deed Book D, page 186 -

March 1, 1750/1 - Sarah Black, Residenter in HAMILTON, aunt of John Allen,
Merchant in HAMILTON, eldest lawful son of the deceased James Allan, mer-
chant in and late Baillie of HAMILTON, thereafter of Spotsylvania County,
Virginia, now also deceased. Whereas said John Allan, by his last will de-
vised certain legacies to his said aunt, Sarah Black. Power of Attorney to
Samuel Ritchie, Archibald Ritchie and John Miller of Essex County, Virginia,
merchants. Witnesses: James Allan, Gaven Roger, William Williamson.
Recorded: September 3, 1751.

Spotsylvania County, Virginia, Records by Crozier, Deed Book D, page 186 -

1 March 1750/1 - Christian Allan, daughter lawful of the deceased James
Allan, merchant, in and late Baillie OF HAMILTON, and sister German of
John Allan, merchant in HAMILTON, eldest lawful son of the deceased James
Allan, thereafter of Spotsylvania County in Virginia. Power of Attorney
to Samuel Ritchie, Archibald Ritchie and John Miller of Essex County in
Virginia, merchants. Witnesses: James Allan, Gaven Roger, William William-
son. Recorded: September 3, 1751.

Ibid - Deed Book E, page 191 -

August 4, 1752 - John Lea and Anne, his wife, of ORANGE COUNTY, NORTH
CAROLINA, sell to Thomas McNeal of St. George Parish, Spotsylvania
County, Virginia, for 24 pounds - 185 acres of land whereon said McNeal
now dwells, it being formerly a patent granted George Carter and given by
said Carter to the said John Lea, his son-in-law, by Deed of Gift, etc.
No witnesses. Recorded: August 4, 1752.

Ibid - Deed Book E, page 199 -

November 16, 1754 - John Williams and Jane, his wife and William Williams
of GRANVILLE COUNTY, PROVINCE OF NORTH CAROLINA, sell to Charles Kennedy
of Hanover County, Virginia for 21 pounds - 100 acres of land in Spotsylvania County conveyed by Ralph Williams to the aforesaid William Williams
and by him conveyed to the aforesaid John Williams. Witnesses: John
Woolfolk, James Wiglesworth, James Crawford, William Davenport. Recorded:
June 3, 1755.

Ibid - Deed Book E, page 203 -

April 29, 1756 - Henry Willis, Gent. of Spotsylvania County, Virginia, sells
to Peter How, Esquire, of WHITEHAVEN IN THE KINGDOM OF GREAT BRITAIN, a
negro slave for 74 pounds 10 shillings 3½ pence. Witnesses: Charles Yates,
William Steward. Recorded: December 7, 1756.

Ibid - Deed Book E, page 205 -

June 11, 1757 - James Tennent of WHITEHAVEN, CUMBERLAND COUNTY (ENGLAND),
Mason, and Elizabeth, his wife - which said Elizabeth is the only sister
living of William Russell, late OF PHILADELPHIA, merchant, deceased - give
their Power of Attorney to William Bragg of Whitehaven aforesaid. Witnesses: Christopher Wilson, Joseph Collin. Recorded October 4, 1757

James Tennant, of WHITEHAVEN, CUMBERLAND COUNTY, Mason, and Elizabeth,
his wife, revoke a former Power of Attorney given to Samuel Bowman, Thomas
Price and Phillip Walker, having decided to send their friend, William
Bragg of Whitehaven aforesaid, to PHILADELPHIA to see as to the Will of
William Russell, late of Philadelphia, deceased. Dated June 11, 1757.
Recorded: October 4, 1757.

Spotsylvania County, Virginia, Records by Crozier, Deed Book E, page 208 -

July 6, 1758 - Fielding Lewis, Esqr. and Betty, his wife, of Fredericksburg sell to Alexander Kennedy, late OF PHILADELPHIA, PENNSYLVANIA, mariner, for 185 pounds - two lots in the Town of Fredericksburg. Witnesses: Charles Dick, William Scott, Daniel Sturges. Recorded: July 5, 1758.

Ibid - Deed Book E, page 209 -

February 3, 1759 - Joseph Hannes OF THE PROVINCE OF NORTH CAROLINA, Gent., to William Waller of Spotsylvania County, Virginia, Gent., - whereas a decree of the Court of Chancery, April 13, 1758, in a suit pending between Joseph Hannes, Plaintiff vs William Waller and Ann, his wife, and Harry Beverley, Gent., Defendants, etc. - mentions slaves and sale and lease of lands, etc. - Also principal of a debt due from Joseph Hannes, deceased (father of the said Joseph, party to these presents) to Robert Beverley, deceased, father to the said Harry, a party to these presents, etc., of 181 pounds, 8 shillings, 4 pence sterling, etc. Witnesses: James Mills, John Waller, William Wood. Recorded: February 6, 1759.

Ibid - Deed Book E, page 209 -

September 14, 1758 - Sarah Hicks of WHITEHAVEN, IN CUMBERLAND COUNTY, executrix of the late William Hicks, Esqr. of the Town and County aforesaid, gives a Power of Attorney to Colonel John Carlyle of Alexandria, Fairfax County, Virginia, merchant, to receive from Jeremiah Aderton of Chicamaxen, IN THE PROVINCE OF MARYLAND, etc. Witnesses: Thomas Benson, Deckar Thompson Recorded: February 6, 1759. (Note by CHH: Whitehaven is a seaport town in the County of Cumberland in England, on the Irish sea near the entrance to Solway Firth.)

Ibid - Deed Book E, page 210 -

January 8, 1759 - James Collins OF NORTH CAROLINA, eldest son and heir-at-law of Joseph Collins, late of Spotsylvania County, Virginia, deceased, sells to Thomas Collins for 20 pounds his interest in the landed estate of the said Joseph Collins, deceased. Witnesses: William Collins, John Collins, Ann Collins. Recorded: May 1, 1759.

Ibid - Deed Book E, page 211 -

October 1, 1759 - George Nelson, Esqr., Alderman of London, in GREAT BRITAIN and Mary, his wife, and Latham Arnold and John Maynard, of London, merchants, sell to Thomas Coleman of Spotsylvania County, Virginia 1395 acres in Spotsylvania County, Virginia - whereas Humphrey Bell, late of CLAPHAM, IN SURRY COUNTY (ENGLAND) and of OLD SWANLANE, IN THE CITY OF LONDON, Merchant, by his last Will and Testament dated February 12, 1757, recorded in Prerogative Court of Canterbury, and thereby did leave his property IN VIRGINIA to the said Nelson, Arnold and Maynard, in trust for purposes stated in said Will and whereas by Deeds dated April 19, 1757 recorded in KING WILLIAM COUNTY (Virginia) the said Bell did convey to said Arnold and Maynard his lands and plantations, etc. in KING WILLIAM; KING & QUEEN; CAROLINE; and SPOTSYLVANIA COUNTIES in Virginia, in trust to sell, convey, etc. Recorded: October 1, 1759.

Spotsylvania County, Virginia, Records by Crozier, Deed Book E, page 212 -

October 1, 1759 - the same parties (see preceding paragraph) also ratify
and convey other property of Humphrey Bell to:

1. Daniel Trigg of Spotsylvania County 500 acres
2. Robert Coleman of Spotsylvania County 2680 acres
3. Thomas McNeil of Spotsylvania County 141 acres
4. John Roan of Essex County 1075 acres

Ibid - Deed Book E, page 222 -

May 14, 1761 - Benjamin Smith, Miles Brenton, Thomas Middleton and Samuel
Brailsford of CHARLESTOWN, PROVINCE OF SOUTH CAROLINA, give a Power of
Attorney to John Champe and James Hunter of Virginia. Witnesses: William
Lowe, Thomas Etherington. Recorded: July 7, 1761.

Ibid - Deed Book E, page 222 -

May __, 1761 - Samuel Wragg, surviving co-partner of Joseph Wragg, Jr.,
of the PROVINCE OF SOUTH CAROLINA gives a Power of Attorney to James
Hunter of Fredericksburg, Virginia. Witnesses: Thomas Etherington,
John Wragg. Recorded: July 1, 1761.

Ibid - Deed Book F, page 225 -

September 8, 1761 - James Compton of SOHO SQUARE, CITY OF LONDON, GREAT
BRITAIN; now in Virginia, Esquire - gives a Power of Attorney to Fielding
Lewis of Fredericksburg, Virginia, Esquire - mentions a tract of 10,000
acres in Culpeper County granted the said Compton by Hon. Thomas, Lord
Fairfax and also that Compton intends leaving the colony. Witnesses:
Charles Dick, William Scott, John Marshall. Recorded: October 5, 1761.

Ibid - Deed Book F, page 238 -

October 1, 1764 - Roger Dixon of Fredericksburg, merchant, and Lucy, his
wife, sell to William Thompson of LONDON, mariner, Captain of the Ship,
John & Presley - for 25 pounds - Lot #251 in the town of Fredericksburg,
etc. No witnesses. Recorded: October 1, 1764.

Ibid - Deed Book F, page 238 -

September 3, 1764 - Roger Dixon of Fredericksburg, merchant, and Lucy,
his wife, sell to Captain Thomas Dixon OF THE CITY OF BRISTOL, GREAT
BRITAIN, Mariner, for 25 pounds - Lot #234 in town of Fredericksburg. No
witnesses. Recorded: October 1, 1764.

Ibid - Deed Book G, page 256 -

May 3, 1767 - Thomas Duncanson of the TOWN AND PARISH OF FORRESS, COUNTY
MURRAY, SCOTLAND, Surgeon to Henry Mitchell of Fredericksburg, Virginia,
merchant - whereas Robert Duncanson of Fredericksburg, deceased, in his
lifetime was seized of certain lots, etc., in the town of Fredericksburg

and being so seized died intestate, whereby the said lots descended to the
said Thomas Duncanson, his heir at law and whereas the said Thomas by his
letter of attorney dated July 7, 1764, constituted and appointed James
Duncanson of Fredericksburg, merchant, his lawful attorney, etc., the said
Thomas Duncanson, by the said James Duncanson, his attorney, for the sum of
66 pounds conveys to said Henry Mitchell, lots 133 and 134 in the town of
Fredericksburg. No Witnesses. Recorded: July 7, 1767.

Ibid - Deed Book G, page 263 -

May 9, 1768 - Pearson Chapman of THE PROVINCE OF MARYLAND, Esqr., makes a
deed of lease to John Dalton of Fredericksburg, Virginia, tailor, to
Elizabeth, his wife, and Walker Dalton, his son, etc. - tenement in the
Town of Fredericksburg late in tenure and occupation of Barbary Jones,
widow, now deceased, etc. for 20 pounds on November 16th annually, etc.
Witnesses: Jonathan Herd, Thomas Walker, Robert Maitland. Recorded:
August 2, 1768.

Ibid - Deed Book G, page 264 -

July 26, 1768 - Joseph Peterson OF THE COUNTY OF ORANGE, PROVINCE OF NORTH
CAROLINA and Lucy, his wife, sell to John Pulliam of Spotsylvania County,
Virginia for 55 pounds - 147½ acres of land in Spotsylvania County, etc.
Witnesses: Larkin Chew, John Carter, Stephen Johnson. Recorded: Septem-
ber 6, 1768.

Ibid - Deed Book G, page 266 -

July 7, 1764 - Thomas Duncanson, Surgeon of FORRESS, COUNTY MURRAY, NORTH
BRITAIN, and brother German to the deceased Robert Duncanson of Fredericksburg, Virginia, merchant. Whereas the said Robert Duncanson sometime since
departed this life in the town of Fredericksburg, Virginia, leaving neither
letter, Will or Testament or disposition of his estate, by which the said
Thomas Duncanson is heir to the said Robert as nearest of kin, etc., and
power of attorney to James Duncanson of Fredericksburg, Virginia, merchant,
etc. Witnesses: John Frazer, Alexander McSween. No date of record.

Ibid - Deed Book G, page 280 -

October 16, 1770 - John Huddleston OF JOHNSTON COUNTY, NORTH CAROLINA, son
and heir of Robert Huddleston, late of Spotsylvania County, Virginia, deceased
to Robert Huddleston, now of Berkeley Parish, Spotsylvania County, Virginia -
Whereas Robert Huddleston, deceased, did by his last will and testament desire that a tract of 113 acres in Spotsylvania County, whereon he formerly
lived, should be sold and the money arising therefrom equally divided amongst
all his children and the said Robert, party to these presents, having purchased the shares of all the said children, and the said John, being
satisfied with his proportionable part, conveys to the said Robert the 113
acres, etc. Witnesses: John Waller, Jr., Lewis Craig, James Chiles, Andrew
Tribble. No date of record.

Spotsylvania County, Virginia, Records by Crozier, Deed Book H, page 287 -

June 18, 1771 - Robert Goodloe and Sarah, his wife, OF BUTE COUNTY IN
NORTH CAROLINA sell to Henry Goodloe, of Caroline County, Virginia - for
35 pounds - 200 acres of land in Berkeley Parish, Spotsylvania County,
Virginia which land was given said Robert Goodloe by his father, George
Goodloe, Gent., deceased, by his last Will and Testament, etc. Witnesses:
Robert Goodloe, William Durrett, James Colquohoon, W. Emmerson. No date
of record.

Ibid - Deed Book H, page 304 -

May 15, 1773 - Phillip Somerby of Fredericksburg, Virginia, sells to
Charles Yates OF THE KINGDOM OF GREAT BRITAIN, but late of Fredericksburg, Virginia, Gent., for 73 pounds 16 shillings 6 pence - a negro man
named Gilbert. Witnesses: John Meals, George Spencer, Tuley Whithourst.
No date of record.

Ibid - Deed Book H, page 305 -

June 7, 1773 - Thomas Estes of Spotsylvania County, Virginia, to his son,
John Estes, OF ORANGE COUNTY, PROVINCE OF NORTH CAROLINA - whereas Thomas
Estes, formerly of Caroline County, Virginia, deceased, by his last Will
and Testament among other things did lend to his daughter, Barbara Rogers
a negro girl .... during the life of the said Barbara and after her death
the said slave to be sold and the money arising from the sale to be
equally divided amongst her children (as by said Will in Caroline Co.) and
since which the said slave having had several children that are now alive
and dispersed in the PROVINCE OF NORTH CAROLINA, etc., and the said Thomas
Estes, the testator, having made no disposition of the increase of the
said slave, the said Thomas Estes, party to these presents, as eldest son
and heir of the said deceased, deeds his right or title in the said increase of the said slave to his son, John Estes, etc. Witnesses: William
Wood, John Holloday, Jr., Rice Curtis, Jr., John Chew, Jr. No date of
record.

Ibid - Deed Book H, page 308 -

March 2, 1774 - John Waller, clerk of Spotsylvania County, Virginia,
having large debts due him by Reuben Vass, who resides IN SOUTH CAROLINA,
gives his Power of Attorney to William Arnold of Caroline County, Virginia
to collect same, etc. Witness: O. Towles. Recorded: March 17, 1774.

Ibid - Deed Book H, page 308 -

March 17, 1774 - George Mitchell of Fredericksburg, merchant, having a
debt due him by John Nall, who resides IN ONE OF THE CAROLINAS, gives
his Power of Attorney to William Arnold of Caroline County, Virginia to
collect same, etc. Witness: John Wiglesworth. Recorded same date.

Spotsylvania County, Virginia, Records by Crozier, Deed Book H, page 309 -

January 31, 1774 - James Sutherland, OF FALMOUTH, COUNTY OF CUMBERLAND, gives his Power of Attorney, to his brother, William Sutherland, of SO. RONALD SHA., ORKNEY ISLES, EUROPE, now residing in Fredericksburg, Virginia. Mentions - our late brother, Dr. John Sutherland, late of Fredericksburg, deceased, etc. Witnesses: Ezra Jordan, George Lowell, John Collier. Recorded: March 17, 1774.

Ibid - Deed Book J, page 316 -

March 8, 1775 - Erasmus Withers Allen and Sarah, his wife, OF THE PROVINCE OF NORTH CAROLINA, sell to Richard Loury of Caroline County - for 250 pounds - 499 acres of land in Spotsylvania County, Virginia, etc. Witnesses: Vincent Vass, Frances Turnley, Benjamin Chapman, Thomas Chapman. Recorded: March 16, 1775.

Ibid - Deed Book J, page 326 -

January 2, 1775 - George Mitchell of Spotsylvania County, Virginia, merchant, of the first part - Thomas Colson and Frances, his wife, of said county, of the second part, convey half a lot in the Town of Fredericksburg, Virginia, to Robert Jardine, late of THE CITY OF LONDON (GREAT BRITAIN), but now of Spotsylvania County, Virginia, merchant, etc. Witnesses: James Mercer, John Munro, John Atkinson. Recorded: December 19, 1776.

Ibid - Deed Book J, page 327 -

August 16, 1776 - Thomas May of SURRY COUNTY IN NORTH CAROLINA sells to Daniel Branham of Spotsylvania County, Virginia, for 100 pounds, 264 acres of land in Spotsylvania County, etc. Recorded: December 19, 1776.

Ibid - Deed Book J, page 333 -

February 5, 1776 - Alexander Spotswood, of Newpost, Spotsylvania County, Virginia, Esqr., grandson and heir-at-law of Butler Spotswood, deceased, late wife of Alexander Spotswood, late of Virginia, Esqr., deceased, which said Butler was one of four daughters and co-heirs of Richard Brayne, LATE OF SAINT MARY'S PARISH, CITY OF WESTMINSTER, Gent., and Anne his wife, before her marriage called Anne Begnold, Spinster, sometime before and on 14 February 1775 entitled to lands in the manors of Greenshall (or Grunshall?) Tower Hill and Grunshall Netty in COUNTY SURRY ENGLAND and in Manor of High Cheer in COUNTY BERKSHIRE IN ENGLAND - and whereas Robert Jardine, now of Fredericksburg, Virginia, merchant, formerly of NEW BOND STREET IN LONDON, etc. agreed to purchase all the lands aforesaid of the said Spotswood. (Note by CHH: Other deeds also identify Alexander Spotswood nephew and heir at law of Diana Brayne and Ann Brayne, deceased, two other daughters and co-heiresses of said Richard Brayne and Ann his wife who was daughter and sole heir of James Begnold, heretofore of SHIERRE, COUNTY SURRY (ENGLAND), and Anne, his wife. No witnesses. Recorded: May 21, 1778.)
    Further note by CHH: Ibid, page 340 - Another deed of interest dated January 10, 1779 is a conveyance of slaves by Alexander Spotswood of Fredericksburg to his brother, John Spotswood of Orange County, Virginia.

Spotsylvania County, Virginia, Records by Crozier, Deed Book J, page 340 -

October 8, 1778 - John Kelly of GRANVILLE COUNTY, NORTH CAROLINA (son and heir of Edward Kelly, of Spotsylvania County, Virginia, deceased) and Nancy, his wife, sell to Benjamin Johnston of Fredericksburg, Virginia for 55 pounds - 150 acres of land in Spotsylvania County, Virginia, fifty acres thereof now held by Edward Bryant Senior in right of his wife who was the widow and relict of John True, from whom the said Edward Kelly, father of the present John (Kelly) purchased and which said Edward died intestate and the said John, as eldest son and heir at law became proprietor thereof, save the dowers in the land, to wit, that of Sarah, the wife of Edward Bryant and Elizabeth, the wife and relict of the said Edward Kelly, etc. Witnesses: William Handley, James Brakley, Edmund Bryant, Fanny Houston. Recorded: February 18, 1779.

Ibid - Deed Book J, page 353 -

June 14, 1780 - William Thompson of Spotsylvania County, Virginia, Gent., to Dr. George French of Fredericksburg, Virginia, and Ann Brayne, his wife. Whereas the said Ann Brayne, jointly with her sister, Dorothea Brayne Benger, as daughters of John Benger, late of Virginia, deceased, are entitled to and seized of a moiety or one-half of an Estate in lands IN THE COUNTY OF SURRY ENGLAND, which came to them on the death of Ann Brayne, late OF THE CITY OF LONDON, ENGLAND sometime deceased; the other one-half of which Estate came or descended to Alexander Spotswood, Esqr., etc. Witnesses: Andrew Buchanan, George Buckner, James Someville. Recorded: June 15, 1780.

Ibid - Deed Book J, page 355 -

March 20, 1780 - William Floid of CASWELL COUNTY, NORTH CAROLINA sells to Thomas Brightwell of Spotsylvania County, Virginia, for 100 pounds - 50 acres of land in Spotsylvania County, Virginia, etc. Witnesses: Charles Jenkins, James Abbett, John Jenkins. No date of record.

Ibid - Deed Book J, page 358 -

August 1, 1780 - William Dawson and Mary, his wife, of Spotsylvania County, Virginia, sell to Zachariah Billingsly of ST. MARY'S COUNTY, MARYLAND - for 3300 pounds - 185 acres of land in Spotsylvania County purchased of Thomas Towles and Mary, his wife, as by deed dated July 10, 1775. Witnesses: David Pulliam, James King, Joseph Pulliam. Recorded: May 17, 1781.

Ibid - Deed Book J, page 359 -

June 6, 1781 - James Head and Sarah, his wife, of Spotsylvania County, Virginia sell to Francis King of MARYLAND for 1595 pounds - 290 acres of land in Spotsylvania County. Witnesses: Thomas Terry, Thomas Turner, James King. Recorded: August 16, 1781.

Ibid - Deed Book J, page 360 -

December 21, 1780 - William Craghill and Elizabeth, his wife, of

Stafford County, Virginia, sell to Jonathan Nixon, Jr. of MARYLAND - for 3000
pounds - 300 acres of land in St. George Parish, Spotsylvania County, Virginia
Witnesses: Harris Hooe, William Craghill, Jr., Betty Craghill, John Chew,
Lodowick O'Neal, John Haydon, John Welch. Recorded: May 17, 1781.

Ibid - Deed Book J, page 364 -

November 17, 1781 - William Dillard of NORTH CAROLINA sells to Thomas Dillard
of Spotsylvania County, Virginia for 35 pounds specie - 100 acres of land
in Spotsylvania County bequeathed said William Dillard by the last Will and
Testament of his father, Thomas Dillard, deceased, and adjoins lands of
Captain Nicholas Payne, Richard Dillard, said Thomas Dillard and others,
etc. Recorded: April 18, 1782.

Ibid - Deed Book K, page 367 -

June 20, 1782 - Lewis Willis and Ann, his wife, of King George County, Vir-
ginia, Gent., and Benjamin Johnston of WASHINGTON COUNTY, PENNSYLVANIA and
Dorothy, his wife, sell to Robert Forsyth of Fredericksburg, Virginia -
Whereas said Willis, being seized of a tract of land adjoining the Town of
Fredericksburg, Spotsylvania County, which he purchased of the Estate of
Roger Dixon, Gent., deceased, did sell 15 acres thereof to the said Johnston,
but before any conveyance was made to him, the said Johnston agreed to the
sale of the said 15 acres to the said Forsyth for 55 pounds, etc. Recorded:
June 20, 1782.

Ibid - Deed Book K, page 367 -

May 21, 1782 - William Bledsoe of LINCOLN COUNTY, VIRGINIA (NOW KENTUCKY)
and Elizabeth, his wife, sell to William McWilliams of Spotsylvania County,
Virginia for 100 pounds - 260 acres near Fredericksburg, Spotsylvania
County, formerly property of Captain William Miller, deceased. Recorded:
June 20, 1782.

Ibid - Deed Book K, page 369 -

August 26, 1782 - Benjamin Johnston and Dorothy, his wife, OF WASHINGTON
COUNTY, PENNSYLVANIA (formerly of Fredericksburg, Virginia) sell to William
Dawson of Spotsylvania County, Virginia - for 20 pounds - 100 acres on East
North East River, in Spotsylvania County, Virginia. Recorded: September 19,
1782.

Ibid - Deed Book K, page 375 -

July 16, 1783 - William Miller Bledsoe and Elizabeth, his wife, of LINCOLN
COUNTY (KENTUCKY) sell to William McWilliams of Fredericksburg, Spotsylvania
County, Virginia for 100 pounds - 261 acres in Spotsylvania County devised
said Bledsoe by his grandfather, William Miller, deceased, being part of a
patent granted John Miller February 9, 1737 and by him conveyed the said
William Miller, etc., said William Miller Bledsoe, son of Joseph Bledsoe,
etc. Recorded: July 17, 1783.

Spotsylvania County, Virginia, Records by Crozier, Deed Book K, page 382 -

May 17, 1784 - John Smith of ORANGEBURG DISTRICT, SOUTH CAROLINA, planter - eldest son and heir at law of John Smith, LATE OF THE SAME PLACE, deceased, sells to Thomas Carr, late of Spotsylvania County, Virginia, for 600 pounds sterling - 4000 acres in Berkeley Parish, Spotsylvania County, Virginia, said tract invested by entailment in Lawrence Smith and after his death in John Smith, heir of said Lawrence and at the death of said John, descended unto John Smith, party to these presents, etc. Witnesses: Peter Stubblefield, James Dawson, B. Dawson, Walter Carr, George Henning, John Brag. Recorded: September 7, 1784. (Note by CHH: John Smith, on the same day, gives a power of attorney to Thomas Carr, late of Spotsylvania County, Virginia, Esquire.)

Ibid - Deed Book K, page 383 -

November 1, 1784 - Thomas Carr of THE STATE OF GEORGIA, and at present in Spotsylvania County, Virginia sells to Robert Hart of Spotsylvania County, Virginia, for 20 shillings, a small parcel of land on Douglass Run, being part of a larger tract which said Carr lately purchased of John Smith, etc. Witnesses: Henry Lane, Thomas Terry, Thomas Turner, William Brock, Thomas Brooks. Recorded: Next Day.

Ibid - Deed Book K, page 384 -

January 4, 1785 - Peter Stubblefield of Spotsylvania County, Virginia but INTENDING TO THE STATE OF GEORGIA gives power of attorney to his brother, George Stubblefield of Spotsylvania County, etc. Witnesses: John Carnahan, John Chew, Jr., Benjamin Holladay, Jr. Recorded same date. (Note by CHH: Another record reveals that Peter Stubblefield has a wife called "Peggy".)

Ibid - Deed Book K, page 393 -

October 8, 1785 - Thomas Carr of THE STATE OF GEORGIA and George Stubblefield and Sally, his wife, of Spotsylvania County, Virginia, sell to John Chandler of Spotsylvania County, Virginia, for 115 pounds 10 shillings - 283 acres of land in Berkeley Parish, Spotsylvania County, etc. Witnesses: T. Dawson, John Day, William Moore, William Taylor. Recorded: November 1, 1785.

Ibid - Deed Book L, page 396 -

March 7, 1786 - Nathaniel ch. Gordon (sic) of WILKES COUNTY, NORTH CAROLINA and Nancy, his wife, sell to William Estes of Spotsylvania County, Virginia for 40 pounds - 95 acres in Spotsylvania County, etc. No witnesses. Recorded same date.

Ibid - Deed Book L, page 399 -

September 5, 1786 - Henry Foster and Mildred, his wife, of THE COUNTY OF FAYETTE (KENTUCKY) sell to Robert Smith of Spotsylvania County, Virginia, Gent., for 30 pounds - 401 acres in St. George Parish, Spotsylvania County, etc. Witnesses: Joseph Brock, Henry Crutcher, William Jones, Richard

Collins, William Herndon. Recorded same date.

Ibid - Deed Book L, page 399 -

September 2, 1786 - Alexander Parker of Caroline County, Virginia, gives Power of Attorney to Robert Beverley Chew of Fredericksburg, Virginia - mentions property in ST NICHOLAS PARISH, CITY OF BRISTOL, GREAT BRITAIN, etc. Witnesses: Larkin Stanard, Edward Peyton, George Scott. No date of record.

Ibid - Deed Book L, page 401 -

September 12, 1786 - Peter Stubblefield and Peggy, his wife, OF THE STATE OF GEORGIA; Evans Long and Lucy, his wife; James Smith and Sally, his wife; Zachariah Lucas and Polly Harrison, his wife; Richard Long and Fanny, his wife (all of Spotsylvania County, Virginia) sell to Thomas Coleman, Jr. - Whereas John Apperson, deceased, did by his last Will devise to his daughter, Peggy, wife to the above named Peter Stubblefield, 200 acres, part of a tract purchased by said Apperson of John Cathrae and James Somerville for her natural life - revision to his other children, viz., Lucy, wife of Evans Long; Sally, wife of James Smith; Polly Harrison who has since intermarried with Zachariah Lucas; Fanny who has since intermarried with Richard Long, etc. convey said land, etc. Witnesses: Stapleton Crutchfield, Joseph Duerson, William Henderson, John Chew, Jr., Nicholas Payne, Henry Pendleton, Jr. Recorded: January 2, 1787.

Ibid - Deed Book L, page 403 -

January 29, 1787 - John Welch and Eleanor, his wife, of BALTIMORE COUNTY, STATE OF MARYLAND sell to David Simons of Fredericksburg, Virginia for 200 pounds - 10 acres of land conveyed by Thomas Carr to Norcut Slaven and by said Slaven to James Frazer and by said Frazer to the said Welch, etc. in Spotsylvania County, Virginia, etc. Witnesses: John Chew, Jr., Joseph Chew, Fontaine Maury. Recorded: February 6, 1787.

Ibid - Deed Book L, page 403 -

December 30, 1786 - John Tankersley of RICHMOND COUNTY, GEORGIA gives a Power of Attorney to Edward Herndon of Spotsylvania County, Virginia, etc. Witnesses: George Cammack, William Orril Brock. Recorded: Feb. 6, 1787.

Ibid - Deed Book L, page 104 -

May 9, 1786 - John Anderson of Spotsylvania County, Virginia to Charles Stewart of NEW JERSEY and Ephraim Blain OF PENNSYLVANIA. In trust, the said Anderson being indebted with one William Wiatt to the said Stuart and Blain, conveys to them 190½ acres of land in WESTMORELAND COUNTY, PENNSYL-VANIA, which was purchased of John Montgomerie and Sarah, his wife, May 30, 1777 - also being entitled to ¼ part of sundry tracts of land IN WESTMORELAND COUNTY, PENNSYLVANIA (which he holds in partnership with William Parr, Owen Biddle and Clement Biddle) also entitled to 1/3 part of about 3000 acres, held in partnership with James Milligan and Hugh Lenox, etc. Witnesses: Joseph Herndon, James Hutchinson, Reuben Straughan, Robert Stubblefield. Recorded: April 3, 1787.

Spotsylvania County, Virginia, Records by Crozier, Deed Book L, page 404 -

January 4, 1787 - Henry Willis of King George County, Virginia, "About to
depart ... and go to THE STATE OF GEORGIA", etc. gives Power of Attorney
to Lewis Willis of Spotsylvania County, Virginia, Gent. Recorded: April 3,
1787.

Ibid - Deed Book L, page 405 -

September 12, 1786 - Thomas Burbridge OF FAYETTE COUNTY, KENTUCKY District
gives Power of Attorney to Daniel Branham of Spotsylvania County, Virginia.
Witnesses: Daniel Branham, Joseph Brock, clk., John Brock, Jr. Recorded:
April 3, 1787.

Ibid - Deed Book L, page 408 -

August 7, 1787 - Francis King and Mary, his wife OF MARYLAND sell to
Ezeriah King of Orange County, Virginia, for 95 pounds - 290 acres in
Spotsylvania County, Virginia. No witnesses. Recorded same date.

Ibid - Deed Book L, page 418 -

March 20, 1788 - John Carter (of Spotsylvania County, Virginia) sells to
his brother, Charles Carter - for 45 pounds - his right, title, and interest
in the estate of their father, Henry Carter, deceased, "the said John
Carter BEING ABOUT TO REMOVE TO KENTUCKY", etc. Witnesses: William
Trigg, William Stears, William Henderson. Recorded: June 3, 1788.

Ibid - Deed Book M, page 424 -

January 13, 1789 - Samuel Bullock of NORTH CAROLINA sells to James Bullock
of Spotsylvania County, Virginia for 25 pounds - 136 acres in Spotsylvania
County, etc. Witnesses: George Shepherd, Joseph Bullock, Daniel Tiller,
John Bullock. Recorded: April 7, 1789.

Ibid - Deed Book M, page 426 -

June 26, 1789 - Samuel Chiles and Sarah, his wife and Catharine Rogers of
Caroline County convey to John Rogers, NOW OF FAYETTE COUNTY, KENTUCKY -
Whereas said John Rogers did by his indenture convey to Thomas Pollard of
Fairfax County, Gent., 645 acres in Spotsylvania County and whereas the
said Samuel Chiles and Sarah, his wife and Catharine Rogers (which said
Sarah and Catharine are daughters of William Rogers, late of Spotsylvania
County, deceased) have a right to a part thereof, etc. Therefore the
said Chiles and wife and Catharine Rogers, for love and affection they
bear and the sum of 25 pounds to each - hereby convey their right thereto
to the said John Rogers, etc. Recorded: July 7, 1789.

Ibid - Deed Book M, page 427 -

September 1, 1789 - Hawes Coleman, of Spotsylvania County, Virginia,
attorney for James C. Goodwin, formerly of Spotsylvania County, Virginia,
NOW OF THE DISTRICT OF KENTUCKY, sells 200 acres of land to Daniel Coleman

of Caroline County, etc. No witnesses. Recorded same date.

Ibid - Deed Book M, page 429 -

January 4, 1787 - Henry Willis, at present in Spotsylvania County, Virginia, "but intending to go to THE STATE OF GEORGIA" sells to John Whitaker Willis, slaves, cattle, etc. mentions a tract of land called Lambs Creek coming to him from Lewis Willis, Gent. Recorded: April 16, 1787.

Ibid - Deed Book M, page 435 -

May 29, 1789 - Joseph Brock, Jr. of Spotsylvania County, Virginia, but intending shortly to go to THE STATE OF SOUTH CAROLINA, gives Power of Attorney to George Stubblefield of Spotsylvania County to sell and convey 600 acres of land in Caroline County, Virginia, etc. Witnesses: William Fox, John Herndon, Jr., Bev. W. Stubblefield, William Herndon. Recorded: June 2, 1790.

Ibid - Deed Book N, page 442 -

March 4, 1791 - William Welch OF THE STATE OF MARYLAND, and John Welch of Spotsylvania County, Virginia to Thomas Towles of Spotsylvania County, Virginia - Whereas William Welch is indebted to Abraham Van Bibber who assigned the same to the said Thomas Towles, on which bond the said John Welch stands as security and whereas the said William and John Welch being possessed of certain properties in the State of Virginia, etc. Witnesses: Larkin Stanard, Stockly Towles, John Blaydes. Recorded: June 7, 1791. (Note by CHH: Another deed dated the day before identifies William Welch of THE STATE OF MARYLAND as the son of John Welch of Spotsylvania County, Va. (page 443) In another deed John Welch of Spotsylvania, is joined in the sale by his wife, Nelly Welch.)

Ibid - Deed Book N, page 444 -

October 15, 1787 - Larkine Perry and Isbal, his wife, of FAYETTE COUNTY (KENTUCKY) sell to James Janell of Spotsylvania County, Virginia - for 64 pounds - 120 acres of land in Spotsylvania County devised the said Perry by Nicholas Hawkins, Jr. as will appear by deed dated August 15, 1782, etc. Witnesses: Richard Todd, John Miller, Daniel Billy Gholson. Recorded: September 6, 1791.

Ibid - Deed Book N, page 445 -

September 15, 1791 - John Reed and Rachael, his wife, and Standish Forde of PHILADELPHIA, PENNSYLVANIA, sell to William Lovell of Fredericksburg, Virginia, merchant - for 750 pounds - Lot #43 in said town. Witnesses: Elizabeth Glentworth, Clement Biddle, Chandler Price. Recorded: November Court 1791.

Ibid - Deed Book N, page 445 -

October 24, 1791 - Willis Hoard of JEFFERSON COUNTY, KENTUCKY, sells to Beverley Stubblefield of Spotsylvania County, Virginia, for 78 pounds 18 shillings, 313 acres part of which was conveyed by the executors of John Battaley, deceased, April 16, 1772 to William Hoard, Jr. and part sold by the Sheriff for taxes in Spotsylvania County, etc. Recorded: March 6, 1792.

Spotsylvania County, Virginia, Records by Crozier, Deed Book N, page 451 -

September 14, 1791 - William Glassell of Fredericksburg, Virginia, to John Minor, Jr. of said town. The said William Glassell by virtue of a Power of Attorney from "John Glassell, Esqr., late of Fredericksburg, but THEN OF COUNTY HADDINGTON IN THAT PART OF GREAT BRITAIN CALLED SCOTLAND" - dated July 19, 1788 - for 460 pounds - conveys to the said John Minor, Jr. a tract of land on Hazel Run in Spotsylvania County containing 28-1/9 acres and 1200 sq. yds., etc. Witnesses: William Lewis, Richard H. Young, Charles Mortimer, William Smock, Benjamin Day, Alexander Roane. Recorded: April 3, 1792.

Ibid - Deed Book N, page 454 -

June 13, 1792 - Thomas Burbridge, Benjamin Robinson, Henry Ealey (Elley) and Tavenor Branham (ALL PARTIES OF THE STATE OF KENTUCKY) - give a Power of Attorney to friends, Robert Smith, Linsfield Burbridge and George Burbridge, to sell a tract of land in Spotsylvania County, Virginia, part of which is claimed by the parties of the first part as legatees of Thomas Burbridge, deceased, etc. Witnesses: Mathew Bridges, Richard Branham, William Parker. Recorded: September 4, 1792.

Ibid - Deed Book N, page 454 -

September 4, 1792 - Edward Herndon and Joseph Brock, acting executors of the last Will and Testament of William Carr, deceased, late of Spotsylvania County, Virginia, give a Power of Attorney to Walter Chiles of Spotsylvania County to receive of Walter Chiles Carr of FAYETTE COUNTY, KENTUCKY, etc. certain slaves who are descendants of a mulatto girl lent to Susannah, the wife of the aforesaid William Carr, deceased, by his Will, for her natural life and which said Susannah is lately dead, etc. No witnesses. Recorded: September 4, 1792.

Ibid - Deed Book N, page 455 -

June 4, 1791 - Oliver Towles, the elder, of Spotsylvania County, Virginia, Attorney at Law to Oliver Towles, Jr., his son, of the same county - Whereas the said Towles, the elder by Indenture received in Spotsylvania County March 2, 1790 conveyed to Archibald Dick of Louisa County, Virginia, merchant, and the said Oliver Towles, Jr. all the said Oliver Towles, the Elder's lands, etc. by warrant or surveys lying on the Western Waters COMMONLY CALLED KENTUCKY, supposed to contain upwards of 7000 acres and it was the whole military bounty lands that he was entitled to, etc., also all the said Oliver Towles, the Elder's commutation, pay and wages that are any way in arrear and underpaid the said Elder Towles as an officer in the late Continental Army, also all debts due the said Towles, the Elder, in trust for saving harmless sundry persons, securities for the said Towles, the Elder and whereas by Indenture dated December 7, 1789 received March 2, 1790, the said Towles, the Elder, conveyed to the said Dick and Towles, the younger, sundry tracts of land and slaves therein described, in trust, in case the first conveyance was not sufficient for the purpose mentioned, to be applied to complete the necessary amount, and also to reimburse and repay the said Dick and Towles, Jr., the sum of 750 pounds and advanced by them for the said Towles, the Elder, etc. Now,

this Indenture witnesseth the said Oliver Towles, the Elder, in consideration
of the sum of 1052 pounds current money, (750 pounds of which is to be applied
towards paying said Dick and Towles, Jr.) - the above mentioned 1440 acres of
land in Spotsylvania County, Virginia - also slaves, goods, chattels, etc.
(436 acres being part of a patent granted Harry Beverley, Gent., deceased,
grandfather to the said Mary, wife of the said Oliver Towles, the Elder, etc.)
Witnesses: Thomas Montague, Gabriel Long, James Richards, Elizabeth Richards,
Recorded: September 4, 1792. (Note by CHH: Full Colonels of the Revolutionary
War received 5,000 to 8,888 acres of Bounty land for their services.)

Ibid - Deed Book N, page 458 -

May 14, 1792 - James Thompson, minister of the Gospel IN THE COUNTY OF AYR
IN NORTH BRITAIN (SCOTLAND), eldest son and heir of William Thompson of Poplar,
near London, Shipmaster, deceased, gives a Power of Attorney to Charles
Mortimer, Esqr. of Fredericksburg, Virginia, to sell lot #251 in Fredericksburg purchased of Roger Dixon and Lucy, his wife, by the said William Thompson,
deceased, during his life time, etc. Witnesses: Thomas Thompson, Thomas
Thompson, Jr. oath of Mr. Thomas Thompson OF THE COUNTY OF AYR, M.G. and Thomas
Thompson, Jr. his son, that they know James Thompson of GRIVAN, M.G. etc.,
as stated above, etc. Witness: John McNeath, Chief Magistrate and Baillie
of the BURGH OF GRIVAN. Recorded: March 6, 1793. (Note by CHH: M.G.
evidently means "Minister of Gospel".)

Ibid - Deed Book N, page 458 -

_____1793 - Richard Bullard of Spotsylvania County, Virginia, gives a
Power of Attorney to Richard Cave OF FAYETTE COUNTY, KENTUCKY, etc. Witnesses:
Joseph Brock, clerk, Robert Branham. Recorded: April 2, 1793.

Ibid - Deed Book N, page 459 -

December 26, 1792 - William Hewell of NORTH CAROLINA to William Herod, 150
acres of land in Spotsylvania County, Virginia which was sold to John Harland
who sold same to William King who sold to the said Herod but no conveyance
ever having been made, etc. Recorded: April 2, 1793.

Ibid - Deed Book N, page 459 -

March 16, 1793 - Robert Smith of Spotsylvania County, Virginia, removing TO
THE STATE OF KENTUCKY gives a Power of Attorney to James Lewis, Gent., of
Spotsylvania County, Virginia. Witnesses: Edward Herndon, Jr., Beverley
Stubblefield, Thomas Bartlett. Recorded: April 1793.

Ibid - Deed Book N, page 460 -

December 17, 1791 - John Proctor OF FAYETTE COUNTY, VIRGINIA (sic) (KENTUCKY),
heir at law of William Proctor, deceased, of Spotsylvania County, Virginia,
having brought suit as heir at law to recover the estate of the said decedent,
etc., gives Power of Attorney to George Mason of Caroline County, Virginia.
Witnesses: John Shackleford, Moses Higgins, Micajah Mason. Recorded:
September 3, 1793.

Spotsylvania County, Virginia, Records by Crozier, Deed Book N, page 461 -

March 29, 1793 - Thomas Lipscomb of Spotsylvania County, Virginia makes a Deed of Gift of two negroes to his son, Joel Lipscomb of EDGEFIELD COUNTY, SOUTH CAROLINA. Witness: Joseph Willoughby. Recorded: September 3, 1793.

Ibid - Deed Book N, page 461 -

_____ 1793 - James Donalson, Lucy Robins, Joanna Robins and Sarah Robins of SCOTT COUNTY, KENTUCKY give a Power of Attorney to James Robins of Spotsylvania County, Virginia, etc. Witnesses: John McEndree, Bartlet Collins. Recorded: September 3, 1793.

Ibid - Deed Book N, page 463 -

October 12, 1793 - Ambrose Dudley and Ann, his wife, of FAYETTE COUNTY, KENTUCKY, sell to Joseph Bullock of Spotsylvania County, Virginia for 218 pounds 15 shillings - 177 acres, being part of a tract purchased by Robert Dudley, deceased, father of the said Ambrose Dudley, of a certain Mr. Goodloe in St. George Parish, Spotsylvania County, etc. Witnesses: Phillip D. Redd, Peter Dudley, James Dudley, Thomas Colson. Recorded: January 7, 1794.

Ibid - Deed Book N, page 463 -

January 7, 1794 - John Lewis of Spotsylvania County, Virginia gives a power of attorney to Richard Terrell OF THE TOWN OF LEXINGTON, IN KENTUCKY. No Witnesses. Recorded: January 7, 1794.

Ibid - Deed Book N, page 464 -

January __, 1794 - Philemon Davis of Spotsylvania County, Virginia, gives a Power of Attorney to William Winslow of the same county to sell his KENTUCKY lands, etc. Witnesses: Robert W. Peacock, William Trigg. Recorded: January 7, 1794.

Ibid - Deed Book N, page 464 -

January 7, 1794 - Thomas Winslow of Spotsylvania County, Virginia, gives his Power of Attorney to William Winslow of said County, to sell lands in the WESTERN COUNTRY (NAME USUALLY GIVEN TO KENTUCKY) OR NORTH WESTERN TERRITORY (COULD BE OHIO, INDIANA, OR ILLINOIS), etc. Witnesses: Benjamin Robinson, John Nelson, Jr., Samuel Robinson. Recorded same date.

Ibid - Deed Book N, page 464 -

February 4, 1794 - Moses Wheeler of Spotsylvania County, Virginia gives a Power of Attorney to William Winslow of said county, to sell LAND IN KENTUCKY to which said Wheeler may be entitled as heir at law of John and William Wheeler, as will appear by patent dated November 18, 1785, etc. Witnesses: Austin Sandidge, John Parrish, James Frazer. Recorded: February 4, 1794.

Spotsylvania County, Virginia, Records by Crozier, Deed Book N, page 470 -

October 6, 1794 - John Wilson of WASHINGTON COUNTY, IN THE STATE OR TERRITORY
SOUTH OF THE OHIO RIVER (note by CHH: WASHINGTON COUNTY, KENTUCKY was formed
1792 from NELSON COUNTY; a John Wilson is listed in the 1790 census OF KEN-
TUCKY IN NELSON COUNTY) gives a Power of Attorney to Thomas Dillard of Spotsyl-
vania County, Virginia to demand and receive of Samuel Luck of Hanover County,
Virginia, Executor of the last Will and Testament of Samuel Luck, late of
Spotsylvania County, Virginia, deceased, the sums owing the said Wilson as
a legacy under the Will of the said Samuel Luck, deceased, etc. Witnesses:
John Crawford, Thomas Dillard, William Buckner, Booker Wilson, Joseph Wilson.
Recorded: December 2, 1794. (Note by CHH: Samuel Luck, Sr. died in 1787
(See W.B. E, page 874) among others was a legacy to his daughter, Ann Wilson.)

Ibid - Deed Book O, page 477 -

February 3, 1795 - Richard Young OF WOODFORD COUNTY, KENTUCKY gives a Power
of Attorney to John Robinson of Fredericksburg, Virginia to make sale of one-
third part of 14,280 acres patented by John Robinson, Benjamin Robinson and
Richard Young; one-half part of 3121 acres patented in the names of John
Stewart and Richard Young; also one-half of 1546 acres patented by William
Richards and Richard Young, etc. No witnesses. Recorded: July 7, 1795.
(Note by CHH: WOODFORD COUNTY, KENTUCKY was formed 1788 from FAYETTE COUNTY.
A Richard Young is listed in the 1790 census of KENTUCKY in 1789 in FAYETTE
COUNTY.)

Ibid - Deed Book O, page 480 -

December 27, 1794 - John Waller Johnston of NELSON COUNTY, KENTUCKY gives
Power of Attorney to Benjamin Childress of Amherst County, Virginia "to enter
upon the agency which I have in trust on the Estate of Henry Johnston of
Spotsylvania County, Virginia as by Indenture there recorded." Witness:
James Harden. Recorded: December 1, 1795.

Ibid - Deed Book O, page 481 -

July 13, 1795 - Richard Noell, formerly of Essex County, Virginia, at present
of Spotsylvania County, Virginia to Robert Crutchfield of Spotsylvania County.
Whereas the said Noell is entitled to his choice of a moiety of 6,000 acres
in the STATE OF KENTUCKY, taken up and located, and as he expects, duly secured
by and through the agency of Joseph Craig, and as acknowledged by his letter
dated September 21, 1793 from Joseph Craig to Richard Noell, Gent. in Essex
County, Virginia, and being desirous of making a reasonable settlement and
provision of same for his creditors and children, this Indenture therefore
witnesseth, that said Noell, in consideration of the premises, etc. conveys
to the said Crutchfield all right, title, etc. in the aforesaid lands, in
trust, for children begotten or to be begotten between the said Richard Noell
and Mary, his present wife, one-third thereof; the remaining two-thirds to be
sold, etc. Witnesses: Robert Lewis, Daniel Trigg, Stapleton Crutchfield,
James Ray, Thomas Crutchfield, Joseph Herndon, Z. Shackleford, Thomas Foster.
Recorded: January 5, 1796.

Spotsylvania County, Virginia, Records by Crozier, Deed Book O, page 482 -

July 9, 1795 - Benjamin Weeks and Aggy, his wife, of Stafford County, Virginia - John Gibson and Mildred, his wife - Norcut Slaven and Nancy, his
wife - ALL OF WILKES COUNTY, GEORGIA - Betsey Wood, widow of John Wood, at
present of Virginia, but intending immediately to remove TO GEORGIA - also
Lucy Holladay and Owen Holladay of THE STATE OF GEORGIA, (parties of one
part) - To Gabriel Long of Spotsylvania County, Virginia,whereas Abram
Simons and Mildred, his wife, and Sarah Holladay by indenture dated
January 6, 1789, did sell to the said Gabriel Long 325 acres in Spotsylvania County, Virginia, and whereas all the wives of the said parties
hereto, as well as Betsy Wood, widow and Lucy and Owen Holladay, are
children and devisees of John Holladay, late of Spotsylvania County,
deceased, and each of them claim, under the said Holladay's Will one-
twelfth part of the land, etc., as aforesaid conveyed by Abram Simons
and Mildred, his wife, and Sarah Holladay, now Sarah Freeman, and whereas
the said several claimants having sold their respective parts to the said
Long and being willing and desirous of relinquishing the same, this indenture therefore conveys, etc. Recorded: January 5, 1796.

Ibid - Deed Book O, page 482 -

December 7, 1795 - John Holladay OF WILKES COUNTY, GEORGIA, one of the
legatees of John Holladay, deceased, late of Spotsylvania County, Virginia
sells to Gabriel Long of Spotsylvania County, Virginia for $40.00 one-
eleventh part of 325 acres in Spotsylvania County, Virginia conveyed to
said Long by Abram Simons and Mildred, his wife (late Mildred Holladay),
etc. Witnesses: William Triplett, Richard Long, Joseph Reynolds,
Benjamin Reynolds. Recorded: February 20, 1796.

Ibid - Deed Book O, page 483 -

March 18, 1796 - William Winslow of Fredericksburg, Virginia, gives
Power of Attorney to Beverley Chew of Fredericksburg, Virginia, and
Richard Terrell of LEXINGTON, KENTUCKY to sell lands IN THE STATE OF
KENTUCKY, ETC. Recorded: April 5, 1796.

Ibid - Deed Book O, page 485-6 -

June 17, 1796 - Agreement between William Champe Carter of Virginia and
William Stanard and Robert Patton of the said State, for sale of one un-
divided eighth part of 26,000 acres of land ON THE DAN RIVER, IN NORTH
CAROLINA, devised by Francis Farley of ANTIQUA to the late James Farley,
and known by the name of Sama Towns, at the price of $2.00 per acre, etc.
Witnesses: John Mercer, Howell Lewis, Go. Lewis. Recorded: July 5,1796.

Ibid - Deed Book O, page 486 -

March 23, 1793 - James Livingston and Thomas Livingston, of EDGEFIELD
COUNTY, SOUTH CAROLINA give a Power of Attorney to Benjamin Wharton of
Spotsylvania County, Virginia. Recorded: July 5, 1796.

Spotsylvania County, Virginia, Records by Crozier, Deed Book O, page 487 -

March 31, 1795 - James Maury, of LIVERPOOL, COUNTY LANCASTER, KINGDOM OF
GREAT BRITAIN, merchant, and Consul of the U.S.A. at the post of LIVERPOOL
aforesaid, gives a Power of Attorney to James Lewis of Spotsylvania County,
Virginia, Gent., to receive from the hands of the executors of the last Will
and Testament of Robert Armistead, late of Louisa County, Virginia, deceased,
father of my late wife, Catharine, all and every legacy due from the estate
of said Armistead, etc. Witness: Joseph Lace, Notary Public, LIVERPOOL, etc.
Recorded: Spotsylvania County, Virginia September 6, 1796.

Ibid - Deed Book O, page 489 -

November 21, 1796 - Thomas Lipscomb and Mary, his wife, of Spotsylvania County,
Virginia sell to Allen Billingsby OF MARYLAND - for 275 pounds - 695 acres
of land in Spotsylvania County, Virginia. Recorded: February 7, 1797.

Ibid - Deed Book O, page 491 -

July 11, 1796 - Richard C. Noel of Spotsylvania County, Virginia, gives a
Power of Attorney to John Berryman of Spotsylvania County mentions a tract
of land IN KENTUCKY, a moiety of which is to be land off to Joseph Craig.
Also land heretofore deeded Robert Crutchfield, etc. Recorded: Feb. 7, 1797.

Ibid - Deed Book O, page 494 -

November 17, 1796 - Thomas Crutcher of NELSON COUNTY, KENTUCKY, conveys to
Anthony Frazer, James Frazer, William Frazer and Reuben Frazer, all of
Spotsylvania County, Virginia, 300 acres of land IN KENTUCKY (NELSON COUNTY)
whereon the said Crutcher now lives to indemnify the said Frazers for stand-
ing bound as security for the said Crutcher, in trust, etc. Witnesses:
Thomas Magee, Thomas Olive, Robert Olive, Thomas Foster. Recorded: July 4,179"

Ibid - Deed Book O, page 496 -

January 20, 1797 - John Partlow of SOUTH CAROLINA sells to Jonathan Clark of
Spotsylvania County, Virginia - for 62 pounds - 62 acres of land devised to
said John Partlow by his father, John Partlow, deceased, in Spotsylvania
County, etc. Witnesses: Thomas Towles, Chris. Crawford, James Crawford,
Elijah Partlow, Lewis Partlow. Recorded: September 5, 1797. (Note by CHH:
John Partlow, Sr. Will Book E, page 975, probated April 6, 1790.)

Ibid - Deed Book P, page 497 -

March 17, 1797 - Samuel Graves, John Graves, and James Graves OF FAYETTE
COUNTY, KENTUCKY, give Power of Attorney to William Graves of Spotsylvania
County, Virginia to collect from and settle with the executor of our grand-
father, Samuel McGee, deceased. Witnesses: Henry Garrett, Jr., William
Alsop. Recorded: September 5, 1797.

Ibid - Deed Book P, page 502 -

May 14, 1798 - John Hall and Eliza Ann, his wife, OF THE CITY OF PHILADELPHIA,
PENNSYLVANIA, sell to _____Towles of the County of _____in Virginia -

for $2,700.00 - 722 acres of land purchased of George Lewis and Catharine, his wife, as by indenture dated October 12, 1797, in Spotsylvania County, Virginia, etc. Witnesses: Bernard Webb, P. Conway. Recorded: July 3,1798.

Ibid - Deed Book P, page 505 -

May 30, 1798 - David Humphries and Elizabeth Moore, his wife, OF FAYETTE COUNTY, KENTUCKY: Charles Scott, Jr. and Fanny, his wife, OF WOODFORD COUNTY, KENTUCKY (late Elizabeth and Fanny Cooke, daughters of Elizabeth Cooke, daughter of John Roberson, deceased) sell to Samuel Sale of Spotsylvania County, Virginia - for 100 pounds - and convey one-half of a tract of 500 acres in Spotsylvania County, Virginia being that tract of land bequeathed by Augustine Moore, deceased of Virginia, in his last Will and Testament to the aforesaid Elizabeth Cooke and to Catharine Throgmorton, formerly Catharine Roberson, daughter of the aforesaid John Roberson, deceased, and which half of the aforesaid tract of land has since been conveyed by John Cooke, father of the aforesaid Elizabeth Humphries and Fanny Scott, to the aforesaid Samuel Sale, by deed dated January 23, 1789. No witnesses. Recorded: December 4, 1798.

Ibid - Deed Book P, page 506 -

February 4, 1799 - Winslow Parker, of THE STATE OF KENTUCKY, Thomas Winslow of Virginia, Susanna Parker, administratrix of William Parker, Jr., deceased, late of Virginia - The aforesaid Winslow Parker, as attorney in fact; Henry Parker and Rowland Thomas and Mary, his wife, of the STATE OF KENTUCKY: William Stubblefield, attorney in fact for Robert Stubblefield and Susanna, his wife; Richard Parker and Thomas Parker, ALL OF THE STATE OF KENTUCKY: Peter Dudley, attorney in fact for Ambrose Dudley OF KENTUCKY sell to James Powell and Benjamin Robinson of Spotsylvania County, Virginia- for 443 pounds 8 shillings 9 pence - 215 acres of land in Spotsylvania County, all that tract of land whereof William Parker, the Elder, of the said county, died seized and possessed, etc. Witnesses: John Nelson, John Alcock, John Day, John Herndon, Isaac Graves. Recorded: February 5, 1799.

Ibid - Deed Book P, page 507 -

May 12, 1798 - Thomas DuVall and Jesse Carpenter, OF FAYETTE COUNTY, KENTUCKY give a Power of Attorney to Zacheus Carpenter to recover the equal parts, etc. of the said Duvall and Jesse Carpenter in the Estate of Jonathan Carpenter, deceased, in Spotsylvania County, Virginia. Witness: Thomas Bodley. Recorded: April 2, 1799. (Note by CHH: September 4, 1798, Elizabeth Carpenter, admrx of Jonathan Carpenter, deceased, gave bond in amount of $6,000.00 with William Trigg - James Ballard - and Clement Montague, her securities.)

Ibid - Deed Book P, page 507 -

June 6, 1798 - Nathan Hawkins and Frances, his wife, OF MADISON COUNTY, KENTUCKY, sell to Thomas Waller of Spotsylvania County, Virginia - for $110.00 - 55 acres in Spotsylvania County, etc. Recorded: July 2, 1799.

Spotsylvania County, Virginia, Records by Crozier, Deed Book P, page 507 -

May 27, 1799 - Francis Coleman, attorney in fact for John Nelson OF CAMPBELL COUNTY, KENTUCKY, sells to Joseph Williams of Spotsylvania County, Virginia - for 75 pounds - 176 acres on Plentiful Run in Spotsylvania County, etc. Witnesses: Charles Burrage, Thomas Olive, William Burnett, Benjamin Robinson, Samuel Robinson. Recorded: July 2, 1799.

Ibid - Deed Book P, page 508 -

June 14, 1799 - Thomas Duvall and Jesse Carpenter OF FAYETTE COUNTY, KENTUCKY, give Power of Attorney to Zacheus Carpenter, Spotsylvania County, Virginia, Gent., to ask, receive, etc. the Estate of Jonathan Carpenter, deceased, our parts of estate, we being legatees of said decedent, this is to say, Frances Carpenter, Nancy Carpenter, and Jonathan Carpenter, orphans who have chosen me, Thomas Duvall, their guardian, etc. Recorded: September 3, 1799.

Ibid - Deed Book P, page 511 -

October 29, 1799 - Richard Collins and Sarah, his wife, OF KENTUCKY, by Henry Collins, their attorney; Moses Quisenberry and Mary, his wife, of Orange County, Virginia; Wharton Schooler and Margaret, his wife, OF KENTUCKY; John Edwards, by Wharton Schooler, his attorney and Henry Gatewood and Ann, his wife of Spotsylvania County, Virginia, heirs of Henry Gatewood, Senior, deceased, sell to Martin Brent of Spotsylvania County, Virginia - for 186 pounds 17 shillings 6 pence - 138 acres of land in Spotsylvania County whereon Henry Gatewood, Senior, lately lived, etc. Witnesses: Henry Towles, Peter Hicks, John Pierce. Recorded: December 3, 1799.

Virginia Genealogist, Volume I - Marriages, Winchester, Virginia (1792-1794)
        (From Bowen's Virginia Centinel & Gazette)

Page 38, 4 April 1792 - William McGuire, Esq. of this town, attorney-at-law, to Miss Polly Little, of BERKELEY (now West Virginia.)

Ibid - 12 April 1792 - Married at PHILADELPHIA, Mr. Warner Lewis to Miss Courtney Norton, both of Virginia.

Ibid - 28 May 1792 - Captain James Stephenson to Miss_____Cunningham, in BERKELEY COUNTY (now WEST VIRGINIA.)

Page 39, 11 December 1792 - Mr. Alexander King of FRANKFORT, merchant, to Miss Sarah McAlister, daughter of Mr. James McAlister in HAMPSHIRE COUNTY, (now WEST VIRGINIA.0

Ibid - 31 December 1792 - Mr. Edward Graham, merchant, of BEDFORD COUNTY (PENNSYLVANIA or VIRGINIA?) to Miss Peggy Alexander of Lexington.

Page 40 - (Week before 18 February 1793) - Mr. James Holliday of this town, merchant, to Mrs. _____Darke in BERKELEY COUNTY (now WEST VIRGINIA.0

Ibid - 14 February 1793 - Mr. Matthew Frame of CHARLESTOWN (probably WEST VIRGINIA) merchant, to Miss Massy Gibbs, near this town. Rev. Mr. Hill, minister.

Virginia Genealogist, Volume I - Marriages, Winchester, Virginia (1792-1794)
(From Bowen's Virginia Centinel & Gazette)

Page 40, 12 March 1793 - Mr. Joseph Longacre of Frederick County to Miss Sally Hite of HARDY COUNTY (now WEST VIRGINIA.)

Page 40 (Edition of 1 July 1793) - In Woodstock, Shenandoah (County, Va.) Mr. Jacob Shrock, of HAGERSTOWN (MARYLAND) to Miss Amelia Heiskell, daughter of Mr. Frederick Heiskell, merchant.

Page 41 - Deed - on Thursday last (1st August 1793) Mr. Francis Raworth. He was a native of OLD ENGLAND.

Page 41, 10 October 1793 - Mr. John Kingan, merchant, of FORT CUMBERLAND to Miss Fanny Walker, daughter of Mr. James Walker, hat manufacturer of this town.

Page 41, 3 February 1794 - Married a few days ago at Woodville, near this town, Alexander Pitt Buchannon, Esq., of BALTIMORE to Miss Sally Hite.

Page 42, 7 July 1794 - Married a few days ago, at German Town, Richard Bland Lee, Esq. of Virginia, to Miss Collins, daughter of Mr. S. Collins, merchant of PHILADELPHIA.

Nottoway County, Virginia, Deed Book 1, page 371 -

Know all men by these presents that I, Peter Stainback of the County of Nottoway and State of Virginia, do by these presents make constitute and appoint Col. John Edwards of COUNTY OF BARBARY (sic) and STATE OF KENTUCKY, my true and lawful attorney for me and in my name to ask demand and sue a certain John Fowler, Jr. now of KENTUCKY on a bond executed by the said Fowler to me the 3rd day of March 1783 for the sum of 2 thousand 2 hundred 45 pounds specie, etc. Dated 3 April 1794 - Peter Stainback, Senior. Recorded same date by Benjamin Pollard, D.C.

Charlotte County, Virginia, Will Book 8, page 226 -

Dated 18 December 1837 and Probated February 1838 - Will of Wood Jones Hamlin of the COUNTY OF HALIFAX, NORTH CAROLINA: To the children of my daughter Martha Powell by her former husband, Blake Baker, the negroes which I have heretofore loaned her being three in number, etc. To the children of my daughter Mary Pearson the negroes now in her possession. To the children of my daughter Eliza Williamson, all the negroes now in her possession. To my son Charles Hamlin, negroes Moses and Frany (?), The land he now has in possession and the tract I purchased of Taylor Allen containing 255 acres lying on Roanoke River. All the balance of my estate to my beloved wife Fanny during her life - and at her death to be given to any or all my children in such portions and manner as she may think proper. Executors: My son Charles Hamlin, my son-in-law James S. Pearson and J. R. J. Daniel. Witnesses: F. Mallory, Benjamin Jenkins.
     Codicil - I give Robert P. Hamlin, Peter, Jack, Harriett, Sally, Alphonso, Allen and Alfred and the tract of land I now live on after the

death of my wife and I give to my son Charles the quarter plantation after
the death of my wife. Witnesses to Codicil: W. S. Jenkins, M. A. Willcox.

Codicil - If any party interested in my property should attempt to up-
set my Will, he or she is to have nothing.

State of North Carolina, County of Halifax - February Court 1838 - This
Will of Wood Jones Hamlin was exhibited in open Court and proved by oaths of
Frances Mallory and Benjamin Jenkins, etc.

State of Virginia, County of Charlotte - Foregoing Will was presented
in Court by Charles Hamlin and James L. Pearson and admitted to record.
September 6, 1841.

Charlotte County, Virginia, Will Book 8, page 226 -

Will of Fanny Hamlin of COUNTY of HALIFAX, STATE OF NORTH CAROLINA (wife of
Wood Jones Hamlin). Dated February 1, 1838 and Probated May 1838: To my son,
William A. Hamlin, one equal share of all my estate Real and Personal and of
all the estate real and personal which I am authorized to dispose of by last
Will and Testament of W. J. Hamlin, deceased. To the children of my daughter
Mary Pearson, one equal share, etc. To my daughter, Eliza Jane Williamson,
one equal share. To James S. Pearson and Charles Hamlin, as trustees for the
sale and only use of my daughter Martha Powell, free and discharged from all
control of her husband, William Morgan Powell, and after her death to the
children of her first marriage with Blake Baker, one equal share. To Charles
Hamlin, one equal share. To my daughter, Euphan W. Hamlin, one equal share.
To Robert P. Hamlin, 1 equal share (not 21 yet). All the lands I own in
Virginia to be sold. All the lands I own in OHIO to be sold. Witnesses:
E. Wilkins, William S. Jenkins, Benjamin Jenkins. James S. Pearson and
Charles Hamlin, Executors. Dated 1 February 1838. Codicial - The two negroes
Hardy and Anthony willed to my son William A. Hamlin are not to be considered
part of his portion or share. Also one negro boy, Lafayette. Probated May
Court 1838.

Bedford County, Deed Book 8, page 2 -

17 March 1787 - I, William Bates, Jr. of COUNTY OF BURKE in the STATE OF
NORTH CAROLINA, do constitute and appoint my brother, James Bates of the
County of ROWAN, STATE OF NORTH CAROLINA, my lawful attorney to transact
all manner of business which relates to me in the County of Bedford, Commonwealth of Virginia, and to particularly ask and demand of Robert Cowan
and William Leftwich, Trustees appointed by the County Court of Bedford, in
my minority to manage my estate, a certain negro lad called Charles, profits
from his hire, etc. Witnesses: Jo. Williams, John McBride, Johnson
Whitaker, John Dowell, Jr. Recorded: Bedford County 28 August 1787.

Halifax County, Virginia, Will Book 9, page 59 -

Will of Elizabeth Moody, dated __October 1809 and probated 27 January 1810:
My lands in STATE OF KENTUCKY to be sold to pay my debts, viz 1000 acres which
John B. Scott has a patent for in his own name and which is first for payment
of several debts which I owe him and also warrants or entries for 2000 more
acres which John B. Scott also has in his hands. To my nephew Edward Moody
Thompson land and slaves. Niece Susanna A. Wallington, slave. Slaves to

representatives of my brother, William Thompson, deceased - my brother, James Thompson. Executors: Henry E. Coleman, William Thompson, and John B. Scott. Witnesses: John B. Cocke, John B. Scott, William T. Scott, William Hall, Jr.

Halifax County, Virginia, Deed Book 11, page 202 -

16 December 1778 - John Scott, Senior of CASWELL COUNTY, NORTH CAROLINA, sells to Robert Scott of Halifax County, Virginia for 50 pounds - that tract of land in County of Halifax on southside of Dan River on the middle fork of Wynn's Creek adjoining lands of Thomas Wilson, William Price, Joseph Gill, William Scott and Josiah Farley, containing 250 acres, etc. Witnesses: Thomas Lipscomb, Caleb Townes, William Lee, William Scott. Recorded: 18 February 1779.

Ibid - page 294 -

16 December 1778 - John Scott, Senior of CASWELL COUNTY, NORTH CAROLINA, sells to John Scott, Junior of Halifax County, Virginia for 50 pounds - 250 acres of land in County of Halifax on south side of Dan River on Wynn's Creek, etc. Same witnesses as above. Recorded: 15 July 1779.
    Note by CHH: There is other proof in Halifax County, Virginia Deeds that the above cited John Scott, Senior, was originally from Lunenburg County, Virginia.

Ibid - page 296 -

_____ 1779 - Thomas Wilson of CASWELL COUNTY, NORTH CAROLINA sells to John Scott, Jr. of Halifax County, Virginia for 160 pounds - 100 acres in Halifax County on south side of Dan River on Winn's Creek adjoining lands of Robert Scott, William Price, Barnet Arnal, Hannah Farley, etc. Witnesses: John Poynor, William Finney, William Scott, Ashwell Stone. Recorded: 20 May 1779.

Goochland County, Virginia, Deed Book 21, page 299 -

24 October 1811 - Henry Holeman and Elizabeth, his wife, OF THE COUNTY OF BARREN, STATE OF KENTUCKY, sell to Thomas Dunnavant of the County of Goochland, State of Virginia - for 265 pounds 12 shillings - a tract of land in said Goochland County containing by late survey 265-3/5 acres adjoining lands of Joseph Duvall, Shadrack Walker, Martin Thacker and Giles Hope - it being the land on which the said Henry Holman last resided in the County of Goochland, etc. Witnesses: William Miller, George W. Watkins, Nat Perkins, Marcellus Smith.

Goochland County, Virginia, Deed Book 23, page 376 -

15 July 1817 - Power of Attorney by Frederick Bates OF THE TOWN OF ST. LOUIS, IN THE TERRITORY OF MISSOURI, to his brother, Edward Bates, OF THE TOWN AND TERRITORY AFORESAID, to attend to any and all business of which he is the lawful proprietor in the State of Virginia (County of Goochland by inference) - Certified by Joseph Charles, Justice of Peace for COUNTY OF ST.LOUIS, MISSOURI and by William Clark, Governor of the Territory. Recorded: Goochland County 19 October 1818.

Virginia Gazette (issue not stated) Williamsburg, Virginia

If William Roughsedge, LATE OF PRESCOT, IN THE COUNTY OF LANCASTER (ENGLAND ?)
who was imported as a transport in the Swaile, Captain John Metcalfe (master)
in the year 1763 and bound to Mr. Burch, of Wicomico, near Pile's warehouse
in CHARLES COUNTY, MARYLAND, be living, he may hear of something to his advantage by applying to me in Williamsburg, Virginia; or whoever can give any
intelligence of him; so that a certificate may be had of his being alive, or
dead, shall be rewarded, by applying to Jacob Allan.

Halifax County, Virginia, Deed Book 22, page 584 -

9 October 1809 - Alexander Cunningham OF THE COUNTY OF PERSON, STATE OF NORTH
CAROLINA, sells to Alexander Posey of the County of Halifax, State of Virginia
for 159 pounds - a tract of land in Halifax County on both sides of Wynn's
Creek containing by estimation 106 acres, etc. Witnesses: Daniel C. Townes,
Richard M. Cunningham, D. Chambers. Recorded: 28 January 1811.

Henry County, Virginia, Deed Book 4, page 71 -

7 September 1789 - William Tanzey OF HENRY COUNTY (see note) STATE OF NORTH
CAROLINA sells to Bennett Posey of the County of Henry, State of Virginia -
for 16 pounds - a tract of land containing 351 acres in said County of Henry
(Va.) on the South fork of Bowen's Creek, etc. Witnesses: Charles _____,
Richard Baker, Isaac Hollensworth.

 Note by CHH: There is no such county as Henry in the State of North
Carolina and this is plainly an error by the Clerk. The 1790 census of
North Carolina should reveal the proper county in North Carolina to which
William Tanzey migrated.

Lee County, Virginia, Deed Book 4, page 32 -

October 18, 1820 - Deed of Gift - David Chadwell, Senior of CLAIBORNE COUNTY,
TENNESSEE, for natural love and affection for his son, David Chadwell, Junior
200 acres of land in Lee County, Virginia, etc.

Lee County, Virginia, Deed Book 5, page 211 -

May 15, 1823 - Deed of Gift - David Chadwell, Senior, of CLAIBORNE COUNTY,
TENNESSEE - 400 acres of land in Lee County, Virginia to (his son-in-law)
James Brittain of Lee County, Virginia, for natural love, affection, and
good will.

Rockingham County, North Carolina, Deed Book R, page 40 -

2nd October 1817 - Indenture in which Alexander Sneed of the COUNTY OF ROCK-
INGHAM, STATE OF NORTH CAROLINA, sells to George Washington Jones, OF THE
COUNTY OF HENRY, STATE OF VIRGINIA - for $50.00 - a certain lot of land in
THE TOWN OF LEAKESVILLE, NORTH CAROLINA, on the north side of Dan River (#9)
containing one-half acre, etc. Recorded October 28, 1817.

Lee County, Virginia, Order Book 5 (1840-6), page 274 -

August 22, 1843 - David Little, Gentleman, who has been duly licensed
to practice the law IN THE COURTS OF THE STATE OF KENTUCKY, on his
motion, has leave to practice in this Court, and thereupon, he took the
oath of an attorney-at-law. (He was age 21 this year. --CHH.)

Comment by CHH: This is Colonel David Yancey Little, son of
Harrington Little, who left Lee County, Virginia and lived awhile in
HARLAN COUNTY, KENTUCKY before settling in MANCHESTER, CLAY COUNTY,
KENTUCKY, where he died. From a photostat copy of the Little Family
Bible, it is disclosed that David Yancey Little was born January 27,
1822, son of Harrington Little and his wife, Susanna Bays (Bayse),
daughter of Peter Bays (Bayse) and his wife, Susanna Barker of Russell
County, Virginia, and that he married first July 18, 1844 Drucilla Posey
Brittain, daughter of General George Brittain, OF KNOX AND HARLAN COUNTIES,
KENTUCKY and his second wife, Nancy Posey, who was a daughter of Benjamin
Posey and his wife, Susanna Chadwell, daughter of Captain David Chadwell.
The Bible further reveals that David Y. Little (Lyttle) and his first wife,
Drucilla Posey Brittain, had the following children:

1. George Brittain Little, born July 19, 1845
2. Dale Carter Little, born June 7, 1847
3. Carlo Brittain Little, born March 10, 1850
4. Louisa M. Little, born April 19, 1852
5. William B. Little, born June 20, 1854
6. Nancy E. A. Little, born August 25, 1856, (married December 23,1875,
   Andrew Jackson Hacker of CLAY CO., KY.)
7. John James Little, born November 20, 1858
8. Sallie Susan Little, born August 22, 1860
9. Robert E. Lee Little, born September 30, 1863
10. Daniel G. Little, born October 25, 1865

David Yancey Little died March 5, 1904, (82 years 1 mo. 8 days)
having had 3 other wives and ten more children, of whose records are also
in my files.

Rockingham County, North Carolina, Deed Book E, page 233 -

29 May 1798 - Indenture in which John Leak, Esq. of the COUNTY OF ROCKINGHAM,
STATE OF NORTH CAROLINA, sells to Terry Hughes OF THE COUNTY OF HENRY, STATE
OF VIRGINIA - for $20.00 - a certain lot of land containing one half-acre
IN THE TOWN OF LEAKESVILLE, STATE OF NORTH CAROLINA (#2B) on the North side
of Water Street and East of Patrick, fronting both streets, etc. Witnesses:
John Gibson, W.(?) Garland. Note by CHH: In subsequent Deeds of Sale in
1799, John Leake, Esq. sells Terry Hughes eight other lots in the TOWN OF
LEAKESVILLE, NORTH CAROLINA.

Ibid - Deed Book M, page 352 -

28 May 1807 (no.1306) John Matlock, Esq., High Sheriff OF THE COUNTY OF
ROCKINGHAM, STATE OF NORTH CAROLINA, sells to Jefferson Hughes,

Letey (Leticia) Hughes, Nancy Hughes, Louisiana Hughes and Polly Hughes, son
and daughters of Terry Hughes OF THE COUNTY OF HENRY AND STATE OF VIRGINIA,
etc. sundry lots in the TOWN OF LEAKESVILLE, NORTH CAROLINA, etc. - to William
Peay, the highest bidder in behalf of the above named children (of Terry
Hughes) etc. (Note by CHH: Henry County, Virginia marriage records prove
the marriage bond in that county of Terry Hughes to Jemima Reamey (Ramey)
daughter of Col. Daniel Reamey (Remy) on November 1, 1796. Other records
reveal that Terry Hughes died in Henry County, Virginia in 1810. (Henry
County Order Book 8, page 95.)

Granville County, North Carolina, Will Book 10, page 256 -

Will of Fanny B. Lyne of GRANVILLE COUNTY, NORTH CAROLINA dated 8 August 1826
and probated November Court 1826. To my sister, Lucy Foster Lyne - slaves.
To my father, Henry Lyne - all my right to any land in the STATE OF TENNESSEE.
To my brother, James H. Lyne - the land bequeath to me by my cousin Henry
Lyne, said land lying in KENTUCKY between Green and Ohio Rivers being one-
sixth (1/6) part of 400 acres which was devised to my father's children by
Henry Lyne, Jr., son of James Lyne, deceased. To my sister, Susan P. Burton -
my right in land in HALIFAX COUNTY, NORTH CAROLINA. My brother-in-law,
Stephen K. Snead to be executor. Witnesses: William H. Owens, James Parrott.

Granville County, North Carolina, Will Book 4, page 304 -

Will of Fanny Vass of Caroline County, Virginia, dated 22 May 1792 and probated May Court 1799: To my honored father, Thomas Vass all that land in
KING & QUEEN COUNTY, VIRGINIA, it being part of a tract given my deceased
mother, by her father, Thomas Foster. Witnesses: Vincent Vass, Caty Vass,
Dorothy Stand.

Granville County, North Carolina Records, Will Book 1, page 246 -

Will of Sarah Leith, late of GLOUCESTER COUNTY, VIRGINIA, dated May 18, 1770
and probated August Court 1779: 500 pounds to Petsoe Parish wherein I formerly resided, for the education of poor and orphan children, etc. Remainder
of my estate to be divided between Thomas Starke and William Starke, my
brothers and Lawrence Smith, Guy Smith, Elizabeth Lewis and Ann Smith. The
last four mentioned are sons and daughters of Constantine Smith and Frankey
Smith, my sisters (sic) - To Dr. William Ridley 500 pounds for professional
services. My executors to make ample satisfaction to Thomas Starke for
bringing me from South Carolina to this place. My brother, William Starke
of KING WILLIAM COUNTY, VIRGINIA, to be executor. Witnesses: Robert Burton,
A. Barker, Richard Edwards.

York County, Virginia Record Book (1760-1771), page 418 -

Will of Sarah Bates: My tract of land sold in NORTH CAROLINA by my son-in-
law, Samuel Jordan to William Burgess, Samuel Williams and John Scarbrough -
to them in case my power of attorney to the said Samuel Jordan is questioned.
June 29, 1750.

Virginia Genealogist, Vol. 6, page 148 - British Mercantile Claims
(1775-1803) - From reports of William W. Hening, 15 June 1802

John Thurmond, Jr. of Albemarle County (Va.) owing 63 pounds 1 shilling by
account, Albemarle Store, Henderson, McCall & Company (pp.2-3) - He removed TO ONE OF THE CAROLINAS shortly after the peace and carried with him
a very good estate consisting of twenty or thirty slaves and other property.
It is supposed he moved to SOUTH CAROLINA NEAR THE GEORGIA LINE.

Ibid -

John Sorrow, Albemarle Co. (Va.) owing 6 pounds 13 shillings 10 pence, by
account, Albemarle Store, Henderson, McCall & Co. (p.3) - He moved to
GEORGIA about 1787 and settled in the upper part of that State. He was
always able to pay his debts. (Item states further that his brother,
William Sorrow (owing 1 pound 5 shillings 5 pence) also moved to GEORGIA
about 1787 and was always able to pay his debts.)

Ibid - page 149 -

John Eades of Albemarle County (Va.) owing 8 pounds 6 shillings 8 pence,
by account, to Albemarle store, Henderson, McCall & Co. (p.5) - He moved
to GEORGIA since the peace and carried with him an estate sufficient to
pay his debts. It is said that he died in that state, in some of the
upper parts of the country, and left a widow with a good estate, who has
since married John Sorrow, who formerly moved from the same neighborhood
in this state.

Ibid, page 150 -

James Hill of Albemarle County (Virginia) owing 9 pounds 12 shillings
1½ pence by account, Donald Scott & Co. (p.10). He removed from Albemarle to Buckingham County (Virginia.) After a few years he moved
to KENTUCKY about 1789 and carried with him an estate sufficient to pay
his debts. (Note by CHH: A James Hill is listed 1789 in Madison County,
Kentucky in 1790 census of Kentucky, page 46.)

Ibid, page 151 -

Abraham Alloway Strange of Fluvanna County (Virginia) owing 38 pounds
6½ pence by account, Thompson, Snodgrass & Co. (p.13) - He moved to
NORTH CAROLINA about 15 years ago in good circumstances. He is living
in BURKE COUNTY on the Yadkin River, still reputed solvent.

Ibid-

William Whitsell of Amherst County (Virginia) owing 30 pounds 16 shillings
6½ pence by specialty and account, Thompson, Snodgrass & Co. (p.13) - He
moved to Bedford County, Virginia about 20 years ago and then to Cumberland River on that part which is since included in TENNESSEE. He has
always been reputed solvent.

88

Virginia Genealogist, Volume 6, page 152 -

Amherst County, Virginia - John Stewart, acting executor of Daniel Buford,
Senior, moved to GEORGIA within a few years past.

Ibid, page 153 -

Orange County (Virginia) - James Barbour, the principal obligator in this
claim (Fredericksburg Store, James Ritchie & Co.) moved to KENTUCKY in 1798
and carried with him property sufficient to pay his debts.

Ibid, page 154 -

Allen Howard's Estate, owing 69 pounds 15 shillings 10½ pence by account,
Albemarle store, George Keppen & Co. (p.25) - He died in 1762 and left a
very valuable estate which descended to his three sons, Benjamin, John and
William. Benjamin died in 1772; John moved TO KENTUCKY about 1794; and
William now resides in Amherst County but has been insane ever since the commencement of the war. (Note by CHH: An Allen Howard's Will was probated
in Goochland County, Virginia in 1761.)

Ibid, page 155 -

George Kennard, Culpeper County (Virginia) owing 3 pounds 5 shillings 2 pence
by account, Robert Jardine. He resided in Culpeper County until about the
termination of the war. He moved to KENTUCKY shortly after the peace and is
said to have died there, insolvent. He was a tailor by trade, very old and
an indifferent workman. (p 28.)

Ibid -

Marble Stone, Amherst County (Virginia) owing 17 pounds 4 shillings 4 pence
by account, Donald Scott & Co. (p.30) - He moved to Franklin County, Virginia
about 8 years ago and then to GEORGIA about a year ago, where he now resides
in ELBERT COUNTY.

Ibid -

Charles Sims, Albemarle County (Virginia) owing 1 pound 10 pence by account,
Donald Scott & Co. (p.31) - He moved to SOUTH CAROLINA during the war, in
good circumstances. He now lives in CHARLESTOWN and is an inspector of
tobacco. Captain John Napier about 12 months past saw him in Fluvanna
County (Virginia). He is supposed still to be able to pay his debts.

Ibid, page 156 -

John Sturgell, Orange County (Virginia) owing 5 pounds 14 shillings 11-3/4
pence by account Donald Scott & Co. (p.32) - He is called John Stodghill in
a claim of John Glassell and his name was always pronounced Sturgeon. He
moved to GREENBRIER COUNTY, VIRGINIA (NOW WEST VIRGINIA) about 1789 or 1790
in good circumstances and from last account still lived there, able to pay
his debts.

Virginia Genealogist, Volume 6, page 156 -

Frost & Snow (sic), Louisa County (Virginia) owing 9 pounds 6 shillings 3-3/4 pence by Account, Donald Scott & Co. (p.33) - He was brother to Ice & Snow (sic). He moved to SURRY COUNTY, NORTH CAROLINA about 15 or 16 years ago and carried with him a good estate. He is still said to be living there and in good circumstances. Richard Snow of Albemarle is a relation. (Note by CHH: The Christian names are actually ICE & and FROST & and the surname is SNOW.)

Ibid -

Francis Grimes, Albemarle County (Virginia) owing 15 pounds 16 shillings 10½ pence by account, Donald Scott & Co. (pp 33-4) - Francis Grayham, generally called Grymes, removed TO GEORGIA in 1778 and carried with him a very good estate. He now lives about 16 miles from COLUMBIA (sic) and is reputed to be in good circumstances. William Michie purchased his land before his removal and paid him 2 negroes in part of the purchase money.

Ibid -

Robert Moorman, Albemarle County (Virginia) owing 12 pounds 2 shillings 11 pence by account Donald Scott & Co. (p.34) - He moved to CHESTER COUNTY, SOUTH CAROLINA about 7 years ago. He is reputed solvent. Charles Moorman of Bedford County, Virginia is his brother.

Ibid, Volume 7, page 13 -

Beverly Winslow, Spotsylvania County (Virginia) owing 1 pound 16 shillings 11 pence Samuel Gest (pp.41-2) - He died in Spotsylvania County about 1792 or 1793 and left a very valuable tract of land and other personal estate sufficient to pay his debts. The executors were his sons, Thomas Winslow and William Winslow. The former (Thomas) removed to KENTUCKY about three years ago and the latter (William) about a year before. They had spent the whole of the estate and their own private property before their removal. The family is insolvent. (Note by CHH: Beverly Winslow's Will was probated in Spotsylvania in 1793. The family probably continues back in Virginia records to Essex County.)

Ibid, page 14 -

Robert and James Slaughter owing 20 pounds by bond, Samuel Gest (pp.44-5) - There were two persons named Robert Slaughter in Culpeper County (Virginia) old enough to have contracted this debt. One was generally distinguished by the appellation of Gentleman Bob and is now living in Culpeper County, but disclaims any knowledge of the debt. The other, generally known by the name of Robin Slaughter, MOVED TO KENTUCKY about 1787 or 1788 and carried with him a good estate. He had not long been in Kentucky before it was said he had conveyed his estate to his children to prevent his liability to pay the debts of his brother, James (Slaughter) for whom he was bound as security for his sheriffalty in Culpeper County and from whom there is still a large balance due the Commonwealth. Robin Slaughter now resides in MERCER COUNTY (KENTUCKY), James Slaughter moved to KENTUCKY about 1795 and died in JEFFERSON COUNTY about 1799, totally insolvent. At the peace (1783) he possessed a good deal of property and though much involved in debt there never was any difficulty of recovering monies due. During 1786 and 1787 he was high sheriff of Culpeper County and in that character became greatly in arrears to the Commonwealth and about 1789 he entirely failed in his circumstances.

Virginia Genealogist, Volume 7, page 15 -

Francis Simpson, Spotsylvania County (Virginia) owing 12 pounds 7 shillings 4 pence by account and 13 pounds 14 shillings 2 pence by bond, John Glassell (p.48) - He died in Spotsylvania County in August 1794 and left a good estate more than sufficient to pay all his debts. His acting executor was Tilley Emmerson of the same county who moved TO KENTUCKY in 1796. He now resides in FAYETTE COUNTY about 12 miles from Lexington. Nearly all the legatees of Francis Simpson have moved to KENTUCKY. He was always reputed a very honest man, remarkably punctual in the payment of his debts. William Simpson of Spotsylvania County is a relation.

Ibid -

Ann Slaughter, Culpeper County (Virginia) owing 27 pounds 9 shillings 3 pence by note, McCall, Smellie & Co. (p.50) - Mrs. Ann Slaughter died in Culpeper long before the peace and left no property. About the commencement of the war she had a very good estate which she divided among her children and after wards lived with Captain William Ball of Culpeper who married one of her daughters. It was said at the time a distribution of her estate took place that her son, Cadwallader Slaughter had undertaken payment of her debts. He moved to JEFFERSON COUNTY, KENTUCKY shortly after the peace and carried with him a good estate. He died in JEFFERSON COUNTY, KENTUCKY about three years ago. Robert Slaughter, Esq. of Culpeper is a relation.

Ibid, page 16 -

Nathaniel Pendleton, Culpeper County (Virginia) owing 50 pounds 11 shillings, balance of judgment, Fredericksburg Store, James Ritchie & Co. (p.55) - He moved to Berkeley County, Virginia (NOW WEST VIRGINIA) since the peace and died there, insolvent. Until about 1787 or 1788 he had some property, etc.

Ibid, page 17 -

William Sherrell, Culpeper County (Virginia) owing 26 pounds 7 shillings 9 pence by judgment, Fredericksburg Store, James Ritchie & Co. (p.56) - He moved to NORTH CAROLINA about 1789 or 1790 and now lives in BURKE COUNTY on John's River, a branch of the Catawba River and was alive in February last and able to pay his debts. Thomas Freeman of Culpeper was at his present residence in February.

Ibid, page 19 -

James Thomas, Culpeper County (Virginia) owing 4 pounds 7 shillings 11 pence

by bond, Culpeper Store, William Cunningham & Co. (pp 64-5) - He moved
to GEORGIA about 1784 and carried with him a very good estate. He settled
in WILKES COUNTY where he still lives, in independent circumstances.

Virginia Genealogist, Volume 7, page 19 -

Mark Thomas, Culpeper County (Virginia) owing 13 pounds 4 shillings 2½
pence by bond, Culpeper Store, William Cunningham & Co. (p.65) - He went
to KENTUCKY about 1779 with Captain George Slaughter to garrison one of
the United States posts at the Falls of the Ohio (Note by CHH: Louisville)
At the time of his removal he possessed but little property and what has
since become of him cannot be ascertained. (Note by CHH: He is shown in
1790 census of Kentucky (p.94) as being on the Tax List August 2, 1790 in
JEFFERSON COUNTY, KENTUCKY.)

Ibid, page 19 -

Samuel Duval, owing 40 pounds 3 shillings 3 pence (Vol.B p.1) He died
about 1793 leaving estate sufficient to pay all just debts. His son,
Claiborne (Duval) is executor and lives in KENTUCKY.

Ibid -

Richard Harvie, Albemarle County (Virginia) - For deduction of war interest
on 69 pounds 17 shillings 11¼ pence (pp 1-3.) He moved to GEORGIA in 1785
and carried with him a very good estate. His residence was in OGLETHORPE
COUNTY where his estate now lies. About 1795 he returned to Albemarle
County and continued there among his friends until 1798 when he died in the
town of Charlottesville. He was never married. By his Will, which was
found after his death deposited with a friend in GEORGIA, he left his estate to his relations in that country. Shortly after his death, his
brother, William Harvie of OGLETHORPE COUNTY, GEORGIA came into Albemarle
County and carried out what little property Richard Harvie brought with
him. (See balance of account in above reference.)

Ibid, page 71 -

Henry Key, Amherst County (Virginia) owing 272 pounds 7 shillings 3½
pence by bond, George Kippen & Co., Amherst and Albemarle Stores (pp 5-8.)
Henry Key, Senior MOVED TO SOUTH CAROLINA in 1774. On 1 December 1773 he
conveyed to Charles Irving, factor for George Kippen & Co., and his relation, Martin Key, eight tracts (of land) in Albemarle and Amherst Counties,
containing 2,153 acres, to secure the payment of his debts, particularly
a debt due Charles Irving, as factor, of 373 pounds 17 shillings 2½ pence.
He died in EDGEFIELD COUNTY, SOUTH CAROLINA IN NINETY-SIX DISTRICT in
August 1776, having on 4 March 1776 made his Will naming his son, Henry
(Key,Jr.) and three others executors. Henry (Key, Jr.) alone qualified.
(See balance of interesting account in above reference.)

Ibid, page 72 -

Giles Harding, owing 3 pounds, 14 shillings 9-3/4 pence (p.13.) He removed to DAVIDSON COUNTY, TENNESSEE about 1797 and was then and still is

reputed able to pay. (Note by CHH: A Giles Harding is listed in 1782 on
Goochland County, Virginia Personal Property Tax Lists with 8 taxable slaves.)

Virginia Genealogist, Volume 7, page 74 -

William Robards. Two accounts, 15 pounds 15 shillings 1 pence (p.18.) He
is dead. His son, George, in KENTUCKY, is his executor. He was able to pay
and by his Will, recorded in Goochland County 15 December 1783, directed all
his debts be paid.

Ibid, page 108 -

Edmund Curd, owing 28 pounds 18 shillings 5½ pence by account, (p.21.) About
1790 has removed from Goochland County to SHELBY COUNTY, KENTUCKY. He was
then very able to pay and still is so, which John Curd and George Underwood
of Goochland County and Jesse Robards OF KENTUCKY can prove.

Ibid, page 109 -

David England, owing 45 pounds 10 shillings 5 pence by account (p.24.) He
removed to KENTUCKY about 1786. He is still in good circumstances and lives
in MADISON COUNTY, KENTUCKY. Jesse Robards can prove him able. (Note by CHH:
A David England is listed on Goochland County Tax List in 1782.)

Ibid -

Stephen Davies, owing 5 pounds, 5 shillings 3½ pence by account. He lives
in FAYETTE COUNTY, KENTUCKY and is known to be able to pay by Jesse Robards
and F. Underwood of Goochland County, Virginia. (Note by CHH: A Stephen
Davis is listed on the 1782 Goochland County Tax List with six taxable slaves.

Ibid, page 111 -

William Robards, Senior, owing 9)pounds 18 shillings 9 pence by account,
September 1775, Richmond and 5 pounds 16 shillings 4 pence by account, 3 March
1776 (p.32.) Debts are paid except war interest. George Robards of MERCER
COUNTY, KENTUCKY, is executor.

Ibid, page 112 -

John Gill, owing 4 pounds 2 shillings 1½ pence by account 3 March 1776
(p.34-5.) He died in Goochland County, Virginia in 1796, insolvent as to
personal estate. He owned lands to greater value than 100 pounds in ROWAN
COUNTY, NORTH CAROLINA. Joseph Watkins, his administrator, says he was
able to pay in 1790, but the estate has since been consumed in the support
of his family.

Ibid -

Samuel Duval, Senior, owing 131 pounds 6 shillings 7-3/4 pence by account
3 March 1774 (p.36.) He died about 1784, able to pay his just debts. His
son, Claiborne, his executor lives in KENTUCKY. (Note by CHH: The Will of
Samuel Duval (d.1784) is recorded in Henrico County, Virginia.)

Virginia Genealogist, Volume 7, page 113 -

Abner Witt, owing 2 pounds 18 shillings 8½ pence by account, Goochland
Store (p.39) - He ran away from Amherst County (Virginia) after the
peace and went to NORTH CAROLINA, IN THE PART SINCE INCLUDED IN TENNESSEE.
He was always a poor man, possessing so little property he was unable to
keep it from the hands of the Sheriff.

Ibid, page 114 -

Augustin Eastin, owing 19 pounds 19 shillings 10½ pence by bond 24 October
1772 (p.42.) He lives in BOURBON COUNTY, KENTUCKY and is able to pay his
debts. (Note by CHH: There was an Augustine Easten listed on Goochland
County 1782 Tax Lists with 5 taxable slaves.)

Ibid, page 177 -

Benjamin Johnson, Fredericksburg, owing 3 pounds 17 shillings 10 pence by
account Falmouth Store and 3 pounds 5 shillings 8 pence by account Culpeper Store; 26 pounds 19 shillings by bond, Fredericksburg Store (p.49.)
He moved to KENTUCKY about the close of the war, (1783 or 1784) He
carried with him property of considerable value but was generally supposed
to be much involved in debt. He greatly improved his estate after he
moved to Kentucky. His residence was in JEFFERSON COUNTY, KENTUCKY.
Thomas Farish of Orange County (Virginia) formerly lived with him.

Ibid -

Robert Stubblefield, owing 45 pounds 6 shilling 0½ pence by judgment (p.52.)
He moved to FAYETTE COUNTY, KENTUCKY in 1787 in good circumstances. From
thence he moved and settled near Limestone in MASON COUNTY, KENTUCKY where
he still resides. Colonel Beverly Stubblefield of Madison County, Virginia
formerly of Spotsylvania County (Virginia) is his brother.

Ibid, page 178 -

Charles Davenport, Culpeper County (Virginia), owing 10 pounds 1 shilling
2¼ pence by account (p.54.) He moved to SOUTH CAROLINA about 1782 and
carried with him a very good estate. He settled in NINETY-SIX DISTRICT
where he still resides and is reputed very rich. Richard Davenport of
Albemarle County, (Virginia) is his brother.

Ibid -

David Kerr, Albemarle, owing 2 pounds 15 shillings 8½ pence by account
(pp 55-6) - He moved to KENTUCKY in 1791 or 1792 in very good circumstances
and now resides in SCOTT COUNTY, KENTUCKY still reputed solvent.

Lunenburg County, Virginia, Deed Book 24, page 418 -

STATE OF SOUTH CAROLINA, 96th DISTRICT - John Glenn of ABBEVILLE and STATE
OF SOUTH CAROLINA, Esquire, reposing special trust and confidence in
Tyree Glenn of LAURENS COUNTY, SOUTH CAROLINA, etc. gives a Power of

Attorney to settle as he thinks fit the Estate of Colonel Lyddal Bacon of
Lunenburg County, Virginia, dec'd., that was left to him by his last Will
and Testament as having married Sally Bacon, daughter of the said Colonel
Lyddal Bacon. Dated 2nd November 1793.

Ibid, page 419 -

I do hereby certify that agreeable to the within Power of Attorney, I have
sold and disposed of all that part of the Estate of Lyddal Bacon, deceased,
to Langston Bacon for 35 pounds current money, that is coming to Colonel
John Glenn by his marrying Sally Bacon, daughter of Lyddal Bacon, deceased.
Witness my hand this 17th December 1793 - (signed) Tyree Glenn.

Loudoun County, Virginia, Deed Book "P" page 307 -

Indenture dated 23rd November 1785 in which Samuel Pearson of the COUNTY OF
BERKELEY, IN SOUTH CAROLINA and Mary, his wife, sell to Thomas and George
Smith of the County of Loudoun, State of Virginia - for 225 pounds - a tract
of land in Loudoun County, Virginia between the short hill and the Blue
Ridge, on a branch called Piney Run, being part of a tract granted Catesby
Cocke by patent for 1726 acres, transferred to Joshua Gore (by said Catesby
Cocke) and by said Gore to said Samuel Pearson 13th May 1760 - containing
470 acres, etc. Witnesses: Ezekiel Potts, Nathan Potts, Samuel Potts, John
Smith, William Smith. Recorded: Loudoun County 12th June 1786.

Bedford County, Virginia, Deed Book 30, page 492 -

24 November 1843 - Indenture in which Thomas Crum, Nancy Crum, Betsy Crum,
Polly Crum, and Elijah Crum, of the COUNTY OF GREENUP, STATE OF KENTUCKY,
(parties of one part) sell to Henry Woodford of the County of Bedford, Vir-
ginia - for $100.00 - a tract of land in the County of Bedford on the north
side of Goose Creek, containing 44 acres, which land formerly belonged to
David Carson, deceased, who left it by a legal Will to the above mentioned
Crums, the children of Gilbert Crum, etc. Witnesses: C. Spangler, A. Crooks.
Signed by: Thomas Crum
             Elijah Crum
             Nancy Towler, formerly Nancy Crum
             Betsy Wilks, formerly Betsy Crum
             Polly Howell, formerly Polly Crum
Signatures certified by the Justices of Greenup County, Kentucky and recorded
Bedford County, Virginia, 25th December 1843.

     Note by CHH: The Will of David Kesson (sic) who married Elizabeth Crum
October 11, 1796, was dated 3 April 1820; probated 27 November 1820 in
Bedford County, Will Book 5, page 232 in which he leaves the above cited 44
acres to Gilbert Crum's children and named them as above. The marriage bonds
of Bedford County, Virginia (p.33) reveal that on March 11, 1809, Gilbert
Crump (sic) married Letty Dixon, daughter of Thomas Dixon.

Granville County, North Carolina, Deed Book 1, page 197 -

1752 - Richard Yancey of LOUISA COUNTY, VIRGINIA purchases 440 acres of land
in Granville County, North Carolina.

Louisa County, Virginia, Deed Book C, page 76 -

Indenture in which William Graves OF GRANVILLE COUNTY, NORTH CAROLINA,
PARISH OF ST. JOHN'S - sells for 20 pounds - John Forsie Junior - 431
acres of land on Beaver Dam Creek, near Nathaniel Williams on the
Albemarle County line, etc. Witnesses: Bartlett Ford, William
Timberlake, Samuel McGehee. Comment: I am sorry but this is an old
notation in my files and I cannot make out the date. Reference to the
cited record should easily reveal same.

Granville County, North Carolina, Deed Book E, page 58 -

1761 - William Moore of Granville County, North Carolina sells John
William Graves OF HANOVER COUNTY, COLONY OF VIRGINIA, 210 acres of land
on both sides of Island Creek, etc. Witnesses: Henry Graves, William
Graves, Benjamin Hendrick.

Ibid, page 12 -

1761 - Zachariah Baker of Granville County, North Carolina, sells William
Graves 592 acres on Grassy Creek, etc.

Louisa County, Virginia, Deed Book U, page 495 -

9th November 1833 - William S. Bates and Huldah, his wife, of the
COUNTY OF MARION AND STATE OF MISSOURI, appoint James Bates, of afore-
said State, attorney to sell slaves decreed to William S. and Huldah
Bates by the Circuit Superior Court for the County of Goochland and
the State of Virginia on the 19th April 1833 in a Chancery Cause in which
James Parrish, administrator do bonis non, with the will annexed of
Booker Parrish, deceased, was Complainant and David M. Parrish, William
S. Bates and Huldah, his wife were defendants, which said Negroes as we
are informed are now in the possession of Horatio G. Winston, Esq. of
Louisa County, Virginia and are seven in number. And James Bates to
sell said slaves and show a bill of sale, etc. Horatio W. Winston was
of Council for the said William S. and Huldah Bates on the above suit.
Whereas Huldah, wife of William S. Bates is entitled to a reversion
interest in the estate of Constant Parrish, her mother, etc.

James Jameson and Samuel C. Reed testify that William S. Bates
and Huldah, his wife, appeared before them in MARION COUNTY, MISSOURI
on 29th November 1833 and acknowledged the same to be their act and
deed for the purpose therein mentioned and desired to Certify the said
acknowledgment to the Clerk of the COUNTY OF GOOCHLAND, VIRGINIA, in
order that the same might be recorded. Huldah was examined privately
and apart from her husband and she acknowledged the same to be her act
and deed. Dated 29 November 1833.

INDEX

States, Countries, or Territories other than Virginia

Arnold (Continued)
John	20[2]
Latham	62,63
Mary	20
V.	46
William	20,65[2]

Arrington
Parham	36

Ashley
Stephen	9
Thomas	3

Askins
Edward	7
John	7

Atkinson
Aaron	51
Anne	51
John	66
Mary	51
Thomas, Sr.	18
Thomas, Jr.	18

Averet
Wilmouth	31

Ayleward
William	3

Babb
Joseph	26

Bacon
Langston	94
Col. Lyddal	18,94[2]
Sally	94

Bagwell
Thomas	4
Thomas, Jr.	4

Bailey
Joshua	51
Peter	46

Baker
Blake	81,82
Mark	49
Martha (Hamlin)	81
Mary	49

Baker (Continued)
Miles	8
Moses	49
Richard	84
Zachariah	46,95

Ball
George	32
John	30
Capt. William	90

Ballard
James	79
John	5
Thomas	2

Barbour
James	88

Barclay
Andrew	44
Elizabeth	44
George	44
Patrick	44

Barker
A.	86
Charles	19
Honour (Cutts?)	19
Jesse	19
John Henry	19
Susanna	85
Capt. William	4[2]

Barnett
William	55

Bartlett
Thomas	74

Barton
Seth	8

Bashford
Elizabeth	33
Grace	32,33
John	32[2],33
Judith	33
Simon	32[2],33[2]

Baskervwyle
John	5

Bass
Burwell	51

Bates
    Charles Fleming   14
    Edward   83
    Frederick   83
    Huldah   95
    James   82,95
    Sarah   86
    William, Jr.   82
    William S.   95

Battaley
    John   72

Baugh
    Rhoda   12

Baylor
    Jon   40
    William   3

Bays (Bayse)
    John   30
    Peter   85
    Susanna (Barker)   85

Beale
    Robert   56

Bean
    John   59

Beauchamp
    John   45
    William   45

Beck(s)
    Benjamin 17^2
    George   18
    Margaret   17

Begnold
    Anne   66
    James   66

Bell
    Humphrey   62,63

Benger
    Ann   67
    Dorothea   67
    John   67

Bennett
    John   17,18
    Mary   17,18
    Peter   11

Benson
    Thomas   34

Bernard
    Robert   14

Berry
    Cara (McChesney)   54,55
    Grace 23^3
    George 23^4
    Hugh   32
    Lawrence   42
    R. A.   54,55
    William 23^2

Berryman
    John   78

Beverley
    Harry   62,74
    Mary   74
    Robert   14,58,62
    William   50

Bibby
    John   22

Biddle
    Clement   70,72
    Owen   70

Bigger
    James B.   8

Billingsly
    Allen   78
    Zachariah   67

Birch
    Richard   23

Bird
    Williamson   6

Black
    Margaret   60
    Sarah   60

Blackburn
    Elizabeth   12
    James   12
    Rhoda (Baugh)   12
    William   39,40

Blain
    Ephraim   70

Blair
    James   13

Bland
    Edward, Jr.   35
    Peter   35,43

Blaydes
    John   72

Bledsoe
    Elizabeth 68^2
    Joseph   68
    William   68
    William Miller   68

Blunt
    John   19

Boatwright
    Benjamin   12
    Elizabeth   12
    James B.   12
    Mary P.   12

Bodley
    Thomas   79

Boggan
    Margaret   20
    Mary (Dabbs)   20
    Patrick   20

Bogle
    William   17,52

Boner
    Witten   1

Borden
    Benjamin, Sr.   16
    Benjamin, Jr.   16
    Magdaline   16
    Martha   16
    Zeruiah   16

Bowden
    William   44

Bowman
    Samuel   61

Bowyer
    Magdaline   16

Boyce
    Richard   43

Bracy
    Thomas   36

Bradford
    Fielding   13

Bradshaw
    Henry   5

Brag(g)
    John   69
    William 61^2

Brailsford
    Samuel   63

Brakley
    James   67

Branch
    Edmund   18

Brandon
    Alexander   6
    Thomas, Jr.   6
    William, Jr.   6

Branham
    Daniel   66,71
    Richard   73
    Robert   74
    Tavenor   73

Brayne
    Ann(e) 66^2,67
    Butler   66
    Diana   66
    Richard   66

Breakhill
    John   4

Brent
    John   26
    Martin   80

Brenton
    Miles   63

Brew
    John   4

Brewer			Brown		
Edmond	26		Adelia	55
Edward	25		Col. Alexander	45
John	20		Ann B.	28
Rease	20		Daniel	59
			Eliza P.	55
Bride			Ermine	28
Thomas	50		Jane A.	55
			John	28
Bridges			John A.	55
Mathew	73		Mary J.	28
Thomas	44,45		William	21

Brewer
    Edmond   26
    Edward   25
    John   20
    Rease   20

Bride
    Thomas   50

Bridges
    Mathew   73
    Thomas   44,45

Briggs   18

Brightwell   67

Brittain
    Drucilla Posey 85
    Gen. George   85
    James   84
    Nancy (Posey)   85

Brizendine
    Isaac   18

Brock
    John, Jr.   71
    Joseph   56,60, 69
                    71,73,74
    Joseph, Jr.   72
    William   69
    William Orril   70

Brodhurst
    Walter   4

Brokenbough
    Dr. John   14

Brook(e)
    Dudley   46
    Elizabeth   46
    George   46
    H.   14
    Joshua   10
    Mary   46
    Robert   14,43
    Sarah   46
    Zachariah   46

Brooks
    Thomas   69

Brown
    Adelia   55
    Col. Alexander   45
    Ann B.   28
    Daniel   59
    Eliza P.   55
    Ermine   28
    Jane A.   55
    John   28
    John A.   55
    Mary J.   28
    William   21

Brumfield
    Obediah   43

Brundett
    John   45

Bryant
    Edmund   67
    Edward, Sr.   67
    Sarah   67
    Silvanus   55

Buchanan
    Alexander Pitt   81
    Andrew   67
    John   7
    William   37

Buckner
    Caroline M.   52
    George   67
    William   76
    William S.   52

Buford
    Daniel   88

Bullard
    Richard   74

Bullitt
    Cuthburt   48

Bullock
    James   71
    John   71
    Joseph   71,75
    Samuel   71

Bulstrode
    Symon   1

Burbridge
George   73
Linsfield   73
Thomas   71,73
Thomas, Sr.   73

Burch
Mr.   84

Burchett
Mary   44

Burgess
William   86

Burk(s)
Henry   9
William   37

Burkett
Jacob   48

Burnett
William   80

Burns
William   56

Burrage
Charles   80

Burton
Jones W.   27
Susan P. (Lyne)   86
Richard   37
Robert   86

Bushrod
Richard   5
Thomas   1

Butler
Joseph   46

Byars
John   54

Cabaness
William   35

Caldwell
John   25,26[2]
William   25,26

Calhoun
Patrick   50

Cameron
John   17

Cammack
George   70

Campbell
Alexander   42
Ann   42
Colin   42
Daniel   42
Dugald   41,42
Duncan   41,42
Elizabeth   42
Henrietta   42
James   14,22,43,54
John   9,14,41,42
Judith   14
Lannce   42
Lucy   42
Mary   27,41,42[2],43
Mary Ann   42
Mumford   42
Neil   42
Prudentia W.   38
Thomas   47
William C.   38
William Newell   42

Canady
Joseph   11

Cannon
James   59

Canterbury
John, Bishop of   41

Car(?)
John   15

Cardwell
Robert   26

Carlyle
Frances   14
Col. John   62
John   14

Carmichael
John   37

Carnahan
    John   69

Carpenter
    Elizabeth   79
    Frances   80
    Jesse   79,80
    Jonathan, Jr.   80
    Jonathan   79,80
    Nancy   80
    Zacheus   79,80

Carr
    Susannah   73
    Thomas 69^3,70
    Walter   69
    Walter Chiles   73
    William   42,73

Carson (See Kesson)
    David   12,94

Carter
    Anne   61
    Charles   71
    George   31,61
    Henry   71
    James   27,43
    John   4,33,64,71^2
    Lucy   31
    Mary   27
    Mary H.   43
    Rachel K.   33
    Robert 4^2
    William   27
    William Champe   77

Cary
    Henry   3
    Patrick   60
    Robert   3

Cates
    Carter   18

Cathrae
    John   70

Cave
    Capt. Benjamin   57
    Richard   56,74

Chadwell
    Capt. David, Sr.   84,85
    David, Jr.   84
    Susannah   85

Chambers
    D.   84

Champe
    John   63
    Col. John   42
    William   42

Chancy
    George W.   7

Chandler
    John   69
    Rachel   10
    Thomas   10

Chapman
    Benjamin   66
    George   19,59
    Giles   43
    Pearson   64
    Thomas   66

Charles
    Joseph   83

Cheaney
    James   46
    Thomas   46

Cheseman
    Edmund   3
    John   2
    Margaret   3
    Thomas   3
    Thomas, Jr.   40

Chesley
    Margaret   3
    Phillip   3

Chew
    Beverly   77
    Henry   60
    Jane   60
    John   68
    John, Jr. $65,69,70^2$
    Joseph   70
    Larkin   60,64
    Robert Beverly   70
    Thomas   4,58

Chicheley
    Sir Henry   5

Chichester	
Jane	5
John	5
Richard	5
Childress	
Benjamin	76
Chiles	
James	64
Samuel	71
Sarah	71
Walter	73
Christian	
James	22
Jordan C.	7
Christmas	
John	47
Clark(e)	
Cary L.	13
Eliza Pinking	55
Elizabeth	35,43
Jonathan	78
John	14
Lew	35,43
Walter B.	55
Gov. William	83
Clay	
Francis	4
Henry	35
William	46
Clayton	
John	3
Cleek	
Mathias	29
Peter	29
Cleever	
James	17
Clutterbuck	
Mary	52
Coats	
John	22
Richard	22
Cobb(s)	
Thomas	46
William	

Cocke	
Catesby	94
John B.	83
Coffey	
William	19
Coffin	
Andrew	34
Coffman	
Martin	25
Michael	25
Cogbill	
Jesse	44
Colbreath	
William	47
Coleman	
Daniel	71
Francis	80
Hawes	71
Henry E.	83
Robert	18,19,59,63
Thomas	62,63
Thomas, Jr.	70
Collier	
John	66
Collins	
Ann	62
Bartlet	75
George	53
Henry	80
James	62
John	62
Joseph	61,62
Miss _____	81
Mackenzie	36
Richard	69,70,80
S.	81
Sarah	80
Thomas	53,62
William	53,62
Colquohoon	
James	65
Colson	
Frances	66
Thomas	66,75

Colvill			Cowper	
Andrew, Sr.	11		Isaac	27,43
Joseph	11		Susanna	27,43
Mary	11		Cox	
Combs			Isabella	30
Joseph	48		Jacob	29
			Nannie K.	30
Compton			Thomas	43
James	63		Craddock	
Connelly			David	26
Sanford	9		Craghill	
			Betty	68
Conway			Elizabeth	67
John L.	24		William	67
P.	79		William, Jr.	68
Cook			Craig	
Capt. Joshua	3		David	12
			Elizabeth	12
Cooke			George W.	31,32
Elizabeth	79		Joseph	76,78
Fanny	79		Joseph, Sr.	11
John	79		Lewis	64
			Mary Ann	32
Coolige			Peggy (Sharp)	31
Judson	14		Robert	12
			Robert, Jr.	28
Cooper			Sally	12
Douglas H.	15		Crawford	
Jonathan	24		Chris	78
			James	61,78
Copeland			John	76
Hervey	49			
			Crocker	
Corbett			Joseph	21
Jone	44^2		William	21
Nathaniel	44^2			
			Crooks	
Cottman			A.	94
Benjamin	59			
Joseph	58		Crosthwait	
			William	59
Coulter				
John	36		Crum	
			Betsy	94
Cowan			Elijah	94
Andrew	32		Elizabeth	94
Clarissa (Sharp)	32		Gilbert	94
James	32		Nancy	94
John	32		Polly	94
Robert	82		Thomas	94

Crump			Dameron	
Gilbert	94		Bartholomew	32,33
Letty (Dixon)	94		Bartholomew, Jr.	32
Richard	51		Elizabeth	32
Susanna	56		George	32
			Thomas, Jr.	33
Crutcher				
Henry	69		Dance	
Thomas	78		William	12
Crutchfield			Daniel	
Robert	76,78		J. M.	38
Stapleton	70,76		J. R. J.	81
Thomas	76		James	45
			John	45
Cryter				
Michael	25		Darke	
			Mrs._____	80
Cummins				
John C.	24		Daubins	
			Thomas	48
Cunningham				
Alexander	53,84		Daughtery	
Jackson	49		James	26
James	26,49			
Jane	49		Davenport	
John	49,51		Charles	93
Miss _____	80		Richard	93
Peggy	49[2]		William	61
Richard M.	84			
Susan	49		Davies	
William & Co.	91		Stephen	92
Curd			Davis	
Edmund	92		Caleb	6
John	92		Nicholas	58
Spencer	8		Philemon	75
			Samuel	4,39
Curtis				
Rice, Jr.	65		Dawson	
			B.	69
			James	69
Dabbs			Mary	67
Elizabeth	20		T.	69
Joseph	20		William	67,68
Josiah	20			
Mary	20		Day	
Nany	20		Benjamin	73
William	20		John	69,79
Dalton			Deakens	
Elizabeth	64		William, Jr.	47
John	64			
Walker	64		Dearry	
			Anthony	57

Delany
    Nancy (Field)   34

Dennis
    Richard 35^2,43

Depp
    John   55

Devauld
    Jacob 29^2,30

Deveraux
    Charles   50

Dew
    William   26

Dick
    Archibald   73,74
    Charles   44,62,63

Dicken(s)
    John 9^2

Dickson
    William   17,52

Dillard
    Richard   68
    Thomas $68,76^2$
    Thomas, Sr.   68
    William   68

Dimmitt
    Elizabeth (Ramey)   10
    James   10

Dixon
    Letty   94
    Lucy 63^2,74
    Roger 63^2,68,74
    Thomas   94
    Capt. Thomas   63

Doby
    John   19

Dodson
    Jaine (Edwards)   39
    James   39
    Joshua   39
    Martin   39
    Oliver   27,43

Donaghe   13

Donaldson
    Henry   59

Donalson
    James   75

Donango
    James   13

Dowell
    John, Jr.   82

Downman
    William   44

Downs
    Henry   59

Drake
    Francis   56

Dryden
    David   28

Duckworth
    Permelia H.   41
    William A.   41

Dudgeon
    Richard   26

Dudley
    Ambrose   75,79
    Ann   75
    James   75
    Peter   75,79
    Robert   75

Duerson
    Joseph   70

Duncan
    John S.   39

Duncanson
    James 64^2
    Robert   63,64
    Thomas $63,64^2$

Dunlap
    Salina   27

Dunlop
    John   58

Dunnavant
    Thomas   83

Dunne
    Charles   2

Dupree
    James   51

Durrett
    William   65

Duval
    Abraham   29
    Claiborne   91,92
    Jacob   29
    Samuel   91
    Samuel, Sr.   92

Duvall
    Joseph   83
    Thomas   79,80

Eades
    John   87
    Widow   87

Ealey
    Henry   73

Early
    John Sharp   32
    Joseph   32

Easley
    Samuel   14

Eastin
    Augustin   93

Eaton
    Mary   23
    William   23

Edmonds
    John, Jr.   19

Edmunds
    Elizabeth Lewis   45
    James Nevil   45[2]

Edmunds, Continued
    Jefferson L.   45[2]
    Lewis   45
    Mary Ann   45
    Polly Clough   45
    Rowland   45

Edmundson
    J. K.   38

Edwards
    Jaine   39
    John   80
    Col. John   81
    Leathy   39
    Richard   86
    Susannah   39
    Thomas R.   39
    Thomas, Sr.   39

Ekerd
    Frederick   29

Eldridge
    Thomas   44

Ellegood
    Hancock   1

Elley
    Henry   73

Ellis
    Bible Records   49
    Elizabeth   49
    Ephraim   49
    Jane (Heath)   49
    Sampson   44

Ellzey
    W.   14

Ely
    Adam   53
    Simon   53

Emmerson
    Tilley   90
    W.   65

Emperor
    Elizabeth   1

England
    David   92

Epperson
    Charles   29
    David   21

Estes
    Barbara   65
    John   65
    Thomas   52,65
    Thomas, Sr.   65
    William   69

Etheridge
    Adam   24
    Andrew   18
    Elizabeth 24^3
    John   17
    Levy   24
    Lydia   24
    Thomas   17

Etherington
    Thomas 63^2

Eudailey
    Moses   43

Ewing
    Samuel   37

Fagan
    Henry   47

Fairfax
    Thomas, Lord   63

Fantleroy
    Colonel   45

Farish
    Thomas   93

Farley
    Francis   77
    Hannah   83
    James   77
    Josiah   83

Faulkner
    Elizabeth   8
    Marcus   :8

Fauntleroy
    Griffin   59

Fawber
    Joseph   27

Fears
    Rebecca M.   6

Featherston(e)
    Burrell $35,43^2$
    Carolus   43
    Charles   35,43
    Charles Hoel   35
    Jesse   35,43
    Lewis   35
    Richard   34,35,43
    Susanna   34
    William $35^2,43$

Fellowes
    Margaret   3
    William   3

Fennie
    William   51

Fernly(?)
    William   16

Field
    Benjamin   34
    Daniel 34^3
    Diana   34
    Elizabeth   34
    George 34^2
    Henry, Jr.   34
    Henry William S. 34^2
    John 34^2
    Joseph   34,56
    Mary 34^2
    Molly   34
    Nancy   34
    Richard H.   33,34
    Sarah   34
    Suze   34
    Thomas   34
    William   34

Fielding
    Edward   23

Finney
    Peter   44
    William   83

Fins(?)
    Rebecca (Marshall) 23

Fisher
    Phillip   55

Fitzhugh
    Lucy   42

Fitzpatrick
    Benjamin   55,56
    Joseph   55,56
    Joseph (dec'd)   55
    Thomas   56
    William   55[2]

Fleming
    William   10

Floid
    William   67

Folson
    Israil   15

Ford
    Bartlett   47,95
    J. T.   38

Forde
    Standish   72

Foreman
    David   7
    Isaac   7

Forsie
    John, Jr.   47,95

Forsyth
    Robert   68

Foster
    A.   59
    Achilles   47
    Benjamin   44
    Henry   69
    Isaac P.   49
    Mildred   69
    Thomas   76,78,86

Fowler
    John,Jr.   81

Fox
    Capt. John   2
    William   72

Frame
    David   12
    Matthew   80

Frazer
    Anthony   78
    James   70,75,78
    John   64
    Reuben   78
    William   78

Freeman
    Sarah (Holladay)   77
    Thomas   90

French
    Ann (Brayne)   67
    Dr. George   67

Friends
    Nathaniel   44

Fuller
    Henry   22

Fulton
    Edward   27
    Andrew   26
    Arthur   30
    James   37
    James (Jones)   30
    Naomi   30

Furlong
    Hubbard   56

Furnine
    John   1

Gaines
    James   29

Galbrath
    Andrew   28

Gale
    Mary (Thomas)   21
    Thomas Whitney   21

Gamble
    John   50

Gamewell
    James   55

Garber			Gilkerson, Continued	
M. Jr.	13		Hugh	38
			Rebecca	38
Garland				
Peter	21		Gill	
W.	85		John	92
			Joseph	83
Garnett				
Capt. Henry	14		Gillum	
			John	56
Garrett				
Henry, Jr.	78		Ginn	
James	39		W. M.	35
Garrison			Glasgow	
Shelly	47		James	37
Gatewood			Glasscock	
Ann	80		Stephen	8
Henry	80			
Henry, Sr.	80		Glassell	
Margaret	80		John	73,88,90
Mary	80		William	73
Sarah	80			
			Glenn	
Gay			Jeremiah	26
John	56		Col. John	93,94
			Sally (Bacon)	94[2]
Geddes			Tyree	26,93,94
Henry	50,51			
			Glentworth	
Gee			Elizabeth	72
John	23			
			Glothlymin (?)	
George			Matthew	15
David	26			
			Gold	
Gest			Daniel	21
Samuel	89[2]		Daniel, Jr.	21
			Elizabeth	21
Gholson			Ephraim	21
Daniel Billy	72		John	21
			Josiah	21,31
Gibbs			Mary	21
Churchill	56		Mealy	21
Massy	80		Moore	21
			Pleasant	21
Gibson			Sarah	21
John	77,85			
Mildred	77		Gooch	
			Joseph	21
Gilchrist				
Robert	17,52		Goodfellow	
			James	37
Gilkerson				
Frances	38		Goodloe	
			George	65
			Henry	65
			Mr._____	75

(16)

Goodloe, Continued
    Robert   65
    Sarah   65

Goodson
    John   54
    Samuel E.   54

Goodwin
    James C.   71

Gordener
    Mastin   3

Gordon
    Eli   48
    Nancy   69
    Nathaniel ch.   69
    Thomas V.   48

Gore
    Joshua   94

Graham
    Edward   80
    John   59

Grame
    John   58
    Katherine   58

Granger
    Richard   17

Grantham
    Thomas   3

Graves
    Asa   56
    Benjamin   58
    Elijah   16,47
    Henry   46,95
    Isaac   79
    James 20^2,78
    John   78
    John William   46,95
    Joseph   20

Graves
    Mary   16,47
    Samuel   78
    Susanna   20
    Thomas   20
    William $46,47^2,78,95^3$
    William, Jr. 20^2

Gray
    Allie   40
    Benjamin   54

Gray, Continued
    Bessie A.   40
    David   11
    David S.   40
    Emma J.   40
    Frederick G.   30
    James   32,33
    Joseph   18,54
    Joseph (dec'd)   54
    Julia Grace   40
    Lula C.   40
    Margaret   30
    Maria Teresa   32
    Mary   30
    Mary J.   40,41
    Nelly G.   40
    R. E.   40
    Robert Emmett   40
    R. M.   40
    Susan Katharine   40
    Thomas   54
    William F.   40

Grayham
    Francis   89

Grayson
    John   59
    Thomas   59
    William   8

Green
    Duff   14
    Elizabeth   15
    Francis   39
    John   43
    Peter   18

Gregory
    Andrew   48

Gresham
    George   6

Griffin
    Mary (Gold)   21
    Peter   21
    Sarah (Gold)   21

Griggs
    Leroy P.   15

Grigsby
    Jacob   9
    Nathaniel   9

Grills
    John   50

Grills, Continued
    John, Jr.   50
    John, Sr.   50

Grim
    Mathew   40

Grimes
    Francis   89
    Mathias   54

Grunty
    John   48

Gunn
    William   36

Gusthart
    John   44

Guthrie
    James   27

Hablett
    William P.   34

Hacker
    Andrew Jackson   85
    Nancy (Little)   85

Hackney
    Benjamin   56

Haisly
    Elizabeth   21
    James   21
    James, Sr.   21

Hale
    Lt. T. W.   48

Haley
    Barney   21
    John   21

Hall
    Eliza Ann   78
    John   78
    Will   5
    William, Jr.   83

Hallman
    Richard   1

Haltxclow
    Jacob   58

Hamblin
    Charles   21

Hamilton
    George   28
    Mary   22

Hamlett
    Mary (Brooke)   46

Hamlin
    Charles   81,82[3]
    Eliza (Jane)   81,82
    Euphan W.   82
    Fanny   81,82[3]
    Martha   81,82
    Mary   81,82
    Robert P.   81,82
    William A.   82[2]
    Wood Jones   81,82[2]

Hammer
    Augustus   54
    Frederick   54
    George   25

Hancock
    Ann   17
    John   17,51
    John, Jr.   17
    Martha   17
    Samuel   17
    William   17

Handley
    William   67

Handsher
    Nicholas   43

Hanna
    James   22

Hannes
    Joseph   62
    Joseph, Sr.   62

Hannis
    Catharine   58
    John   58

Hansbrough
    Elijah   24

Harden
    James   76

Hardin
    Mark   11

Harding
Giles 91,92
Richard 23

Hardyman
Francis 44

Hargrave
Austin 51
Hartwell 51
Joseph, Sr. 51
William 51
William, Sr. 51

Harker
Erasmus 49
J. W. 49

Harkins
George W. 15

Harland
John 74

Harman(s)
Dr. John 27,43
Mary 27^2,43
Mrs. Mary 43
Susanna 27,43

Harrelson
Alexander 52^3
Anne 36,37
Gideon 52
John 52
Lea 53
Nanna 37^2
Peter 52
William $36^2,37^2$

Harrie
Samuel 23

Harrington
Joseph 46

Harris
Christopher 2
Hardy 19
Nathaniel 54
Tabitha 14

Harrison
Burr 11
Cuthbert 11
Polly (Apperson) 70

Harry
Jacob 49

Hart
Robert 69

Harvey
Martha (Hawkins) 16
Robert 16

Harvie
Richard 91
William 91

Harwood
James 54^2

Hatchett
Jane 5,6
William 5,6

Hatfield
David 18

Hawkins
Benjamin 16
Frances 79
Joseph 53
Martha 16
Nathan 79
Nicholas, Jr. 72

Haydon
John 68

Hayes
D. H. 55

Hays
Joseph 11

Hayton
George 53
John 53
Margaret 53

Head
James 67
Sarah 67

Heath
Jane 49
Samuel 32

Hedges
Solomon 48

Heiskell
Amelia 81
Frederick 81

Helvie
Adam 50

(19)

Henderson	28	
McCall & Co.	87	
William	70,71	
Hendrick		
Benjamin	46,95	
Hendrix		
Thomas	37	
Hening		
William W.	87	
Henning		
George	69	
Hensley		
Samuel	19	
Herd		
Jonathan	64	
Herndon		
Edward	70,73	
Edward, Jr.	74	
John	79	
John, Jr.	72	
Joseph	6,70,76	
Sallie	6	
William	70,72	
Herod		
William	74	
Hess		
G. W.	55	
Jacob C.	55	
Hewell		
William	74	
Hewitt		
James	56	
Susanna (Crump)	56	
Hewlett		
John	4	
Hickes		
Escamues	2	
Katherine	2	
Hickey		
Mary Jane	41	
Permelia	41	
William	41	
William, Jr.	41	
W. M. Jr.	41	

Hicks		
Peter	80	
Sarah	62	
William	62	
Higgins		
Moses	74	
Highsmith		
Anne	17	
Daniel	17	
Hill		
Edmund W.	45	
Herbert	36	
James	87	
Littleton	48	
Rev.	80	
Hite		
Lt. T. W.	48	
Sally	81^2	
Hoard		
William, Jr.	72	
Willis	72	
Hobbs		
Mrs. Susan E.	41	
Hobson		
John	59	
Hodges		
Thomas	56	
Hoggett		
Nathaniel	20	
Nancy	20	
Hogshead		
John S.	40	
Nelly G.	40	
Holdercrost		
Henry	44	
Holeman (Holman)		
Elizabeth	83	
Henry	83	
Holladay		
Aggy	77	
Benjamin, Jr.	69	
Betsey	77	
John	77^2	
John, Sr.	77	
Lucy	77	
Mildred	77^2	

Holladay, Continued		
Nancy	77	
Owen	77	
Sarah	77	
Hollensworth		
Isaac	84	
Holliday		
James	80	
Holloday		
John, Jr.	65	
Holloway		
Whit	53	
Holmes		
Gabriel	13	
James	13	
Home		
G.	59	
Hooe		
Harris	68	
Hope		
Giles	83	
Hopkins		
John	8	
Wi(?)	45	
Horsley		
William	19	
Houck		
Susan	35	
Susanna	35	
Houston		
Fanny	67	
How		
Peter	61	
Howard		
Allen	88	
Benjamin	88	
James	52	
John	88	
William	88	
Howell		
John	50	
Polly (Crum)	94	
Hubbard		
Benjamin	44	

Huddleston		
John	64	
Robert	64	
Robert, Jr.	64	
Huff		
Daniel	36	
James	36^2	
Julius	36	
Lewis	36	
Mary	36	
Rebecca	36	
William	36	
Hughes		
Jefferson	85	
Leticia	27,86	
Louisiana	86	
Nancy	86	
Polly	86	
Stephen	22	
Terry	$52,85,86^2$	
Thomas	7	
Hume		
James	59	
Humphries		
David	79	
Elizabeth Moore	79	
Hunter		
James	$4,63^2$	
John	56	
Hutcherson		
Collier	46	
Sarah	46	
Hutchinson		
James	70	
Imboden		
John A.	48	
Ingles		
Thomas	50^2	
Ingram		
John	23^2	
Irving		
Charles	91	
Ivey		
Adelia	55	
Benjamin C.	55	

1xem	
Frederick	1
Jackling	
Edward	3
Jackson	
Christopher	3
Margaret	59
Thomas	27,56,59
Jaffery	
George	16
James	
Abigail	15
Alsey	151 15
Asa	15
Benjamin	15,16
Elgira	15
Elizabeth	15
George	15,16
Harriet	15
Henry	15
John	15,16
Joseph	15,16
Keziah	15
Mary Ann	15
Nancy	15
Robert	15
Roda	15
Susanna	15
Thomas	15,45
William	12,15[2]
Jameson	
James	95
Janell	
James	72
Janney	
Jane	45
Jardine	
Robert	66[2],88
Jerkins	
Benjamin	81,82[2]
Charles	67
John	67
W. S.	82
William S.	82
Johns	
Richard	47

Johnson	
Benjamin	36,93
Jane	49
Joshua	49
Samuel	51
Stephen	64
Unity	23
William	4,58[2]
Johnston	
Benjamin	67,68[2]
Dorothy	68[2]
Henry	76
John	13
John Waller	76
William	13
Zachariah	13
Jones	
A.	30
Abner	15
Dr. Adolphus D.	27[2]
Agnes	9
Allen	36
Ann	9
Mrs. Barbary	64
Dr. Benjamin	27
Caroline (Reamey)	27
Charles	20
Churchill	15
Edmund	9
Elizabeth	1,2,9,47
Elizabeth (Powell)	20
Elizabeth (Ramey)	27
Fanny	15
Frederick	47
Frederick, Jr.	47
George Washington	27[2],84
Henry	9
Jane	9,47
James	19
Joseph	9
Col. Joseph	52
Martha	47
Mary (Melton)	19
Minitree, Jr.	14,15,20,30
Minitree, Sr.	15[2],30
Mosias	47
Naomi	30
Nelson Powell	20
Phillemon	9
Phillip Edward	50
Rebecca	47
Richard	1,2
Robert	1,35

Jones, Continued

Robert, Jr.	23
Salina	27
Sarah	9,50
Thomas	4,47
Thomas, Jr.	8
Thomas, Sr.	8
William	19,69
William Harding	47

Jopling

John	19

Jordan

Abner	51
Benjamin S.	51
Ezra	66
Hannah Dawson	51
Hezekiah	51
Jane Smith	51
Mary	51^2
Samuel	86
Thomas	52
William	45
(?) Bates	86

Keller

Ida E.	40

Kelly

Edward	67
Elizabeth (True)	67
Giles	23
John	67
Nancy	67

Kemper

John	8

Kennard

George	88

Kennedy

Alexander	62
Benjamin	38
Charles	61
Elizabeth B. (Markham)	38

Kenner

Mary	6
Matthew	6
Sarah	6
Sophia	6

Kennerly

Samuel, Jr.	60
Samuel, Sr.	60

Keppen

George & Co.	88,91

Kerns

George	35,36

Kerr

Andrew	35
David	93
Susan (Houck)	35,36
Susanna	35

Kesson (See Carson)

David	94
Elizabeth (Crum)	94

Key

Henry	91
Henry, Sr.	91
Isham	10
Martin	91

Keyes

Humphrey	48

Kidd

James	5
William	5

Kieth

James W.	45

Kilpatrick

Samuel	49

King

Alexander	80
David	32,53
Elizabeth	28
Ezeriah	71
Francis	67,71
James	67^2
James, Sr.	55
John	21
Jonathan	28,32
Mary	71
William	28^2,29,53,74

Kingan

John	81

Kinney

Jefferson	49^2
William, Jr.	54

Kirk

James	14

Klugh
Michael 33
Rachel 33
Reuben 33

Kyle
Alexander 25
Charles 13
Gabriel 25
James 13
John 13,25
William 13

Lace
Joseph 78

Lamphier
Going 14
Venus 14

Lane
Henry 69

Lanier
William 51

Laning
Charles 50

Larimore
Caty 52
James 52

LaRue
Clarissy 10
James 10
John 10
Mary 10
Phebe 10
Samuel 10

Lauberger
Michael 43

Laughton
Alexander 28
John 28

Lea
Anne 61
Deborah 10
John 61
Stephen 10

Leak
John 85

Leason
Samuel 26

Lee
Elizabeth 56
George 2
Hancock, Jr. 56
Capt. John 56
Maj. John 56
Mary 56
Peter 20
Richard Bland 81
William 38,83

Leftwich
William 82

Leith
Sarah (Smith) 86

Lenox
Hugh 70

Leseur
Martel 20

Lewes (Lewis)
Henry, Sr. 5

Lewis
Betty 62
Catharine 79
Edward 38
Elizabeth (Smith) 86
Fielding 62,63
Gabriel 8
Go: 77
George 79
Howell 77
James 74,78
John 8,75
John Z. 20
Mary M. 38
Robert 20,76
Thomas 37
Warner 80
Warner Washington 8^2
William 73

Light
George 1

Lilly
John 3

Linch
Charles 48

Lindemood
George 53

Lindsay
Joshua	57
Reuben	53
Taylor	57

Lipscomb
Joel	75
Mary	78
Thomas	75,78,83

Little (Lyttle)
Carlo Brittain	85
Dale Carter	85
Daniel G.	85
David	7,85
Col. David Yancey	85
Drucilla P. (Britain)	85
George Brittain	85
Harrington	30,85
James	30
John	7
John James	85
Louisa M.	85
Nancy E. A.	85
Polly	80
Robert E. Lee	85
Sallie Susan	85
Susanna	85
William	7
William B.	85

Livingston
Frances	50
James	26,77
John	13,14
John, Jr.	50
Capt. Muscoe	14
Susannah (Walker)	13,14
Thomas	26,77

Lockett
Ann	21

Lockey
Edward	2,5
Elizabeth Freind	5
True Freind	5

Loften   44

Long
Armistead	5
Elizabeth	17
Mrs. Elizabeth	51,52
Evans	70
Fanny	70
Gabriel	74,77[2]

Long, Continued
John	27
Joseph	17,51
Lucy	70
Richard	70,77

Longacre
Anne (Sharp)	31
Iveson	31,32
John Sharp=	32
Joseph	81

Longbride
J. A.	48

Longman
Richard, Jr.	2
Richard, Sr.	2

Loury
Richard	66

Lovell
William	72

Lowe
William	63

Lowell
George	66

Lucas
Polly Harrison	70
Zachariah	70

Luck
Ann	76
Samuel	76
Samuel, Sr.	76

Lyle
John	16

Lymbrey
John	2

Lynch
Jacob	29,32

Lyne
Fanny B.	86
Henry	86
Henry, Jr.	86
James	86
James H.	86
Lucy Foster	86
Susan P.	86

McAlister
James	80
Sarah	80

McBride
    John   22,82

McBridge
    James   50

McAll
    Smellie & Co.   90

McCargo
    James   5,6
    Prudence   5,6

McChesney
    Amanda J.   54
    Bessie A.   40
    Cara   54,55
    C. H.   40,41
    D. W.   40,41
    Elizabeth   13,30[3]
    Hugh   28[2]
    Hugh A.   30,40,41
    Ida W.   40
    Isabella   29
    J. B.   54,55
    J. C.   30
    J. Craig   30
    James   16,25
    James Z.   38
    Jennie   54,55
    John   29,49[3]
    Julia   30
    Julia A.   40
    L. J.   38
    L. M.   30
    Leander   30
    Mary G.   30
    Mary J.   40
    Nannie K.   30
    Paul S.   41
    Dr. R. A.   54,55[2]
    Robert   13,16,24,25[2]
    S. J.   41
    Sally (Sharp)   31,32
    Samuel   16,28
    Susan E.   41
    Susan Katharine   40
    Thomas   28[2],29,31,32
    Thomas J.   41
    W. L.   41
    W. S.   55
    Walter   16
    Zachariah   25

McClanahan
    Alexander   37

McClung
    Charles   50

McClure
    Halbert   54

McConkey
    Betsey   32
    Clarissa   32
    Harriet   31
    Jane (Sharp)   31,32
    John   31,32
    John, Sr.   32
    Maria Teresa   31,32
    Merissa   32
    Peggy   32
    Salina   32
    Samuel   32[2]

McConnell
    John Sharp   32
    Sally Merissa   32

McConner
    Thomas   32

McCormick
    John   11

McCoy (McKoy)
    George   7
    Robert   7[2]

McCudon (?)
    Thomas   7

McCullough
    Nancy (Miller)   37

McDowell
    Joseph   24
    Samuel   16

McEndree
    John   75

McGehee
    Samuel   47,95

McGraw
    Samuel   11

McGuire
    William   80

McKean
    Samuel   54

McLaughlan
    Duncan   55

McNeal	
Thomas	61
McNeath	
John	74
McNeil	
Thomas	63
McNutt	
Alexander	7
McPherson	
Archibald	58
McQuay (Macquay)	
Sarah (Brooke)	46
William	46
McQuie	
Elizabeth (Rice)	12
John	12,46
McReynolds	
Samuel	54
McSween	
Alexander	64
McWilliams	
William	68^2
Mackey	
Ribart (sic)	7
Robert	7
Mackie	
William	55
Mackmath	
John	58^2
Maclin	
Henry	23
Magee	
Samuel	78
Thomas	78
Maghews	
John	14
Mahain	
Dorothy	33
Samuel	33
Mahood	
Bible Records	49
Alexander	49
Elizabeth (Ellis)	49
George	49
Jane	49

Maitland	
Robert	64
Mallory	
Ann (Jones)	9
F (rancis)	81,82
Malone	
A.	23
Drury	52^2
George, Jr.	31^2
George, Sr.	31
James	23,31
Lucy	31^2
Manlove	
C.	44
Mann	
Beverly	26
Manzey	
John	48^2
Markham	
Allen Waller	38
Anne	38
Elizabeth	38
Elizabeth Boswell	38
George	44
Jane	38^2
James	38
John	38
John, Jr.	38
Lewis	38
Mary	38
Peggy	38
William	38
Marr	
Gideon	25
Marshall	
Alexander K.	10
Becky	22
Charles	38
Jack	23
Jane	22
Jesse	22
John	4,31,63
Lucy	31
Rebecca	23^2
Samuel	22
Samuel, Jr.	22^2
Spain	22,23
William	22,23
Unity J.	23
Martin (Martyn)	
Andrew W.	30

Martin, Continued
    Ganaway   6
    Henry, Jr.   45[2]
    Henry, Sr.   45

Mason
    Daniel   51
    George   9,74
    Micajah   74
    Peter   13

Massey
    John   19,20
    Joseph   19,20
    William   19

Massie
    Joseph   24
    Mary   24
    Rebecca   24

Matlock
    John   85

Maury
    Catharine   78
    Fontaine   70
    James   78

May(s)
    Elizabeth L. (Edmunds) 45
    George   34
    George S.   45
    Thomas   66
    William   43

Mayle
    Charles   17

Maynard
    John   62,63

Meals
    John   65

Mercer
    J.   59
    James   66
    John   77
    Margaret (Becks) 17

Meriwether
    David   47
    Ni: 52

Merrest
    Richard   2

Metcalfe
    Gilbert   1
    Capt. John 84

Michie
    William   89

Middleton
    Thomas   63

Miller
    Eliza   37
    George C.   37
    Hannah   37
    Henry   37
    James   17,52
    James Henry 37
    John   17,29,51,60[2],61,72
    Martha   37
    Nancy   37
    Nicholas   16
    Robert Grattan 37
    Samuel   37,38
    William   37,38,68,83
    Capt. William 68

Milligan
    James   70

Mills
    Ann   42
    James   62

Milton
    Daniel   19
    Eli   19
    Mary   19
    William   19
    William (Sr.) 19

Minor
    John, Jr.   73

Mitchell
    George   65,66
    Henry   63,64
    James   16
    Richard   27
    Robert   23,31
    Thomas   56

Mitchelson
    John   44

Moffett
    George   38
    George, Sr. 38
    Rebecca   38

Moncure
    John   59

Montague
    Clement   79
    Thomas   74

Montgomerie			Moss	
John	70		Edward	5
Sarah	70		Mound	
			William	18
Montgomery				
Alexander	11		Mountjoy	
Elizabeth (Craig)	12		William	38
John	12,50			
Joseph	50		Muhlenburg	
Michael	11		Gen.Peter	11
			Mulkey	
Moody			John	58
Benjamin	36		Sarah	58
Elizabeth	82			
William	36		Mumford	
			William	41,42
Moon(e)				
Alexander B.	26,28[2]		Munro	
John	26,28		John	66
William	48			
			Murray	
Moore (See More)			John	18
Alexander	22		William	53
Augustine	79			
Capt. J. H.	48		Murrell	18
John	37,47			
Lewis	48		Muscoe	
William	22,46,53,69,95		Frances	50
			Salvatore	50
Moorman			Sarah	50
Charles	89			
Robert	89		Nall	
			John	65
More (See Moore)				
William	44		Nance	
			John	21
Morison				
Alexander	60		Napier	
Jean	60		Capt. John	88
John	60		P(atrick)	55
Patience	60			
			Neele	
Mornson			Richard	14
George	29			
			Neely	
Mortimer			George	50,51
Charles	73,74		John	50[2]
Morton			Nelson	
George B.	10		Elisha	36
John	17		George	62,63
Robert	46		John, Jr.	75,79,80
			Mary	62,63
Mosby			Samuel	10
Littlebury	14			
			Netherland	
Moseley	44		Richard	32
Rebecca	36		Wade, Sr.	14
Samuel	36[3]			

Nevitt
William 2

Newell
Jonathan 2

Newport
John 25

Nichols
George 53

Nixon
Jonathan, Jr. 68

Noble
Thomas 12

Noell
Mary 76
Richard 76
Richard C. 78

Norton
Courtney 80

Norwood
Samuel 37

Nuckolls
Ezra 15

Oden
Elizabeth (Markham) 38
Harriet 38
Mary M. 38

Olive
Robert 78
Thomas 78,80

Oliver
John 24
Reason H. 24

O'Neal
Lodowick 68

Osborne
Benjamin 44
Reps 46

Overby
Buckner 23
Henry 46

Owens
Nathaniel 8
Rebecca 8
William H. 86

Pamplin
James 19

Park
John 14

Parker
Alexander 70
Henry 79
John 4
Joseph 58
Richard 79
Susanna 79
Thomas 79
William 73,79
William, Jr. 79
Winslow 79

Parr
William 70

Parrecke
John 52

Parrish
Booker 95
Constant 95
David M. 95
Huldah 95
James 95
John 75

Parrott
James 86
William 26,28

Parsell
Thomas 11

Partlow
Elijah 78
John 78
John, Sr. 78^2
Lewis 78

Patterson
Betty 14
Susannah 14
Thomas 14
William 14

Patteson
David 22

Patton
James 37
James D. 35
Robert 8,77

Paxton
John 22

Payne
George H. 8
George W. 5
Jane 4
John, Sr. 5
Nicholas 70
Capt. Nicholas 68,70
Robert 5

Peacock
Robert W. 75

Pearson
James 81,82[3]
Mary 94
Mary (Hamlin) 81,82
Samuel 94
William 1

Peay
William 86

Pemberton
Benjamin 32
Marianna (Sharp) 32
Merissa 32
William 11

Pendleton
Edmund 53
Henry, Jr. 70
Nathaniel 90

Penn
John 19

Pennington
Jack 22
John 23

Perine
David M. 54[2]

Perkins
Ezekiel 55
Nat 83

Perrin
Joel 36,37[2]

Perry
Evans 30
Isbal 72
Larkine 72
Micajah 3

Peterson
Joseph 64
Lucy 64

Pettit
Catey 24
John H. 12,13,24[2]
Keturah 13,24
Nancy 24
Nathaniel 8,24
Obadiah 8,12,24
Rebecca 8
Samuel 12,24
Thomas 12,24[2]
William 12,24

Pettus
John W. 20
Susannah 20
William, Jr. 20
William, Sr. 20[2]

Petty
George 34
George, Sr. 35[2]

Peyton
Edward 70
Henry, Jr. 14

Phelps
Edward 39
Edward, Sr. 39,40

Phillips
Cald(?) 3
Hartwell 18
John 18
Richard 45

Pickett
Reuben 52

Pierce
John 80

Pilcher
Moses 38

Pincham
Richard 35

Pine
Lazarus 8

Pitcairn
Dr. David 41

Platt
Elizabeth 44
James 44
Mary 44
Randle 44
Samuel 44
William 44[2]

(31)

Pleasant(s)
  John   44

Pollard
  Benjamin   81
  Thomas   71

Pool
  Edward

Portlock
  John   6
  Joseph   18
  Seth   17

Posey
  Alexander   84
  Benjamin   85
  Bennett   84
  Nancy   85
  Susanna   85

Poston
  Elias   48

Poteet
  Brittain.   30

Potter
  Cuthbert   46
  Solomon   29

Potts
  Ezekiel   94
  Nathan   94
  Samuel   94

Powell
  Elizabeth   20
  James   79
  Martha (Hamlin)   81,82
  William Morgan   82

Poynor
  John   83

Prescott
  Moses   13

Preston
  Francis   29
  Jane (Ramey)   10
  John   10
  Sarah B.   29

Pretlow
  Thomas   51

Price (See Prise)
  Anjer(?)   36
  Chandler   72

Price, Continued
  Frances   36,37[2]
  Richard   36,37[2]
  Thomas   61
  William   33,83[2]

Prichard (See Pritchard)
  John   51

Prise (Price)
  John   1

Pritchard (See Prichard)
  Samuel   48

Proctor
  John   74
  William   74

Prupecker
  John   25

Pugh
  Edward   1

Pulliam
  David   67
  John   64
  Joseph   67

Pumphary
  Nathan   58
  Silvanus   58

Purvis
  John   13

Puryear
  Elijah   31

Quincey
  William   4

Quinn
  Benjamin   57
  Frances   57
  John   57
  Thomas   57[3]
  William   57

Quinney
  William   60

Quisenberry
  Mary   80
  Moses   80

Ragland
  L.   53

Ramey (See Remey, Reamey)
Catharine 10
Col. Daniel 86
Deborah 9
Elizabeth 10
Jacob 5,9
Jacob, heirs of 9
Jane 10
Jemima 86
Nancy 10
Sanford 9,10
Sanford, Jr. 10
Sanford, Sr. 10
Widow 9

Raworth
Francis 81

Ray
James 76

Read
Thomas 46

Reamey (See Ramey, Remey)
Caroline L. 27
Elizabeth 27
James Sanford 27
James 53
Letitia (Hughes) 27

Red(d)
John 59
Philip D. 75

Reed (Reid)
Andrew 16
John 72
Rachael 72
Samuel C. 95
Thomas 20

Remey (Remy) See Ramey, Reamey
Daniel 54
John 54
William 54
William, Jr. 54

Rennolds (See Reynolds)
Elizabeth 17[2],51
Mrs. Elizabeth 51
Frances 17,52
Henry 57
John 17,51,57
Mary 17,51

Revell
James 9

Reynolds (See Rennolds)
Benjamin 77
Joseph 77

Rhea
William 28

Rice
Elizabeth 12

Richards
Elizabeth 74
James 74
William 76

Richardson
Aaron 10
Benjamin 11
Caley 11
Daniel 10
James 4
John 10,17
John, Jr. 11
Laviney 11
Patty 11
Sarah 10
Thomas 11
William 11

Riddell
George 44

Ridley
Bromfield 19
James 19
William 19
Dr. William 86

Rinker
Casper 47,48

Rister
John 14
Mary 14

Ritchie
Archibald 60[2],61
James & Co. 88,90
Samuel 60[2],61

Roan(e)
Alexander 73
John 63

Robards
George 92[2]
Jesse 92[3]
William 92
William, Sr. 92

Roberson
 Catharine 79
 Elizabeth 79
 John 79

Roberts
 Bartholomew 5,6
 Benjamin 34
 Francis 5,6
 Jane 6
 John 5,6
 Martha 6
 Prudence 6
 Rebecca 5
 Richard, Sr. 3
 Robert 24
 Susanna 5
 Thomas 6,12

Robertson
 Alexander 60
 George 44
 William, Jr. 20

Robins
 James 75
 Joanna 75
 Sarah 75

Robinson
 Benjamin 58,73,75,76,79,80[2]
 Fanny (Uphame) 14
 John 7,14,15,58,76
 Joseph 15
 Phanney (Fanny) 15
 Richard 5
 Samuel 75,80
 William 24

Robison
 A. 46

Rogers
 Barbara 65
 Catharine 71
 Gaven 60[2],61
 Hugh 25
 John 26,71
 Peter 52
 Col. Peter 52
 Sarah 71
 William 71

Roman
 Jacob 54

Rosan
 Dr. John 39

Rose
 John 42

Ross
 William 27

Roughsedge
 William 84

Rowe
 James Benn 4

Rowlen
 Martin 29

Rowzee
 Edward, Jr. 50

Royster
 Jacob, 47
 John 47

Russell
 Andrew 11,12,29
 Elizabeth 61[1]
 William 58,61[2]

Sale
 Samuel 79

Sams
 William 53

Sanders
 John Wynell 19,59
 Nathaniel, Jr. 18,19,59
 Nathaniel, Sr. 19,59

Sandige
 Austin 75

Sargent
 William 21

Sarratt
 Mary 21

Sarveer (Sarver)
 Mrs. Jane 18

Scarbrough
 John 86

Scasey
 William 3

Scelton (Skelton)
 John 59

Schooler
 Margaret 80
 Wharton 80

Scorey
    William   1

Scott
    Charles, Jr.   79
    Donald & Co.   87,88,89
    Fanny   79
    George   70
    J. D.   24
    John, Jr. 83^2
    John, Sr. 83^2
    John B.   82,83
    Robert $7,83^2$
    William $62,63,83^3$
    William T.   83

Selser
    Mathias   25

Semmes
    Ignats   59

Shackleford
    John   74
    Z.   76

Sharkey
    Henry   5
    John   5

Sharp(e)
    Anne   31
    Benjamin   53
    Clarissa   32
    Elizabeth   31
    Jane   31
    John   28,31,53
    John, Sr.   53
    Marianna   32
    Peggy   31
    Sally   31,32
    Simon   35

Shelton
    Mary Ann (Edmunds)   45
    Samuel   45

Shepherd
    George   71

Sherrell
    William   90

Sherrer
    Eleanor   21
    Elizabeth   21

Shimm (or Shinn)
    George   24,25

Shipwash
    John   22

Short
    William   20

Shrock
    Jacob   81

Sibley
    Judith   10
    Leonard   10

Sidwell
    Hugh   43

Silvester
    Henry   4

Simms (See Sims)
    Peter   59

Sims
    Charles   88
    John   22
    Thomas S.   33

Simons
    Abram 77^2
    David   70
    Mildred 77^2

Simpson
    Francis   90
    William   90

Skelton
    Elizabeth 46^2
    Isaac   46
    Mark   46
    Powell   46
    William   46

Slaughter
    Ann   90
    Cadwallader   90
    Capt. George   91
    James 89^2,90
    Robert   89,90
    Robin   89,90

Slaven
    Nancy   77
    Norcut   70,77

Slayden
    Stokley   39

Sleet (?)
    Weeden   57

Smith
    Ann   86
    Benjamin   63
    Constantine   86
    Daniel   40
    Edwin   49
    Elizabeth   86
    Frankey   86
    George   94
    Guy   86
    Henry 51^2
    James   70
    John   94
    John, Jr.   69
    John, Sr.   69
    John A. W.   8
    Lawrence   2,5,69,86
    Lodemia   8
    Marcellus   83
    Pouncey   8
    Robert   69,73,74
    Samuel $18,57^2$
    Sarah   86
    Solomon   51
    Thomas $4^2,94$
    William   17,39,94

Smock
    William   73

Snead (See Sneed)
    Evan   39
    Francis   39
    James   39
    Stephen K.   86

Sneed
    Alexander   84

Snow
    Frost and (sic)   89
    Ice and (sic)   89
    Richard   89

Somerby
    Phillip   65

Somerville
    James   67,70

Sorrow
    John   87
    William   87

Spangler
    C.   94

Spencer
    George   65
    Robert   1
    Samuel, Sr.   19

Spooner
    John   60

Spotswood
    Alexander $58^2,66,67$
    Butler   66
    John   66

Stainback
    Peter, Sr.   81

Stanard
    Larkin   70,72
    William   77

Stand
    Dorothy   86

Stanfield
    Benjamin   53
    Robert   53

Stanton
    Capt. Thomas   2

Starke
    Sarah   86
    Thomas 86^2
    William 86^2

Stears
    William   71

Steele
    Andrew   26,27
    Elizabeth   26
    George   48
    James   27
    Robert   25
    Samuel $25^3,26$
    Samuel, Sr.   25
    Sarah   24

Stell (See Still)
    Angeline   35
    Frances 35^3
    Jeremiah   35
    John 35^2

Stephenson
    Capt. James   80
    John   21

Stevenson   18

Steward		**Stubblefield, Continued**	
William	61	Peter	69[2],70
Stewart		Robert	70,79,93
Charles	70	Sally	69
John	76,88	Susanna	79
Still (See Stell)		William	79
Anna	34	**Sturgell**	
Frances	34	John	88
George	34	**Sturgeon**	
James	34	John	88
Jeremiah	43	**Sturgis**	
Joel H.	34	Daniel	62
John	34[2]	**Sugg**	
Josiah	34	Aquila	22
Stodgell (Sturgell)		George	18,22
John	88	**Sullivan**	
Stokely		Daniel	4
John	30	**Sullivant**	
Stokes		Charles	26
Allen	18	Hewlet	26
William	46	Milly	26
Stone		Moses	26
Ashwell	83	**Sutherland**	
Ludwick	25	James	66
Marble	88	Dr. John	66
Stout		William	66
John	29	**Swanke**	
Strange		George	49
Abraham Alloway	87	**Swepson**	
Stratton		John	46
Benjamin	47	Richard, Jr.	46
Straughan		**Symonds**	
Reuben	70	John	2
Street		**Talbot**	
Anthony	18	Richard	7
Struman		**Tankersly**	
Richard	43	John	70
Stuart		**Tanzey**	
Alexander	33	William	84
Stubblefield		**Tarrant**	
Beverley	72,74	James	36
Col. Beverley	93	Leonard	36
Beverley W.	72	**Taylor**	
George	69[2], 70	Charles	50
J. S.	7	Elizabeth	6
Peggy	69,70		

Taylor, Continued
    Francis, Jr.   6
    John   50
    Margaret   6
    Nancy   6
    Septimus, Jr.   6
    Septimus, Sr.   6
    William   24,47,69
    Zach.   3

Teals
    Edward   58

Tennent
    Elizabeth 61^2
    James 61^2

Terrell
    Richard   75,77

Terry
    Thomas   67,69

Thacker
    Benjamin   56
    Martin   56,83

Thomas
    Eleanor   21
    Elizabeth   21
    James   90
    John 21^2,32
    Capt. Lewis   11
    Mark   91
    Mary   21,79
    Phillip   43
    Richard   21
    Rowland   79
    Samuel   21

Thompson   67
    Deckar   62
    Edward Moody   82
    Elizabeth   83
    James   9,83
    Rev. James   74
    John   22,59
    Joseph   24
    Snodgrass & Co.   87
    Thomas   74
    Thomas, Jr.   74
    William $74,83^2$
    Capt. William   63

Thomson
    Andrew   60
    Capt. John   60
    Laurence   54

Thornton
    Francis   60
    Jane   52
    John   52

Thorpe
    Timothy   19

Throgmorton
    Catharine   79

Thruston (Thurston)
    John   47

Thurmond
    John, Jr.   87

Thurston
    John   47

Tiller
    Daniel   71

Timberlake
    William   47,95

Timpson
    Samuel   3

Tiner (?)
    Lewis   50

Todd
    James   13
    Richard   72

Towler
    Nancy (Crum)   94

Towles
    _____   78
    Mary   67,74
    O.   65
    Oliver   73,74
    Oliver, Jr.   73,74
    Stockly   72
    Thomas   67,72,78

Towne(s)
    Alfred   9
    Caleb   83
    Daniel C.   84
    George   35

Trail
    George   60

Trewitt
    (See Truewhitt)

Tribble
    Andrew   64

Trigg
Adam — 50
Daniel — 63,76
William — 71,75,79

Trim
Mathew — 40

Trimble
James — 22

Triplett
William — 77

Troughton
William — 44

True
Elizabeth — 67
John — 67

Truewhitt
Levi — 18

Tucker
Elizabeth — 1
George — 1
John — 1
Mathew — 19
Robert, Jr. — 17

Tudor
Thomas — 12

Tunstall
John — 50
Thomas, Jr. — 50

Turner
Elizabeth — 17
James — 17
Thomas — 59,67,69
Col. Thomas — 60

Turnley
Frances — 66

Twitty
Thomas — 20

Tyler
Charles — 4,58
Thomas — 4,58

Underwood
F. — 92
George — 92
Jacob — 18

Van Bibber
Abraham — 72

Vass
Caty — 86
Fanny — 86
Reuben — 65
Thomas — 86
Vincent — 66,86

Vaughan
George — 45
John — 15,35,43
Lucy — 35,43
Polly C. (Edmunds) — 45
William — 16,30

Vaulx
Robert — 2

Vause
Capt. William — 48

Vawter
John — 57

Vernon
Anthony — 56[2],57[2]
Fanny — 56[2],57[3]
Richard — 56[2],57[2]
Richard, Jr. — 57
Tinsley — 56,57

Voss
R. B. — 34

Wady
James — 9

Waggoner
Harriet — 8
Jacob — 8

Wakcome (?)
John — 16

Walden
Francis — 24
John — 24
Nancy (Pettit) — 24

Walker
Alexander — 3
Elizabeth — 22
Fanny — 81
George Minge — 7
James — 81
James C. — 27

Walker, Continued		Watkins	
John	14,42	George W.	83
Joseph	3	John	52
Mondingo	7	Joseph	92
Phillip	22,61	Thomas	6
Robert C.	7		
Samuel	14	Wayland	
Shadrack	83	Abraham	54
Stephen D.	7	Lewis	54[2]
Thomas	14,64	Webb	
Thomas, Jr.	53		
Thomas W.	7	Bernard	79
William	7,22	James	20
Wyatt	6	Nancy (Dabbs)	20
		Weeks	
Wallace		Agnes	77
David	60	Benjamin	77
James	16		
Patience	60	Welch	
Peter	25	Eleanor	70
		John	68,70
Waller		John, Sr.	72
Ann	62	Nelly	72
Benjamin	59	William	72
Edmund	59		
John	58,59[2],62,65	Westall	
John, Jr.	64	Daniel	3
Thomas	79		
William	62	Whaley	
		Mary	3
Wallington			
Susanna A.	82	Wharton	
		Benjamin	26,77
Wallis		Valentine Long	26
Aquila	22	Wheeler	
John	6	Ignatius	12
		John	75
Walsh		Mariana	12
Catharine	13	Moses	75
Cornelius	13	William	75
Mary Ann	13		
William	13	Whiden	
		John	52
Walton			
Edward	46	Whitaker	
Richard	5	James	46
True	5	Johnson	82
Ward		White	
Thomas	4	John	51
		Joseph	13
Wardley			
Anne	2	Whitehaire	
Eleanor	2	Robert	2[2]
Joane	2		
Thomas	2	Whitehead	
		Jonathan	55
Watson			
Joseph	48		

Whiteman	
Peter	26,27
Whiteside	
John B.	25
Whithourst	
Tuley	65
Whithy	
John	45
Whitney	
John	52
Whitnor (See Widener)	
Henry	29
Lewis	29,30
Whitsell	
William	87
Whitworth	
John	13
Mary Ann	13
Sallie	13
Wiatt (Wyatt)	
William	11,70
Widener (See Whitnor)	
Henry	29,30
Lewis	30
Wier	
Asa	9
Wiglesworth	
James	61
John	65
Wilcox (See Willcox)	
John	29
Phebe	29
Wilkins	
E.	82
Wilks	
Betsy (Crum)	94
Willard	
Hugh	10
Willcox (See Wilcox)	
M. A.	82
Williams	
Elizabeth	24
Frankey	6
James	8
Jane	61

Williams, Continued	
Jo:	82
John	8,56,59,61
John, Jr.	59
Joseph	6,80
Judith	8
Nathaniel	95
Oliver	48
Prudence	24
Rachel	7^2
Ralph	61
Robert	24
Samuel	86
W. G.	13
William	7^2,61
Williamson	
Eliza (Hamlin)	81,82
William	60^2,61
Willis	
Ann	68
Henry	59,61,71,72
Col. Henry	56
John Whitaker	72
Lewis	68,71,72
Mary	56
Willoughby	
Joseph	75
Wallace	28
William	28
Willox	
Mary	42
William	42
Wills	
Jacob	29
John	29
Thomas	16
Wilson	
	13
Ann	76
Booker	76
Christopher	61
George	3
John	76
Joseph	76
Katherine	13
Robert R.	28
Thomas	83^2
William, Sr.	7
Winders	
James	45

Winegar		Woodford	
David	29^2	Henry	94
Frederick	29^2	Thomas	52
Peter	29^2	Woodson	
Winlock		Jesse	9
Gen. Joseph	11	Sam	9
Winslow		Wook	
Beverly	89	John	1
Thomas	75_3,79,89	Woolfolk	
William	75^3,77,89	John	61
Winston		Wooten	
Horatio G.	95	Samuel	46
Wirt		Samuel, Jr.	46
Elizabeth	33	Word	
William	33	Thomas	60
Wise		Wormington	
James	23,24	Abram	17
John	23	Wragg	
Mary	23,24	John	63
Rebecca	24	Joseph, Jr.	63
Richard	23	Samuel	63
Thomas	23^2,24	Wright	
Withers		Daniel	30
Anne (Markham)	38	Elizabeth	30^2
Daniel	8	John	22
Withey		John David	30
Augustine	45^2	Richard	4
John	45^2	Robert	55^2
Witt		Thomas	22
Abner	93	Yancey	
Wolf(e)		Lewis Davis	59
Catharine	10	Richard	94
Elizabeth	10	Yates	
George	10	Charles	61,65
Jacob	54	Young	
John	10	Henry	10
Lewis, Jr.	10	Richard	76
Lewis, Sr.	10	Richard H.	73
Polly	10	Samuel	46
Thomas	10	Younger	
Wood		Joseph	47
Andrew	10		
Betsey	77		
Gen. James	11		
John	1,77		
Joshua	18		
Thomas	43		
William	62,65		

THEY WENT
THATAWAY

Volume 2

Dedicated to

the loving memories

of my father,
Charles Hughes Hamlin, Senior,
born Danville, Virginia, son of
Captain Francis Mallory Hamlin, and his wife,
Sarah Elizabeth Arney

and of my mother,
Sallie Bell Hacker, born
Manchester, Clay County, Kentucky,
daughter of
Andrew Jackson Hacker and
Nan E. A. Lyttle, his wife

"For inquire, I pray thee, of the former age
and prepare thyself to the search of their
forefathers."
--Job 8:8

TABLE OF CONTENTS

FOREWORD

"This is the place, stand still, my steed
    Let me review the scene,
And summon from the shadowy past
    The forms that once have been."

                    --Longfellow--

    Without very much humility but with a great deal of appreciation
for the many individuals, libraries, historical societies, etc. who
purchased Volume I of this series and for their many kind expressions
of encouragement, this compiler is very grateful. Indeed, without
their past and future support, this second volume would not have been
possible.

    This second volume, then, continues with abstracts of original
records and in each case the citation to the source or authority.
These records were obtained from court records, wills, deeds of
purchase or sale, church, marriage, census, bible, library accessions,
etc. Also, in every record, is proven the migration to or from
Virginia to other states, territories, or countries. They are,
therefore, "migration links" primarily, but in most cases they also
comprise "genealogical links" in that they also reveal various degrees
of relationships with other individuals. In this connection, where
this compiler has found additional information in his files, he has
attempted to add it to the cited records in the form of comments or
notes following the abstract.

    As for our courageous and often reckless ancestors; they set
forth in an irresistable tide southward and westward. Their migration
held an epic significance and nothing could halt it permanently. Ever
beyond the boundless horizon was an empire in the making and the
deathless dream of our ancestors was to build this empire, and within
it their own little private kingdoms in which to accumulate land,
possessions, liberty, independence, and the education of their progeny.
May this dream and the pursuit thereof never die out or be legislated
out of our country.

Dale Van Every, in his monumental history of our Pioneers (Ark of Empire), states that some evidence of our ancestors inexhaustible vitality may be gained by a glance at the timetable of the western movement. That in the first 158 years after the settlement of Jamestown in 1607, settlement had progressed or spread to New River, 220 miles to the westward. (This seems to average about one and one-third miles per year.) But only nine years later (after 1766) the settlement of Harrodsburg, 220 miles further west, had been accomplished, and in only 23 more years Daniel Boone had resettled on the Missouri, another 350 miles farther west. There was the little matter of the Revolutionary War in this interim.

Someone has stated that history needs a skeleton just as the human body does. Genealogy provides this skeleton for history, and makes it exceedingly interesting because history is made by people. It becomes much more interesting when we have been able to trace and prove the names of our own specific ancestors and can determine the part they played or something of the events which occurred in their own lifetime and in each generation.

You will be amazed to discover also that our ancestors lived, propagated, fought and died and had very much the same ideas, desires, faults and virtues that we also have. Primarily, they were very human.

This foreword should, therefore, be concluded with another biblical quotation, i.e.,

"And God blessed Noah and his sons and said unto them, be fruitful and multiply and replenish the earth." --Gen.9:1

This commandment was obviously taken as a personal mandate by our colonial Virginia forefathers and their descendants now number in the millions. Let us therefore be diligent and seek them out.

--Charles Hughes Hamlin

P.O. Box 3525
Richmond 34, Virginia
May 1965

THEY WENT THATAWAY

Lunenburg County, Virginia, Order Book 1, page 50 -

August Court 1746: James Dockery, last from Bristol in the Kingdom of Great Britain, came into court and made oath that he had been an inhabitant of this colony 15 years (thus since 1731) and that this is the first time of his claiming his importation right which is ordered to be certified.

Ibid -

August Court 1746: Henry Sage, last from London, in the Kingdom of Great Britain, came into court and made oath that he had been an inhabitant of this colony 13 years (thus since 1733) and this is the first time of his claiming his importation right which is ordered to be certified. [See note.]

Ibid -

August Court 1746: George Ireland, last from Shropshire, in the Kingdom of Great Britain, came into court and made oath that he had been an inhabitant of this colony 10 years (thus since 1736) and that this is the first time of claiming his importation right, which is ordered to be certified.

Ibid -

August Court 1746: John Freeman, last from Worcestershire in the Kingdom of Great Britain, came into court and made oath that he had been an inhabitant of this colony 14 years (thus since 1732) and that this is the first time of his claiming his importation right; which is ordered to be certified. [See note below.]

Orange County, Virginia, Order Book 6, page 236 -

25 May 1756 - John Rigby made oath that he was imported into this colony immediately from Great Britain and that this is the first time of his making oath to the same to entitle him to a right to 50 acres of land in this colony which right he assigns over to Hono(?) Powell.

Note by C.H.H.: As a matter of interest it is noted that in Torrence's Wills before 1800, there is listed the will of a Henry Sage in Mecklenburg County, Virginia in 1797, who may be the same listed above. The will of an Arthur Freeman (1753) is recorded in Lunenburg County, Virginia, who may have been of some relationship to John Freeman, cited above.

Orange County, Virginia, Order Book 6, page 237 -

25 May 1756 - Elizabeth Stokes, Anne Brown, John McDonald, and Thomas
Walker made oath that they were imported into this colony immediately from
Great Britain and that this is the first time of either of their making
oath to the same in order to entitle each of them to a right to 50 acres
of land in this colony, which right they assign to Hono(?) Powell.

Augusta County, Virginia, Order Book 2, page 59. -

19 August 1748 - James Porteus and Patrick McDonald came into court and
made oath that they were immediately imported into this colony (Porteus
from London and McDonald from Ireland) and that this is the first time
of proving their importation in order to partake of his Majesty's bounty
to a right to 50 acres of land (to each) which said rights were in open
court assigned over to Valentine Sevier.

Caroline County, Virginia, Order Book (1732-1740) page 400 -

Proof of Importations

11 February 1736 - James Vaughn made oath that this is the first time of
proving his right for his importation into this colony and that he assigned
the same over to Richard Taliaferro, Gent.

Ibid -

11 February 1736 - Richard White made oath that this is the first time of
proving his right for his importation into this colony and that he assigned
the same over to Richard Taliaferro, Gent.

Ibid -

11 February 1736 - William Barns made oath that this is the first time of
proving his right for his importation into this colony and that he assigned
the same over to Richard Taliaferro, Gent.

Ibid -

11 February 1736 - David Dixon made oath that this is the first time of
proving his right for his importation into this colony and that he assigned
the same over to Richard Taliaferro, Gent.

Ibid -

11 February 1736 - Henry Nichols made oath that this is the first time of
proving his right for his importation into this colony and that he assigned
the same over to Richard Taliaferro, Gent.

Ibid -

11 February 1736 - John Wallis Sumers made oath that this is the first time
of proving his right for his importation into this colony and that he assigned
the same over to Richard Taliaferro, Gent.

Ibid -

11 February 1736 - Thomas Price made oath that this is the first time of
proving his right for his importation into this colony and that he assigned
the same over to Richard Taliaferro, Gent.

Ibid -

11 February 1736 - Thomas Sanders made oath that this is the first time
of proving his right for his importation into this colony and that he
assigned the same over to Richard Taliaferro, Gent.

Ibid -

11 February 1736 - Sarah Tibbu made oath that this is the first time
of proving her right for her importation into this colony and that she
assigned the same over to Richard Taliaferro, Gent.

Ibid -

11 February 1736 - Mary Nichols made oath that this is the first time
of proving her right for her importation into this colony and that she
assigned the same over to Richard Taliaferro, Gent.

Ibid -

11 February 1736 - James Atkins made oath that this is the first time of
proving his right for his importation into this colony and that he assigned
the same over to Richard Taliaferro, Gent.

Ibid -

11 February 1736 - Thomas Elliott made oath that this is the first time
of proving his right for his importation into this colony and that he
assigned the same over to Richard Taliaferro, Gent.

Ibid, page 409 -

11 March 1736 - George Brassfeild, Edward Savage, Elizabeth Savage, John
Green, Manuel Penn, James Hearn, Benjamin Haws, Patrick Welch, made oath
that this is the first time of proving their right for their importation
into this colony and who assigned the same over to George Brassfeild.

Ibid, page 432 -

10 June 1737 - George Marsh made oath that this is the first time of
proving his right for his importation into this colony.

4

Ibid, page 432 -

10 June 1737 - Joseph Bates made oath that this is the first time of
proving his right for his importation into this colony and that he assigned
the same over to George Marsh.

Orange County, Virginia, Deed Book 39, page 126 -

17 May 1843 - Power of Attorney from Mary Quisenberry of the COUNTY OF
SALINE, STATE OF MISSOURI. Whereas George Rhoades, late of [Orange County]
Virginia, deceased, did leave a legacy of money and negroes to me, Mary
Quisenberry, by his last Will and Testament [note by C.H.H.: Orange County
Will Book 9, page 324, probated 26 December 1842] of which Will, John
Rhoades and Catlett Rhoades of [Orange Co.] Virginia are joint executors -
Now then, I do herewith constitute and appoint George Rhoads of MISSOURI
[Saline County] my true and lawful attorney to obtain the legacy given and
bequeathed to me, etc. (Then follows several certifications from the
Clerk and Justices of Saline Co., Missouri, etc.) Recorded Orange County,
Virginia, 26 June 1843.

> Comment: The above cited Mary Quisenberry was the daughter of
> George Rhoades, died Orange Co., Virginia 1842, and his wife,
> Nancy Wright, daughter of William Wright, Sr., of Orange Co., Va.
> (W.B.7, page 560.) Mary Rhoades, daughter of George, married
> December 10, 1812 Daniel Quisenberry in Orange County, Virginia.
> She was a double first cousin of her attorney, George Rhoades,
> cited in above record, who was born in Orange County, Virginia in
> 1803 and was the son of Richard Rhoades (W.B. 9, page 216) of
> Orange County, Virginia, and his wife, Lucy Wright, also a
> daughter of William Wright, Sr., whom he had married 9 February 1793
> in Orange County, Virginia

Cumberland County, Virginia, Deed Book 21, page 432 -

5 June 1834 - Deed of Trust in which Robert Starkey of County of Cumberland,
being justly bound with his sisters Permelia, Sally, Mary, and Martha
Starkey, together with Thomas and Joseph Starkey in two bonds, to wit, one
for $582.60 and the other for $250.49 and to provide for his portion of
the payment of the said debts and also to protect and keep harmless his
said sisters who are jointly bound with him - mortgages, convey, etc. his
undivided interest in all the estate, real and personal of which his
father, William Starkey, died seized and possessed, being one-eighth part
of the whole estate and one-half of one-eighth part purchased by him of
his brother, William Starkey, NOW OF OHIO, etc. Recorded same date.

Ibid, page 495 -

15 September 1834 - Deed of Gift by Thomas Starkey of Cumberland County
of his undivided interest in the Estate of William Starkey, deceased, for
natural love and affection to his sisters, Pamela, Sally, Mary, and
Martha Starkey, etc.

Ibid, page 241 -

6 April 1833 - William Starkey sells his portion (1/8) part of his father, William Starkey's Estate to his brothers, Robert and Thomas Starkey for $220.00, etc.

Ibid, Deed Book 24, page 101 -

1 September 1840 - Deed of Trust in which Joseph Starkey - to secure a debt by Bond in amount of $553.10 - mortgages his undivided 1/8 part of Estate of William Starkey, deceased, consisting of land, slaves, etc. Recorded 9 September 1840.

Frederick County, Virginia, Deed Book 20, page 117 et seq. -

1 December 1775 - Indenture in which Peter Richards and Mary Richards of BUDLEIGH IN THE COUNTY OF DEVON, children of Peter Richards, of the same place, deceased, by their attorney, John Lee, whose authority is executed and recorded IN THE COUNTY OF FREDERICK, Colony of Virginia, and which John Lee is NOW OF THE CITY OF BURLINGTON, AND WESTERN DIVISION OF NEW JERSEY, and Alice, his wife, which Alice is one other of the daughters of the said Peter Richards, deceased - parties of the first part - and Thomas P. Hewings of the CITY OF BURLINGTON, Esq., of the second part - whereas John Richards late of the County of Frederick, deceased, was in his lifetime lawfully seized of several tracts of land in Frederick County, Colony of Virginia and made his last Will and Testament 28 November 1749 - and therein did give and devise unto his brother, Peter's children, all his estate, real and personal to be equally divided between them, but in case one of his brother Peter's sons comes over to this country then he gave him one-half his estate, real and personal, another half to be divided between his brother Peter's children, etc. and soon after died. And whereas Henry Richards, one of the sons of the said Peter Richards came over to this country and whereas Jonathan Richards, one other of the sons of the said Peter Richards, did constitute and appoint the said Henry Richards his attorney to sell and dispose of the said estate - and whereas the said Henry Richards in right of himself and also in right of his brother, Jonathan, and the said John Lee in right of his said wife, and also as attorney for Peter and Mary Richards, did mutually agree to submit their several claims to the arbitrament of Joseph Fawcett and William Russell, both of Frederick County, Virginia, etc.

Note: The land involved consisted of two tracts for 353 acres and 150 acres, a total of 503 acres. Recorded 6 April 1784 (ibid, page 121) 13 October 1776 Thomas P. Hewlings, Esq. of CITY OF BURLINGTON, WESTERN DIVISION OF NEW JERSEY, sells the two above cited tracts of land to Henry Richards of Cedar Creek in County of Frederick, Colony of Virginia, planter, for Ł264 sterling money of Great Britain, etc. Recorded 6 April 1784.

Halifax County, Virginia, Deed Book 13, page 89 -

29 March 1784 - Isaac Ball of the COUNTY OF WILKES, STATE OF GEORGIA, Administrator of the Estate of James Armstrong, deceased, late of the STATE OF SOUTH CAROLINA, gives Power of Attorney to his friend William Peters Martin of County of Halifax, State of Virginia, to recover for him, the said Isaac Ball, Administrator, all that is or will be due the said James Armstrong, deceased from the Estate of the late William Armstrong, deceased, etc. Witnesses: Mary Dudley, Susannah Baker, Sarah Snelson. Recorded 21 October 1784.

Halifax County, Virginia, Deed Book 18, page 211 -

8 July 1799 - Ann Palmer of COUNTY OF WILKES, STATE OF GEORGIA, gives her Power of Attorney to her trusty friend, Robert Echols of said County and State to recover her portion of her father, John Palmer, deceased, estate, willed to him by her grandfather Joseph Palmer, deceased. [Note by CHH: Joseph Palmer's Will dated 21 March 1749.] Certificates follow from WILKES COUNTY, GEORGIA-(page 212)-- Robert Echols transfers his Power of Attorney to Evan Echols of Halifax County, Virginia, to act in his stead for Ann Palmer. Recorded 23 September 1799.

Halifax County, Virginia, Deed Book 18, page 237 -

15 October 1799 - Indenture in which Daniel Palmer of the STATE OF SOUTH CAROLINA and COUNTY OF UNION, sells to Elias Palmer of the State of Virginia and County of Halifax - for L60 -- a tract of land in Halifax Co., Virginia, on the waters of Terrible Creek, containing 100 acres, etc. Witnesses: William Nance, Jr., Jeffry Palmer, Watkins Brown, Ephraim Crews, James Brown. Recorded 28 October 1799.

Halifax County, Deed Book 32, page 176 -

30 September 1823 - Mary Palmer of COUNTY OF CHRISTIAN, STATE OF KENTUCKY, late Mary Faulkner, widow and relict of Drury Palmer, deceased, being en-titled to a part of the estate of her father, Jacob Faulkner, deceased, late of the County of Halifax, State of Virginia, by virtue of his last Will and Testament, gives her Power of Attorney to her son, Drury Palmer of said COUNTY OF CHRISTIAN and STATE OF KENTUCKY, etc. Certified before Justices of CHRISTIAN COUNTY, KENTUCKY and Recorded Halifax County, Virginia 22 March 1824.

    Note by C.H.H.: Halifax County marriages by Knorr, page 71:
    26 January 1795, Drury Palmer to Mary Faulkner, daughter of
    Jacob Faulkner.

Halifax County, Virginia, Deed Book 32, page 178 -

28 January 1824 - Robert L. Ranson, Jeremiah P. Ranson, James B. Ranson and

Armistead R. Ranson of the COUNTY OF HANCOCK, STATE OF GEORGIA, give
Power of Attorney to John W. Ranson of the COUNTY OF WILKES, STATE OF
GEORGIA, to recover and secure from Aaron (or Amos?) Hardwick of Halifax
County, State of Virginia, Administrator of the Estate of Mary Hardwick,
deceased, the legacies bequeathed to us by James Hardwick, deceased, of
Halifax County, Virginia, etc. Recorded 22 March 1824.

Note by C.H.H.: These surnames may ·be Runson or Ronson

Halifax County, Virginia, Deed Book 33, page 510 -

8 October 1824 - Benjamin Estes and Fanny his wife of COUNTY OF WILSON,
STATE OF TENNESSEE, sell to Sterling L. Haley of County of Halifax, State
of Virginia, for $50.00, a tract of land in Halifax County on Buckskin
Creek containing 50 acres, adjoining the land belonging to the legatees
of Bartlett (or Bartell?) Estes, deceased. Recorded 22 January 1826.

Virginia State Library, Accession #22625

Will of Nicholas Long of Halifax County, North Carolina, dated 13 June
1797 and probated February session 1798:

£5 to children of my late son, Gabriel Long, deceased, in
addition to what I gave their deceased father.

To my grandson, Nicholas Long, son of Gabriel, 600 acres of land in
STATE OF GEORGIA in lieu of 130 acres sold by me to John Miller of State
of Virginia in Caroline County. [See note.]

To my son, Nicholas Long, slaves named Nanny, and Hercules (NOW IN
GEORGIA) besides what I have already given him. Also one-fourth my land
and land warrants in the STATE OF GEORGIA.

To my son, Lunsford Long, 200 acres of land in NORTHAMPTON COUNTY on
Roanoke River [note - this is probably in North Carolina] which I purchased
of Thomas Edward Sumner. Also to him several slaves, all named.

To my son, Richard Harrisson Long, 200 acres of land in HALIFAX
COUNTY, NORTH CAROLINA, near Roanoke River whereon his negroes now are,
being part of the land I purchased of Henry Montfort and all the land I
purchased of John Branch on Lake George. Also slaves, named.

To my daughter, Mary Stith, slaves (named).

To my son, John Joseph Long, 200 acres in HALIFAX COUNTY (N.C.) called
Denson's Place which I purchased of Henry Montfort. Also slaves (named).

To my son, Lemuel Long, remaining part of land I purchased of Henry
Montfort on Roanoke River containing 200 acres more or less. Also slaves
(named).

To my son, McKennie Long, one-half all rest of my land on Roanoke
River called my Ferry Plantation. Also slaves (named).

Will of Nicholas Long, continued -

To my son, George Washington Long, plantation whereon I now live (underage) also to him and my son, Lemuel, all my estate in STATE OF GEORGIA, that I have not already given away in this Will.

Names his children with reversionary rights from son George Washington Long as Lunsford Long, Richard Harrison Long, Mary Stith, John Joseph Long, Lemuel Long, McKennie Long, and Martha Elizabeth Long.

To my daughter, Mary Elizabeth Long, land and other items (under age)

My beloved wife, Mary Long, for her natural life, etc.

My grandchildren, sons and daughters of Ann and William Martin, £5 each besides what I have already given them, deceased father and mother.

Whereas there is 5,000 acres surveyed on the WESTERN WATERS to each of my two sons, Nicholas Long and Lunsford Long, therefore the residue of my lands on WESTERN WATERS to my other surviving children.

To Bassett Stith, my son-in-law - land.

Executors, my wife, Mary Long, and sons, Nicholas Long, Lunsford Long, Richard Harrison (Long) and son-in-law, Bassett Stith.

Witnesses: Peter Isbell, William Walston, P. Haile, J. J. Pastuer. (Will Book 3, page 292.)

Note by C.H.H.: This is probably the Nicholas Long who was living in Caroline County, Virginia in 1783 with 6 taxable slaves.

Brunswick County, Virginia, Wills, Deeds, etc. #1, 1732-1740, page 206 -

2 July 1735 - Indenture in which Philip O'Riley of Brunswick County, near Roanoke River, sells to Richard Washington of NORTH CAROLINA, one-tenth part of a tract of land in Brunswick County on Roanoke River for £20 being the one-tenth part of a survey of land for Cornelius Cargill containing 100 acres, named Copper Hill, by patent dated 9 June 1735. Witnesses: Edward Hood, Henry Bedingfield. Recorded 3 July 1735.

Ibid, page 210 -

28 June 1735- John Lynch of NORTH CAROLINA sells to John Betty of Brunswick County, Virginia, clerk, a tract of land on the Southside of Meherring River in Brunswick County, containing 200 acres, for £30 , etc. Witnesses: Nathaniel Parrott, George Hicks, John Douglas, John Wall. Recorded 3 July 1735.

Ibid, page 360 -

1 July 17__ - Indenture in which Thomas Vinson of Parish of St. Andrews, County of Brunswick, sells to Walter Long of said Parish and County, for

Ł20, 100 acres on southside of Fountains Creek in said county, on Linches Branch, Gum Branch, adjoining land of John Vinson, etc. Recorded 4 August 1737. Witnesses: Mary Peterson, Mary Wall, Michael Wall, John Crosland.

Surry County Orders 1691-1713, page 357 -

February 25, 1710 - Certificate is granted Christopher Moring to the Secretary's office for fifty acres of land for the importation of himself into this colony, he having made oath as the law directs, being free when he came in.

Ibid -

February 25, 1710 - Certificate is granted David Andross to the Secretary's office for 50 acres of land for importation of himself into this colony, he having proved the same according to law, being free when he came in.

Southampton County, Virginia, Deed Book 1, page 81 -

Indenture dated 12 April 1750 in which Thomas Williams and Sarah, his wife, of the PROVINCE OF NORTH CAROLINA, sell to John Bowen, Jr. and Mary, his wife; Hardy Hart and Jane, his wife; Arthur Hart and Martha, his wife, all of the PROVINCE OF NORTH CAROLINA, of the second part and John Holding of the County of Southampton in Virginia, of the third part - for Ł 36 - a certain tract of land containing 180 acres in County of Southampton on southside of Lightwood Swamp, being a part of a patent granted Bartholomew Andros for 320 acres by date 16 June 1714 and by said Andros conveyed to Robert Warren, Jr., Thomas Warren and John Warren 26 October 1719, etc. devised by Will of Thomas Warren to his wife Sarah Warren and after her death to his son, Thomas Warren, and his heirs; but said Thomas [Jr.] dying an infant with no heirs, the said land has devolved to his four sisters, Mary, Jane, Martha and Patience Warren, and whereas said Sarah Warren, relict of said Thomas, hath intermarried with said Thomas Williams and they being willing to sell their right, being the first part, etc. and whereas the said Mary, Jane and Martha Warren hath intermarried with the said John Bowen, Jr., Hardy Hart and Arthur Hart, etc. Recorded same date.

> Note by C.H.H.: Ibid, page 138 - Thomas Williams in another sale of land is shown to be of NORTHAMPTON COUNTY, PROVINCE OF NORTH CAROLINA, which was part of two patents granted to him dated 16 June 1727 and 2 August 1736.

Southampton County, Virginia, Deed Book 7, page 173 -

26 November 1788 - In which John Williams of the COUNTY OF HALIFAX in STATE OF NORTH CAROLINA sells to Amos Stephenson of the County of Southampton, Virginia, for Ł 45 - all that parcel or tract of land given to Jacob Williams by Thomas Williams, deceased, in his last Will and

Testament and descended to the said John Williams by the death of Jacob
Williams, being situated on southside of Nottoway River in County of Southampton and on northside of Togathunting Swamp containing 100 acres, etc.
Witnesses: John T. Blow, Sr., John T. Blow, Jr., George Blow. Recorded
11 December 1788.

Surry County, Virginia, Deed Book 5, page 153 -

20 October 1747 - Indenture in which Thomas Tarver of the COUNTY OF NORTH-
AMPTON IN NORTH CAROLINA sells to Arthur Long of the County of Isle of
Wight, Colony of Virginia, for Ⱡ28, a tract of land containing 200 acres
in the County of Surry, Virginia, which land was conveyed by Samuel Tarver
by deed on Proctor's Branch, adjoining land of George Briggs - Nottoway
Indians old line - Robert Long, etc. Witnesses: Anselm Bailey, Jr.,
Thomas Davis, James ___?___. Recorded 20 October 1747 and Sarah, wife
of said Thomas Tarver, relinquishes her right of dower.

Ibid - page 354 -

20 March 1749 - Arthur Long and Elizabeth, his wife, of County of Isle of
Wight, sell the above land to Robert Long of Surry County, Virginia for
Ⱡ36.

Surry County, Virginia, Deed Book 10, page 69 -

23 August 1770 - Indenture in which Joshua Barker of the PROVINCE OF NORTH
CAROLINA, COUNTY OF ALLEFAX [sic] sells to Amos Sledge of the Parish of
Albemarle, County of Sussex [Va.] for Ⱡ126, a tract of land in County of
Surry [Va.] on the Northside of Otterdam Swamp, containing 150 acres ad-
joining land of Major Collin Campbell, etc. Recorded September 18, 1770.

Surry County, Deed Book 10, page 92 -

20 November 1770 - Indenture in which Benjamin Champion and Elizabeth,
his wife, and William Champion of the COUNTY OF HALIFAX IN THE PROVINCE
OF NORTH CAROLINA, sell to Joseph Holleman of the Parish of Southwark and
County of Surry in Virginia - for Ⱡ65 - a tract of land on the southside
of the Main Black Water Swamp in the County of Surry [Va.] adjoining land
of Hart Champion and others - containing 340 acres, it being the land
which formerly belonged to Benjamin Champion of the said County of Surry,
Grandfather of the said Benjamin and William [Champion] etc. Witnesses:
Benjamin Bailey, David Holleway, Sr., Joel Thompson. Recorded same date.

Surry County, Deed Book 10, page 115 -

21 January 1771 - Indenture in which Samuel Sorsby of the PROVINCE OF
NORTH CAROLINA, COUNTY OF EDGECOMBE, sells to Stephen Sorsby of the
Province [sic] of Virginia and County of Surry - for Ⱡ65.10.6 - a

tract of land in County of Surry [Va.] containing 300 acres, etc.
Witnesses: James Kee, Jr., David Putney, Lewis Putney. Recorded May
21, 1771.

Surry County, Virginia Deed Book 10, page 132 -

17 November 1769 - Indenture in which Joshua Moor(e) and Hannah, his
wife, of PERQUIMANS COUNTY IN NORTH CAROLINA, sell to Michael Bailey of
Surry County in Virginia - for Ł13.10. - 50 acres of land, etc. Witnesses: Selia Hargrave, Anselm Hargrave, Joseph Hargrave, Sr., Michael
Hargrave. Recorded August 20, 1771.

Surry County, Deed Book 10, page 208 -

19 September 1772 - Indenture in which Hart Champion of HALIFAX COUNTY,
NORTH CAROLINA, sells to Charles Champion of Surry County, Virginia - for
Ł40 - a tract of land containing 100 acres, which land is part of a
patent granted to James Allen April 25, 1701 for 1400 acres, which said
100 acres John Champion purchased of Robert Savedge and bequeathed to
the said Hart Champion in his last Will and Testament, being in Surry
County, Virginia, etc. Recorded September 22, 1772.

Surry County, Deed Book 10, page 262 -

21 December 1771 - Indenture in which John Gray of the Province of NORTH
CAROLINA, IN EDGECOMBE COUNTY, sells to Hartwell Cocke of the Colony of
Virginia and County of Surry for Ł200 - a tract of land in Surry County,
containing 100 acres, being all the land purchased by Gilbert Gray, father
of the said John Gray of William Gray of New Kent County by deed dated
1741 - on Grays Creek, etc. Recorded June 24, 1772.

Surry County, Deed Book 10, page 296 -

20 April 1773 - Indenture in which Thomas Wilson of BUTE COUNTY, PROVINCE
OF NORTH CAROLINA sells to William Evans of Surry County [Va.] - for Ł75-
a tract of land containing 271 acres in the County of Surry on the southside of the main Black Water Swamp (Reserves about 20 feet square, it being a graveyard) etc. Witnesses: Michael Bailey, Richard Wren, Lewis
Pulley. Recorded April 27, 1773.

Surry County, Deed Book 10, page 301 -

22 May 1773 - Deed of Trust in which John Barker of County of Surry, Colony
of Virginia, being indebted to Thomas Reekes of the COUNTY OF GRANVILLE,
PROVINCE OF NORTH CAROLINA - in the amount of Ł85 - for 196 acres of land
the said Reekes sold him 4th of May last, etc. Witnesses: Harmon Bishop,
John Shuffel, William Justiss. Recorded May 25, 1773.

Surry County, Virginia, Deed Book 10, page 369 -

5 November 1773 - Indenture in which James Maddera of NORTHAMPTON COUNTY, NORTH CAROLINA, sells to Mary Carrell of the County of Surry in Virginia - for Ł15 - all his right title and interest and claim to a tract of land in Southwark Parish in Surry County, containing 30 acres adjoining land of Zachariah Maddera and others being part of the land that Zachariah Maddera, deceased, and William Smith bought of John Deborix, which said land came to the possession of the said James Maddera by other conveyance, etc. Witnesses: John Davis, Sr., Thomas Davis, Nathan Davis. Recorded November 23, 1773.

Surry County, Virginia, Deed Book 10, page 500 -

1 December 1776 - William Bailey of HALIFAX COUNTY, NORTH CAROLINA sells to Mary Bailey of Surry County, Virginia - for Ł40 - two negroes named Harry and Janny, etc. Witnesses: John Bailey, Mary Bailey. Recorded January 28, 1778.

Surry County, Virginia, Deed Book 10, page 503 -

5 July 1776 - Archibald Campbell of Surry County, Colony of Virginia, gives bond in the full sum of Ł666.13.4 to Jane Copeland of the same county. Whereas Mary Clear, late of the TOWN OF NEWBERN IN NORTH CAROLINA did by her last Will and Testament dated 23 September 1775 [among other things] devised unto Jane Copeland, niece of the said testatrix, ten negores or Ł500 proclamation money of NORTH CAROLINA and whereas the said Archibald Campbell, nephew and residuary legatee of the said Mary Clear, etc. Witnesses: James Belsches, Colin Campbell. Recorded March 25, 1777.

Surry County, Deed Book 10, page 531 -

20 May 1777 - Indenture in which Samuel Rose of the COUNTY OF BUTE IN NORTH CAROLINA, sells to James Kee of County of Surry of Virginia - for Ł35 - a tract of land in the County of Surry, containing 100 acres, which said land descended unto William Rose, Junior by deed from Lemon Shell, and which descended unto the said Samuel Rose as heir at law of the said William Rose, deceased, etc. Witnesses: Rebekah Kee, Dorley Kee, Robert Lanier, Stephen Grantham. Recorded December 23, 1777.

Norfolk County, Virginia, Wills and Deeds Book 2, page 403 -

13 April 1663 - Bill of Sale from Henry Hudson, NOW OF MARYLAND, Merchant, owner of ye good barque, formerly called_____, of the burthen of 40 tons or thereabouts to Henry Goodricke (Goodrich) - now riding in the Potowmack River - for a valuable sum - etc. Witnesses: John Damrill, Henry _____, Francis Doser, Thomas Smith.

    Note: (Ibid) 20th December 1663 - Henry Goodrick assigns his right to above ship to William Carver - and on 10th May 1664 William Carver sells and assigns his right to David Anderson.

Norfolk County, Virginia, Deed Book 9, page 291 -

19 February 1713/14 - Richard Sanderson, OF NORTH CAROLINA, Gent. sells
to George Newton of County of Norfolk, Colony of Virginia, all his right,
title and interest in the plantation Mr. Thomas Mason, deceased, gave and
left to his widow, Mrs. Elizabeth Mason, by his Will, since which I, the
said Richard Sanderson, have intermarried with the said Elizabeth and also
my right in the cattle, sheep, horses, mares on said plantation, and also
in two gold rings, silver flagon, silver hilted sword, a gun and a pair
of pistols which was a legacy that was given unto Lemuel Mason by the Will
of his father, Mr. Thomas Mason, deceased, etc. Witnesses: Ann Furlong,
Frances Tucker, Mary Mason. Recorded 19 February 1713/14 after Captain
Richard Sanderson came into court and acknowledged the above deed and on
the motion of Captain George Newton was admitted to record.

Land Patent Book 13, page 362 -

September 28, 1728 - Patent for 152 acres of land in Nansemond County,
Virginia, granted to Aaron Blanchard OF NORTH CAROLINA, adjoining land of
George Spivey, etc.

Land Patent Book 14, page 296 -

June 26, 1731 - 388 acres of land granted to Richard Parker of NORTH
CAROLINA - in Nansemond County, Virginia, adjoining his own and Joseph
Horton's land.

Land Patent Book 14, page 137 -

September 28, 1730 - Patent for 399 acres of land in Nansemond County,
Virginia, granted to Richard Parker of NORTH CAROLINA, in the upper
Parish, adjoining his own land, land of Thomas Odum and to the county
line.

Land Patent Book 15, page 67 -

June 20, 1733 - Patent for 371 acres of land in Nansemond County,
Virginia, granted to John Parker of the PROVINCE OF NORTH CAROLINA, in
the upper Parish, adjoining his own land and the land of John Knight.

Elizabeth City County, Will, Deeds, etc. 1684-1699 (Transcript) -
        Pages 439-440 - Ref. to pps. 237-238 -

22 March 1697/8 - Sir Edmond Andros, Knt., his Majesties Lieutenant
and Governor of Virginia, grants naturalization papers to Bertram
Servant, a NATURAL BORN SUBJECT OF YE KINGDOM OF FRANCE, of ye age
of sixty and six years; settled and resided thirty and eight years
in Elizabeth City County, Colony of Virginia, etc. Recorded 28 November
1698 by Charles Jennings, clerk.

Note by C.H.Hamlin: See Will of William Harris of Elizabeth City
(Ibid page 402, ref. to page 209) dated 14 December 1695, who makes
his loving friend Mr. Bertram Servant his sole executor and leaves
legacies of £6 to each of the following children of Bertram Servant:
Madaline Servant, Frances Servant, and Mary Servant. In addition,
he leaves 2/3rd of his estate to his wife, Judah Harris and the other
1/3 to his daughter (name unknown) having been born since he left.
He also leaves legacies to George Walker and Madaline Kelly. Will
probated 18 May 1696.

Knox County, Tennessee, pages 104-105 (Deed Book not given) -

10 October 1808 - Indenture in which Jacob Loomis OF THE COUNTY OF KNOX
STATE OF TENNESSEE, sells to the heirs of Jacob Neff, deceased, of the
COUNTY OF SHENANDOAH, STATE OF VIRGINIA, for $400.00 - a tract of land
in the County of Knox, State of Tennessee, containing 132 acres, etc.
Registered and recorded October 11, 1808 by John Gamble, Deputy Clerk of
Knox County, Tennessee. [Note by C.H.H. See below cited Will.]

Shenandoah County, Virginia, Will Book H, page 268 -

Last Will and Testament of Francis Neff dated 14 September 1812, pro-
bated 12 October 1812: To my son, John Neff, my land and plantation,
being the same as willed me by my father, John Henry Neff, deceased,
(See Will Book B, page 101) - To George Grabuc(?) husband of my oldest
daughter, Anna - My eldest son, Jacob Neff, deceased, in his lifetime
I paid for him $400.00 for land he bought near KNOXVILLE in the
TENNESSEE STATE, to his children, etc. Executors, my son John Neff and
Benjamin Gaines; witnesses, Samuel Hupp, Aaron Gaines, Peter Good.

Early Records of Hampshire County (1782-1860) by Sage and Jones, p.125 -

Last Will and Testament of Elizabeth Machir of Washington, MASON COUNTY,
KENTUCKY, dated January 6, 1830 and probated August 27, 1832:

Nephews	Nieces	Brother	Sisters
John Brough (Exor.)	Nancy Richie	John Machir	Jane Brough
Franklin Brough	Lillian Kennedy		Maria Mitchell
Charles M. Brough	Rachel Machir		

Will mentions THE ESTATE IN SCOTLAND of deceased brother, John Machir,
and also mentions: Mr. W. M. Kennedy, David N. Richey, Joseph Foreman,
M. W. Owens, Elijah Berry, Lawrence Butler, and Angus W. McDonald
(relationship not stated.) Witnesses: Sally Rannels, B. W. Wood.

Northumberland County, Virginia, Order Book 1753-56, page 126 -

Last Will and Testament of Tunstall Hack dated 29 August 1757, codicil dated
30 August 1757, probated 12 September 1757: To Ann Gordon, daughter of

Colonel James Gordon, of Lancaster County - slaves.
    To _____Conway, son of Captain George Conway of Lancaster - slave.
    To brother, Spencer Hack's children - each a slave.
    To Sarah Conway McAdams - a ring.
    To friend, Doctor Joseph McAdams - a ring.
    To brother Spencer Hack's son, Peter John Tunstall - plantation and
           land.
    My son, John Tunstall Hack - (underage) -
    Brother, Peter Spencer and his wife, Sarah Ann -
    To John Wright - 500 pounds of tobacco -
    To Ann Yop, alias Floyd - 700 lbs. tobacco
    To my wife - (not named) -
Executors: Colonel James Gordon, Mr. Samuel Blackwell, Colonel Spencer
Ball and Captain Richard Hull.
    Codicil - In case my son, John Tunstall Hack should die without law-
ful issue - my brother, Spencer Hack to have no right to my estate, or
power in its management but his children to claim as if he were dead, etc.
Witnesses: Giles Webb, Joseph McAdams and Ann Floyd.

Northumberland County, Virginia, Order Book 1753-56, page 127 -

31 August 1757 - Joseph McAdams and Ann Floyd swear an affidavit that it
was Mr. Hack's will and desire on his death bed that the child, Betty
Holebrook, and also the child which Molly Way had by him should each have
a little negro when they arrive at the age 21 or married.

Northumberland County, Virginia, Order Book 1753-56, page 128 -

29 August 1757 - Memorandum of matters taken from Mr. Hack's mouth relating to his affairs - signed by Joseph McAdam, Ann Floyd and John
Wright -
    (1)   Mr. Ephraim King and John Waters bound to him by
          Bond for ₤120 MARYLAND currency and they received
          ₤100 of money from Joshua Calwell, which sums have
          never been settled.
    (2)   2 old negroes I left on the Eastern Shore.
    (3)   My tract of land on HEAD OF WICCOCOMOCO IN MARYLAND
          containing 300 acres called "Shitten Hill"

Northumberland County, Virginia, Record Book 6, 1762-1766, page 139 -

Last Will and Testament of William Kenner, mariner of WHITEHAVEN
COUNTY OF CUMBERLAND (ENGLAND) dated 11 December 1758, probated
9 November 1762 -
    My cousin (nephew?) Richard Kenner of Northumberland County in
Virginia ₤100 -
    My son, John William Hicks Kenner (underage) -
    Sister-in-law, Mrs. Elizabeth Hall, all my late wife's clothing,
which is now in possession of her brother, Mr. William Hicks of MARYLAND,

merchant.

Custody and tuition of my son to my friend, Mrs. Sarah Hicks of
WHITEHAVEN, widow. She to continue him at some school in ENGLAND -
reversion of 1/2 my estate to my cousin (nephew?) Richard Kenner - the
other part to the children of my brothers and sisters, Matthew Kenner,
Francis Kenner, Elizabeth and Nancy - share alike -

Sarah Hicks, executrix as long as she lives, then my friend, Henry
Ellison OF WHITEHAVEN, merchant. The said William Hicks (OF MARYLAND)
and Richard Hull and Thomas Jones of Northumberland County (Va.) to have
government and tuition of my son in his minority. Witnesses: James
Wherry, James Wherry, Jr., John Finlay.

True copy taken from original Will of William Kenner in possession
of Mrs. Sarah Hicks and compared at WHITEHAVEN this 21st day of April
1762 by Henry Littledal, Publick Notary, Administration granted to
Francis Kenner.

Northumberland County, Virginia, Record Book 6, 1762-66, page 317 -

Last Will and Testament of David Straughan of HALIFAX COUNTY, PROVINCE OF
NORTH CAROLINA, dated 27 November 1763, probated ___?___ : My estate
to my wife, Elizabeth, and son, John (underage) to be equally divided when
he is 21 years of age. After her death, the whole to son, John. Reversion
to David Straughan, son of my brother, Richard Straughan, except ₤10 to
my sister, Margaret Straughan. Executors: Wife, Elizabeth and brother,
Richard Straughan, and friend William Tarte. Witnesses: Giles Boggess,
Hannah Cox, Keziah Boggess.

Northumberland County, Virginia, Record Book 6, 1762-66, page 507 -

Last Will and Testament of Edward Coles of St. Stephen's Parish, dated
15 November 1764, probated 10 December 1764: To my brother, John Cole's
daughter, Elizabeth Wise - 4 negroes for life, then to her children.
To cousin (niece?) Esther and John Hughlett - slave. To cousin (niece?)
Alce and James Conway - slave. To Francinah Conway - chest of drawers.
To Peter Hack's son, George, upon the Eastern Shore, one seal skin trunk.
To Sarah Carpenter and all her children, for life - may live upon my land
and not be disturbed. To cousin (nephew?) John Coles - all my land for
his life, then to his three sons, Edward, William and Richard Coles. The
Estate belonging to me in ENGLAND to be equally divided between my four
cousins, (nephews and nieces?) John Coles, Eliza Wise, Esther Hughlett,
and Alce Conway. Cousin John Coles, Executor. Witnesses: John Corbell,
John Span Webb.

Northumberland County, Virginia, Record Book 7, 1766-70, page 84 -

Last Will and Testament of John Alexander, dated 27th July 1765, probated
8 June 1767: Son, John Sheldon Alexander, one lot of land LYING IN SNOW
HILL TOWN, IN WORCESTER COUNTY, MARYLAND and two negro slaves. Reversion
to my wife, Sarah Alexander, and to her a slave named Fortan. My son
should go to my friend, Solomon Townsend in WORCESTER COUNTY, MARYLAND, and

be bound to a house carpenter and house joyner. I disinherit a child that
my former wife had in my absence, called Ann, with one shilling sterling.
My wife (Sarah) executrix. Witnesses: Thomas Airs, Mary Enser.

Northumberland County, Virginia, Record Book 11, (1780-82), page 118 -

Last Will and Testament of David Boyd of St. Stephen's Parish dated 7 May
1781, probated 10 December 1781:
    I confirm my late precious daughter, Margaret Smith's Will in every
part of it (evidently living at "Shooter's Hill" in Middlesex Co. in 1774.)
    To my grandson, Augustine Jacqulin Smith, son of my said daughter,
all my land in Fairfax County. Reversion to David McCullock, son of John
McCullock of TARHOUSE, and Mary, his wife, my youngest sister of the
SHIRE OF WIGTON IN NORTH BRITAIN (SCOTLAND) - further reversion to James
McCullock, son of John McCullock and Agnes, his wife, late of the ISLE OF
MAN. Also to grandson, other land in Fairfax and in Loudoun County.
    To my grandaughter, Mary Jacqulin Smith, my dwelling plantation and
a small tract of land I purchased of the widow of John Nichols on which
Henry Self now lives.
    Two-thirds of my slaves to my above grandson. One-third of my slaves
to my above grandaughter, and to her all my plate, because her mother gave
her brother, Augustine, her plate.
    To my wife, the use of my home plantation and the negroes thereon,
cattle, oxen, hogs, sheep and hourses, chariot, etc.
    My estate in NORTH BRITAIN to my sister, Mary McCullock and her
eldest surviving son, and to the eldest child, male or female, of my late
sister, Agness McCullock -
    Grandson may be brought to the profession of a physician and liberally
educated and TO BE SENT TO SCOTLAND for that purpose to one of the colleges
in ABERDEEN and then to EDINBURGH and he to visit LONDON, LIGDEN AND PARIS.
    My wife having perused my Will, and not being satisfied, I hereby void
every gift to her.
    Balance of my estate to my two grandchildren and if both die before
age 21, or marriage, to my two sisters Agnes McCullock and Mary McCullock
and their heirs.
    My land in Loudoun County containing 1500 acres (the courses will give
1750 acres) for tobacco rent till my grandson comes of age.
    Grandson to carry my bones, those of his mother, and of his uncle,
Alexander Boyd, to SCOTLAND and have them buried by my father and mother
in the CHURCHYARD OF THE TOWN OF WIGTON.
    Colonel John Smith of Frederick County, Rev. M. Thomas Smith of West-
moreland County, guardians to my grandchildren and with Richard Mitchell
of Lancaster County. Captain David Ball and one siphorus Harvey of Northumberland County, John Sydnor, Captain Williamson Ball, William Miskell,
and Major Charles McCarty of Richmond County, and William Taylor of Northumberland County, my executors.

    Note by C.H.H.: Presented in court by the widow, Margaret Boyd,
the executors refusing to act, administration granted to the
widow.

    Further note: This is such an interesting document I think it well to supplement it with the Will of his wife, Margaret, which follows:

Last Will and Testament of Margaret Boyd, of St. Stephen's Parish, dated 22 April 1782, probated 10 June 1782 - [Record Book 11, page 200.]

My daughter Millie Hall - furniture, china, trunks, clothes, etc.

My granddaughter, Mary Jacqulin Smith - furniture, etc. and a mourning ring that was formerly Alexander Boyd's - also my religious books.

My grandson, Augustine Jacqulin Smith - large gilt looking glass, china, and the mourning ring of my father, Thomas Pinckard.

My four grandchildren, Mary Jacqulin Smith, Augustine Jacqulin Smith, Milly Pinckard Hall, and Horatio Gates Hall - the remainder of my estate and all the slaves given to me by my father, Thomas Pinckard by deed of gift.

To Nancy Haynie - a cow and calf.
To Bridgar Haynie and Sarah, his wife, each £10 specie.

Executors: Thomas Gaskins, Sr., James Gordon, Edwin Conway and Bridgar Haynie. Witnesses: Bridgar Haynie, William Lansdell and Enoch Potts.

Northumberland County, Virginia, Record Book 3 (1753-56), page 227 -

Last Will and Testament of Alexander Boyd, dated 11 July 1755, probated 9 September 1755 -

All my estate both real and personal in the Colony of Virginia, SCOTLAND, OR ELSEWHERE, to my brother, David Boyd of Northumberland County, Colony of Virginia, and he to be my executor. [Proved by oath of George Ker.]

Northumberland County, Virginia, Record Book 8 (1770-1772), page 532 -

Last Will and Testament of Margaret Watson of Wiccomoco Parish, dated 22 February 1772, probated 8 June 1772 -

To nephew, John Barr, plantation and slaves.
To nieces, Agness Rodment and Janet Rodment, IN NORTH BRITAIN (SCOTLAND) - £15 sterling each.
Nieces Margaret and May Davidson, IN NORTH BRITAIN, £15 sterling each - daughters of William Davidson.
To nephew John Barr, my tract of 79 acres called Scotland, which my deceased husband purchased of David Lattimore. If nephew marry a native of Virginia, she is not to enjoy my estate after his death. He to be my executor.
Cow and calf to Agness Eston.
Witnesses: William Brown, Ezekiel Hudnall

Northumberland County, Virginia, Record Book 14 (1787-1793), page 342 -

Last Will and Testament of Henry Barnes, of Wiccomoco Parish, dated
29 March 1789, probated 12 April 1790 -

Wife, Mary Barnes, land, etc. for natural life.
Granddaughter, Betsy Barnes Marsh -
Grandson, Gideon Hammonds Marsh - land - reversion to granddaughter
Betsy Barnes Marsh - reversion from her to Spencer Snow, son of Elisha
Snow.

Reversion legacy to Joseph Spencer Snow OF NORTH CAROLINA, son of
Samuel Snow - also to John Snow, son of Elisha Snow.

Executors: Wife, Mary Barnes, and friends, Isaac Basye and Ezekiel
Haydon. Witnesses: Betty Edwards, Judith Edwards, Robert Short.

Augusta County, Virginia, Deed Book 19, page 94 -

20 November 1772 - Indenture in which Christopher Vickrey and Hannah, his
wife, OF GUILDFORD COUNTY, NORTH CAROLINA, sell to Andrew Bird of Augusta
County, Virginia - for ₤155 - a tract of land in Augusta County being part
of a tract of 210 acres originally granted out of his majesties office to
a certain Samuel Newman by patent dated 29th August 1757 and which the
said Samuel Newman sold to Jacob Hodgh 21 June 1763, and the aforesaid
Hannah, wife of the aforesaid Christopher Vickrey, being sister and heir
at law of the aforesaid Jacob Hodgh, containing 105 acres on Smith's
Creek, etc. Witnesses: John Lilly, John Benson, Jances West. Recorded
same date.

Augusta County, Virginia, Deed Book 20, page 352 -

6 April 1774 - Indenture in which Adam Stephen OF THE COUNTY OF BERKELEY,
COLONY OF VIRGINIA (NOW WEST VIRGINIA) sells to Mark Bird and Henry Miller
of the COUNTY OF BUCKS IN THE PROVINCE OF PENNSYLVANIA - for ₤110 -
Pennsylvania money - a tract of land in Augusta County on Mossy Creek
containing 212 acres, it being the land the said Adam Stephens purchased
of William Minter, etc. Witnesses: Abram Smith, Peter Hog, Gabriel
Jones. Recorded 18 May 1774.

Note: Adam Stephen sells Mark Bird and Henry Miller another
tract of land, the same date (ibid p.356) containing 170 acres
which he had purchased of Henry Smith.

Augusta County, Virginia, Deed Book 23, page 23 -

26 April 1779 - Indenture in which Mark Bird, Esquire and Mary, his wife,
OF THE TOWNSHIP OF UNION IN THE COUNTY OF BERKS AND STATE OF PENNSYLVANIA,
sell to Henry Miller of the Parish and County of Augusta in Virginia,
Ironmaster - his interest in the above cited land. Mentions he and Henry

Miller had entered into a co-partnership 1 June 1774 to carry on the art and mystery of Iron Masters and they had erected the necessary forges, furnaces and mills, for L15,000 for his moiety or share, etc. Witnesses: Jesse Potts, David Davis, Sarah Lincoln. Certified in Berks County, Pennsylvania and recorded in Augusta County, Virginia, May 19, 1779.

Essex County, Virginia, Deeds and Wills 13, page 118 -

10 August 1708 - John Waggoner, aged 65 years, of Essex County, being examined and sworn at the request of Phillip Pendleton, deposeth and saith - That on or about the year 1674 FROM ENGLAND, came consigned to Captain Edmund Crask, two reputed brothers called and known by the name of Nathaniel Pendleton and Phillip Pendleton, and the said Nathaniel was reputed a minister, and soon after his arrival sickened and dyed and that this deponent was with his wife and several other neighbors at the funeral of the said Nathaniel Pendleton and that he never heard that the said Nathaniel had either wife or child and that the said Phillip Pendleton, when he had served out his time WENT FOR ENGLAND AND RETURNED HITHER again and is since marryed and has several children, all now resident in King and Queen County in Virginia.

Essex County, Virginia, Deeds and Wills 13, page 118 -

10 August 1708 - George Ward, aged 57 years, being sworn deposed that - same as above, except he states the two brothers, Nathaniel Pendleton and Phillip Pendleton were sent by their mother in a ship whereof was Master Captain John Plover - and that the said Phillip went FOR ENGLAND after five years servitude and CAME TO VIRGINIA again the same year.

Washington County, Virginia, Will Book 2, page 46 -

Last Will and Testament of Charles McDonald of Washington County, State of Virginia - not dated, probated August 9, 1794.

Mentions beloved wife, Margaret McDonald.

To my sons, John Viney McDonald and Bartholomew Jude McDonald, plantation where I now live in the Rich Valley joining lines with John Kincade and Robert Wallis.

To my son James McDonald MY LAND ON THE OHIO LYING ON THE NORTH FORK OF GREEN CREEK, joining lines with David Jonas and Morgan Jonas.

To my daughters: Hannah McDonald, Azuba McDonald, Anny (or Amey?) McDonald - to each - L20.

Executors: Beloved wife, Margaret, and John McHenry. Witnesses: William Mobeley, John Moffett, Andrew Ullam(?).

Augusta County, Virginia, Deed Book 8, page 199 -

20 November 1759 - Indenture in which John Burk of the County of Augusta, Colony of Virginia, sells John McDonald of the COUNTY OF ORANGE, in NORTH CAROLINA - for Ⱡ35 - a tract of land in the County of Augusta, Virginia, containing 108 acres on Boons Run, a branch of the Main River of Shenandoah, etc. Recorded November 21, 1759.

Augusta County, Virginia, Deed Book 20, page 448 -

16 November 1774 - Indenture in which William Patterson and Mary, his wife, of CUMBERLAND COUNTY, PROVINCE OF PENNSYLVANIA, a tract of land in Augusta County, Colony of Virginia, which tract is the joint property of four sisters, heirs of Randall McDonald, patented to John Hope 5 September 1749 and by him conveyed to Randall McDonald who died intestate and Mary, wife of William Patterson became invested in one-fourth part, etc. [See record below.]

Augusta County, Virginia, Order Book 8, March 1769 -

Fowler vs Skidmore - Bill in chancery filed 1764-5, John Fowler and Margaret, his wife, William Patterson and Mary, his wife, Patrick Quin and Jane, his wife - which said Margaret, Mary, Jane - together with Sarah, since intermarried with James Skidmore were sisters and co-heirs of Randolph McDonald of Augusta County. Said Randolph died intestate, unmarried and without children. His mother was Jane (Jeanet) McDonald. Randolph, age 26 when he died.

Culpeper County, Virginia, Deed Book QQ, page 518 -

22 July 1822 - John Slaughter of the COUNTY OF WOODFORD, STATE OF KENTUCKY, appoints his friend, Thomas Brooks, of the STATE OF MISSOURI, his true and lawful attorney to settle and receive his one-sixth portion or share as one of six heirs of his mother, Franky Slaughter, (late Horde) in that part of my grandfather Horde's estate which descended to my said mother as one of his heirs - the said estate lying in the County of Culpeper, State of Virginia, etc. Certified to before two Justices of COUNTY OF WOODFORD, STATE OF KENTUCKY, same date. Recorded Culpeper County 5 June 1824.

Culpeper County, Virginia, Deed Book QQ, page 520 -

20 December 1823 - Lawrence Slaughter and Mary Slaughter of COUNTY OF WOODFORD, STATE OF KENTUCKY, give Power of Attorney to their trusty friend Thomas Brooks to collect, receive, sell and convey, concerning all kinds of estate they possess in the State of Virginia. Certified before Justices

of WOODFORD COUNTY, KENTUCKY same date. Recorded Culpeper County,
5 June 1824.

Culpeper County, Virginia, Deed Book QQ, page 521 -

23 August 1813 (sic) - Robert Brooks, Alexander Brooks and William Brooks,
all of the COUNTY OF WOODFORD AND STATE OF KENTUCKY, give Power of Attorney
to our trusty friend and brother, Thomas Brooks to collect, sell, convey,
etc. all kinds of estate we possess in the State of Virginia. Certified
before two Justices of COUNTY OF WOODFORD (KY.) same date. Recorded
Culpeper County, 5 June 1824 (sic)

Culpeper County, Virginia, Deed Book VV, page 102 -

24 December 1828 - Whereas Daniel Garwood, late of LOGAN COUNTY AND STATE
OF OHIO, now deceased - he, the aforesaid Garwood, being in possession of
a tract of 50 acres of land in the State of Virginia, County of Culpeper,
which land was sold in his life time by his agent, Henry Miller of the
County of Culpeper, at public sale in the Town of Washington, County of
Culpeper, to David Coxe, now deceased, of said town. No deed of conveyance having been made to said Coxe or his widow, now know ye that we,
Jose H. Garwood and Angeline, his wife; Daniel Garwood and Elizabeth, his
wife; Daniel Stokes and Patience, his wife (late Garwood); John Bishop
and Sarah, his wife (late Garwood); and Jonathan Garwood, legal heirs of
Daniel Garwood, deceased - all of the COUNTY OF LOGAN, STATE OF OHIO -
give power of attorney to Henry Miller of the County of Culpeper to ex-
ecute and convey to Ann Coxe, the widow of the above named David Coxe,
deceased, and being the legal heirs of the late Mary Bishop, now Mary
Garwood, late of the County of Culpeper, Virginia, deceased, she being the
daughter and legal heir of Jonathan Bishop, late of the County of Culpeper, now deceased, and Patience, his wife, late of LOGAN COUNTY, OHIO,
now deceased, and being the legal heirs of Daniel Garwood, deceased, to
one-eighth part of all the real estate in the County of Culpeper of
Jonathan Bishop and his wife, now both deceased, etc. Witnesses: David
Ripley, Rebecca Speers, Certified before Justices of LOGAN COUNTY, OHIO
named Alex Long and Isaiah Garwood. Recorded Culpeper County 16 February
1829.

Land Patent Book 12, page 515 -

7 July 1726 - 130 acres in Brunswick County, Virginia, granted to John
Davis "THE WELCHMAN" on the north side of Maherin River.

Prince George County, Virginia, Land Patent Book 10, page 40 -

8 April 1711 - Patent for 2208 acres of land in Prince George County, Virginia, granted to John Sadler, CITIZEN AND GROCER OF LONDON and Rev. Joshua
Richardson, Clerk, and husband of Ellenor Richardson, Executor of Thomas

Quiny(?) - called Merchants Hope on James River and Powells Creek.

Prince George County, Virginia, Land Patent Book 10, page 40 -

8 April 1711 - Patent for 5037 acres of land in Prince George County,
Virginia, granted to John Sadler, CITIZEN AND GROCER OF LONDON and Rev.
Joshua Richardson, Clerk, and husband of Ellenor Richardson, Executor
of Thomas Quiny(?) - beginning at mouth of Hackey Creek on James River
and Chippokes Creek, including Tappahannah Marsh, etc.

Brunswick County, Virginia, Deed Book 4 - last section at end of book, page 35 -

Account of Benjamin Sims, orphan of John Sims, deceased, with Peter
Randle, his guardian -

This is an itemized account of debits and credits commencing January 1779
through 1782 - containing such items as 1 year's board with William
Randle in 1779 - one year's board in 1780 with William Finch - one year's
board in 1781 with Bartlet Sims.

The account was sworn to be correct on the 24th day of November 1784 by
Peter Randle of MONTGOMERY COUNTY, STATE OF NORTH CAROLINA, Guardian of
Peter Sims, orphan of John Sims, deceased, before Mark Allen, a Justice
of the Peace. Recorded in Brunswick County, Virginia 26 August 1785.

> Note by C.H.H.- Ibid, page 47 - In 1784 and 1785 Benjamin Sims,
> orphan of John Sims, deceased, is under the guardianship of John
> Sims of Brunswick County, Virginia, who returns an account which
> is recorded 26 August 1785.

Brunswick County, Virginia, Deed Book 4, page 92 -

Account of Lizzie Mahaney, orphan of Thomas Mahaney, deceased, with
Thomas Spain - 1787 through 1790 - signed by Thomas Spain and Susannah,
his wife, of WAKE COUNTY [NORTH CAROLINA] and recorded in Brunswick
County, Virginia, January 24, 1791 by John Jones, Clerk, who states that
Thomas Spain had intermarried with [Susannah] guardian of Lizzey Mahaney.

Brunswick County, Virginia, Deed Book 5, page 221 -

20 November 1751 - Indenture in which William Huggins and John Huggins
of the COUNTY OF CRAVEN, PROVINCE OF SOUTH (SIC) CAROLINA, sell to John
Randle of the County of Brunswick, Colony of Virginia - for Ł30 - a
tract of land in Brunswick County on the south side of Meherrin River on
the lower side of Coldwater Run, containing 200 acres, more or less, which
is part of 290 acres formerly granted to Adam Sims by patent and by him
conveyed to William Huggins, the Elder, etc. Recorded 23 June 1752.

> Note by C.H.H.- Craven County is in NORTH CAROLINA.

Henry County, Virginia, Deed Book 4, page 71 -

7 September 1789 - William Tanzey of HENRY COUNTY AND STATE OF NORTH
CAROLINA (sic) sells to Bennett Posey of County of Henry, State of
Virginia - for £16 - 351 acres of land in County of Henry as by patent
dated 9 February 1781 may appear - on south fork of Bowens Creek.
Witnesses: Charles Hibbert, Richard Baker, Isaac Hollinsworth. No
date of recording.

Henry County, Deed Book 5, page 128 -

25 August 1794 - Power of Attorney from Thomas Posey who intermarried
with Elizabeth Hobert, daughter of Harrison Hobert and Jean, his wife,
and Savarah Hobert, daughter of said Harrison and Jean Hobert, of the
County of Henry, Virginia, appointing their trusty and well beloved
friend, John Hobert of said County their true and lawful attorney to ask
and demand of the executor of Asa King, deceased, of the County of CHARLES
IN THE STATE OF MARYLAND, all legacy or legacies left to us by the last
Will and Testament of the said Asa King, deceased, etc. Signed by Thomas
and Elizabeth Posey and Saberah Hobert. Recorded 25 August 1794.

Henry County, Virginia, Deed Book 4, page 133 -

27 July 1790 - Elisha Wallen of HAWKINS COUNTY, STATE OF NORTH CAROLINA,
gives Power of Attorney to his truly faithful beloved friend, Stephen
Lyon of the County of Henry, State of Virginia, to recover by law a
certain negro man slave by the name of Jack, which negro was plundered
from John Roberts in the time of the last war (Revolutionary) by Daniel
Carlin of Henry County, Virginia. No witnesses and no date of recording.

Early Records of Hampshire County, Virginia (now West Virginia)
1782-1860 by Sage and Jones (1939) page 60 -

4 December 1764 - Jacob Westfall and Judith, his wife, of HAMPSHIRE
COUNTY sell to Peter Reeves of PHILADELPHIA, PENNSYLVANIA - 140 acres of
land on Luneys Creek. Witnesses: David Scott, William Westfall,
Benjamin Scott, Mathew Kuykendall.

    Note: In the time period 1760 through 1784, there are deeds of sale
by Cornelius, John and William (wife Elizabeth) in Hampshire County.

Prince George County, Virginia -

Mary Bland Graveyard (6 miles from Disputanta, Virginia, 3/4 mile from
road) - A marker at one grave:

Sacred to the memory of
Mary Bland, consort of John Bland, Esq.
formerly of LONDON who departed
this life March 27, 1826 in the
71st year of her age [thus born 1755]

Fauquier County, Virginia, Deed Book 15, page 565 -

25 January 1804 - James Harris, late of Fauquier County, State of Virginia,
now a soldier in the 1st Regt. of Infantry in the Army of the United States,
in the TOWN OF EDYVILL, COUNTY OF LIVINGSTON, IN THE STATE OF KENTUCKY,
gives Power of Attorney to his father, William Harris of Fauquier County,
Virginia to collect monies and debts owing him and also in his behalf all
estate, both real and personal, in the property of Joseph Barbee of
Fauquier County, as the only son and heir of his daughter, Bersheba Barber,
late Bersheba Harris, etc. Certified same date before Justices of Livingston County, Kentucky. Recorded Fauquier County, Virginia, 27 March 1804.

Petersburg Husting Court Marriage Bonds, etc. (originals) -

21 February 1846 - Peter H. Cocke of NORTHAMPTON (CO.) NORTH CAROLINA,
to Miss Elizabeth W. Lee. H. B. Cowles, minister.

21 December 1843 - William Stiles of Petersburg, Virginia, to Sarah T.
Jenkins. Belfield Stiles, Security. Consent of Thomas T. Jenkins of
WARREN COUNTY, NORTH CAROLINA, father of Sarah T. who signed at War-
renton, N. C. 28 November 1843. Belfield Stiles and John J. Vaughan,
witnesses to consent.

23 May 1843 - Thomas McConnell to Miss Margaret Kennaday. H. Bright,
Security. Margaret signs own consent stating that she is upwards of
22 years and was a FORMER RESIDENT OF PHILADELPHIA (PENNSYLVANIA).
Jane Hannah also certifies her to be of age.

18 August 1837 - Joel Sturdivant of Prince George County, Virginia, to
Frances L. Womack. Joel Sturdivant of Petersburg, Virginia, Security.
Consent of J. D. Lunsden of OXFORD, NORTH CAROLINA to Frances L. Womack's
marriage, relationship not stated.

13 May 1811 - Edward Dillard to Minerva Ruffin. James Wright, Security.
Minerva signs own consent stating she was FORMERLY OF ROCKINGHAM COUNTY,
NORTH CAROLINA.

30 April 1828 - Rev. William G. H. Jones of FAYETTEVILLE, NORTH CAROLINA
to Frances C. Allison of Petersburg, Virginia, daughter of John Allison,
who consents.· Richard T. Spotswood, Security.

22 July 1846 - John Burns to Miss Sarah A. L. Ellis. John Stevens,
Security. G. D. Lumsden of GREENSBORO, NORTH CAROLINA, guardian of
Sarah, signs consent with Charles Lumsden, his witness (dated June 27,
1846.

26

If James Feskin, a Weaver by Trade, who sailed from PORT GLASGOW the latter
End of last year, or at the beginning of this, for Virginia, will apply
to the subscriber, at Mr. Robert Nicolson's, he will hear of something to
his satisfaction.   --Peter Feskin

If any of the Descendants of John Hellier, who came to Virginia many years
ago, from BRISTOL, IN GREAT BRITAIN, and settled on the Freshes of Rappahannock River, will apply to me in Fredericksburg, they be informed of a
particular inquiry made after them, perhaps much to their advantage. ---
I have received Information of a family of the Name of Hilliard, who came
from BRISTOL, and formerly settled in the neighbourhood of the late
Colonel Turner, on Rappahannock. If any of that family are alive, perhaps
they may be able to reconcile the difference of the name from convincing
circumstances, as there is so great a similitude in the sound.--Roger
Dixon.

Augusta County, Virginia, Deed Book 28, page 446 -

25 February 1795 - Indenture in which William Floyd of COUNTY OF CHESTER,
STATE OF PENNSYLVANIA, being the right heir at law of Charles Floyd,
deceased, sells to William McKenny of the County of Augusta, State of
Virginia - for £100 - a certain tract of land in the County of Augusta
containing 90 acres, etc. Witnesses: James McKenny, Charles Hogshead,
Richard Roche. Recorded December Court 1795.

Augusta County, Virginia, Deed Book 29, page 100 -

10 December 1796 - Power of Attorney given by John McKittrick of WASH-
INGTON COUNTY, STATE OF KENTUCKY to his trusty friends, James Hogshead
and John McGlamming(?) of Augusta County, State of Virginia, to dispose
of a tract of land in County of Augusta, Virginia, it being a tract of
land devised to me and my two brothers, William and James McKittrick
by the last Will and Testament of our father, Robert McKittrick, deceased.
Witnesses: Charles Hogshead, Thomas Shanklin. Recorded Augusta Court
December 20, 1796.

Augusta County, Virginia, Deed Book 29, page 100 -

26 December 1795 - Indenture in which James Cooper and Hannah, his wife,
of THE COUNTY OF YORK IN THE STATE OF PENNSYLVANIA, sell to John McKenny
of Augusta County, State of Virginia, for £110 - a parcel of land containing 110 acres in the County of Augusta, Virginia, on both sides of
the north River of Shenandoah, etc. Witnesses: William McKenny, Eleanor
McKenny, William Walker, Jr.

   Certified as their act and deed before John King, one of the
justices of the peace of YORK COUNTY, PENNSYLVANIA on the above date -
Recorded Augusta County, Virginia, December 21, 1796.

Augusta County, Virginia, Deed Book 32, page 1 -

26 September 1802 - Indenture in which Samuel Buchannan and Elizabeth,
his wife, John Edmondson and Jinnet, his wife, of DAVIDSON COUNTY; David
Craig and Mary, his wife, of BLOUNT COUNTY; John McKinney and Jane, his
wife, of WILLIAMSON COUNTY AND STATE OF TENNESSEE - by James Craig,
their attorney in fact and James Brownlee and Florence, his wife, of
Augusta County, Virginia, heirs and legatees of Andrew Duncan, deceased,
of the one part, sell to John Craig Baskins of the County of Augusta,
Virginia of the other part - for $450.00 - a tract of land containing
165 acres in County of Augusta, State of Virginia, etc. Recorded
September 27, 1802.

> Note by C.H.H.- (Ibid, page 11) - The Power of Attorney mentioned
> in the above deed denotes that all the above counties except
> Augusta County, were IN THE STATE OF TENNESSEE, and also shows
> that James Craig, the attorney in fact, was also of Blount County,
> State of Tennessee. This Power of Attorney also particularly
> specifies that all of the wives cited above were the daughters
> and heirs of Andrew Duncan, Senior, deceased. Dated 15 July 1802.
> Recorded Augusta County, Virginia, 27 September 1802.

Augusta County, Virginia, Deed Book 33, page 516 -

14 May 1805 - Commission from Commonwealth of Virginia to Oliver Williams
and Nicholas Seales, Gentlemen, Justices of WILLIAMSON COUNTY, TENNESSEE,
to take the acknowledgment of dower by Margaret Crawford, wife of John
Crawford who had sold a tract of land in August Acounty, Virginia
10 October 1804, containing 285 acres to Alexander Crawford, etc. (note -
complied with) Recorded Augusta County, Virginia, 24 December 1806.

Augusta County, Virginia, Deed Book 42, page 149 -

7 January 1812 - John Hawk and Abraham Hawk of the County of Augusta,
Virginia, attornies in fact for Frederick Hawk of THE COUNTY OF GREEN,
STATE OF KENTUCKY, sell to Henry Cease of Augusta, for $600.00, a
tract of land in Augusta County, Virginia, in what is called Beverley
Manor, containing 120 acres, being the same land purchased by the said
Frederick Hawk 6 October 1800, etc. Witnesses: Samuel Clacke, John D.
Grimes, Joett(?) Tapp, Vincent Tapp, William Kinney, Jr.

> Note: The Justices of GREEN COUNTY, KENTUCKY, certified that
> Sally Hawk, wife of Frederick, relinquished her right of dower
> 8 October 1817

Augusta County, Virginia, Deed Book 56, page 157 -

11 December 1833 - William C. McKanney of the COUNTY OF ROANE, STATE
OF TENNESSEE, sells to Richard H. Dudley of County of Augusta, State of
Virginia, for $20.00 a certain tract of land in the County of Augusta,

Virginia being Lot #35 in the Town of Mercersville in said county and State, etc. Certified by Justices of the Peace of ROANE COUNTY, TENNESSEE 11 December 1833. Recorded Augusta County, August Term 1834.

Augusta County, Deed Book 58, page 254 -

27 October 1836 - Andrew McKamey, Attorney in fact for Nancy McKamey as by Power of Attorney dated 8 September 1836, all of the COUNTY OF ANDERSON, STATE OF TENNESSEE of one part, sell to William C. McKamey and James McKamey of County of Augusta, State of Virginia - for $300.00 - all the right, title and undivided interest in and to the estate both real and personal of John McKamey, deceased, and Eleanor McKamey, his wife, deceased. Recorded 7 November 1836.

Chesterfield County, Virginia, Deed Book 2, page 305 -

29 April 1755 - William Eppes of SALEM IN THE PROVINCE OF MASSACHUSETTS BAY, Gentleman, and Abigal, his wife, sell to Peter Randolph of Chatsworth in the County of Henrico and Colony of Virginia, Esquire, for ₤2000 current money of Virginia, a certain tract of land containing 5,000 acres in the County of Chesterfield on the north side of the Appomattox River, adjoining land of William Kennon and the said Eppes, Robert Hancock, William Moseley, Thomas Tanner, Samuel Goode, which land was granted to Frances Eppes, father of the said William Eppes by patent dated 8th February 1733, etc. Witnesses: Richard Royall, Benjamin Harris, Alexander Diack, William Watkins, Jr. Recorded 7 June 1755

> Comment: According to the latest information available, this William Eppes was of the fifth generation in Virginia, and died in 1765. He was a son of Francis Epes[4] (Francis[3], Francis[2], Francis[1]) He married 1750 Abigail Pickman (1733-1780) of Salem, Massachusetts.

CHARLES CITY COUNTY, Virginia, Records 1766-1774, page 175 -

27 July 1769 - William Holt and Mary, his wife, of City of Williamsburg, sell to Charles Jeffry Smith, Master of Arts of LONG ISLAND IN THE PROVINCE OF NEW YORK - for ₤875 - three tracts of land in County of Charles River on Chickahominy River, containing by estimation 1,738 acres more or less, which includes all the land the said Holt bought of Richard Christian, John Soane Marston and wife, and Turner Hunt Christian and wife, etc. Witnesses: Nathaniel Gordon, William Douglass, Thomas Shore. Recorded 3 January 1770.

Charles City County, Virginia, Records 1766-1774, page 218 -

22 May 1770 - John Jolley OF THE PROVINCE OF NORTH CAROLINA, sells to Robert Pleasants of the County of Henrico, Colony of Virginia - for ₤20 - 100 acres of land in the County of Charles City, which land was given

him by his father, Edward Jolly in his Will in Charles City County, bounded
on other lands given to Thomas Jolly by the said Edward Jolly and now in
the possession of Captain John Atkinson, etc. Witnesses: Thomas Jolly,
Thomas Childers, Thomas Pleasants, Jr., William Binford, Robert Pleasants,
Jr. Recorded 5 December 1770. (William Binford and Thomas Pleasants
"affirmed" being Quakers.)

CHARLES CITy County, Virginia, Records 1766-1774, page 41 -

2 November 1767 - John Brooks of the COUNTY OF ORANGE, PROVINCE OF NORTH
CAROLINA, sells to John Brooks of the County of Northampton - for 2,500
pounds of tobacco - 100 acres of land bounded as in my father's Will, in
Charles City County in Virginia, etc. Witnesses: James Hockady, Warwick
Hockady, Joab Brooks, John Brooks, Jr. Recorded 2 March 1768. (States
that both John Brooks' were of North Carolina.)

Charles City County, Virginia, Records 1766-1774, page 125 -

1 May 1769 - Edward Munford (Montfort) and Betty, his wife, of COUNTY OF
HALIFAX, PROVINCE OF NORTH CAROLINA, sell to Paul Jones of the County of
Charles City, Colony of Virginia - for ₤100 * a certain tract of land in
the County of Charles City devised by the last Will and Testament of Edward
Broadnax to his daughter, Betty Broadnax, now Betty Munford (Montfort)
for her natural life, etc. Witnesses: W. M. Hulme, Jacob Carter,
Benjamin Bradley. Recorded 3 May 1769.

Charles City County, Virginia, Records 1766-1774, page 259 -

17 December 1770 - John Brookes of the COUNTY OF NORTHAMPTON, PROVINCE
OF NORTH CAROLINA, sells to John Riddlehurst of County of Charles City,
Colony of Virginia - for ₤161 - a tract of land whereon the said John
Brooks formerly lived in the said County of Charles City - 300 acres,
etc. Witnesses: Richard Riddlehurst, William Lennard, Robert Drake,
Susanna Edwards. Recorded 2 January 1771.

Henrico County, Virginia, Deeds and Wills #2 (1725-1737) page 664 -

26 June 1736 - John Hatcher formerly of Henrico County in Virginia, but
now of EDGECOMBE PRECINCT ON PAMPLICO RIVER IN NORTH CAROLINA and John
Hatcher (Jr.) eldest son of the aforesaid John Hatcher of the said precinct,
planters - sell to Tarlton Woodson, eldest son and heir apparent of John
Woodson, deceased, of Henrico County, Virginia, Gent. - for ₤200 - 460
acres in Henrico County, Virginia, at a place called Neck-a-land, on the
south side of James River and also particularly 42 acres and 2/3 of an
acre of land given by Edward Hatcher, Sr. to John Hatcher by Deed of Gift
dated 30th day of the 9th month 1694, etc. Witnesses: Thomas Sessoms,
John Hall, Sarah Evans, Charles Evans, Charles Woodson, Tarlton Woodson,Jr.,
Jacob Woodson. Recorded October 1737.

Henrico County, Virginia, Deeds and Wills #2 (1725-1737) page 620 -

1 August 1735 - John Grills of NORTH CAROLINA sells to Mathew Ligon of C
County of Henrico, Virginia for £10, a certain lot of land in Bermuda
Hundred taken up and surveyed by Richard Grills, Senior, lying between
William Gay's lot and Alexander Marshall's lot. Witnesses: Joseph
Allfriend, Robert Elam, Jr., Will: Ligon. Recorded June Court 1737.

Henrico County, Virginia, Deeds and Wills #2 (1725-1737) page 148 -

30 September 1727 - Indenture in which Charles Evans, formerly of Virginia, but now of MORATTICK (SIC) RIVER IN NORTH CAROLINA sells to
Henry Stokes of Henrico County in Virginia - all the run of my land
unsold containing 400 acres more or less being part of a patent of land
granted unto me, Charles Evans, for 788 acres bounded as by patent
dated 13 August 1723 for £5. Witnesses: George Thomas, Charles Allen,
Sylvannus Stokes. Recorded November Court 1727.

Henrico County, Virginia, Deeds and Wills 1725-1737, page 134 -

25 August 1727 - John Soane of Burtee Precinct in ALBEMARLE COUNTY IN
NORTH CAROLINA, but now in Virginia of one part and Tarlton Woodson of
Henrico County of Virginia of the other part - for £10 sells the said
Tarlton Woodson one tract of land in Henrico County on south side of
James River bounded on lands of Robert Elam, Doctor John Bowman, dec'd.,
and others, containing 200 acres being that land bought by William Soane,
father of the aforesaid John Soane of Timothy Allen, etc. Witnesses:
Hutchins Burton, John Wood, Mich:(?) Holland, Baldwin Rockett, Ann
Rockett.

Henrico County, Virginia, Deeds and Wills 1725-1737, page 104 -

Will of William Finney of the UNIVERSITY OF GLASGOW, MASTER OF ARTS, AND
MINISTER, of Henrico Parish. Dated 3 February 1726/7 and probated 5 June
1727. To my son, William, my plantation called the World's End, and the
easternmost half of my plantation in St. James Parish and two negroes.

To my daughter, Mary, the westernmost half of my plantation in St. James
Parish (Henrico County) and three negroes. [Both children under 21 years.]

Reversion to loving wife, Mary. Estate to be valued by Col. Francis Epes,
Major Thomas Randolph, and Henry Wood. My loving wife, Mayy, my sole
executrix. Witnesses: Tarlton Woodson (a Quaker) and Henry Wood.

Mecklenburg County Deed Book 27, page 080-

10 August 1837 - John Moss and Rebecca, his wife, of the COUNTY OF McMINN
AND STATE OF TENNESSEE, sell to Henry C. Moss of County of Mecklenburg,

State of Virginia, for $250.00 - all the interest which the said John Moss
now holds in the real estate which was allotted to Jane Moss, widow and
relict of Ray Moss, deceased, as well as that part which he is entitled
to receive at the death of his mother, etc. Recorded 11 August 1837.

Mecklenburg County, Virginia, Deed Book 19, page 364 -

5 February 1822 - Power of Attorney in which Abraham Buford of Nottoway
County, Virginia, owning a tract of land in the COUNTY OF MORGAN, STATE
OF GEORGIA, in the Fifth District, formerly Baldwin, now Morgan County,
on the waters of Lunday Creek, containing 202½ acres adjoining lands of
Presley Burton, Margaret Snead, John Morris, Jonathan Day and John
Burton. Appoints and constitutes John D. Moss, his attorney, to sell for
him said land, etc. Recorded Mecklenburg County 15 February 1822.

Mecklenburg County, Virginia, Deed Book 21, page 124 -

6 September 1824 - Indenture in which John H. Hardie of County of
Mecklenburg, State of Virginia, conveys to John Moss OF THE COUNTY OF
CABARRAS AND STATE OF NORTH CAROLINA. Whereas, Henry C. Moss did by deed
dated 30 March 1824 convey to the said John H. Hardie in trust to secure
a debt owing Josiah Daley, his reversionary interest in the Dower Estate
of Jane Moss and the said Hardie having at public auction and the said
John Moss being the highest bidder became the purchaser for $120.00.
Therefore, does convey to the said John Moss the right, title and interest
of the said Henry C. Moss in the dower estate of Jane Moss. Recorded same
date.

Mecklenburg County, Virginia, Deed Book 18, page 491a -

1821 - Burwell B. Moss of County of Mecklenburg, State of Virginia, for
$200.00 sells, assigns, etc. to Mary Moss, the widow of Ray Moss, deceased,
[Note by C.H.H: This is an error by the clerk as will appear later, she
being the widow of William Moss, deceased.] all his right title claim,
etc. purchased of James Crook of said County and State, which he had purchased of Robert Oliver of said county and which Robert Oliver purchased
of Asa Oliver of FRANKLIN COUNTY, STATE OF TENNESSEE, and which Asa Oliver
purchased of William Moss, late of Mecklenburg County, Virginia, in and
to the estate held by Jane Moss, his mother, as her dower of the estate
of her late husband, Ray Moss, deceased, which interest, claim, etc.
Now to the aforesaid Mary Moss, widow, etc. Recorded 19 February 1821.

Mecklenburg County, Virginia, Deed Book 18, page 492 -

19 February 1821 - Power of Attorney from Abraham Buford of County of
Nottoway, Virginia, and John Buford of County of Mecklenburg, Virginia,
to John D. Moss of County of Mecklenburg - to take possession of the
negroes, stock, etc. as by a Deed of Trust of record in County of Pittsylvania, Virginia and also in the COUNTY OF MORGAN, STATE OF GEORGIA, which

is now in the possession of William Buford in the COUNTY OF MORGAN, STATE
OF GEORGIA, said deed executed to Abraham C. and John Shelton of Pittsylvania
County, Virginia, etc. Recorded same date.

Accomack County, Virginia, Wills and Deeds 1676-1690, page 487 -

7 June 1676 - Daniel Jennifer of Accomack County, Gent., gives a receipt
and a deed of sale for 400 acres of land in said county to Matt Norwood of
LONDON IN THE KINGDOM OF ENGLAND, Marriner, etc. which record is followed
by a record signed by John Wise, Gent. in which he acknowledges to have
received the original of the above copy for the use of Matt Norwood and
also what assurement shall be made by Capt. Daniel Jenefer to Matt Norwood
by means of which the land herein mentioned shall be delivered to the
said Matt Norwood, his heirs or assigns upon demand, or kept by me [John
Wise] for his use until demanded. Signed 26 June 1676. Witnesses:
William Anderson, Mathew Scarbrough.

Surry County, Virginia, Deed Book 5, page 153 -

20 October 1747 - Thomas Tarver of the COUNTY OF NORTHAMPTON IN NORTH
CAROLINA, sells to Arthur Long of the County of Isle of Wight in Virginia,
for ₤28, 200 acres of land in the County of Surry, Virginia which lands
were conveyed to Samuel Tarvery by deeds recorded in Surry County, etc.
Witnesses: Anselm Bailey, Jr., James Stanford, Thomas Davis. Recorded
same date and Sarah, wife of Thomas Tarver, relinquished her right of
Dower.

Surry County, Virginia Deeds and Wills #5 (1694-1709), page 131 -

6 July 1697 - John King of LITTLE RIVER IN THE COUNTY OF ALBEMARLE IN
NORTH CAROLINA - for ₤22.10s, sells to Stephen Main Waring of Poquoson
River of said County, all his right, title, inheritance, etc. in 100
acres of land on Chipoakes Creek in Surry County, Virginia, and also a
tract of land containing 117 acres in Surry County, Virginia, purchased
in 1688, etc. Witnesses: William Pettway, Elizabeth Pettway. Recorded
same date.

Surry County, Virginia, Deeds and Wills #10 (1754-1768) page 185 -

Last Will and Testament of Benjamin Harrison of the County of Surry,
dated 14 November 1758, probated 20 March 1759.

To my son, Nathaniel Harrison, silver tankard, plate and spoons
and gold watch.

Daughters, Susanna Harrison, Hannah Harrison, and Ludwell
Harrison -

My beloved wife, Susannah Harrison -

To my loving son, Peter Cole Harrison, all my land in NORTH CAROLINA IN GRANVILLE COUNTY, on the south side of Roanoke River, also slaves now in NORTH CAROLINA.

Executors: Wife, Susannah, and brother (Col.) Nàthaniel Harrison. Witnesses: Anne Bozman, Anne Rispis, William Moring.

Shenandoah County, Virginia, Will Book A, page 59 -

Last Will of James Carnagie of the Town of Woodstock in County of Shenandoah, Commonwealth of Virginia, dated 11 August 1780 and probated August Court 1780.

To my brother, Andrew Carnagie, 8000 pds. current money in paper currency, 12 pds. in specie, etc.

I give and bequeath to John Machir, Junior, my house and lot and 32 pds. specie out of which he shall remit 100 pds. as soon as possible to be equally divided among his brothers and sisters IN SCOTLAND. If impossible, the whole is vested in him.

To the children of my cousin Alexander Machir to be equally divided, the remainder of the sales of my effects after my debts are paid.

My executors, Alexander Machir and Col. Tavener Beale, Gent. Witnesses: Rebecca Campbell, John Huffman, Peter Wolfin.

Shenandoah County, Virginia, Will Book C, page 176 -

Will of Alexander Machir dated 2 March 1790 and probated 26 June 1790.
My loving children, Scota Machir, Margaret Machir, Betsy Machir, Sarah Machir, Angus Machir, Henry Machir - Ŀ150 each - it being the legacies left them by James Carnagy, deceased.

To my beloved son, John Machir - L150 - to make him equal with my other children who have that sum from my kinsman, James Carnagy, dec'd.

Bequest to son, Angus Machir -
To beloved wife, Magdalena Ann - Ŀ100, etc.
Executors: Mr. John _____of Woodstock, Mr. John Machir of KENTUCKY, Mr. James Machir of Moorefield and Mr. William Clayton Williams. Executor's Bond required - Ŀ10,000.

Culpeper County, Virginia, Deed Book E, page 571 -

5 September 1768 - George Roberts and Elizabeth, his wife, of County of Culpeper, sell to Joseph Burt of COUNTY OF CUMBERLAND, PROVINCE OF PENNSYLVANIA and William Green of County of Culpeper, Virginia, 184 acres of land in Culpeper, etc. Witnesses: Benjamin Roberts, William Delany, Joseph Roberts. Recorded 15 September 1768.

34

Albemarle County, Virginia, Deed Book 13, page 112 -

19 December 1796 - STATE OF GEORGIA - Indenture in which William Speers
of County of ELBERT, OF STATE AFORESAID, sells to John Sneed of County
of Albemarle, Commonwealth of Virginia - whereas, James Spears, father
of the above said William Speers, possessed 100 acres of land in County
of Albemarle devised to him in 1757 by the Will of Peter Jefferson, and
the said James Spears dying intestate, the property devolved on the said
William Spears, he being the only son of the said James Spears. Now, for
sum of $50.00 sells to said John Sneed the said 100 acres of land whereon
the said James Spears formerly lived, etc. Witnesses: M. Woods, J.P
Thomas Cook,J.P., R. Hunt, J.P. - (of Elbert Co., Georgia)

   Note by C.H.H.- John Sneed sold this 100 acres 12 Nov. 1798 for
   $100.00 to Richard Johnson of Albemarle County, Va. (Ibid, p.121)

Wythe County, Virginia, Deed Book 2, page 442 -

22 September 1798 - Indenture in which Jarvis Smith and Nancy, his wife,
OF THE COUNTY OF WILKES, STATE OF NORTH CAROLINA, sell to Jacob Wells of
the County of Wythe, State of Virginia, for $18.00, a tract of land in the
County of Wythe on the Waters of the South Fork of the Holston River,
containing 42 acres, etc. Witnesses: James Daugherty, Jacob Heck, John
Smyth, Moses Wells. Recorded 8 January 1799.

Surry County, Virginia Deeds #8 (1730-1738) pages 34-37 -

23 July 1730 - Indenture in which Thomas Haynes of the County of Charles
City and Thomas Haynes, Jr., his son, of THE PROVINCE OF NORTH CAROLINA,
of the one part, sell to Thomas Judkins of the County of Surry, Colony of
Virginia, of the other part, a tract of land in Surry County, Virginia,
containing 180 acres, etc. Recorded Aug. 19, 1730.
   Comment: This deed is torn and much faded in spots.

Surry County, Virginia Deeds #8 (1730-1738) page 146 -

17 September 1731 - Indenture in which George Norwood of the COLONY (SIC)
OF NORTH CAROLINA, sells to Joseph Wytherington of the County of Surry
(Colony of Virginia), a tract of land containing 114 acres in the Parish
of Southwarke, County of Surry, etc. Witnesses: Nicholas Maget, Joseph
Nicolson. Recorded Nov. 17, 1731.

   Note by C.H.H. - Ibid, page 147 - 17 Sept. 1731, same date, George
   Norwood of NORTH CAROLINA sells William Blackburn of Surry County,
   Virginia, a tract of land containing 114 acres adjoining the land
   above described.

Surry County, Virginia, Deeds #8 (1730-1738) page 213 -

14 August 1732 - Indenture in which Richard More (Moore) of Bertye

Precinct, ALBEMARLE COUNTY, NORTH CAROLINA sells Thomas Avant of Surry
County, Virginia, one parsell (sic) of land containing 120 acres on the
south side of Nottoway River in the Parish of Lawnes in the County of
Surry, Virginia, etc. Recorded 16 August 1732. Witnesses: William
Huggins, Thomas Eldridge.

Surry County, Virginia, Deeds #8 (1730-1738) page 339 -

20 November 1733 - Indenture in which William Rutter and Sarah, his
wife, late of the County of Nansemond, Colony of Virginia and now of
PROVINCE OF NORTH CAROLINA, sell to William Sumner of the County of
Nansemond, Virginia for ₤40, a tract of land in Surry County, Virginia,
adjoining Colonel Harrison's mill dam, belonging to the said William
Rutter by right of his wife, Sarah, --[faded out]-- her father - or her
grandfather, Edward Scarborough, etc. Recorded November 21, 1733.

Surry County, Virginia, Deeds #8 (1730-1738), page 902 -

Last Will and Testament of John Gillum of Surry County, Virginia, dated
9 August 1738, probated 20 September 1738. Legatees:
    To my son, John, my plantation IN CARRALINO ON ROANOKE [RIVER] and
all the lands thereto belonging and also to him a negro garle (sic) named
Pheb.
    To son, Hinche - land.
    To son, Burrell - land
    To son, Levi - land
    Wife, Sarah, land for life and slaves
    Daughter, Sarah - slave
    Daughter, Amy
    Daughter, Mary
    Daughter, Milley
    My son, Isom and Hansill and daughters, Tabitha and Leada -
Executors: Son, John, and wife Sarah. Witnesses: John Dunn, Thomas Dunn,
Moses Johnson.

Surry County, Virginia, Deeds #8 (1730-1738), page 906 -

20 June 1738 - William Bridges of County of Surry, Virginia and Susanna,
his wife, and Joseph Bridges of BERTIE PRECINCT IN NORTH CAROLINA, of one
part, sell to William Dancy of said County of Surry - 500 acres of land
on the north side of Nottoway River in County of Surry, etc. Witnesses:
John Mason, Joseph Mason, William Jones. Recorded 17 January 1738/39.

Mecklenburg County, Virginia, Deed Book #8, page 386 -

Certificate setting forth that on the 9th day of February 1794, John
Somerville, Esquire, hath lately removed OUT OF THE STATE OF NORTH
CAROLINA and hath removed with him into this state [Mecklenburg County,

Virginia] the following slaves (names 74 slaves) - and makes oath that his removal to this State was with no intention to evade the act for preventing the further importation of slaves within this Commonwealth and that he has no intent of selling them, nor have any of these slaves been imported from Africa or the West Indies Islands since 1 November 1778. Recorded 10 February 1794.

Mecklenburg County, Virginia, Deed Book #8, page 386 -

9 February 1794 - A similar certificate concerning Howell Moss who hath lately removed to Mecklenburg County, Virginia FROM NORTH CAROLINA and hath removed with him into this State seven slaves - (named) - Recorded 10 February 1794.

Mecklenburg County, Virginia, Deed Book 15, page 101 -

12 February 1813 - Power of Attorney by William Moss of the STATE OF SOUTH CAROLINA, COUNTY OF FAIRFIELD, to Thomas Moss of County of Mecklenburg, State of Virginia, to secure all moneys now due or owing to me from the estate of Joshua Moss, deceased, as a legatee of the estate of the said Joshua Moss, deceased, or any part thereof, etc. Witnesses: Charles Hamblin, Stephen Worsham, Aaron Butler. Recorded 15 February 1813.

> Note by C.H.H.- Joshua Moss of Mecklenburg County, Virginia, dated his Will 14 April 1809, which was probated 8 January 1810 (W.B.6, p.285) His legatees were: Wife, Elizabeth, sons, John Moss, William Moss, Wiley Moss, Thomas Moss, Bracie Moss, Edmund Moss, and Lewis Moss (provided he does not marry a certain Nancy Franklin). Daughters, Patsy O'Briant, Elizabeth Coke, [Additional note by C.H.H.- Lewis Moss married Nancy Franklin May 15, 1815 (Bond) with his brother, Thomas Moss, his security.]

Isle of Wight County, Virginia, Deed Book 6, page 374 -

23 May 1744 (sic) - Indenture in which Ezekiel Fuller and Solomon Fuller OF THE COUNTY OF BARTIE (BERTIE) IN CAROLINA, planters, of the one part, sell to James Turner of the Parish of Newport, County of Isle of Wight in Virginia, planter, for £12 - a tract of land containing by estimation 400 acres in Newport Parish, County of Isle of Wight, which is the same land sold by James Bragg and Mary, his wife, to Ezekiel Fuller May __, 1717 - and devised by the said Ezekiel in his last Will to his two sons, Ezekiel and Solomon Fuller, etc. Witnesses: Thomas Woodley, John Batten, John Turner. Recorded April 23, 1744 (sic).

> Note by C.H.H.- The last paragraph of the above deed of sale names the wife of Ezekiel, Jr. as Sarah, and the wife of Solomon as Mary Fuller. The Will of Ezekiel Fuller, Sr. may be found in Isle of Wight Will Book II, page 133, dated 19 November 1722, probated 24 June 1723.

Bedford County, Virginia, Deed Book 12, page 152 -

21 July 1806 - Joel Starkey and Jane (or Jean) his wife sell to Joshua
Halley, their share and proportion to which they are entitled to as heirs
of Jarvis Jackson, deceased, in a tract of land containing 25 acres, etc.
Recorded 27 October 1806.

> Note by C.H.H.- The Will of Jarvis Jackson dated 1796 names Jane
> (or Jean) Starkey as his daughter. The Justices of Bedford County,
> Virginia write the Justices of BUNCOMBE COUNTY, NORTH CAROLINA, to
> secure consent of Jane Starkey to sale of this land, which was
> complied with, proving that this Joel Starkey and his wife had
> migrated to NORTH CAROLINA. Further note (Ibid, p.162) - Joel
> and Jane Starkey also sell (from BUNCOMBE COUNTY, NORTH CAROLINA)
> to Francis Halley, their interest in 100 acres of land as heirs
> of Jarvis Jackson, deceased, in Bedford County, Virginia. Recorded
> 27 October 1806.

Greensville County, Virginia, Will Book 3, page 58 -

Last Will and Testament of Isham Harwell dated 23 September 1816,
proved 1 September 1817 at HANCOCK COUNTY, GEORGIA. Recorded Greensville
County, Virginia 8 December 1817.

> HANCOCK COUNTY, GEORGIA - "Being about to take a long journey and
> knowing it is ordained for all men to die --" etc.

> Alexander J. Harwell to have six negroes - (named)

> To Mrs. Harwell's four children, namely, Thomas G., Alexander J.,
> Mark G. and Polly Mason Harwell - all my estate in Virginia to be
> equally divided - (all underage)

> My executor and guardian to the above named children, Green
> Mitchell.

Witnesses: Edmund Butts, Jesse G. Butts, Thomas C. Butts.

> Note by C.H.H.- Southampton County, Virginia Marriages by Knorr,
> p.31 - 26 June 1811 - Isham Harwell married to Mildred Turner,
> widow of John Blunt Turner, son of John and Priscilla (Blunt)
> Turner.

Greensville County, Virginia, Deed Book 1, page 376 -

20 December 1790 - Know all men by these presents that I, Hannah Rieves
of the County of Greensville (Virginia) have sold to Simon Rieves of
the STATE OF SOUTH CAROLINA, a negor boy named Will - for £20 - the
delivery of the said negro being made to Mr. Absalom Harris in behalf of
the said Simon Rieves, etc. Witnesses: Isaac Rowell, Burgess Bass,
Mathew Mayes. Recorded 26 May 1791.

38

Louisa County, Virginia, Deed Book L, page 284 -

21 February 1810 - Indenture in which Sarah Landrum, widow and relict of
Francis Landrum, deceased, John Landrum and Mary, his wife, of County of
Louisa, Virginia, Thomas Landrum and Dorothy, his wife, William Shelton
and Sarah, his wife, of the COUNTY OF CLARKE, STATE OF KENTUCKY, Reuben
Landrum and Martha, his wife, of the COUNTY OF CUMBERLAND, STATE OF [blank]
Paul Talbert and Elizabeth, his wife, Samuel Landrum and Francis Landrum,
of the County of Louisa, Virginia - all parties of one part, sell to Thomas
Ellis of the County of Orange, State of Virginia, of the other part - for
£124 - a tract of land in the County of Louisa, State of Virginia, containing by late survey 155 acres - (all of the parties of the first part
being legal heirs and representatives of Francis Landrum, deceased.)
Recorded 10 December 1810.

> Note by C.H.H.- William Shelton and Sarah, his wife, and Thomas
> Landrum and Dorothy, his wife, acknowledged their act and deed
> before two Justices of Clarke County, Kentucky.

> Marriages of Louisa County, Virginia by Williams, reveals the follow-
> ing:
> > 10 July 1809 - William Shelton to Salley Landrum (over 21)
> > Paul Talbot, Surety.   page 90.
>
> > 12 May 1799 - Thomas Landrum to Doney Parrish.   Surety, Joel
> > Parrish.   Married 14 May by Rev. John Lasley who says Dolly -
> > (Nickname for Dorothy.)   page 62.

Louisa County, Virginia, Deed Book L, page 589 -

12 January 1810 - The Commonwealth of Virginia to the Gentlemen Justices of
ELBERT COUNTY, STATE OF GEORGIA - whereas, John Tate and Sally, his wife,
Rachael Tate Rice (sic) and Sally, his wife, Enos Tate Junior and Mary,
his wife, Beverley Martin and Jane, his wife, and Enos Tate (minor) have
by their indenture sold to John Graves a tract of land in the County of
Louisa on the waters of Hickory Creek, containing 160 acres and the said
Mary Tate, wife of Enos Tate, Junior, and Jane Martin, wife of Beverley
Martin, cannot conveniently travel to our Court of Louisa, etc. do empower and require you to obtain their relinquishment of dower rights,
etc. Signed John Poindexter, clerk, 12 April 1811. (Complied with
14 September 1811 by Justices of Elbert County, Georgia.) Recorded 12
November 1811.

> Note by C.H.H.- Marriages of Louisa County by Williams reveals -

> > 12 March 1799 - John Tate to Sally Poindexter, daughter of
> > William Poindexter. Surety, Benjamin Bibb. p.98.

> > 9 September 1772 - Enos Tate and Elizabeth Tate (under 21 years)
> > daughter of James Tate. Surety, Uriah Tate. Witness: Robert
> > Tate. [This was probably Enos Tate, Senior.] p. 97.

Louisa County, Virginia, Deed Book L, page 623 -

25 November 1811 - Indenture in which William D. Gooch of the COUNTY OF LINCOLN, STATE OF KENTUCKY, attorney-in-fact for Dabney Gooch and Ruth W., his wife, of the County and State aforesaid, sell to James Turner of County of Louisa, Virginia, a tract of land in the County of Louisa on the head-waters of Harris Creek, containing 62 acres which said land was allotted to the said Dabney Gooch in right of the said Ruth W., his wife, under the last Will and Testament of William Hughes, deceased, late of the said County of Louisa, etc. - Recorded 18 January 1812.

> Note by C.H.H. - Marriage records of Louisa County, Virginia by Williams:
>
> > 24 March 1813 - William D. Gooch and Matilda Chiles. Surety, John Chiles. page 42.
>
> > 11 June 1804 - Dabney Gooch and Ruth Dunn. Sureties, Liner Gooch and Martin Dunn. page 41.
>
> > 27 February 1792 - James Turner and Mary Gooch. Surety, John Fleeman. page 106.

Augusta County, Virginia, Deed Book 60, page 59 -

4 October 1838 - James Kinsolving and Margarette, his wife, of County of Cabell, State of Virginia, sell to William B. Wood of JOHNSON COUNTY, STATE OF ILLINOIS - for $75.00 - one moiety of an undivided tract of land in Augusta County, Virginia, containing 1000 acres, known as the Dowell tract, which he, the said James Kinsolving, inherited as one of the heirs of James Kinsolving, deceased, etc. Recorded 4 February 1839.

> Note by C.H.H. - Albemarle County, Virginia Marriage Register records the marriage of William B. Wood to Martha Kinsolving, 22 December 1817. He [Wood] is shown as one of the twelve heirs and legatees of James Kinsolving, deceased [of Albemarle Co., Va.] in 1829 and is thus a brother-in-law of the above James Kinsolving (Jr.)

Mecklenburg County, Virginia, Will Book 1, page 140 -

Will of Thomas Taylor, Sr. dated 24 October 1772 and probated 9 October 1773. Mentions wife, Penelope; sons, Thomas, John, William, Goodwyn, David, James, Jones. Daughters, Mary Taylor, Susanna Taylor, Elizabeth Watson. Grandchildren, Jesse, Thomas, son of Thomas.

Refers to land on Jeneto and Flatt Creeks in Mecklenburg County and land on both sides of Broad River in SOUTH CAROLINA. Executors, sons, William, James and David Taylor. Witnesses: Nathaniel Edwards, Thomas Malone, Amey Malone.

40

Mecklenburg County, Virginia, Order Book 8, page 212 -

Dr. John Francis Joseph Quinichett, a physician and a NATIVE OF FRANCE, who has resided in this county for several years, personally appeared in court and took the Oath of Fidelity to this Commonwealth and is thereby admitted to the rights of citizenship. 9 December 1793.

Mecklenburg County, Virginia, Deed Book 6, page 535 -

11 December 1782 - John Taylor, Jr. OF THE STATE OF NORTH CAROLINA sells to Richard Taylor of County of Mecklenburg, State of Virginia - for 1000 lbs. of tobacco, 170 acres of land adjoining his own land in the County of Mecklenburg, etc. Witnesses: John Lewis, Edmund Taylor, Jr. Recorded 9 January 1786.

Mecklenburg County, Virginia, Deed Book 6, page 89 -

26 August 1780 - James Lewis and Susanna, his wife, of County of Mecklenburg, Colony of Virginia, sell to Richard Taylor of COUNTY OF GRANVILLE, STATE OF NORTH CAROLINA, for 100,000 pds. current money of Virginia - a tract of land in the County of Mecklenburg, containing 570 acres adjoining land of Charles Lewis, John Taylor, Michaux_____ on Roanoke River, etc. Witnesses: Edmund Taylor, Joseph Taylor, Ann Taylor. Recorded 11 September 1780.

Frederick County, Virginia, Superior Court, Deed Book 6, page 484 -

1 July 1811 - Robert Higgins of the COUNTY OF CLERMONT, STATE OF OHIO (to secure James Machir of the COUNTY OF HARDY, STATE OF VIRGINIA, now West Virginia) - a tract of land at the mouth of White Oak Creek in the County of Clermont, Ohio, containing about 900 acres. Also one undivided third part of a tract of land in the County of Frederick, State of Virginia, containing 209 acres, being the land devised by the last Will of Amos Jolliffe, deceased, to Guillalima Maria Higgins, John Jolliffe and Eliza Higgins, children of the said Robert Higgins - the said third part being the part of Elizabeth Higgins who died sometime after the death of the said Amos Jolliffe, the said Robert Higgins being father and heir-at-law to the said Eliza, etc. There follows a document in which the county court of Frederick appoints as guardian, Robert Higgins, to his infant children, John Jolliffe Higgins and Guillalima Maria Higgins, with James Machir his security. Recorded 30 September 1811.

Frederick County, Virginia, Deed Book 21, page 197 -

31 October 1785 - Andrew Vance and Ann, his wife, of LINCOLN COUNTY, IN THE SETTLEMENT OF KENTUCKY sells to Alexander Machir of the County of Shenandoah, State of Virginia, for £300 - a tract of land in the counties of Frederick and Shenandoah, on Cedar Creek, on Gravelly Creek - containing

183 acres which is part of a greater tract of 400 acres which was granted
to Andrew Vance, Sr., 6 March 1752, and by the last Will of said Andrew
Vance, of record in Frederick County, the part above mentioned was devised to the said Andrew Vance, Jr. Recorded 6 December 1785.

Grayson County, Virginia, Deed Book 1, page 411 -

24 January 1801 - William Chalfant and Ruth, his wife, Meredith Shockley
and Sarah, his wife, John Worrell of Grayson County, Virginia, parties of
one part - sell to Jesse Bond of GUILFORD COUNTY, STATE OF NORTH CAROLINA,
of the other part - whereas the Commonwealth of Virginia by their patent
dated 24 June 1785, granted to a certain Richard Shockley 360 acres of land
by survey dated 24 October 1782, lying in the County of Grayson, then
Montgomery County, on Little Reed Island Creek, which patented land has
by various sales and conveyances has become vested - (91 acres to John
Worrell, and the balance thereof between William Chalfant and Gainer
Pierce) - and whereas also was granted to Meredith Shockley 28 May 1796
100 acres in said County of Grayson, then Montgomery County, adjoining
said Richard Shockley's land - parties of first part for $335.00 sell to
party of second part - above described lands - containing the whole of
225-3/4 acres, etc. Recorded March Court 1801.

Accomack County, Virginia, Deeds, etc. (1737-1746), page 381 -

1 February 1743 - Indenture in which Samuel Wise of WORCESTER COUNTY IN
THE PROVINCE OF MARYLAND, sells to Thomas Newbold of SOMERSET COUNTY IN
PROVINCE OF MARYLAND - for £15 - one-half or moiety of a certain Island
being and lying in Accomack County (Colony of Virginia) - commonly called
Foxes Island, etc. Witnesses: Will: Arbuckle, George Drummond, Thomas
Teackle. Recorded same date.

Accomack County, Virginia, Deeds, etc. 1737-1746, page 441 -

30 January 1744 - Indenture in which Ambrose Willet of WORCESTER COUNTY
IN PROVINCE OF MARYLAND, sells to Thomas Wise of County of Accomack,
Colony of Virginia - "Shipwright" - for £30 - a tract of land in Accomack
County, near the head of Hunting Creek, containing 145 acres of land,
being the land bequeathed to a certain Elizabeth Willet by the last Will
of William Willet, deceased, as by said Will it may more at large appear,
etc. Witnesses: Han (sic) Neckless, Will. Arbuckle, Josiah Lewis.
Recorded same date.

Accomack County, Virginia, Deeds #9, page 131 -

19 May 1797 - Edmund Custis of TOWN OF BALTIMORE, STATE OF MARYLAND, and
Garrot Topping of Accomack County, Virginia - of one part - sell to John
Wise, Tully R. Wise, and George Gillett of said county - whereas, a certain John Bradford, late of Accomack County did on 28 April 1783 convey
unto said Edmund Custis, Garret Topping and a certain (Col.) Levin Joynes,

houses and lots in the Town of Port Scarburgh, commonly called Onancock, in trust to secure certain debts which was afterwards sold to a certain Abraham Outten, now deceased, etc. Recorded 31 October 1797.

Accomack County, Virginia, Deeds & Wills 1715-1729, part I, page 465 -

Will of Matilda Wise of Accomack County [widow] dated 6 September 1721 and proved 6 March 1722. Recorded 25 March 1723: To my son, John Wise, one negro man named Latcharah. To son, Thomas Wise, a negro man named Lazah. To my daughter, Elizabeth Wise, a negro George. To my daughter named Mary Cade Scarburgh, a negro woman Nancy. To my daughter, Hannah Scarburgh, negro girl Esther. Whereas, my deceased husband by his last Will appointed me to sell his part of Foxes Island land and his part of Smith Island land and marsh in SOMERSET COUNTY, MARYLAND and the proceeds of sale to our son, Samuel and I having sold the land of Smith Island aforesaid to John Caldwell of SOMERSET COUNTY, MARYLAND, for about the value of ₤50. Now if my son will discharge my executor and for a negro boy named Daniel and one-half of my thirds of my said husband's estate to me given by his last Will, etc., the other half of my third to my son, Thomas Wise, and he is to take his brother Samuel and sister Hannah into his custody and care.

The balance of my estate to all my children, viz, John, Thomas, Samuel, Mary Cade, Elizabeth and Hannah Scarburgh. My son, Thomas to be executor. Witnesses: Charles Snead, James Davis, Henry Davis, Jonathan West.

Accomack County, Virginia, Deeds and Wills 1729-1737, part I, page 199 -

27 January 1730 - Power of Attorney from Obadiah Cookson OF BOSTON, COUNTY OF SUFFOLK IN PROVINCE OF MASSACHUSETTS BAY IN NEW ENGLAND, to his trusty and well beloved friend, John Wise, of Accomack County, Colony of Virginia, merchant, to collect all debts or dues coming to him and to say, do, act, transact, and finish and settle all matters and things whatsoever. Witnesses: John Haristey, Thomas Wise. Recorded 2 May 1732.

Shenandoah County, Virginia, Deed Book E, page 435 -

23 February 1786 - Power of Attorney from Mounce Bird of Shenandoah County to his beloved son, Abraham Bird. Having procured 3000 acres of land on THE KENTUCKY, indifferent tracts, 1750 acres laying on the waters of Licking River, part of a tract of 2000 acres of which Isaac Ruddle is to have 250 acres. Also 1250 acres, being the one-half of a quantity of land surveyed by Green Clay and being desirous that the said lands should be divided between my three sons, Abraham, John and William Bird, etc. Recorded same date.

Shenandoah County, Virginia, Deed Book I, page 183 -

22 May 1793 - Indenture in which Abraham Bird and Mary, his wife, John Bird

and Elinor, his wife, John Moore and Sarah, his wife, Isaac Goare and
Ingobo(?) his wife, Cornelius Newman and Mary, his wife, John Taylor and
Magdalene his wife, of one part - all being heirs of Mounce Bird, de-
ceased, late of County of Shenandoah, Virginia, to William Bird and
Mounce Bird, sons of Mounce Bird, deceased, of said county, of the other
part for £1000, two tracts of land in CCounty of Shenandoah on Smith's
Creek containing 360 acres, the other tract of 250 acres on easktside of
Smith's Creek, etc.

Page 187 - Acknowledgments of the above deed were signed by
Abraham Bird and Mary, his wife, of THE STATE OF KENTUCKY; John and Sarah
Moore of Rockingham County, Virginia; Isaac Goare and Ingobo, his wife,
of Shenandoah County, Virginia - dated 22 June 1793.

On page 188 follows a release of acknowledgment by Cornelius and Mary
Newman of COUNTY OF GREEN, TERRITORY OF U.S. SOUTH OF THE OHIO RIVER
[i.e., KENTUCKY] Recorded 11 September 1793.

Page 427 - 9 September 1794 - John Byrd and Elinor, his wife, of the
COUNTY OF BOURBON, STATE OF KENTUCKY assign to William and Mounce Byrd of
Shenandoah County, their portion of the Estate of Mounce Bird, deceased.

Shenandoah County, Virginia, Deed Book E, page 434 -

20 February 1786 - Power of Attorney by Jacob Rupp of LANCASTER COUNTY,
STATE OF PENNSYLVANIA to Frederick Woolfard of the County of Shenandoah,
State of Virginia, to demand and receive of Ulrick Miller and Christian
Miller, administrators of the Estate of Jacob Miller, deceased, all sums
of money due him from said decedents estate. Signed Jacob Roop. Witnesses: Samuel Clayton, John Anderson, Philip Williams. Recorded 23 February 1786.

Shenandoah County, Virginia, Deed Book F, page 187 -

28 September 1786 - Power of Attorney from Mounce Bird of County of
Shenandoah, State of Virginia, to his son, Abraham Bird [Junior] -
whereas, I have procured a quantity of land IN THE KENTUCKY COUNTRY in
partnership with Isaac Ruddell and now being desirous that said land should
be divided, etc. Signed, Mounce Byrd. Recorded same date.

Shenandoah County, Virginia, Deed Book F, page 527 -

6 September 1783 - Power of Attorney from Isaac Ruddell of County of
Shenandoah, Commonwealth of Virginia, to his trusty and well beloved
friends, Col. Abraham Byrd and Capt. Isaac Bowman, to settle his accounts,
he INTENDING TO MOVE IMMEDIATELY TO KENTUCKY, etc. Witnesses: George
Ruddle, Mounce Byrd, John Beall. Recorded 26 October 1787.

Louisa County, Virginia, Deed Book R, page 22 -

5 December 1826 - Power of Attorney from Henry Hall of the COUNTY OF

JACKSON, STATE OF TENNESSEE to James A. Hall, his brother, of the County
and State aforesaid, late of the County of Buckingham, State of Virginia
to receive for him what may be owing him from George Harris, Executor of
the last Will and Testament of David Hall, deceased, late of Louisa County,
Virginia, as one of the legatees of the said David Hall, etc. Recorded
8 January 1827.

> Note by C.H.H.- Louisa Marriages by Williams, page 46 -
> 27 August 1796 (Bond) David Hall to Sarah McGehee. William
> Cooke, Surety.

Louisa County, Virginia, Deed Book Q, page 21 -

4 December 1819 - Indenture in which Dabney McGehee and Esther, his wife,
of ABBEVILLE DISTRICT IN THE STATE OF SOUTH CAROLINA, sell to Oswell
McGehee of the County of Louisa, State of Virginia, a tract of land in the
County of Louisa, containing 61½ acres, it being the same tract of land
allotted to the said Dabney in the division of the lands of which his
father, Edward McGehee died seized, - and also his share in the land
assigned to Frances McGehee, his widow, as her dower and also all the
right, title and interest of him, the said Dabney McGehee, as one of the
distributees of Edward McGehee, deceased, in and to that tract of land
devised by the Will of John McGehee, deceased, to his three daughters,
Molly, Sarah, and Agnes McGehee for life and at their deaths, then to
Edward McGehee, his son, etc. Witnesses: Jo: F. Dabney, John H.
Hillman, John O. Harris. Recorded April 11, 1820.

> Note by C.H.H.- Louisa Marriages by Williams, page 67 -
> 28 August 1781 (Bond) Edward McGehee to Frances Lunsden. Surety,
> George Lunsden [also spelled Lumsden]
>
> Ibid, page 68 - 25 October 1813 - Oswell McGehee to Martha Cooke,
> daughter of W. Cooke. Surety, Edward N. Cooke. Married 30 October
> by Rev. William Cooke. [Many other McGehee marriages in this
> county.]

Greensville County, Virginia, Deed Book 2, page 492 -

14 May 1798 - Indenture in which Green Turner of County of Greensville,
State of Virginia, sells to Thomas Dupree of NORTHAMPTON COUNTY, STATE
OF NORTH CAROLINA - for ₤223 - a certain tract of land in the said
county of Greensville on south side of Meherrin River, adjoining land of
Thomas Dupree, containing 89¼ acres, etc. Witnesses: Henry Hayley,
Isham Fennell, James Hayley, Lewis Dupree. Recorded September Court
1798.

Greensville County, Virginia, Deed Book 3, page 90 -

19 December 1801 - Indenture in which John E. Dawson and Annabella, his
wife, of Greensville County, sells to Thomas Dupree of the COUNTY OF

NORTHAMPTON, STATE OF NORTH CAROLINA - for £1171.16 - a tract of land containing 976½ acres, adjoining lands of Henry Harrison and Mrs. Ross, Cane Branch to Fountain's Creek, Peter Peterson, Jaconiah Parks, etc. Recorded January Court 1802.

Greensville County, Virginia, Deed Book 4, page 443 -

15 February 1814 - Indenture in which Benjamin Stewart and Farthy, his wife (formerly Farthy Dupree) of THE COUNTY OF FRANKLIN, STATE OF NORTH CAROLINA - John Justice and Mary, his wife, (formerly Mary Dupree) - and Hannah H. Mayes (formerly Hannah H. Dupree) - of the County of Greensville, State of Virginia of the one part, sell to Henry Dupree of County of Greensville, Virginia for $3,000, the right we have to two tracts of land in the County of Greensville - one containing 200 acres and the other 100 acres, being land devised to said Henry by his father, Lewis Dupree, etc. Recorded 13 February 1815.

> Note: Followed by a relinquishment by Henry Dupree to the above named parties of the 1st part of his right and claim in the estate of his father, Lewis Dupree, due to his mother, Elizabeth Dupree, deceased.
>
> Marriage Records of Greensville County, Virginia by Knorr:
> 7 March 1798 - Benjamin Stewart to Phatha Dupree. page 67
> 30 November 1787 - John Justice to Mary Dupree, daughter of
>   Lewis Dupree, Jr. page 40
> 28 January 1790 - Joshua Mayes and Hannah Hill Dupree, daughter
>   of Elizabeth Dupree. page 48

Greensville County, Virginia, Deed Book 5, page 203 -

12 January 1820 - Power of Attorney from Briton Bynum of the County of Greensville, State of Virginia, to Lugass(?) Turner, Junior, to settle, etc. and to receive his distributive share of the estate of his brother, Francis Bynum, late of the STATE OF LOUISIANA, deceased, etc. Recorded same date.

Greensville County, Virginia, Deed Book 4, page 204 -

12 January 1820 - Deed of Gift from Charlotte (?) Spence of County of Greensville, Virginia, for love and affection to (her ?) son, Joseph Spence OF THE COUNTY OF MADISON, STATE OF ALABAMA of a negro girl slave now in the possession of her son Solomon Spence of the COUNTY OF MADISON, STATE OF ALABAMA, etc. Recorded same date.

Franklin County, Virginia, Deed Book 4, page 238 -

20 July 1801 - Power of Attorney from Sarah Thompson, of Knox County, State

OF TENNESSEE, appointing her trusty friend, Michael Kelly of the County
and State above mentioned to recover or receive from Thomas Thompson of
Franklin County, State of Virginia, one negro slave named Esther, between
14 and 15 years of age, etc. (her mark +) Witnesses: Thomas Wallace,
John Sawyers, _____ Kelley. Recorded August Court 1801.

Montgomery County, Virginia, Deed Book E, page 245 -

14 December 1811 - Indenture in which Edward Choat, Senior, of the County
of ROBINSON, STATE OF TENNESSEE, sells to Garland Wade of the County of
Montgomery, State of Virginia - for Ł130 current money of Virginia - a
tract of land containing 155 acres of land by survey, in the County of
Montgomery, on Greasy Creek, Waters of Big Reed Island, a branch of New
River, adjoining land of Jonathan Isom and James Callaway, etc. Witnesses:
John Dobyns, Edmund Vancel, John Rentfrow, William Keeth, William
Simmons, Charles Simmons. Recorded April Court 1812.

Halifax County, Virginia, Deed Book 22, page 115 -

18 October 1808 - Indenture in which Blackmon Ligon of the County of
Greensville in the STATE OF SOUTH CAROLINA sells to Thomas Ligon of the
County of Halifax in the State of Virginia for Ł100, a tract of land in
the County of Halifax, Virginia, on the north side of the Dan River, etc.
[Clerk left out the acreage.] Witnesses: James Ligon, Moses Paris,
Stephen Easley. Recorded Halifax County, 26 June 1809.

> Note by C.H.H. - 18 October 1808 - James Ligon made an affidavit
> before a Justice of Greensville District, SOUTH CAROLINA as to the
> signature of Blackmon Ligon. Further note: The above Blackmon
> Ligon was a Revolutionary Soldier from Halifax County, Virginia,
> as is proved in the Will of his father, Joseph Ligon [Will Book 1,
> page 309, Halifax County; probated 18 May 1780.]

Halifax County, Virginia, Deed Book 23, page 433 -

6 March 1812 - Power of Attorney from James Ligon of HENDERSON COUNTY,
STATE OF KENTUCKY, appointing John Ligon of Halifax County, State of
Virginia his true and lawful attorney to recover for him everything due
him from Jackonias Overby and Peter Overby, his surety, and from John
Wilson, his former attorney (deceased). Certified before Ambrose Barbour,
Clerk of Court of Henderson County, Kentucky, and recorded in Halifax
County, Virginia 27 May 1812.

Halifax County, Virginia, Deed Book 21, page 53 -

24 January 1806 - Power of Attorney from Thomas Yuille of the County of
Halifax, State of Virginia, by the Power of Attorney he had from George
Yuille, late merchant in Manchester, County of Chesterfield, Virginia,
bearing date 17 January 1798 to settle all accounts due to George Yuille,

of DEARBITH (?) and James Murdock and George Murdock of GLASGOW IN SCOT-
LAND, GREAT BRITAIN, in this and adjoining states by these presents do
appoint James Logan (or Ligon?) of THE STATE OF KENTUCKY, COUNTY OF
LIVINGSTON, his lawful attorney, etc. Recorded 27 January 1806.

Halifax County, Deed Book 21, page 444 -

20 March 1807 - Power of Attorney from Henry Ligon of County of Halifax,
State of Virginia, appointing his beloved brother, John Ligon, his lawful
attorney to sell some land to pay a debt and from or if any surplus be to
pay it to James Ligon, Junior, of the COUNTY OF GRANVILLE, STATE OF NORTH
CAROLINA, Etc. Witnesses: James Ligon, Senior, Susanna Ligon, Judith
Ligon, James Stuart, William Puryear. Recorded 22 June 1807.

Halifax County, Virginia, Deed Book 21, page 670 -

1 April 1808 - Power of Attorney from James Ligon of the County of Halifax,
State of Virginia, being about to start to the STATE OF KENTUCKY, do
appoint John Wilson of said county my true and lawful attorney to settle
all my unfinished business of every description. Recorded 25 July 1808.

   Note: Marriages of Halifax by Knorr: 25 June 1789 - James Ligon
   married Judith Church. Rev. Henry Lester, minister. page 57.

Halifax County, Virginia, Deed Book 11, page 138 -

16 May 1776 - Indenture in which William Hardin and Phebe, his wife, of
the PROVINCE OF NORTH CAROLINA, COUNTY OF ORANGE, sell to Roger Atkinson,
Gent., of the County of Dinwiddie and Colony of Virginia - for £80 - a
tract of land in the County of Halifax, Colony of Virginia, on both sides
of Holts Mill Creek, containing 383 acres, etc. Witnesses: Isaac Johnson,
John Rogers, Jr., Peter Rogers, Ben Cotnam. Recorded 21 November 1776.

Henrico County, Virginia, Records. Notes by W. G. Stanard (unpublished)

Page 85, ref. to page 240 - October 1746 - Power of Attorney from Richard
Worsham, Senior, of CATERET COUNTY, NORTH CAROLINA, to his kinsman, Richard
Ward of the same county, to make sale of land called Sheffield, in Henrico
County, Virginia, left him by his father, Richard Ward, deceased.

Ibid, page 10, ref. to page 24 - 1 April 1679 - Deed from William Beauchamp,
citizen and vintner of LONDON; brother and heir of John Beauchamp, of James
River, merchant; all the plantation of John Beauchamp in Henrico County.
Witnesses: John Munford, William Byrd, John Ruddes, Charles Dyose.

   Note by C.H.H. - Deed of same parties for 300 acres in Henrico,
   adjoining land of John Greenough and John Woodson.

Henrico County, Virginia Records.   Notes by W. G. Stanard (unpublished)

Page 34, ref. to page 99 - 1 December 1686 - Deed from Richard Lee of
LONDON, Gent. to Henry Ayscough, for 150 acres of land at the falls of
James River in Virginia [now Richmond, Va.] formerly belonging to Peter
Lee, deceased, brother of Richard Lee.

Ibid - 1 December 1686 - Power of Attorney from Richard Lee of LONDON,
formerly of Virginia, Gent., to William Byrd and William Randolph.

Spotsylvania County, Virginia, Deed Book EE, page 87 -

13 February 1789 - Indenture in which James Jack and Peggy, his wife,
of WILKS COUNTY, STATE OF GEORGIA, sell to Abraham Simons of Spotsylvania
County, Virginia, 300 acres of land in Spotsylvania County, adjoining land
of Benjamin Webster and Thomas Carson, which land was granted to the said
James Jack in 1787.

Culpeper County Deed Book R, page 260 -

20 May 1793 - William Kabler of County of Culpeper, State of Virginia,
gives Power of Attorney to his trusty friend, Thomas Stubblefield Long
of said County and State to sell, lease or demise a certain tract of land
containing 400 acres, being IN THE STATE OF NORTH CAROLINA on the waters
of New River, etc. Recorded same date.

Culpeper County, Virginia, Deed Book R, page 261 -

20 May 1793 - Power of Attorney from Mary Henry and Catharine Thompson of
the County of Madison, State of Virginia, to their trusty friend Thomas
S. Long of County of Culpeper, Virginia, to sell, lease, or demise a
certain tract of land in the STATE OF NORTH CAROLINA on the south side of
New River, opposite the mouth of Fan River near the Town of Bath, containing 150 acres and also another tract adjoining the above oontaining 59
acres, etc. Witnesses: John Walker, Jr., Gabriel Kay, James Kay. Recorded
20 May 1793.

Culpeper County, Virginia Deed Book U, page 169 -

27 November 1798 - Whereas, John Bond of the County of Culpeper did on
the 16th November 1769 convey unto Thomas Parks, Jr. two negro slaves,
Hannah and her child Phillis, in trust for the benefit and advantage of
his two daughters, Elizabeth and Mary, now know ye that I, John Long, of
the OOUNTY OF FRANKLIN, STATE OF KENTUCKY, one of the heirs and devisees
of Bromfield Long, deceased, who was formerly the husband to the aforesaid
Elizabeth (Bond) - have for the sum of ₤90 sold to Benjamin Long of the
County of Culpeper all my estate, right, title and interest in and to the

slaves, their increase, etc. Witnesses: Robert B. Long, Thomas Long, Robert Latham, Jr. Recorded 21 January 1799.

Culpeper County, Virginia, Deed Book Y, page 336 -

22 December 1803 - Indenture in which Joseph Sture and Eleanor, his wife, now of CENTRE COUNTY, PENNSYLVANIA, sells to John Holland of the County of Culpeper, Virginia - for £220 - 228 acres of land in the County of Culpeper, etc. Witnesses: John Bennor, James Sture, Certified before James Potter, Esq. one of the Judges in the County of Centre, State of Pennsylvania. Recorded Culpeper County Court 16 January 1804.

Culpeper County, Virginia, Deed Book CC, page 61 -

18 December 1807 - Indenture in which Gabriel Long and Elizabeth, his wife, of County of Culpeper, to John Shackelford of said county, and Thomas S. Long of said county of the 3rd part - Whereas, the said Thomas S. Long hath sold the said John Shackelford a tract of land for $2763.00, which land was given the said Thomas by the said Gabriel, his father, who hath not conveyed to him the legal title therein. Wherefore, the said Gabriel Long and Elizabeth, his wife, now sell and convey the said land to said John Shackelford, etc. containing 307 acres which the said Gabriel had purchased of John Apperson and Alice, his wife, 21 January 1793, etc. Recorded 21 December 1807.

Note by C.H.H.- Deed Book FF, page 137 dated 19 May 1812, a release in connection with the above sale of land reveals that Gabriel Long, a party to the deed, is still living in Culpeper County, but that Thomas S. Long IS NOW LIVING IN THE STATE OF KENTUCKY.

Culpeper County, Virginia, Deed Book FF, page 342 -

15 February 1813 - Power of Attorney from John Williams, Senior, of the County of Culpeper, State of Virginia, authorizing and appointing Nimrod Long of the County of Shenandoah, State of Virginia, his true and lawful attorney to receive in his name all money, etc. from John Machir (or Maclin ?) of MASON COUNTY, STATE OF KENTUCKY, his former attorney, transacting business for him IN THE STATE OF KENTUCKY and to reach a proper settlement with him, etc. and to sell and dispose of his lands in Kentucky, etc. Recorded same date.

Culpeper County, Virginia, Deed Book SS, page 78 -

October 1821 - I, Sarah Brown, now a widow and formerly Sarah Long, widow of Brumfield Long - for natural love and affection for my son, Thomas Long, of the COUNTY OF FRANKLIN, TOWN OF FRANKFORT, IN THE STATE OF KENTUCKY, give, grant, etc. all my right of dower and all my share and interest what soever in and to the Estate, real and personal and mixed, of my deceased

husband, Brumfield Long who died in Culpeper County, Virginia, and also
my right share and interest in the said estate derived by purchase of
Richard Chism and Ann, his wife, one of the children of the said Brumfield
Long, as more fully recited executed by said Chism and wife 19 June 1780,
recorded in said County of Culpeper, Virginia and do moreover appoint my
said son, Thomas Long, my attorney-in-fact, etc., that he may have the
benefit of this mother's gift to her dutiful and affectionate son. Done
at Frankfort, in the COUNTY OF FRANKLIN, STATE OF KENTUCKY, being the
county wherein I reside, etc. Certified before two Justices of the Peace
of Franklin County, Kentucky. Recorded Culpeper County, 16 October 1821.

> Note by C. H.H. - Thomas Long of Frankfort, Kentucky, transferred
> his right, title and interest in the foregoing Deed of Gift, con-
> veyed by his mother, Sarah Brown, of her dower interest, etc. to
> Armistead Long of the County of Culpeper, State of Virginia.
> Recorded Culpeper Court 18 July 1825.

> Culpeper Marriages by Knorr, page 11:   26 April 1786 - Sarah Long
> married Hezekiah Brown.

Culpeper County, Virginia, Will Book K, page 386 -

Will of Gabriel Long - dated 7 December 1824 and probated 19 March 1827.
My just debts to be immediately paid by my son, William Ball Long.

To son, Thomas S. Long, all the slaves I have given him and now in
his possession and also 450 acres of land near HOPKINSVILLE IN THE STATE
OF KENTUCKY whereon he now lives, being part of a larger tract which I
had formerly conveyed to him.

I give to the children of my son, Reuben Long, a tract of land containing 1000 acres lying and being in the District set apart for the
officers and soldiers of the Virginia Continental line in the COUNTY OF
HOPKINS, STATE OF KENTUCKY, adjoining lands of John McDowell and John B.
Johnston, which patent was granted to me for 800 acres, and one hundred
acres to Samuel Wise and one hundred acres to John Blackwell - all included in the same patent I purchased of the said Blackwell, etc. Also
my right and title to several lots of ground IN THE CITY OF BALTIMORE
which were conveyed to me by my said son, Reuben Long. Also, slaves now
in my son Reuben's possession to my said grandchildren. The whole of
the said land and slaves to my daughter-in-law, Maria Long, and her
children by my said son, Reuben Long, her husband, and to have the use
and benefit of during the life of my said son Reuben Long, and after his
death, then my daughter-in-law, Maria Long, is to have 1/3 part of the
profits or rents of the aforesaid lots IN BALTIMORE and 1/3 part of the
aforesaid slaves during her natural life.

To my son, John Slaughter Long, all the slaves he now has and also
the land IN KENTUCKY I have already conveyed to him.

To the children of my son, Gabriel Long, deceased, the remainder of
my tract of land IN CHRISTIAN COUNTY, KENTUCKY near Hopkinsville, not

already conveyed by me to Thomas S. Long and others which land was granted
to me by patent dated 11 December 1797 ON THE MIDDLE FORK OF LITTLE RIVER
near CHRISTIAN COURTHOUSE, also the half of 336 acres in MECKLENBURG COUNTY,
KENTUCKY and likewise a tract of 716 acres in the STATE OF KENTUCKY on the
East fork of Pond River - these being military lands.

To the children of my son, Nimrod Long, deceased, the tract of land
conveyed to their father by my son Thomas S. Long at my request. Also the
slaves and other property in his possession at his death.

To my daughter Frances Slaughter Ball (sic) wife of John Slaughter
(sic) several slaves [named] now in possession of John Slaughter, my said
daughter's husband, in lieu of a legacy left to my said daughter by John
Hackley, deceased. Also to my said daughter Frances Slaughter Ball, wife
of John Slaughter, several slaves [named.]

To my son, William B. Long, the tract of land whereon I now live in
Culpeper County. Also several slaves, stock and furniture.

Executors: My son, William Ball Long and my friend Phillip Slaughter.

Codicil - 7 September 1826: Gives further instructions as to the land in
KENTUCKY devised to the children of his son Reuben Long and his wife, Maria
Long. Also mentions his son John S. Long and his nephew, James Kay. He
also makes a further bequest of 375 acres of land on the WEST FORK OF RED
RIVER IN KENTUCKY to his daughter Frances S. Ball Slaughter, wife of John
Slaughter which land was conveyed to him by John Tutt.

Second Codicil - 8 September 1826: Referring to the slaves he left the
children of his son, Reuben Long, and whereas the said children live IN
THE STATE OF MARYLAND and cannot carry the said slaves to that State
(Maryland) the said slaves to be sold at public auction or private sale
by his son, William Ball Long, and the money put out on land security and
the interest paid annually to his daughter-in-law, Maria Long, wife of
his son Reuben Long, and her children.

Third Codicil - December 1826:-Absolves his son William B. Long of any
obligation to pay $1000 collected for the benefit of the creditors of
Zoller Koffer and Long and paid to his son, Reuben Long, IN BALTIMORE
May 31, 1823 and who has retained the said $1000.00.

Culpeper County, Virginia, Deed Book G, page 237 -

21 April 1774 - Reuben Long and Mary, his wife, of Parish of St.Mark's
County of Culpeper, sell to James Inskeep OF THE PROVINCE OF THE JERSEYS,
for ₤45, that tract of land in said parish and County of Culpeper, con-
taining 19 acres, adjoining Carter's old line, Long's corner, etc.
Witnesses: William Williams, John Long, N. Pendleton, Samuel Stigler.
Recorded 16 May 1774.

Bounty Warrants -

Reuben Long (Soldier)

This may certify that the bearer, Reuben Long, a soldier belonging to
Captain Gabriel Long's Company, Inf. the Rifle detachment, did produce
a certificate to me signed by the said Captain Long wherein it appears
that the said Reuben Long's time of service did expire the 21 day of
this instant and being desirous of returning to Virginia he is therefore
hereby discharged from the service. Given under my hand at FORT SULLIVAN
August 25, 1779.

                                        -- Will Butler, Lt.Col.

All commissaries are desired to
supply the bearer with provisions
till he arrives at home in Virginia.

Virginia Revolutionary War Land Bounty Warrants by Wilson -

Page 45: Warrant #2202 Gabriel Long, 4000 acres, Captain, Virginia
Cont. Line, 3 years. Dec. 23, 1783.

Page 47: Warrant #4225 Reuben Long, Pvt. Va. Cont. Line, 3 years,
100 acres. Nov. 15, 1786.

Page 45: Warrant #1570 Reuben Long, Lieut. Cont. Line, 3 years,
2666-2/3 acres. Aug. 14, 1783.

Bounty Warrants (originals, Virginia State Library -

Gabriel Long, Captain

In the House of Delegates 12 December 1783 - Resolved that the petition
of Gabriel Long praying to be allowed the same Bounty in land as is by
law given to Captains in the Continental Service is reasonable -

                                        --Teste   John Berkeley
1783 December 16th
Agreed to by the Senate

Reuben Long, Lieutenant

2 September 1782 - Christian Febiger, Colonel, certifies that Lt.Reuben
Long was appointed an officer in the 11th Regiment prior to 1 May 1777
and stands now a First Lieutenant in the 3rd Regiment from 10 May 1779, etc.

Lieutenant Reuben Long - (Land Office 19 April 1809)

It also appears that a military bounty land warrant was issued to Reuben
Long 14 August 1783 for 2666-2/3 acres for his services three years in
the Continental Line as a Lieutenant and that on 1 November 1786 a warrant
was issued to Reuben Long for 100 acres for his services as a private in

the Continental Line three years. The above are the only military bounty
warrants that appear to have been issued.

--William G. Pendleton, Clerk

Louisa County, Virginia, Deed Book K, page 145 -

15 February 1804 - Indenture in which Joseph Bunch and Mary, his wife, of
the STATE OF SOUTH CAROLINA, sell to James Armstrong of the County of
Louisa, State of Virginia, for ₤100, a tract of land in the County of
Louisa on both sides of one of the forks of Foster's Creek containing
148 acres, etc. Witnesses: Turner Anderson, Nathaniel Anderson, Nelson
Anderson. Recorded 14 October 1805.

Louisa County, Virginia, Deed Book K, page 146 -

25 October 1805 - Indenture in which Joseph Ore and Elizabeth, his wife,
of the COUNTY OF GRAINGER, STATE OF TENNESSEE, sell to William Walker of
the County of Louisa, State of Virginia, for ₤60 - a tract of land in the
County of Louisa upon the waters of Camp Creek, containing 273 acres, etc.
Witnesses: Thomas Diggs, Jesse Walker, Thomas Whitlock, Thomas Walker,
John Edwards, John Lipscomb. Recorded 9 December 1805.

> Note by C. H. H. - Grainger County, Tennessee Tax Lists for 1810
> a Joseph Oar with 540 acres and also a William Oar who is tithable
> but owns no land.

Louisa County, Virginia Deed Book BB, page 510 -

This is to certify that the within named persons are my lawful legitimate
children by both of my husbands. The first five named, three sons and two
daughters, were by my first husband, Zachariah Arnett, deceased. The last
named daughter is by my second husband, John Lovelace, now living and residing in SCOTT COUNTY, KENTUCKY: James Arnett, deceased, the widow of
whom is Sarah Arnett now living in LEESBURGH, HARRISON COUNTY, KENTUCKY;
Jefferson Arnett and Robert Arnett, both residing in BEACH GROVE, RUSH
COUNTY, INDIANA; Eliza Arnett married Robert Coleman, residing in BURBON
COUNTY, KENTUCKY; Louisa Jean Arnett married John W. Forbes, residing in
SCOTT COUNTY, KENTUCKY; and Angelina E. M. Lovelace married Ephriam B.
Doll, residing in SCOTT COUNTY, KENTUCKY. Given under my hand and seal
this 2nd day of February 1848. /s/ Nancy Lovelace

Fauquier County, Virginia, Will Book 2, page 58 -

Will of (Captain) Robert Knox of THE STATE OF MARYLAND (COUNTY OF CHARLES),
dated 21 September 1781.

To my son, John Knox, tract of land in the State of Virginia called
Summer Dusk, containing about 5,000 acres. Also negroes, cattle, stock,

thereupon said plantation. Also to my said son, John Knox, all my estate I have in SCOTLAND.

To my son, Robert Dade Knox, all my lands in the STATE OF MARYLAND with negroes, stock thereupon.

To my daughter, Elizabeth Knox, 500 acres of land in the State of Virginia, four negroes, stock, etc.

To my daughter, Jannett Knox, land to be taken out of Summer Dusk (in Virginia) four slaves, stock, etc.

To my wife, Rose Townshend, whatever is customarily given to widows in the part of the world where my estate lies.

Mentions his share in the co-partnership of Knox and Baillie. Mentions brother, John, and brother William. Executors: Wife, Rose Townshen, Col. Robert Hooe, Andrew Baillie, Alexadder B. Martin.

15 February 1782 - Codicil: Whereas my beloved wife, Rose Townshend, is now with child, etc. - ₿800 sterling to said child - also appoints William Allison of Fauquier County one of his executors.

Proved Charles County, MARYLAND 30 October 1782 by oath of Rose Townshend Knox, widow of Robert Knox, deceased (copy taken from records of the Orphans Court for Charles County, Maryland 29 August 1783. Recorded Fauquier County, Virginia, 25 July 1785.

St. Andrew's Cemetery, Hale County, Alabama -

Tombstone: George Richard Collins
                  Born Caroline Co., Virginia
                      November 21, 1841
                      Died January 19, 1890

Augusta County, Virginia, Deed Book 1A, page 300 -

31 December 1799 - John Jack of the CITY OF PHILADELPHIA IN STATE OF PENNSYLVANIA, Physician and Lettis, his wife, to George Thompson and Edward Thompson of the CITY OF PHILADELPHIA, PENNSYLVANIA, merchants - for $1.00 - convey two tracts of land in the State of Virginia - one containing 10,000 acres in the County of Rockbridge on the Big Mary and Irish Creeks, branches of James River [gives bounds] - exclusive of 3600 acres held by former grants included in the boundaries of this tract and hereby excepted - and the other tract containing 10,000 acres being in the County of Augusta and Albemarle, the greater part thereof in Augusta lying on several South East branches of the South River of Shenandoah [gives bounds] - exclusive of 50 acres held by a former grant included in the boundaries of this tract and hereby excepted - It being the same premises granted unto Joseph Grubb of Peter's Township in the County of Franklin, PENNSYLVANIA, Yeoman, by his attorney, James Irwin of Miersburg,

in the same County, merchant, by letter of attorney dated 19 May 1795, conveyed to said John Jack by deed dated 14 June 1796 in fee simple, etc. Witnesses: Samuel Porter, John C. Wells, Cynthia Mahany. Certified before Robert Wharton, Esq., Mayor of City of Philadelphia, 6 January 1800. Recorded Staunton District Court 2 April 1800.

Orange County, Virginia, Deed Book 29, page 348 -

22 September 1821 - George Bledsoe and Joannah, his wife, of the County of Orange and Jonathan Pitcher of WOODFORD COUNTY, STATE OF KENTUCKY, all of the one part - sell to Alexander Pitcher of the County of Orange, Virginia, of the other part for $160.00, all their right, title, interest and claim to land of which William Pitcher, late of the said County of Orange died seized and which title was vested in them by the last Will of the said William Pitcher, deceased, etc. Witnesses: John Mallory, Thomas Row, William Cox. Recorded 27 May 1822.

    Note: This name is later spelled Peacher by the Justices and
    Recording Clerk. However, a John Pitcher died testate in
    Culpeper County in 1774.

Orange County, Will Book 4, page 16 -

Will of John Bledsoe dated 12 September 1800 - probated 27 July 1801 -
    To nephew, George Bledsoe, son of my brother, George, ₤20
    To nephew, John Bledsoe, son of my brother George, ₤20
    To nephew, Moses Bledsoe, son of my brother George, ₤20

    To my brother George and his wife, Lucy, $20.00 annually for life
    To my brother William's sons, John, Joseph, James, Benjamin, William,
Abraham, Isaac and Jacob Bledsoe, ₤20 to each.

    To Elizabeth Mallory, daughter of Uriel Mallory, slave -

    Beloved wife, Elizabeth Bledsoe - 2 slaves and one sorrel mare I had
of Larkin Wright.

    To my brother William's eight sons above mentioned, all my lands in
the STATE OF KENTUCKY except 100 acres which I give to John Perry, son of
Puree Perry, deceased.

Executors: My wife, Elizabeth Bledsoe and my friends, Uriel Mallory and William Mallory. Witnesses: George Perry, Ambrose Richards, John B. Johnson [Executors Bond $10,000 - 175 slaves in inventory of Estate - Total value of personal estate as by appraisal and inventory ₤1390.9.3.

Fairfax County, Virginia, Will Book B1, page 299 -

Will of Ann Mason dated 9 August 1761: To John Evans, an orphan, ₤10
To Elizabeth Ramsay, daughter of William Ramsay, ₤30. To Charles Roch,

an orphan boy now living with me, ₤10 and he to be put to school for three years. To Ann Longden now living with me ₤25 - and three years schooling. To Sarah Masterson ₤5.

To my loving brother, Jonathan Gooding living in OAKHAM, COUNTY OF RUTLAND IN ENGLAND, remainder of my real and personal estate. Reversion to my sister Sarah Gooding with further reversion to my brother, Robert Gooding.

My executor to write my friends AT OAKHAM and make them acquainted with this my will, so that if no claim is made in two years then the said remainder of my estate to Elizabeth Dalton, daughter of John Dalton.

Executors: My friends, John Carlyle and John Dalton. Witnesses: Robert Loxham, Joseph Watson, Robert Dalton.

Fairfax County, Virginia, Will Book F#1, page 95 -

Will of George Mason of Gunston Hall, dated 20 March 1773 - probated 16 October 1792.

To be buried by the side of his dear and ever lamented wife.

All his lands, slaves, etc. both in Virginia and MARYLAND to be kept intact until his children come of age or marry.

My four daughters - Ann Mason, Sarah Mason, Mary Mason, and Elizabeth Mason - slaves. Also confirms title to a slave girl given to each of them by their grandfather, Mr. William Eilbeck, deceased. Also to each of my daughters ₤600 sterling.

To my eldest son, George Mason, my mansion house, Gunston Hall, and land adjoining, being between five and six thousand acres. Also to him all my stock or lands in THE OHIO COUNTY. [Mentions his son, George, will soon be of age.]

To my son, William Mason, lands in CHARLES COUNTY, MARYLAND - slaves, etc. reversion to youngest son, Thomas Mason.

To my son, Thomson Mason, land [about 3300 acres] slaves, etc. and one moiety of the land devised me by my grandfather, Col. George Mason, deceased, to his daughters Elizabeth and Rosanna - Reversion to youngest son, Thomas Mason.

To my son, John Mason, land - about 2000 acres - slaves, etc. - Reversion to youngest son, Thomas Mason.

To my youngest son, Thomas Mason, land and the Occoquean Ferry which has been vested in me and my ancestors since the first settlement of this part of the country, and long before the land there was taken up or patented - in general, all my land in Prince William County and land IN CHARLES COUNTY, PROVINCE OF MARYLAND. [Mentions his mother, Mrs. Ann

Mason - Reversion to son, William Mason.] Also slaves and £600 sterling.

Mentions sundry tracts of land he also owns in COUNTY OF HAMPSHIRE, (Va.) and in the COUNTY OF FREDERICK, PROVINCE OF MARYLAND, near FORT CUMBERLAND.

Mentions his brother, Thomson Mason.

To Mrs. Heath, wife of Thomas Heath of Stafford County, 40 shillings a year, and her son, Mr. Richard Hewitt, my old school fellow from my childhood -

To Mr. John Moncure, a mourning ring and one also to my old and long tried friends the Rev. Mr. James Scott and Mr. John West, Jr. Also to my friend and relation the Rev. Mr. Lee Massey.

My cousins Mrs. Cockburn and Miss Bronaugh -

Executors: My son George Mason and friend Mr. Martin Cockburn. Executors bond £20,000.

Fairfax County, Virginia, Will Book G#1, page 254 -

Will of George Mason of Lexington, Parish of Truro, County of Fairfax, dated 17 April 1795 and probated 19 December 1796.

Body to be buried at Gunston Hall.

To wife, Elizabeth, my mansion house and seat called Lexington, slaves, etc.

To sons, George and William (under age) - To George a silver beaker given him by his grandfather, Col. George Mason.

My three daughters (all underage) - Betsy, slaves, etc.; Nancy, slaves, etc.; Sally, slaves, etc.

My wife's father, Mr. Gerrard Hooe, deceased, property in hands of his wife, Mrs. Sarah Hooe.

Mentions Mrs. Mason, widow of my late father, my lands IN THE KENTUCKY COUNTRY to be divided between my two sons, George and William.

A mourning ring to each of my friends and brothers-in-law, Mr. Daniel McCarty, Col. John Cooke and Mr. William Thornton.

Executors: My brothers, William, Thomson, John and Thomas

Codicil - 4 May 1795: Further instructions concerning his wife and upkeep of his estates.

Codicil - 28 June 1795:- To his three daughters the five lots he has purchased in the CITY OF WASHINGTON, D.C. (described.)

Codicil - 3 November 1796: Situation now altered by his wife being now
pregnant - then to him or her - all my lands in KENTUCKY. Also, slaves
and $500.00 cash.

Fairfax County, Virginia, Will Book M#1, page 130 -

Will of Thomson Mason of Hollin Hall. Dated 15 April 1797, probated
21 November 1820.

    Wife, Sarah McCarty Mason -

    My father, Col. George Mason, deceased -

    My three daughters, Sarah Chichester Mason, Elizabeth Mason, and Ann
Elbeck Mason, (all underage). Title to a slave confirmed, given her by
her grandfather, Mr. Richard Chichester.

    Sons, Thomson, George William Mason, William Mason, Richard Chichester
Mason (all underage) - 8,000 acres in STATE OF KENTUCKY to my four sons.

    My wife, now pregnant, etc. Executors: Brothers William, John and
Thomas.

EXTRACTS FROM THE FILES OF THE VIRGINIA GAZETTE

Files of 1773: The three following Tenements in the City of Williamsburg,
which formerly belonged to the Honourable Phillip Ludwell, and are now held
by William Lee, Esquire, OF THE CITY OF LONDON: namely, the large wooden
House, on the Back Street, next Door but one to Mr. Speaker's; the Brick
House on the Main Street, where Mrs. Rind lives; and the House called the
Blue Bell, below the Capitol, opposite to the Playhouse, and in which Mr.
Brammer formerly lived, together with all the Lots and their Appurtenances.
The Terms may be known of the Subscribers.

                                      Richard Henry Lee
                                      Francis L. Lee
                                      Ro. C. Nicholas

The files of 1773: Princeton, NEW JERSEY - The Publick is hereby informed
that AT THE COLLEGE HERE young Gentlemen are instructed in all the
Branches of Literature, with the utmost Care. There is also a Grammar
School, in which young Boys are perfected in the English, and taught the
Latin and Greek Languages, Writing and Arithmetick, preparatory to the
College.

The Expense of Board and Education will not exceed twenty Pounds a Year, to which must be added Clothes, Books, and Pocket Money, which Gentlemen may estimate for themselves, according to the Way in which they choose their Children should be supported.

The files of 1773: A young gentleman who has recently taken his Bachelor's Degree at NASSAU HALL COLLEGE, in NEW JERSEY, would be glad of Employment as a Private or Publick Tutor, and will wait on any Gentleman, on Notice being given by Letter directed to Mr. William Carr, Postmaster at Dumfries if the Terms proposed are approved.

The Files of 1773:

JONATHAN PROSSER,
Tailor,
WILLIAMSBURG,

Returns Thanks to his Customers, and others from whom he has received Favours, and begs Leave to acquaint them that he continues his Business in all its Branches, which, from many Years Experience IN LONDON, he is bold to say he understands as well as any Man IN EUROPE, and has given the greatest Satisfaction to all Gentlemen of Fashion and Dignity who have been pleased to employ him in Virginia. In Order to enable him the better to fulfill his Engagements, as well as to support his Family, he gives this publick Notice, that he is determined to work for none but such as choose to pay him upon the Delivery of their Clothes. The many bad Payments he has laboured under induce him to take this Method, on account of which he has suffered by Lawsuits, as well as for Family Necessaries, which are almost innumerable, and demand immediate Cash. If any Gentlemen please to employ him upon these Terms they shall have their Business well executed, without any Disappointments; and those who are indebted to him are desired to make immediate Payment, to prevent Suits being commenced against them.
* * * I will pay twelve Shillings and Sixpence weekly to Journeymen who understand their Business well.

--Jonathan Prosser

The Files of 1771-1772:

I intend for SCOTLAND in a short Time.

--John Hook

The Files of 1773:

WANTS EMPLOYMENT,

An English Farmer, who HAS BEEN IN AMERICA Upwards of eight years, and came in with a Gentleman to EAST JERSEY, where he managed for him four Years, since which he has served Lewis Burwell, Esq., of Gloucester County. He understands the raising of all Kinds of Grain, the Culture of Tobacco, raising and fattening of Stock, etc. Whoever wants such a Person may apply for my Character to the above Gentleman. N.B. He is a married Man, and has one Child.

--Robert Mountain.

The Files of 1774: Whereas I intend shortly to remove from the Place where
I now live in FINCASTLE COUNTY, ON THE WESTERN WATERS, [Kentucky] it is ex-
pected that all these Gentlemen who have Business to do with me will attend at the Raleigh Tavern in Williamsburg, where I shall be from the 15th
of April next to the 25th of the said Month, in order to have all those
Accounts which are now unsettled properly adjusted.

--Israel Christian

The Files of 1774: Run away from the Subscriber, near Baltimore Town,
MARYLAND, on the 10th of February last, an IRISH indented Servant Lad
named Patrick Malone, about twenty Years of Age, five Feet five or six
Inches high, well set, with short brown hair, speaks quick and a good
Deal on the Brogue. Whoever secures him so that I may get him again
shall have Fifty Shillings if he is taken in the County, and the above
Reward if out of the Province, besides all reasonable Charges for bring-
ing him home.

--James Franklin

The Files of 1774: It gives me Concern to inform those indebted to
Captain John Gawith of LIVERPOOL that their long Neglect in Payments
has determined him to come to Virginia this Spring, in Hopes to prevent
farther Delay. I must therefore entreat them to make immediate Provision
for paying him when he arrives, that he may not long be detained from his
Family through their farther Default.

--Edmund Pendleton

The Files of 1774: The Subscriber intends for the WEST INDIES soon, and
to return in a few Months.

-- Robert Taylor

The Files of L774: The Subscriber hereby informs his Customers that he
intends to LEAVE THIS COLONY early in the Fall, and hopes all those indebted to him will make immediate Payment, to prevent Suits being commenced
against them. Those to whom he is indebted are desired to send in their
Accounts, that they may be properly settled.

-- Jonathan Prosser

The Files of 1771-1772: Run away from the Subscriber, in Bedford County,
on Great Falling River, an IRISH SERVANT Man named Michael Kelly, about
five Feet Inches high, with short black Hair, wears a cut brown Wig, a
blue Broadcloth Coat, spotted Flannel Jacket, and a Pair of old patched
Breeches. Also an Irish Servant Woman named Margaret Kelly, Wife to the
said Michael. She wore a blue Calimanco Gown and Petticoat. They both
speak IRISH, but neither of them are known to speak ENGLISH. I will give
Five Pounds Reward on their being delivered to me, and Fifty Shillings if
they are securdd in any Jail in this colony, upon Information of the same
given to   --William Hayth

<u>The Files of 1771-1772:</u> Run away from Hobb's Hole, on the 24th of March
last, a white Servant Boy named William Cox, BORN IN LONDON, about seventeen Years of Age, five Feet five or six Inches high, stoops much, of a
pale Complexion, and most villainous Countenance, was clothed in a Drab
coloured Cloth upper Jacket with Metal Buttons, and lined with white
Plaid, an under jacket of blue broadcloth much worn, with yellow Metal
Buttons, a pair of Thickset Breeches, Stockings and Shoes. He was seen,
soon after he went off, at or near Mr. William Meredith's Plantation in
King and Queen County, and very probably may be thereabouts yet. Whoever
takes him up, and conveys him to me, at my Plantation near Hobb's Hole,
shall have Twenty Shillings Reward, besides what the law allows.

--Andrew Crawford

<u>The Files of 1771-1772:</u> The Subscriber, having served a regular Appren-
ticeship to the noted Mr. Joseph Carncross, of the CITY OF DUBLIN, Coach-
maker, and for many Years past carried on the Coach-Making Trade, in all
its different Branches, in IRELAND, and in NEW YORK, where he had the
Honour of making a Coach, Pheton, and Chaise, for his Excellency the Right
Honourable the Earl of Dunmore, is now removed, with his Family, from
NEW YORK to Palace Street, in this City, where he proposes to make and
repair all Sorts of Coaches, Landaus, Chariots, Post Chaises, Petons,
Curricles, Chaises, and Chairs, with Harness of every Sort; also Steel
Springs, and Iron Work of every Kind relative to the Coach-making Trade;
likewise Painting, Gilding, and Japanning. The Subscriber being determined
to do all his Work in the best Manner, and on the lowest terms, humbly
hopes those Gentlemen that are pleased to employ him will pay Cash, at
least for any Piece of new Work, on Delivery of the same; and will be truly
thankful to every Gentleman or Lady who will employ him to repair Car-
riages, even if the Repairs do not exceed Half a Bit. The utmost Care
and Despatch of Business, shall be the constant Study of the Publick's
most humble Servant,

--Elkanah Deane

<u>The Files of 1771-1772:</u> I intend for GREAT BRITAIN soon.

-- John Rowsay

<u>Issue of April 11, 1766:</u> If Robert Burrough (son of Richard Burrough, of
the city of LONDON, bookseller, who died in the year 1728, or thereabouts)
who was a carver, and resident in the parish of ST. MARY'S ROTHERITHE,
SURRY in the year 1731 went to live at CHEYNES IN BUCKINGHAMSHIRE, and from
thence went beyond the seas, as is apprehended, to the island OF JAMAICA,
or to some other part of AMERICA, be living, and will apply by letter or
in person to Mr. Thomas Winchley in ESSEX COURT, MIDDLE TEMPLE, LONDON;
Mr. Thomas Weston, of WALLERSCOAT, near NORTHWICH in CHESHIRE; Mr. Peck-
ance, Attorney at Law in LIVERPOOL; Mess. Campbell and Hayes, of said
place, merchants; or to the subscribers in NORFOLK, VIRGINIA, may hear of
something to his or their advantage: Or if any person or persons can
give an account of the death of the said Robert Burrough, with or without
issue, and will apply as above, it will be a favour done to the family,
and their expenses will be generously paid.

--Bolden, Lawrence & Co.

EPITAPHS OF GLOUCESTER AND MATHEWS COUNTIES

IN TIDEWATER VIRGINIA THROUGH 1865

(Published by Virginia State Library 1959)

Note by C.H.H. - This is a 152-page book, well indexed, describing the various gravestones, family plots, location of cemeteries, etc. with very interesting and valuable information of a genealogical nature. This compiler has abstracted only the epitaphs denoting prior origin or death elsewhere than Virginia. Any record pertaining to Gloucester County is particularly valuable as most of the records are lost or destroyed.

Page 18:
                In memory of Richard Coke
                Born November 16, 1790
                Died March 31, 1851
          Beloved in Life, lamented in Death
       The best consolation of his friends
        is their hope of his mortality

A note following states that Richard Coke was the uncle of Senator Richard Coke OF TEXAS.

Page 18:
          Under this Stone lyes the Body of
          Captain William Blackburne who was
          Born in THE TOWN OF NEW CASTLE ON TYNE IN
          GREAT BRITAIN on the 17th of September 1653.
          He departed this Life the 18th day of October
          in the year of our Lord 1714 In hopes of a Joyful
                    Resurrection

Page 19:
          To the lasting memory of Major Lewis Burwell of the
          County of Gloucester, in Virginia, Gentleman, who
          descended from the Ancient family of the Burwells,
          OF THE COUNTIES OF BEDFORD AND NORTHAMPTON, in ENGLAND,
          who nothing more worthy in his Birth than Virtuous in
          his life, exchanged this life for a better one the
             19th day of November in the 33rd year
               of his age A.D. 1658

Note: Ancestor of the Burwell Family in Virginia. There are many other Burwell tombstones and their inscriptions including one of the wife of Major Lewis Burwell who was Lucy Higginson, (d. Nov. 6, 1675) only daughter of Captain Robert Higginson.

Page 26:
                    Cornelius Donovan
        BORN IN COUNTY CORK, IRELAND, April 1793
               Migrated to Virginia May 1818
                    Died March 19, 1856
                     (and of his wife)
              Elizabeth, daughter of Warner
                 and Nancy Bain - wife of
             C. Donovan, born May 20, 1798
                  Died December 14, 1838

Page 33:
               Here lies ye Body of Will Potter,
               A WILTSHERE (sic) MAN who departed
               this Life in ye Seting (sic) of ye
               Evening on Monday the 25 of January,
               Aged 56 years and was buried ye Friday
               following ye 29 January 1703.

Page 42:
        Here lies John Randolph Bryan, Born ON
        WILMINGTON ISLAND, GEORGIA, March 23, 1806.
        Educated under John Randolph of Roanoke,
        Midshipman in U.S. Navy 1823-1831. Married
        Elizabeth Tucker Coalter January 30, 1830.
        Resided here 1831-1862. Died at the University
        of Virginia September 13, 1887. Strong in body,
        mind and convictions. Inflexible in Integrity,
        a Patriot in Peace and War. A friend of the Poor.
        He early joined the church at Abingdon and was for
        fifty years an earnest follower of Christ and for
        all His mercies by Sea and Land he blessed and
        praised God to his life's End.

Note: His wife died in 1856 and the above inscription was written by his
sons, Mr. Joseph Bryan and Rev. Corbin Braxton Bryan.

Page 43: (Man with arms spread, sitting on top of a helmet)

        Here lieth interred ye body of Thomas Booth, Gent., who was born
        IN LANCASHIRE but lived most of his days in Gloucester County,
        Ware Parish, in Virginia where he departed this life on the 11th
        of October, Ann Dom., 1736 in the 74th year of his age. This
        monument is erected as the last Duty paid to the memory of a
        tender and loving father by the Sons and Daughters of the said
        deceased as a memento for us to follow the steps he trod, know-
        ing we and all must die, so saith ye Lord. But death this
        loanly cave(?) why need we fear, if we but live and die as he
        that lyeth here who only waits the Savior's call to rise again
        as he did fall, and then receive the Glorious crown for which
        his life so freely he laid down. So let us his example follow
        and fear not if we die tomorrow.

Thomas Booth's stone continued -

Note: There is also a monument to his wife Mary Booth (died January ye 21st 1723) who was the daughter of Mordecai Cooke, Gent., of Ware Parish, Gloucester County, Va.

Page 61:   Here quietly reposes the body of William Smart,
                   BORN IN ENGLAND of William and Mary Smart on the
                   20th of July 1784. In early life he emigrated to
                   the United States and after sustaining an
                   irreproachable reputation and a life of unexceptional
                   (sic) piety, he died in certain hopes of the resur-
                   rection of the just and eternal life, on the 10th
                   day of February 1840. "Let me die the death of the
                   righteous and let my last end be like his."

Note by C.H.H. - Also noted is the headstone of his wife, Louisa, who departed this life October 7th, 1828 in the 34th year of her age.

Page 70:   Underneath this stone lyeth the body of Mr. John Richards,
                   late Rector of NETTLESHEAD AND VICAR OF TESTON, IN THE
                   COUNTY OF KENT IN THE KINGDOM OF ENGLAND, and minister of
                   Ware in the County of Gloucester and Colony of Virginia,
                   who after a troublesome passage through the various changes
                   and chances of this mortal life at last reposed in this
                   silent Grave in expectation of a joyful Resurrection to
                   Eternal Life. He died the twelfth day of November in the
                   year of our Lord MDCCXXXV (1735) aged XLVI (46) years.

Note by C.H.H. - By his side is the grave of his wife, Amy Richards (died
21st of November 1725) aged 40 years.

Page 80:   Lucy Alice T. Dugan, wife of
                   Hammond Dugan, OF BALTIMORE, MARYLAND
                   Daughter of John H. Tabb, Gloucester
                   County, Virginia, born March 7, 1836 -
                   Married June 14, 1859. Died December 28th,
                                    1859.

Note by C. H. H. - The above dates are correctly copied.

Page 85:   Eliza C. Tabb, wife of
                   Thomas Todd Tabb, and daughter of William
                   and Jane Forman OF BALTIMORE, MARYLAND who
                   departed this life July 1, 1851 in the 53rd
                   year of her age. "Blessed are the dead who
                           die in the Lord."

Note by C. H. H. - There are many other "Tabb" tombstones listed.

Page 90:   Here lyeth the body of James Clack, the
                  youngest son of William and Mary Clack, who
                  was born IN THE PARISH OF MARDEN ... MILES
                  FROM THE DEVIZES IN THE COUNTY OF WILTS. He
          came out of ENGLAND in August 1678. Arrived in Virginia
          upon New Year's Day following. Came into this Parish of
          Ware on Easter where he continued minister near forty-five
          years till he dyed. He departed this life on the 20th day
          of December in the year of our Lord God 1723 in hopes of a
          Joyful Resurrection to Eternal Life which God Grant him for
                  his Blessed Redeemer's Sake. Amen.

Page 97:   Warner Lewis, Eldest son of Warner Lewis, Esq. and
                  Eleanor Gooch, widow of William Gooch, and daughter
                  of James Bowles, Esq., of MARYLAND. Died the 30th
                  of December 1791, aged 24 years.

Page 97:   This is to the memory of James J. McLanahan, eldest son
                  of John and Elizabeth McLanahan OF FRANKLIN COUNTY,
                  PENNSYLVANIA. Born November 15, 1791, died October 16,
                  1881. "His worth could not be properly appreciated but
                  by those who were most nearly connected with him."

Page 98:   Here lieth interred the body of John Lewis (BORNE IN
                  MONMOUTHSHIRE) died the 21st of August 1657, aged 63
                  years. The Anagram of his name I shew no ill.
                  [The remainder of the anagram is missing.]

Page 99:   ARMS
                  Here lyeth interred the body of Captain Edward Lewis,
                  the son of Major John Lewis and his wife, Isabelah,
                  who was grandson of John Lewis OF MONMOUTH SHIRE and
                  was born near this place the 5th of September 1667 and
                  departed this life the 11th of February 1713 (aged 47
                          years, 5 months and 6 days.

Note by C.H.H. - Many other "Lewis" epitaphs listed in this cemetery and
also "Warners."

Page 105: Captain Archibald Willey, born in DORCHESTER COUNTY, MARYLAND
           September 12, 1816. Died in Gloucester County, Virginia,
           February 22, 1874. "A span is all that we can boast, an inch
           or two of time, man is but vanity and dust in all his flower
           and prime.

Note by C. H. H. - Also listed are the graves of his 2nd wife, Ann Maria
(died Aug. 1863) in her 45th year and of his 3rd wife, Georgianna Smith,
born September 15, 1849. Died December 20, 1871.

66

Page 111:   (Carving of hand pointing upward)
            Sacred to the memory of Dr. John Catlett, son of
            Jeff W. and Ann W. C. Stubbs, born in Gloucester
            County, Virginia, April 20, 1848. Died of Typhoid
            Fever IN BALTIMORE, MARYLAND, November 13, 1874.
            He was a devoted son, a fond and loving brother,
            a constant friend, a devoted christian, and many
            mourn his loss.

Note by C. H. H. - Many other "Stubbs" tombstones listed. Among them that
of "our mother, Ann Walker Carter Stubbs," wife of Jefferson W. Stubbs,
Esq., and eldest daughter of Captain James Baytop and Lucy Taliaferro
Catlett. Died 22 September 1894 in the 78th year of her age, and 60th
of her marriage, etc.

Page 129:   In memory of Charles Ormsby [Guion] son of Abram G. and
             Sarah Guion. Born in RYE, NEW YORK, August 3, 1837.
             Died in Mathews, Virginia, December 23, 1889. "The
             beloved of the Lord shall dwell in safety."

Page 129:   Samuel Wright, born in LONG ISLAND, NEW YORK, July 4, 1798
             Died in Mathews County, July 18, 1870.

Page 129:   Anna Matilda [Guion] daughter of Abram G. and Sarah Guion
             Born in WESTCHESTER COUNTY, NEW YORK, November 3, 1848.
             Departed this life in Mathews County, Virginia, July 19, 1876.

                        + + +
                         + +
                          +

THE OHIO SOCIETY OF THE SONS OF THE REVOLUTION PROCEEDINGS
1909-1919 (Published 1920)

Note by C.H.H. - This 174-page book was printed by the above Society for
the benefit of its members in 1920. There are probably very few left in
existence at this late date. The Ohio Society amalgamated and merged with
the Sons of the American Revolution, State of Ohio, in 1930. The applications showing proven descent of its members from Revolutionary War soldiers
are now in the custody and safe keeping of the Cincinnati Society of the
Sons of the American Revolution, Ohio Society, in Cincinnati, Ohio. These
members, whose ancestors migrated to Ohio, are descendants of soldiers
who served variously from all the thirteen colonies. From this list the
following short biographical sketches were selected and abstracted by this
compiler.

List of (Virginia) Ancestors of the
Ohio Society Sons of the Revolution
(Pages 124 through 174)

Anderson, Richard Clough - (1750-1826) Virginia, Kentucky
    Captain 5th Virginia Regiment Continental Line and Major 1st Virginia
    Regiment, C.L.; Major 6th Virginia Regiment C.L.; Lt-Col. 1st Vir-
    ginia C.L.; Brigadier-General Virginia Militia; Aide-de-Camp to
    General Lafayette; original member of the Society of the Cincinnati.
    (Edward Lowell Anderson, Cincinnati, Ohio, second in descent.)

Ashby, John (1755-1815) - Virginia
    Fauquier County, Virginia. Captain in 3rd Virginia Regiment, C.L.
    from March 18, 1776 to October 30, 1777.

Ballard, William (1732-1799) Virginia
    Culpeper County, Virginia. Lieutenant of Artillery, Virginia Line.
    In service three years. Reference, certified copy of Warrant 160,
    Book 1, page 28, Land Office Records, Richmond, Virginia.
    (Descendant, 4th in descent, Edward McClure Ballard, Cincinnait,
    Ohio, elected 1897.)

Blackburn, William (_____ - 1780) Virginia
    Lieutenant in Captain Craig's Company of Colonel Campbell's Regiment
    of Virginians. Ref. to page 405 of Drapers Heroes of King's
    Mountain. "Fought bravely, losing his Lieutenant William Blackburn."
    Also page 304, same book. (Selby Frame Vance of Cincinnait, Ohio
    fourth in descent, elected 1916.)

Brent, Hugh (1739-1813) Virginia
    Stafford County, Virginia. Captain of Militia from Prince William
    County, Virginia. Ref. Oouncil Journal of Virginia showing payroll
    of the Prince William County militia. (Harry Brent Mackay,

Covington, Kentucky, fourth in descent, elected 1895.) Note by C.H.H.-
Another record states Captain Hugh Brent was born in Stafford County,
Virginia and died in Mason County, Kentucky.

Brent, William (1742-1802) Virginia
Captain of Militia from Prince William County, Virginia. Ref. Certi-
fied abstract from Council Journal of Virginia showing payroll of the
Prince William County militia.

Brooking, Vivian (1738-1808) Virginia
Graduated from W. & M. College in 1753. Lt.-Col. of the Commissary
Department, Army of Virginia, stationed at Richmond, Virginia. He
owned a tract of land near Valley Forge, the building of which were
used for storage of supplies for the Army. Lord Cornwallis paid him
a visit during the winter at Valley Forge and told him that only his
personal presence prevented the destruction of the plantation by
fire. Purchased 2217 acres of land August 12, 1763 in Amelia County,
Virginia. (Alex Brooking Davis, Cincinnait, Ohio, fourth in descent,
elected 1918.)

Brown, John (_____- 1830) Virginia
Captain in Colonel Sampson Matthews Regiment of Virginia Militia.
Ref. certificate from U. S. Commissioner of Pensions.

Buckner, Phillip (1747-1820) Virginia
Captain Phillip Buckner was a man of large means and acted as Commissary for entire period of Revolutionary War. Received large grants
of land in Kentucky on Land Office Treasury Warrants. Removed himself
and his family to Kentucky in 1783. From 1799 to 1810 he represented
the County of Bracken as its first Senator and Representative. Ref.
to Records of Land Office Grants, Caroline County, Virginia, and to
Collins History of Kentucky, page 772. Also, Littels History of
Kentucky, Vol. 1, page 37. (Herman Armstrong Bayless, Cincinnati,
Ohio, fourth in descent, elected 1916.)

Cunningham, John - Virginia
Ensign in 7th Virginia Regiment May 8, 1776.

Dowdell, James (1758-1800) Virginia
Served as Cadet in Peter Bryan Bruin's Company, 11th Virginia Regiment, commanded by Col. Daniel Morgan. Enlisted November 27, 1776
and his name appears last on the Muster Roll dated August 5, 1777.
(Richard Mulford Stanley, Norwood, Ohio, fourth in descent, elected
1918.)

Evans, Peter (1758-1814) Virginia
   Prince William County, Virginia. Enlisted 1776 in Captain
   Theodorick Bland's Company of Virginia Light Dragoons. Commissioned
   Captain of Militia May 1, 1780 under Col. Wheeden. Present at York-
   town. Ref. Certificate from Bureau of Pensions.)

Faulconer, Joseph - Virginia
   Made application for pension on March 30, 1833 at which time he was
   75 years of age and resided in Fayette County, Kentucky. Served
   18 months, 21 days as a private. Enlisted in Spotsylvania County,
   Virginia, and served under Captain Childs and Colonel Logan. His
   widow, Frances, received a pension on his services. (Marcus
   Clinton Smith, Norwood, Ohio, fourth in descent,,elected 1919.)

Freeman, John (1756-1848) Virginia
   Culpeper County, Virginia. Private in Captain John Green's Company,
   1st Virginia Regiment, served 12 months, re-enlisted in 1777 in
   Captain Richard Taylor's Company, Col. John Green's 1st Virginia
   Regiment, served three years.

Fuqua, Moses (1725-1813) Virginia
   Bedford County, Virginia. Sworn in as 2nd Lieutenant of Bedford
   County Militia February 28, 1780. (Harry Brent Mackay, Covington,
   Kentucky, descendant and Morton Mackay Lyons of Wayne, Pennsylvania
   also a descendant.)

Gall, George (1766-1832) Virginia
   Enlisted January 1781 as private in Captain James Buchanan's Company
   of Col. Boyers Regiment of Virginia Troops. Served three months and
   re-enlisted in September 1781 as private in Captain Charles Campbell's
   Company (afterwards Capt. William Moore's) of Col. Vance's Regiment.
   Served three months. Was at Battle of Yorktown. Ref. Bureau of
   Pensions.

Garth, John (1762-1835) Virginia, Kentucky
   Albemarle County, Virginia. Private in Captain Leak's Company, Col.
   Lindsey's Regiment Virginia Troops. Ref. certificate from Bureau of
   Pensions.

Gill, Samuel (1750-1822) Virginia
   Ensign, 4th Virginia Regiment 10 February 1776. 1st Lieutenant
   November 1776. Captain, January 1777. Retired September 14, 1778.
   (Lloyd Bates Johnson, of Raton, New Mexico sixth in descent, elected
   1918.)

Harrison, John (1754-1821) Virginia
Louisville, Kentucky. Ensign 13th Virginia Regiment December 16, 1776.
2nd Lieutenant January 1777, 9th Virginia Regiment, 1st Lieutenant
October 1778. Transferred to 7th Virginia Regiment October 12, 1781.
Served to close of Revolutionary War. (John P. Harrison Brewster,
Covington, Kentucky, fourth in descent, elected 1917.)

Hart, James - Virginia, Kentucky and Ohio
Private in the Virginia [Continental] Line as evidenced by a record
in the Virginia State Library which is a list of the enumerations of
names of soldiers receiving final pay. James Hart migrated to Virginia from County Tyrone, Ireland. (DeJohn Hart Macready, Cincinnati,
Ohio, descendant, elected 1902.)

Hathaway, John (1733-1786) Virginia
Captain of a Company of Militia of Fauquier County, Virginia in the
Continental Service from October 25, 1779 to May 26, 1783. Continued
in the Civil Service, holding office of Associate Justice of the
Court of Common Pleas of Fauquier County until his death, April 19,
1786. (Edwin Wilson Kemper, Cincinnati, Ohio, fourth in descent,
elected 1908.)

Jameson, David (_____ - 1812) Virginia
Enlisted in Captain Matthew Arbuckle's Company, 12th Virginia Regiment, September 12, 1775 and continued in service until October 10,
1778. (Henry Craig Yeiser, Cincinnait, Ohio, fourth in descent,
elected 1907.)

John, James - Virginia
Private in John Overton's Company, 10th Virginia Regiment commanded
by Col. William Davis. Enlisted October 1, 1777 for three years.
Ref. to Pension Office Certificate.

Johnson, Robert (1745-1815) Virginia and Kentucky
Orange County, Virginia. Member of the Virginia Assembly in 1782.
His family were inhabitants of Bryants Station, Kentucky when Girty
attacked that place August 14, 1782, and his wife, Jemima Suggett
Johnson, was one of the matrons who passed the Indian lines to
secure water. Was in expedition of Gen. George Rogers Clark August
1780 against the Shawnees. Commanded a Company under Clark in
Fall of 1782 in march on Piqua, Ohio.

Julian, John (1738-1788) Virginia
Dr. John Julian commissioned a surgeon in the Virginia Continental
Line June 5, 1776, and continued to close of the War. Detailed by
Washington, after the Battle of Yorktown, to take care of British
sick and wounded upon request of Lord Cornwallis, etc. (William

Alexander Julian, Cincinnati, Ohio, third in descent, elected 1916.)

Kemper, Charles (1756-1841) Virginia
Served 20 days in 1777 as a private in Virginia State Troops under
Captain Hezekiah Turner; August 1777 served 7 months as a private in
Virginia Artillery under Captain Elias Edmonds; May 1781 served four
months as Sergeant and Ensign under Captain William Jennings and
Col. Elias Edmonds, Virginia Troops. Record from Bureau of Pensions.
(Edwin Wilson Kemper, Cincinnati, Ohio, 4th in descent, elected 1908.)

Kincaid, James (1762-1840) Virginia
Albemarle County, Virginia. Private in General George Rogers Clark's
Regiment. Ensign under Captain Joseph Kincaid (his brother) at
Battle of Blue Licks August 1782. Lieutenant under General Charles
Scott.

Langhorne, Maurice (_____ -1791) Virginia
Cumberland County, Virginia. Member of Committee of Safety from Febru-
ary 18, 1775 to September 23, 1776. (Harry Brent Mackay, Covington,
Kentucky, fifth in descent, elected 1895.)

Lewis, Thomas (1718-1790) Virginia
Augusta County, Virginia. Member of the House of Burgesses and of
the Conventions of 1775 and 1776. (Charles Lewis, Cincinnati, Ohio,
4th in descent, elected 1910. Charles Birk Lewis, Cincinnait, Ohio,
6th in descent, elected 1918. Harry Kemper Lewis, Cincinnati, Ohio,
4th in descent, elected 1917. Henry Thompson Lewis, Cincinnati, Ohio,
5th in descent, elected 1913.) Note by C.H.H.- Another record states
Thomas Lewis married Jane Strother.

McDonald, Benjamin John (1746-1827) Virginia
Enlisted in Virginia Continental Line September 4, 1781. Discharged
July 6, 1783. Ref. to Virginia Land Office Vol. 2, page 150. (James
Hamilton Cather, RFD, Zanesville, Ohio, 3rd in descent, elected 1913.)

McDowell, Joseph (1756-1801) Virginia and North Carolina
Quaker Meadows, Burke County, North Carolina. Major in Burke County
Regiment commanded by his brother, Col. Charles McDowell in February
1776; the same year served in Rutherford's Campaign against the
Cherokees, was on the Stone expedition in 1780; was in the Victory
at Ramsour's Mill in the spring of 1781; in 1782 he led an expedition
against the Cherokees. Ref. Drapers King Mountain and Lossings
History.)

Massie, John (1765-_____) Virginia
Enlisted at age 16 from New Kent County, Virginia, and served until
1781 as Cornet in the Continental Dragoons. He was transferred in
1782 to Bayless' Consolidated Regiment of Dragoons and served until

the close of the War. His name is among the officers of Virginia entitled to half-pay. (John Upshaw Byrd, Newport, Kentucky, 4th in descent, elected 1914.)

Matthews, Sampson Virginia
    Sworn in as Lieutenant-Colonel Augusta County, Virginia Militia May 9, 1778. (Ben Barrere Nelson, Cincinnati, Ohio, 4th in descent, elected 1916.)

Metcalfe, John (1724-1799) Virginia
    Fauquier County, Virginia. On the first call for soldiers, Captain John Metcalfe raised a Company of Volunteer Infantry in Fauquier County, Virginia. Served throughout the War. (Alfred Metcalfe Davies, Cincinnati, Ohio, 4th in descent, elected 1910.)

Mills, John (_____-1800) Virginia and Kentucky
    Ensign in the 9th Virginia Regiment 1779. Lieutenant 1781.

Nicholas, George (1755-1799) Virginia
    Hanover County, Virginia. Captain 2nd Virginia October 3, 1775. Major, 10th Virginia November 13, 1776. Lieutenant-Colonel 11th Virginia September 26, 1777. Resigned November 27, 1777. Raised at his own expense the original company commanded by him, which helped to drive Dunmore from Virginia, and for which his heirs were re-imbursed by Congress without their solicitation. Assisted in defense of Richmond against Arnold. Member of House of Delegates and of Convention which ratified Constitution of U. S.

Nicholas, Robert Carter (1715-1780) Virginia
    Member of Committee of Correspondence appointed by House of Burgess dissolved by Lord Dunmore, which afterwards assembled at Raleigh Tavern. Member of Committee of Safety and Financier of that Committee. Chairman pro tem of Committee which met in 1775 for adoption of State Constitution [can this be right?] Judge of Chancery and Appeals 1779-1780. Died at Hanover County, Virginia 1780. [Note by C. H. H.- DAR lineages give him the title of "Colonel" and state he was married to Ann Cary.]

Norman, Thomas (1758-1838) Virginia
    Culpeper County, Virginia. Private in Captain Robert's Company. Col. Crockett's Regiment, Virginia Troops. Ref. Pension List of 1835.

Patton, George (1757-1813) Virginia
    Falmouth, Virginia [Stafford County] Sergeant in Captain William Wallace's Company. Col. Fowler's Regiment 1777-1778. Ref. Pension

Office Certificate. (John Blaine Patton, New York City, 4th in descent, elected 1907.)

Payne, Edward (1726-1806) Virginia
Fairfax County, Virginia. Member of Committee of Safety. Commanded a Company of Virginia Troops in Revolution.

Pendleton, Nathaniel (1746-1821) Virginia and New York
Ensign, 10th Continental Infantry January 1, 1776; 1st Lieutenant 11th Virginia July 23, 1776; Captain March 13, 1777; taken prisoner at Fort Washington November 16, 1776; exchanged October 18, 1780; transferred to 3rd Virginia Regiment February 1781; Aide-de-Camp to General Greene to close of War.

Peyton, Yelverton (1735-1794) Virginia
Member of Committee of Safety of Stafford County, Virginia. Prepared an address expressing sympathy with the people of Boston, Mass. Also member of the permanent Committee of Sixty-Nine. Ref. Force's Archives, Vol. 1, page 618.

Phillips, Mourning (1758-1831) Virginia
May 1776 enlisted under Capt. James Harvey in the 2nd Virginia Regiment for 3 years. Honorably discharged in Spring of 1779 at Philadelphia, Pa. Served in Command of General LaFayette in 1781 until the surrender at Yorktown October 19, 1781. Twice married, 1st wife, Miss Payne 1780; 2nd wife, Elizabeth Kendricks, whom he married March 23, 1808, who petitioned for a pension on his services. (Walter Dabney Phillips, Cincinnati, Ohio, fourth in descent, elected 1911.)

Posey, Zephariah (1752-1826) Virginia
Served as private in Captain Charles Gallahun's Company, 11th Virginia Regiment, commanded by Col. Daniel Morgan. He enlisted November 5, 1776 to serve three years, was transferred to Capt. George Rice's company, 11th and 15th Virginia Regiments, commanded by Lt.-Col. John Cropper and Col. Daniel Morgan about June 1778 and to Captain Phillip Slaughter's Company, known as Lieutenant James Wright's Company 7th Virginia Regiment. Discharged November 1779. Was pensioned in Hamilton County, Ohio June 23, 1819 as Sergeant in Virginia Continental Troops. Ref. U. S. Pension Certificate.

Robeson, William (1762-1839) Virginia
Was a member of the State Militia of North Carolina and while very young (about 18) fought in the Battle of Kings Mountain, October 7, 1780. Not married for about eight years after. After the Revolution settled in the western part of the state in Buncombe County. (Lewis Robeson Akers, Sebring, Ohio fourth in descent, elected 1917.)

Rochester, Nathaniel (1752-1831) Virginia, North Carolina, Maryland, New York
    In 1775 was appointed a member of the Committee of Safety for Orange
    County, North Carolina. In August 1775 was appointed a Major of one
    of four Regiments of Continental Troops raised in North Carolina and
    as such attacked and captured 500 troops raised among the "Royalists"
    of North Carolina for the British. In May 1776 was appointed Com-
    missary General (with the rank of Colonel) for the ten Regiments of
    North Carolina. The City of Rochester, New York named after him.
    (See Rochester and Western New York by Henry O'Reilly, page 407.)

Stephenson, James (_____ - 1813) Virginia
    Berkeley County (now West Virginia) Captain and Paymaster of 13th Vir-
    ginia Regiment December 16, 1777. (John Parker Hanna, Cincinnati,
    Ohio, fourth in descent. Died April 21, 1918.) Note by C.H.H.-
    Another record states he was married to Rachel McKeever.

Taliaferro, Nicholas (1757-_____) Virginia
    Ensign 10th Vigginia Regiment August 15, 1777 - 2nd Lieutenant,
    November 15, 1777. Regiment designated as 6th Virginia September 14,
    1778. Taken prisoner at Charleston May 12, 1780 and later exchanged.
    1st Lieutenant February 18, 1781 and served to close of war.

Tallman, Benjamin (1745-1820) Virginia, Pennsylvania
    Member of the 5th Battalion of Militia of Berks County, Pennsylvania
    under Captain John Bishop and Col. Jacob Weaver. Between 1777-1778
    he paid for exemption and removed to Virginia about 1780, where he
    enlisted as a private in the 4th Troops of the First Partisan Legion
    under Capt. Claudius de Bert and Col. Armand, Marquis de la Roubirie,
    a portion of Amando Corps that was credited to Virginia. A list
    shows that Benjamin Tallman (Tollman) #39 on the list was entitled
    to 100 acres of land for his service.

Thompson, Roger (1700 - _____) Virginia
    Captain of a company of Minutemen from 1775-1776. Stationed at
    Burwell's Ferry, James River July 2, 1776; ordered to North Carolina
    with his company June 4, 1776 with Captain Nicholas Lewis. (Brent
    Arnold, Cincinnait, Ohio, third in descent, elected 1895.)

Trimble, James (1753-1804) Virginia
    Captain in a company in Regiment commanded by Col. George Mathews.
    Ref. Certificate of County Clerk of Augusta County, Virginiae

Trotter, James (_____ - 1836) Virginia
    Augusta County, Virginia. Served in Virginia Troops during Revolution.
    After moving to Kentucky, performed efficient frontier service against
    the Indians. Ref. Appletons Encyclopedia of American Biography, Vol.6
    page 182.

Upshaw, James (_____ - 1807) Virginia
    Lieutenant in Continental Line and Captain of Militia. Member of the
    Society of the Cincinnati and was a "Signer" of the famous Westmore-
land land Resolutions written in 1776. (John Upshaw Byrd, Newport, Kentucky,
    fourth in descent, elected 1914.) Note by C.H.H.-James Upshaw married
    Mary (Molly) Martin.

Van Metre, Abraham (1721-1783) Virginia
    Soldier of the Revolution. Erected Fort Van Metre on Short Creek,
    Ohio County, West Virginia, called the Court House Fort and 1777-
    1782 was under command of Major Samuel McCullogh. Was with Squire
    Boones, Shelby County, Kentucky in 1779 and with Capt. Harrods
    party at the Falls of the Ohio in 1780. (Willis Vincent Van Metre,
    Marietta, Ohio, fifth in descent, elected 1915.)

Vaughan, Reuben (1740-1808) Virginia
    Captain in Virginia Militia from 1777 to close of war. Ref. certi-
    fied copy of his Commission as Captain.

Waggener, Thomas (1762-1842) Virginia
    Culpeper County, Virginia. Sergeant in Captain Stanton's Company,
    Col. Thornton's Regiment, Virginia Line. Ref. certificate from
    Bureau of Pensions.

Webb, Isaac (1758 - _____0 Virginia
    Ensign, 7th Virginia Regiment September 1776; 2nd Lieutenant,
    January 13, 1777; transferred to 5th Virginia September 14, 1778;
    1st Lieutenant, October 30, 1778. (Bifchard Austin Hayes, Toledo,
    Ohio, third in descent, elected 1894.)

West, John (1758-1808) Virginia
    Served as private in Virginia Service. Was paid on April 8, 1782
    forty-seven pds. the full amount of his pay due him. (Eckenrode,
    page 464.) (Clarence Clifford West, Cincinnati, Ohio, fourth in
    descent, elected 1916.)

Williams, David (1750-1831) Virginia
    Lieutenant, 8th Virginia Regiment, Continental Line. Served
    through the war; 2nd Lieutenant, 12th Virginia Regiment; 1st Lieuten-
    ant, 12th Virginia Regiment. (Brent Arnold, Cincinnati, Ohio, third
    in descent, elected 1895.)

Wilson, James (1763-1829) Virginia
    Caroline County, Virginia. Private in Captain Nicholas Long's Com-
    pany, Colonel Johnson's Regiment, Virginia Troops; Participated in
    the Battles of Camden, Guilford Courthouse, Yorktown. Certificate
fro   from Bureau of Pensions. (James Alpheus Collins, Cincinnati, Ohio
    third in descent.)

* * *

CONTRIBUTIONS BY OTHERS

This compiler is extremely gratified and pleased to
exhibit the following records which have been furnished
him by his friends, and to thank them for their
interest and energy.

The following abstracts were contributed by Mrs. Frank F. Byram, 145 Chilean
Avenue, Palm Beach, Florida:

Henry County, Virginia, Deed Book 6, page 493 -

29 November 1803 - David Alexander and wife, Unity, of ROCKINGHAM COUNTY,
NORTH CAROLINA, to John Pratt of Henry County, Virginia, land in Henry
County, Virginia. Witnesses: John Rice, Aron Seanoy(?), Robert Ross.
Recorded 26 March 1804.

Amherst County, Virginia, Deed Book F, page 62 -

2 September 1785 - John Farrar and John Wammock of CASWELL COUNTY [no
state given but later shown to be NORTH CAROLINA,] executors of John
Lyons, and Richard Tankersley Lyon, heir-at-law, to Bennett Nalley,
350 acres on Rich Cove, part of 400 acres sold to John Lyon by Capt.
Charles Lewis of Goochland Co., Virginia, [this earlier deed 1750,
Albemarle County, Virginia,] adjoining lines of Benjamin Moore, Capt.
John Dawson, Peter Lyon, John Burns.

Amherst County, Virginia, Deed Book F, page 158 -

2 May 1787 - Samuel Anderson to James Turner, 150 acres called the Mill
Tract, which Samuel Anderson, son-in-law of John Lyon late of CASHWELL
[sic] COUNTY, NORTH CAROLINA, was empowered by the will of 23 April 1784
of the said John Lyon to sell at the best price. Adjoining lines of
Benjamin Moore, Samuel Anderson (land given him in said will of said
John Lyon), Terisha Turner's spring, O. Pearce.

Amherst County, Virginia, Deed Book I, page 410 -

30 August 1789 - John Spencer, attorney in fact for Edward Lyon of
WASHINGTON, NORTH CAROLINA, to Joseph Nichols, 150 acres on Stovall, adjoining lines: Martin Bibb, John Merritt, Benjamin Rucker, Peter Day,
dec'd. Witnesses: Zach. Dawson, Thomas Day, John Wood, William
Mayfield, Robert D. Dawson.

Patrick County, Virginia, Deed Book 1, page 391 -

30 April 1796 - Stephen Lyon of Patrick County to Matthew Moore of
STOKES COUNTY, NORTH CAROLINA. Elley Lyon, wife of Stephen Lyon, consents.

Patrick County, Virginia, Deed Book 4, page 57 -

13 April 1814 - Jacob and Jane Lyon of Patrick County, and John
Mitchell [Deed 4:273 shows his wife as Patsy Mitchell] of HAWKINS COUNTY,
TENNESSEE, to Joseph Gray of Patrick County.

Patrick County, Virginia, Deed Book 2, page 91 -

22 May 1801 - Robert Harris of SURRY COUNT, NORTH CAROLINA, to Thomas
Sumner of STOKES COUNTY, NORTH CAROLINA, land on Blue Ridge Mountain in
Virginia. Witnesses: Moses Grigg, Joseph Sumner, Bezaleel Harris.

Patrick County, Virginia, Deed Book 2, page 271 -

__November 1803 - James Harris of ROCKINGHAM COUNTY, NORTH CAROLINA to
Reuben Harris of Patrick County, 2 tracts of land on Wiggon Creek.

Patrick County, Virginia, Deed Book 2, page 305 -

14 January 1804 - George Rogers of HAWKINS COUNTY, TENNESSEE to William
Harris of Patrick County. Witnesses: Amos Askew, William Askew,
Thomas Rhodes, Alex. Askew, Rebecca Harris Mumford.

Patrick County, Virginia, Deed Book 5, page 73 -

11 November 1817 - Daniel Booth of LAWRENCE COUNTY, OHIO, and John Massey
and Samuel Harris of Patrick County, to William Ayers of Patrick County.
Witnesses: Abijah Booth, Wm. Alexander, Jr., Ruben Harris.

Patrick County, Virginia, Deed Book 8, page 90 -

21 April 1832 - Reuben Harris, Jr. of JACKSON COUNTY, MISSOURI, to Alex.
Wood of Patrick County, land on Smith's River, Widgeons Creek. Witnesses:
Wm. McAlexander, Wm. Price, Reuben Harris.

Patrick County, Virginia, Deed Book 7, page 405 -

24 September 1830 - William McAlexander of Patrick County to Edmund
McAlexander of SALINE COUNTY, MISSOURI and John McAlexander, Sr. of
Patrick County, land on Widgeon Creek where said John McAlexander, Sr.
now lives.

Patrick County, Virginia, Deed Book 10, page 489 -

20 September 1841 - Power of Attorney from Nathan [signed Nathaniel]
McAlexander, Nancy Wilson, William McAlexander, John McAlexander, Jane
Mannon, David McAlexander, John McAlexander agent for Onea Harmer,
all of CHAMPAIGN COUNTY, OHIO, to John Hall, to obtain legacy from
the estate of John Hall, dec'd. of Patrick County.

Patrick County, Virginia, Deed Book 12, page 395 -

28 February 1845 - Power of Attorney from Daniel McAlexander of BATH
COUNTY, KENTUCKY to William J. Robertson, for all transactions concerning legacy from will of father William McAlexander, dec'd. of
Patrick County, Will dated 19 December 1820. [Probated March Court
1822.]

Patrick County, Virginia, Deed Book 8, page 352 -

28 September 1833 - James Tuggle of JACKSON COUNTY, MISSOURI, one
heir of John Tuggle, Sr., dec'd, with the rest of the heirs and legatees to Solomon Washington of Patrick County, land on Rockcastle
Creek. Acknowledge Jackson Co., Mo., 10 February 1834.

Patrick County, Virginia, Deed Book 8, page 354 -

23 November 1833 - Henry Tuggle, Reuben Burnett and wife Nancy,
Shadrach Brammer and wife Frances, William Brammer and wife Lucy,
all of WAYNE COUNTY, KENTUCKY, some of the heirs of John Tuggle, Sr.,
dec'd., with the rest of the heirs and legatees to Solomon Washington
of Patrick County, land on Rockcastle Creek.
[Note for Deeds 8:352 and 8:354: The rest of the heirs of John
Tuggle Sr., dec'd., who remained in Patrick County, made a similar
deed 4 March 1834, 8:353.]

Patrick County, Virginia, Deed Book 13, page 294 -

13 October 1837(sic) [From context and study of the family this date
seems erroneous and most likely 1847. --M.B. Byram] - Power of
Attorney from John A. Tuggle, William D. Tuggle, James J. Tuggle,
Henry P. Tuggle, James and Elizabeth (Tuggle) Beets, Henry L. and
Mary Ann (Tuggle) Lyon, Edmund L. Tuggle, and Robert Shelton,
guardian of William L. Shelton, Mary J. E. Shelton and James C. Shelton

the infant heirs of Nancy W. (Tuggle) Shelton, dec'd, all of VAN BUREN
COUNTY, MISSOURI, and heirs of James Tuggle, dec'd late of VAN BUREN
COUNTY, MISSOURI to Henry Tuggle of Patrick County, for all transactions
concerning legacy from estate of John Tuggle dec'd of Patrick County,
their grandfather, due them by reason of being the heirs of James Tuggle,
dec'd. Acknowledged Van Buren County, Missouri, 13 October 1847, by
John A. Tuggle, William D. Tuggle, James J. Tuggle, and Henry P. Tuggle.
Acknowledged Van Buren County, Missouri, 10 January 1848, by Robert
Shelton and Edmund L. Tuggle. Acknowledged Van Buren County, Missouri,
2 December 1847, by Henry L. and Mary Ann Lyon.

Patrick County, Virginia, Deed Book 4, page 446 -

9 January 1815 - Power of Attorney from Thomas Bristow, Peyton Bristow,
Henry Bristow, and James Atwood, all of PREBLE COUNTY, OHIO, Jasper
Bristow of SHELBY COUNTY, _____(?), Sarah Bristow widow of Benjamin
Bristow, dec'd and her children James Bristow, Joseph Lewis, John Harris,
Sarah Bristow, Jr., and Samuel Bristow heirs of Benjamin Bristow, dec'd,
all the above persons being heirs of William Bristow, dec'd, to James
Bristow, for all transactions concerning land in Patrick County.
[Shelby County, Ohio was organized 1819, so above Shelby County might be
Kentucky since in deed 5:323, 9 September 1817, are mentioned some of
these and other names, called of Kentucky and Ohio, heirs of William
Bristow, dec'd.]

+ + +

The following abstract was contributed by Mr. James F. Lewis,
Kilmarnock, Virginia:

Northumberland County, Virginia - Found in the loose papers in chancery
suit Gough vs Lucas Common Law Court Papers. Ended at September 1789
and April 1790 -

The Deposition of Toulson Parker aged 49 years or thereabout taken at
Fairfield Tavern the Twenty fifth day of February 1790 upon oath do say
that Abner Neale of the STATE OF NORTH CAROLINA was at his house in March
in 1782 and Affirm'd to him that Shappliegh Hudnall was dead and that he
died at his father's house, Christopher Neale, in Newburn Town in the
state of North Carolina and farther the deponant Sayeth not
Test: Geo. Blackwell and Wm. Nelms.

+ + +

The following abstracts were contributed by Mrs. Dewey W. Huggins,
Professional Genealogist, of Raleigh, North Carolina:

Northampton, North Carolina Deed Book 1, page 182 -

John Long was "of Brunswick County, Virginia" on May 20, 1745 when he
purchased his first tract of land in Northampton County, North Carolina,
from William Finnie of Isle of Wight County, Virginia. The acreage was
not given, but a later deed of sale shows that it was for 50 acres. The
tract "beginning at a beach in the Cypress Swamp, along a line of marked

trees to the old country line, along the country line to Cypress Swamp and up to the first station." There were no names of witnesses listed, but the deed was recorded in May 1745.

Northampton, North Carolina, Deed Book 1, page 438 -

On February 28, 1749, John Long was "of Brunswick County, Virginia," purchasing 200 acres of land from Samuel Strickland of Northampton County, North Carolina. This had been a grant to William Boon. The land was on the south side of the Meherrin River, "beginning at a white oak a corner between Joseph Strickland and a line of marked trees to the upper line and courses of a former deed from Boon to Strickland." Witnesses were John Brittle and Joseph Strickland, and the deed was recorded in August 1750 court.

Northampton, North Carolina, Deed Book 2, page 58 -

On May 3, 1751 John Long was "of Surry County, Virginia, planter," selling the 50-acre tract purchased on May 20, 1745, to Francis Hutchins of Surry County, Virginia, carpenter. No witnesses were listed. John Long signed his name and acknowledged the deed of sale at the February term of court, in 1752.

Northampton, North Carolina, Deed Book 2, page 58 -

On the same date of May 3, 1751, John Long "of Surry County, Virginia, planter," sold another tract to the same man. This was 100 acres on the south side of the Meherrin River, "beginning at the old county line, a line of marked trees to a white oak in a slack (?), down to a pine at William Hill's line, along said line to the Cypress Swamp, part of patent granted Richard Wall in 1743. There were no names of witnesses listed. John Long signed his name and acknowledged the deed of sale at the February term of court, in 1752.

Northampton, North Carolina, Deed Book 2, page 301 -

On May 9, 1755, John Long was "of Northampton County, North Carolina" taking up a Lord Granville grant of 350 acres in the county, "beginning at Nicholas Tyner's . . . on Little Swamp . . . (He came from Virginia 1754 to May 9, 1755.)

Northampton, North Carolina, Deed Book 3, page 344 -

On December 12, 1764, John Long "of Northampton County, North Carolina," sold the 200 acres (granted William Boon in 1723) to Nicholas Judkins of the county, "beginning at a white oak a corner between Joseph Strickland (See book 1, page 438.)

The aforementioned deed was signed by John Long and acknowledged in
court, and witnesses were a Drewry and a Deberry, first names not legible.
This is the last conveyances by John Long of Brunswick County, Virginia
of May 20, 1745, and February 28, 1749, of Surry County, Virginia of
May 3, 1751, of Northampton County, North Carolina of May 9, 1755 to December 12, 1764. (There are several other deeds of purchase and sale to
the name of John Long, but this was John Long, born 1730 who married
Joyce Washington (1732-1799), daughter of James Washington.)

Northampton County, North Carolina, Book 7, page 361 -

Joseph Long was of Greensville County, Virginia in 1785 when he bought
land that he sold in 1787 of Northampton County, North Carolina. He was
not in the county in 1790.

+ + +

The following article was contributed by the late
Mr. Lundie Barlow of Richmond, Virginia:

SOME VIRGINIA SETTLERS OF GEORGIA, 1773-1798

In 1773 the Creek and Cherokee Indians ceded to the Colony of Georgia
a large tract of land lying between Augusta and the present site of Athens,
and extending from the Savannah River on the north to the Ogeechee on the
south. Comprising some 3500 square miles, this territory was organized
in 1777 as Wilkes County. Three years later its court-house village of
Washington was established.

Over the period from 1790 to 1828 five counties were cut off and set
up from the original Wilkes area, namely, Elbert, Hart, Lincoln, Madison
and Oglethorpe, together with the northern parts of Greene, Taliaferro and
Warren. The early records of Wilkes refer therefore to people whose lands,
and the evidences of whose descendants, are now to be found in one or more
of these nine counties as presently constituted.

From about 1773 to the turn of the century this vast extent of land
was settled, principally by Virginians and Carolinians, upon the headright
system and by grants of bounty land for Revolutionary War service. It is
the "Gone With the Wind" country made universally beloved by Margaret
Mitchell. Aside perhaps from a few of the older communities along the
coast, it was, and is, the cultural and social center of all Georgia.

Except for those designated CLC (for the records of the Court of Land
Commissioners), now in the State Archives; and those denoted LP (for the
loose papers) and MR (for a small book of mixed records), in the County
Court House; all of the abstracts which follow are from the deed and will
books (AA, BB, CC, etc.) of Wilkes. For convenience of reference they
have been arranged alphabetically by the names of the emigrants from Virginia, regardless of date, source, or location of land. A full copy of
any CLC grant may be obtained from the Secretary of State, Atlanta; and
of any of the other items from the Clerk of the Superior Court, Washington,
Georgia.

Grant to BENJAMIN ARNOLD of Virginia: himself, wife, 10 sons and 2 daughters aged 18 to 2 years, headrights; 100 acres "formerly entered by Pettycrew who has given it up;" 10 Oct. 1774. CLC, 19.

Deed to THOMAS ATKINS, SENIOR, of Mecklenburg Co., Va., from William Wilder and wife Winnie of Wilkes; 200 acres on waters of Long Creek granted said Wilder in 1784; Thomas Atkins and William Pitchfor, witnesses; 3 Feb. 1785. AA, 15.

Estate inventory of JAMES AYCOCK, deceased: due from John Bradford to William Aycock "about the year 1745 for one horse lent in Virginia;" due from Mr. Henry Pope to William Aycock "about 1757 for a mare in Virginia, about 1749 to bed and furniture, about 1757 for a cow;" 4 January 1778. MR, 11.

Grant to RICHARD AYCOCK of Virginia: himself, wife, son aged 4 years, son aged 9 months, headrights; 200 acres on Chickasaw Creek adjoining land of Holman Freeman; 27 Sept. 1773. CLC, 1.

Deed to LEWIS BARRETT of Virginia from Jacon Autry and wife Elizabeth of Wilkes; 300 acres on Little Beaverdam Creek; Joel Terrell and David Meriwether, witnesses; 9 Aug. 1785. AA, 146.

Deed to ROBERT BEESLEY of Lunenburg Co., Va., from John Harvey of Wilkes; 537½ acres on Fishing Creek; Thomas Grant, Daniel Grant, Fanny Grant, witnesses; 7 Jan. 1785. CC, 57.

Deed to WILLIAMSON BIRD of Prince Edward Co., Va., from Joseph Williams and wife Frances of Wilkes; 400 acres on Uptons Creek; Ganoway Martin and George Gresham, witnesses; 26 Jan. 1785. Deed Book 1784-85, 87.

Deed to NEWMAN BROCKENBROUGH of Essex Co., Va., from Francis Smith and wife Lucy of Wilkes; 226 acres on White Marsh Swamp adjoining Vincent Hudson and said Smith; Jesse Heard, J.P., witness; 21 Nov. 1786. AA, 122.

Deed from JAMES BUFORD of Bedford Co., Va., to Jacob Early of Wilkes; 500 acres, part of tract purchased from William Hammett; Buckner Harris, witness; 15 Aug. 1786. AA, 183.

Deed from JAMES BUFORD of Bedford Co., Va., to Jeffrey Early of Wilkes; land on Beaverdam Creek; A. Cummins, witness; 15 Aug. 1786. AA, 164.

Deed from JAMES BUFORD of Bedford Co., Va., to Thomas Stark of Wilkes; 200 acres on Shoulderbone Creek granted said BUFORD in 1784; Bernard Kelly and Bedfor Brown, witnesses; 16 May 1789. DD, 224.

Deed to JAMES BUFORD (BEWFORD) of Bedford Co., Va., from Bernard Kelly of Wilkes; 500 acres on waters of Hammocks Creek; William Moore, J.P., and Benjamin Bragg, witnesses; 4 June 1789. HH, 101.

Deed of gift from MARY BUNKLEY of Wilkes, late of Charlotte Co., Va., widow of Joshua Bunkley, to son-in-law James Lucas and son Jesse Bunkley;

8 Negro slaves; Benjamin Thompson, Israel Burnley, Andrew Frazer, witnesses; 4 Nov. 1789. DD, 217.

Grant to JOHN BURKS OF Virginia; himself, wife, 5 sons and 3 daughters aged 13 years to 3 months, headrights; on waters of Little River; Douglas Watson, Thomas Baldwin, Thomas Nelms, Jr., witnesses; 4 Jan. 1791. HH, 199.

Promissory note of JOSHUA DAVIS of Mecklenburg Co., Va., to George Lumpkin of Wilkes; $1222; John Lumpkin and Vines Collier, witnesses; 25 Feb. 1785. LP.

Deed to JESSE DUNCAN of Pittsylvania Co., Va., from Robert McCrory of Wilkes; 530 acres on Little River; Polly Mounger, Nancy Mounger, Henry Mounger, witnesses; 5 May 1789. EE, 104.

Bill of sale from JESSE DUNCAN of Pittsylvania Co., Va., to Robert McCrorie; two Negro slaves; Polly Mounger, Nancy Mounger, Henry Mounger, witnesses; 8 May 1789. EE, 75.

Deed from ABRAHAM EADES and wife Sarah of Albemarle Co., Va., to Thomas Stephens of Wilkes; 200 acres on Goose Pond Creek; Thomas Hopper and John Tiller, witnesses; 10 Dec. 1789. HH, 328.

Power of attorney from MARTIN ELAM of Wilkes to Francis Barnes of Charlotte Co., Va., to sell 500 acres on Great Bluestone Creek in Charlotte, part of tract William Elam lived on and deeded by him to said MARTIN ELAM, adjoining lands of Almon and Edward Elam; John Sims and Frederick Sims, witnesses; 28 April 1790, EE, 139.

Power of attorney from CHARLES FINCH to Micajah Anthony to convey 2 tracts in Henry Co., Va., to George Hareston, adjoining land sold said Hareston by William Finch, son of said CHARLES FINCH; Sydnor Cosby, J.P., and William Rogers, J.P., witnesses; 1 Aug. 1791. HH, 294.

Grant to GEORGE FREEMAN of Virginia: himself, wife and 1 slave, headrights; 100 acres "above the Goose Ponds;" 10 Oct. 1774. CLC, 18.

Grant to HOLMAN FREEMAN of Virginia; himself, wife, 2 sons and 3 daughters aged 20 to 12 years, headrights; tract on Chickasaw Creek; 27 Sept. 1773. CLC, 1.

Affidavit by DANIEL GAINES of Virginia: "John and Joseph Hawkins were Commissioners for supplying troops in Virginia during the Revolutionary War ... Joseph Morton acted for them ... deponent does not know whether said Morton was a partner with the said Hawkins;" undated. LP.

Letter from DANIEL GAINES of Amherst Co., Va., to "the Honorable Walton Harris near Wilkes Court House, Ga."; "The bearer hereof, James Stewart, carries out my slaves to make a crop on the plantation I bought of you ... disappointed here in receiving money to discharge the first payment for the land ... expect Mr. Stewart will receive it in South Carolina ... if he fails, to let you have my negroes agreeable to what

passed between us at Savannah ... Mr. Thomas Gilbert, who goes out with
Mr. Stewart, means to become a citizen of Georgia ... to follow the
business of Surveyor ... recommend him to your good offices ... he will
show you a petition to your Assembly signed by a number of respectable
gentlemen ... hope you will support it ... my most respectful compliments
to Mrs. Harris;" 29 Dec. 1783. LP.

Deed to DANIEL GAINES of Amherst Co., Va., from Commissioners of
Confiscated Estates; 500 acres on Broad River adjoining land of Dempsey
Hinton, formerly held by James Gordon; John Talbert, J.P., and Job
Pray, witnesses; 10 Jan. 1784. HH, 24.

Deed to DANIEL GAINES of Amherst Co., Va., from Commissioners of Confiscated Estates; 500 acres adjoinging land of Drury Cade and 500 acres
at "Brewton Cabbins" formerly held by James Gordon; 15 Jan. 1784. HH, 26.

Bond from DANIEL GAINES of Amherst Co., Va., to Walton Harris of
Wilkes; Henry Mounger, Sampson Harris, Joel Harris, witnesses; 20 Aug. 1787.
LP.

Power of attorney from DANIEL GAINES (GAINS) of Wilkes executor under
will of Henry Gilbert, sometime of Hanover Co., Va., but late of Amherst
Co., Va., deceased, to William Goode, to collect debt from estate of
Stephen Terry, late of Craven Co., S.C., deceased; John Crutchfield, J.P.,
witness; 7 July 1788. DD, 91.

Deed to FELIX GILBERT of Virginia from John Ray and wife Mary; 400
acres on Uptons Creek; James Lane and Stephen Clement, witnesses; 17 Oct.
1786. EE, 171.

Deed to THOMAS GORDON, Merchant, of Virginia, from Richard Call and
wife Alethea Anderson of Washington Co., Ga.; 900 acres in Wilkes granted
said Call in 1786; Charles Odingsells, J.P., of Chatham Co., Ga., Robert
Montford, Nathaniel Pendleton, witnesses; 8 Oct. 1787. EE, 12.

Deed to ANTHONY GRIFFIN of Lunenburg Co., Va., from William Starke
of Wilkes; 200 acres granted said Starke in 1784; J. H. Foster and John
Wingfield, witnesses; 8 June 1785. Deed Book 1784-5, 25.

Judgment against ARCHELAUS HARRIS, obtained in Louisa Co., Va., in
favor of Edward Herndon as assignee of Thomas Wingfield; 11,000 pounds of
tobacco; 13 April 1784. LP.

Bill of Sale from ARCHELAUS HARRIS to John Talbot; livestock, personalty,
and interest in estate left to said HARRIS and wife by her mother, Frances
Smith, of Hanover Co., Va.; property in possession of Bartlett Smith of
Hanover; Hickerson Cosby and Price Bird, witnesses; 3 July 1788. DD, 196.

Inventory of estate of ARCHELAUS HARRIS, deceased; 3 volumes of
Wesley's Notes, Hymn Book, Prayer Book, Bible, a bay mare, etc., all in
State of Virginia; 27 Nov. 1792. LP.

Receipt from HOWELL HARRIS of Virginia to Nicholas Long; Ł 4.4.0 due said HARRIS by estate of David Coleman of Wilkes, deceased; 19 Feb. 1793. LP.

Deed to RICHARD HARVIE of Virginia from Henry Candler, administrator of estate of William Candler, deceased, of Richmond Co., Ga.; 300 acres on Broad River; Thomas Napier, J.P., and John Moore, witnesses; 3 Oct. 1787. BB, 2.

Deed to JOSEPH HUBBARD of Cumberland Co., Va., from John Reed and wife Caty of Wilkes; 180 acres on Macks Creek adjoining land of Thomas Moody; John Griffin, Robert Smith, Thomas Moody, witnesses; 3 May 1791. HH, 351.

Deed to NICHOLAS JOHNSON of Virginia from Bernard Kelley of Wilkes; 90 acres on Clouds Creek; David Ward and Samuel Gardner, witnesses; 1789. EE, 108.

Deed to NICHOLAS JOHNSON of Virginia from James Tate and wife Rebecca of Wilkes; land on waters of Clouds Creek; Samuel Gardner and Thomas N. Gilmore, witnesses; 10 Sept. 1789. EE, 110.

Deed to JOHN KING of Gloucester Co., Va., from Robert Middleton of Wilkes; 1000 acres on waters of Ogeechee River, part of 2150 acre tract granted to Benjamin Few; James Alford and John Rutherford, witnesses; 21 June 1785. AA, 176.

Deed to FRANCIS KIRTLY of Virginia from Benjamin Hart and wife Ann of Wilkes; 450 acres on Broad River granted said Hart in 1786; Joh Moore, J.P., witness; 10 Dec. 1790. HH, 308.

Deed to DAVID LOCKETT of Buckingham Co., Va., from Richard Fretwell and wife Frances of Wilkes and William Fretwell of Cumberland Co., Va.; 250 acres in Wilkes purchased by said Richard Fretwell in 1784; William Byram, Leonard Fretwell, James Wootten, James Alexander, William Hamilton, witnesses; 28 Sept. 1784. Deed Book 1784-5, 36.

Will of JOHN MARKS: wife Lucy; son John Haistens Marks; daughter Polly Garland Marks; to nephews Haistens and Peter Marks, sons of testator's brother Peter Marks, 1000 acres "on the western waters of Virginia, being part of 4000 acres due me for my service in the Continental Arme, if it be procured;" friends John Gilmer and Nicholas Johnson, executors; Henry Tyler, Thomas Meriwether, William Johnson, Francis Meriwether, witnesses; 22 March 1791. Will Book DD, 250.

Grant to DOUGLASS MARTIN of Virginia: himself, wife, son and 2 daughters aged 6 years to 4 months, headrights; 100 acres on waters of Little River; 13 Jan. 1775. CLC, 20.

Power of attorney from JOHN MOODY of Lunenburg Co., Va., to Peter Tatum of Wilkes to receive all lands said Moody may have in Georgia by grants or bonds; Howell Tatum, Wyatt Williams, John Williams, witnesses; 16 Nov. 1785. EE, 12.

Power of attorney from LITTLEBERRY MOSBY, JUNIOR, of Powhatan County, Va.
to John Talbot of Wilkes to convey all land held by said MOSBY in Georgia
to Thomas Glascock of Richmond Co., Ga.; Richard Mosby and Thomas Murray,
witnesses; 8 Sept. 1786. CC, 26.

Power of attorney from WILLIAM MURRAY to Matthew Talbot, junior, to
convey 265 acres of land in Bedford Co., Va.; John Talbot, J.P., Thomas
Talbot, John Baker, witnesses; 7 Oct. 1789. HH, 11.

Grant to JOSEPH NEAL of Virginia: himself, wife, 5 sons and 3 daughters
aged 16 to 1 years, headrights; 200 acres on Broad River "whereon the widow
Clark lives," resigned by Captain William Candler; 10 Oct. 1774. CLC, 19.

Grant to NEWDEGATE OWSLEY of Loudon Co., Va.: himself, wife, 3 sons
and 2 daughters aged 11 years to 3 months, headrights; 200 acres on Fishing Creek; 27 Sept. 1773. CLC, 1.

Promissory note from JOSEPH PANNILL and MICAJAH ANTHONY of Henry Co.,
Va., to William Mills of Hanover Co., Va.; 40 barrels of corn for rent of
a plantation on Matry Creek; 1 Dec. 1781. LP.

Grant to JOSHUA PARKS of Virginia: himself, wife, son and 2 daughters
aged 6 years to 4 months, headrights; 100 acres on waters of Little River;
13 Jan. 1775. CLC, 20.

Petition of John Wingfield that JOHN, CHARLES, and STEPHEN PETTUS
(PETTICE), sons of STEPHEN PETTUS, deceased, late of Hanover Co., Va., be
placed under guardianship of Garland Wingfield; March Court 1789. DD, 197.

Bond of Garland Wingfield as guardian of JOHN, CHARLES, and STEPHEN
PETTUS, sons of STEPHEN PETTUS, deceased, late of Hanover Co., Va.; John
Wingfield, surety; H. Mounger, witness; 5 Sept. 1789. LP.

Claim of NICHOLAS PORTER, JUNIOR, against Nicholas Porter, Senior; cash
paid Whitehead Coleman and William Grimes for hauling tobacco to Fredericksburg, Va., in 1773; sworn to in Botetourt Co. Va., 28 Oct. 1794. LP.

Estate account of NICHOLAS PORTER, deceased; affidavit of Hugh Walker
that said PORTER gave a bond in 1786, when said Walker lived in Orange
Co., Va., and that Joseph Porter paid the bond; 20 March 1793. LP

Deed of gift from JOSEPH ROBERTS of Pittsylvania Co., Va., to Daniel
Roberts; 10 Negro slaves, cattle and household goods; A. Bedell, J.P.,
and Thomas Watts, witnesses; 2 Dec. 1789. HH, 223.

Deed to ABRAHAM SIMONS of Spotsylvania Co., Va., from James Jack and
wife Peggy of Wilkes; 300 acres of land adjoining Benjamin Webster and
Thomas Carson, granted said Jack in 1787; William Barnett, witness; 13 Feb.
1789. EE, 87.

Power of attorney from FREDERICK SIMS of Wilkes to Drury Stith, Esq.,
of Brunswick Co., Va., to sell 543 acres of land on Meherrin River in
Brunswick to William Edwards Broadnax; 14 March 1788. DD, 32.

Power of attorney from CHARLES SMITH of Wilkes to George Smith "to settle all amounts due said CHARLES SMITH in Virginia;" Josiah Doss and Thomas Reynolds, witnesses; 3 Oct. 1785. Deed Book 1784-5, 43.

Power of attorney from FRANCIS SMITH of Wilkes to friend Francis Webb of Essex Co., Va., "to attend to all business in Virginia;" Jesse Heard, J.P., witness; 21 Nov. 1786. AA, 121.

Deed to GRIFFIN SMITH of Nottoway Co., Va., from John McClain and wife Marney of Wilkes; 200 acres on waters of Fishing Creek, in occupancy of Richard Heard; Acquilla House, Martha House, Richard Heard, witnesses; 16 Feb. 1791. HH, 278.

Bill of sale from RICHARD THOMPSON of Amherst Co., Va., to John Ross of Amherst; cattle and personalty; Richard Gilbert and Joshua Doss, witnesses; 29 Jan. 1787. DD, 3.

Grant to ELIJAH THURMOND of Virginia: himself, wife, son and 6 daughters aged 16 years to 10 months, headrights; tract on Pistol Creek, "the place where he now lived;" 10 Oct. 1774. CLC, 19.

Deed to JOHN THURMOND (THURMAN) of Chesterfield Co., Va., from Joseph Catching of Wilkes; 200 acres on Little River granted said Catching in 1784; Benjamin Catching, J.P., and Milly Catching, witnesses; 21 Sept. 1785. Deed Book 1784-5, 41.

Grant to GILES TILLETT of Virginia: himself, wife, 4 sons and 3 daughters aged 29 to 9 years, headrights; 500 acres at forks of Broad River; 16 Nov. 1773. CLC, 9.

Affidavit of ROBERT TOOMBS "of the State of Georgia," made in Culpeper Co., Va.; said TOOMBS entitled to 5 negro slaves by right of marriage with Sarah Catlett of Culpeper, and desires to remove said Negroes to Georgia; 15 Oct. 1798. LP.

Grant to JOHN WALKER of Virginia: himself and 2 slaves, headrights [page mutilated]; Feb. 1775. CLC, 21.

Grant to JOHN WEBB of Virginia: himself, wife, 5 sons and 2 daughters aged 20 to 3 years, headrights; 400 acres on Broad River adjoining land of John Coleman; 15 Oct. 1773. CLC, 5.

Grant to JOHN WESTBROOK of Mecklenburg Co., Va.: himself, wife, 3 sons and 4 daughters aged 20 to 2 years, headrights; 100 acres on Cootis Creek and Broad River; 13 Oct. 1773. CLC, 6.

Grant to THOMAS WILLIAMS of Virginia: himself, wife, 5 sons and 3 daughters aged 18 to 3 years, headrights; 350 acres on waters of Ogeechee River; 4 Nov. 1773. CLC, 7.

Bill of sale to THOMAS WINGFIELD, SENIOR, JOHN WINGFIELD, JUNIOR, and JOHN GRIMES, all of Hanover Co., Va., from George Walton "of the State of Georgia;" 1150 acres adjoining "Washington Town;" William Terrell and John

Wingfield, witnesses; 24 July 1783. Deed Book 1784-5, 86.

Deed to THOMAS WINGFIELD of Virginia from Michael Cupp and wife Barbary of Wilkes; tract on Rocky Creek; John Wingfield, J.P., James Smith, E. Butler, witnesses; 15 Dec. 1785. Deed Book 1784-5, 81.

Estate account of JOHN WINGFIELD, deceased, late of Wilkes: receipt of John Darracott and J. Hardin Foster for their proportionate parts of proceeds of sale of land in Virginia which said WINGFIELD left to his daughters; 1796. LP.

Deed to JESSE WITT of Henry Co., Va., from George Lumpkin and wife Ann of Wilkes; 400 acres on waters of Long Creek; Holman Freeman, Joseph Cook, John Hardiman, Robert Lumpkin, witnesses; 5 Jan. 1789. HH, 55.

Deed to GEORGE YOUNG of Virginia from George Lumpkin and wife Ann; 400 acres on Buffaloe Creek granted to said Lumpkin in 1785; 1786. CC, 4.

Note: Mr. Barlow's article as above appeared in The Virginia Genealogist, Vol. 2, No. 1, January-March 1958.

* * *
* *
*

The following was contributed by Mr. Thomas P. Hughes, Memphis, Tennessee:

VOLUME 26 - EAST TENNESSEE, HISTORICAL SOCIETY PUBLICATIONS 1954

1806 KNOX CO., TENN., TAX LIST FOOTNOTES
People who had Virginia connections and migrated to Tennessee

Townsend Dade by James Trimble (an Attorney from King George Co., Va. who returned.)
Fleshart Francis from Botetourt Co., Va., where he married 5-6-1794, Elizabeth Wysong.
John Hillsman, native of Amelia Co., Va.
Pleasant M. Miller, native of Campbell Co., Va. d. Gibson Co., Tenn. 4-26-1849.
Josiah Dodd m. Mary, daughter of Richard Luttrell of Amherst Co., Va.
John Witt, Sr., Rev. Sol. from Amherst Co., Va. (1740-1825)
John Childress who drew a pension for service in Va.
Curd Cox, b. 1762 in Charlotte Co., Va., S 3169
Abraham Hankins, Rev. Sol. who drew pension for Va. Militia
William Anderson, Rev. War Sol. Rockbridge Co., Va., 12-17-1830 died.
Moses Brooks, son of John Brooks and Ann Irwin, b. 4-1-1760 Augusta Co., Va.
Geo. McNutt, b. Ireland 1751; lived in Rockbridge Co., Va., Kings Mt. Men.
Gideon Cruise, Rev. Sol. from Amherst Co., Va. S 39371
William Dunn drew pension for service in Va. Militia.
Francis Merryman, pension for service in Va. Militia.
Cornelius Hickey, son of John Hickey whose will was pr. 12-25-1784
Abner Witt, desc. of French Hue. d. Rhea Co., Tenn.

David Clap, b. Orange Co., N. C., m. 4-22-1793 in Montgomery Co., Va.
    Betsy, daughter of Boston Graves and Sarah Ephland.
Robert Johnston (perhaps the man who drew pension for service in Va.
    Militia.)
Bostian Nosler from Montgomery Co., Tenn., see Summers.
Absalom Rutherford, Wythe Co., Va., Rev. Sol.
Samuel Sharp drew pension for Rev. Sol.
Roger Barton (7-9-1747 - 6-4-1822) native of Augusta Coo, Va.
Peter Bennett R 754, m. in King William Co., Va., ca 1773 Elizabeth P
    Pomfret.
Nicholas Bartlett, a Quaker from Greenbrier Co., Va.
James Price, Rev. Sol. for Virginia Service.
William Tipton, b. 2-13-1761, Shenandoah Co., Va. Rev. Sol. pension.

* * *
* *
*

CHARLES HUGHES HAMLIN AND HIS DAUGHTER, VICKI

HAMLIN EXCURSUS

This branch of the Hamlin family, whose records are
treated of in this section, migrated from Virginia to
North Carolina. Some of them later returned to Virginia
(among them, this compiler's branch.) Others migrated
to Kentucky, Georgia, etc., and their descendants are
now living in Ohio, Arizona, California, and most of
the other States.

To those who might think that this collection of records
of the author's own family is an imposition, I would like
to state that this chapter is an extra addition to
Volume 2, and the contents hereof are above and beyond
the contents contemplated originally.

THE BELL BIBLE AND THE HAMLIN BIBLE

There are two ancient, torn and tattered bibles in the carefully guarded possession of my aunt, Miss Martha Reamey Hamlin of Danville, Virginia. They have been much used by the elder generations and much abused by the uncontrolled little hands of four generations of children. In spite of their worn and shattered condition it is evident that they were once very handsome, expensive looking books. They have been known and called by members of the family for nearly 140 years, "the old BELL Bible" and "the old HAMLIN Bible."

A sheet in the middle of the "Bell"BBible indicates that it was "Published and Sold by Daniel D. Smith at the Franklin Juvenile Book and Stationery Store, No. 190 Greenwich Street and also by the Principal Book Sellers in the United States." Stereotyped by E. White, New York - 1820. A similar sheet in the "Hamlin" Bible is torn in half and the publisher and date is lost.

The original owners of the "Bell" Bible were Benjamin Bell (1790-1839) and his wife, Lydia Tucker (1795-1834) of Greenville, Pitt County, North Carolina (See Note 1). The Bible's next owner was their daughter, Sarah Ann, (1818-1872) who married first in 1841, Danial Arney, a Quaker from Philadelphia who settled in Rockingham County, N. C. Sarah Ann's second husband was Captain George W. Peay of Rockingham County who helped rear the only surviving child, Sarah Elizabeth, of the first union. This child, Sarah Elizabeth Arney (1848-1919) married 1866 Captain (CSA) Francis Mallory Hamlin of Rockingham County, N.C. and were the parents of thirteen children. She was the next owner of the "Bell"Bible and she and her husband were the original owners of the "Hamlin" Bible. There are naturally some duplication of entries in the Birth, Marriage, Death record sheets in the two Bibles. There are forty entries in the "Bell" Bible and sixty-three in the "Hamlin". The records of both Bibles are yellowed with age, the paper is brittle, the ink has turned a dark brown color, the entries seem to have been made in at least three different handwritings. In spite of the evident age of all the entries, the writing is remarkably clear and legible. It therefore gives this writer great pleasure to certify to all whom it may concern that the following transcript of the birth, marriage, and death records are true and correct copies of the original records as contained in the above mentioned Bibles. [Re-arranged by me.]

THE BELL BIBLE - MARRIAGES

Benjamin Bell and Lydia Tucker was married the 15th of January 1818.

Dannel Arney and Sarah Ann Bell was married the 19th of January 1837.

Joseph B. Bell and Jeffie Crutchfield were married December 12th, 1865.

Francis M. Hamlin and Sarah E. Arney were married Sept.25 [torn] (note 1866)

Barclay A. Hamlin and Mary Pace Talbott were married November 22, 1892.

James Turner   Hamlin and Mary N. Brown were married at Richmond Feb. 14, 1894.

Charles E. Hughes and Sallie Bell Hamlin were married August 5, 1895.

F. M. Hamlin Jr. and Daisy (White) have been married ( ) ( ) ( ) ( ) -

BIRTHS

Sarah, the daughter of Benjamin Bell and Lydia, his wife, was born the 19th October 1818 (Margin - died 21 March 1872 - 53 yrs 5 mo 2 days)

George, the son of Benjamin Bell and Lydia, his wife, was born the 11th day of Feby 1820 - (Margin - died 30 Aug 1823)

James Montgomery, the son of Benjamin Bell and Lydia, his wife, was born the 21st November 1821.

Samuel, the son of Benjamin Bell and Lydia, his wife, was born the 7 Octr. 1823.

Henry, the son of Benjamin Bell and Lydia, his wife, was born 9th May 1825.

George, the son of Benjamin Bell and Lydia, his wife, was born 23rd Feby. 1827.

Elias, the son of Benjamin Bell and Lydia, his wife, was born 25th Sept. 1828.

Joseph Benjamin, the son of Benjamin Bell and Lydia, his wife, was born 18th July 1833.

Benjamin Bell, the FATHER of Sarah, George, James, Samuel, Henry, George, Elias,and Joseph Bell, was born December 2, 1790. [This entry and the next were evidently made by Sarah Ann Bell after she married Daniel Arney and came into possession of the bible.]

Lydia Tucker was born February 19, 1795.

Barclay Arney, the son of Daniel Arney and Sarah, his wife, was born the 19th of September 1847.

Charlotte Ann Arney, the daughter of Daniel and Sarah, his wife, was born on the 12th day of August 1845.

Sarah Elizabeth Arney, the daughter of Daniel Arney and Sarah, his wife, was born February 14, 1848.

Barclay Arney Hamlin, the son of F. M. Hamlin and Sarah E. Hamlin, his wife, was born on Saturday night, the 5th of October 1867 - signed F. M. Hamlin.

J. Turner Hamlin born 13th of March 1869 - signed (FMH)

Francis Mallory Hamlin, Jr. was born the 14th of September 1870.

Sallie Bell Hamlin was born the 17th of April 1872.

Martha Reamey Hamlin was born August 23rd 1874 - Sunday morning 9 o'clock.

George Vance Hamlin was born Thursday (?) September 9th, 1876 -
(notation in same handwriting and ink that looks like "Centennial Boy".)

DEATHS

George Bell, son of Benjamin Bell and Lydia, his wife, departed this
life 30hh August 1823.

Lydia Bell, wife of Benjamin Bell departed this life the 10th day of
August 1834.

Benjamin Bell departed this life on the 2nd day of August 1839 being in
the 50th year of his life.

George Bell, son of Benjamin Bell and Lydia, his wife, departed this life
30th June 1857.

Charlotte Ann Arney, daughter of Daniel Arney and Sarah, his wife, departed this life 26th May 184_(?).

Barclay Arney, son of Daniel Arney and Sarah, his wife, departed this
life ( ) of December 1854.

Daniel Arney departed this life on the 22nd day of October 1856 being
about 49 years 6 months (0)? days of age.

Henry Bell, son of Benjamin Bell and Lydia, his wife, departed this life
the 15th of October 1859.

James Bell, the son of Benjamin Bell and Lydia, his wife, departed this
life 12 June 1860.

Samuel Bell departed this life August 21, 1869.

Sarah A. Peay died 21 March 1872 - Thursday 10 P.M. aged 53 years 5 mo.
2 days.

Francis Mallory Hamlin Jr. died Danville, Vigginia, July 7th, 1919 aged
48 years 9 months 24 days.
                [This is the last entry in the "Bell" Bible.]

THE HAMLIN BIBLE - MARRIAGES

What God hath joined together let not man put asunder. This certifies that the Rite of Holy Matrimony was celebrated between Francis Mallory Hamlin of Leaksville, North Carolina and Sarah E. Arney of Leaksville, North Carolina, on September 25, 1866 at George W. Peay's home by Mr. Dan Fields, Leaksville, North Carolina.

Barclay Arney Hamlin and Mary Pace Talbott were married November 22, 1892.

James Turner Hamlin and Mary Newell Brown were married Feb. 14, 1894.

Charles E. Hughes and Sallie Bell Hamlin were married August 5, 1895.

F. M. Hamlin Jr. and Daisy White were married October 15, 1901.

Charles Hughes Hamlin and Sallie Bell Hacker were married July 9, 1906.

Ella Bell Hamlin and Raleigh C. Gilliam were married August 29, 1906.

Kate Lay Hamlin and William Button McNeal were married June 3, 1908.

Sarah Arney Hughes and Richard Wilcox Taylor married Sept.(?) 1918

Edward Reamey Hamlin married Helen Norwood Oct. 30, 1923, South Boston, Va.

Charles Hughes Hamlin Jr. married Hallie Inez Williams Oct. 29, 1932, Marion, S.C.

Mary Elisabeth Hamlin, daughter of Charles H. and Sallie H. Hamlin, married Hugh Thomas Williams March 18, 1933 at Danville, Va.

Daisy Bell Hamlin, daughter of Charles H. and Sallie H. Hamlin married Reginald L. Wood June 8, 1935 at Danville, Va.

Talbott Barclay Hamlin, son of Barclay Arney and Mary Talbott Hamlin married Gladys M. Didawick September 10, 1936 at Richmond, Va.

Charles Edwin Hughes,III married Jeanette Kaufman _____(?)

Charles Hughes Hamlin Jr. married 2nd Anna Diltz Holton September 4, 1948 at Cincinnati, Ohio.

BIRTHS

Barclay Arney Hamlin, the son of Francis M. Hamlin and Sarah E. Arney was born on Saturday night, October 5, 1867.

James Turner Hamlin was born March 13, 1869.

Francis Mallory Hamlin, Jr. was born September 14, 1870.

Sallie Bell Hamlin was born April 17, 1872.

Martha Reamey Hamlin was born August 23, 1874.

George Vance Hamlin was born September 9, 1876.

Mary Virginia Hamlin was born January 16, 1878.

Charles Hughes Hamlin was born March 30, 1880.

Jeffie Bell Hamlin was born March 14, 1882.

Thomas Hamlin was born August 16, 1884.

Kate Ley Hamlin and Ella Bell Hamlin - our twins - were born Friday, May 20, 1887.

Edward Reamey Hamlin was born November 19, 1889 (?)

Talbott Barclay Hamlin, son of Barclay A. and May Talbott Hamlin was born August 29, 1893.

May Talbott Hamlin, daughter of Barclay A. and May T. Hamlin was born August 5, 1894.

James Turner Hamlin Jr., son of James T. and Mary B. Hamlin was born Nov. 6, 1896.

Sarah Arney Hughes, daughter of Charles E. and Sallie Hamlin Hughes was born July 6, 1897.

Charles E. Hughes, Jr., son of Charles E. and Sallie Hamlin Hughes was born July 1, 1899.

Elizabeth Arney Gilliam, daughter of Raleigh C. and Ella Bell Hamlin Gilliam was born June 13, 1907.

Charles Hughes Hamlin Jr., son of Charles H. and Sallie Hacker Hamlin was born August 25, 1907 at Barbourville, Kentucky.

Daisy Bell Hamlin, daughter of Charles H. and Sallie Hacker Hamlin was born July 1, 1908 at Manchester, Ky.

Mary Elisabeth Hamlin, daughter of Charles H. and Sallie Hacker Hamlin was born March 12, 1910 in Danville, Va.

William Hamlin McNeal, son of William B. and Kate Hamlin McNeal was born February 3, 1911.

Frank Hamlin McNeal, son of William B. and Kate Hamlin McNeal was born October 28, 1914.

Elizabeth Arney Taylor, daughter of Richard W. and Sarah Hughes Taylor was born June 10, 1919 at Asheville, N. C.

Charles Edwin Hughes III, son of Charles E. and Bernice Wyatt Hughes was born August 4, 1921 at Asheville, N. C.

Richard Wilcox Taylor Jr. son of Richard W. and Sarah Hughes Taylor was born February 24, 1923 at Asheville, N. C.

Hugh T. Williams Jr., son of Hugh T. and Mary Hamlin Williams, was born Decmmber 2, 1934 at Danville, Virginia.

Vicki Hamlin, daughter of Charles H. Hamlin Jr. and his wife, Hallie Inez Williams was born September 21, 1936 at Mullins, South Carolina.

Mary Dale Williams, daughter of Hugh T. and Mary Hamlin Williams was born April 19, 1937 at Danville, Va.

Sandra Susan Hughes, daughter of Charles E. Hughes III and his wife, Jeanette Kaufman was born December 7, 1946 at Palo Alto, Calif.

Sandra Kay Williams, daughter of Frank Hamlin Williams and his wife, Ovella Hardy was born March 13, 1955.

Hugh Thomas Williams III, son of Hugh T. Williams Jr. and his wife, Barbara (Batten) was born May 27, 1957.

HAMLIN - DEATHS

Daniel Arney died October 22, 1856 - aged 49 years plus.

Sarah A. Peay died March 21 (?) 1872 - aged 53 years 5 mo and 2 days.

Jeffie Bell Hamlin died at Danville, Va. June 15th 1884 - aged 2 yrs
    3 mo 1 day.

John C. Garrant died March 18, 1884 (?)

Lizzie Guerrant died June 8th, 1884.

George W. Peay died Feb. 24th, 1887 - aged 79 years and 16 days.

Thomas Hamlin died September 15, 1892 - 8 years and one month.

Mary Talbott Hamlin, wife of Barclay Arney Hamlin, died Oct. 11, 1894.

May Hamlin, daughter of Barclay A. and Mary T. Hamlin, died Aug. 21 (?)
    1895.

Sarah Arney Hamlin, wife of Francis M. Hamlin died Dec. 8, 1919 age 71 years.

Sallie Hacker Hamlin, wife of Charles Hughes Hamlin, died July 29, 1927.

Francis Mallory Hamlin, son of Thomas Hamlin and his wife, Martha Ann Reamey, died July 14, 1929, age 82 yaars 2 months 11 days [note: born May 3, 1847.]

Charles Hughes Hamlin, son of F. M. Hamlin and his wife, Sarah, died
May 19, 1938, at Danville, Va.

Charles E. Hughes, Jr., died Phoenix, Arizona, July 3, 1944.

This ends the recordings as revealed by both the old "Bell" Bible
and the old "Hamlin" bible. It is to be regretted that there are several
marriages, deaths, and births which have not been recorded and which
should properly be included. However, all the available space has been
utilized and it would be impossible to add further to these records.
There are a dozen or more newspaper clippings relative to events not
recorded which have evidently been placed there for future reference.

Note 1: Refer to an article by this compiler titled, "A letter of
Proposal" which appeared in The North Carolinian of March 1957, pps.
261-2, which treats of Benjamin Bell and his wife, Lydia Tucker, the
original owners of the "Bell" bible.

> Certified to be a true, correct and accurate
> copy of the contents of the two bibles, above
> described.
> -- Charles Hughes Hamlin

* * *

The following records were not contained within the pages of the
Hamlin Bible as three generations completely filled the available
pages. However, they were kept in meticulous note form along with
many newspaper clippings, etc. The dates have been re-checked and
confirmed and have been re-arranged by the compiler for easier com-
prehension.

James Turner Hamlin, Senior, born March 17, 1869, Leakesville, N.C.
died July 17, 1955, Danville, Virginia (see Bible record) married
February 14, 1894 to Mary Newell Brown, daughter of Colonel John
Thompson Brown (C.S.A.) Their only child -

Col. James Turner Hamlin, Jr. (W.W. 1 and W.W. 2 Veteran) born November 6,
1896, Danville, Virginia, married November 10, 1925, to Ellen Chester
Davis (called Nell) in Fernandina, Florida, who was born January 15, 1900,
Crandall Plantation, Nassau County, Florida, daughter of Charles
Jefferson Davis (b. Feb. 15, 1861) and his wife, Nellie Snow Davis
(b. July 10, 1872.) Their three children -

1. Dr. James Turner Hamlin III, born February 6, 1929, Danville, Virginia,
   graduated VMI 1951 (B.S.) Graduated Pre-med, University of Virginia.
   Married June 9, 1955 to Mary Gaston Caperton of Slab Fork, West
   Virginia, daughter of S. Auston Caperton and Helen Mason, his wife.
   Issue:

    a.   Helen Austin Hamlin, born August 18, 1957
    b.   Mary Davis Hamlin, born June 17, 1959
    c.   James Turner Hamlin IV, born December 11, 1964

2. Nell Marie Hamlin, born August 28, 1930, Danville, Virginia. Graduatedated Randolph-Macon Woman's College, Lynchburg, Virginia 1952. Married William Hundley Jefferson, Jr., September 2, 1961, son of William Hundley Jefferson, Sr. and Alice Gunn, his wife. Issue:

    a.   William H. Jefferson III, born August 6, 1962.
    b.   Nell Turner Jefferson, born October 1, 1963.

3. Jefferson Davis Hamlin, Lt. (jg) U. S. Naval Reserve, born March 27, 1932, Danville, Virginia. Graduate University of Virginia. Married Maude Winborne Leigh 27 June 1959, daughter of Dr. Southgate Leigh (M.D.) and Maude Winborne, his wife. Issue:

    a.   Jefferson Davis Hamlin, Jr., born March 3, 1964.

Mary Elisabeth Hamlin, attorney, daughter of Charles Hughes Hamlin, Sr. and Sallie Bell Hacker, his wife, born March 12, 1910, Danville, Virginia. Married March 18, 1933 Hugh Thomas Williams, attorney, Danville, Virginia (see Bible record). Their three children:

1. Hugh Thomas Williams, Jr., born December 19, 1933, Washington, D.C. (Lieutenant, Senior Grade, U. S. Navy Coast Guard) Married Barbara Anne Batten, July 5, 1956. Issue:

    a.   Hugh T. Williams, III, born May 27, 1957, Danville, Virginia.

2. Frank Hamlin Williams, born December 2,,1934, Danville, Virginia. Professional Accountant. Married Ovella Gay Hardy, April 24, 1954. Issue:

    a.   Sandra Kay Williams, born March 13, 1955, Danville, Va.
    b.   Robin Leslie Williams, born January 18, 1962.
    c.   Frank Hamlin Williams, Jr., born July 13, 1964.

3. Mary Dale Williams, born April 19, 1937, Danville, Virginia. Married William Duane Kaufman, March 18, 1959. Issue:

    a.   Mary Theresa Kaufman, born December 23, 1960.
    b.   Kathryn Anne Kaufman, born June 12, 1963.

* * *

ROCKINGHAM COUNTY, NORTH CAROLINA - RECORDS -

Deed Book Y, page 212 -

Sixth Monday after the fourth Monday in March 1824 - In the petition of Robert Menzies and others, heirs-at-law of John Menzies, dec'd., for the sale and distribution of real estate - the following decree was made (to wit) - To expose to public sale a certain tract of land, etc. - and whereas the same was sold on the third day of September (1824) to THOMAS HAMBLIN for $6100.00 - Now conveys to THOMAS HAMBLIN OF THE COUNTY OF CHARLOTTE, COMMONWEALTH OF VIRGINIA, a certain tract of land in the County of Rockingham, State of North Carolina - on the Dan River, at the mouth of Matrimony Creek - crossing Buffalo Creek, etc. - containing 609 acres, etc. - Recorded December session 1824.

COMMENT: The above cited Thomas Hamlin (SENIOR) (born 1765) was the son of Charles Hamlin Junior (died 1786) of Lunenburg County, Virginia and his wife, Agnes Cocke (died 1800) who was the daughter of Abraham Cocke Senior of Amelia County, Virginia. We have seen records of this Thomas Hamlin (Senior) in Lunenburg and Brunswick Counties, Virginia, and now he is denoted as being of "Charlotte County, Va." It will be remembered that Thomas Hamlin (Senior) had married first, Elizabeth Cross, who died in 1806 or 1807 and that he married secondly, Mary Ligon Stainback in 1808. Issue by both marriages.

Deed Book Z, page 80 -

May 10, 1825 - Indenture in which George D. Winston of the County of Rockingham, North Carolina sells to THOMAS HAMLIN OF THE SAID COUNTY AND STATE - for $8478.75 - a tract of land in said county containing 997½ acres - adjoining lands of Joseph Martin - en the Island ford road - on the lines of Webster - Thomas Barnett - Winston - Martin, etc. Witnesses: JAMES DILLARD - James Kyle - Recorded: May Session 1825.

Deed Book "2nd C" page 103 -

Indenture dated 11th August, 1831 in which THOMAS HAMLIN (Senior) of the County of Rockingham, State of North Carolina - gives, grants, conveys, sells, etc., to JOHN HAMLIN (SON OF THE SAID THOMAS HAMLIN) - of the same County and State - for the natural love and affection which he hath and beareth unto the said JOHN HAMLIN, HIS SON, and also for the better maintainance and preferment of the said JOHN HAMLIN - a tract of land in said County - on the east side of Smith's River and the North side of Dan River, it being one half of a tract of 997½ acres of land the said THOMAS HAMLIN purchased of George Winston - which half is the western part and contains 498-3/4 acres, etc. Witnesses: G. L. Coleman, A. A. Moris.

COMMENT: The above cited John Hamlin was the son of Thomas Hamlin (Senior) and his first wife, Elizabeth Cross (d. 1806-7). John Hamlin married in 1829 Elizabeth (called 'Betsy') Moman Dillard, daughter of James Dillard Senior (died 1859) of Rockingham Co., N.C. (see his will in said County - Will Book C, page 289.)

Deed Book "2nd E" page 126 -

Indenture dated ..... 1832 in which THOMAS HAMLIN (SENIOR) of
Rockingham County, North Carolina conveys, sells, etc., to PETER S.
HAMLIN, SON OF THE SAID THOMAS HAMLIN, OF THE SAME COUNTY AND STATE -
for $500.00 - a tract of land in said county - adjoining lands of
James Aiken - Col. Joseph Martin - JOHN HAMLIN - Winston's line,
etc. containing 498-3/4 acres, etc.

COMMENT: The above cited Peter Stainback Hamlin was the son of
Thomas Hamlin Senior and his second wife, Mary Ligon Stainback. He
was born in 1808 or 1809, died 1891 - married Virginia Ann Michaux
(1812-1889) daughter of Richard W. Michaux and his wife, Mary Mayo
Macon. Peter Stainback Hamlin and his wife, Virginia Ann, removed
to Calloway County, Kentucky in 1838 and became the progenitures of
the Hamlin Branch there. (Of this, more later.)

Deed Book "2nd H" page 312 -

Deed of Gift dated 30 August 1837 in which THOMAS HAMLIN SENIOR
of the County of Rockingham, North Carolina conveys to CHARLES HAMLIN,
SON OF THE SAID THOMAS HAMLIN, of the same County - for natural love
and affection and for the better maintanence and preferment of the
said Charles Hamlin, his son, and for $1.00 - a certain tract of land
situated and being in THE COUNTY OF MONTGOMERY, STATE OF TENNESSEE - on
the waters of Cumberland River, adjoining lands of Edward Niblett -
J. Martin, and others - it being the same tract of land purchased by
the said Thomas Hamlin Senior of STEPHEN COCKE and containing 360 acres,
etc. Witnesses: William M. Michaux - James M. Shelley - P. S.
Hamlin. Recorded August term 1837.

COMMENT: The above cited Charles Hamlin (died 1899 Rockingham Co.,
N. C.) was son of Thomas Hamlin Senior and his 2nd wife, Mary Ligon
Stainback. He never married.

Deed Book "2nd I" page 82 -

Indenture dated 26th October 1838 in which PETER S(TAINBACK)
HAMLIN of the County of Rockingham, N. C. sells to THOMAS HAMLIN
SENIOR of the same County and State - for $5000.00 - a tract of
land containing by estimate 498-3/4 acres, etc. Witnesses: George
L. Aiken - D. W. Tinsley - Richard Johnston. Recorded: November
term 1838.

COMMENT: Thus we see that Peter Stainback Hamlin is selling back
to his father for $5000.00 the same land which was given to him
in 1832 for a token payment of $500.00 and is evidently preparing
to take his family on the long trip west into Kentucky. He was
thirty years of age at this time. The next record indubitedly con-
nects him with Rockingham County, N.C. from Calloway County, Ky.

Deed Book "2nd N" page 294 -

Indenture dated 28th November 1843 in which Peter Stainback Hamlin
OF THE COUNTY OF CALLOWAY, STATE OF KENTUCKY sells to Charles Hamlin of
the County of Rockingham, N. C. - for $100.00 - his interest of one-third
of a certain town lot and house in the Town of Leakesville, N. C. on
Washington Street - it being the same lot purchased by Thomas Hamlin,
George L. Aiken, and Peter Stainback Hamlin - trading under the name,
style, and firm of 'Hamlin, Aiken and Company' and purchased from
William P. Adams, etc. Witnesses: John D. Grogan, Jesse W. Michland (?).

Deed Book "2nd S" page 10 -

Deed of Gift dated 25 June 1852 in which THOMAS HAMLIN SENIOR of
Rockingham County, N.C. gives and conveys to THOMAS HAMLIN JUNIOR of
the same county and state - "for natural love and affection" which he
hath and bears unto his son, the said THOMAS HAMLIN JUNIOR and for $1.00
a certain tract of land called "The Meadows" - on the road from Leakesville to Danville - it being the same tract of land once given to and
then repurchased from Peter S. Hamlin by the said Thomas Hamlin Sr.,
containing 498-3/4 acres of land and does also give to the said Thomas
Junior the following named slaves, viz., William and Rhoda and her two
children, etc. Recorded February term 1853.

COMMENT: The above cited Thomas Hamlin Junior was the son of Thomas
Hamlin Senior and his second wife, Mary Ligon Stainback and was born in
1810 as shown by the 1850 Census of Rockingham County, N. C. (he died
in 1859 - see abstract of his will, later). It should be noted here that
there is recorded in the original marriage bonds of Rockingham County in
the Archives of the North Carolina Historical Commission, Raleigh, N.C.
(page 102) the marriage bond of Thomas Hamlin Junior to Sarah Jane
McCormick, dated December 16, 1835 - Francis J. Lawson, Security and
J. Holderby, Clerk. It is strongly suspected by this compiler that this
is a first marriage of our ancestor altho there is no mention or reference
to it among the family papers. She must have died shortly after the
marriage. Thomas Hamlin Junior married 2ndly (?) in 1844 Martha Ann
Reamey (1818-1875) daughter of James Sanford Reamey and his wife, Letitia
Hughes, of Henry County, Virginia. This was also the second marriage of
Martha Ann Reamey who had married first (in 1839) Dr. Erasmus D. Jones,
son of George Washington Jones. There was one child of her first marriage, namely, Mary Eleanor Jones.

Deed Book "2nd S" page 110 -

Deed of Gift from THOMAS HAMLIN SENIOR (dated April 7, 1853) to
CHARLES HAMLIN, HIS SON, both of Rockingham County, N. C. - for natural
love and affection and $1.00 - a certain tract of land in said county,
on the south side of Dan River and also the following slaves (to wit) -
Henry, Richmond, Archer, George, Davy, Lucy, Tence, Winny, Mary, Nelly,
Nash, and Benton, etc. Witnesses: George L. Aiken, James Dillard.
Recorded: September 7, 1853.

Deed Book "2nd S", page 111 -

Deed of Gift dated 7th April 1853 (same date as above D of G)
from THOMAS HAMLIN SENIOR of Rockingham County, N. C. to HIS DAUGHTER,
LUCY HAMLIN, "for natural love and affection" a tract of land, including
"The Island", on the north side of Dan River, known as "The Scotland
Tract" purchased by the said Thomas Hamlin from MENZIE'S heirs and also
fhe following negro slaves (to-wit) - Daniel, Robin, Maurice, Peter,
Thomas, William, Maria, Belgy, Dolly, Clara, Sam, Blackwell, and Louisa,
etc. Recorded September 7, 1853.

COMMENT: Lucy Hamlin was the daughter of Thomas Hamlin Senior and his
2nd wife, Mary Ligon Stainback and died in 1899. Like her brother,
Charles Hamlin, she never married. In neither of the two above cited
deeds of gift is the number of acres involved shown. It has however been
shown above that the 'Menzie' heirs had sold him in 1824, 609 acres of
land.

Deed Book "2nd O" page 449 -

Indenture dated 12th August 1846 in which JOHN HAMLIN of the County
of Rockingham, N. C. sells to THOMAS HAMLIN JUNIOR of the same County
and State - for $4500 - a tract of land in what is commonly called "The
Meadows" - adjoining the lands of George W. Peay - said Thomas Hamlin Jr.,
Leakesville,road - Broadnax line - to Blue Creek, etc. containing 498-3/4
acres of land - it being the same land given to the said JOHN HAMLIN BY
HIS FATHER, THOMAS HAMLIN SENIOR, etc. Witnesses: George L. Aiken,
Drury C. Dillard. Recorded: May Term 1847.

COMMENT: The above cited John Hamlin was the half brother of the above
Thomas Hamlin Junior. After making the above sale of land, John Hamlin
removed to Rockford, in Surry County, N. C. with his family and remained
there until 1861 when he moved to Yadkin County, N. C. (Booneville).

1850 Census, Rockingham County, N. C. -(No. 28 - Eastern District)

THOMAS HAMLIN (JR), white, male, born in Va., age 40
    (thus born 1810) estate valued $10,000.00)
MARTHA HAMLIN, white, female, born in Va., age 30-
M. E. JONES, white, female, age 10,born in N. C.
T. HAMLIN, white, male, age 4, born in N. C.
F. H. HAMLIN, white, male, age 3, born in N. C.
M. L. HAMLIN, white, female, age 1, born in N. C.

COMMENT: The above cited individuals are identified as follows:
    Martha Hamlin, wife of Thomas Hamlin, was formerly Martha
    Ann Reamey.

    M. E. Jones was the daughter of her lastmarriage to Dr. Erasmus
D. Jones and was named Mary Eleanor Jones.

T. Hamlin was Thomas Hamlin the third (eldest son)
F. M. Hamlin was Francis Mallory Hamlin (2nd son)
M. L. Hamlin was Mary Ligon Hamlin (3rd child)

Will Book C, page 309 -

Will of THOMAS HAMLIN (JUNIOR) of Rockingham County, N. C. dated
August 20, 1859 - (no date of probate given.)

Leaves bequests to his wife, Martha A. Hamlin and to his step-
daughter, Mary Eleanor Jones -

The following children named (all to share and share alike) -

Thomas Hamlin

Francis Mallory Hamlin

Mary Ligon Hamlin

Charles S(anford) Hamlin

James H(ughes) Hamlin

Edward R(eamey) Hamlin

Executors: brother, Charles Hamlin, and wife, Martha A. (Ann)
Hamlin. Witnesses: George L. Aiken and George W. Peay.

Deed Book "2nd Y", page 94 -

Division of the lands of THOMAS HAMLIN (JR) DEC'D., February
Term 1868 (The land was evidently held together until all the
children had arrived at legal age.)

Mrs. Martha Hamlin	161 acres	$1500.00
Thomas Hamlin	150 acres	1500.00
Francis M. Hamlin	161 acres	1500.00
Mary L. Guarrant, wife of Jno. C. Guarrant	179 acres	1500.00
Charles S. Hamlin	150 acres	1500.00
James H. Hamlin	175 acres	1700.00

Tenants in common of the real estate divided to them as the
children of the late Thomas Hamlin, dec'd.   Signed -

George L. Aiken
George W. Peay
John W. Brodnax
J. Turner Morehead

Recorded May Term 1868.

COMMENT: The last named child ; in the will of Thomas Hamlin, i.e.,
Edward Reamey Hamlin, must hat have survived as he is not shown in the
above division. Note that the number of acres in the division amounted
to 976 acres.

Deed Book "2nd V", page 596 -

Indenture dated 20 February 1859 in which LUCY HAMLIN of the
County of Rockingham, N. C. sells to R. R. Robinson of the same county,
for $537.50, a tract of land on the waters of Buffalo Creek, adjoining
the lands of P. J. Carter - said R. R. Robinson (formerly John Grogan's)
on the road from Leakesville to Madison - containing 30-3/4 acres, etc.
Witnesses: John M. Reynolds, Thomas Reynolds. Recorded August Term 1860.

Will Book F, page 138 -

Will of Lucy Hamlin, dated 26th March 1899 - probated May 2, 1899.

To my brother, Charles Hamlin, all of my property of every kind,
both real and personal - to be held and used by him as long as he shall
live - after his death, I desire that said property so willed shall be
the property of Charles S. Hamlin and James H. Hamlin, my nephews and
my niece, Lucy Hamlin Guerrant, to be held by them in equal parts and
shares. My old servant, Mariah, shall be supported during her life.
Witnesses: R. N. Howard, John D. Martin.

Deed Book A, page 179 -

Indenture dated 4th October 1786 in which Michael Henderson of the
County of Surry, N.C. sells to GEORGE HAMBLIN OF ROCKINGHAM COUNTY, N.C.
for 100 pds., a tract of land on the west fork of Upper Hogan's Creek,
adjoining lands of Williams and Brasher, containing 165 acres, etc.
Witnesses: William Williams, James Reagan, JOSEPH HAMBLIN.

COMMENT: The above cited George and Joseph Hamblin have not been
identified by this compiler as yet. They may have been descendants of
George Hamlin of Worcester County, Maryland who moved to Charlotte
County, Virginia about 1776.

Will Book C, page 289 -

Will of James Dillard, Senior of Rockingham County, N. C., dated
15 July 1853. Probated February Court 1859.

To my beloved wife (not named but known to be Lucy C.) - one
third part of my lands, six slaves, $500.00 in money, etc.

TO MY DAUGHTER, BETSY HAMLIN, a negro girl, Malinda, and her
increase from this day, besides Dilce and all her offspring,
which last woman and her children are already in her possession.

To my daughters: Lucy Jane Aiken - Martha R. Martin - Ruth Martin - Agness (?) -

To my sons: John - Drury - James - all my land subject to the life of their mother -

To Richard Johnson, a negro boy, Charles, now in his possession and at his death to my granddaughter, Mary Ann Reynolds.

Executors: son-in-law, George L. Aiken and son, John H. Dillard.

Witnesses: James W. Burton and CHARLES HAMLIN.

Will Book C , page 338 -

Will of Drury C. Dillard of Rockingham County, N. C. dated 20th April 1860, probated August Court 1860.

To my mother, Lucy C. Dillard - (Mentions terms of the will of his father, James Dillard, dec'd.)

To Doctor R. R. Robinson the refusal of my negro girl, Emity, and her increase at cash valuation in accordance with my penal bond in his possession.

To my brothers - (not named) -

To Bettie W. Aiken, my saddle horse known by the name of Sam Patch.

CODICIL - dated May 1, 1860 - George L. Aiken to be my executor and Trustee for my mother - The word legatee in the above will and testament applies only to those who are living at this time and their representatives - To John H. Dillard - James P. Dillard - E.M. Hamlin- L. J. Aiken - M.R.D. Martin ÷ A. M. Robinson - (evidently his brothers and sisters) -

To my sister, E. M. HAMLIN (Elizabeth Moman Hamlin) my buggy or vehicle that I ride in, provided I have one at the time of my death. If there is not one on hand, I give to her $150.00 or $75.00 over an equal share to purchase one for her, etc.

CODICIL - To pay for and neat gilt frames of three portraits - one for my sister, L. J. Aiken - one to M. R. Martin and one to Agnes M. Robinson - To Dr. Robinson my medical books and instruments. It is my earnest desire that my heirs make every reasonable effort, in view of past services, to get Wade back to Tampa with his wife, even make a sacrifice, etc.

Proved by the oaths of James W. Burton - CHARLES HAMLIN - Thomas Reynolds.

COMMENT: The two above cited wills of James Dillard Senior and of his son, Drury Dillard, are shown as they prove the identity of the wife of John Hamlin (son of Thomas Senior and his 1st wife, Elizabeth Cross) as being Elizabeth Moman Dillard, daughter of James Dillard Senior and sister of Dr. Drury Dillard.

PITTSYLVANIA COUNTY, VIRGINIA - RECORDS -

1880 Census, Pittsylvania County, Va. (City of Danville):

Fourth Ward, page 29, Paxton Avenue, house No. 256, family #273 -

FRANK M. HAMLIN	W M age 32 Grocer - b NC, parents born Va.
Sarah E.	B F age 32 wife	b NC " " N.C.
Barkley	W M age 12 son
J. Turner	W M age 11 son
Frank M.	W M age 9 son
Sallie B.	W F age 8 daughter
Martha R.	W F age 5
George V.	W M age 3 son
Mary V.	W F age 2 daughter
CHARLES H.	W M age 2/12 son
Terry Lawson	B F age 21 servant

Ibid - (Next house - #255, #272)

JOHN C. GUERRANT	W M age 39 Lumber Merchant b. Va., parents N.C.
Mary L.	W F age 30 wife	b.N.C., parents Va.
William	W M age 12 son	b.N.C.
Lucy	W F age 10 daut.	b.N.C.
Peter	W M age 8 son	b. N.C.
Pattie	W F age 3 daut.	b. Va.
Carrie	W F age 42 sister	b. N.C.
Ann Brown	B F age 30 servant	b. N.C.

Third Ward - Main Street (page 5, #62 - 75)

THOMAS HAMLIN	White Male age 32 Lawyer, single, born N.C.
William Harris	White Male age Lawyer - (Boarder)

Page 20 - #174 - 260:

EDWIN HUGHES	White male age 51 - Saloon Keeper - b.N.Y.parents N.Y.
Jennie	White female 44 - wife b. Mass.,parents Mass.
Charles	White male 7 - son b. Va.,parents NY, "

COMMENT: I think these are the parents of Charles E. Hughes who married Sallie Bell Hamlin, daughter of Francis M. Hamlin, and his wife, Sarah Elizabeth Arney. Hold for future reference.

The Thomas Hamlin, Lawyer, as cited on page 107, is the elder brother of Captain Francis Mallòry Hamlin.

Mary Ligon (Hamlin) Guerrant cited above is the sister of Thomas add Captain Francis Mallory Hamlin.

* * *

ORIGINAL MARRIAGE BONDS OF ROCKINGHAM COUNTY, NORTH CAROLINA IN THE ARCHIVES OF THE NORTH CAROLINA HISTORICAL COMMISSION, RALEIGH, NORTH CAROLINA (NOTE: ROCKINGHAM COUNTY FORMED 1785 FROM GUILFORD COUNTY, N.C.

page 102 - THOMAS HAMLIN JUNIOR TO SARAH JANE McCORMICK, BOND DATED DECEMBER 16, 1835 - Francis J. Lawson, Security - J. Holderby, C. C.

COMMENT: This record must be a first marriage of which we know nothing. He married secondly, Martha Ann Reamey (Jones).

page 102 - FRANCIS M. HAMLIN TO SARAH E. ARNEY, BOND DATED 24th SEPTEMBER 1866, SURETY, JOHN C. GUENNANT (GUERRANT) (NOTE: THEY MARRIED SEPTEMBER 25, 1866.)

page 99 - MARY L(IGON) HAMLIN TO JOHN C. GUERRANT BOND DATED 18th DECEMBER 1866 - A. B. GALLAWAY, SURETY - A. P. SMITH, CLERK - MARRIED 20th DECEMBER 1866 by C. C. DODSON, M.G. NOTE: This was the sister of grandpa (Francis Mallory Hamlin.)

page 132 - MARTHA A. RANEY (SHOULD BE RAMEY) TO ERASMUS D. JONES, SEPTEMBER 25, 1839, WILLIAM P. ADAMS, SURETY - WILLIAM M. ELLINGTON, WITNESS. (NOTE: THIS IS THE FIRST MARRIAGE OF MARTHA ANN RAMEY, WHO MARRIED SECONDLY, THOMAS HAMLIN JR.. - MARY ELEANOR JONES IS THE ONLY CHILD BORN OF THE FIRST MARRIAGE.)

page 131 - CAROLINE L. REAMEY TO ADOLPHUS D. JONES, 18th FEBRUARY 1843 - JAMES C. WALKER, SURETY - T. B. WHEELER, CC. NOTE: Caroline L. Reamey was a sister of Martha Ann Reamey and they both married b brothers. They were daughters of JAMES SANFORD REAMY AND HIS WIFE, LETITIA HUGHES, OF HENRY COUNTY, VIRGINIA. The Jones brothers whom they married, i.e., Erasmus D., and Adolphus Dorsett, were both physicians and were the sons of George Washington Jones and his wife, Salina Dunlap, of Henry County, Virginia. George Washington Jones was the son of DR. BENJAMIN JONES and his wife, Elizabeth Ramey.

* * *

Thomas Hamlin, Senior, born circa 1765-6 (1850 census) in Lunenburg County, Virginia, died November 8, 1857 in Rockingham County, North Carolina, was the son of Charles Hamlin, Junior (died 1786, Lunenburg County, Virginia) and his wife, Agnes Cocke, daughter of Abraham Cocke, Senior, and his wife, Mary (maiden name unproven.)

Thomas Hamlin, Senior, married twice. First, to his first cousin, Elizabeth Cross, daughter of John Cross, who had married in 1765 in Amelia County, Elizabeth Cocke, also a daughter of Abraham Cocke, Senior and his wife, Mary. He married, secondly, May 5, 1807, Mary Ligon Stainback, daughter of Peter Stainback, Senior. Issue by both marriages as follows:

Issue by first wife, Elizabeth Cross:

1. William Hamlin - dsp
2. Jane Hamlin - dsp
3. John Hamlin, married 1829 Elizabeth Moman Dillard (b.1811) and removed to North Carolina with his father, Thomas Hamlin, Sr. issue six children.*

Issue by second wife, Mary Ligon Stainback:

4. Peter Stainback Hamlin - removed to Kentucky
5. Charles Hamlin - dsp 1897
6. Lucy Hamlin - dsp 1897
7. Thomas Hamlin - (1810-1859) married Martha Ann Reamey (Jones) (1818-1875), daughter of James S. Reamey and Letitia Hughes, his wife, of Henry Co., Virginia, issue five children:

    a. Thomas Hamlin
    b. Mary Ligon Hamlin
    c. Captain Francis Mallory Hamlin
    d. Charles Sanford Hamlin
    e. James Hughes Hamlin

*-Note: The issue of John Hamlin and his wife, Elizabeth M. Dillard were:

    a. Jane Cross Hamlin, b. 1831
    b. Sally Jane Hamlin, b. 1832
    c. Mary Ann Hamlin, b. 1836
    d. Thomas Hamlin, b. 1838
    e. Lucy Dillard Hamlin, b. 1844
    f. James Dillard Hamlin, b. 1847

Lunenburg County Will Book 3, page 252 -

Last Will and Testament of Charles Hamlin, Junior of the Parish of Cumberland, County of Lunenburg, dated 5 March 1786, probated 14 September 1786.

Legatees:

Wife, Agnes Hamlin, land in Lunenburg and Amelia
counties, slaves, etc.
Son, John Hamlin (underage) - land, slaves
Daughter, Tabitha Batte
Daughter, Lucy Hamlin
Daughter, Mary Hamlin
Daughter, Martha Hamlin
Son, Thomas Hamlin - land (1150 acres in Lunenburg
county) slaves, etc.
Executors, son, Thomas Hamlin and friends, Stephen Cocke
and John Cross.

Comment: The above Charles Hamlin, Junior[6] (Charles[5], Captain John[4],
Captain John[3], Stephen[2] Stephen Hamlin[1]) was born 1734 and married in
Amelia County, December 28, 1757, Agnes Cocke[5] (1737-1800) daughter of
Abraham Cocke[4] (Stephen Cocke[3], Captain Thomas Cocke[2], Lt.Col. Richard
Cocke[1] of Henrico County.)

The marriages of the above cited children of Charles and Agnes
(Cocke) Hamlin are as follows - (not listed in order of birth):

1. John Hamlin married Mary Williams 1809

2. Thomas Hamlin (married twice as cited above)

3. Tabitha Hamlin married 1785 James Batte, son of Captain
   William Batte and his wife, Sarah Parham.

4. Lucy Hamlin married first Michael McKie (d. 1797)
   (one child, Martha Cocke McKie, b. 1787 who married
   William Hewett Powell in 1802. Lucy Hamlin (McKie)
   married secondly in 1801, Warning Peter Robertson
   (died testate 1814), no known issue.

5. Mary Hamlin married 1798 William Colgate Boswell.

6. Martha Cocke Hamlin married 1800 Thomas Taylor of
   Mecklenburg County, Virginia.

CHART 1
HAMLIN FAMILY OF VIRGINIA

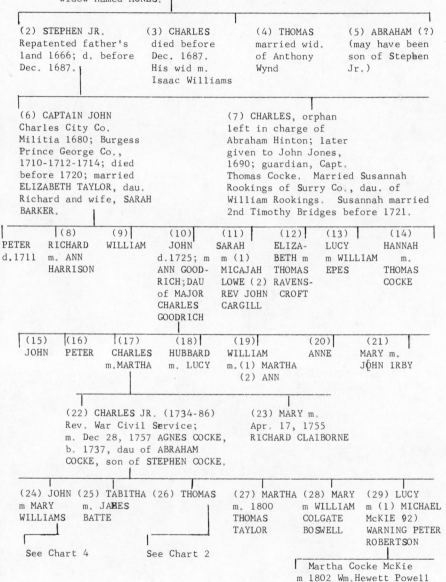

(1) STEPHEN HAMELYN (qv) Emigrant to Virginia before 1638;
died before August 23, 1665; Burgess from Charles City
County 1654, again 1663; Justice of County Court; Left
widow named AGNES.

(2) STEPHEN JR.
Repatented father's
land 1666; d. before
Dec. 1687.

(3) CHARLES
died before
Dec. 1687.
His wid m.
Isaac Williams

(4) THOMAS
married wid.
of Anthony
Wynd

(5) ABRAHAM (?)
(may have been
son of Stephen
Jr.)

(6) CAPTAIN JOHN
Charles City Co.
Militia 1680; Burgess
Prince George Co.,
1710-1712-1714; died
before 1720; married
ELIZABETH TAYLOR, dau.
Richard and wife, SARAH
BARKER.

(7) CHARLES, orphan
left in charge of
Abraham Hinton; later
given to John Jones,
1690; guardian, Capt.
Thomas Cocke. Married Susannah
Rookings of Surry Co., dau. of
William Rookings. Susannah married
2nd Timothy Bridges before 1721.

PETER
d.1711

(8)
RICHARD
m. ANN
HARRISON

(9)
WILLIAM

(10)
JOHN
d.1725; m
ANN GOOD-
RICH;DAU
of MAJOR
CHARLES
GOODRICH

(11)
SARAH
m (1)
MICAJAH
LOWE (2)
REV JOHN
CARGILL

(12)
ELIZA-
BETH m
THOMAS
RAVENS-
CROFT

(13)
LUCY
m WILLIAM
EPES

(14)
HANNAH
m.
THOMAS
COCKE

(15)
JOHN

(16)
PETER

(17)
CHARLES
m.MARTHA

(18)
HUBBARD
m. LUCY

(19)
WILLIAM
m.(1) MARTHA
(2) ANN

(20)
ANNE

(21)
MARY m.
JOHN IRBY

(22) CHARLES JR. (1734-86)
Rev. War Civil Service;
m. Dec 28, 1757 AGNES COCKE,
b. 1737, dau of ABRAHAM
COCKE, son of STEPHEN COCKE.

(23) MARY m.
Apr. 17, 1755
RICHARD CLAIBORNE

(24) JOHN
m MARY
WILLIAMS

(25) TABITHA
m. JAMES
BATTE

(26) THOMAS

(27) MARTHA
m. 1800
THOMAS
TAYLOR

(28) MARY
m WILLIAM
COLGATE
BOSWELL

(29) LUCY
m (1) MICHAEL
McKIE 92)
WARNING PETER
ROBERTSON

See Chart 4

See Chart 2

Martha Cocke McKie
m 1802 Wm.Hewett Powell

112

CHART 2
HAMLIN FAMILY OF VIRGINIA

(26) THOMAS HAMLIN, son of CHARLES and AGNES (COCKE) HAMLIN, born
in Lunenburg Co., Va. ca 1765, died in Rockingham Co., N. C. in
1857. Married 1st in Charlotte Co., his first cousin ELIZABETH
CROSS, who died and he married 2nd, MARY LIGON STAINBACK, daughter
of PETER STAINBACK and his wife, MARY LIGON. Issue by both
marriages:-

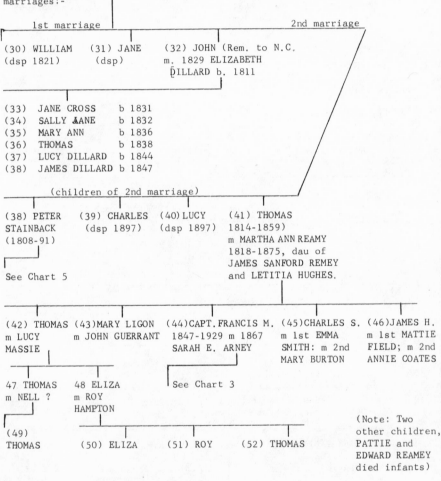

1st marriage   2nd marriage

(30) WILLIAM   (31) JANE   (32) JOHN (Rem. to N.C.
(dsp 1821)   (dsp)   m. 1829 ELIZABETH
                             DILLARD b. 1811

(33) JANE CROSS   b 1831
(34) SALLY JANE   b 1832
(35) MARY ANN   b 1836
(36) THOMAS   b 1838
(37) LUCY DILLARD   b 1844
(38) JAMES DILLARD b 1847

(children of 2nd marriage)

(38) PETER   (39) CHARLES   (40) LUCY   (41) THOMAS
STAINBACK   (dsp 1897)   (dsp 1897)   1814-1859)
(1808-91)   m MARTHA ANN REAMY
                                             1818-1875, dau of
                                             JAMES SANFORD REMEY
See Chart 5   and LETITIA HUGHES.

(42) THOMAS (43) MARY LIGON   (44) CAPT. FRANCIS M. (45) CHARLES S. (46) JAMES H.
m LUCY   m JOHN GUERRANT   1847-1929 m 1867   m 1st EMMA   m 1st MATTIE
MASSIE   SARAH E. ARNEY   SMITH: m 2nd   FIELD; m 2nd
                                                      MARY BURTON   ANNIE COATES

47 THOMAS   48 ELIZA   See Chart 3
m NELL ?   m ROY
             HAMPTON
                                                      (Note: Two
(49)   other children,
THOMAS   (50) ELIZA   (51) ROY   (52) THOMAS   PATTIE and
                                                      EDWARD REAMEY
                                                      died infants)

CHART 3
HAMLIN FAMILY OF VIRGINIA

(44) CAPTAIN FRANCIS MALLORY HAMLIN, born Rockingham County, North Carolina
May 3, 1847 died Danville, Va. July 14, 1929. Served in Confederate Army
in Co. "K", 3rd Regt., 72nd N. C. Troops, Armisteads Brigade, Hokes Div.,
Johnstons Army. Married Sept. 25, 1867 SARAH ELIZABETH ARNEY, born Feb. 14,
1848, died Danville, Va. Dec. 8, 1919, daughter of DANIEL ARNEY of Philadelphia, Pa. and Rockingham Co., N. C. and his wife, SARAH BELL, dau. of
BENJAMIN BELL and LYDIA TUCKER.

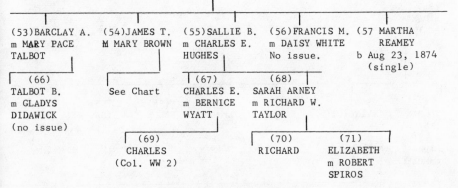

(53)BARCLAY A.   (54)JAMES T.   (55)SALLIE B.   (56)FRANCIS M.   (57 MARTHA
m MARY PACE   M MARY BROWN   m CHARLES E.   m DAISY WHITE   REAMEY
TALBOT   HUGHES   No issue.   b Aug 23, 1874
                                                               (single)

(66)   (67)   (68)
TALBOT B.   See Chart   CHARLES E.   SARAH ARNEY
m GLADYS   m BERNICE   m RICHARD W.
DIDAWICK   WYATT   TAYLOR
(no issue)

          (69)   (70)   (71)
          CHARLES   RICHARD   ELIZABETH
          (Col. WW 2)   m ROBERT
                                                      SPIROS

CHILDREN OF CAPTAIN FRANCIS MALLORY HAMLIN CONTINUED:

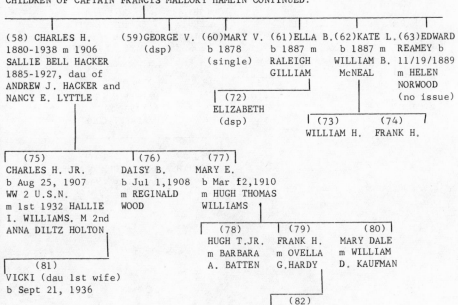

(58) CHARLES H.   (59)GEORGE V.   (60)MARY V.   (61)ELLA B.(62)KATE L.(63)EDWARD
1880-1938 m 1906   (dsp)   b 1878   b 1887 m   b 1887 m REAMEY b
SALLIE BELL HACKER   (single)   RALEIGH   WILLIAM B. 11/19/1889
1885-1927, dau of   GILLIAM   McNEAL   m HELEN
ANDREW J. HACKER and   NORWOOD
NANCY E. LYTTLE   (72)   (no issue)
                                    ELIZABETH
                                    (dsp)   (73)   (74)
                                                          WILLIAM H.   FRANK H.

   (75)   (76)   (77)
CHARLES H. JR.   DAISY B.   MARY E.
b Aug 25, 1907   b Jul 1,1908   b Mar f2,1910
WW 2 U.S.N.   m REGINALD   m HUGH THOMAS
m 1st 1932 HALLIE WOOD   WILLIAMS
I. WILLIAMS, M 2nd
ANNA DILTZ HOLTON   (78)   (79)   (80)
                                   HUGH T.JR.   FRANK H.   MARY DALE
   (81)   m BARBARA   m OVELLA   m WILLIAM
VICKI (dau 1st wife)   A. BATTEN   G.HARDY   D. KAUFMAN
b Sept 21, 1936
                                               (82)
                                             SANDRA

NOTE: TWO OTHER CHILDREN, (64) JEFFIE B. and (65) THOMAS DIED in early childhood.

114

CHART 4
HAMLIN FAMILY OF VIRGINIA

(24)
JOHN HAMLIN, son of CHARLES HAMLIN JR., and his wife, AGNES
COCKE, married MARY WILLIAMS: Issue -

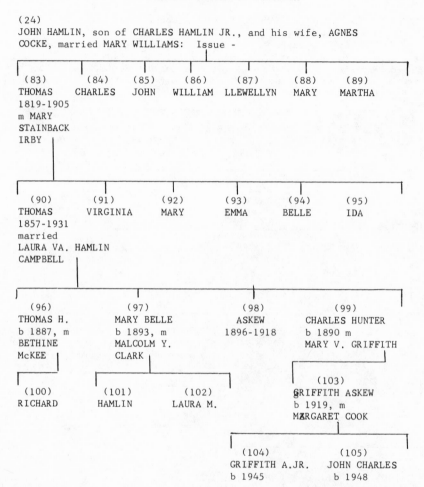

(83)   (84)   (85)   (86)   (87)   (88)   (89)
THOMAS   CHARLES   JOHN   WILLIAM   LLEWELLYN   MARY   MARTHA
1819-1905
m MARY
STAINBACK
IRBY

(90)   (91)   (92)   (93)   (94)   (95)
THOMAS   VIRGINIA   MARY   EMMA   BELLE   IDA
1857-1931
married
LAURA VA. HAMLIN
CAMPBELL

(96)   (97)   (98)   (99)
THOMAS H.   MARY BELLE   ASKEW   CHARLES HUNTER
b 1887, m   b 1893, m   1896-1918   b 1890 m
BETHINE   MALCOLM Y.   MARY V. GRIFFITH
McKEE   CLARK

                                                      (103)
(100)   (101)   (102)   GRIFFITH ASKEW
RICHARD   HAMLIN   LAURA M.   b 1919, m
                                            MARGARET COOK

                                          (104)   (105)
                                          GRIFFITH A.JR.   JOHN CHARLES
                                          b 1945   b 1948

CHART 5
HAMLIN FAMILY OF VIRGINIA

(38) PETER STAINBACK HAMLIN, born 1808, died 1891, son of
THOMAS HAMLIN and his wife, MARY LIGON STAINBACK, married
VIRGINIA ANN MICHAUX, born 1812, died 1889, daughter of
RICHARD W. MICHAUX and MARY MAYO MACON, Moved from Rock-
ingham County, N. C. to Calloway County, Kentucky in 1838.

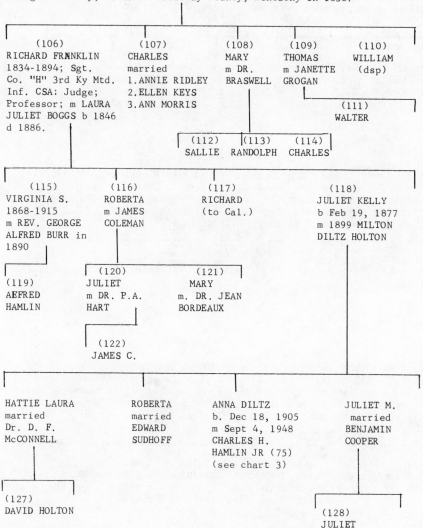

(106)
RICHARD FRANKLIN
1834-1894; Sgt.
Co. "H" 3rd Ky Mtd.
Inf. CSA: Judge;
Professor; m LAURA
JULIET BOGGS b 1846
d 1886.

(107)
CHARLES
married
1. ANNIE RIDLEY
2. ELLEN KEYS
3. ANN MORRIS

(108)
MARY
m DR.
BRASWELL

(109)
THOMAS
m JANETTE
GROGAN

(110)
WILLIAM
(dsp)

(111)
WALTER

(112)   (113)   (114)
SALLIE   RANDOLPH   CHARLES

(115)
VIRGINIA S.
1868-1915
m REV. GEORGE
ALFRED BURR in
1890

(116)
ROBERTA
m JAMES
COLEMAN

(117)
RICHARD
(to Cal.)

(118)
JULIET KELLY
b Feb 19, 1877
m 1899 MILTON
DILTZ HOLTON

(119)
AEFRED
HAMLIN

(120)
JULIET
m DR. P.A.
HART

(121)
MARY
m. DR. JEAN
BORDEAUX

(122)
JAMES C.

HATTIE LAURA
married
Dr. D. F.
McCONNELL

ROBERTA
married
EDWARD
SUDHOFF

ANNA DILTZ
b. Dec 18, 1905
m Sept 4, 1948
CHARLES H.
HAMLIN JR (75)
(see chart 3)

JULIET M.
married
BENJAMIN
COOPER

(127)
DAVID HOLTON

(128)
JULIET

CHART 6
HAMLIN FAMILY OF VIRGINIA

(38) JAMES DILLARD HAMLIN, son of JOHN HAMLIN (32) and his wife,
ELIZABETH DILLARD, was born in Surry County, N. C. Feb. 20, 1847.
Married in Forsythe Co., N.C. August 1875 MOLLIE L. FALGER,
daughter of MILTON Y. AND BETTY (GRAY) FALGER. He was a merchant,
planter, and for four years was sheriff of Yadkin Co.

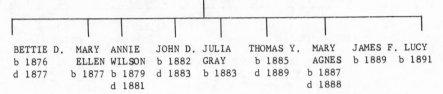

BETTIE D.	MARY	ANNIE	JOHN D.	JULIA	THOMAS Y.	MARY	JAMES F.	LUCY
b 1876	ELLEN	WILSON	b 1882	GRAY	b 1885	AGNES	b 1889	b 1891
d 1877	b 1877	b 1879	d 1883	b 1883	d 1889	b 1887		
		d 1881				d 1888		

* * * * * *

(46) JAMES HUGHES HAMLIN, son of THOMAS HAMLIN (41) and MARTHA ANN
REAMEY was born in Rockingham County, N.C. in 1853. He married 1st in
that county, MARY (or MATTIE) daughter of THOMAS FIELD. She died in
1881. No issue. He married 2nd in 1885, ANNA, daughter of DANIEL
COATES (or COURTS) of Reidsville, N. C.

(138)	(139)	(140)	(141)	(142)
THOMAS	FRANCIS	JAMES	MARY LIGON	"BROWNIE"
b 1885				
(died)				

* * * * * *

(43) MARY LIGON HAMLIN, daughter of THOMAS HAMLIN (41) and MARTHA ANN
REAMEY was born 1849 in Rockingham Co., N. C. and married there on
Bond 18 Dec 1866 to JOHN C. GUARRENT who was born in Pittsylvania Co.,
Va. ca 1844. He was a mechanical genius and invented a tobacco steam-
ing machine, the patent of which was considered of great value. He d
died in March 18__

(143)	(144)	(145)	(146)	(147)	(148)	(149)	(150)
WILLIAM	LUCY	PETER	JOHN	MARY	MARTHA	LIZZIE	JOHN C. JR.
ROULETT	b 1869	DUTAY	twin	twin	REAMY	b 1880	b 1884
b 1867		b 1871	died	died	(PATTIE)	d 1884	
					B 1875		

CHART 7

HAMLIN FAMILY OF VIRGINIA

(Col.) James Turner Hamlin, Jr., born November 6, 1896, son of James
Turner Hamlin Sr., (see Chart 3) and Mary Newell Brown, his wife,
married November 10, 1925, Ellen Chester Davis, born January 15, 1900,
daughter of Charles Jefferson Davis, (born Feb. 15, 1861) and his wife,
Nellie Snow, (born July 10, 1872.)

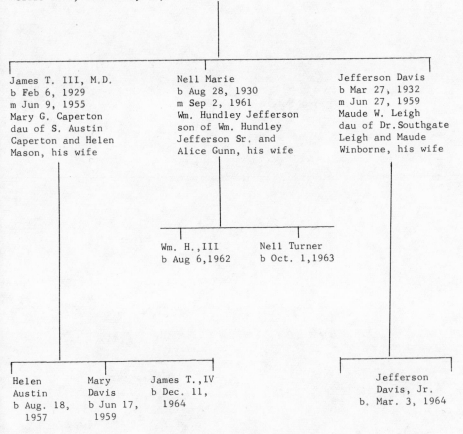

James T. III, M.D.
b Feb 6, 1929
m Jun 9, 1955
Mary G. Caperton
dau of S. Austin
Caperton and Helen
Mason, his wife

Nell Marie
b Aug 28, 1930
m Sep 2, 1961
Wm. Hundley Jefferson
son of Wm. Hundley
Jefferson Sr. and
Alice Gunn, his wife

Jefferson Davis
b Mar 27, 1932
m Jun 27, 1959
Maude W. Leigh
dau of Dr. Southgate
Leigh and Maude
Winborne, his wife

Wm. H., III
b Aug 6, 1962

Nell Turner
b Oct. 1, 1963

Helen
Austin
b Aug. 18,
1957

Mary
Davis
b Jun 17,
1959

James T., IV
b Dec. 11,
1964

Jefferson
Davis, Jr.
b. Mar. 3, 1964

(1)

Kentucky (continued)

Bourbon	43,53
Bracken	68
Bryants Station	70
Calloway	101,102
Christian	6,50,51
Clarke	38
Covington (City)	68,69,71
Fayette	69
Franklin	48,49,50
Green	27,43
Harrison	53
Henderson	46
Hopkins	50
Hopkinsville (Town)	50
Leesburgh (Town)	53
Lincoln	39,40
Livingston	25,47
Louisville (City)	70
Manchester (Clay Co.)	96
Mason	14,49,68
Mecklenburg	51
Newport (City	72,75
Scott	53
Shelby	75,79
Washington	26
Wayne	78
Western Waters	8,60,85
Woodford	21,22,55

Louisiana

Not specified	45

Maryland

Not specified	12,15,16,51
	54,56,65
Baltimore (City)	41,50,51
	60,64,66
Charles	24,53,54,56
Dorchester	65
Fort Cumberland	57
Frederick	57
Somerset	41,42
Snow Hill Town	16
Worcester	16,41,105

Massachusetts

Boston	42,73
Salem	28
Suffolk	42

Missouri

Not specified	21
Jackson	77,78

Missouri (continued)

Saline	4,78
Van Buren	79

New Jersey

Not specified	51
Burlington	5
East Jersey	59
Nassau Hall College	59
Princeton	58
Western Division of	5

New Mexico

Raton	69

New York | 61,73

Jamaica	61
Long Island	28,66
New York City	73
Rochester	74
Rye	66
Westchester	66

North Carolina

Not specified	8,9,12,13,19
	28,30,34,35,36,40
	48,73,79,109
Albemarle	30,32,35
Asheville (City)	96,97
Bertie	34,35,36
Buncombe	37,73
Burke	71
Bute	11,12
Cabarras	31
Caswell	76
Cateret	47
Craven	23
Edgecombe	10,11,29
Fayetteville	25
Franklin	45
Granville	11,33,40,47
Greensboro	25
Greenville	92
Guildford	19,41
Halifax	7,9,10,11,12,16,29
Hawkins	24
Leakesville	95,98,102
Montgomery	23
Marrattic River	30
Newbern	12
Northampton	7,9,10,12,25
	29,32,44,45,79,80,81
Orange	21,29,47,74
Oxford	25

North Carolina (continued)
```
    Pitt                      92
    Quaker Meadows            71
    Raleigh                   79
    Rockingham    25,76,77,92,100,101
       102,103,104,105,106,108,109
    Stokes                    77
    Surry                 77,103
    Wake                      23
    Warren                    25
    Washington                77
    Wilkes                    34
    Yadkin                   103
```

Ohio
```
    Not specified         4,20,56
    Champaign                 78
    Cincinnati    67,68,69,70,71,72
                       73,74,75,95
    Clermont                  40
    Hamilton                  73
    Lawrence                  77
    Logan                     22
    Marietta                  75
    Norwood                68,69
    Piqua                     70
    Preble                    79
    Sebring                   73
    Toledo                    75
    Zanesville                71
```

Pennsylvania
```
    Berks                  19,74
    Bucks                     19
    Centre                    49
    Chester                   26
    Cumberland             21,33
    Franklin               54,65
    Lancaster                 43
    Miersburg                 54
    Philadelphia           24,25,54
                           55,73,92
    Union Township            19
    Wayne                     69
```

South Carolina
```
    Not specified     6,37,39,53,83
    Abbeville District        44
    Craven                    84
    Fairfield                 36
    Greensville               46
    Marion                    95
    Mullins                   97
    Union                      6
```

Tennessee
```
    Anderson                  28
    Blount                    27
    Davidson                  27
    Franklin                  31
    Grainger                  53
    Gibson                    88
    Hawkins                   77
    Jackson                   44
    Knox             14,46,88,89
    McMinn                    30
    Memphis                   88
    Montgomery            89,101
    Rhea                      88
    Roane                  27,28
    Robinson                  46
    Williamson                27
    Wilson                     7
```

Texas   62

Virginia
```
    Not specified     67,68,69,70
    71,73,74,75,82,83,84,85,86
                           87,88
    Accomack             32,41,42
    Albemarle     34,39,54,69,71
                           76,83
    Amelia     68,88,100,109,110
    Amherst   76,77,83,84,87,88
    Augusta     2,19,20,21,26,27
       28,39,54,71,72,74,88,89
    Bedford      37,60,69,82,86
    Berkeley (W.Va.)      19,74
    Botetourt              86,88
    Brunswick        8,9,22,23
              79,80,81,86,100
    Buckingham             44,85
    Cabell (W.Va.)            39
    Campbell                  88
    Caroline     2,3,4,7,8,68,75
    Charles City       28,29,34
    Charles River             28
    Charlotte  82,83,88,100,105
    Chesterfield       28,46,87
    Culpeper    21,22,33,48,49
       50,51,55,67,69,72,75
    Cumberland        4,5,71,85
    Danville        92,94,95
       96,97,98,99,102,107
    Dinwiddie                 47
    Eastern Shore         15,16
    Elizabeth City        13,14
    Essex              20,82,87
```

(3)

Virginia (continued)

Fairfax	17,55,56,57,58,73
Falmouth	72
Fauquier	25,53,54,67,70,72
Fincastle	60
Franklin	45,46
Frederick	5,17,40
Fredericksburg	26,86
Gloucester	59,62,63
	64,65,66,85
Goochland	76
Grayson	41
Greenbrier (W.Va.)	89
Greensville	37,44,45,81
Halifax	6,7,46,47
Hampshire (W.Va.)	14,24,57
Hanover	72,84,86,87
Hardy (W.Va.)	40
Henrico	28,29,30,47,48,110
Henry	24,76,83,86
	88,102,108,109
Isle of Wight	10,32,36,79
Kilmarnock	79
King & Queen	20,61
King George	88
King William	89
Lancaster	15,17
Loudoun	17,86
Louisa	38,39,43,44,53,84
Lunenburg	1,82,84
	85,100,109,110
Lynchburg	99
Madison	48
Mathews	62,66
Mecklenburg	1,30,31,35,36
	39,40,82,83,87,110
Mercersville	28
Middlesex	17
Montgomery	46,89
Nansemond	13,35
New Kent	11,71
Norfolk	13,35,61
Northumberland	14,15,16
	17,18,19,79
Nottoway	31,87
Ohio (W.Va.)	75
Orange	1,2,4,38,55,70,86
Patrick	77,78,79
Petersburg	25
Pittsylvania	32,83,86,107
Powhatan	86
Prince Edward	82
Prince George	22,23,24,25
Prince William	67,68,69

Richmond	17
Richmond (City)	72,93,95
Rockbridge	54,88
Shenandoah	14,33,40,42
	43,49,89
Southampton	9,10,37
South Boston	95
Spotsylvania	48,69,86
Stafford	57,68,72,73
Surry	9,10,11,12
	32,34,35,80
Sussex	10
Washington	20
Westmoreland	17
Williamsburg	28,59,60,61
Wythe	34,89
Yorktown	69,70

Washington, D.C.	58,99
West Indies	60
West Virginia (See Virginia)	
Slab Fork	98

GENERAL INDEX

Atkinson		Ballard	
(Capt.) John	29	Edward McClure	67
Roger	47	(Lieut) William	67
Atwood		Barbee (Barber)	
James	79	Bersheba (Harris)	25
		Joseph	25
Autry			
Elizabeth	82	Barbour	
Jacon	82	Ambrose	46
Avant		Barker	
Thomas	35	John	11
		Joshua	10
Aycock		Sarah	111
James	82		
Richard	82	Barlow	
William	82	Lundie	81
Ayers		Barnes (See Barns)	
William	77	Francis	83
		Henry	19
Ayscough		Mary	19
Henry	48		
		Barnett	
Bailey (see also Baillie)		Thomas	100
Anselm, Jr.	10,32	William	86
Benjamin	10		
John	12	Barns (See Barnes)	
Mary	12	William	2
Michael	11		
William	12	Barr	
		John	18
Baillie (see also Bailey)			
Andrew	54	Barrett	
		Lewis	82
Bain			
Elizabeth	63	Bartlett	
Nancy	63	Nicholas	89
Warner	63		
		Barton	
Baker		Roger	89
John	86		
Richard	24	Baskins	
Susannah	6	John Craig	27
Baldwin		Bass	
Thomas	83	Burgess	37
Ball		Basye	
(Capt.) David	17	Isaac	19
Isaac	6		
(Col.) Spencer	15	Bates	
(Capt.) Williamson	17	Joseph	4

Blanchard
Aaron 13

Bland
John (Esq.) 24
Mary 24
(Capt.) Theodrick 68

Bledsoe
Abraham 55
Benjamin 55
Elizabeth 55
George 55
George, Jr. 55
Isaac 55
Jacob 55
James 55
Joannah 55
John 55
John, Jr. 55
Joseph 55
Lucy 55
Moses 50
William 55

Blow
George 10
John T., Sr. 10
John T., Jr. 10

Boggess
Giles 16
Keziah 16

Boggs
Laura Juliet 115

Bolden
Lawrence & Co. 61

Bond
Elizabeth (Long) 48
Jesse 41
John 48

Boon(e)
Squire 75
William 80

Booth
Abijah 77
Daniel 77
Mary (Cooke) 64
Thomas 63,64

Bordeaux
(Dr.) Jean 115
Mary (Coleman) 115

Boswell
Mary (Hamlin) 110,111
Wm. Colgate 110,111

Bowen
John, Jr. 9
Mary 9

Bowles
Eleanor 65
James 65

Bowman
(Capt.) Isaac 43
(Dr.) James 30

Boyd
Agnes 17
Alexander 17,18
David 17,18
Mary 17
Margaret 17
Millie (Hall) 18

Boyer
Colonel 69

Bozman
Anne 33

Bradford
John 41,82

Bradley
Benjamin 29

Bragg
Benjamin 82
James 36
Mary 36

Brammar, (Mr.) 58

Brammer
Frances (Tuggle) 78
Lucy (Tuggle) 78
Shadrack 78
William 78

Branch
John 7

Brassfeild			Bronaugh	
George	3		(Miss)	57
Brasswell			Brookes (See Brooks)	
Charles	115		John	29
(Dr.)	115		Brooking	
Mary (Hamlin)	115		(Lt.Col.) Vivian	68
Randolph	115			
Sallie	115		Brooks (See Brookes)	
			Alexander	22
Brent			Ann (Irwin)	88
(Capt.) Hugh	67		Joab	29
(Capt.) William	68		John	29,88
			John (2nd)	29
Brewster			John, (Jr.)	29
John P. Harrison	70		Moses	88
			Robert	22
Bridges			Thomas	21,22
Joseph	35		William	22
Susanna	35			
Susanna (Hamlin)	111		Brough	
Timothy	111		Charles M.	14
William	35		Franklin	14
			Jane	14
Briggs			John	14
George	10			
			Brown	
Bright			Ann (Col.svt.)	107
H.	25		Anne	2
			Bedford	82
Bristow			Hezekiah	50
Benjamin	79		James	6
Henry	79		(Capt.) John	68
James	79		(Col.) John Thompson	98
Jasper	79		Mary Newell	93,95,98,113,117
John Harris	79		Sarah (Long)	49,50
Joseph Lewis	79		Watkins	6
Peyton	79		William	18
Samuel	79			
Sarah	79		Brownlee	
Sarah (Jr.)	79		Florence (Duncan)	27
Thomas	79		James	27
William	79			
			Bruin	
Brittle			(Capt.) Peter Bryan	68
John	80			
			Bryan	
Broadnax			(Rev.) Corbin Braxton	63
Betty	29		Elizabeth T. (Coalter)	63
Edward	29		John Randolph	63
John W.	104		Joseph	63
Wm. Edwards	86			
			Buchanan	
Brockenbrough			Elizabeth (Duncan)	27
Newman	82		(Continued)	

(9)

Buchanan, continued
    (Capt.) James   69
    Samuel   27

Buckner
    (Capt.) Phillip   68

Buford
    Abraham   31
    James   82
    John   31
    William   32

Bunch
    Joseph   53
    Mary   53

Bunkley
    Jesse   82
    Joshua   82
    Mary   82

Burk(s)
    John   21,83

Burnett
    Nancy (Tuggle)   78
    Reuben   78

Burnley
    Israel   83

Burns
    John   25,76
    Sarah A.L.   25

Burr
    Alfred Hamlin   115
    (Rev.) Geo. Alfred 115
    Virginia S. (Hamlin) 115

Burrough(s)
    Richard   61
    Robert   61

Burt
    Joseph   33

Burton
    Hutchins   30
    James   106
    John   31
    Mary   112
    Presley   31

Burwell
    Lewis   59
    (Maj.) Lewis   62
    Lucy (Higginson)   62

Butler
    Aaron   36
    E.   88
    Lawrence   14
    (Lt.Col.) Wm.   52

Butts
    Edmund   37
    Jesse G.   37
    Thomas C.   37

Bynum
    Briton   45
    Francis   45

Byram
    Mrs. Frank F.   76
    William   85

Byrd (See Bird)
    John Upshaw   72,75
    William   47,48

Cade
    Drury   84

Caldwell
    John   42

Call
    Alethea Anderson   84
    Richard   84

Callaway
    James   46

Calwell
    Joshua   15

Campbell
    Archibald   12
    (Capt.) Charles   69
    Colin   12
    (Maj.) Collin   10
    Colonel   67
    Hayes and   61
    Laura V.H. Hamlin 114
    Rebecca   33

Candler	
Henry	85
William	85
(Capt.) Wm.	86
Caperton	
Helen (Mason)	98,117
Mary Gaston	98,117
S. Austin	98,117
Cargill	
Cornelius	8
(Rev.) John	111
Sarah H. (Lowe)	111
Carlin	
Daniel	24
Carlyle	
John	56
Carnagie	
Andrew	33
Angus	33
James	33
Sarah	33
Carncross	
Joseph	61
Carpenter	
Sarah	16
Carr	
William	59
Carrell	
Mary	12
Carson	
Thomas	48,86
Carter	
Jacob	29
P.J.	105
Carver	
William	12
Catching	
Benjamin (J.P.)	87
Joseph	87
Milly	87
Cather	
James Hamilton	71

Catlett	
Ann Walker Carter	66
(Capt.) James Baytop	66
Lucy Taliaferr	66
Sarah	87
Cease	
Henry	27
Chalfant	
William	41
Champion	
Benjamin	10
Benjamin, Sr.	10
Charles	11
Elizabeth	10
Hart	10,11
John	11
William	10
Chichester	
Richard	58
Childers	
Thomas	29
Childress	
John	88
Childs	
Captain	69
Chiles	
John	39
Matilda	39
Chism	
Ann (Long)	50
Richard	50
Choat	
Edward, Sr.	46
Christian	
Israel	60
Richard	28
Turner Hunt	28
Clack(e)	
James	65
Mary	65
Samuel	27
William	65
Claiborne	
Mary (Hamlin	111
Richard	111

Clap
Betsy (Graves)	89
David	89

Clark(e)
(Gen.) George Rogers	70
Hamlin	114
Laura M.	114
Malcolm Y.	114
Mary B. (Hamlin)	114
widow	86

Clay
Green	42

Clayton
Samuel	43

Clear
Mary	12

Clement
Stephen	84

Coalter
Elizabeth Tucker	63

Coates
Anna	112,116
David	116

Cockburn
Martin	57
Mrs.	57

Cocke
Abrham (Sr.)	100,109,110,111
Agnes	100,109,110,111
Elizabeth	109
Elizabeth W. (Lee)	25
Hannah (Hamlin)	111
Hartwell	11
Mary	109
Peter H.	25
(Lt.Col.) Richard	110
Stephen	101,110,111
Thomas	111
(Capt.) Thomas	110,111

Coke
Elizabeth (Moss)	36
Richard	62
(Sen.) Richard	62

Coleman
David	85
Eliza (Arnett)	53
G. L.	100
James	115
John	87
Juliet	115
Mary	115
Robert	53
Roberta (Hamlin)	115
Whitehead	86

Coles
Edward	16
Edward, Jr.	16
Elizabeth	16
John	16
Richard	16
William	16

Collier
Vines	83

Collins
George Richard	54
James Alpheus	75

Conway
Alce	16
Edwin	18
Francinah	16
(Capt.) George	15
James	16

Cook(e)
Edward N.	44
(Col.) John	57
Joseph	88
Margaret	114
Martha	44
Mary	64
Mordecai	64
Thomas	34
W.	44
William	44
(Rev.) Wm.	44

Cookson
Obadiah	42

Cooper
Benjamin	115
Hannah	26

(continued)

Cooper (continued)			Cropper	
James	26		(Lt.Col.) John	73
Juliet	115		Crosland	
Juliet M. (Holton	115		John	9
Copeland			Cross	
Jane	12		Elizabeth	100,109
Corbell			Elizabeth (Cocke)	109
John	16		John	109,110
Cornwallis			Cruise	
Lord	68,70		Gideon	88
Cosby			Crutchfield	
Hickerson	84		Jeffie	92
Sydnor (J.P.)	83		John (J.P.)	84
Cotnam			Cummins	
Ben	47		A.	82
Cowles			Cunningham	
(Rev.) H.B.	25		(Ens.) John	68
Cox(e)			Cupp	
Ann	22		Barbary	88
Curd	88		Michael	88
David	22			
Hannah	16		Custis	
William	55,61		Edmund	41
Craig			Dabney	
David	27		Jo: F.	44
James	27			
Mary (Duncan)	27		Dade	
			Townsend	88
Crask				
(Capt.) Edmund	20		Daley	
			Josiah	31
Crawford				
Alexander	27		Dalton	
Andrew	61		Elizabeth	56
John	27		John	56
Margaret	27		Robert	56
Crews			Damrill	
Ephraim	6		John	12
Crockett			Dancy	
Colonel	72		William	35
Crook			Darracott	
James	31		John	88

(13)

Daugherty
James   34

Davidson
    Margaret   18
    May   18
    William   18

Davies
    Alfred Metcalfe   72

Davis
    Alex Brooking   68
    Charles Jefferson   98,117
    David   20
    Ellen Chester   98,117
    Henry   42
    James   42
    John   22
    John, Sr.   12
    Joshua   83
    Nathan   12
    Nellie (Snow)   98,117
    Thomas   10,12,32
    (Col.) Wm.   70

Dawson
    Annabella   44
    (Capt.) John   76
    John E.   44
    Robert D.   77
    Zach: 77

Day
    Jonathan   31
    Peter   77
    Thomas   77

Deane
    Elkanah   61

DeBert
    (Capt.) Claudius   74

Deborix
    John   12

Delany
    William   33

De La Roubirie
    Marquis   74

Diack
    Alexander   28

Didawick
    Gladys M.   95,113

Diggs
    Thomas   53

Dillard
    Agness   106
    Betsy   105
    (Dr.) Drury C.   103,106,107
    Edward   25
    Elizabeth Moman   100,107,109
                           112,116
    James   100,102,105,106,107
    James P.   106
    John H.   106
    Lucy C.   106
    Lucy Jane   106
    Martha R.   106
    Minerva   25
    Ruth   106

Dixon
    David   2
    Roger   26

Dobyns
    John   46

Dockery
    James   1

Dodd
    Josiah   88
    Mary (Luttrell)   88

Dodson
    C.C.   108

Doll
    Angelina (Lovelace)   53
    Ephraim B.   53

Donovan
    Cornelius   63
    Elizabeth (Bain)   63

Doser
    Francis   12

Doss
    Joshua   87
    Josiah   87

Douglas
    John   8
    William   28

(14)

Dowdell			Early	
James	68		Jacob	82
			Jeffrey	82
Dudley				
Mary	6		Easley	
Richard H.	27		Stephen	46
Dugan			Echols	
Alice T.	64		Evan	6
Hammond	64		Robert	6
Duncan			Edmonds	
Andrew	27		(Col.) Elias	71
Elizabeth	27			
Florence	27		Edmondson	
Jane	27		Jennet (Duncan)	27
Jesse	83		John	27
Jinnet	27			
Mary	27		Edwards	
			Betty	19
Dunlap			John	53
Salina	108		Judith	19
			Nathaniel	39
Dunmore			Susanna	29
Earl of	61			
			Eilbeck	
Dunn			William	56
John	35			
Martin	39		Elam	
Ruth	39		Almon	83
Thomas	35		Edward	83
William	88		Martin	83
			Robert	30
Dupree			Robert, Jr.	30
Elizabeth	45		William	83
Farthy	45			
Hannah Hill	45		Eldridge	
Henry	45		Thomas	35
Lewis	44-45			
Lewis, Jr.	45		Ellington	
Mary	45		William M.	108
Phatha	45			
Thomas	44		Elliott	
			Thomas	3
Drake				
Robert	29		Ellis	
			Sarah A. L.	25
Drummond			Thomas	38
George	41			
			Ellison	
Dyose			Henry	16
Charles	47			
			Enser	
Eades			Mary	17
Abraham	83			
Sarah	83			

(15)

Epes (Eppes)
    Abigail (Pickman)   28
    Francis   28
    (Col.) Francis   30
    Lucy (Hamlin)   111
    William   28,111

Ephland
    Sarah   89

Estes
    Ann   8
    Arthur   10
    Bartlett   7
    Benjamin   7
    Fanny   7

Eston
    Agnes   18

Evans
    Charles   29,30
    John   55
    (Capt.) Peter   68
    Sarah   29
    William   11

Falger
    Betty (Gray)   116
    Milton Y.   116
    Mollie L.   116

Farrar
    John   76

Faulconer
    Frances   69
    Joseph   69

Faulkner
    Jacob   6
    Mary   6

Fawcett
    Joseph   5

Febiger
    (Col.) Christian   52

Fennell
    Isham   44

Feskin
    James   26
    Peter   26

Few
    Benjamin   85

Field(s)
    Daniel   95
    Mary   116
    Mattie   112,116
    Thomas   116

Finch
    Charles   83
    William   23,83

Finlay
    John   16

Finney
    Mary   30
    Mary (Sr.)   30
    William   30
    William, Jr.   30

Finnie
    William   79

Fleeman
    John   39

Floyd
    Ann   15
    Charles   26
    William   26

Forbes
    John W.   53
    Louisa Jean (Arnett)   53

Foreman
    Joseph   14

Forman
    Eliza C.   64
    Jane   64
    William   64

Foster
    J. Hardin   84,88

Fowler
    Colonel   72
    John   21
    Margaret (McDonald)   21

Francis
    Elizabeth (Wysong)   88
    Fleshart   88

Franklin
James 60
Nancy 36

Frazer
Andrew 83

Freeman
Arthur 1
George 83
Holman 83,88
John 1,69

Fretwell
Frances 85
Leonard 85
Richard 85
William 85

Fuller
Ezekiel 36
Ezekiel, Jr. 36
Mary 36
Sarah 36
Solomon 36

Fuqua
(Lt.) Moses 69

Furlong
Ann 13

Gaines
Aaron 14
Benjamin 14
Daniel 83,84

Gall
George 69

Gallahun
(Capt.) Charles 73

Gallaway
A. B. 108

Gamble
John 14

Gardner
Samuel 85

Garth
John 69

Garwood
Angeline 22
Daniel 22
Elizabeth 22
Isaiah 22
Jonathan 22
Jose H. 22
Mary (Bishop) 22
Patience 22
Sarah 22

Gaskins
Thomas, Sr. 18

Gawith
(Capt.) John 60

Gay
William 30

Gilbert
Felix 84
Henry 84
Richard 87
Thomas 84

Gill
(Capt.) Samuel 69

Gillett
George 41

Gilliam (Gillam)
Amy 35
Burrell 35
Ella Bell (Hamlin) 95,96,113
Elizabeth Arney 96,113
Hansell 35
Hinche 35
Isom 35
John 35
John, Jr. 35
Leada 35
Levi 35
Mary 35
Milley 35
Raleigh C. 35
Sarah 35
Sarah (Jr.) 35
Tabitha 35

Gilmer
John 85

(17)

Gilmore			Grantham	
Thomas N.	85		Stephen	12
Girty			Granville	
(Simon)	70		Lord	80
Glascock			Graves	
Thomas	86		Betsy	89
			Boston	89
Goare			John	38
Ingobo (Bird)	43		Sarah (Ephland)	89
Isaac	43		Gray	
Gooch			Gilbert	11
Dabney	39		John	11
Eleanor (Bowles)	65		Joseph	77
Liner	39		William	11
Mary	39			
Matilda (Chiles)	39		Green(e)	
Ruth (Dunn)	39		General	73
Ruth W. (Hughes)	39		John	3
William	65		(Col.) John	69
William D.	39		William	33
Goode			Greenough	
Peter	14		John	47
Samuel	28			
William	84		Gresham	
			George	82
Gooding				
Ann	55,56		Griffin	
Jonathan	56		Anthony	84
Robert	56		John	85
Sarah	56			
			Griffith	
Goodrich			Mary V.	114
Ann	111			
(Maj.) Charles	111		Grigg	
Henry	12		Moses	77
Gordon			Grills	
Ann	14		John	30
James	18,84		Richard	30
Col. James	15			
(against) Lucas	79		Grimes	
Nathaniel	28		John	87
Thomas	84		John D.	27
			William	86
Grabuc (?)				
Anna	14		Grogan	
George	14		Janette	115
			John D.	102,105
Grant				
Daniel	82		Grubb	
Fanny	82		Joseph	54
Thomas	82			

Guerrant
    Carrie   107
    John   116
    John C.   97, 104
            107,108,112,116
    John C., Jr.   116
    Lizzie   97,116
    Lucy   107,116
    Lucy (Hamlin)   105
    Mary   116
    Mary L. (Hamlin) 104,107
              108,112,116
    Martha Reamey (Pattie) 107
                       116
    Peter   107
    Peter Dutay   116
    William   107
    William Roulett   116

Guion
    Abram G.   66
    Charles Ormsby   66
    Sarah   66

Gunn
    Alice   99

Hack
    George   16
    John Tunstall   15
    Peter   16
    Peter John Tunstall 15
    Sarah Ann   15
    Spencer   15
    Tunstall   14

Hacker
    Andrew J.   113
    Nancy (Lyttle)   113
    Sallie Bell   95,113

Hackley
    John   51

Haile
    P.   8

Haley
    Sterline L.   7

Hall
    Mrs. Elizabeth   15
    David   44
    Henry   43
    (continued)

Hall (continued)
    Horatio Gates   18
    James A.   44
    John   29
    John Sr.   78
    John Jr.   78
    Millie (Boyd)   18
    Milly (Pinckard)   18
    Sarah (McGehee)   44

Halley
    Francis   37
    Joshua   37

Hamblen (Hamblin)
    See Hamlin

Hamilton
    William   85

Hamlin (Hamblin, etc.)
    Abraham   111
    Agnes (1st)
    Agnes (Cocke)   100,109
           110,112,113,114
    Ann   111
    Ann (Goodrich)   111
    Ann (Morris)   115
    Anna D. (Holton) 95,113
    Annie (Ridley)   115
    Annie (Wilson)   116
    Askew   114
    Barclay Arney 92,93,95
           96,97,107,113
    Belle   114
    Betsy (Dillard)   105
    Bettie D.   116
    "Brownie"   116
    Charles 101,102,103,104,105
      106,109,111,112,113,114,115
    Charles (Sr.)   36,110
    Charles (Jr.) 100,109,110
           111,112,113,114
    Charles Hunter   114
    Charles Hughes (Sr.) 95,96,97
            98,99,107,113
    Charles Hughes (Jr.) 95,96
            97,98,113
    Charles Sanford 104,105,109
    Daisy Bell   95,96,113
    Daisy (White)   93,113
    Ella Bell   95,96,113
    Ellen Chester (Davis) 98,117
    Ellen (Keys)   115
    (continued)

Hamlin (continued)

Eliza	112
Edward Reamey	95,96,104
	105,112,113
Elizabeth	111
Elizabeth (Cross)	100,107,112
Elizabeth Morman (Dillard)	
	100,106,107,109,112,116
Elizabeth (Taylor)	111
Emma	114
Francis	116
(Capt.) Francis Mallory	92,93
	95,97,98,103,104
	107,108,109,112,113
Francis Mallory (Jr.)	93,94
	95,107,113
George	105
George Vance	94,96,107,113
Gladys M. (Didawick)	95,113
Griffith Askew	114
Griffith A. Jr.	114
Hallie Inez (Williams)	95,97
	113
Hannah	111
Helen Austin	99,117
Helen (Norwood)	95,113
Hubbard	111
Ida	114
James	116
James Dillard	109,112
James F.	116
James Hughes	104,105,109,116
James Turner (Sr.)	93,94
	95,96,98,107,113,117
(Col.) James Turner, Jr.	96
	98,117
(Dr.) James Turner,III	98,117
James Turner,IV	99,117
Jane	109,112
Jane Cross	109,112
Janette (Grogan)	115
Jefferson Davis	99,117
Jeffie Bell	96,97,113
John	100,101,103,107
	109,110,111,112,114,116
John Charles	114
John D.	116
(Capt.) John (1st)	110,111
(Capt.) John (2nd)	110
Joseph	105
Julia Gray	116
Juliet Kelly	115
Kate Lee	95,96,113
Laura Juliet (Boggs)	115

Hamlin (continued)

Llewellyn	114
Lucy	103,105,109
	110,111,112,116
Lucy Dillard	109,112
Margaret (Cook)	114
Martha	110,111,114
Martha Ann (Reamey)	97,102,103
	104,108,109,112,116
Martha Cocke	110
Martha Reamey	92, 94,96,107,113
Mary	110,111,114,115
Mary Agnes	116
Mary Ann	109,112
Mary Belle	114
Mary Davis	99,117
Mary Elisabeth	95,96,99,113
Mary Ellen	116
Mary G. (Caperton	98,117
Mary Ligon	103,104
	108,109,112,116
Mary Ligon (Stainback)	100
	101,102,103,112,115
Mary Newell (Brown	93,95,96
	98,113,117
Mary Pace (Talbott)	92,95
	96,97,113
Mary V. (Griffith)	114
Mary Virginia	96,107,113
Mary (Williams)	113
Maude W. (Leigh)	99,117
May Talbott	96,97
Mollie (Falger)	116
Nell	112
Nell Marie	99,117
Pattie	112
Peter	111
Peter Stainback	101,102
	109,112,115
Richard	111,114,115
Richard Franklin	115
Roberta	115
Sallie Bell	93,94,95,113
Sallie Bell (Hacker)	95,96
	97,99,107,113
Sally Jane	109,112
Sarah	111
Sarah Elizabeth (Arney)	92,93
	97,98,107,108,112,113
Sarah Jane (McCarmick)	102,108
Stephen (1st)	110,111
Stephen (2nd)	110,111
Susanna (Rookings)	111
Tabitha	110,111
Talbott Barclay	95,96,113

Hamlin (continued)
Thomas   96,97,103,104,108
    109,111,112,113,114,115,116
Thomas (Sr.) 100,101,102,103
        107,109,110,111,112
Thomas (Jr.)   102,103,104
        105,108,109,116
Thomas H.   114
Thomas Y.   116
Vicki   97,113
Virginia   114
Virginia Ann (Michaux)101,115
Virginia S.   115
Walter   115
William   109,111,112,114,115

Hammett
William   82

Hampton
Eliza (Hamlin)   112
Roy   112
Roy, Jr.   112
Thomas   112

Hancock
Robert   28

Hankins
Abraham   88

Hanna
John Parker   74

Hannah
Jane   25

Hardie
John H.   31

Hardiman
John   88

Hardin
Phebe   47
William   47

Hardwick
Aaron (?)   7
James   7
Mary   7

Hareston
George   83

Hargrave
Anselm   11
Joseph Sr.   11
Michael   11
Selia   11

Haristey
John   42

Harmer
Onea   78

Harris
Absalom   37
Archelaus   84
Benjamin   28
Bersheba (Barber)   25
Bezaleel   77
Buckner   82
George   44
Howell   84
James   25,77
Joel   84
John O.   44
Judah   14
Reuben   77
Reuben, Jr.   77
Robert   77
Sampson   84
Samuel   77
(Hon.) Walton   83,84
William   14,25,77,107

Harrison
Benjamin   32
Colonel   35
Hannah   32
Henry   45
(Lieut.) John   70
Ludwell   32
Nathaniel   32
(Col.) Nathaniel   33
Peter Cole   33
Susanna   32,33

Harrod
Captain   75

Harvie
Richard   85

Harvey
John   82

(21)

Harwell
Alexander J.	37
Isham	37
Mark G.	37
Polly Mason	37
Thomas G.	37

Hart
Ann	85
Arthur	9
Benjamin	85
Hardy	9
James	70
James C.	115
Jane	9
Juliet (Coleman)	115
Martha	9
(Dr.) P.A.	115

Hatcher
Edward Sr.	29
John	29
John Jr.	29

Hathaway
(Capt.) John	70

Haydon
Ezekiel	19

Hayes
Birchard Austin	75

Hayley
Henry	44
James	44

Haynes
Thomas	34
Thomas, Jr.	34

Haynie
Bridgar	18
Nancy	18
Sarah	18

Hayth
William	60

Hawk
Abraham	27
Frederick	27
John	27
Sally	27

Hawkins
John	83
Joseph	83

Haws
Benjamin	3

Heard
Jesse (J.P.)	82,87
Richard	87

Hearn
James	3

Heath
Mrs.	57
Thomas	57

Heck
Jacob	34

Hellier (?)
John	26

Henderson
Michael	105

Henry
Mary	48

Herndon
Edward	84

Hewings
Thomas P.	5

Hewitt
Richard	57

Hibbert
Charles	24

Hickey
Cornelius	88
John	88

Hicks
George	8
Mrs. Sarah	16
William	15,16

Higgins
Amos	40
Elizabeth	40

(continued)

Higgins (continued)

Guillalima Maria	40
John	40
John Joliffe	40
Robert	40

Higginson

Lucy	62
(Capt.) Robert	62

Hill

William	80

Hillman (Hillsman)

John	88
John H.	44

Hinton

Abraham	111
Dempsey	84

Hobert

Elizabeth	24
Harrison	24
Jean	24
John	24
Savarah	24

Hockady

James	29
Warwick	29

Hodgh

Hannah	19
Jacob	19

Hog

Peter	19

Hogshead

Charles	26
James	26

Holderby

J.	102

Holding

John	9

Holebrook

Betty	15

Holland

John	49
Michael	30

Holleman
Joseph

Holleway

David Sr.	10

Hollinsworth

Isaac	24

Holt

Mary	28
William	28

Holton

Anna Diltz	95,113,115
Hattie Laura	115
Juliet K. (Hamlin)	115
Juliet M.	115
Milton Diltz	115
Roberta	115

Hood

Edward	8

Hooe

Elizabeth	57
Gerrard	57
(Col.) Robert	54
Sarah	57

Hook

John	59

Hope

John	21

Hopper

Thomas	83

Horde

Franky	21

Horton

Joseph	13

House

Acquilla	87
Martha	87

Howard

R. N.	105

Hubbard

Joseph	85

Johnson			**Justice**	
Colonel	75		John	45
Isaac	47		Mary (Dupree)	45
Jemima Suggett	70		**Justiss**	
John B.	55		William	11
Lloyd Bates	69			
Moses	35		**Kabler**	
Nicholas	85		William	48
Richard	34,106			
Robert	70		**Kaufman**	
William	85		Jeannette	95
			Kathryn Anne	99
Johnston			Mary Dale (Williams)	99,113
John B.	50		Mary Theresa	99
Richard	101		William Duane	99,113
Robert	89			
			Kay	
Jolley			Gabriel	48
Edward	29		James	48,51
John	28			
Thomas	29		**Kee**	
			Dorley	12
Jolliffe			James	12
Eliza	40		James, Jr.	11
			Rebeckah	12
Jonas				
David	20		**Keeth (Kieth)**	
Morgan	20		William	46
Jones			**Kelley**	
(Dr.) Adolphus D.	108		Bernard	85
(Dr.) Benjamin	108			
Caroline (Reamey	108		**Kelly**	
Elizabeth (Ramey)	108		Bernard	82
(Dr.) Erasmus D.	102,103,108		Madaline	14
Frances C.	25		Margaret	60
Gabriel	19		Michael	46,60
George Washington	102,108			
John	23,111		**Kemper**	
Martha Ann (Reamey)	102,108		(Ens.) Charles	71
Mary Eleanor	102,103,104,108		Edwin Wilson	70,71
Paul	29			
Salina (Dunlap)	108		**Kenneday**	
Thomas	16		Lillian	14
William	35		Margaret	25
(Rev.) Wm. G. H.	25		W. M.	14
Joynes			**Kenner**	
(Col.) Levin	41		Elizabeth	16
			Francis	16
Judkins			John Wm. Hicks	15
Nicholas	80		Mathew	16
Thomas	34		Nancy	16
			Richard	15
Julian			William	15,16
(Dr.) John	70			
Wm. Alexander	71			

Kennon			Landrum	
Willia,	28		Dolly	38
			Doney (Parrish)	38
Ker(r)			Dorothy	38
George	18		Elizabeth	38
			Francis	38
Keys			Francis, Jr.	38
Ellen	115		John	38
			Martha	38
Kincade			Mary	38
John	20		Reuben	38
			Salley	38
Kincaid			Samuel	38
(Lieut.) James	71		Sarah	38
(Capt.) Joseph	71		Sarah, Jr.	38
			Thomas	38
King				
Asa	24		Lane	
Ephraim	15		James	84
John	26,32,85			
			Langhorne	
Kinney			Maurice	71
William Jr.	27			
			Lanier	
Kinsolving			Robert	12
James, Sr.	39			
James, Jr.	39		Lansdell	
Margarette	39		William	18
Martha	39			
			Lasley	
Kirtly			(Rev.) John	38
Francis	85			
			Latham	
Knox & Ballie	54		Robert, Jr.	49
Knox			Lattimore	
Elizabeth	54		David	18
Jannett	54			
John	53,54		Lawson	
John (2nd)	54		Francis J.	102
(Capt.) Robert	53,54		Terry (Col.svt.)	107
Robert Dade	54			
Rose Townshend	54		Leak	
William	54		Captain	69
Kuykendall			Lee	
Mathew	24		Alice	5
			Elizabeth W.	25
Kyle			Francis L.	58
James	100		John	5
			Peter	48
Lafayette			Richard	48
General	67		Richard Henry	58
			William	58

Leigh			**Lipscomb**	
Maude Winborne	99,117		John	53
Maude (Winborne)	99,117		**Littledal**	
(Dr.) Southgate	99,117		Henry	16
Lennard			**Lockett**	
William	29		David	85
Lester			**Logan**	
(Rev.) Henry	47		Colonel	69
			James	47
Lewis				
Charles	40,71		**Long**	
(Capt.) Charles	76		Alexander	22
Charles Birk	71		Ann	50
(Capt.) Edward	65		Armistead	50
Eleanor (Bowles)	65		Arthur	32
Harry Kemper	71		Benjamin	48
Henry Thompson	71		Bromfield	48,49,50
Isabelah	65		Elizabeth	10,48,49
James	40		Frances Slaughter Ball	51
James F.	79		Gabriel	7,49,50
Jane (Strother)	71		(Capt.) Gabriel	52
John	40,65		Gabriel, Jr.	50
John, Sr.	65		George Washington	8
(Maj.) John	65		John	48,51,79,80,81
Josiah	41		John Joseph	7,8
(Capt.) Nicholas	74		John Slaughter	50,51
Susanna	40		Joseph	81
Thomas	71		Joyce (Washington)	81
Warner (Sr.)	65		Lemuel	7,8
Warner (Jr.)	65		Lunsford	7,8
			McKennie	7,8
Ligon			Maria	50,51
Blackmon	46		Martha Elizabeth	8
Henry	47		Mary	7,8,51
James	46,47		Nicholas	7,8,84
James Sr.	47		(Capt.) Nicholas	75
James Jr.	47		Nicholas (Jr.)	7,8
John	46,47		Nicholas,III	7
Joseph	46		Nimrod	49,51
Judith (Church)	47		Reuben	50,51,52
Mathew	30		(Lieut.) Reuben	52
Mary	112		Richard Harrison	7,8
Susanna	47		Robert	10
Thomas	46		Robert B.	49
Will:	30		Sarah	49
			Thomas	49,50
Lilly			Thomas Stubblefield	48,49
John	19			50,51
			Walter	8
Lincoln			William Ball	50,51
Sarah	20			
			Longden	
Lindsey			Ann	55
Colonel	69			

(27)

Loomis			Lyttle		
Jacob	14		Nancey E.A.	113	
Lovelace			McAdams		
Angelina E.M.	53		Joseph	15	
John	53		(Dr.) Joseph	15	
Nancy (Arnett)	53		Sarah Conway	15	
Lowe			McAlexander		
Micajah	111		Daniel	78	
Sarah (Hamlin)	111		David	78	
			Edmund	78	
Loxham			John	78	
Robert	56		John Sr.	78	
			Nathaniel	78	
Lucas			William	77,78	
James	82				
			McCarty		
Ludwell			(Maj.) Charles	17	
(Hon.) Phillip	58		Daniel	57	
Lumpkin			Machir		
Ann	88		Alexander	33,40	
George	83,88		Betsy	33	
John	83		Elizabeth	14	
Robert	88		Henry	33	
			James	33,40	
Lumsden			John	14,33,49	
Charles	25		John, Jr.	33	
G. D.	25		Magdalena Ann	33	
			Margaret	33	
Lunsden			Rachel	14	
Frances	44		Scota	33	
George	44				
J. D.	25		McClain		
			John	87	
Luttrell			Marney	87	
Mary	88				
Richard	88		McConnell		
			(Dr.) D. F.	115	
Lyon(s)			David Holton	115	
Edward	77		Hattie L. (Holton)	115	
Elley	77		Margaret	25	
Henry L.	78,79		Thomas	25	
Jacob	77				
Jane	77		McCormick		
John	76		Sarah Jane	102,108	
Mary Ann (Tuggle)	78,79				
Morton MacKay	69		McCrory		
Peter	76		Robert	83	
Richard Tankersley	76				
Stephen	24,77		McCullock		
			Agnes	17	
Lynch			David	17	
John	8		James	17	

McCullock (continued)
John	17
Mary	17

McCullough
(Maj.) Samuel	75

McDonald
Angus W.	14
Anny (Amey?)	20
Azuba	20
Bartholomew Jude	20
Benjamin John	71
Charles	20
Hannah	20
James	20
Jane	21
(Jeanet?)	21
John	21
John Viney	20
Margaret	20,21
Mary	21
Patrick	2
Randall	21
Randolph	21
Sarah	21

McDowell
(Col.) Charles	71
John	50
(Maj.) Joseph	71

McGlamming (?)
John	26

McGehee
Agnes	44
Dabney	44
Edward	44
Esther	44
Frances	44
Frances (Lunsden)	44
John	44
Martha (Cooke)	44
Molly	44
Oswell	44
Sarah	44

McHenry
John	20

McKamey (See McKenny)
Andrew	28
Eleanor	28
James	28

McKamey (continued)
John	28
Nancy	28
William C.	27,28

MacKay
Harry Brent	67,69,71

McKeever
Rachel	74

McKenny (See McKamey)
Eleanor	26
James	26
John	26
William	26

McKie
Lucy (Hamlin)	110,111
Martha Cocke	110,111
Michael	110,111

McKinney
Jane (Duncan)	27
John	27

McKittrick
James	26
John	26
Robert	26
William	26

McLanahan
Elizabeth	65
James	65
John	65

McNeal
Frank Hamlin	96,113
Kate Lee (Hamlin)	95,96,113
William Burton	95,96,113
William Hamlin	96,113

McNutt
George	88

Macready
DeJohn Hart	70

Macon
Mary Mayo	101,115

Maddera
James	12
Zachariah	12

Maget
    Nicholas   34

Mahaney (Mahany)
    Cynthia   55
    Lizzie   23
    Susannah   23
    Thomas   23

Mainwaring
    Stephen   32

Mallory
    Elizabeth   55
    John   55
    Uriel   55
    William   55

Malone
    Amey   39
    Patrick   60
    Thomas   39

Mannon
    Jane   78

Marks
    Haistens   85
    John   85
    John Haistens   85
    Peter   85
    Peter, Jr.   85
    Polly Garland   85

Marsh
    Betsy Barnes   19
    George   3
    Gideon Hammonds   19

Marshall
    Alexander   30

Marston
    John Soane   28

Martin
    Ann   8
    Alexander B.   54
    Beverley   38
    Douglas   85
    Ganoway   82
    Jane   38
    John D.   105
    Joseph   100
    (Col.) Joseph   101
      (continued)

Martin (continued)
    Martha R(Dillard)   106
    Mary (Molly)   75
    Ruth (Dillard)   106
    William   8
    William Peters   6

Mason
    Ann   56
    Mrs. Ann   56
    Ann (Eilbeck)   58
    Ann (Gooding)   55
    Betsy   57
    Elizabeth   56,57,58
    Mrs. Elizabeth   13
    Elizabeth (Hooe)   57
    George   56,57
    George, Jr.   56
    (Col.) George   56,57,58
    George William   58
    Helen   98,117
    John   35,56,57,58
    Joseph   35
    Lemuel   13
    Mary   13,56
    Nancy   57
    Richard Chichester   58
    Rosanna   56
    Sally   57
    Sarah   56
    Sarah Chichester   58
    Sarah McCarty   58
    Thomas   13,56,57,58
    Thomson,   56,57,58
    Thomson, Jr.   58
    William   56,57,58

Massey (Massie)
    John   71,77
    Lee   57
    Lucy   112

Masterson
    Sarah   55

Mathews
    (Col.) George   74
    (Col.) Sampson   68,72

Mayes
    Hannah H. (Dupree)   45
    Mathew   37

Mayfield
    William   77

Menzies			Mitchell (continued)	
John	100		Maria	14
Robert	100		Patsy	77
			Richard	17
Meredith				
William	61		Mobeley	
			William	20
Meriwether				
David	82		Moffett	
Francis	85		John	20
Thomas	85			
			Moncure	
Merritt			John	57
John	77			
			Montford (Montfort)	
Merryman			Henry	7
Francis	88		Robert	84
Metcalfe			Moody	
(Capt.) John	72		John	85
			Thomas	85
Michaux				
Mary Macon	101,115		Moore	
Richard W.	101,115		Benjamin	76
Virginia Ann	101,115		Hannah	11
William M.	101		John	43,85
			John (J.P.)	85
Michland (?)			Joshua	11
Jesse W.	102		Matthew	77
			Sarah (Bird)	43
Middleton			Richard	34
Robert	85		William (J.P.)	82
			(Capt.) William	69
Miller				
Christian	43		Morehead	
Henry	19,20,22		J. Turner	104
Jacob	43			
John	7		Morgan	
Pleasant M.	88		(Col.) Daniel	68,73
Ulrick	43			
			Moring	
Mills			Christopher	9
(Lieut.) John	72		William	33
William	86			
			Morris	
Minter			A.A.	100
William	19		Ann	115
			John	31
Miskell				
William	17		Morton	
			Joseph	83
Mitchell				
Green	37		Mosby	
John	77		Littleberry, Jr.	86
Margaret	81		Richard	86
(continued)				

Moseley			Neal(e)	
William	28		Abner	79
			Christopher	79
Moss			Joseph	86
Bracie	36			
Burwell B.	31		Neckless	
Edmund	36		Han. (sic)	41
Elizabeth	36			
Elizabeth (Jr.)	36		Neff	
Henry C.	30,31		Anna	14
Howell	36		Francis	14
Jane	31		Jacob	14
John	30,31,36		John	14
John D.	31		John Henry	14
Joshua	36			
Lewis	36		Nelms	
Mary	31		Thomas Jr.	83
Nancy	36		William	79
Patsy	36			
Ray	31		Nelson	
Rebecca	30		Ben Barrere	72
Thomas	36			
Wiley	36		Newbold	
William	31,36		Thomas	41
Mounger			Newman	
H.	86		Cornelius	43
Henry	83,84		Mary (Bird)	43
Nancy	83		Samuel	19
Polly	83			
			Newton	
Mountain			George	13
Robert	59		(Capt.) George	13
Mumford (Munford)			Nicholas	
Betty	29		Ann Cary	72
Edward	29		(Col.) George	72
John	47		Robert Carter	58,72
Rebecca Harris	77			
			Nichols	
Murdock			Henry	2
George	47		John	17
James	47		Joseph	77
			Mary	3
Murray				
Thomas	86		Nicolson	
William	86		Joseph	34
			Robert	26
Nalley				
Bennett	76		Norman	
			Thomas	72
Nance				
William Jr.	6		Norwood	
			George	34
Napier			Helen	95,113
Thomas (J.P.)	85		Matt	32

Nosler			Pannill		
Bostian	89		Joseph	86	
O'Briant			Parker		
Patsy (Moss)	36		John	13	
			Richard	13	
Odingsells			Toulson	79	
Charles (J.P.)	84				
			Parham		
Odum			Sarah	110	
Thomas	13				
			Paris		
Oliver			Moses	46	
Asa	31				
Robert	31		Parks		
			Elizabeth	48	
Ore (Oar)			Jaconiah	45	
Elizabeth	53		Joshua	86	
Joseph	53		Mary	48	
William	53		Thomas,Jr.	48	
O'Reilly			Parrish		
Henry	74		Dolly	38	
			Doney	38	
O'Riley			Dorothy	38	
Phillip	8		Joel	38	
Overby			Parrott		
Jackonias	46		Nathaniel	8	
Peter	46				
			Pasteur		
Overton			J. J.	8	
(Capt.) John	70				
			Patterson		
Outten			Mary (McDonald)	21	
Abraham	42		William	21	
Owens			Patton		
M. W.	14		(Sgt.) George	72	
			John Blaine	72	
Owsley					
Newdegate	86		Payne		
			Edward	73	
Palmer					
Ann	6		Pearce		
Daniel	6		O.	76	
Drury	6				
Drury,Jr.	6		Peay		
Elias	6		(Capt.) George W.	92,95	
Jeffry	6			97,103,104	
John	6		Sarah Ann Bell (Arney)	92, 94	
Joseph	6			97	
Mary	6		Peckance		
			Mr.	61	

Pendleton
    Edmund   60
    N.   51
    Nathaniel   20,84
    (Capt.) Nathaniel 73
    Phillys   20
    William G.   53

Penn
    Manuel   3

Perry
    George   55
    John   55
    Puree   55

Peterson
    Mary   9
    Peter   45

Pettus
    Charles   86
    John   86
    Stephen   86
    Stephen, Jr.   86

Pettway
    Elizabeth   32
    William   32

Peyton
    Yelverton   73

Phillips
    Elizabeth (Kendricks) 73
    (?) Payne   73
    Mourning   73
    Walter Dabney 73

Pickman
    Abigail   28

Pierce
    Gainer   41

Pinckard
    Margaret (Boyd) 18
    Thomas   18

Pitcher (or Peacher?)
    Alexander   55
    Jonathan   55
    John   55
    William   55

Pitchfor
    William   82

Pleasants
    Robert   28,29
    Thomas, Jr.   29

Plover
    (Capt.) John   20

Poindexter
    John   38
    Sally   38
    William   38

Pomfret
    Elizabeth   89

Pope
    Henry   82

Porter
    Joseph   86
    Nicholas, Sr. 86
    Nicholas, Jr. 86
    Samuel   55

Porteus
    James   2

Posey
    Bennett   24
    Elizabeth (Hobert) 24
    Thomas   24
    (Sgt.) Zephariah 73

Potter
    James   49
    Will: 63

Potts
    Enoch   18
    Jesse   20

Powell
    Honor (?)   1,2
    Martha C. (McKie) 110,111
    William Hewett 110,111

Pratt
    John   76

Pray
    Job   84

Rice (continued)

John	76
Rachel Tate	38
Sally	38

Richards

Alice	5
Ambrose	55
Amy	64
Henry	5
Jonathan	5
John	5
(Rev.) John	64
Mary	5
Peter	5
Peter (Sr.)	5

Richardson

Ellenor (Quiny?)	22,23
(Rev.) Joshua	22,23

Richie

David N.	14
Nancy	14

Riddlehurst

John	29
Richard	29

Ridley

Annie	115

Rieves

Hannah	37
Simon	37

Rigby

John	1

Rind

Mrs.	58

Ripley

David	22

Rispis

Anne	33

Robert

Captain	72

Roberts

Benjamin	33
Daniel	86
(continued)	

Roberts (continued)

Elizabeth	33
George	33
John	24
Joseph	33,86

Robertson

Lucy H. (McKie)	110,111
Warning Peter	110,111
William J.	78

Robeson

William	73

Robinson

Agnes M.	106
(Dr.) R. R.	105,106

Roch(e)

Charles	55
Richard	26

Rochester

(Col.) Nathaniel	74

Rockett

Ann	30
Baldwin	30

Rodment

Agnes	18
Janet	18

Rogers

George	77
John Jr.	47
Peter	47
William (J.P.)	83

Rookings

Susannah	111
William	111

Rose

Samuel	12
William, Jr.	12

Ross

John	87
Mrs.	45
Robert	76

Row

Thomas	55

(36)

Rowell	
Isaac	37
Rowsay	
John	61
Royall	
Richard	28
Rucker	
Benjamin	77
Ruddell (Ruddle)	
George	43
Isaac	42,43
Ruddes	
John	47
Ruffin	
Minerva	25
Rupp (Roop)	
Jacob	43
Russell	
William	5
Rutherford	
Absalom	89
John	85
Rutter	
Sarah	35
William	35
Sadler	
John	22,23
Sage	
Henry	1
Sanders	
Thomas	3
Sanderson	
Elizabeth	13
(Capt.) Richard	13
Savage	
Edward	3
Elizabeth	3
Robert	11
Sawyers	
John	46

Scarborough	
Edward	35
Scarbrough	
Mathew	32
Scarburgh	
Mary Cade (Wise)	42
Scott	
Benjamin	24
(Gen.) Charles	71
David	24
(Rev.) James	57
Seales	
Nicholas	27
Seanoy (?)	
Aron	76
Self	
Henry	17
Servant	
Bertram	13,14
Frances	14
Madaline	14
Mary	14
Sevier	
Valentine	2
Shockley	
Meredith	41
Richard	41
Sarah	41
Shore	
Thomas	28
Short	
Robert	18
Shuffel	
John	11
Simmons (See Simons)	
Charles	46
William	46
Simons (See Simmons)	
Abraham	48,86

Sims
- Adam   23
- Benjamin   23
- Frederick   83,86
- John   23,83
- Peter   23

Skidmore
- James   21
- Sarah (McDonald)   21

Slaughter
- Frances S. Ball (Long)   51
- Franky   21
- John   21,51
- Lawrence   21
- Mary (Horde)   21
- Phillip   51
- (Capt.) Phillip   73

Sledge
- Amos   10

Smart
- Louisa   64
- Mary   64
- William   64
- William, Sr.   64

Smith
- A. P.   108
- Abram   19
- Augustine Jacquilin   17,18
- Bartlett   84
- Charles   87
- Charles Jeffry   28
- Daniel D.   92
- Emma   112
- Frances   84
- Francis   82,87
- George   87
- Griffin   87
- Henry   19
- James   88
- Jarvis   34
- (Col.) John   17
- Lucy   82
- Marcus Clinton   69
- Margaret   17,18
- Mary Jacquilin   17,18
- (Rev.) M. Thomas   17
- Nancy   34
- Robert   85
- Thomas   12
- William   12

Smyth
- John   34

Snead (Sneed)
- Charles   42
- John   34
- Margaret   31

Snelson
- Sarah   6

Snow
- Elisha   19
- John   19
- Joseph Spencer   19
- Nellie   117
- Samuel   19
- Spencer   19

Soane
- Joun   30
- William   30

Somerville
- John   35

Sorsby
- Samuel   10
- Stephen   10

Spain
- Susanna (Mahaney)   23
- Thomas   23

Speers
- James   34
- Rebecca   22
- William   34

Spence
- Charlotte (/)   45
- Joseph   45
- Solomon   45

Spencer
- John   77
- Peter   15
- Sarah Ann   15

Spiros
- Elizabeth A. (Taylor)   113
- Robert   113

Spivey
- George   13

Spotswood
  Richard T.   25

Stainback
  Mary Ligon   100,109,112,115
  Peter (Sr.)   109,112

Stanford
  James   32

Stanley
  Richard Mulford   68

Stanton
  (Captain)   75

Stark(e)
  Thomas   82
  William   84

Starkey
  Jane (Jean) Jackson   37
  Joel   37
  Joseph   4,5
  Martha   4
  Mary   4
  Permelia   4
  Robert   4,5
  Sally   4
  Thomas   4,5
  William, Sr.   4,5
  William, Jr.   4,5

Stephens
  Adam   19
  John   25
  Thomas   83

Stephenson
  Amos   9
  (Capt.) James   74
  Rachel McKeever   74

Stewart
  Benjamin   45
  Farthy (Dupree)   45
  James   83,84
  Phatha (Dupree)   45

Stigler
  Samuel   51

Stiles
  Belfield   25
  Sarah T.   25
  William   25

Stith
  Bassett   8
  Drury   86
  Mary   7,8

Stokes
  Daniel   22
  Elizabeth   2
  Henry   30
  Patience (Garwood)   22
  Sylvanus   30

Straughan
  David   16
  Elizabeth   16
  John   16
  Margaret   16
  Richard   16

Strickland
  Joseph   80
  Samuel   80

Stuart
  James   47

Stubbs
  Ann Walker Carter   66
  Jefferson C.   66
  (Dr.) John Catlett   66

Sturdivant
  Frances L.   25
  Joel   25
  Joel (2nd)   25

Sture
  Eleanor   49
  James   49
  Joseph   49

Sudhoff
  Edward   115
  Roberta (Holton)   115

Sumers
  John Wallis   3

Sumner
  Joseph   77
  Thomas   77
  Thomas Edward   7
  William   35

Sydnor
  John   17

Tabb
    Alice T. 64
    Eliza C. 64
    John H. 64
    Thomas Todd 64

Talbert
    Elizabeth (Landrum) 38
    John (J.P.) 84
    Paul 38

Talbot(t)
    John 84,86
    John (J.P.) 86
    Mary Pace 92,95,113
    Matthew, Jr. 86
    Thomas 86

Taliaferro
    (Lieut.) Nicholas 74
    Richard 2,3

Tallman
    Benjamin 74

Tanner
    Thomas 28

Tanzey
    William 24

Tapp
    Joett(?) 27
    Vincent 27

Tarte
    William 16

Tarver
    Samuel 10
    Sarah 10,32
    Thomas 10,32

Tate
    Elizabeth 38
    Enos (Sr.) 38
    Enos (Jr.) 38
    Enos (minor) 38
    James 38,85
    John 38
    Mary 38
    Rebecca 85
    Robert 38
    Sally 38
    Uriah 38

Tatum
    Howell 85
    Peter 85

Taylor
    Ann 40
    David 39
    Edmund 40
    Edmund Jr. 40
    Elizabeth 39,111
    Elizabeth Arney 96,113
    Goodwyn 39
    James 39
    Jesse 39
    John 39,40,43
    John, Jr. 40
    Jones 39
    Joseph 40
    Magdalene (Bird) 43
    Martha C. (Hamlin) 110,111
    Mary 39
    Penelope 39
    Richard 40,111
    (Capt.) Richard 69
    Richard Wilcox 95,96,97,113
    Richard Wilcox, Jr. 97,113
    Robert 60
    Sarah Arney (Hughes) 95,96
        97,113
    Sarah (Barker) 111
    Susanna 39
    Thomas 110,111
    Thomas Sr. 39
    Thomas Jr. 39
    Thomas,III 39
    William 17,39

Teackle
    Thomas 41

Terrell
    Joel 82
    William 87

Terry
    Stephen 84

Thomas
    George 30

Thompson
    Benjamin 83
    Catharine 48
    Edward 54
        (continued)

Vaughan (Vaughn)
    James   2
    John J.   25
    (Capt.) Reuben   75

Vickrey
    Charistopher   19
    Hannah (Hodgh)   19

Vinson
    John   9
    Thomas   8

Wade
    Garland   46

Waggener
    (Sgt.) Thomas   75

Waggoner
    John   20

Walker
    George   14
    Hugh   86
    James C.   108
    Jesse   53
    John   87
    John Jr.   48
    Thomas   2,53
    William   53
    William Jr.   26

Wall
    John   8
    Mary   9
    Michael   9
    Richard   80

Wallace
    Thomas   46
    (Capt.) William   72

Wallen
    Elisha   24

Wallis
    Robert   20

Walston
    William   8

Wammock
    John   76

Ward
    David   85
    George   20
    Richard, Sr.   47
    Richard, Jr.   47

Warren
    Jane   9
    John   9
    Martha   9
    Mary   9
    Patience   9
    Robert, Jr.   9
    Sarah   9
    Thomas   9
    Thomas Sr.   9

Washington
    (Gen.) George   70
    James   81
    Joyce   81
    Richard   8
    Solomon   78

Waters
    John   15

Watkins
    William Jr.   28

Watson
    Douglas   83
    Elizabeth (Taylor   39
    Joseph   56
    Margaret   18

Watts
    Thomas   86

Way
    Molly   15

Weaver
    (Col.) Jacob   74

Webb
    Francis   87
    Giles   15
    (Lieut.) Isaac   75
    John   87
    John Spann   16

Webster
    Benjamin   48,86

Welch
    Patrick   3

Wells
    Jacob   34
    John C.   55
    Moses   34

West
    Clarence Clifford   75
    Jances   19
    Jonathan   42
    John   75
    John, Jr.   57

Westbrook
    John   87

Westfall
    Cornelius   24
    Elizabeth   24
    Jacob   24
    John   24
    Judith   24
    William   24

Weston
    Thomas   61

Wharton
    Robert   55

Wheeden
    Colonel   69

Wheeler
    T.B.   108

Wherry
    James   16
    James, Jr.   16

White
    Daisy   93,95,113
    E.   92
    Richard   2
    Thomas   53

Wilder
    William   82
    Winnie   82

Willet
    Ambrose   41
    Elizabeth   41
    William   41

Willey
    Ann Maria   65
    (Capt.) Archibald   65
    Georgiana Smith   65

Williams
    Barbara (Batten)   97,99,113
    (Lieut.) David   75
    Frances   82
    Frank Hamlin   97,99,113
    Frank Hamlin, Jr.   99
    Hallie Inez   95,97,113
    Hugh Thomas, Sr.   95,97,113
    Hugh Thomas, Jr.   97,99,113
    Hugh Thomas, III   97,99
    Isaac   111
    Jacob   9,10
    John   9,10,85
    John, Sr.   49
    Joseph   82
    Mary   110,111,113
    Mary Dale   97,99,113
    Mary E. (Hamlin) 95,97,99,113
    Oliver   27
    Ovella Gay (Hardy) 97,99,113
    Phillip   43
    Robin Leslie   99
    Sandra Kay   97,99,113
    Sarah   9
    Thomas   9,87
    William   51,105
    William Clayton   33
    Wyatt   85

Wilson
    James   75
    John   46,47
    Nancy   78
    Thomas   11

Winborne
    Maude   99,117

Winchley
    Thomas   61

Wingfield
    Garland   86
    John   84,86,88
    John, Jr.   87
    Thomas   84,88
    Thomas, Sr.   87

Winston
    George D.   100

(43)

Wise
    Elizabeth   16,42
    John   32,41,42
    Hannah Scarburgh   42
    Matilda   42
    Mary Cade   42
    Samuel   41,42,50
    Thomas   41,42
    Tully R.   41

Witt
    Abner   88
    Jesse   88
    John, Sr.   88

Wolfin
    Peter   33

Womack
    Frances L.   25

Wood
    Alexander   77
    B. W.   14
    Daisy B. (Hamlin)   95,113
    Henry   30
    John   30,77
    Martha (Kinsolving)   39
    Reginald L.   95,113
    William B.   39

Woodley
    Thomas   36

Woods
    M.   34

Woodson
    Charles   29
    Jacob   29
    John   29,47
    Tarlton   29,30
    Tarlton, Jr.   29

Woolfard
    Frederick   43

Wooten
    James   85

Worrell
    John   41

Worsham
    Richard Sr.   47
    Stephen   36

Wren
    Richard   11

Wright
    James   25
    (Lieut.) James   73
    John   15
    Larkin   55
    Lucy   4
    Nancy   4
    Samuel   66
    William Sr.   4

Wyatt
    Bernice   97

Wynd
    Anthony   111

Wysong
    Elizabeth   88

Wytherington
    Joseph   34

Yeiser
    Henry Craig   70

Yop
    Ann   15

Young
    George   88

Yuille
    George   46
    Thomas   46

Zollerkoffer & Long   51

THEY WENT
THATAWAY

Volume 3

Dedicated to

My fellow genealogists and colleagues

whose combined knowledge of Virginia
genealogy and history is immense,
amazing and wonderful.

        Batte, R. Bolling Col.
        Dorman, John Frederick
        Elliott, H. A. Mr. & Mrs.
        King, George H. S.
        Knowles, W. Herbert Mrs.
        Lewis, James F.
        Lindsay, Joyce H. Mrs.
        Livingston, Virginia Mrs.
        Matheny, Emma R. Mrs.
        Reddy, Anne Waller Miss.
        Woodson, Robert F. Mrs.
        Wright, Phyllis Bates Mrs.
        Yates, Helen K. Mrs.

TABLE OF CONTENTS

Section 1

Section 2

Section 3

FOREWORD

"Bring me men to match my mountains,
Bring me men to match my plains.
Men with empires in their purposes
And new eras in their brains."

- Sam Foss

Come, journey along with me in this third volume of our ex-
hilarating and fascinating quest for knowledge of our migrating
and adventurous Virginia ancestors.

These records continue to bridge the gap between former Virginia residents and their new places of settlement. Also bridging
a gap are many records of former residents of other States, Colonies, and European countries who migrated to Virginia. The Oxford Universal Dictionary defines a colony as a settlement in a
new country. Therefore, these personages should be called and
known as "Virginia Colonizers" whether they came to or went from
Virginia.

These men, who were from all walks of life and of all ages,
had the foresight and the fortitude to endure unspeakable hard-
ships and danger in what they eventually proved was a golden
opportunity to build a new life of freedom and fortune in new
lands. Above all other things they sought, maintained and cher-
ished their independence and their equality before the law.

A large majority of them undoubtedly had a far better knowledge of their ancestry and of their exact relationship with others
of their "kin", (both paternal and maternal,) than the average person of to-day possesses. Blood was ever thicker than water with them,
even to remote degrees of relationship. They passed on their knowledge of their family history to their off-spring in quiet evenings
around the fireside after the day's labor was done.

There is also no doubt that many of the historical and biographical details of their stories of their ancestry were not only
fancifully but luridly embellished. This was very natural and normal
in those days and still is as we all love to hear and to tell a good
and an interesting story.

Except in very rare instances they carried with them no actual
proof of their ancestry or thought it was necessary. However, as
they acquired land, slaves, cattle, and other possessions they were
generally very careful to record the necessary legal documents in
order to be able to prove their own right and title and in order to
be able to devise and allot it to their progeny.

In like manner, proof of descent has existed for many hundreds of years in parish, church and vestry records; military records; birth, death and marriage records; Wills; Deeds of Gift; Estate Settlements; law suits; court orders; orphan and guardianship records; Bible records; cemetery records; Tax and Census records; et cetera. On the other hand, it is very lamentable that many of these records have been forever lost or destroyed by war, fire, rot, neglect, and general carelessness and ignorance.

When and where a family has remained in a specific or the same general locality for many years or generations it is very possible and indeed comparatively easy to trace the lineage of the family, either in the whole or in the direct line. However, when a member of the family removes to a distant locale (even to-day) it becomes extremely difficult and often impossible to be able to identify and positively prove that a certain individual (now deceased) who may have lived in several different sections of the country is the same identical personage who was born in such and such a State, Country, or Colony and in a specific town or county thereof.

As is now fairly well recognized, the compilation of the type of records found in the first three volumes of this series are designed to afford the "connecting link" which proves legally and without question the identity and origin of the subject individual. In most cases this is the hardest and most difficult part of the assignment or research. It is also the part which is most often unsuccessful.

In this latter connection, I have been a trifle disturbed by the counsel and friendly advice of one or two friends that it did not look quite right to them to include records (in a few instances) which have previously appeared in print. Personally I can see no harm in so doing if the records are in the Public Domain and are so cited. It is my sincere belief that any record of sufficient quotable authority, whether formerly in print or newly discovered and which is a public document, is of much more benefit and of easier finding for reference in a concentrated effort such as this series than a record dispersed among many various type books and publications which consist of hundreds of other and different type records of genealogical importance. In addition to this I know of no individual and of only two libraries in the United States that possibly could have all the books written on the subject.

I cannot help but believe that most people will agree that since it is absolutely necessary and essential to provide full proof of the identity and origin of a migratory ancestor, that all such "connecting links" from whatever source, provided they are authentic and acceptable as proof, should be gleaned from all possible founts and sources.

Charles Hughes Hamlin
March 1966

P.O. Box 3525 - Richmond, Va.

VIRGINIA COLONIAL MILITIA SIZE ROLLS

These records are contained in 19 muster rolls of seventeen officers of the First Virginia Regiment, including Colonel George Washington, for the years 1756 - 1757. Captain Joshua Lewis and Captain Henry (Harry) Woodward have two different dated rolls. Four of the rolls are undated but they undoubtedly belong in this same year period.

The originals of these records are to be found among the Washington Papers in the Department of State, Washington, D. C. and were printed in full 72 years ago by the Virginia Magazine of History and Biography in Volume I of its Quarterly series. All of these names are therefore included in Swem's Index.

However, very few people, other than Virginia genealogists and historians, are aware of these records and a full set of The Virginia Magazine together with Swem's Index is available in only a few of the largest genealogical libraries in the United States.

This compiler has rearranged these rolls to appear alphabetically by the names of the officers and has rearranged each of the individual rolls also alphabetically by the names of the soldiers. This was quite a tedious task as there are 986 names included.

These rolls are considered to be very valuable inasmuch as they not only name the soldier but also indicate his age, place of birth, and in most instances his place of enlistment. This does not necessarily prove his county of residence but for want of other data gives a good clue or lead to commence further research. It will be found that quite a few of these names are repeated by reason of later re-enlistments and that sometimes their names or ages or places of birth, cannot be reconciled with each other. In such cases, both records should be cited.

In addition to the information compiled herein most of these rolls also give other very useful knowledge such as the size of the soldier in feet and inches (hence called size-rolls) his trade, actual date of enlistment, etc.

The age of the individual soldiers ranged from age 13 to age 60 but the majority were in their late 'teens' and early 'twenties'. Their trades were usually those of planter, blacksmith, tanner, weaver, etc., but also included were laborer, gentleman, schoolmaster, surgeon, sailor, soldier, hunter, etc. Many claimed the trade of

I.

tailor which greatly mystified me and of which I am somewhat dubious
as I do not believe we have as many tailors in Virginia even today.
Having been an enlisted man in military service myself I believe
this trade may have been certified in the hope of avoiding arduous
manual labor. I doubt if it worked if this was so. I have compiled
a very interesting summary of these rolls which is herewith submitted

SUMMARY OF COLONIAL MILITIA SIZE ROLLS AND
ANALYSIS OF BIRTHPLACES SPECIFIED

Officer	Va.	Other Colonies	Europe	Not Specified	Total
Ashby, John	12	8	12	-	32
Bell, David	2	-	16	-	18
Cocke, William	4	5	14	1	24
Gist, Christopher	1	42	25	-	68
Harrison, Henry	21	5	16	-	42
Lewis, Andrew	36	7	49	3	95
Lewis, Charles	27	-	12	-	39
Lewis, Joshua	9	-	16	11	36
Lewis, Joshua	41	2	42	2	87
Mc Kenzie, Robert	41	6	37	5	89
Mercer, George	35	4	36	-	75
Peachy, William	22	-	13	6	41
Spotswood, Robert	20	1	18	-	39
Stephens, Adam	14	-	14	11	39
Stewart, Robert	4	7	23	-	34
Waggoner, Thomas	42	3	44	-	89

-2

Officer	Va.	Other Colonies	Europe	Not Specified	Total
Washington, George	8	2	15	1	26
Woodward, Harry	14	-	24	2	40
Woodward, Henry	31	3	34	5	73
19 Rolls -	384	95	460	47	986

2nd Company of Rangers of Captain John Ashby[1]

Dated October 21, 1757

Name	Age	Born	Enlisted
Ambries, Freeman	23	Maryland	-
Arnold, Moses	22	Virginia	-
Barlow, Benjamin	21	Virginia	-
Bell, James	20	Maryland	_
Bolton, Richard	48	England	-
Cockren, Thomas	20	Pennsylvania	_
Conway, Timothy (see note)	40	Ireland	-
Cooper, Job	23	Virginia	-
Diaper, William	22	Virginia	-
Dodson, William	24	Virginia	-
Doolen, Thomas	28	Ireland	-
Farrel, Samuel	19	Dutch	-
Field, William	40	Ireland	-
Frazer, James	35	"Highlander"	-
Goldsbarry, Robert	19	Maryland	-
Goldsbarry, William	21	Maryland	-
Harper, Leonard	28	Virginia	-
Homan, Robert	46	England	-
Hooper, Innes	19	Virginia	-
Howell, Thomas	26	Virginia	-
Istobe, William	43	England	-
Jinkins, Owen	21	Pennsylvania	-
Jinkins, George	28	Pennsylvania	-
Marr, Nathan	25	Virginia	-
Morgan, Daniel	25	Pennsylvania	-
Oldham, Jesse	21	Virginia	-

-3

Name	Age	Born	Enlisted
Piper, John Henry	30	Dutch	-
Rodes, Henry John	23	Virginia	-
Sanders, George	30	England	-
Tate, Samuel	24	Ireland	-
Turner, Thomas	24	England	-
Rouse, John	20	Virginia	-

Note 1: Captain John Ashby had command of a small fort on Patterson Creek, located about 9 miles south of Cumberland, Maryland. All of the men on this Roll are shown to have enlisted in this Company between August 18th and October 17, 1755. Their place of enlistment is not designated.

Timothy Conway is very probably the same as Timothy Conoway noted and commented on elsewhere. Army life evidently agreed with "Irish Tim" as he gets younger every year.

Ranger Company of Captain David Bell[1]
Dated, Maidstone, May 12, 1756
(Place of Enlistment not Designated)

Name	Age	Born	Enlisted
Austin, Edward	39	England	-
Bassett, Robert	23	England	-
Childs, Edward	22	England	-
Coffield, Phillip	17	Dutch	-
Collins, David	21	Ireland	-
Coltbert, William	22	Scotland	-
Cummings, Samuel	21	Virginia	-
Hooper, James	35	England	-
Hooper, John	35	England	-
Keen, Richard	22	England	-
Mullen, Peter	23	Ireland	-
Penmore, John	26	England	-
Sherrod, Henry Francis	40	England	-
Smith, William	25	England	-
Stanley, Daniel	26	Ireland	-
Sullivan, Timothy	20	Ireland	-
Thomas, John	20	Virginia	-
Thompson, James	26	England	-

Note 1: Captain David Bell is listed among the officers of the

Virginia Regiment October 10-December 27, 1755 in the journal of
Captain Charles Lewis.

Ranger Company of Captain William Cocke[1]
Dated October 21, 1755

Name	Age	Birth	Enlisted
Adcock, Thomas	27	England	-
Bennet, Thomas	24	Virginia	-
Borden, Joseph Cpl.	22	West Jersey	_
Carr, Thomas	40	Scotland	-
Gill, John	24	Ireland	-
Goldon, George	17	Virginia	-
Higgins, Lawrence	40	Ireland	-
Hill, George	30	Ireland	-
Jones, John Sgt.	26	Pennsylvania	-
Johnson, Richard	24	Maryland	-
Lamb, Thomas	16	England	-
Lane, Abraham	-	-	-
Lasley, Daniel	27	Scotland	-
Linch, Matthew	21	Ireland	-
McNamara, Dennis	25	Ireland	-
Matthews, Barry	24	Virginia	-
Patton, James	34	Pennsylvania	-
Perkins, Valentine	18	Virginia	-
Sherman, John	33	Dutch	-
Simmons, John	40	England	-
Smith, William	45	England	-
Watts, Thomas Cpl.	33	England	-
Whipple, John	20	Pennsylvania	-
Wood, James Sgt.	32	Ireland	-

Note 1. - The place of enlistment is not designated. Colonel
George Washington rented a house for 40 pds. per annum, from
Captain William Cocke, in the Town of Winchester, (Frederick
Co.) in 1756, of which he made a record of in his Ledger A,
Folio 32.

Company of Captain Christopher Gist[1]
Dated July 13, 1756

Name	Age	Born	Enlisted
Adams, Thomas	23	Maryland	Baltimore
Ashby, William	27	England	"
Barnett, James	24	Maryland	"
Barrett, John	22	Ireland	Fredksbrg, Va.
Brothers, Francis	21	Maryland	Baltimore
Brown, Thomas	20	Maryland	"
Burgess, John	21	Maryland	"
Carpenter, John	19	Maryland	"
Chapman, Cornelius	19	Maryland	"
Clifts, James	24	England	"
Connell, William	21	Virginia	Fredksbrg, Va.
Conner, John	21	Tipperary(Ire.)	Lancaster, Penn.
Constantine, Edw. Tully	19	Maryland	Baltimore
Constantine, Patrick	18	Maryland	"
Craghead, Robert	21	Maryland	"
Crawley, John	28	Ireland	Fredksbrg, Va.
Creswell, Robert	22	Maryland	Baltimore
Cross, John	20	Maryland	"
Davidson, John	24	Maryland	"
Davis, Richard	22	Maryland	"
Dawson, David	31	England	Lancaster, Penn.
Dyer, Thomas	29	England	" "
Fowler, Mathew	20	Maryland	Baltimore
Francis, Henry	22	Maryland	Fredksbrg, Va.
Garsnell, Mordicai	22	Maryland	Baltimore
Gowen, Zadock	24	Maryland	"
Grammer, John J. Peter	26	Germany	"
Hagerly, Mathew	31	Ireland	Fredksbrg, Va.
Hall, John	17	Maryland	Baltimore
Hammond, Thomas	19	Maryland	"
Henley, Cornelius	21	Ireland	Lancaster, Penn
Hodson, John	25	England	Baltimore
Hudson, Thomas	27	England	"
Hughes, Patrick	22	Ireland	Lancaster, Penn.
Hurley, Jeremiah	24	Ireland	Fredksbrg, Va.
Jackson, George	31	England	" "
Jefferson, Henry	22	Maryland	Baltimore
Little, John	19	Maryland	"
Logan, Colloe	30	Ireland	Lancaster, Penn.
Lynch, James	26	Ireland	Baltimore

-6

Name	Age	Birth	Enlisted
McDonald, Robert	25	Dublin, Ireland	Lancaster, Penn.
McMath, William	40	Ireland	Baltimore
Mason, William	20	Maryland	"
Moore, John	28	Ireland	Fredrksbrg, Va.
Pardoe, John	22	Maryland	Baltimore
Patterson, William	24	Maryland	"
Posey, Richard	22	Maryland	Fredrksbrg, Va.
Pritchard, Thomas	20	Pennsylvania	" "
Reese, Henry	22	Germany	Baltimore
Rice, Richard	19	Pennsylvania	Lancaster, Penn.
Roberts, Joseph	27	Jerseys	Fredrksbrg, Va.
Saunders, Samuel	22	Maryland	Baltimore
Socketts, Phillip	27	Pennsylvania	Lancaster, Penn.
Stewart, Asael	17	Maryland	Baltimore
Stockstill, William	17	Maryland	"
Summers, William	23	New England	Lancaster, Penn.
Talbot, William	22	Maryland	Baltimore
Tole, Timothy	23	Maryland	Fredrksbrg, Va.
Tooth, Jno. Christopher	21	Germany	Baltimore
Tuder, Thomas	24	Ireland	"
Turnbull, Alexander	35	Ireland	Lancaster, Penn.
Vaughn, Gist	21	Maryland	Baltimore
White, Thomas	28	England	"
Williams, Peter	20	Maryland	"
Wilson, Aquilla	21	Maryland	"
Wilson, Samuel	19	Maryland	"
Wittaker, Abraham	19	Maryland	"
Wittaker, Isaac	21	Maryland	"

Note I:- Captain Christopher Gist (ca 1706-1759 was a veteran
frontiersman, experienced surveyor, etc., who explored the Ohio
Valley region for the Ohio Company in 1750 and served as a guide
on Braddocks expedition. He established a small trading post
called Gist's Station, west of the mountains on Chestnut Mountain
between Ft. Necessity and Great Meadows, Penna. Washington placed
implicit trust in him and used his Company as a company of scouts
based variously at Ft. Cumberland and Ft. Loudoun.

Company of Captain Henry Harrison[1]
July 13, 1756

Name	Age	Born	Enlisted
Bedgood, Joseph	22	Virginia	Isle of Wight
Bevin, Peter	25	Virginia	Prince George
Buckridge, James	28	Virginia	" "
Buffen, Joseph	27	Virginia	Suffolk
Champion, Henry	21	Virginia	"
Clements, John	25	Virginia	Cumberland
Cockeril, John	30	Virginia	Richmond Co.
Coe, Barnard	23	Ireland	Baltimore
Cook, Thomas	20	England	"
Cotton, Benjamin	24	New England	Suffolk
Dacres, John	20	England	Cumberland
Daviss, James	23	Ireland	Lancaster, Penn.
Deer, William	20	Ireland	Middlesex
Deloack, Michail	37	Virginia	Isle of Wight
Dudding, John	45	England	Richmond Co.
Fear, William	22	Virginia	Charles City
Ferguson, Duncan	24	Scotland	Winchester
Frazier, John	19	Scotland	Cumberland
Hains, James	22	Virginia	Fredckbrg, Va.
Hill, James	26	New England	Norfolk
Jones, Jesse	23	Virginia	Isle of Wight
Kelly, John	24	Ireland	Fairfax
Key, John	39	Virginia	Surry
McPherson, William	29	Scotland	Goochland
Moreland, Francis	22	Virginia	Surry
Norvell, James	23	Virginia	Charles City
O'Conner, William	26	Ireland	Prince George
Parks, Will	18	Maryland	Baltimore
Price, Joseph	21	Virginia	Cumberland
Pulling, Robert	34	England	Norfolk
Rawls, James	22	Virginia	Suffolk
Rosser, John	30	Virginia	Isle of Wight
Seal, Thomas	32	Maryland	Suffolk
Thompson, Will	22	Virginia	Charles City
Walden, Samuel	18	Virginia	Middlesex
Walker, Francis	26	England	Suffolk
Warden, Will	33	Virginia	Prince George
Waters, William	48	England	Richmond Co.
Williams, Will	25	Virginia	Surry
Wilson, Will	18	Maryland	Baltimore

Name	Age	Born	Enlisted
Wright, Thomas	26	England	Petersburg
Wyley, Alex	31	England	Baltimore

Note 1: - Colonel George Washington placed Captain Henry Harrison in command of Fort Edwards, "if it could be reached" on Cacapon River in Hampshire County (now West Virginia) which was about 20 miles from Winchester.

Company of Major Andrew Lewis[1]
No Date

Name	Age	Born	Enlisted
Adams, Francis	24	England	Augusta
Adderson, Joseph[2]	23	No. Carolina	Accomack
Aliot, Robert	30	England	Augusta
Blankenship, Henry	22	Virginia	Chesterfield
Blanton, William	22	Virginia	Caroline
Bledcer, Abraham	45	Virginia	Culpeper
Body, William	30	Scotland	Augusta
Bradford, Thomas	30	England	Westmoreland
Brannin, Thomas	30	Ireland	Augusta
Bromley, William[2]	25	Virginia	Accomack
Brooks, John	20	Virginia	Hanover
Brown, John	26	Manksman[3]	Augusta
Burns, Michael	35	Ireland	Lunenburg
Campbell, John	31	Scotland	Alexandria
Cooper, Samuel	23	Pennsylvania	Augusta
Curls, John	22	Jersey	Nansemond
Currie, David	20	Virginia	Albemarle
Davis, John	31	Jersey	Louisa
Davis, Thomas	23	England	Augusta
Deadman, Nathaniel	45	Virginia	Fairfax
Debord, David	41	Virginia	Culpeper
Dehay, David	45	England	Cumberland
Donald, John	22	Virginia	Sussex
Donally, John	17	Virginia	Augusta
Donally, Mark	30	Ireland	Augusta
Easdale, Samuel	35	Ireland	Frederick
Evans, Abram	22	Pennsylvania	Augusta
Edwards, William	18	Virginia	Westmoreland
Faubous, William	25	Scotland	King & Queen
Ferguson, Duncan	20	Scotland	Prince William

-9

Name	Age	Born	Enlisted
Fowler, Andrew	22	Scotland	Fairfax
French, William	32	England	Lunenburg
Gailor, Edward	36	England	Augusta
Garoine, Moses	27	Ireland	"
Gillions, Branden	38	Virginia	Accomack
Gillions, Elyan[2]	22	Virginia	"
Gilmore, John	27	Ireland	Augusta
Goodin, John	20	Jersey	Frederick
Goss, Benjamin	20	Virginia	Prince George
Govern, John	21	Virginia	Caroline
Green, John	30	Ireland	Augusta
Gwin, Peter	22	Virginia	Bedford
Hart, John	24	Ireland	Fairfax
Hicks, Joseph	20	Virginia	Hanover
Hingham, Joseph	23	Virginia	Caroline
Holland, William	30	Ireland	Frederick
Humphreys -	(See Umphries)		
Hunter, Thomas	21	England	Lunenburg
Kegan, Thomas	26	Ireland	Augusta
Kelly, Lawrence	30	Ireland	Brunswick
Johnston, John	37	Virginia	Fairfax
Lain, Thomas	21	England	Augusta
Larmour, Levin	25	Virginia	Accomack
Leak, John	40	England	Frederick
Low, Beverly[2]	18	Virginia	Albemarle
Lucaner, William	27	Ireland	Augusta
McEntire, John	25	Ireland	"
McHenery, William	-	-	-
McPike, Patrick	53	Ireland	Fairfax
Mander, William	43	England	Augusta
Martain, Richard	21	Virginia	King William
May, Jessy	24	Virginia	Amelia
Mitchell, John	19	Ireland	Brunswick
Murphy, Robert	23	Ireland	James City
Perkisson, Thomas	23	England	Augusta
Picket, Henry	19	Virginia	"
Ponty, John	20	Maryland	"
Raby, Moses	25	Virginia	Nansemond
Rafferty, Thomas	22	Ireland	"
Rigg, Thomas	26	Virginia	Westmoreland
Riley, Barnard	23	Ireland	Fairfax
Riley, John	26	Ireland	Augusta
Roberts, Joseph	30	Ireland	"

10

Name	Age	Born	Enlisted
Rogers, Benjamin	22	Virginia	Nansemond
Rogers, Francis	32	England	"
Royalty, Daniel	29	Virginia	Albemarle
Scully, Michael	44	Ireland	James City
Shifflet, Thomas	21	Virginia	Louisa
Simpson, William	23	Virginia	Accomack
Smith, John	30	Ireland	Augusta
Smith, Levi	16	Virginia	"
Smith, William	27	Virginia	Prince Wm.
Swinburn, John	40	England	Spots.
Swiney, Terence	40	Ireland	Augusta
Tapman, Joseph	22	Virginia	Accomack
Tate, David	40	Ireland	Augusta
Tegan, John	23	Scotland	Fairfax
Thompson, Henry	-	-	-
Umphries, John	23	England	Yorktown
Waters, John	41	England	Nansemond
Wildridge, John[2]	19	Virginia	Accomack
Williams, James	21	England	Augusta
Williams, James	-	-	-
Willow, Joseph	24	Virginia	Henrico
With, Edward	34	Virginia	Westmoreland
Wright, Thomas	26	England	Hanover

Note 1:- Major Andrew Lewis was age 35 in 1755 (thus born 1720). Colonel Washington placed him in charge of the frontier at Fort Dinwiddie, Augusta County, in September 1755. As a Brigadier General he was in command at the Battle of Point Pleasant, October 10, 1774.

Note 2:- Deserted

Note 3:- John Brown, "Manksman" probably means he was from the Isle of Man in the Irish Sea, owned by Scotland and the Earls of Derby until 1827.

Company of Captain Charles Lewis[1]
July 13, 1756

Name	Age	Born	Enlisted
Anderson, John	32	Scotland	Fredrksburg
Austin, John	18	Virginia	Gloucester
Barnett, William	26	Virginia	"
Bassford, Alexander	21	Virginia	Westmoreland
Burford, William	19	Virginia	Gloucester
Caillian, Charles	23	France	Alexandria
Carson, James	24	England	King & Queen
Crittenden, Abraham	24	Virginia	Gloucester
Crouch, Jacob	48	Virginia	Hanover
Eaton, Thomas	42	England	Smithfield
Edmondson, Thomas	25	Virginia	Essex
Edzer, Joseph	20	Virginia	Westmoreland
Flowers, John	23	England	Spots.
Franklin, Sampson	20	Virginia	Caroline
Gardner, Thomas	23	England	Richmond Co.
Harmon, Richard	21	Virginia	Westmoreland
Harris, Reuben	25	Virginia	Hanover
Harriss, John	18	Virginia	"
Harwood, John	30	England	Maryland
Hazan, William	28	Ireland	Williamsburg
Hendrin, John	21	Virginia	Richmond Co.
Howard, Shiplet	31	Virginia	Gloucester
Joins, Joseph	18	Virginia	Northampton
Kingston, Francis	25	Virginia	Dinwiddie
Little, Thomas	19	Virginia	"
Loffman, Edward	18	Virginia	Chesterfield
Loffman, John	20	Virginia	"
Meggs, John	17	Virginia	Gloucester
Mitchell, William	19	England	Hanover
Palmore, George	24	Virginia	Dinwiddie
Perkins, George	26	Virginia	Gloucester
Quisenberry, Nicholas	21	Virginia	Westmoreland
Ratcliffe, James	19	England	Stafford
Richardson, Ezekiel	20	England	Spots.
Roundtree, William	34	Virginia	Gloucester
Smith, Charles	18	Virginia	Essex
Stephenson, Nathaniel	22	Scotland	Northampton
Tarriss, William	20	Virginia	Spots
Thomas, Francis	18	Virginia	King William

Note 1:- Captain Charles Lewis, Gent., was commissioned Captain in
Spotsylvania Co. and took the oath September 4, 1753 (Ord. Bk.1749-55)
He was promoted to Major in Spots. Co. October 4, 1757 (Ord. Bk 1755-65)
His original Journal is now in the Library of Congress and contains
much of value in this period. I believe he was the Col. Charles
Lewis killed at the Battle of Point Pleasant Oct. 10, 1744 but
this should be verified.

Company of Captain (Joshua) Lewis[1]
July 13, 1756
(#1 Roll)

Name	Age	Born	Enlisted
Allberry, Thomas	17	Gibraulter	Warwick
Ballen, Edward	20	Virginia	Maryland
Best, Christopher[2]	26	Virginia	Nansemond
Best, James*	-	-	-
Brock, William	35	Ireland	Winchester
Carrier, Henry[2]	25	England	"
Carrier, Thomas[2]	23	England	"
Emmerson, Henry	60	England	"
Fashee, Nathan	21	Virginia	Fredcksburg
Fines, William*	-	-	-
Fogg, Obediah	20	Virginia	Nansemond
Foster, Richard*	-	-	-
Francis, John*	-	-	-
Freeman, Edward	22	Virginia	Fredcksburg
Gender, John	23	Holland	Frederick
Gill, Edward*	-	-	-
Hall, Thomas*	-	-	-
Hickman, Burton	20	Virginia	Eastern Shore
Hook, John	31	Holland	Winchester
Jenkins, William	28	Ireland	Maryland
Johnston, John[2]	35	England	Marylnad
Kelly, James*	-	-	-
Kennedy, Anthony	25	Ireland	Winchester
McDonald, Patrick	52	Ireland	Fredcksburg
Paul, Aaron	26	England	Winchester
Pope, Ephraim[2]	23	Virginia	Nansemond
Quisenberry, Humphrey	24	Virginia	Fredcksburg
Rawls, David	46	England	Annapolis
Shermon, William*	-	-	-
Smith, James	31	England	Belhaven[2]
Spann, Thomas*	-	-	-

Name	Age	Born	Enlisted
Stephens, James*	-	-	-
Stillts, Anthony[2]	26	Holland	Frederick
Townsend, Tom*	-	-	-
Vaughn, Andrew	25	Virginia	Belhaven[2]
Wells, Joseph	26	England	Quantico

Note 1:- I cannot find anything definite on Capt. Joshua Lewis
in the most readily available sources except that he is one of
the officers of the Virginia Regiment contained in the Journal
of Captain Charles Lewis as being in the Expedition against the
French Oct. 10 - Dec. 27, 1755.

* "On Command" - I assume this means they were members of the
Company but remained at home until the company received orders
for active duty.

Note 2:- More later. See next Company Roll.

Seventh Company of Captain (Joshua) Lewis[1]
No Date
(#2 Roll)

Name	Age	Born	Enlisted
Ashwell, Richmond	32	Virginia	Sussex
Atkinson, James	21	Virginia	Southampton
Austin, William	27	England	Stafford
Bailey, Thomas	22	England	Richmond Co.
Baldock, Richard	20	Virginia	King & Queen
Basset, John	28	Scotland	Stafford
Benson, John	25	Virginia	Accomack
Best, Christopher[2]	27	Virginia	Nansemond
Blankenship, Stephen	22	Virginia	Chesterfield
Boswell, James	18	Ireland	Stafford
Bridge, Joseph	21	Virginia	Gloucester
Butcher, Samuel	24	Virginia	Amelia
Butler, James	-	-	-
Bryant, Jessy	20	Virginia	Richmond Co.
Carrier, Henry[2]	42	England	Frederick
Carrier, Thomas[2]	22	England	"
Campbell, Douglas	30	Scotland	Ft Cumberland*
Carwig, John	43	Ireland	Northumberlnd
Clark, George	23	England	Petersburg

14

Name	Age	Born	Enlisted
Clark, John	25	Virginia	Isle of Wight
Cooper, James	24	Virginia	Norfolk
Covey, Durret	28	England	Augusta
Croswell, William	18	Virginia	Northumberland
Davis, David	23	Virginia	Bedford
Delaney, Thomas	40	Virginia	King & Queen
Donaldson, James	28	Scotland	Stafford
Edwards, Thomas	27	Wales	King William
Farrow, Thomas	34	England	Bedford
Francis, John	35	Maryland	Frederick
Frye, Christopher	26	Holland	South Branch
Gill, Edward[2]	24	Virginia	Stafford
Godfrey, Anthony	31	England	Bedford
Gowing, Daniel	27	Virginia	Stafford
Grant, John	20	Ireland	Williamsburg
Halslop, Abram	22	Virginia	Southampton
Hall, Richard	29	Virginia	Gloucester
Hall, Thomas[2]	25	England	Westmoreland
Halloway, John	22	Virginia	York
Hinchey, Michail	22	Virginia	Hanover
Holloway, James	25	Virginia	York
Hope, Thomas	33	England	Ft.Cumberland*
Jenkins, James	22	England	Williamsburg
Jessee, William	20	Virginia	King & Queen
Johnson, John[2]	33	England	Maryland
Johnston, Charles	23	Virginia	Gloucester
Kirkland, Isham	23	Virginia	Prince George
Lamb, Joshua	20	England	Williamsburg
Lamb, William	22	Virginia	Prince George
Liptrot, James	22	Virginia	Nansemond
Loakey, John	23	Maryland	Accomack
Londren, William	40	England	Gloucester
McFarling, John	18	Virginia	Richmond Co.
McWilliams, Brd't.	25	Virginia	King William
Marsh, James	32	England	Stafford
Maxom, Henry	30	England	Petersburg
May, Martin	31	Ireland	Amelia
Mitchell, James	18	England	Brunswick
Moon, Abraham	40	Virginia	Orange
Pate, Thomas	-		-
Peed, Philip	23	Virginia	Gloucester
Petersonbrough, Peter	30	Germany	
Pope, Ephraim[2]	22	Virginia	Nansemond
Porter, Daniel	25	Virginia	Westmoreland

Name	Age	Born	Enlisted
Purdue, Joseph	23	Virginia	Amelia
Rainger, Garr't.	28	Holland	Frederick
Robottom, Matthew	25	Virginia	Charles City
Rowt, Andrew	30	Germany	Frederick
Rutherford, Ad'm.	40	Virginia	Louisa
Simpson, Thomas	38	Virginia	Ft Cumberland*
Stewart, Alexander	20	Scotland	Stafford
Stilts, Anthony[2]	28	Germany	Frederick
Sullivan, Daniel	27	Ireland	Port Royall*
Suple, Morris	26	Ireland	Norfolk
Thomas, James	31	Scotland	Alexandria
Townsend, Thomas[2]	23	Virginia	Nansemond
Venable, James	19	Virginia	Spots
Walters, Robert	22	Scotland	Northumberland
Ward, John	21	England	
Wells, Josiah	33	England	Prince William
White, William	47	Scotland	Ft Cumberland*
Williams, Henry	26	Ireland	Frederick Town
Williams, John	16	Wales	Ft Cumberland*
Wilson, Benjamin	30	Virginia	King & Queen
Wimbrow, Abram	26	Virginia	Accomack
Winn, Charles	42	Virginia	Sussex
Wire, William	24	England	Frederick

Note 1:- This and the preceding Roll are designated by this compiler as Company Roll[1] of Captain Joshua Lewis. Actually, this roll is listed as Captain J. Lewis and the preceding roll as of Captain Lewis. As far as my own research can determine, the only Captain Lewis in this period who has a first name beginning with the initial "J" is Captain Joshua Lewis.

This roll is evidently of a slightly later date than the preceding roll as this roll has the enlistment date of 22 of these men as between the dates of January 7, 1754 and October 8, 1756. The preceding roll was dated July 13, 1756. This roll was therefore in the latter part of 1756 or the early part of 1757.

Note 2:- Both these rolls are assumed by this compiler to be companies of Captain (Joshua) Lewis because the names of the following nine men are common to both rolls. (To wit)- Christopher Best, Henry Carrier, Thomas Carrier, Edward Gill, Thomas Hall, John Johns(t)on, Ephraim Pope, Anthony Stilts and Thomas Townsend.

* - Fort Cumberland, now Cumberland, Maryland is about 115 miles

16

Northwest of Washington, D. C. and 10 miles south of the Pennsylvania boundary.   Port Royal is or was on the Rappahannock.

Company of Captain Robert McKenzie[1]

Name	Age	Born	Enlisted
Adams, John Cpl	28	Scotland	Caroline
Afflack, Peter Cpl	20	Scotland	Isle of Wight
Ale, Joseph	34	England	Prince William
Anderson, James	21	Virginia	Gloucester
Batten, Nathan	19	Virginia	Isle of Wight
Belcher, Isham	24	Virginia	Amelia
Best, John	25	Virginia	Middlesex
Blackbourn, Edward	26	Virginia	Frederick
Britton, John	30	Ireland	Westmoreland
Brooks, William*	-	-	-
Brown, Philip Combs	20	Virginia	Westmoreland
Brown, Thomas	23	Maryland	Northumberland
Bruce, Charles	23	Scotland	Frederick
Burkham, Roger	58	Maryland	Hampshire
Burrill, Phillip	48	England	"
Campbell, Absalom	20	Scotland	Baltimore
Campbell, John	34	Scotland	Talbot Co.,Md.
Carr, Thomas	56	Scotland	Hampshire
Chapple, Edward	23	Virginia	Henrico
Cinclair, John	24	England	Frederick
Clark, James	23	Virginia	Surry
Clarke, John	54	England	Isle of Wight
Colbert, William	22	Virginia	Westmoreland
Connor, John	30	Ireland	Cumberland, Pa.
Cotton, Thomas	21	Virginia	Westmoreland
Curtice, George*	-	-	-
Davis, John	23	Virginia	Amelia
Evans, John	30	Virginia	King & Queen
Ferguson, Thomas*	-	-	-
Fields, Stephen	21	Virginia	Albemarle
Glinn, Patrick	40	Ireland	Frederick
Golding, George	18	Virginia	Hampshire
Green, Lewis	30	Virginia	Dinwiddie
Hartwell, David Cpl	21	Virginia	Albemarle
Hatfield, James	28	England	Dinwiddie
Higgins, Lawrence	56	Ireland	Hampshire
Hogan, William	38	Ireland	Spots.
Hughes, Henry	54	Ireland	Chesterfield

17

Name	Age	Born	Enlisted
Hughes, Thomas	18	Virginia	Chesterfield
Jenkins, John	19	Pennsylvania	Frederick
Kemp, John	37	Virginia	King & Queen
Lamb, Thomas Cpl	18	England	Ft Washington
Land, Edward	26	Virginia	Albemarle
Lynch, Matthew	22	Ireland	Hampshire
McCloud, William	26	Scotland	New Kent
McCoy, Elijah	28	Virginia	Brunswick
McLane, Daniel	27	Scotland	Winchester
McNamarra, Dennis	26	Ireland	Ft Washington
Malone, James	31	Ireland	Isle of Wight
Maxedent, James	21	Virginia	Sussex
Morgan, David	19	Virginia	Orange
Morris, Jacob	24	Virginia	Albemarle
Morton, George	37	England	Nansemond
Mosely, Jacob	22	Virginia	Brunswick
Munday, James	16	Maryland	Baltimore
Nuland, Thomas	49	Penna.	Nansemond
Patterson, William	38	Virginia	Richmond Co.
Penmore, John	26	England	York
Proctor, George	27	Virginia	Isle of Wight
Quinn, Thomas	24	Ireland	Frederick
Ragsdale, William	18	Virginia	Amelia
Riddle, Richard	30	Virginia	King & Queen
Rilie, James	21	England	Dinwiddie
Robinson, James Sgt	22	Scotland	King George
Roberts, Thomas	26	Jersey	Fairfax
Roe, James	33	Virginia	Isle of Wight
Scott, Charles Sgt	20	Virginia	Albemarle
Shields, George	28	England	Dinwiddie
Sigriff, Hugh*	-	-	-
Simmonds, Joel	18	Virginia	Norfolk
Sinclair -	See Cinclair		
Solomon, Peter	21	Virginia	Sussex
Sweeny, Aron	21	Virginia	Albemarle
Thompson, Charles*	-	-	-
Thompson, James	27	England	York
Thorn, Robert	20	Virginia	Caroline
Tiller, John	28	Virginia	Charles City
Tillery, Samuel	26	Virginia	Richmond Co.
Timmons, John	45	England	Hampshire
Truly, Peter	29	Ireland	Caroline
Turner, James	25	Virginia	Albemarle
Underwood, Thomas	21	Virginia	Sussex

18

Name	Age	Born	Enlisted
Ward, Barnard	41	Holland	Frederick, Md.
Warner, James Cpl.	21	Ireland	Albemarle
Watts, Thomas, Sgt.	32	England	Ft Washington
White, Thomas, Sgt.	28	England	Baltimore
Williams, Walter	28	England	Westmoreland
Wimbrough, John	17	Virginia	Accomack
Wright, William	35	Virginia	Nansemond

Note 1:- Captain Robert McKenzie is among the list of officers of the Virginia Regiment contained in the Journal of Captain Charles Lewis in the Expedition against the French October 10-December 27, 1755. The name of Robert McKenzie is also among the signatures of other officers of the Virginia Regiment who indited an address, dated at Fort Loudoun December 31, 1758 to George Washington, Esq., on the occasion of his retirement as Commander of Virginia troops December 27, 1758 (Virginia Col Militia, Crozier, Page 21).

* - "Not yet joined".

Company of Captain (George?) Mercer[1]
August 2, 1756

Name	Age	Born	Enlisted
Adams, John	28	England	Spots.
Askins, John	26	Virginia	Prince William
Askins, Philemon	22	Virginia	" "
Banner, Peter	25	England	Suffolk
Barrett, Benjamin	24	Ireland	Prince George
Barrett, Nathaniel[1]	20	Virginia	Northumberland
Bedient, William	33	England	Fairfax
Bevans, Daniel	21	England	Gloucester
Brumley, William	21	Virginia	Spots.
Burton, Samuel	26	Virginia	Frederick
Carroll, John	25	Virginia	Caroline
Coine, John	40	Ireland	Fairfax
Colston, William	47	England	York
Combs, Thomas	32	Maryland	Culpeper
Cotling, John	24	Virginia	Richmond Co.
Corvin, Samuel	21	England	Caroline
Dillard, Joseph	21	Virginia	"
Dodson, William	22	Penna.	Chester
Donnabough, Thomas	25	Ireland	Alexandria

19

Name	Age	Born	Enlisted
Edwards, Ignatius	24	Maryland	Stafford
Edwards, John	20	Virginia	Albemarle
Evans, Edward[1]	22	Scotland	Frederick
Farmour, Francis	22	England	Fairfax
Fling, Matthew	29	Ireland	"
French, Samuel Cpl	27	Maryland	"
Gaile, John	46	England	Norfolk
Gill, Edward	20	Ireland	Dinwiddie
Grinnaway, John	26	Virginia	Frederick
Guinnon, John Sgt	19	Virginia	Stafford
Handcock, Joseph	32	Virginia	Chesterfield
Harres, William	40	Virginia	Southampton
Hedgman, John	20	Virginia	Stafford
Jones, John	26	England	Fredrksburg
Juggins, John	21	England	Stafford
Keaton, John	24	Virginia	Caroline
Kenniss, Andrew	22	Scotland	Spots.
King, William	24	Virginia	Caroline
Lattin, Thomas	24	Ireland	Prince William
Lilvy, John	24	England	Richmond Co.
Lockard, Archibald	23	Scotland	Prince William
Long, Ambrose	20	Virginia	Caroline
McDonald, Angus Sgt	21	Scotland	King George
McGennett, David	42	Ireland	Frederick
Mannen, Edward	31	Ireland	Fairfax
Mathews, John Sgt	43	England	Dinwiddie
Mills, James	23	Virginia	Alexandria
Mingeese, Peter	20	Scotland	Chesterfield
Morgan, John	19	Virginia	Caroline
Morris, Joseph	32	Virginia	Spots.
Munjoy, Thomas	22	Virginia	Stafford
Murray, Duncan	28	Scotland	Fairfax
Nealy, Matthew	24	Ireland	"
Nevil, Gabriel	24	Virginia	Prince William
Nevil, Henry	20	Virginia	" "
Organ, John	24	Virginia	Amelia
Orme, Henry	21	England	Stafford
Perry, Joseph	16	Virginia	Caroline
Pope, John Cpl	18	Virginia	Prince William
Power, James	13	Virginia	Winchester
Price, Joseph	24	Ireland	Goochland
Ross, Andrew	26	Virginia	Caroline
Salmon, John	21	Virginia	"
Scully, Chris	38	Ireland	Frederick

Name	Age	Born	Enlisted
Seaman, Robert	43	England	Frederick
Seaton, George	17	Virginia	Prince William
Snipes, Thomas	23	Virginia	Dinwiddie
Sommerville, James	25	Scotland	Frederick
Stark, Benjamin	18	Virginia	Stafford
Stripling, Samuel	33	Virginia	Caroline
Swain, William	29	Ireland	Cumberland
Thomas, Samuel	41	England	Prince George
White, John	27	Ireland	Alexandria
Williams, James	28	Virginia	Chesterfield
Williams, Joseph	22	Virginia	Amelia

Note I:- I believe this Roll can be identified as the Company of
Captain George Mercer by the inclusion of the names of Nathaniel
Barret and Edward Evans. These two soldiers had been named in a
report signed by Captain "G" Mercer as "fit for duty", July 9, 1755
after the Battle of Great Meadows. In the payroll of the Virginia
Regiment 29th May - 29th July 1754 George Mercer is the only one
of the surname with the rank of captain. In December 1755, in the
Journal of Captain Charles Lewis, are found both John and George
Mercer with the rank of captain. In Crozier's Colonial Militia
(page 33) is a very interesting application for land bounty made
March 22, 1780 by James Mercer Esq. as attorney for George Mercer,
in which he recites that George Mercer and John Fenton Mercer were
his brothers; that both commanded companys in the old Virginia
Regiment; that John Fenton Mercer was killed by the enemy and that
George was promoted to Lt. Colonel in the 2nd Virginia Regiment;
and that the said Col. George Mercer is the heir at law of the said
John Fenton Mercer, etc.

Company of Captain William Peachy[1]
July 13, 1756

Name	Age	Born	Enlisted
Anderson, Alexander	26	Ireland	Baltimore
Baker, William	-	Virginia	Richmond Co.
Bins, James	20	Virginia	"
Bossman, John	18	Virginia	"
Brann, Jacob	21	Virginia	Essex
Brooks, Bibby	22	Virginia	Richmond Co.
Burn, Aquillo	18	Virginia	"
Burn, Joseph	21	Virginia	"

21

Name	Age	Born	Enlisted
Cathrim, John	-	-	-
Cofflin, John	-	-	-
Collom, Jeremiah	25	England	Winchester
Conoway, Timothy	45	England	Baltimore
Dodson, William	-	_	-
Due, Thomas	15	Virginia	Richmond Co.
Fenley, Patrick	26	Ireland	Essex
Gale, Richard	30	England	Essex
Gaskins, John Cpl	20	Virginia	Richmond Co.
Gutridge, James	29	England	Northumberland
Hathaway, Francis	19	Virginia	Richmond Co.
Jefferson, Henry	26	Virginia	Baltimore
Jones, John	31	Virginia	Essex
Leland, John	-	-	-
Lewis, Jacob	25	Virginia	Northumberland
Lowry, William	17	Virginia	Richmond Co.
McDuell, Samuel	25	Virginia	Essex
Magennett, David	-	-	-
Marshall, William	27	England	Essex
Moss, Thomas	22	England	"
Newil, William	22	Virginia	Winchester
Nonery, Griffith	-	-	-
Parsley, Augustine	28	Virginia	New Kent
Redman, Chris	46	England	Baltimore
Robinson, John	30	England	Essex
Robinson, William	22	Virginia	Northumberland
Ryon, James	30	Ireland	Spots.
Sawer, Joseph	19	Virginia	Winchester
Smith, Thomas	23	Virginia	Essex
Sparks, John	30	England	Baltimore
Thompson, Edward	23	England	Essex
Vass, Reuben, Sgt	24	Virginia	"
Williams, John	19	Virginia	New Kent

Note I:- March 6, 1780 - Richmond Co., Virginia, William Peachey, Gent., received land bounty for his services as Captain in regiment commanded by Col George Washington in 1755, 1756 and 1757 and continued in same till it was reduced.

William Peachey, Gent., served as Lieut-Colonel commanding, of the Frontier Battalion in 1759 until same was properly discharged.
- Va Col Militia, Crozier P. 32.

22

Company of Captain Robert Spotswood[1]
July 13, 1756

Name	Age	Born	Enlisted
Alexander, John	23	Virginia	King William
Alley, Thomas	34	England	Fredrcksburg
Barrack, John	46	Scotland	Ft Cumberland
Bates, Thomas	22	England	"
Bear, William	41	Virginia	Prince William
Blakely, William	24	Virginia	Caroline
Bludoe, Joseph	18	Virginia	Fredrcksburg
Bosswell, John	22	Virginia	"
Donally, John	36	Ireland	Conocochiege
Douglas, Thomas	24	Scotland	Fredrcksburg
Dunn, Richard	49	England	Northumberland
Fletcher, Joseph	19	England	Stafford
Garland, John	32	Virginia	North Carolina
Gilliam, William	19	Virginia	Stafford
Good, Richard	23	Virginia	Caroline
Growter, David	16	Virginia	Northumberland
Lare, Edward	20	Ireland	Williamsburg
Lockart, Andrew	19	Virginia	Hampshire
Lyle, James	24	Scotland	Williamsburg
McDonald, John	23	Scotland	Caroline
McEntyre, Daniel	22	Scotland	Fredrcksburg
Maynard, William	28	Virginia	Williamsburg
Moody, William	18	Virginia	Northumberland
Morris, Thomas	21	Virginia	Caroline
Muckelroy, Robert	36	Ireland	Orange
Nott, Walter	20	Virginia	Spots.
Pedder, John	46	England	"
Pike, Richard	38	Scotland	King William
Poor, Jeremiah	19	Virginia	Hampshire
Powers, Richard	21	Ireland	Suffolk
Robinson, Samuel	22	Virginia	Caroline
Ross, William	24	Scotland	"
Ryley, John	49	Ireland	Fredrcksburg
Sale, John	24	Virginia	Caroline
Taylor, John	16	No. Carolina	North Carolina
Thomas, William	26	England	Suffolk
Thorn, Edmond	23	Virginia	-
Thorp, William	22	Virginia	Caroline
Wright, John	21	Virginia	Culpeper

23

Note I:- Robert Spotswood is listed as a captain in the Virginia Regiment in the Journal of Captain Charles Lewis, in the Expedition against the French October 10 - December 27, 1755. Douglas Southall Freeman in Vol 2 of his Life of George Washington discloses that Captain Robert Spotswood led a small party on a scout towards Logstown and was apparently killed in the Spring of 1757.

Company of Lieut-Col (Adam) Stephens[1]
July 13, 1756

Name	Age	Born	Enlisted
Alenthorp, John	-	-	-
Baldock, Richard	19	Virginia	Essex
Barringer, Isaac, Cpl	31	England	Belhaven
Beazeley, Gowan	20	Virginia	Caroline
Bridgman, Roger	40	England	Frederick
Brown, Samuel	42	Virginia	Stafford
Buckley, John	40	Ireland	Winchester
Carter, Thomas Sgt	-	-	-
Coffland, Will	35	Ireland	Stafford
Cole, John	30	Virginia	Caroline
Collis, Kellis	18	Virginia	King & Queen
Cox, William	40	England	Stafford
Cram, Peter	24	Scotland	Stafford
Davis, George	26	Virginia	Accomack
Deekens, Thomas	20	Virginia	Hanover
Graham, John Sgt	31	-	-
Hazel, David	25	Scotland	Stafford
Heaslup, Abner	-	-	-
Heaslup, Albert	-	-	-
Hogan, William	-	-	-
Jones, Samuel	-	-	-
Loflan, Morgan	24	Virginia	Northampton
Nugent, Will	21	Ireland	Marlbrough, Md.
Perry, John	31	Wales	Caroline
Phipps, Thomas	-	-	-
Price, John	21	England	Stafford
Robinson, Daniel	19	Virginia	Prince William
Robinson, John	-	-	-
Saunders, Francis	20	Virginia	Stafford
Saunders, John	42	England	Pennsylvania
Saunders, John	-	-	-
Sparks, Edward	20	Virginia	Belhaven
Spencer, Zekel	21	Virginia	Isle of Wight
Taylor, Jerry	-	-	-

24

Name	Age	Born	Enlisted
Tell, Robert	29	England	Norfolk
Thompson, John	26	Ireland	Stafford
Waters, Philemon, Cpl	22	Virginia	Isle of Wight
Willet, Benjamin	17	Virginia	"
Wilson, Robert	30	England	Stafford

Note I:- Col Adam Stephens was second in command under Washington in the Expedition against the French October 10, 1755. (Crozier-Page 120). He had been a major at the time of Braddock's Defeat (1755). He was living in Frederick Co. March 8, 1780 when he received land bounty for his services. (Crozier pp 35-36). (Further note: He was in chief command of the Virginia Regiment raised in 1762.)

Lighthorse Troop of Captain Robert Stewart[1]
At Ft Maidstone, May 11, 1756

Name	Age	Born	Enlisted
Baxter, Samuel	20	England	-
Broughton, William,Cpl	23	Virginia	-
Brown, John	25	England	-
Buchanan, James	20	Scotland	-
Burns, John	26	Ireland	-
Clancy, George	23	Maryland	-
Cornelius, Robert	21	Virginia	-
Craig, John	24	Ireland	-
Eleonar, John	24	Germany	-
Glendening, David	35	Scotland	-
Govers, James	34	England	-
Hill, John	20	Virginia	-
Skelton, John	22	England	-
Smerrer, John	26	Germany	-
Speake, George	21	Virginia	-
Thompson, Thomas	32	Scotland	-
Turnstile, Robert	30	Yorkshire	-
Wilson, George	19	Pennsylvania	-
Winterbuttom, John Cpl	27	England	-

Note I:- Captain Robert Stewart had a company of Light Horse at Braddock's Defeat July 9, 1755 and was one of two officers and the General's servant who helped carry Braddock from the field of battle

after he was wounded.   He was later promoted to Major in the 1st
Virginia Regiment and commanded a Company of regulars in Col. William
Byrd's 2nd Vairginia Regiment.   The place of enlistment of the sold-
iers in this Roll are not designated.

Company of Captain (Thomas) Waggoner[1] at
Fort Holland, on ye South Branch. (No date)

Name	Age	Born	Enlisted
Austin, Francis, Sgt	49	England	Prince William
Barnet, John	22	England	Sussex
Bearcroft, William	22	Virginia	Northumberland
Biggers, James	31	Virginia	King William
Bond, Christopher	21	Virginia	Albemarle
Bowles, Doctor	24	England	Prince William
Brooks, Bibby Sgt	22	Virginia	Essex
Burn, Equilia	19	Virginia	Richmond Co.
Chiswell, William	45	Virginia	Spots.
Cole, John Cpl	21	Scotland	Prince William
Collom, Jeremiah	27	England	Orange
Combs, William	39	Virginia	James City
Conaway, Timothy	43	Ireland	Frederick
Cotham, Thomas	25	Virginia	"
Creock, John Sgt	25	Ireland	Stafford
Crickmore, James	26	Virginia	Norfolk
Davis, Edward	21	Virginia	Culpeper
Davis, James	24	England	Lancaster
Dexter, Samuel	20	England	Henrico
Ellot, Robert	35	Ireland	Essex
Farmer, Job	24	Ireland	Hanover
Fenley, Patrick	26	England	Essex
Fielding, Christian	31	England	Culpeper
Fisher, Richard	24	England	Dinwiddie
Fitzgeffries, William	47	Virginia	Amelia
Franklin, John Cpl	26	New Eng.	Prince William
Frazier, James	24	Scotland	King & Queen
Gale, Richard Cpl	32	England	Essex
Gardener, John	21	Virginia	Lancaster
Grana, Alexander	23	Scotland	Culpeper
Grimes, Edward	27	Virginia	Fairfax
Guttroy, James	29	England	Richmond Co.
Hally, John	24	Virginia	Prince William
Hamilton, Joseph	24	Virginia	Hanover
Hanna, John	49	Ireland	Elizabeth City

26

Name	Age	Born	Enlisted
Hitchcock, Thomas	38	England	Essex
Jenkins, George	19	Virginia	Frederick
Jones, David	21	Virginia	Amelia
Jones, Edward	48	Virginia	King George
Jones, John	36	Virginia	Essex
Kitchin, John	49	England	Richmond Co.
Leland, John	46	Virginia	Northumberland
Lewis, Jacob	25	Virginia	"
Lewis, Henry	24	Virginia	Amelia
Ludwick, Edward	35	Ireland	Elizabeth City
McDoel, Samuel	26	Ireland	Augusta
Major, John	41	Virginia	King & Queen
Manns, John	20	England	Frederick
Miles, James	24	Ireland	"
Mills, Emanuel	22	England	Stafford
Morgan, Richard	22	Virginia	Gloucester
Moss, Thomas	22	England	Essex
Murphy, John	24	Ireland	Bedford
Newell, William	20	England	Caroline
Nicholls, Edward	20	England	Surrey
Pendergrass, John	21	Virginia	Northumberland
Perrit, Edward	40	Virginia	Nansemond
Poe, Samuel Sgt	26	England	Northumberland
Pompey, James	22	Virginia	Sussex
Powell, George	24	Virginia	Goochland
Pruit, Thadeus	25	Virginia	Caroline
Purcell, Edward	26	Ireland	Hampshire
Redmayne, Charles	46	England	Baltimore
Rigby, Lawrence	23	New York	Norfolk
Rine, Daniel	37	Wales	Dinwiddie
Roberts, James	27	Virginia	Caroline
Robinson, William	26	Virginia	Northumberland
Rogers, William	19	England	Charles, Md.
Rounday, David	34	England	Stafford
Ryan, James	35	Ireland	Spots.
Sawyer, Joseph	20	New Eng.	Norfolk
Scople, Willis	48	Virginia	Norfolk
Short, William	21	Ireland	Brunswick
Simpson, Solomon	34	Virginia	Accomack
Smith, Thomas	22	Virginia	Essex
Smith, William	21	Virginia	Hanover
Solomons, George Cpl	30	Scotland	Stafford
Stewart, Robert	21	Scotland	"
Taylor, Jeremiah	20	Virginia	Accomack

Name	Age	Born	Enlisted
Thompson, Edward	23	England	Prince William
Warton, Anthony	30	England	Fairfax
Whitehead, Matthew	18	Virginia	Sussex
Williams, George	24	Virginia	Richmond Co.
Williams, John	19	Virginia	New Kent
Williams, Thomas	40	Wales	Essex
Willis, Richard	23	Virginia	Brunswick
Willimore, James	18	Virginia	King & Queen
Wright, Daniel	22	Virginia	Culpeper
Young, Ezekiel	20	England	Prince William

Note I:- I have been unable to locate any reference to Ft Holland (specifically by name) but the South Branch is of the Potomac River, Northwest of Winchester and according to Douglas Southall Freeman, the Virginians built two forts thereon in circa 1756.

Captain Thomas Waggoner was a veteran of Fort Necessity in 1754 and was at the Battle of Great Meadows (Braddock's Defeat July 9,175

A comparison of the Company Roll with the Roll of the Company of Captain William Peachy, dated July 13, 1756 reveals at least 17 name (possibly 19) which are common to the two rolls. This Roll of Captain Waggoner is not dated as is the Roll of Captain Peachy. In my opinion, this Roll is probably a later Roll but is probably so only by a few months. Please note the name of Bibby Brooks, age 22 in Captain Peachy's Roll, is still age 22 in this Roll but has been pro moted to sergeant. Aquillo (Equilia) Burn is 18 in 1756 and 19 in this Roll; Jeremiah Collom age 25 versus age 27; Timothy Conoway age 45 from England in 1756 reduces his age to 43 and admits that he is actually from Ireland in the later Roll. Patrick Fenley age 26 in both Rolls is mixed up as to whether he was born in England or Ire land but he first and secondly enlisted from Essex Co., Virginia. Richard Gale advances from age 30 to age 32 and to the rank of cor poral; James Gutroy, age 29, is very probably the same as James Gutridge, age 29; John Jones is 31 in 1756 and 36 in this Roll, whic age 31 I believe must be an error for age 35; Samuel McDoel, age 25 vs age 26 is very probably the same as Samuel McDuell and it would seem that this Roll corrects his birthplace from Virginia to Irelan Thomas Moss remains the same age of 22 in the 2 Rolls; Chris Redman and Charles Redmayne, age 46 in both Rolls, of England and enlisted from Baltimore should very probably be Charles instead of Chris. James Ryan (Ryon) evidently thought it necessary to fib a little abc his age (30 vs 35); Thomas Smith becomes a year younger (age 22) anc Edward Thompson does not age at all; likewise John Williams.

Company of Colonel George Washington
August 1, 1756*

Name	Age	Born	Enlisted
Belford, John	25	Ireland	Ft Cumberland
Briggs, Joseph	21	Penna	Maidstone
Brown, Thomas	22	Ireland	Charles City
Campbell, James	-	-	Stafford
Davis, James	20	Ireland	Maidstone
Dent, Arthur	35	England	Stafford
Gallard, John	25	Virginia	Richmond Co.
Hill, George	29	Ireland	Winchester
Hill, John	26	England	"
Hughs, Saunder	18	Virginia	"
Langworth, Samuel	25	Jersey	Norfolk
McLean, Lochland	24	Scotland	Prince William
McMillon, John	33	Virginia	Westmoreland
Mason, Abel	23	Virginia	Accomack
Napp, Thomas	23	England	Williamsburg
Nash, Robert	25	Virginia	Winchester
Nugent, John	23	Ireland	Maidstone
Packet, Wm. Stuart	25	Virginia	Richmond Co.
Roberts, Francis	22	Virginia	Amelia
Robinson, John	21	England	Winchester
Robinson, John Jr.	20	Scotland	Fredrcksburg
Robinson, Simon	24	England	Stafford
Smith, Benjamin	27	England	Williamsburg
Trigg, John	25	Virginia	King & Queen
Tully, Peter	32	Ireland	Winchester
Whitehead, Edward	25	Ireland	Norfolk

*   The majority of these men enlisted between March 1754 and July 1756.

Company of Captain Harry Woodward[1]
July 13, 1756

Name	Age	Born	Enlisted
Amos, Absalom*	45	England	Westmoreland
Carmichael, James*	19	Scotland	Prince George
Carroll, Matt*	24	Ireland	Spots
Chandler, John	23	Virginia	Richmond Co.
Cockrill, Joseph*	23	Virginia	Westmoreland

Name	Age	Born	Enlisted
Cope, James	23	Virginia	Westmoreland
Croxton, Thomas	32	England	Richmond Co.
Daugherty, Edward*	24	Ireland	New York (1753)
Dunn, Abram Mashaw	30	Swiss	Augusta
Evans, Thomas*	21	Virginia	Essex
Evans, William*	23	England	Albemarle
Gupton, William	23	Virginia	Orange
Harden, Peter	23	Virginia	Westmoreland
Harwood, John	32	England	Maryland
Heath, William*	-	-	-
Jones, Abraham	26	Virginia	King George
Jones, John	31	Virginia	Richmond Co.
Jones, Thomas	29	England	Essex
Kelsey, John*	25	Ireland	Winchester
Lowry, John*	21	Scotland	Essex
McCloud, Mordecai*	32	Scotland	Westmoreland
McDaniel, Terence*	22	Virginia	Amelia
McKenzie, John*	22	Scotland	Westmoreland
McMasters, William*	24	Scotland	St Marys, Md.
Mills, James	24	Scotland	Leeds Town
Moran, Dominick*	22	Virginia	King George
Murray, Richard	32	England	Frederick
Neal, James	-	-	-
Pratt, Nathaniel	20	Virginia	Eastern Shore
Raingers, Garrett	40	Dutch	Alexandria
Richardson, James*	26	Virginia	Lancaster
Roberts, Edward*	25	Ireland	Frederick
Sandy, William	24	Virginia	Westmoreland
Scattergood, William	29	England	Stafford
Scott, John*	25	Ireland	Westmoreland
Tent, Joseph	24	England	Northampton
Troy, Simon	20	Ireland	Essex
Whitecotton, George	-	Virginia	Stafford
Williams, John	24	England	Baltimore
Wright, Robert	29	Ireland	Richmond City

Note 1:- Henry (Harry) Woodward is listed as a Captain in the Virginia Regiment Oct. 10-Dec. 27, 1755 in the Journal of Captain
Charles Lewis and he was one of the officers whose signatures appear
on an address, dated at Fort Loudoun December 31, 1758, to George
Washington, Esq., on his retirement as Commander of Virginia troops
27 December 1758.

*   The names of these 18 men also appear on a later (1757) Roll of
Captain Henry Woodward, which Roll follows this one.   See also note
later.

Company of Captain Henry Woodward
September 21, 1757

Name	Age	Born	Enlisted
Adams, John	25	Virginia	Prince George
Amos, Absalom*	47	England	Westmoreland
Arnold, Anthony	21	Virginia	Caroline
Brooks, Francis	17	Virginia	Chesterfield
Brown, Edward	23	Virginia	Hampshire
Brown, Thomas	19	Virginia	Essex
Bryant, John	29	Ireland	Fairfax
Campbell, George	25	Ireland	Augusta
Carmichael, James*	20	Scotland	Prince George
Carroll, Mathew*	26	Ireland	Spots
Clark, John, Cpl	26	England	"
Cockrill, Joseph*	24	Virginia	Westmoreland
Colman, Cornelius	25	Ireland	Prince William
Cook, Reuben	18	Virginia	Sussex
Cowen, Samuel	22	England	Cambridge
Dean, William Sgt.	-	-	-
Denny, Richard	30	Virginia	Northumberland
Dothery, Edmond*	25	Ireland	York
Downey, John	45	England	Northumberland
East, Josiah	21	Virginia	Louisa
Evans, Thomas*	21	Virginia	Essex
Evans, William*	24	England	Albemarle
Farmer, Charles	-	-	-
Fendley, Briant	23	England	Augusta
Fent, Joseph Sgt	-	-	-
Ferrall, John	35	Virginia	King & Queen
Fields, Henry	22	Ireland	Augusta
Fisher, John	20	Virginia	Accomack
Fitzpatrick, John	50	Ireland	Fairfax
Gales, John	24	Virginia	Orange
Guptor, William	23	Ireland	Augusta
Heath, William*	20	Virginia	Hampshire
Hilton, George	26	England	"
Hook, William	25	England	Frederick
Hornback, Joel	56	New York	Chester (Pa?)
Hunt, William	41	England	Belhaven

31

Name	Age	Born	Enlisted
Huts, Jacob	30	Germany	Hampshire
Ingeram, James	18	Virginia	Spots
Kelsey, John*	24	Ireland	Middlesex
Ketcham, John	22	Virginia	Amelia
Lacey, John	28	Penna.	Winchester
Linsie, Daniel Crawley	19	Virginia	Richmond Co.
Lovit, John	23	Virginia	Northumberland
Lowrey, John*	22	Scotland	Dinwiddie
McCloud, Mordicka*	34	Scotland	St Marys, Md.
McCormick, Adam	23	England	Northumberland
McDonald, Terence*	23	Ireland	Westmoreland
McKenzie, John*	32	Scotland	King George
McMasters, William*	25	Scotland	Hampshire
Macksfield, Wilby	22	Virginia	Westmoreland
Moorin, Dominick*	24	Ireland	Essex
Nash, John Sgt	-	-	-
Naughty, John	24	England	Amelia
Neall, James	24	Ireland	Belhaven
Pratt, Marshall	22	Virginia	Stafford
Quisenberry, Humphrey	24	Virginia	Hampshire
Remeshall, John	25	Virginia	Dinwiddie
Reynolds, John	24	Maryland	Spots
Reynolds, Thomas	25	Virginia	Albemarle
Richinson, James*	27	Virginia	Lancaster
Roberts, Edward*	26	England	Orange
Robinson, Hamblet	22	Virginia	Northampton
Ross, William	26	Scotland	Caroline
Rowell, Jacob	23	Virginia	Accomack
Scott, John*	39	Scotland	Prince William
Shaw, Abraham	44	England	Augusta
Sheperson, William	40	Virginia	Hanover
Sinks, Jacob	31	Low Dutch	Augusta
Smith, Richard	23	Virginia	Princess Ann
Sutliff, John	18	Virginia	Essex
Tolley, Dudley	19	Virginia	Essex
Trotter, Richard Sgt	-	-	-
Wallace, William	27	Virginia	Frederick

*   These 18 men can possibly be identified as being soldiers who appeared in the preceding earlier (1756) Roll of Captain Harry Woodward although in some instances the names are spelled a little differently, their ages are not reconcilable, or their birthplaces are listed differently. In any further or future research on any of these individuals both records should be cited.

The following Colonial Militia soldiers were left out of the preceding Rolls by error and are herewith added under the name of their Company Captain.

Soldier	Age	Born	Enlisted
Captain Joshua Lewis (# 2)			
Hutson, Thomas	27	England	Lancaster
Captain Robert McKenzie			
Smith, Thomas	29	Virginia	Northumberland
Captain George Mercer			
Clatterbuck, John	17	Virginia	Caroline
Captain Robert Stewart			
Hill, Samuel	32	Ireland	-
Huff, John	28	Maryland	-
Hughes, William Sgt.	26	England	-
Kelly, Daniel	26	Pennsylvania	-
Ketting, John	23	Ireland	-
Linn, William	24	Ireland	-
McKay, Phinley	27	Scotland	-
Martial, William	27	England	-
Murphy, Patrick	21	Pennsylvania	-
Powell, Jacob	23	Pennsylvania	-
Rowe, Thomas	21	Maryland	-
Salser, George	26	Holland	-
Sarbuck, John	22	Germany	-
Shepherd, Thomas	25	England	-
Shriver, George	23	Germany	-

Revolutionary War Size Roll (After Sept. 1, 1780)

Chesterfield (County, Va.) Supplement - Virginia State Library Accession #23816-

Frontispiece - (Quote) - "This book is a supplement to 'papers concerning the Army of the Revolution,(?) I, Executive Department' and in order, precedes Benjamin Harrison's mission to Philadelphia 1781 - Size Roll of Troops joined at Chesterfield Courthouse since Sept. 1, 1780 (Signed) - Captain Joseph Scott". (End Quote)

Comment by C. H. Hamlin:

These records give the name of the soldier, his age, his size in feet and inches, his trade, where born, place of residence, color of hair, eyes and complexion.

The ages of the soldiers given in this roll very probably are their ages in the latter part of the year 1780 when the roll was evidently initiated and it might be well to estimate the year of birth as, circa 1780, from which deduct the ages given for the year of birth.

From the list, which will be treated of below, it would seem that this company or regiment was a Foreign Legion outfit, from their places of birth as given, but in actuality they composed only about 25 percent of the total of this muster roll. I have not listed the soldiers claiming Virginia as their birthplace. A full list, including the Virginia born, is being currently serialized by the Virginia Genealogical Society in their Quarterly Bulletin.

Although this record is called the Chesterfield County Supplement and most people think it is therefore a company of soldiers recruited from residents of Chesterfield County I was struck by the very singular and noteworthy fact that less than one percent of these men claimed Chesterfield County as their birthplace or place of residence.

There seem to be several possibilities for surmise inherent herein. (1) These men may have been recruited in various sections of the State and all brought together or concentrated at Chesterfield Courthouse to form a new company or (2) They may have been the remnants or remaining portions of several other regiments and companies brought together from various sections for the purpose of re-organization into full strength.

33

I have done no research at all to decide if this is so or not. Very probably the military records or pension applications of some of the individuals contained in this list could be checked and further very important historical facts determined or disclosed.

At any rate, this muster or size roll cannot properly be claime by Chesterfield County beyond the fact that this company was evident ly organized and encamped here at one time. My last observation is that this is a truly remarkable, important and valuable record and of a very rare type.

Revolutionary War Size Roll - After Sept. 1, 1780

Name	Age	Place of Birth	Residence
Ambler, George	40	England	Spotsylvania C
Adcock, William	26	Windsor, England	Albemarle Co.
Adkinson, Wm	25	London, " -	Fauquier Co.
Archer, Evan	25	Hertford, N.C.	Norfolk, Va.
Balies, William	25	Birmingham, Eng.	Leesburg, Va.
Beal, John	18	Maryland	Pittsylvania C
Butler, Lewis	17	France	Princess Ann,C
Baley, William	40	Ireland	Surry Co.
Bradey, John	28	Scotland	Westmoreland C
Buckhannon, John	36	"	Caroline Co.
Bryan, Barrack	23	Maryland	Prince Wm. Co.
Brown, Thomas	47	England	" " "
Butcher, Daniel	21	"	" " "
Branin, Daniel	16	Ireland	Richmond City
Brown, John	35	England	Amherst Co.
Boy, Jacob	32	Penna.	Loudoun Co.
Braddock, Peter	22	France	Isle of Wight
Brown, George	25	Maryland	Loudoun Co.
Burn, Thomas	20	London, Eng.	Prince Wm. Co.
Brown, David	25	England	Baltimore, Md.
Connel, John	20	Ireland	Williamsburg
Cahill, Barnaby	60(sic)	"	Fairfax Co.
Carr, Thomas	39	Maryland	Bedford Co.
Cousins, Peter	18	France	Princess Ann C
Colwell, Robert	42	England	Fauquier Co.
Connelley, John	24	Ireland	Spots. Co.
Conner, Lawrence	26	"	Botetouct Co.
Church, John	20	Bristol, Eng.	Maryland

34

Name	Age	Place of Birth	Residence
Craft, John	26	England	Culpeper Co.
Chapman, Thomas	19	Maryland	Loudoun Co.
Charlott, John	19	France	Isle of Wight
Carr, Joseph	42	England	Caroline Co.
Cole, George	28	"	Fauquier Co.
Crane, William	40	"	" "
Crook, John	33	"	" "
Caugan, Ralph	20	New Jersey	Culpeper Co.
Collins, John	30	Ireland	" "
Carson, Matthew	17	Maryland	Berkeley Co.
Chalkly, Thomas	25	England	Fauquier Co.
Campin, William	27	Ireland	Henrico Co.
Clayton, John	28	England	Chesterfield Co
Coleman, John	27	Amelia Co.,Va.	Warren Co.,N.C.
Dickson, George	21	Maryland	Stafford Co.
Dickson, William	29	Ireland	Delaware
Dunnivant, Michal	22	"	-
Duddleston, Thomas	32	England	See Note 1
Driver, Edward	22	"	See Note 2
Duestan, John	19	France	Amelia Co.
Dispain, Peter	17	No. Carolina	Montgomery Co.
Duncan, Solomon	39	" "	Princess Ann Co
Dounstanham, John	21	Maryland	Prince Wm. Co.
Dumont, James	20	France	Isle of Wight
Duvall, Thomas	24	"	" " " Co.
Dixon, Samuel	24	England	Prince Wm. Co.
Dixon, John	21	"	Culpeper Co.
Elwell, Thomas	29	New Jersey	See Note 3
English B---	23	Ireland	See Note 4
Fowler, Robert	35	England	Hampshire Co.
Fram, John	24	New Britton(Note 6)	Charlotte Co.
Franklayn, John	22	Ireland	King Wm. Co.
Fitzgrel, George	40	Maryland	Henrico Co.
Fields, Michael	30	England	Hanover Co.
Fonton, Lewis	31	France	Amelia Co.
Forest Hampton, John	18	France	" "
Frost, Joshua	24	England	Prince Wm Co.
Folks, Thomas	21	"	Richmond
Farren, Thomas	23	Italy	King & Queen Co

Name	Age	Place of Birth	Residence
Gough, Adam	24	Maryland	Loudoun Co.
Glimp, Abraham	39	Prussia	Chesterfield C
Giddins, John	38	England	New Kent Co.
Grinins, James	26	"	Westmoreland C
Grant, William	30	Scotland	Montgomery Co.
Garner, George	20	Maryland	See Note 5
Green, Joseph	20	"	Fauquier Co.
Grayham, Arthur	32	Ireland	Fairfax
Hamlin, Job	19	Maryland(Western)	Pittsyl. Co.
Hood, Edw.	23	Dublin, Ireland	Montgomery Co.
(Herry?)Henry, James	24	England	Hampton, Va.
Holledge, William	27	"	Amelia
Hill, John	22	Ireland	Bedford
Hale, John	30	England	Frederick
Heath, William	40	Ireland	Ft Pitt, Va.
Hickson, James	17	Jersey(Middlesex)	Prince Wm.
Hallicia(?),Thomas	25	Italy	Isle of Wight
Hill, Edmund	-	England	Berkeley
Hughes, Thomas	45	"	Culpeper
Harvey, Edward	28	"	Prince Wm.
Hawkins, William	30	"	Fauquier Co
Huff, James	18	Jersey(Sussex)	Loudoun Co
Harriss, James	36	Md. (P. Geo.)	Fauquier
Heson, Samuel	18	London, Eng.	"
Hawkes, John	34	England	Norfolk
Hays, Vachal	15	Dorset, Md.	Dorset, Md.
Holebrook, James	37	England	Montgomery,Md.
Hicks, David	24	No. Carolina	Washington,N.C
Harris, William	24	Pennsy (York)	Loudoun
Harrison, Solomon	20	Maryland	Montgomery
Jackson, Peter	24	Germantown,Penna	Henrico Co.
Johnson, Samuel	22	England	Augusta
Johnson, John	18	N.C. (Roane)	Washington
Jones, Thomas	21	England	Newburn, N.C.
Jones, William	27	"	Loudoun
Jordan, Thomas	29	"	Culpeper
Kelley, Thomas	22	Ireland	Williamsburg
Kelley, James	25	"	Stafford
Kinsor, Michael	22	Pennsylvania	Montgomery
Knox, John	37	Ireland	-
Klotz, John	36	France	Virginia

36

Name	Age	Place of Birth	Residence
King, Sabbert	19	Maryland	Albemarle
Kaddock, James	26	"	Fairfax
Kennaday, William	21	England	Culpepper
Loftis, John	28	Ireland	Cumberland
Lairy, William	-	"	Loudoun
L----, Thomas	22	London, Eng.	Fairfax
L----, George	23	Penna, (Burks)	Augusta
Lowe, Henry	19	Maryland	Montgomery
Lour, Andrew	22	"	"
Librook, Henry	21	Lancaster, Penna	"
Loyd, John	22	England	"
Lingo, James	42	Maryland	Essex
Lewis, Fretus(?)	22	London, Eng.	Loudoun
Lenox, Charles	26	Glasgow, Scot.	Prince Wm.
Latour, John	32	France	Isle of Wight
Lang, John	22	Md. (P. Geo.)	" " "
Lane, William	22	Bristol, Eng.	Augusta
Lion, Samuel	21	Jersey(Morris)	Rockbridge
Lessley, William	25	Ireland	Boston
Lilley, John	27	No. Carolina	No. Carolina
Linaham, Jer.	26	Ireland (Cork)	Montgomery, Md.
Mathews, James	39	Ireland (Down)	Dutches
McQuin, John	25	Ireland	Loudoun
Merchant, Thomas	32	England	Louisa
Morris, Lewis	22	France	Hampton, Va.
McCoy, Patrick	42	Ireland	" "
Murrough, Lewis	18	France (Nantz)	Princess Ann
Meeke(?), John	24	Norfolk, Eng.	Botetouct
Mitchell, Thomas	32	England	James City
Merritt, Samuel	20	Jersey(Sussex)	Loudoun
McCaul, John	42	France	Isle of Wight
Marshall, Richard	-	Maryland	Albemarle
Murphy, Michael	-	Ireland(Cork)	"
McKinley, John	33	Chester, Penna	Fauquier
McDade, James	21	Hampshire(W.Va.)	Hampshire
Mattson, John	20	Jersey(Hopewell)	King George
McClanon, John	22	Prin. Ann (Va.)	Currutuck, N.C.
Newman, Walter	26	Pennsylvania	Montgomery
Nequale, John	-	France	-
Needum, Isaac	17	Maryland	Westmoreland
Nowel, Batt	27	Italy	Isle of Wight

Name	Age	Place of Birth	Residence
Nekum, Peter	21	Newburn, N. C.	?
Newton, William	30	England	Loudoun
Newman, Thomas	21	"	Fairfax
Newell, Ben	27	"	Culpepper
Osborn, Thomas	24	England	Hanover
Owens, James	34	Belfast, Ireland	Augusta
Orsborn, Elisha	24	Jersey(Trent town)	Loudoun
Petree, Alexander	35	Elgin, Scotland	King Wm.
Pardo, James	22	Boston, Mass.	King. Wm.
Palmer, Thomas	43	Portsmouth, Eng.	Hanover
Plowman, Robert	59	England	Chesterfield
Parmore(?), Thomas	22	London, Eng.	Fairfax
Piper, George	23	Burks, Penna.	Augusta
Prichard, James	52	England	Prince Wm.
Pearce, Edward	28	Ireland	-
Potter, William	18	(?) Island	Montgomery
Pharnhouse, Thos.	22	London, Eng.	"
Parker, William	24	England	Augusta
Parks, Daniel	23	Hampshire,W.Va.	Loudoun
Price, Elinzer	37	Jersey(Burlington)	Isle of Wight
Perry, William	21	England	Westmoreland
Pugh, Richard	21	Longon, England	Rockingham
Parsons, Jerry	24	Md. (Charles)	Stafford
Powers, Thomas	30	Dublin, Ireland	Dublin, Ire.
Pidgeon, Jno.Leonard	21	York, Penna.	Washington
Prue, Humphrey	26	Culpepper Co,Va.	Wilks Co.N.C.
Right, Thomas	17	N. Y. (Burlington)	Loudoun
Rogers, Cornelius	17	Ireland	Princess Ann
Rowe, William	28	Phila., Penna.	Hartford,Md.
Roberts, Evan	27	" "	Amelia
Rhodes, John	26	Maryland	Culpepper
Robertson, David	19	"	Middlesex
Rawden, John	40	York, England	Fauquier
Syms, William	23	Scotland	Williamsburg
Spragg, John	22	Maryland	Lunenburg
Sharplin, James	21	Britain(Middlesex)	Lunenburg
Smith, John	35	England	Stratsburg
Still, Jno Alexdr.	42	Scotland	Hanover
Sikes, William	21	No. Carolina	N. C.
Shearg(?), John	22	Ireland	Virginia

Name	Age	Place of Birth	Residence
Sridder(?), Martin	21	Burks, Penna.	Montgomery
Shepler, Conrod	35	Germany	Washington
Snider, Fred	18	Lancaster, Penna.	Montgomery
Soleleather(?), Philip	54	Germany	Richmond
Sadler, Samuel	33	Maryland	Montgomery
Stephens, Richard	53	England	Essex
Smith, Thomas	20	Maryland	Stafford
Stout, Reubin	19	Jersey(Ammel)	Prince Wm.
Stanley, Samuel	-	London, Eng.	Albemarle
Smith, Jacob	-	Berlin, Germany	"
Sharpe, William	-	Ireland	"
Steward, George	-	London, Eng.	Augusta
Smith, William	43	England	Nansemond
Smiler, James	28	"	Williamsburg
Smith, Samuel	22	Jersey	Culpepper
Straton, Seth	18	"	"
Stephenson, George	35	London, Eng.	"
Scarbrough, James	30	England	Loudoun
Sidwell, Stephen	18	Bucks, Penna.	Fauquier
Soons, John	24	England	Loudoun
Steward, James	28	Scotland	Richmond Co,N.C.
Turnbull, Peter	21	Scotland	-
Taffe, James	28	Dublin, Ireland	Guilford Co,N.C.
Thornton, William	22	Maryland	Hampton, Va.
Tanner, Paul	24	Dublin, Ireland	Alexandria,Va.
Tannes (?), Peter	24	Frankfort, Ger.	Montgomery
Trinon, James	23	Dublin, Ireland	"
Turnbull, John	25	London, England	Stafford
Turner, John	26	England	Augusta
Taylor, James	21	London, England	Edenton, N.C.
Tomlin, William	36	Baltimore, Md.	Richmond, Va.
Trotman, Samuel	19	England	Fairfax
Vicker, John	22	Portsmouth, N.E.	Portsmouth
Vanpelf, Samuel	17	Phila., Penna.	Fauquier
Vernon, Joseph	17	New Castle, Penna	Charlotte
White, John	16	Burlington,N.J.	Brunswick
Works, James	24	Penna (York)	Prince George
Weaner, Christian	23	Charleston,S.C.	Hampton, Va.
Walthall, William	22	Ireland	Amelia
White, Caleb	22	Jersey (Essex)	"
Wilson, Joseph	38	England	"

Name	Age	Place of Birth	Residence
White, John	19	Ireland, (Dary)	Mecklenburg
Woody, Richard	17	Louisa Co.,Va.	Washngton Co.N.
Windledurk(?),Geo.	32	Penna, (Burk)	Albemarle
Walsh, Thomas	34	Waterford, Ire.	Montgomery
Walta, George	41	Lancaster, Penna	"
Wilkins, Thomas	24	England	Loudoun
Wallace, William	49	Dublin, Ireland	Prince Wm.
White, John	45	" "	" "
Ward, Joseph	33	Maryland	Albemarle
West, William	18	Salem, Penna.	Portsmouth,Va.
Woomple, Peter	23	Phila., Penna.	Loudoun
Wilson, Edward	27	England	"
Wealch, Jeremiah	32	Ireland	York
Wise, (Chas.?)	27	London, Eng.	Chesterfield
Walston(?), Jonathan	30	Pr.Anne Co.,Va.	Currytuck,N.C.

NOTES

1. A Thomas Duddleston on Hanover Co. Tax List in 1782.

2. Families of surname "Driver" were living in York - Isle of Wight-
Gloucester - Powhatan Counties in 1782. For Edward Driver see
Echenrode (1911) p. 144.

3. Thomas Elwell, res. of Maryland - had Virginia Cont. Service - removed to Ohio. His widow, Elizabeth, applied for pension (#W7096)
Bounty Warrant for Services #695-100 (per Hoyts Index).

4. This may be Batt English - See Echenrode (1911) p. 154.

5. See Echenrode (1911) p. 175. The name Garner - Gardner - Gardiner
are often misspelled for each other.

6. I cannot identify New Britton but it may be referring to New
Britain, Connecticut. Hoyt's Index shows a John Fram (or Fame)
with Virginia Service and who applied for pension (#541526).

PALMER

Pension application of James Howard, Virginia Service File #S20406 - (National Archives, Washington, D. C.)

He was born in Virginia circa 1761, moved to South Carolina in his 18th or 19th year - served 18 months as private. Allowed pension by State of South Carolina. Died in Union District, South Carolina, November 24, 1843 leaving no widow, but the following children:

Patty Howard
Henry Howard
Elizabeth, wife of Elisha Palmer
Laodicia (called Dicy), wife of Samuel W. Tucker.
Sarah Howard
Thomas Howard (died before father.)

Henry Howard, (above) later lived in Pickens Dist., S. C.

Laodicia Tucker was of Spartanburg, S. C. in 1852.

Note: In an attempt to identify Elisha and Elizabeth Palmer, refer to Halifax County Deed Book 18, page 237 - 15 Oct. 1799 Daniel Palmer of County of Union, State of South Carolina sells 100 acres of land in Halifax County, Virginia to Elias Palmer of Halifax Co., Virginia. (Note - a Daniel Palmore (Palmer) married in Halifax Co. 10 May 1781 Elizabeth Nance). An older Elisha Palmer (Rev. War) (Son of Thomas Palmer Sr.) married in Halifax Co., Virginia 4 July 1782 Nancy Legrand, daughter of John Legrand) and later married secondly Ann ---. This older Elisha Palmer (born Oct. 15, 1755 by his pension application) died testate 1842 in Halifax Co., Virginia.

Application for Pension of John Owsley (or Ousley) or Housely) - File # R-16894 - Virginia Service - Signed by Mark (x) John Ousley but family records are OWSLEY - application dated March 19, 1833 in Claiborne Co., Tennessee - age 76 (thus born 1757), enlisted 1776 while residing in Loudon Co., Virginia. Gives his various enlistments, officers, etc. Total service more than 13 months.

His Family Bible Records are as follows:

John Owsley married Charity Barten (born 11-6-1757) 8-16-1778. Their children:

Tabitha - born March 15, 1780
John Jr. Born March 17, 1783 (later called John Lynch Owsley)

41

```
Isaac    - Born April 27,1785
Stephen  - Born June 24, 1787
Mathew   - Born Sept. 23, 1789
Ann      - Born April 9, 1796
```

The widow, Charity Housely, age 95, made application for pension October 16, 1846. Husband (John) died 19 December 1845. Husband received pension of $43.33 per annum commencing 3-4-1831. (Note by C. H. H. - One of the daughters named above married James Blackburn of Maury Co., Tennessee.

Application of Samuel Dean - R2808 - A resident of Henry Co., Kentucky, age 85 - dated Feb. 26, 1846 - states he enlisted as a private in the army in 1779 for 18 months, from Loudoun Co., Va. with William Housley, under Jonas Dunkin, etc.

Application for Revolutionary War Pension

Virginia Service of Joseph Ligon (Son of Capt. Joseph Ligon), National Archives, Washington, D. C. (File #S132).

Declaration was made January 8, 1807 in Halifax Co., Virginia.

It appears from the papers on file in Claim S132 based upon disability of Joseph Ligon, incurred while in service during the War of the Revolution.

Joseph Ligon of Halifax County, Virginia, served as private in Capt. John Thompson's Company, Colonel Nathaniel Cooke's Virginia Regiment and while in line of duty March 15, 1781 at the battle of Guilford Court House, he was wounded by a musket ball passing through his right shoulder. The date of his enlistment is not given

His name was transferred from the Virginia Pension Agency to the West Tennessee Agency. In 1833 he was a resident of Montgomery County, Tennessee.

The papers on file in this claim contain no discernible data in regard to the family of the soldier, Joseph Ligon.

There were several letters in this file from the following persons: Mrs. Charles B. Ferman, Attalla, Alabama, 1929; Miss Minnie McWherter, 115 Church St., Winder, Georgia 1930; Mrs. H. K. Brewster, 592 2nd St., Brooklyn, New York 1939

Application for Revolutionary War Pension - Virginia Service
of Blackman Ligon and Elizabeth, National Archives, Washington, D.C.
File # W9132.

Declaration was made November 14, 1818 in Greenville, Greenville District, South Carolina, age 61 (born 1757) by said Blackman
Ligon, son of Capt. Joseph Ligon. It appears from the papers in
the Revolutionary War Pension Claim W9132, that Blackman Ligon enlisted in Halifax Co., Virginia, February 12, 1776, served as a
private in Capt. Nathaniel Cooke and William Moseley's companies,
Colonels William Dangerfield and Alexander McClannahan's 7th Virginia Regiment, that he was in the battles of Brandywine and Germantown and at the "Affair at Cootes' Bridge", and was discharged
Feb. 12, 1780 by Colonel Christian Febiger.

In Feb. 1781, he volunteered and was at the Battle of Guilford, where he received a musket ball wound in the thigh.

He married about 1780 to Elizabeth, maiden name not stated.
She was born April 28, 1753. She was allowed pension 1841. She
died Oct. 15, 1842

In 1821 the soldier referred to his children, John T., age
29, Elizabeth, age 25 and Blackman, age 22 and to his grandsons,
James B. Roseman, or Rosemond, age 9 and Joseph Ligon, age 4. His
eldest child was a girl, name not stated and his second, was Mrs.
Nancy T. Moore, or Moon, who was born Nov. 1, 1784. She and her
brother, John T., resided in Greenville District, South Carolina
in 1841.

Application for Revolutionary War Pension - Virginia Service
of William Ligon, National Archives, Washington, D. C., File
S13764.

Declaration was made in Owen County, Kentucky, August 17,1832
by said William Ligon.

He was born November 24, 1762 in Powhatan Co., Virginia and
while a resident of Powhatan Co., William Ligon enlisted and served
as private with the Virginia troops as follows: in 1779, three
months in Capt. Richard Crump's Company in Col. Parker's Regiment;
he next served three months as an express rider and carried an express from General LaFayette to General Wayne; next served three
months in Capt. Robert Hughes' Company in Col. Beverly Randolph's
or Col. John Holcombe's Regiment and was in the battle of Guilford

43

Court House, next served three months in Capt. Littlebery Mosby's Co. in Col. Caul's Regiment and was in the battle of Petersburg.

After the Revolution, he lived in Cumberland Co. and in Prince Edward Co., Virginia - in Wilson Co., Tennessee and about 1816 he moved to Owen County, Kentucky.

In 1897 it was stated that William Ligon's daughter, Mrs. Martha H. Morgan, was age 87 (?). The last digit not clearly written, years of age. There is no further data relative to soldier's family in these files.

Application for Revolutionary War Pension - Virginia Service of John Ligon, National Archives, Washington, D. C. File #S4555.

Declaration was made by John Ligon, September 4, 1832, in Smith County, Tennessee, for 18 years previous to which time he had resided in Halifax Co., Virginia.

The data which follow were found in pension Clain S4555, based upon service of John Ligon in the Revolutionary War.

John Ligon was born 1761 in Chesterfield Co., Virginia - the day of his birth and the names of parents are not shown.

While a resident of Halifax Co., Virginia he enlisted 1780 or early 1781 and served 20 days as a private in Capt. James Hill's Virginia Company, from which he was discharged near Petersburg. He enlisted next in 1781, served as a private in Capt. Powell's and Richard Gaines' Company, Col. Fleming's Virginia Regiment, marched to different places but was stationed most of the time near Suffolk, and was discharged there at the expiration of service of three months. He enlisted a third time, served as a private in Capt. John Carr's Company - Col. John Purnell's Virginia Regiment, marched to Prince Edward Court House, crossed the James River and left the service June 22, 1781 on account of illness. He did not return until a "considerable time" after the surrender of Cornwallis and received his discharge from Capt. Clark. His entire service amounts to six months and 20 days.

John Ligon made no reference to wife or children.

In 1832 William Ligon was a resident of Smith County, Tenn. but no relationship between him and John Ligon was stated.

44

His (John Ligon's?, William Ligon's ?) pension certificate is #19199, issued 8-13-1833, Rate $22.22 per annum, commenced March 4, 1831, Act. of June 7, 1832, Tennessee Agency.

Bounty Warrant for Revolutionary War Services - (Original in Virginia State Library)

Issued to John Forester who states he is of the County of Barren, State of Kentucky and gives his Power of Attorney to Nathaniel Sawyer of Frankfort, County of Franklin, State of Kentucky, to secure any bounty land warrant due him for military services by him performed as a soldier in the Virginia Line, upon Continental Establishment in the Revolutionary War - dated 22 August 1818.

John Forester states on the reverse side of the above that he enlisted in the year 1776 in the Company of Capt. John Ashby in the Third Virginia Regiment, Continental Establishment and served three years. At the expiration he then re-enlisted for one year in the Company of Capt. Triplett belonging to Morgan's Regiment in said Virginia Line - (front of document - allowed Land Bounty as a private for three years).

NOTE BY C.H.H.: There is a record in 1820 stating that John Forrester (File #S35948) of Barren Co., Ky. was 81 years old, a farmer, and had no family except his wife, Mary Forrester, age 84.

Land Bounty Warrant of Thomas Owsley, Soldier (Rev. War)(Virginia State Library - original)

17 June 1821, made application from Rock Castle Co., Kentucky, stating he had enlisted in Virginia Continental Service in Capt. Charles Slaughter's Co. of Col. Daniel Morgan's Regiment for duration of the War in 1776 and served until the Battle of Germantown when he was taken prisoner. Twelve months later he was exchanged and continued in Service until the year 1783 at the end of the war, at which time he was honorably discharged in Loudown Co., Virginia.

He gives P of A to John Watkins of Richmond, Virginia to receive his land warrant when issued.

22 June, 1821, John Clark of Garrard Co., Kentucky made a deposition under oath that he was well acquainted with Thomas Owsley

in the Revolutionary War and was a prisoner with him in the jail in Philadelphia.

On the back is a notation - Thomas Owsley's Petition - Land Claim July 25, 1821, allowed as private for the War.

ORIGINAL RECORDS - ABSTRACTS

Culpeper County, Virginia, Deed Book R, Page 319-

3 April 1792 - James Hickman Senior, living in KENTUCKY, of one
part and John Minor of CULPEPER COUNTY, VIRGINIA, of the other
part - Whereas the said James Hickman Sr., before he moved to
Kentucky did appoint James Hickman Jr. and William Roberts of
Culpeper County his true and lawful attorneys. (Note by C.H.H.):
See Culpeper Deed Book O, page 309) to sell and convey land be-
longing to him; therefore sell 48 acres of land to said John
Minor, etc. - Recorded 17 September 1792.

COMMENT: The above James Hickman Senior was devised land
in Culpeper County by will of his father, Edwin Hickman of
Albemarle County, Virginia, dated 4 February 1758, probated November Court 1769 (Will Book 2, Page 248) A James Hickman is on
1790 Kentucky Census in Fayette County.

Orange County Will Book 3, Page 190-

Will of Thomas Burras, dated 2 October 1788, probated 23 March 1789

To beloved wife, Frances Burras, my whole estate, real and
personal for her life or widowhood, then to be divided amongst my
children hereafter named:

To Son Thomas, 500 acres of land in KENTUCKY, (first choice)
To Son William Tandy Burras, 500 acres in KENTUCKY,(2nd choice)
To my Son Roger Burras, 500 acres in KENTUCKY, (3rd choice)
To my Grandson, Thomas Burras, son of Thomas, one negro boy,
Absalom.
To Daughter, Morning Burras, negro woman Nan (under age).
To Daughter, Fanny Embry, a negro girl, Suckey
To Daughter, Mildred Embry, a negro boy, Ben
To Daughter, Elizabeth Brockman, negro boy Duke
To Daughter, Sarah Tribble, negro girl, Agnes
To Daughter, Jane Quisenberry, negro girl, Dinnah
To Granddaughter, Frances Quisenberry, daughter of Jane
Quisenberry, a negro girl, named (Nan?)
To my Daughter, Frances Tandy Bush, negro girl, Alce

Balance of my land in KENTUCKY (500 acres) to my daughters,

Fanny Embry, Mildred Embry, Sally Tribble, Jane Quisenberry and
Frances T. Bush; to my Granddaughters and grandsons, Elizah Perry,
Dicey Perry and Harry Perry.

Executors: Wife, Frances, Henry Tandy and Thomas Burras.
Witness: Caleb Lindsay, Thomas Bell, James Daniel.

Will Book 4, Page 122 - Settlement of Estate of Thomas Burrus
deceased, by Henry Tandy and Thomas Burrus.

Distribution

To William Tandy Burrus 51 pds, 12 sh. 11 pence
Roger Burrus   "   "   "
Roger Burrus for James Quisenberry, 51 pds, 12 sh., 11 pe.
To John Brockman   "   "   "
To Thomas Burrus   "   "   "
To Thomas Burrus for Joseph Embry "   "   "
To Thomas Burrus for John Embry   "   "   "
To Thomas Burrus for children of Molly Perry, dec.
                                   51 pds, 12 sh., 11 pe.
To William T. Bush for William Bush "   "   "
To Thomas Graves   "   "   "
Due to Andrew Tribble: legatees   "   "   "
                                   641   17   4

Returned November 24, 1800
Recorded 28 January 1805

Accession # 21765 Virginia State Library, Richmond, Virginia

Last Will and Testament of (Mrs) Frances Burrus*of the State
of Kentucky and County of Christian - (dated 25 January 1816- Probated Christian County, Kentucky January Term 1817.

**

To my three sons, Thomas Burrus, William T. Burrus and Roger
Burrus $400.00.
To son in law, Andrew Tribble, 20 pounds
To daughters Sally Tribble and Frances T. Bush, 60 pounds
To granddaughter, Sally Ellen Burrus, daughter of my son,
Roger Burrus, bed and furniture.
To Joseph Mills Burrus, son of Nathaniel Burrus, bed & furniture
Executors - friend: William Tandy and Nathaniel Burrus
Witnesses - William Daniel - Anderson Preuitt, Charles H. Mills

Note: *Frances was the widow of Thomas Burrus (1722-89) of Orange Co.,
       Virginia, a Revolutionary War Soldier.

48

Note: **The middle initial T. in William's name probably stands for
Tandy as this name descends in the family.

AMHERST COUNTY, Will Book 3, Page 246-

15 October 1792 - Joseph Burrus and Fanny Penn, administrators
of Estate of Joseph Penn, deceased, gave bond in sum of 3,000 pds.
to make a true and perfect inventory Benamms Stone and Charles
Burras, their Sec.

Will Book 3, Page 407

Will of Charles Burrus - Dated 1 May 1795, Probated 16 Jan.1797

To Son, Joseph, land where he now lives (400 Acres) and 1200
Acres of land in KENTUCKY (beginning part of 2000 acres) and also
200 acres in CAINTUCKY, also slaves (all named)-

To children of my deceased daughter Fanny Penn, Slaves-
To my daughter, Molley Ann Crawford, slave
My four children, Joseph, Elizabeth Pickett, Pamelia Burrus,
Fanny Penn, Children
Grandson, Charles Burrus Pickett - daughter Lucy Camden-
mentions among his children Carolus Burrus - land I now live on
containing 1000 acres and 800 acres in Caintuckie - my beloved
wife Agenteel maintenance with my son Charles.
Executors - sons Joseph and Carolus & fried Philip Johnson
Witnesses - George Dillard - James Dillard - Wratt Smith -
Martin Bibb

AMHERST Will Book 3, Page 479-

Court allots and assigns to Sarah Burrus, widow of Charles
Burrus, deceased, her dower in the personal estate of said deceased, etc. Recorded 18 June 1798.

LEE COUNTY, VIRGINIA, Deed Book 9, Page 320-

27 April 1844 - Indenture in which Jacob Fisher of LIMESTONE
COUNTY, STATE OF ALABABA by John D. Sharp and Elizah Hill, his
attorneys, in fact OF THE COUNTY OF LEE, STATE OF VIRGINIA - of
one part - sell to Arthur Blankenship of Lee County, Virginia, for
$120.00 - a tract of land in the said County of Lee on Trading
Creek (Acreage not given)- Recorded same date -Witnesses not listed.

49

Augusta County, Virginia - Deed Book 28, Page 421-

18 August 1795 - Power of Attorney by Mary Francis, widow of
John Francis, deceased - Ann Hind - Samuel Hind and Jane, his wife,
Alexander Hind and Martha, his wife - devisees of the said John
Francis whereas the said John Francis bequeathed a tract of land
in Augusta County - 1/3 to Mary Francis, his widow and 2/3 to his
four daughters: Ann, now wife of William Hind; Jane, wife of
Samuel Hind; Martha, wife of Alexander Hind and Margaret, wife of
John Hogshead - constitutes and appoint William Hind as their
true attorney to sell their several proportions to Martin Coiner
etc. -
Witnesses: Samuel Dillen, William Wright, Jane Wright, Proven
by the witnesses in the County of Bourbon, State of KENTUCKY before Thomas Arnold, Clerk of Court.
Recorded: Augusta County, Virginia, October Court 1795.

Comment: (Another record -Ibid Page 426 - specifies they are
            selling 150 acres which is part of a patent of 400
            acres granted to John Francis 25 November 1743). This
            original patent therefore, was in Orange County in
            that section which was later Augusta County.

            John Francis died testate 1786 - named wife, Mary,
            Daughters, Ann, Margaret, Martha, Jean, Elizabeth,
            Agnes, Mary, Son in laws, James McKamey and John
            Gardner.

Deed Book 35 - Page 98-

26 April 1808 - James McKemmy and Nancy, his wife, of County
of Augusta sell to Joseph Woodell of County of Bath, Wirginia, for
400 pds - 4 parcels of land in BATH COUNTY on an east branch of
Greenbrier River, called Dur Creek - one parcel contained 214
acres, part of a tract of 350 acres conveyed by Thomas Cartmell to
Abram Ingram, 13 June 1789 and by him conveyed to James McKemmy
and Joseph Wood, 9 June 1801. The second parcel containing 40
acres, part of 200 acres granted to Abraham Ingram, 29 July 1800
and by him conveyed to James McKemmy and Joseph Woodell, 9 June
1801. The 3rd contains 60 acres, part of a tract of 150 acres
granted to James McKemmy and Joseph Woodell 3 June 1802. The 4th
tract contains 138 acres granted to Abraham Ingram 1st January 1795.
Recorded: April 26, 1809.

<u>Augusta County Deed Book 36, Page 444</u>-

24 June 1811 - James McKemy and Nancy, his wife, of County of
Augusta, State of Virginia, sell to James Curry of the same County
for 200 pds - a certain tract of land in 2 surveys being in the
<u>County of Pendleton</u> (<u>now WEST VIRGINIA</u>) on the N W branch of the
Bullpasture River, joining the lands of Joseph Malcolm and Petter
Hull Jr. - one containing 161 acres, the other containing 200
acres - etc. Recorded September 23, 1811.

Ibid - Page 446 - 24 June 1811 - James McKemy and Nancy, his wife
of County of Augusta sell to John McKemy of said County, for
100 a tract of land in said County on the wates of North River
containing 358 acres being part of a tract of 945 acres whereon
the said James McKemy now lives etc.
Witnesses: John Hogsett - James McKamey - Jacob Sheets. Recorded
September 23, 1811.

Comment by C.H.H.: This James with wife Nancy must be son of John.
Died 1792.

<u>Caroline County Deeds (1758-1845) page 181</u>

12 October 1821 - Judith Kenner <u>of the STATE OF TENNESSEE</u>
of one part - Mackenzie Beverley of Caroline County, Virginia
of 2nd part and <u>William Gray of Town of Port Royal, Virginia</u> of
3rd part - Whereas said Mackenzie Beverley hath instituted suit
against the representative of Rodham Kenner in County Court of
Westmoreland for the purpose of recovering damages for a fraud
supposed to have been practiced on said Beverley by said Rodham
Kenner and said Judith Kenner is entitled to estate of said Rodham by virtue of his will recorded in Westmoreland. (her brother)-
etc. said <u>William Gray</u> is to collect the rents as they are due.
etc.
Witnesses- <u>James Gray</u>, Richard C. Borbin, Daniel Turner (?).-

<u>Henrico County, Virginia - Wills & Deeds (1714-1718) page 129</u>-

Last Will and Testament of Samuel Knibb - dated (?) October
1716 - probated 7 January 1716/17.

To my two brothers, three pounds apiece and my mare, Jenny,
to my brother, John and I give my brother, Thomas, Jenny's foal
which she had last.

51

To my loving wife, Elizabeth, my negroes and all the rest of my estate, both in England and Virginia - and she my whole and sole executrix.
Witnesses: - John Worsham, William Worsham.

LOUISA COUNTY, VIRGINIA, Deed Book D½, Page 541 -

Indenture dated 23 October 1773 in which John Moore,Jr. of the County of Roane, of North Caroliner (sic) and Sarah, his wife, sell to Joseph Carver of the County of Louisa, Colony of Virginia for 30 pds- all that tract of land in Louisa County containing 400 acres on both sides of Sycamore Fork Creek adjoining land of Charles Hopkins, etc.

Witnesses:- Becknell Alvarson, Samuel Bunch, Joseph Carver,Jr.
Recorded 8 November 1773.

HALIFAX COUNTY, VIRGINIA - Deed Book 29, Page 229-

30 September 1820 - William Terrell, Administrator of the Estate of Evi Desmukes, deceased, of the County of Person, State of North Carolina, appoints and constitutes William Walden of the County of Halifax, State of Virginia, his true and lawful attorney to recover and receive all such monies, etc. due and owing to the Estate of the said Evi Desmukes, deceased, and to make sale of the property of the said estate, etc.

Witnesses:- John Terrell, James L. Overby.
Recorded: 26 March 1821.

Note by C. H. H. The will of John Desmukes dated 23 April 1801, Probated 26 April 1802 names as legatees his wife, Betsey Desmukes and his three children, Evynard Desmukes , John Desmukes and Mildred Ragsdale, also his daughter, Patsy Dunnaho. (WBook 6, Page 346) Halifax County marriages by Knorr, Page 78, reveals that Mildred Desmukes, daughter of John Desmukes (who consents) married Benjamin Ragsdale 24 December 1800 (Bond).

HALIFAX COUNTY, VIRGINIA, Deed Book 16, Page 536-

25 January 1796. Indenture in which Benjamin Echols of
County of Halifax, State of Virginia sells to Elisha Desmukes
of the County of Granville, State of North Carolina- for 100 pds.
400 acres of land in the County of Halifax being the land which
William McDaniel, deceased, gave to Obediah Echols and Catherine,
his wife, for life of the said Catherine, by Deed of Gift dated
16 May 1771, etc.
Witnesses:- Martin Farmer, Alexander Irvine, Elisha Desmukes,
           R. Tompkins.
Recorded:- 22 February 1796.

GRAYSON COUNTY, VIRGINIA, Deed Book 2, Page 312-

7 January 1807- Indenture in which William Joshua and
Arthur Parker and Susanna Bryant of Grayson County, Virginia
and John Parker of the County of Surry, State of North Carolina
and Joseph Parker of the County of White, State of Tennessee-
all parties of one part sell to Samuel Parker of the County of
Grayson, State of Virginia (party of the 2nd part)-for 100 cents
(sic)- a tract of land containing 209 acres by survey in the Co.
of Grayson, on the waters of Meadow Creek a branch of New River-
adjoining land of Robert Muckolls - etc.
Witnesses:- David Noblett, Daniel Austin, Garner Bryant.
Recorded:- June Court 1807.

Note by C. H. H. Samuel Parker sells this land for $666.66
                 4 November 1816 to Joseph Elliott (Deed Bood 3
                 page 479).

GRAYSON COUNTY, VIRGINIA- Deed Book 2, Page 313-

1807, Indenture in which Joseph Parker and Elizabeth, his
wife, of the County of White, State of Tennessee, William Parker
of the County of Grayson, State of Virginia, Susanna Bryant of
the County of Grayson, State of Virginia, John Parker of the Co.
of Surry, State of North Carolina and Joshua Parker, Samuel Parker
and Arthur Parker, each of the County of Grayson, State of Virginia-
parties of one part- sell to Robert Nuckolls of the County of Grayson, State of Virginia for $525.00 a tract of land containing 87
acres, 2 roods, 24 poles in the County of Grayson on Meadow Creek
and Campfork waters of New River, etc. Witnesses: John Robinson,
David Noblett, Garner Bryant, Recorded June Court 1807.

GRAYSON COUNTY, VIRGINIA- Deed Book 2-Page 318-

21 February 1807- Indenture in which William Gregg of the
County of Stokes, State of North Carolina, sells to Lemuel Parker
of the County of Surry, State of North Carolina- for $300.00 a
tract of land in the County of Grayson, State of Virginia, on the
lead branches of Grassy Creek a south branch of Big Reed Island,
the waters of New River containing 118 acres, etc.
Witnesses:- Joseph Ballard, Levi Burcham, John Ballard
Recorded July Court 1807.

Note: Lemuel Parker sells this land (118 acres) in April 1810
to Jonathan Harrald (Deed Book 2, Page 532.)

GRAYSON COUNTY, VIRGINIA- Deed Book 2, Page 319-

26 February 1807 - Indenture in which Thomas Leonard of the
County of Guilford, State of North Carolina, sells to Abraham
Wolfington of the County and State aforesaid for $100.00, a tract
of land containing 50 acres in the County of Grayson, State of
Virginia, on the waters of Chestnut, a branch of New River, etc.
Witnesses:- John Blair, William Leonard, George Leonard.
Recorded July Court 1807.

HENRICO COUNTY, VIRGINIA- Deed Book 22, Page 338-

Indenture dated 16 October 1820 in which Austin Porter and
Frances Porter, his wife, of the County of Madison, State of Ala-
bama, sells to Yancy Thompson of the County of Henrico, State of
Virginia for $300.00 one undevided eighth part of five certain
islands in James River in the County and State aforesaid, being
known by the name of Bull Island - Little Shad Island - Gordons
Island - Long or Big Shad Island - and Little Eddy Island, etc.
Witnesses:- John Martin, Thomas Humes- (J. P's Madison Co. Ala.)
Certified before and by acting Justices of Madison County, Alabama, 17 October 1820 (Frances Porter is called Fanny Porter
therein)-
Recorded:- Henrico County, Virginia 11 November 1820.

Marriage Notices from the Richmond Enquirer-

January 31, 1807-(Sat.) In North Carolina, on Monday evening last, Mr. David Timberlake to the amiable and much accomplished Miss Sarah Hill, only daughter of James Hill, Esq. of Hanover County, Virginia.

December 30, 1817 (Tuesday) on the 18th instant, Major John Wyatt, of Fayette County, Kentucky to Miss Patsey Harris, of Hanover County, Virginia.

Richmond Whig and Public Advertiser-

February 6, 1857 (Friday) - On Thursday, 29th of January, at the residence of Mr. W. F. Wickham, in Hanover County, Virginia by the Rev. Mr. Peterken - Mr. Julius T. Porcher, of South Carolina and Miss Mary Fannie - and Mr. George H. Byrd of Baltimore, and Miss Lucy Carter, daughters of the late Mrs. E. F. Wickham.

Richmond Semi-Weekly Examiner-

May 19, 1857 (Tuesday) On May 7th, in Darlington. District, South Carolina, by the Rt. Rev. Mr. Spain, Dr. Benjamin C. Norment of Hanover, Virginia to Miss Lori H., daughter of Gen. J. B. Nettles of Darlington, South Carolina.

ALBEMARLE COUNTY, VIRGINIA, Deed Book 20, Page 116-

August 1, 1815 - Gideon Fitz of the Parish of St. Landrey, State of Louisiana gives his Power of Attorney to Archelaus Carver and William Meriwether, Esquires of the County of Albemarle, State of Virginia to ask for, demand, receive, etc. from William Fitz and Elizabeth Fitz of Albemarle County, Virginia his portion of the Estate of his late father, John Fitz, deceased, etc. Certified before George King, Judge and Ex-officio Notary Public of Parish of St. Landrey, State of Louisiana, the same date and recorded Albemarle County, Virginia 5 June 1816.

NORFOLK COUNTY, Deed Book 22- Page 76-

25 October 1764 - John Warden of the County of Norfolk, Virginia sells to William Parr of the County of Currituck, North Carolina - for 15 pounds - a tract of land containing 44 acres lying and being in County of Norfolk, it being the one half the said John Warden had of Urias Simonons, etc - known by name of the acre.
Witnesses- Absalom West, Caleb Comings, Robert Parker
Recorded 21 March 1765.

IBID - Deed Book 28 - Page 20-

2 September 1783 - Isaiah Parr and Mary, his wife, of the County of Currituck, State of North Carolina, sell to Abner Turbon of the same County and State - for 40 pounds silver money a tract of land in Norfolk County, Virginia, known by the name of the acre, being part of a patent containing 88 acres granted 17 August 1720 - this tract being for 44 acres, etc.
Witnesses: Willoughby Marchant, William Murden, James Fentress
Recorded 18th September 1783.

HALIFAX COUNTY, VIRGINIA, Deed Book 49, Page 514-

20 April 1843- Power of Attorney from James Snead and Frances, his wife, of County of St. Charles, State of Missouri appointing as their lawful attorney, their friend, John S. Duncan of Lincoln County, Missouri, to secure for them their portion in the estate of their deceased father, Jacob Anderson, late of the County of Pittsylvania, State of Virginia and also their share in the estate of their late father, Evan Sneed, deceased, of Halifax Co., Virginia or which may have been devised to him by his mother, if dead.

NOTE: This record followed by several affidavits from officials of Lincoln County, Missouri and recorded in Halifax Co., Virginia 25 May 1844.

PRINCE EDWARD COUNTY, Deed Book 6, Page 312-

24 June 1780- Indenture in which Munford Dyarnett and Elizabeth, his wife, of Prince Edward Co., Virginia sell to Samuel Elbert, Esq., late from the State of Georgia for 25,000 lbs of

inspected tobacco, a tract of land in Prince Edward Co., on both
sides of Mountain Creek, containing 169 acres and a half being
that tract of land on which the said Dejarnett now lives, etc.
Witnesses:- William Watts, Thomas Scott, Christopher Dejarnett
Recorded October Court 1780.

RICHMOND COUNTY, VIRGINIA, Deed Book 23, Page 402-

11 March 1833 - Power of Attorney from Einnifred Newsom,
the mother of Aretta Dobyns, deceased - Joseph B. Kelsick who
intermarried with Parthenia Dobyns - Thomas Jasper who intermarried with Margaret N. Dobyns - Elizah Swope who intermarried
with Brunetta W. Dobyns - James Swope who intermarried with Mary
M. Dobyns, sisters of the above named Aretta Dobyns, deceased
and children of Abner Dobyns, deceased - of the County of Spencer
and State of Kentucky - do appoint our friend, George H. Dobyns
of the County of Essex in the State of Virginia our true and
lawful attorney to receive of Thomas Dobyns of the County of
Richmond, State of Virginia, guardian on our said sister, Aretta
Dobyns, deceased, all money and estate of the said Aretta now in
the hands of Thomas Dobyns, her Guardian, etc.

    Comment:- All the above heirs signed the Power of Attorney
         in Spencer Co., Ky. and which was certified there-
         to by the Justices of the County.
         Recorded in Richmond Co., Va. 5 August 1833.

RICHMOND COUNTY, VIRGINIA Deed Book 27, Page 437-

20 August 1849 - Power of Attorney from Samuel B. Neasome
to George Wallens, as his true and lawful attorney to collect a
legacy left him by Samuel W. Neasome, deceased, late of the County
of Richmond, State of Virginia, etc. Sworn and certified to by
the Justices of Davidson Co., State of Tennessee.
Recorded: Richmond County, Virginia 5 October 1849.

Comment: - (The name Neasome, Neasom, Neasum and Newsom or New-
         some are the same in Virginia Records). George
         Wallen, Attorney, settles the above estate 9 October
         1849 in the net amount due of $654.41 with William I.
         Newsome, deceased, who is therein specifically stated
         to have been the father of Samuel B. Newsom and also
         mentions him as heir of his sister, Catherine A. New-
         som, deceased (Deed Book 27, Page 468). Recorded 2 Jan 1850.

Further Comment: Richmond County Marriages by King - Page 145-
12 September 1811 - Samuel W. Neason married
to Nancy Baker.

RICHMOND COUNTY, VIRGINIA, Deed Book 16, Page 41-

17 February 1789 - Indenture in which John Lawson and Ann,
his wife, of Dobbs County in the State of North Carolina sell
to Robert Neasom of Richmond County, State of Virginia, for 65
pounds all their right, title, interest, claim and demand in
and to one-fifth part of the lands formerly possessed and
occupyed (sic) by Epaphroditus (blotted out) deceased, etc.
Recorded 6 April 1789. (The next record gives us the blotted
out name).

RICHMOND COUNTY, VIRGINIA   Deed Book 16, Page 82-

26 September 1789 - Indenture in which Robert Degges of
Edgecombe County, North Carolina sells to Robert Neasom, of
Richmond County, Commonwealth of Virginia - for 65 pds. all his
right, title, claim etc. in and to one-fifth part of the lands
formerly belonging to Epaphroditus Lawson, deceased in said Co.
of Richmond, etc.
Witnesses: Abner Dobyns, James Alderson, Thaddeus Williams,
             Giles Sydner, John Holt, W. Williams, John Kirkham.
Recorded: 5 October 1789.

RICHMOND COUNTY, VIRGINIA, Deed Book 17, Page 471-

7 December 1801 - Indenture in which Peter Brown, heir at
law of Vincent Brown, deceased, of the State of South Carolina-
sells to William Forester of the County of Richmond, Virginia -
for 247 pds., 10 shillings, 330 acres of land in Richmond Co.,
Virginia, adjacent land of said Forester and others, etc.
Witnesses: Edward Saunders, William Bragg, George Saunders,
             B. McCarty.
Recorded: Same date.

RICHMOND COUNTY, Deed Book 18, Page 93-

5 December 1803 - Indenture in which Vincent Brown of the State of South Carolina sells to William Forester of the County of Richmond, Virginia for $206.00, one-fourth part of the land purchased. Francis H. Christian and the Deed made to Peter Brown, considered to be my portion of the said tract of land amounting in the whole to 440 acres, the 1/4 portion herewith conveyed, being 110 acres, etc.
Witnesses: Benjamin N. Garland, Peter Brown, George Pursell, Thomas F. Reynolds.
Recorded: Same Date.

RICHMOND COUNTY, VIRGINIA, Deed Book 13, Page 129-

9 April 1804 - Indenture in which Peter Brown, Vincent Brown (for himself) and the said Vincent Brown, as Attorney for Lucy Wright (formerly Lucy Brown) and Richard Wright, her husband and Molly Tims (formerly Molly Brown) and Joseph Tims, her husband, all of the State of South Carolina, the said Browns being the children of Vincent Brown, of Richmond County, Virginia, deceased, of the one part, sell to William Forester of County of Richmond, Virginia, for 24 pds., 10 shillings - a tract of land in the County of Richmond, Va. containing by survey 330 acres.
Recorded: 4 June 1804.

RICHMOND COUNTY, VIRGINIA, Deed Book 18, Page 34-

6 July 1768 - Indenture in which Daniel Everett of the County of Halifax, Province of North Carolina, sells to Robert Forrester of the County of Richmond, Colony of Virginia, for 40 pds. Current money - a tract of land in the County of Richmond, Va. containing 106 acres on the Flower Branch, etc.
Witnesses: Robert Clarke, William Forrester, Gabriel Smithers, John Routt, William Miskell.
Recorded: 1 August 1768.

Note by C.H.H.: (This record is followed by another record in which Daniel Everett gives bond in sum of 80 pds. that Frances, his wife, will relinquish her right of dower). Recorded 1 August 1768.

25 December 1813, Power of Attorney from James Dozier and
Mary Dozier (formerly Mary Randall) of the County of Lewis and
State of Kentucky to their true and trusty son, Tomblin Dozier,
of said County and State to recover and receive all they are entitled to in the State of Virginia and Maryland in right of my
wife, Mary Dozier (formerly Mary Randall) as heir of George
Randall, deceased, of King William Co., Virginia, and he also, to
sell 260 acres of land in the County of Richmond which I claim in
the right of my wife, Mary Dozier (formerly Mary Randall) and do
further authorize my said attorney to receive from John Randall,
of the Town of Annapolis, State of Maryland, the value of a negor man, named Will, which he moved from the State of Virginia,
etc. Certified by Joseph Robb, Clerk of Court of Lewis, Co.,
Kentucky. Recorded Richmond Co., Virginia 7 February 1814.

Note by C. H. H.: This is an abstract of an original deed (sealed
                  with red wafers) in my possession which was made
                  to my Grandmother, Sarah Elizabeth Arney, at
                  that time,"of Rockingham Co., North Carolina"
                  and later, after her marriage to my Grandfather,
                  Capt. Francis Mallory Hamlin, "of Danville, Va."
                  The said Sarah Elizabeth Arney was the daughter
                  of Daniel Arney, a quacker formerly of Philadel-
                  phis, who married 19 January 1837 Sarah Ann Bell,
                  who married secondly, Capt. George W. Peay, of
                  Rockingham County, North Carolina.

The State of South Carolina

27 August 1860 - Deed of Gift from George W. Peay of the State of
North Carolina and Sarah, his wife, Nee Bell - Whereas Henry Bell,
a brother of the said Sarah, late of Ocala, in the State of Florida,
departed this life, intestate, leaving a widow, and the said Sarah,
of his next of kin, him surviving and entitled to a distributive
share of his estate and whereas James M. Bell, also a brother of the
said Sarah, late of Little River, in the State of South Carolina,
departed this life intestate, leaving the said Sarah, one of his
next of kin him surviving and entitled to a distributive share of
his estate. Now these presents witness that the said George W.
Peay and Sarah, his wife, for natural love and affection which
they have and bear for and to Sarah E. Arney, a child of the said
Sarah aforesaid by a previous marriage with one Daniel Arney - do
give, grant, confirm, etc. unto the said Sarah E. Arney all right,

title, interest, claim, etc. in the estate of the late Henry Bell, deceased and the estate of the said James M. Bell, deceased, etc.
Witnesses: Samuel Bell, George V. Bell.
Recorded: <u>Horry District, South Carolina</u> September 3, 1860, proven by affidavit of Samuel Bell before J. A. Thompson, Clerk of Court. (Book N, Pages 752-753.

AMELIA COUNTY, VIRGINIA, Deed Book 9, Page 137-

Indenture dated 26 December 1766 in which Henry Blanchet <u>of the Province of North Carolina</u>, tho late <u>of the County of Amelia, in the Colony of Virginia</u>, sells to Reuben Palmer of County of Amelia, Va. for 60 pds - a tract of land in County of Amelia containing 90 acres, adjoining (among others named) land of William Hall, who purchased from John Blanchet, brother to the aforesaid Henry Blanchet, etc.
Witnesses: Humphrey Bickley, John Belcher, Holdcroft Nowell.
Recorded: 28 May 1767.

Comment: Robert Palmer of Richmond County, Virginia in his will dated 25 February 1732 named among his 7 sons and 3 daughters, Reuben and Parmenas Palmer, both of whom are revealed as living in Amelia County. Parmenas was later in Lunenburg County and Reuben in Prince Edward.

EARLY KENTUCKY WILLS by J. E. S. King, Page 147-

LINCOLN COUNTY, KENTUCKY, Will Book A (1781-1790 -

Last Will and Testament of John Bowman, dated February 5, 1784 - probated August 17, 1784.
       Wife, Elizabeth
       Son, John Bowman
       Brothers, Abraham and Isaac Bowman
       Sisters: Mary Stephens
               Elizabeth Ruddle
               Sarah Wright
               Regina Durley
               Rebecca Brinker
Executors: Wife, Elizabeth, Brothers, Abraham and Isaac Bowman.
Witnesses: Joseph Love, James Cox, Richard Foley, Wilson Maddox.

Comment: The above John Bowman was a son of George Bowman, who died testate in Frederick County, Virginia (Will Book 3, Page 431) who dated his will 3 November 1764; probated March 2, 1768, who named wife, Mary, and Sons, John, Jacob, Abraham, Joseph, Isaac, George Bowman and Daughters, Mary Stephens, Elizabeth Ruddle, wife of Isaac Ruddle, Sarah Right (Wright), Regina Durley, and Rebecca Bowman. He also named grandsons, George William Stephens, Jacob Stephens, Isaac Stephens, Joseph Stephens and Adam Stephens.

The daughter, Sarah (Bowman) Right (Wright) married before 1764 George Wright Junior (or the younger) born at least by 1730 or before). Sergeant of Colonial Militia 1758 of Frederick Co., Virginia, who later migrated with his family (after 1772,before 1779) to 96 District, South Carolina (Frederick Co., Deed Book 18, Page 271 shown elsewhere in this Vol.)

Land Patent Book 13, Page 362-

September 28, 1728 - Patent for 152 acres of land in Nansemond County, Virginia granted to Aaron Blanchard of North Carolina - adjoining land of George Spivey, etc.

Ibid - Book 14, Page 137-

September 28, 1730 - Patent for 399 acres of land in Nansemond County, Virginia granted to Richard Parker of North Carolina, in the upper parish, adjoining his own land thence to a pine in the county line, adjoining land of Thomas Odum.

Ibid - Page 296-

August 25, 1731 - Patent for 388 acres of land in Nansemond County, Virginia granted to Richard Parker of North Carolina adjoining his own and Joseph Horton's land.

Book 15, Page 67-

June 20, 1733 - Patent for 371 acres granted to John Parker of the Province of North Carolina - in Nansemond County, Virginia in the upper Parish, adjoining his own land and John Knight's.

Land Grant Book 44, page 334-

February 27, 1800 - Patent for 355 acres of land in Nansemond

County, Virginia granted to James Knight of Gates County, State of North Carolina - in the upper Parish adjoining lands of Abraham Riddick and Kedar Wiggins.

Bedford County, Will Book A-I, Page 401-

Will of John Kennedy dated 22 February 1781. Probated 24 September 1781.

Whereas in the course of the winter 1780, while I was in Kentucky, I found it to be to the united advantage of my brother, Joseph Kennedy of Maryland and myself to contract with Mr. James Rucker and Reuben Coward to clear out and procure the Grants to us for 2 tracts of land being Preemption Rights of 1,000 acres each. One of which grants to issue in the name of Joseph Kennedy and the other in my own name, etc.

As soon as Grants are obtained for the 3 following warrants - 1) for 750 acres and (2) for 1,000 acres each, all dated 16 October 1779. My executors to lay off 1,000 acres to Joseph Kennedy and 750 acres to Peter Kelly - they paying to my heirs Major Daniel Boon's charge for locating and surveying the said warrants-

To Esther, my beloved wife, her thirds and balance to all my children (not named) - my lands in Bedford County to be sold. Executors: My wife, Esther and friend, Thomas Logwood. Witnesses: Thomas Williams, John Hardwick, John Hardwick,Jr. Executors Bond was 500,000 pounds.

Stafford County, Virginia,- Leber "M" (1729-48) Page 337-

Last Will and Testament of Samuel Bowman, of the City of Glasgow, Mariner.

All my estate of what nature or kind to my beloved wife, Eleanor, during her natural life and after her decease it to be equally divided between my sons, Richard and Samuel Bowman.

To my Grandson, (not named), the son of my deceased son, William Bowman, a ring of 20 shillings value.

Executors: My sons, Richard and Samuel Bowman, signed and sealed in Stafford County 18 June 1742.
Witnesses: Robert Rose, William Alliso, Thomas Bogle, John Short, John Stark.

Codicil: Whereas I have several effects in Virginia and Maryland which cannot be got in and disposed of and remitted home without authority from my executors within named, I hereby appoint by good friends, Duncan Graham and Thomas Atchison, Executors of such of my estate as lies in America.
Witnesses: John Moncure, J. Mercer, William Allison.
Probated: September 14, 1742.

Frederick County, Virginia, Deed Book I, Page 352-

    11 January 1747 - Indenture in which Richard Lean of the County of Frederick, Colony of Virginia (but formerly of the Township of New Brunswick, in the County of Middlesex in the East Jerseys - sells to Andrew Bowman of the County and Parish of Frederick Colony of Virginia, for 100 pds, a tract of land in the Co. of Middlesex in the Corporation of Brunswick, containing 350 acres more or less, conveyed by Deed from William Creed to Richard Lean, etc.
Witnesses: John Forwood, Charles Demoss.
Recorded 1st March 1747.

Frederick County, Virginia, Deed Book I, Page 389-

    11 February 1747 - Emanuel Grub of Brandewine Hundred, County of Newcastle on Delaware, Province of Pennsylvania, sells to Benjamin Grub of County of Frederick, Colony of Virginia, for 100 pds., 255 acres of land in County of Frederick, Virginia, on North side of Shenandoah River, said land having been conveyed by deed from Jost Hite to Emanuel Grubb of NewCastle Co.; adjoining dividing line of John Grubbs, etc.
Recorded 5 April 1748.

Albemarle County, Virginia - Deed Book 3, Page 32-

    20 August 1760 - Indenture in which John Wright, of the County of Orange in North Carolina sells to Thomas Jopling of the County of Albemarle, Virginia, for 100 pds current money of Va. a tract of land containing 400 acres in the County of Albemarle on the north side of Rockfish River, being part of 800 acres John Wright purchased of Col. John Chiswell, etc.
Witnesses: Jo. Ramsay, James Nevil, Michael Thomas, Robert
              Johnston.
Recorded: 12 March 1761.

64

Frederick County, Virginia- Deed Book 18, Page 271-

7 September 1779 - Indenture in which George Wright, late of
the 96 Hundred in the State of South Carolina, sells to David
Wright (sic) of Frederick County, State of Virginia - for 270 pds.
a tract of land in County of Frederick - containing 615 acres, being the same land which was granted unto the said George Wright by
the Northern Neck Proprietors, 30 August 1751 unto the said David
Right (sic) - excepting the sum of 150 pds. secured to William
Ewing and Joseph Vance by an indenture of mortgage dated 4 August
1772, etc. Signed - George Right (sic)-
Witnesses: J. Peyton Jr., William Glascock, Robert Kite.
Recorded: Same date.

Note by C. H. H.: (Ibid page 273) - Same date George Wright, late
                  of 96 Hundred, South Carolina sells Adam Kline
                  of Frederick County, Virginia, for 120 pounds,
                  400 acres granted him 10 October 1754. Signed by
                  George Right (sic) Recorded Same date.

Campbell County, Virginia - Deed Book 4, Page 156-

28 March 1797 - James Miller and Frances, his wife, of Campbell County, Virginia, sell to Anthony and John Kennedy of the
Town of Baltimore, State of Maryland, for 1450 pounds - the following parcels of land in Campbell County: (1) 15½ acres laid out in
lots at Campbell County Courthouse (2) 13½ acres on head branches
of Molly's Creek, adjoining the lots aforesaid, (3) 1½ acres adjoining the 13½ acres, (4) 60 acres adjoining the lots at Campbell
Courthouse, (5) 75 acres adjoining the above, (6) 400 acres adjoining the above patented by John Hay, 5 June 1765 and by him
conveyed to James Shearer and by said Shearer and Mary, his wife,
conveyed to said James Miller by deed dated 2 June 1791, (7) 200
acres in said County on Beaver Creek, etc.
Witnesses: Francis Miller, Donald Warrand, Terrence O'Brien.
Recorded: April 6, 1797.

Campbell County, Virginia, Deed Book 16, Page 1-

19 February 1827- John Kennedy and Nancy C., his wife, of
County of Jefferson, State of Virginia, sell to Anthony Kennedy,
of County of Philadelphia, State of Pennsylvania - Whereas by deed
dated 28 March 1797 in Campbell Co., Va., a certain James Miller
and Frances, his wife, conveyed to the above Anthony and John

Kennedy, then of the Town of Baltimore, State of Maryland, several parcels of land, etc. - containing in all about 800 acres of land. Said John and Nancy C. Kennedy, by these presents release and quit claim all their right title claim, etc. to said Anthony Kennedy, etc.

Witnesses: Ana Kennedy, John Kennedy.
Recorded: Campbell Co., July 9, 1827.

Note by C. H. H.: Deed Book 18, page 109 - Refers to above deed of release and states Anthony Kennedy died testate in 1828 in City of Philadelphia, his will duly proven 7 October 1828 and did therein devise to John Kennedy for his natural life 750 acres and 17 town lots in the County and Town of Campbell, Va. and names him as his brother - and after his decease to his 4 children, namely, John, Andrew, Pendleton and Anthony Kennedy, etc. Later he names the children more specifically as: John P. Kennedy, Andrew Kennedy, Philip Pendleton Kennedy and Anthony Kennedy, tenants in common, etc. Said Anthony, the youngest, still a minor and will not have completed his full age before 21st December 1831 - do appoint Chiswell Dabney, Esq. of the Town of Lynchburg in Virginia their true and lawful attorney, etc. - signed and sealed 10 Sept. 1830 by John P. Kennedy. Philip Pendleton Kennedy and Anthony Kennedy at Baltimore, Maryland and by John Kennedy and Andrew Kennedy 27 Sept. 1830 at Jefferson Co., Va. (Certified by various Justices at both places). Recorded Feb. Court 1831.

Further Note: Later deeds reveal that John P. Kennedy had a wife, Elizabeth. Andrew Kennedy, a wife, Mary Ann, who co-signed with them.

Campbell County, Virginia - Deed Book 19, Page 40-

24 December 1831 - Indenture in which John Kennedy, John P. Kennedy and Elizabeth, his wife, Andrew Kennedy and Mary Ann, his wife, Philip Pendleton Kennedy and Anthony Kennedy, parties of one part, sell to Josiah Shepperson of Campbell County, Virginia, for $250.00 a tract of land in Campbell Co. on the head branches of Beaver Creek - containing 200 acres - which land was conveyed by James Miller 28 March 1797 to Anthony and John Kennedy and of record in the County Court of Campbell, etc. Signed.

66

Acknowledged and certified before Thomas W. Griffith and John F. Harris, two Justices of the Peace of the City of Baltimore, Baltimore County, State of Maryland on 3 February 1832 by John P. Kennedy, Elizabeth, his wife, Phillip P. Kennedy and Anthony Kennedy.

John Kennedy and Andrew Kennedy and Mary Ann R., wife of Andrew Kennedy acknowledged the deed to be their act before two justices of of the Peace of Jefferson County, Virginia who certified the same. Recorded: Campbell County, Virginia December 10, 1832.

Halifax County, Deed Book 47, Page 143-

I September 1841- Thomas Moore and Elizabeth, his wife, of the County of Hardiman, State of Tennessee, appoint and constitute their son, William A. Moore of Said County and State their lawful attorney to apply for every part and portion of the estate of William H. Bates, deceased, late of Halifax Co., Virginia and to secure the same from Jonathan B. Stovall, Administrator of said estate, whither our undivided portion of said estate consists of lands, negroes, money, etc. Witnesses: Jacob Grave, Joseph Crews, Certified by Justices of Hardiman Co., Tenn. and Recorded Halifax Co., Virginia II October 1841.

Bedford County, Virginia - Deed Book II, Page 253-

(Not dated)- Power of Attorney by George Rucker of Bedford Co., State of Virginia to John Rucker of Woodford County, Kentucky and Thomas Canady (Kennedy) of Bourbon County, Kentucky to collect rents and arrears of rents from Benjamin Penn of Bourbon County, Kentucky and other tenants of a tract of land belonging to me in Bourbon Co., Kentucky, etc. Recorded 22 September 1800.

Northampton County, Virginia - Will Book 27, Page 281-

Will of George W. Denham Forester, dated 12 February 1785. Probated 17 June 1785.

Describes himself in preamble of will as "Of County of Kent in the State of Maryland". 60 acres of land called Free Gift and known by name of the Meadow given me by will of my deceased father, William Forrester (which is mortgaged to Mr. Blackstone Wilmer).

Remainder of my land to my wife, Temperance, for her natural life and at her death to my son, George William, reversion to my two

67

daughters, Mary Wilmer and Henrietta Elizabeth.
Executors: My wife, Temperance and friend, Mr. James Pierce.
Witnesses: Margaret Fulwell, Victor A. Fulwell, John Harmanson,
           Griffin Stith.

Richmond County, Virginia - Deed Book 17, Page 471-

   7 December 1801 - Peter Brown, heir at law of Vincent Brown,
deceased, of the State of South Carolina, sells to William Forester
of the County of Richmond, State of Virginia, for 247 pds. 10 shillings, a tract of land in the County of Richmond containing by survey
24 January 1801, 330 acres-adjoining land of the said Forester,
Peter Brown, etc.
Witnesses: Edward Saunders, William Bragg, George Saunders, B.
           McCarty,
Recorded: Same Date.

Richmond County, Virginia- Deed Book 18, Page 93-

   5 December 1803 - Vincent Brown of the State of South Carolina
sells to William Forester of County of Richmond, State of Virginia,
for $206.00 - one fourth part of the land purchased of Frances H.
Christian and Deed made to Peter Brown which is considered to be my
portion amounting in the whole to 440 acres - the part conveyed being 110 acres.
Witnesses: Benjamin N. Garland, Peter Brown, George Pursell, Thomas
            T. Reynolds. Recorded - same date.

Richmond County, Virginia - Deed Book 18, Page 129-

   9 April 1804 - This indenture by Peter Brown, Vincent Brown,
for himself and as attorney in fact for Lucy Wright (formerly Lucy
Brown) and Richard Wright, her husband; Molly Tims (formerly Molly
Brown) and Joseph Tims, her husband, all of the State of South Carolina, the said Browns being children of Vincent Brown of Richmond
Co., Virginia, deceased, of the one part - sell to William Forester
of the County of Richmond, State of Virginia - for 247 pds, 10
shillings, 330 acres in the said County of Richmond, the particu-
lars of which are expressed in a Deed of Sale by Peter Brown to
William Forester 7 December 1801 being the same tract therein conveyed, etc.
Witnesses: Thomas Plummett, Richard Street, Rodham Davis, Richard
           Claughton. Recorded 4 June 1804.

68

Note by C. H. H.:   Torrence Index to Wills reveals that an inventory
of the Estate of Vincent Brown (Sr.) was made in
Richmond County, Virginia in 1788.

Accomack County, Virginia, Deed Book 12, Page 187-

13 July 1808 - Deed in which Thomas Savage of the County of
Accomack, State of Virginia, sells to Severn Savage, Merchant, of
the City of Baltimore, for 490 pds. the following parcel of land
which the said Thomas Savage drew as his share in the division of
his father's plantation on Metompkin, whereon William S. Custis
and Margaret, his wife, now dwell, containing 81 2/3 acres -
bounded on north by lott #5 of Ann Savage, etc.
Recorded: 20 September 1808.

Note by C.H.H.: The above Severn (Eyre) Savage and Thomas (Waters)
Savage were sons of Major John Savage (died testate
Accomack Co. in 1792) and his wife, Margaret (said
to have been Waters) who remarried 2ndly William Smith
Custis.   Major John Savage is fully documented with
records of proof back to his emigrant ancestor, En-
sign Thomas Savage, in Virginia in 1608, in my files.
This pedigree is one of the oldest proven English
pedigrees in Virginia and therefore of North America.
Will of Thomas W. Savage follows:

Accomack County Wills (1809-1812) page 416-

Last Will and Testament of Thomas Waters Savage dated
22 November 1810- Proven Worcester Co., Maryland 14 October 1811-
Recorded Accomack County, Virginia 24 February 1812-

States that he is of Worcester County, Maryland -

All my estate, real and personal, to be sold and the proceeds
to be divided as follows:
2/3 to my brother, William Savage.
1/3 to my brother, Joseph Savage-
and they to be my executors.

Augusta County, Virginia, Deed Book 21, Page 475-

20 May 1777- Patrick Campbell and Agnes, his wife, sell to John Burk of Philadelphia, Pennsylvania, a tract of land boutht by Patrick Campbell, deceased, from Beverley 21 February 1738 which deed was recorded in Orange County, Colony of Virginia.

Caroline County, Virginia (Deeds 1758-1845) Page 243-

9 March 1809 - Indenture in which Elijah Catlett of the State of Kentucky, Mary Catlett, Sally Catlett, Edward Jones and Judity, his wife, of the County of Caroline and State of Virginia, parties of one part, sell to William Peake of Caroline Co., Va. for $830.00, he, the said Elijah Catlett as trustee under a deed of trust dated 20 January 1802, recorded in Caroline County, all that tract of land conveyed by Benjamin Catlett to the said Elijah Catlett, in trust, in Caroline Co., Virginia, containing 166 acres, etc. (Ends here).

Caroline County, Virginia (Deeds 1758-1845) Page 236-

7 March 1842 - Indenture in which Thomas Woodford of the County of Montgomery, State of Kentucky, sells to Edward H. Didlake, of the County of Clarke - Robert Ewing of the County of Bath - Thomas Huffman - John Crawford, Jr. - James Turley - William Ragan - Alexander Barnes - Benjamin T. Bott - Robert Evans - Joseph Russel and Miller Hatheway, of the County of Montgomery, and State aforesaid (Kentucky) - witnesseth, said Thomas Woodford is bound as security of William S. Buckner to the said parties of the second part - and to secure them - mortgages his estate, real and personal, etc.
Witnesses: H. B. Wren, William Edmonson, Certified before James
        Howard, Clerk of County Court of Montgomery Co., Ky., same
        date.   Recorded Caroline County, Virginia 11 April 1842.

Nottoway County, Virginia - Deed Book 1, Page 371-

3 April 1794 - Power of Attorney from Peter Stainback (Sr.) of County of Nottoway, State of Virginia, to Col. John Edwards of County of Barbary (sic) State of Kentucky to demand, sue, etc. a certain John Fowler Jr., now of Kentucky, on a Bond executed to me by said Fowler 3 March 1783 for sum of 2245 Pds specie, etc. Recorded: 3 April 1794.

70

Note by C.H.H.: A John Edwards is in Bourbon County, Kentucky in the 1790 Census. In the same census A John Fowler is in Fayette in 1789 and he, or another, is in Woodford County in 1790.

Accomack County, Virginia - Deeds #10, Page 431-

27 October 1803 - Deed in which Cassia Wise, Elizabeth Wise and Mary Outten of the Parish of St. George, County of Accomack, Virginia of one part, sell to Daniel Jones Sr., Samuel Gillet, Benjamin Aylett, and William Aylett, all of Worcester Co., State of Maryland, of the other part - for 7 pds 10 shillings - a certain parcel of land and marsh of Chincoteague Island which they hold in common, with others under a devise from a certain Agnes Parrish, deceased, the quantity being conveyed being 20 acres,etc. Witnesses: William Gillett, Charles Snead, Samuel Waples. Recorded: October 31, 1803.

Comment: Cassia Wise, Elizabeth Wise and Mary Outten were children of Major John Wise, who died testate in Accomack Co. in 1770 and his wife, Margaret (called Peggy), Douglas (died testate as Peggy Gillett in 1808) who was the daughter of Colonel George Douglas and his wife, Tabetha Drummond). Accomack Marriage Bonds (micro) Feb. 2, 1785 Abraham Outten to Mary Wise, Peter Hack, Security. The Agnes Parrish, referred to above, died testate 1771 and was another daughter of Col. George & Tabetha (Drummond) Douglas. She married 1st James Rule and (2nd) (?)Parrish.

Isle of Wight County, Virginia - Deed Book 5, Page 163-164-

21 October 1737 - John Cain of the County of Edgecombe in North Carolina sells to William Jones of County of Isle of Wight, in Virginia - for sum of one likely negro boy, 4 ft,2 inches high, a tract of land on the southside of Nottoway River in Isle of Wight Co., containing 225 acres, bounded according to a patent granted to the said John Cain dated 31 October 1726, etc. Witnesses: John Dunklay, Thomas Atkinson. Recorded: 24 October 1737.

71

King George County, Deed Book 8, Page 6-

11 October 1794 - William Cash of County of Wilkes, State of North Carolina sells to John Carver of County of King George, State of Virginia, whereas James Cash, grandfather of the said William Cash, party to these presents, late of County of King George did possess 2 tracts of land, did by his last will devise the said land to his son, John Cash, for his natural life and then to William and Thomas Cash, sons of said John Cash - said land containing 220 acres in County of King George, etc.
Witnesses: Mathen King, William Suttles, Bennett Knight, Reuben Suttles. Recorded 1 January 1795.

York County Deeds #6 (1755 - 1763) Page 53-

10 February 1756 - Jane Hardman of Liverpoole in County of Lancaster, widow, relict and executrix of last will and testament of John Hardman, late of Liverpoole aforesaid, Esq., deceased - gives power of attorney to Divid Jameson of the Province (sic) of Virginia, merchant, in my name and the name of Jane Hardman of Rochdale in said County, widow, and James Percival of Liverpoole, aforesaid, Merchant, the other executor and executrix of the said will to secure and receive from (several persons named) all of Va., such debts, etc, whatsoever, which were due and owing, etc.
Witnesses: Henry Twentyman, William Reynolds, Recorded: 17 May 1756.

(This letter of Attorney was proved by the oath of Henry Twentyman, a witness threto and ordered to be recorded). (Please note that he signed as a witness in Liverpool and proved same in York County, Virginia Court).

Virginia Historical Magazine (Vol. 13) - page 405--

Virginia Gleanings in England. Ref. to Parker, 88-

Thomas Stacie of Maidstone, Co. Kent, Gentleman - Will dated 31 August 1619 - proved 13 September 1619.

To my nephewe, William Joye, sonne of my brother in law, Roberte Joye, all my lands, tenements, etc. situated and being in Virginia, to him and his heirs forever. To the said Robert Joye all my goods and chattels in whose hands soever as well in England as in Virginia or elsewhere, which said Robert Joye I make my Exetr.

72

Witnesses: Thomas Ayerest, Thomas Skelton.

Comment: (William Joy was living at Elizabeth City, census of Feb-
    ruary 1623. Thomas Stacy was a member of the Virginia County
    and paid 25 pds. (for his shares). Mr. Robert Stacy was Bur-
    gess for Martins Brandon in the first Virginia Assembly in
    1619.

Brunswick County, Virginia - Deed Book 20, Page 171-

    28 April 1807 - Thomas Stacy mortgages his interest in slaves
belonging to his father, John Stacy, after the death of his said
father which slaves were bequeathed to the said John Stacy in Will
of Simon Stacy dated 17 March 1784 for his life and then to said
Thomas Stacy and which negroes are at this time in North Carolina.
Recorded: September 28, 1807.

Comment: It seems obvious that his father, John Stacy, Son of Simon
    (of Sussex Co., Virginia) had removed to North Carolina.

Charlotte County, Virginia-Deed Book 8, Page 120-A-

    20 September 1798 - Deed of Gift from Susannah Cardwell of
Charlotte County of Virginia - for love, good-will and affection
for her loving daughter, Mary Anne Chism (Chisolm) of Warren Co.,
State of Kentucky, of one negro girl named Druciler and her future
increase, etc. -
Recorded: 1 October 1798.

Ibid - Page 227-A-

    7 October 1799 - Taylor Harris and Syntha (sic) Harris of the
State of North Carolina, of the one part, sell to Samuel Fugua, of
Charlotte County, Virginia. Whereas Joel Farmer, late of said Co.
of Charlotte died intestate, seized of 200 acres in said county and
leaving 4 daughters, (to wit) (1) Polly, who hath intermarried with
John Fouqurean, (2) Elizabeth, who hath intermarried with William
Parker, (or Partein?) (3) Frances, who hath intermarried with William Smith and (4) Syntha, who hath intermarried with Taylor Harris,
etc. - daughters and only children of said Joel Farmer - do herewith sell their share or portion, for 150 pds., in said 200 acres to
Samuel Fuqua, etc. Recorded 7 April 1800.

Charlotte County, Virginia - Deed Book 9, Page 254-

. 15 December 1798 - Beverly Callicott and Precilla, his wife, of the County of Randolph, State of North Carolina, sell to Thomas Brooke and Traverse Brooke, heirs of George Brooke, deceased, of the County of Charlotte, State of Virginia, of the other part, for 200 pds., a tract of land in County of Charlotte, Virginia, containing 240 acres on a branch of Sandy Creek, etc.
Witnesses: Dixon Loggins, Bibby Brooke, James Callicott -certified (1 February 1799 and recorded 5 September 1803.

Pittsylvania County, Virginia - Deed & Will Book #5, Page 147-

24 December 1777- Charles Ward and Elizabeth, his wife, of County of Pittsylvania, sell to Jonathan Montgomery Church of the Province of Maryland, County of (blank) for 150 pds. a tract of land in County of Pittsylvania on north side of Dan River, on upper fork of Double Creek containing 330 acres, etc.
Witnesses: John Chadwell, John Marnick, Nemehiah Trahern.

Essex County, Virginia Wills, etc. #3 (1717-1721), page 220-

Last Will & Testament of Joseph Baker of South Farnham Parish, County of Essex, Merchant. - Dated 20 September 1720, Probated 16 November 1720.

For use of the Upper Church of South Farnham Parish one silver salver of 5 pds. sterling price.

To Thomas Boarn - 1/2 the tobacco he now owes me.

To George Treble all the tobacco he oweth me.

To Thomas Dix - the widow Olive and the Widow Aires, 1/2 the tobacco each oweth me.

To Peter Godfrey, for his care and trouble of me, all the medicines I have now sent for to England, and my best saddle & bridle.

To John, the son of Peter & Elizabeth Godfrey, 10 pds. sterling after decease of my beloved wife, Amy.

To Elizabeth Bradbourn, 200 pds. of tobacco.

74

To my sister, Ann White, 20,000 lbs of tobacco to be shipped to her and her husband, Richard White, living in London.

To my sister, Elizabeth Hart, 20,000 lbs of tobacco to be shipped to her.

My sister, Anne, living in Cow Lane in West Smithfield, London with Richard White, a coach-maker (or coat ? maker). My sister, Elizabeth, living with him.

To my Godson, Joseph Gatewood, my negro, Tom and negro girl, Sue.

To William Gatewood, 2 cows and calves. (William is son of Gohn Gatewood, deceased).

To John Farguson, one gold ring.
To Henry Gatewood, new suit of clothes
To James Gatewood, my son-in-law, land I bought of Thomas Wheeler (means Step-son).

To all the rest of my wife's children not herein before mentioned, a gold ring.
To Thomas Bell - 1/2 tobacco he owes me.
To Anthony North, my best suit of wearing apparel.

Beloved Wife, Amy and John Gatewood, my Executors.
Witnesses: Anthony North, John Alt C. Godfrey.

Sussex County, Virginia, Deed Book H, Page 423-

31 December 1795 - Indenture in which Stephen Stacy of Rockingham County, State of North Carolina, sells to Edmond Stacy of County of Sussex, State of Virginia - for 13 pds 5 shillings, all his right, title and interest in his part or portion that is due from his father's estate at his Mother-in-law's decease, etc. Signed by Stephen Stacy and Susan (x) Stacy. Witnesses: William Harrison, Nicholas Stacy, William Lamb. Recorded: 4 February 1796.

Note by C.H.H.: Albemarle Parish Reg. shows a Steven Stacey, son of Simon & Elizabeth Stacey, born 7/31/1761 and Edmund Stacey, son of Simon & Catherine Stacey, born 11/23/1766 (Mother in law above therefore means Step-mother). Nicholas Stacey, son of Simon & Mary Stacey was born 3/28/1774.

Mecklenburg County, Virginia, Deed Book 5, Page 167-

(blank) 1777 - James Kidd and Winny, his wife of Mecklenburg
County sell to George Wilson of Bute County, North Carolina, a tract
of land in the County of Mecklenburg, Colony of Virginia, on the
county line, containing by estimation 100 acres. (no witnesses
listed. Recorded 12 January 1778.

Mecklenburg County, Virginia, Deed Book 6, Page 464-

26 November 1784 - James Kidd of County of Mecklenburg sells to
John Tanner of the County of Warren, State of North Carolina, for
125 pds. - a tract of land in County of Mecklenburg, Va., containing
200 acres, etc.
Witnesses: William Kidd, John Kendrick, John Kendrick,Jr.,
Recorded: 9 May 1785 and Winney, wife of James Kidd relinquishes
her right of dower.

Note by C.H.H.: Will of Robert Hudson of Mecklenburg Co. dated
17th February 1787 names (among other legatees) his
daughter, Winny Kidd (Will Book 3, Page 337). (Will
probated 11 April 1796.

Mecklenburg County, Virginia, Will Book 3, Page 367-

Last Will and Testament of Thomas Carter, dated 21 Dec. 1795.
Probated: 8 August 1796.

To my son, John Carter, 150 acres of land in Granville County
(North Carolina) joining the land whereon I now live, and to my son,
Charles Carter, 150 acres joining land I have willed my son, John -
on Nutbush Creek. To my natural son, Thomas Carter, 100 acres of
land, part of which I now live on. To my natural son, Charles Carter
100 acres whereon he now lives. To beloved wife, Mary, balance of
land for her life or widowhood and then to my son, John Carter. To
daughter, Elizabeth Johnson, slave. To my daughter, Judith Kidd, a
negro man named Cato. To my daughter, Sally Johnson, slave, a negro
boy to Secretary Carter and Sarah Carter, children of Robert Carter.
To my daughter, Mary Freeman, 10 pounds.
Executors: sons John and Thomas Carter.
Witnesses: William Hendrick, Stephen Hendrick, Jesse Carter, Secretary Carter.
(Mecklenburg County Marriages by Elliott, Page 77 - October 8, 1781 -
William Kidd to Judy Carter).

76

Mecklenburg County, Deed Book 7, Page 132-

8 June 1787 - Deed of Gift from Mary Stevens of County of Mecklenburg to her beloved grandson, William Kidd, for natural love and affection, of 200 acres of land in said County, near Nutbush Creek, adjoining land of James Kidd, the County line - John Tannor's line, etc. Recorded 11 June 1787.

(Note): Deed Book 9, Page 407 - William Kidd sells this 200 acres 21 August 1797 (whereon he now lives and which formerly belonged to Mary Stevens) to John Tanner of County of Warren, State of North Carolina - and Judy, wife of William Kidd, relinquished her right of dower).

Mecklenburg County, Deed Book 10, Page 13-

James Kidd of the County of Oglethorpe, State of Georgia, gives Power of Attorney to his son, William Kidd, of Mecklenburg Co., Virginia, to sell his land in Mecklenburg Co., etc. Dated 1 September 1798. Recorded 8 October 1798.

Note by C.H.H.: (Ibid P 376) James Kidd was still of Mecklenburg County, Virginia on November 11, 1795 when he sold 220 acres of land in that County to William Hendrick, at which time his wife, Frances, cosigned with him.

Mecklenburg Marriage: Elliott P. 77. August 8, 1795. James Kidd to Frances Robertson.

Hoyts Index - James H. Kidd, Virginia (born in Va.) S 16436.

Report of Secretary of War 1835 - Pension Rolls Vol 3, Pt. 1, Page 514 -
County of Jackson,Georgia
James H. Kidd, Private - $36.66 Annual Allowance. Sums received - $109.98 - Virginia Service - Militia. Placed on Pension Roll Sept. 14, 1833. Pension commenced March 4, 1831, age 69.

Oglethorpe County, Georgia

William Kidd, Private - Annual Allowance $39.00. Received $117.00. Virginia Militia Service. Placed on Pension Roll March 18, 1833. Commenced pension March 4, 1831. Age 72. (Hoyts Index S31796.

77

William Kidd, born Mecklenburg County, Virginia, December 16,
1763. Will made 1843, probated January 27, 1845 - moved to Ogle-
thorpe County, Georgia 1799 where he died. Was a Revolutionary War
Soldier. Served in Virginia Army in Capt Anderson's Company.
Wounded 1780. Enlisted again 1781 in Capt Swepton's Company, Col.
Munford's Regiment. Allowed pension in Oglethorpe Co., Ga, 1832.
Married October 8, 1781, Judith (called Judy) Carter. She died
before 1843.

Children mentioned in Will -
1. William, married Dec. 20, 1813 Nancy Carter
2. Mary, married Edward Carter
3. Lucy, married Johnson Wright
4. Elizabeth, married Dean Tucker
5. Webb, married Malinda Kidd.
Ibid - Page 105 - also says:
6. Carter

Georgia's Roster of the Revolutionary War - Knight, Vol 4, page 420-

The Harvey List - certified List of Rev. War Soldiers -
James H. Kidd
William Kidd
Page 442 - Revolutionary Pensioners - James H. Kidd, Jackson Co., Ga.
Page 451 - Revolutionary Pensioners - William Kidd Sr., Oglethorpe, Ga

Bedford County, Virginia - Deed Book 11, Page 254-

(not dated) Power of Attorney by George Rucker of Bedford Co.,
Virginia to John Rucker of Woodford County, Kentucky and Thomas
Canady (Kennedy) of Bourbon County, Kentucky, to collect rents and
arrears of rents from Benjamin Penn of Bourbon Co., Kentucky and
others on his land in Bourbon County, Ky. Recorded 22 Sept. 1800.

Pittsylvania County, Virginia - Deed Book 12, Page 246-

25 August 1800 - Marlin Young of the County of Sumner, State
of Tennessee, sells to Augustine Smith and George Robins of the
County of Pittsylvania, State of Virginia, for 130 pds., 196 acres
of land in County of Pittsylvania on the waters of the Corn Branch,
etc.

78

Witnesses: John Smith, Lewis Smith, Jacob Vance, George Young, Casper
             Mess. Recorded: January 19, 1801.

Note by C.H.H.: Pittsylvania County Marriages by Knorr, Page 99.
             May 1, 1792 (Bond) Marlin Young married Tabitha Witcher,
             daughter of Daniel Witcher.

             The Will of William Young dated 1 January 1805, pro-
             bated 19 April 1813 in Pittsylvania County, Virginia,
             (D & W #11, Page 378) names among his other children
             this son, Marlin Young (spelled in the records, Merlin
             Young). This 196 acres of land had been sold 19 April
             1790 (Deed Book 8) by William Young to (his son,
             Marlin Young) and on the same date, William Young
             sold 2 other tracts of land in Pittsylvania Co. to
             2 other sons, Archibald Young (201 acres) and Milton
             Young (246 acres).

Land Tax Records of Hanover County, Virginia - 1814
Absentee Landowners

NAME	ACRES	PRESENT RESIDENCE
Eliza & Mariah Bullock	231	Kentucky
James Cason	22½	Tennessee
Joseph Hawkins	444	Kentucky
Robert Morris	1128	Philadelphia
Henry H. Mallory	20	Kentucky
Samuel Richardson	616	Louisiana
William O. Winston Jr.	323	New Orleans
Samuel Gist	2337	England
John Glazebrook, Son of James Glazebrook	126	Kentucky
John J. Grosjean Estate	-	Kentucky
John Hendley, Guardian for Peter Martin & Sarah Martin	34 45	Tennessee

****

CONTRIBUTIONS BY OTHERS

The following was Contributed by Mrs. Catherine L. Knorr, Pine Bluff, Arkansas. (Thanks, "Kitty").

Pittsylvania County, Virginia - Deed Book 44, page 283-

27 September 1837 - Power of Attorney by Gabriel May, of the County of Tippah and State of Mississippi. To Thomas W. Still of Tennessee - to collect for me any monies due me from the estate of (Mrs) Elizabeth Still of Pittsylvania County, Virginia. Recorded Pittsylvania Co., V. 21 December 1860 (sic).

Comment: It is interesting to note that Tippah County had just been formed in 1836 from the Chickasaw Cession of 1832. Ripley, Miss. is the county seat. I am informed that there are extant similar documents to the above from members of the Still family of Williamson County, Tennessee. Mrs. Knorr has records to prove that Gabriel May, (son of John May and Susanna Porter, his wife) was born 8 December 1793; died ca 1864/5 and who married in Pittsylvania Co., Va. 14 January (or June?) 1817 Elizabeth Still, (born 6 March 1794) who was the daughter of John and Elizabeth Still. Gabriel May and his wife, Elizabeth must have left Virginia after the 20 October 1836 for on that date they sold to Josiah Still and Izbell Still, of Pittsylvania Co. their 1/3 share or interest in the the land of John Still, Sr., deceased. (Ref: Deed Book 39, Page 198).

The following was contributed by Mrs. Emma R. Matheny, Prof. Genealogist, Richmond, Virginia. (Thanks, Emma).

TOMBSTONE INSCRIPTIONS

Milton Public Cemetary, Caswell County, North Carolina
John Epperson
Born Jan. 31, 1776 Hanover Co., Va.
Died June 3, 1852.

Ibid -

Bettie E. Royer, Wife of W. P. Royer
Born Halifax Co., Virginia (ca 1844)
Died April 6, 1919, age about 75 years.

Family Cemetary, Cunningham Farm, Person County,
North Carolina, (State Route 1318)

Alexander Cunningham
Born Feb. 27, 1776 Lombardy Grove, Mecklenburg Co., Va.
Died October 12, 1849.

Wills, Invs., Etc., Warren Co., North Carolina, Will Book I
(1764-1783), Pages 105-109, 112. Original in Wake County Court
House. Transcript Hall of History and Archives, Raleigh, N. C.

WILL of THOMAS CHRISTMAS (of Hanover County, Virginia)

Names Sons: John Christmas, his son Thomas Christmas
Daughter: Elizabeth Paulett, John Christmas, son of Elizabeth
                Paulett
Daughter: Caty Higgason
Daughter: Rachel Chrisholm
Son: Thomas Christmas, his wife, Temperance and their children
                Viz: John, Mary, Thomas, Richard and William.

Grandchildren: Charles, James, Thomas and Nathaniel Whitlock.
                Mary Jones, Anne Austin, John, Nancy, Mary and Riella
                Sanders, Elizabeth Simms.

Executors: My Son John Christmas and John Higgason.

Sealed and Delivered in the presence of: David Anderson, Richard
Higgason, John Higgason.

Offered for proof at a Court held for Hanover County, Virginia on
Thursday, the 7th day of September 1769 and ordered to be recorded
by: William Pollard C. H. C.

A copy of the above will has been given to Hanover C. H., Virginia
State Library and National DAR Library, Washington, D. C.

****

82

PROOF OF IMPORTATIONS

Charles City County, Virginia, Orders (1672-1673)Page 514)-
(Library Accessions #22345)

April 3, 1673 - Capt Otho Southcott hath proved right to 500 acres of land for the Charge of Importation of Thomas Mason - Polidore Prichard - Richard Patnam (or Patram?) - Joseph Davis - John Adams-Elizabeth Seabrooke - Henry Roberts - Thomas Hindmars - Oliver Davenport and Elizabeth Wise and hath assigned the same to William Harrison Jr.

Henrico County Order Book 5, Page 610 -

7 October, 1793 - George Gardner, Merchant, William Goodwin and Patrick Braney, Mariners - migrating into this Commonwealth, the said Gardner from Scotland. The said Goodwin from England, and the said Braney from Ireland, who have resided within the limits and jurisdiction of the United States for the term of two years and within this State for one year, etc. - having taken the oath, etc. - are thereupon admitted citizens of the same.

Brunswick County, Virginia - Order Book 4, Page 182-

May Term 1752 - Thomas Bull, of the County, came into Court and made oath that he imported himself into this Colony of Virginia directly from the Kingdom of Great Britain about 31 years since (thus arriving about 1721) and that this was the first time of proving such importation which is ordered to be certified.

Ibid - Order Book 6, Page 51-

March Court 1750 - Thomas Stone came into Court and made oath that in the year 1740 he imported himself directly from the Kingdom of Great Britain into this Colony and that this is the first time of his proving such importation. (IBID) - John Macinvale makes the same oath that he imported himself directly from the Kingdom (sic) of Ireland in the year 1727.

Henrico County, Virginia - Minute Book (1827-29) Page 38-

14 August 1827 - "I, William Bates, make the following report of myself to the County Court of Henrico in the State of Virginia, that is to say: I report that I was born at Dublin in the Kingdom of Great Britain on the 1st day of April 1804, being now in the 24th year of my age, that I am a subject of the King of Great Britain, owing allegiance to that Monarch, and none other. That I migrated from England to the United States in the year 1822 and that I intend to settle myself in Virginia, one of the United States".
                              (Signed) William Bates.

Note: Ibid, Page 40 is found his oath of allegiance to the United States, becoming a citizen.

Loudoun County, Virginia - Superior Court, Deed Book A (1809-1844) Page 121-

2 April 1824 - Report of Simon Smale, an alien, who was born in the Parish of Uhridge (?), County of Devonshire, aged 43 years, of Great Britain, migrated from the County of Devonshire and intends settling in Leesburg, Loudoun County, Virginia, etc. Recorded: same date.

Loudoun County, Superior Court, Deed Book A (1809-44) Page 122-

3 April 1824 - Report of George Washington Smyth, an alien, who was born in Moneymore County of Londonderry, of Ireland, about 23 years of age, owing allegience to the King of Great Britain (quote) "if birth in his Dominion makes me owe allegience" (end quote) - Migrated from the County of Dublin and intends settling in Leesburg, Loudoun County, Virginia. Recorded same date.

IBID, Page 122 - April 5, 1824. A report of John Burton, an alien, who was born in Rothwell County, Yorkshire, England, aged about 46 years, owing allegience to the King of Great Britain - (quote) "if birth in his Dominion makes me owe allegience" (end quote). Migrated from Liverpool, Lancaster County and intends settling in Loudoun County, Virginia. Recorded same date.

IBID, Page 123 - 7 April 1824 - Report of Michael Morallee, an alien who was born in the Parish of Longhasley, County of Northumberland, England, owing allegiance to the King of Great Britain, about 26 year

84

of age. Migrated from County of Northumberland and intends settling in the Town of Leesburg, Loudoun County, Virginia. Recorded
same date.

Loudoun County, Virginia, Superior Court Deed Book A (1809-1844)
Page 124-

September 1, 1824 - A report of John S. Pearce, an alien, who was
born in the Parish of St Snoder, County of Cornwall, England -
about 29 years of age, owing allegience to the King of Great Britain. Migrated from the County of Cornwall and intends residing
in Leesburg, Loudoun County, Virginia. Recorded Same date.

IBID, Page 124- 6 September 1824 - a report of Peter Wetherly, an
alien, who was born in the Parish of Cockburn Path, County of Berwickshire, upon the Tweed, Scotland, age 29 years. Migrated from
Berwickshire, Scotland and intends settling in Loudoun County, Va.
near Leesburg, Recorded same date.

IBID- Page 125- 31 July 1826- a report of Thomas Lobey (?) -or
Sobey, (?), an alien, who was born in the Parish of Roach in the
year 1786, of Great Britain, owes allegience to the King of England. Migrated from the County of Cornwall and intends settling
in Loudoun County, Virginia. Recorded same date.

IBID - Page 125 - July 31, 1826. A report of John Hocking, an
alien, who was born in the Parish of Roach in the year of 1786,
of Great Britain, owing allegience to the King of England. Migrated from the County of Cornwall and intends settling in the
County of Loudoun, Virginia. Recorded same date.

IBID- Page 126- August 1, 1826, A report of Henry Moon, an alien,
age 47 years, produced a certificate from the USA District of Columbia, County of Alexandria, by George Deneale, Clerk of the U. S.
Circuit Court, certifying that on 23 July 1812, Henry Moon of Bolton, in Kingdom of Great Britain, came personally before the said
Court and made oath that it was bonafide his intention to become a
citizen of the United States and to renounce forever all allegience
and fidelity to any foreign Prince, State, etc. and particularly
the King of Great Britain, etc. (Further - "Liverpool, 10 August
1809, Received from Henry Moon, twenty one guineas for his family's
passage in the steerage of the W & John, he finding provisions to
Virginia". and having resided several years in the Town of

Alexandria and for the last five years in the State O Virginia, the last two years in this County, etc. and the said Henry Moon is a man of good moral character, etc. Recorded same date.

Loudoun County, Virginia, Superior Court Deed Book A (1809-44) P. 12⁹

May 16, 1829- James D. Kirwan, an alien, exhibited a certificate of the Clerk of the Superior Court for the County of Berkeley (now in Virginia) dated 17 May 1824 that it was his bonafide intention to become a citizen of the United States and renounced his allegience to George IV, King of Great Britain and it being proved by the testimony of Charles Lewis that he has resided in this State one year at least and is a man of good moral character, etc. and thereupon the said James D. Kirwan is admitted a citizen of the United States.

IBID, Page 137- 17 February 1830, a report of John Barrett, an alien, who states that he was born 17 March 1796 (being now in the 34th year of my age) in the County of Tyrone, in the North of Ireland and owe allegience to the King of Great Britain. That he migrated from the said Kingdom (County Tyrone) to the United States in the year 1814 and intends to settle in the County of Loudoun, Virginia, etc. Recorded same date.

86

<u>CEMETERY RECORDS</u>

SHOCKOE HILL CEMETERY
Richmond, Virginia

<u>INFORMATION FROM CEMETERY RECORDS</u>:_

JOHN CASKIE - Range 12 - Section 4 - Quarter 1 - Row 2 - Grave 2 -
Retired merchant - buried September 15, 1867 - died of heart
disease.

On the same plot are:

> Reuben R. Caskie (7 - 15 - 1837)
> Mrs Harrison's still born -
> Martha J. Caskie
> Reuben Norwell

<u>FROM TOMBSTONE INSCRIPTIONS</u>:-

IN MEMORY OF JOHN CASKIE - BORN IN (See note below) AYRSHIRE,
SCOTLAND, February 17, 1790 - Died in Richmond, Virginia 13th
September 1867 - Blessed are the dead which die in the Lord.

This is a long, wide, table top slab lying flat on the ground.
Next to him is the grave of -

MARTHA JANE, WIFE OF JOHN CASKIE, born January 16, 1798 - died
December 2, 1844 - The Sacrifices of God are a broken spirit; a
broken and contrite heart, O God thou wilt not despise - Psalm
51:17.

This is a long, wide, raised table-top slab, enclosed all around,
about one foot high and six feet long.

<u>Note by C.H.H.</u>: From other records we know that she was MARTHA
JANE NORWELL, daughter of REUBEN NORWELL (of whom
more later) - From other records we also know that
the birthplace of JOHN CASKIE (almost obliterated
on his monument) was STEWARTON, AYRSHIRE, SCOTLAND.

REUBEN NORVELL (NORWELL ?) - born August 6, 1769 - died June 17, 1852.

This is a four foot tall, two foot wide upright slab with a Masonic
emblem on the top portion.

<u>Note by C.H.H.</u>: The 1850 Census shows Reuben (NEWELL ?) age 87, blind, as living in the household of John Caskie that year.

MATTIE J. (OR MARTHA J. ?) Daughter of JOHN CASKIE, born September 24, 1829 - died September 28, 1854.

ANOTHER MONUMENT I CANT DECIPHER - born February 18, 1831 (?) - died January 2, 1854 (?) -

REUBEN K (or R ?) - infant son - (cant deciper) died 15 July 1837 - age 6 months (?) days -

<u>INFORMATION FROM CEMETERY RECORDS</u>:-

ROBERT HUTCHINSON - Range 13, Section 9, Quarter 4, Row 2, Grave second from carriage way. (Section Book I shows grave 3) -

JAMES CASKIE - Same Plot - (original records show James Caskie owned one-half of plot) -
Buried on this plot are:
        Robert Hutchinson*
        James Caskie
        Eliza K. R. Caskie
        Eliza Caskie
        Ellen L. Hutchinson
        Nancy Caskie
        Harriet A. Scott
        Henneta (sic) Caskie
        Nannie E. Caskie

* Robert Hutchinson, age 60, died May 17, 1861 (or buried this date) Congestion of bowels - Merchant

<u>FROM TOMBSTONE INSCRIPTIONS</u>:-

ROBERT HUTCHINSON OF SAVANNAH - <u>Born in Glasgow, Scotland</u> - April 5, 1802 - Died in Savannah, Georgia (faded out - looks like May 17th 1861 - This is a tall, beautiful monument with a large urn on top. In the grave next to him is -

ELLEN LAURA, WIFE OF ROBERT HUTCHINSON, (on one side-) This Memorial dedicated by her grateful and sorrowing husband (another side -) She died at Savannah just one week after giving birth to an only child, a daughter, on Monday 22 March 1858 - aged 22 years and 16 days -

This is another tall, beautiful, draped monument with a tall slender urn on top.

ROBERT HUTCHINSON - JAMES CASKIE - TOMBSTONE INSCRIPTIONS, continued -

To the dearly beloved memory of NANNIE EUPHEMIA CASKIE - Born in Virginia August 31, 1831 - Died in Florence, Italy April 21, 1893 - This monument is of a beautiful, kneeling angel on a large table top type raised and enclosed chest like stone. The caretaker told me that the monument was shipped from Italy. I noticed that all the letters of the inscription were chisled very beautifully and had lead inserts in each letter.

ELIZA K. R. CASKIE - Born June 18, 1797 - died September 19, 1861.

Note by C.H.H.: From other records we know that she was ELIZA KENNON RANDOLPH PINCHAM, WIFE OF JAMES CASKIE.

This is a large $3\frac{1}{2}$ foot high - 5 foot wide tablet like monument divided in two sections - on the other half is: -

JAMES CASKIE - Born May (?) 1792 - died October 11, 1866 -

HARRIET AUGUSTA CASKIE, DAUGHTER OF JAMES AND ELIZA KENNON RANDOLPH CASKIE - Wife of JOHN SCOTT OF FAUQUIER COUNTY, VIRGINIA. Born February 6, 1833 - died April 1, 1892. This is a beautiful granite stone monument about two feet by three feet.

There are also two small children head stones, writing obliterated.

INFORMATION FROM CEMETERY RECORDS:-

MRS. MARY C. HUTCHINSON, buried July 4, 1852 - Range 21 - Section 6 Quarter 2, Row 2, Grave 2 -

MARY CASKIE HUTCHINSON, same as above but Grave 1 - died (or buried) December 15, 1851 -

Note by C.H.H.: This is a HARRISON Burial Plot and other monuments are to Caskie Harrison - Edmund Caskie Harrison - Margaret Caskie Harrison - Lucy Norvell Harrison.

89

FROM TOMBSTONE INSCRIPTION:-

MARY CASKIE, DAUGHTER OF JOHN CASKIE AND WIFE OF ROBERT HUTCHINSON
OF SAVANNAH, GEORGIA - born (obliterated) - died December (?) 1852.

The inscription continues with something about a daughter (which
cannot be deciphered) died 1851 - who must be Mary Caskie Hutchinson as named in the Shockoe Hill Cemetery records.

This is a large coffin shape monument about three feet high and
about six feet long.

Note by C.H.H.: Richmond Virginia Marriage Bonds by Reddy, page 99-
          October 31, 1848 ROBERT HUTCHINSON of Savannah,
          Georgia to MARY M(ARGARETHA) CASKIE, DAUGHTER OF
          JOHN CASKIE, ESQ.

Ibid, page 87 -

September 25, 1845 - Nannie E. Caskie, daughter of John Caskie, to
Samuel J. Harrison.

Comment: The above Mary Margaretha Caskie, daughter of John
          Caskie, was the second (?) wife of Robert Hutchinson of
          Savannah, Georgia and he married (thirdly ?) her first
          cousin, Ellen Laura Caskie, daughter of James Caskie.

Further Comment: It was particularly noticed that all three sub-
          ject burial plots were inscribed "for perpetual care" and
          were in extremely beautifully kept condition. The care-
          taker for the past 20 years, Mr. Wade, was most helpful,
          obliging and courteous.

****

90

CENSUS RECORDS

1850 Census of Harlan County, Kentucky-
House #223, Family 224-

George Brittain, Age 82 (1768) - Born in Virginia
Nancy (Posey) Brittain, Age 54 (1796) -Born in Georgia
Nancy Lankford, Age 25 - Born in Tennessee
Mary Lankford, Age 21 - Born in Tennessee

1850 Census of Harlan County, Kentucky-

#218-218 - David G. Lyttle, Age 30 - Born in Virginia
James Lyttle, Age 17 - Born in Virginia

#219-219 Benjamin Posey, Age 43 - Born in Georgia
Lucy Posey, Age 39 - Born in Virginia

#223-223 - Carlo B. Brittain, Age 30 - Born in Kentucky
Sally Brittain, Age 25 - Born in Virginia

#225-225 - Carr Brittain, Age 51 - Born in Kentucky
Caroline Brittain, Age 49 - Born in Virginia

#247-247 - Harrington Lyttle, Age 49 - Born in Virginia
Mary A. Lyttle, Age 24 - Born in Virginia
Catherine Smith, Age 4 - Born in Virginia
Rebecca F. Smith, Age 2 - Born in Virginia
George Lyttle, Age 14 - Born in Virginia

Lee County, Virginia, Deed Book 2 - Page 26-

3 November 1804 - Indenture in which Henry Brackbell, now of
Lee County, Virginia, acting by virtue of a Power of Attorney for
Jacob Eshlemore, Sr., of the State of Pennsylvania - sells to
George Brittain of the County of Knox, State of Kentucky, for $500
a tract of land lying and being in the County of Knox, on both
sides of the south fork of Cumberland River, three miles above the
mouth of Crank's Creek, etc.
Witnesses: Hercules Whaley, (?) Fulkerson, Thomas Knotts, James
F. Sharp, Joseph Ewing.

Ibid - Page 164-

23 December 1808 - Indenture in which George Brittain and Mary, his wife, of Knox County, State of Kentucky - sell to Daniel Dickerson, of Lee County, Virginia - for $500 - a tract of land in said County of Lee, on the head of the Glade Spring branch of the Waters of Powell River, which land was granted to Aaron Lewis by Patent Dated 27 December 1787 - containing by survey 300 acres, etc.
Witnesses: John McKoon, H. Rice, Joab Matlock, John Boyd.
Recorded: February Court 1809.

1850 Census of Coles County, Illinois-

Upper Okaw Precinct - September 13, 1850 -

53-53 - David Romine, Age 49, farmer - Born in Virginia
        Naomi Romine, Age 45 - Born in Pennsylvania
        Nancy Romine, Age 17 - Born in Ohio
        Joanah Romine, Age 15 - Born in Ohio
        Levi Romine, Age 12 - Born in Ohio
        William Romine, Age 9 - Born in Illinois or Indiana
        Sarah J. Romine, Age 6 - Born in Illinois or Indiana

63-63 - Elias Romine, Age 39 - Born in Ohio
        Nancy Romine, Age 33, Born in Ohio
        Mary Romine, Age 8 - Born in Illinois (?)
        Sarah Romine, Age 6 - Born in Illinois
        Daniel Romine, Age 4 - Born in Illinois
        Rebecca Romine, Age 10/12 - Born in Illinois
        Joseph Romine, Age 10/12 - Born in Illinois
        Elias Romine, Age 17 - Born in Ohio
        Abram Romine, Age 12 - Born in Ohio
        Jonah Romine, Age 68 - Born in Virginia

115-115 - With family of J. F. Henderson-
        Elizabeth Romine, age 18 - Born in Indiana

1880 Census of Champaign County, Ohio - Goshen Township-

Page 218   James Romine, 75, farmer, born Ohio (Father born N.Jersey
                                                (mother born (unknown)
           Sarah J. Romine, 60, Born Ohio (father born, unknown -
                                            Mother born, unknown)
           Ella Romine, 19 Born in Ohio
           James Romine,Jr., 45, Born Ohio (father born Virginia)
                                            (mother born in ")
           Mary J. Romine, 44, Born in Ohio (father born Virginia)
                                             (Mother born Virginia)
           William J. Romine, 16, Born in Ohio (father born Ohio)
                                                (Mother born Ohio)

Page 219   Eli Romine, 50, farmer, Born in Virginia (Father born Va.)
                                                      (Mother born in Va.)
           Rebecca Romine, 52, Born Pennsylvania (father born Penna.)
                                                  (Mother born in Penna.)

1850 Census of Nansemond County, Virginia-

House #106 - Samuel Ward, Age 44, Shoemaker, Born in North Carolina
             Margaret Ward, Age 50, Born in North Carolina
             George Ward, Age 10, Born in North Carolina
             Kenneth R. Ward, Age 9, Born in North Carolina

                        ****

E R R A T A

Page 10 - Change _Elyan_ Gillions to _Elijah_ Gillions.

Page 13 - Change Battle of Point Pleasant from October 10, _1744_ to October 10, _1774_.

Page 13 - Change William _Sherman_ to William _Shennon_.

Page 14 - Change Joseph _Wells_ to Joseph _Wills_.

Page 15 - Change Abram _Halslop_ to Abram _Haeslop_.

Page 18 - Change John _Penmore_ to John _Pinmore_.

Page 19 - Add the rate of Corporal after the name of Benjamin Barrett.

Page 19 - Change Thomas _Donnabough_ to Thomas _Donnahough_.

Page 26 - Spell 2nd _Vairginia_ Regt. as 2nd _Virginia_ Regt.

Page 25 - Change John _Smerrer_ to John _Smerver_.

Page 40 - Change George _Walta_ to George _Walter_.

Page 53 - Change Robert _Muckolls_ to Robert _Nuckolls_.

Page 56 - Change Munford _Dyarnett_ to Munford _Dejarnett_.

Page 57 - Change _Elizah_ Swope to _Elijah_ Swope.

Page 60 - Under the note by CHH: Change Daniel Arney, a _quacker_, to Daniel Arney, a _Quaker_.

Page 73 - Under comment, change Thomas Stacy, Member of the Virginia _County_ to Thomas Stacy, Member of the Virginia _Company_.

INDEX

Atchison
Thomas 64

Atkinson
James 14
Thomas 71

Austin
Anne 82
Daniel 53
Edward 4
Francis 26
John 12
William 14

Ayerest
Thomas 73

Aylett
Benjamin 71
William 71

Bailey
Thomas 14

Baker
Amy 74
Ann 75
Elizabeth 75
Joseph 74
Nancy 58
William 21

Baldock
Richard 14,24

Baley
William 34

Balies
William 34

Ballard
John 54
Joseph 54

Ballen
Edward 1

Banner
Peter 19

Barlow
Benjamin 3

Barnes
Alexander 70

Barnett
James 6
John 26
William 12

Barrack
Bryan 34
John 23

Barrett
Benjamin 19,94
John 6,86
Nathaniel 19,21

Barringer
Isaac 24

Barten
Charity 41

Bassett
John 14
Robert 4

Bassford
Alexander 12

Bates
Thomas 23
William 84
William H. 67

Batten
Nathan 17

96

Baxter		
Samuel	25	
Beal		
John	34	
Bear		
William	23	
Bearcroft		
William	26	
Beazely		
Gowan	24	
Bedgood,		
Joseph	8	
Bedient		
William	19	
Belcher		
Isham	17	
John	61	
Belford		
John	29	
Bell		
Capt David	2,4	
George V.	61	
Henry	60,61	
James	3	
James M.	60,61	
Samuel	61	
Sarah Ann	60	
Thomas	48,75	
Bennet		
Thomas	5	
Benson		
John	14	

Best		
Christopher	13,14,16	
James	13	
John	17	
Bevans		
Daniel	19	
Beverley		
Mackenzie	51	
Bevin		
Peter	8	
Bibb		
Martin	49	
Bickley		
Humphrey	61	
Biggers		
James	26	
Bins		
James	21	
Blackbourn		
Edward	17	
Blackburn		
James	42	
Blair		
John	54	
Blakely		
William	23	
Blanchard		
Aaron	62	
Blanchet		
Henry	61	
John	61	

Blankinship
    Arthur   49
    Henry   9
    Stephen   14

Blanton
    William   9

Bledcer
    Abraham   9

Bludoe
    Joseph   23

Boarn
    Thomas   74

Body
    William   9

Bogle
    Thomas   63

Bolton
    Richard   3

Bond
    Christopher   26

Boon(e)
    Maj. Daniel   63

Borbin
    Richard C.   51

Borden
    Joseph   5

Bossman
    John   21

Bosswell
    John   23

Boswell
    James   14

Bott
    Benjamin T.   70

Bowles
    Doctor   26

Bowman
    Abraham   61,62
    Andrew   64
    Eleanor   63
    Elizabeth   61,62
    George   61,62
    Isaac   61,62
    Jacob   62
    John   61,62
    John, Jr.   61
    Joseph   62
    Mary   61,62
    Rebecca   61,62
    Regina   61,62
    Richard   63
    Samuel   63
    Samuel, Jr.   63
    Sarah   61,62
    William   63

Boy
    Jacob   34

Boyd
    John   92

Brackbell
    Henry   91

Bradbourn
    Elizabeth   74

Braddock
    Gen. Edward   7,25
    Peter   34

Bradey
    John   34

Bradford
Thomas   9

Bragg
William   58,68

Braney
Patrick   83

Brann
Jacob   21

Bran(n)in
Daniel   34
Thomas   9

Brewster
Mrs. H.K.   42

Bridge
Joseph   14

Bridgman
Roger   24

Briggs
Joseph   29

Brittain
Carlo B.   91
Caroline   91
Carr   91
George   91,92
Mary   92
Nancy (Posey)   91
Sally   91

Britton
John   17

Brock
William   13

Brockman
Elizabeth   47
John   48

Bromley
William   9

Brook(e)(s)
Bibby   21,26,28,74
Francis   31
George   74
John   9
Thomas   74
Traverse   74
William   17

Brothers
Francis   6

Broughton
William   25

Brown
David   34
Edward   31
George   34
John   9,11,25,34
Lucy   59,68
Molly   59,68
Peter   58,59,68
Phillip Combs   17
Samuel   24
Thomas   6,17,29,31,34
Vincent   58,59,68,69

Bruce
Charles   17

Brumley
William   19

Bryant
Garner   53
Jessy   14
John   31
Susannah   53

Buckhan(n)an
James   25
John   34

Buckley		Burras	
John	24	Agenteel (?)	49
		Carolus	49
Buckner		Charles	49
William S.	70	Elizabeth	47,49
		Fanny	47,48,49
Buckridge		Frances	47,48
James	8	Frances Tandy	47,48
		Jane	47,48
Buffen		Joseph	49
Joseph	8	Joseph Mills	48
		Lucy	49
Bull		Mildred	47,48
Thomas	83	Molly	48
		Molly Ann	49
Bullock		Nathaniel	48
Eliza	80	Morning	47
Mariah	80	Pamelia	49
		Roger	47,48
Bunch		Sally Ellen	48
Samuel	52	Sarah	47,48,49
		Thomas	47,48
Burcham		Thomas Jr.	47
Levi	54	William Tandy	47,48,49
Burford		Burrill	
William	12	Phillip	17
Burgess		Burton	
John	6	John	84
		Samuel	19
Burk			
John	70	Bush	
		Frances Tandy	47,48
Burkham		William	48
Roger	17	William T.	48
Burn(s)		Butcher	
Aquillo	21	Daniel	34
Equilia	26,28	Samuel	14
John	25		
Joseph	21	Butler	
Michael	9	James	14
Thomas	34	Lewis	34

Byrd
    George H.   55
    Col. William   26

Cahill
    Barnaby   34

Caillian
    Charles   12

Cain
    John   71

Callicott
    Beverley   74
    James   74
    Precilla   74

Camden
    Lucy   49

Campbell
    Absalom   17
    Agnes   70
    Douglas   14
    George   31
    James   29
    John   9,17
    Patrick   70
    Patrick Sr.   70

Cardwell
    Mary Anne   73
    Susannah   73

Carmichael
    James   29,31

Carpenter
    John   6

Carr
    Capt John   44
    Joseph   35
    Thomas   5,17,34

Carrier
    Henry   13,14,16
    Thomas   13,14,16

Carroll
    John   19
    Matt(hew)   29,31

Carter
    Charles   76
    Edward   78
    Elizabeth   76
    Jesse   76
    John   76
    Judith   76,78
    Mary (wife)   76
    Mary (daut)   76
    Mary (Kidd)   78
    Nancy   78
    Robert   76
    Sally   76
    Sarah   76
    Secretary   76
    Thomas   24,76
    Thomas Jr.   76

Cartmell
    Thomas   50

Carson
    James   12
    Matthew   35

Carver
    Archelaus   55
    John   72
    Joseph Sr   52
    Joseph Jr   52

Carwig
    John   14

Cash
    James   72
    John   72
    Thomas   72
    William   72

Caskie
Eliza	88
Eliza,K.R.	88,89
Ellen Laura	90
Harriet Augusta	89
Henneta	88
James	88,89,90
John	87,88,90
Martha Jane	87,88
Mary	90
Nancy	88
Nannie Euphemia	88,89,90
Reuben R.	87,88

Cason
James	80

Cathrim
John	22

Catlett
Benjamin	70
Elijah	70
Judity	70
Mary	70
Sally	70

Caugan
Ralph	35

Caul
Colonel	44

Chadwell
John	74

Chalkly
Thomas	35

Champion
Henry	8

Chandler
John	29

Chapman
Cornelius	6
Thomas	35

Chapple
Edward	17

Charlott
John	35

Childs
Edward	4

Chism
Mary Anne	73

Chiswell
Col. John	64
William	26

Chrisholm
Rachel	82

Christmas
Caty	82
Elizabeth	82
John	82
John Jr.	82
Rachel	82
Richard	82
Temperance	82
Thomas	82
Thomas Jr.	82
Thomas III	82
William	82

Cinclair
John	17

Christian
Francis H.	59,68

Church
Jonathan Montgomery	74
John	34

Clancy
    George   25

Clark(e)
    Captain   44
    George   14
    James   17
    John   15,17,31,45
    Robert   59

Clatterbuck
    John   19,32B

Claughton
    Richard   68

Clayton
    John   35

Clements
    John   8

Clifts
    James   6

Coe
    Barnard   8

Cocke
    Capt William   2,5

Cockeril(l)
    John   8
    Joseph   29,31

Cockren
    Thomas   3

Coffield
    Phillip   4

Coffland
    Will   24

Cofflin
    John   22

Coine
    John   19

Coiner
    Martin   50

Colbert
    William   17

Cole
    George   35
    John   24,26

Coleman
    John   35

Collins
    David   4
    John   35

Collis
    Killis   24

Collom
    Jeremiah   22,26,28

Colman
    Cornelius   31

Colston
    William   19

Coltbert
    William   4

Colwell
    Robert   34

Combs
    Thomas   19
    William   26

Comings
    Caleb   56

Conoway
   See Conway

Connel(l)
   John   34
   William   6

Connelley
   John   34

Conner
   John   6,17
   Lawrence   34

Connor
   See Conner

Constantine
   Edward Tully   6
   Patrick   6

Conway
   Timothy   3,4 ,22,26,28

Cook(e)
   Capt Nathaniel   43
   Reuben   31
   Thomas   8

Cooper
   James   15
   Job   3
   Samuel   9

Cope
   James   30

Cornelius
   Robert   25

Corvin
   Samuel   19

Cotham
   Thomas   26

Cotling
   John   19

Cotton
   Benjamin   8
   Thomas   17

Cousins
   Peter   34

Covey
   Durret   15

Coward
   Reuben   63

Cowen
   Samuel   31

Cox
   James   61
   William   24

Craft
   John   35

Craig
   John   25

Craighead
   Robert   6

Cram
   Peter   24

Crane
   William   35

Crawford
   John Jr.   70
   Molly Ann   49

Crawley
   John   6

Creed			Currie	
William	64		See Curry	
Creock			Curry	
John	26		David	9
			James	51
Creswell			Curtice	
Robert	6		George	17
Crews			Curtis	
Joseph	67		See Curtice	
Crickmore			Custis	
James	26		Margaret	69
Crittenden			William Smith	69
Abraham	12		Dabney	
Crook			Chiswell	66
John	35		Dacres	
Cross			John	8
John	6		Dangerfield	
Croswell			Col William	43
William	15		Daniel	
Crouch			James	48
Jacob	12		William	48
Croxton			Daugherty	
Thomas	30		Edward	30
Crump			Davenport	
Capt Richard	43		Oliver	83
Cummings			Davidson	
Samuel	4		John	6
Cunningham			Davis(s)	
Alexander	82		David	15
			Edward	26
Curls			George	24
John	9		James	8,26,29
			John	9,17
			Joseph	83

Davis(s) continued
 Richard 6
 Rodham 68
 Thomas 9

Dawson
 David 6

Deadman
 Nathaniel 9

Dean
 Samuel 42
 William 31

Debord
 David 9

Deekens
 Thomas 24

Deer
 William 8

Degges
 Robert 58

Dehay
 David 9

Dejarnett
 Christopher 57
 Elizabeth 56
 Munford 56,57,94

Delaney
 Thomas 15

Deloack
 Michail 8

Demoss
 Charles 64

Deneale
 George 85

Denny
 Richard 31

Dent
 Arthur 29

Derby
 Earl of 11

Desmukes
 Betsey 52
 Elisha 53
 Evi 52
 Evynard 52
 John 52
 John Jr. 52
 Mildred 52
 Patsy 52

Dexter
 Samuel 26

Diaper
 William 3

Dickerson
 Daniel 92

Dickson
 George 35
 William 35

Didlake
 Edward H. 70

Dillard
 George 49
 James 49
 Joseph 19

Dillen
 Samuel 50

Dispain
 Peter 35

Dix			Dounstanham	
Thomas	74		John	35
Dixon			Downey	
John	35		John	31
Samuel	35		Dozier	
Dobyns			James	60
Abner	57,58		Mary	60
Aretta	57		Tomblin	60
Brunetta W.	57			
Einnifred	57		Driver	
George H.	57		Edward	35,40
Margaret N.	57			
Mary M.	57		Drummond	
Parthenia	57		Tabitha	71
Thomas	57			
			Dudding	
Dodson			John	8
William	3,19,22			
			Duddleston	
Donald			Thomas	35,40
John	9			
			Due	
Donaldson			Thomas	22
James	15			
			Duestan	
Donally			John	35
John	9,23			
Mark	9		Dumont	
			James	35
Donnahough				
Thomas	19,94		Duncan	
			John S.	56
Doolen			Solomon	35
Thomas	3			
			Dunkin	
Dothery			Jonas	42
Edmond	31			
			Dunklay	
Douglas			John	71
Agnes	71			
Col. George	71		Dunn	
Margaret	71		Abram Mashaw	30
Tabitha	71		Richard	23
Thomas	23			

Dunnaho		Eleanor	
Patsy	52	John	25
Dunnivant		Elliott	
Michael	35	Joseph	53
Durley		Ellot	
Regina	62	Robert	26
Duvall		Elwell	
Thomas	35	Elizabeth	40
		Thomas	35,40
Dyer			
Thomas	6	Embry	
		Fanny	47,48
Easdale		John	48
Samuel	9	Joseph	48
		Mildred	47,48
East			
Josiah	31	Emmerson	
		Henry	13
Eaton			
Thomas	12	English	
		B----	35
Echols		Batt	40
Benjamin	53		
Catharine	53	Epperson	
Obediah	53	John	81
Edmondson		Eshlemore	
Thomas	12	Jacob	91
William	70		
		Evans	
Edwards		Abram	9
Ignatius	20	Edward	20,21
John	20	John	17
Col. John	70,71	Robert	70
Thomas	15	Thomas	30,31
William	9	William	30,31
Edzer		Everett	
Joseph	12	Daniel	59
		Frances	59
Elbert			
Samuel	56		

Ewing
    Joseph   91
    Robert   70
    William   65

Farmer
    Charles   31
    Elizabeth   73
    Francis   73
    Job   26
    Joel   73
    Martin   53
    Polly   73
    Syntha   73

Farmour
    Francis   20

Farquson
    John   75

Farrel
    Samuel   3

Farren
    Thomas   35

Farrow
    Thomas   15

Fashee
    Nathan   13

Faubous
    William   9

Fear
    William   8

Febiger
    Col Christian   43

Fendley
    Briant   31

Fenley
    Patrick   22,26,28

Fent
    Joseph   31

Fentress
    James   56

Ferguson
    Duncan   8,9
    Thomas   17

Ferman
    Mrs. Charles B.   42

Ferrall
    John   31

Field(s)
    Henry   31
    Michael   35
    Stephen   17
    William   3

Fielding
    Christian   26

Fines
    William   13

Fisher
    Jacob   49
    John   31
    Richard   26

Fitz
    Elizabeth   55
    Gideon   55
    John   55
    William   55

Fitzgeffries(sic)
    William   26

Fitzgrel (sic)
George 35

Fitzpatrick
John 31

Fleming
Colonel 44

Fletcher
Joseph 23

Fling
Matthew 20

Flowers
John 12

Fogg
Obediah 13

Foley
Richard 61

Folks
Thomas 35

Fonton
Lewis 35

Forester
George W. Denham 67
George William 67
Henrietta Eliz. 68
John 45,64
Mary 45,68
Robert 59
Temperance 67,68
William 58,59,67,68

Foresthampton
John 35

Foster
Richard 13

Fouqurean
John 73
Polly 73

Fowler
Andrew 10
John Jr. 70,71
Mathew 6
Robert 35

Fram
John 35,40

Francis
Agnes 50
Ann 50
Elizabeth 50
Henry 6
Jane 50
John 13,15,50
Margaret 50
Martha 50
Mary 50

Franklayn
John 35

Franklin
John 26
Sampson 12

Frazier
James 3,26
John 8

Freeman
Douglas S. 24,28
Edward 13
Mary 76

French
Samuel 20
William 10

Frost		Garsnell	
Joshua	35	Mordecai	6
Frye		Gaskins	
Christopher	15	John	22
Fugua		Gatewood	
Samuel	73	Mrs Amy (Baker)	75
		Henry	75
Fulkerson		James	75
(?)	91	John	75
		Joseph	75
Fulwell		William	75
Margaret	68		
Victor A.	68	Gender	
		John	13
Gaile			
John	20	Giddins	
		John	36
Gailor			
Edward	10	Gilmore	
		John	10
Gaines			
Capt Richard	44	Gill	
		Edward	13,15,16,20
Gallard		John	5
John	29		
		Gillet	
Gale(s)		Peggy	71
John	31	Samuel	71
Richard	22,26,28	William	71
Gardner		Gilliam	
George	83	William	23
John	26,50		
Thomas	12	Gillions	
		Branden	10
Garland		Elijah	10,94
Benjamin N.	59,68		
John	23	Gist	
		Capt Christopher	2,6,7
Garner		Samuel	80
George	36		
		Glascock	
Garoine		William	65
Moses	10		

111

Glazebrook			Govern	
James	80		John	10
John	80			
			Govers	
Glendening			James	25
David	25			
			Gowen	
Glimp			Zadock	6
Abraham	36			
			Gowing	
Glinn			Daniel	15
Patrick	17			
			Graham	
Godfrey			Duncan	64
Anthony	15		John	24
Elizabeth	74			
John	74		Grammer	
John Alt C.	75		John J. Peter	6
Peter	74			
			Grana (sic)	
Goldsbarry			Alexander	26
Robert	3			
William	3		Grant	
			John	15
Golding			William	36
George	17			
			Grave(s)	
Goldon			Jacob	67
George	5		Thomas	48
Good			Gray	
Richard	23		James	51
			William	51
Goodin				
John	10		Grayham	
			Arthur	36
Goodwin				
William	83		Green	
			John	10
Goss			Joseph	36
Benjamin	10		Lewis	17
Gough			Gregg	
Adam	36		William	54

Griffith		Haeslop	
Thomas W.	67	Abram	15,94
		See Heaslop	
Grimes			
Edward	26	Hagerly	
		Mathew	6
Grinins			
James	36	Hains	
		James	8
Grinnaway			
John	20	Hale	
		John	36
Grosjean			
John J.	80	Hall	
		John	6
Growter		Richard	15
David	23	Thomas	13,15,16
		William	61
Grub			
Benjamin	64	Hallicia (?)	
Emanuel	64	Thomas	36
John	64		
		Halloway	
Gwin		John	15
Peter	10	See Holloway	
Guinnon		Hally	
John	20	John	26
Gupton		Hamilton	
William	30	Joseph	26
Guptor		Hamlin	
William	31	Capt Francis M.	60
		Job	36
Gutridge		Sarah Elizabeth	60
James	22		
		Hammond	
Guttroy		Thomas	6
James	26,28		
		Handcock	
Hack		Joseph	20
Peter	71		
		Hanna	
		John	26

Hardin
  Peter   30

Hardman
  Jane   72
  John   72

Hardwick
  John   63
  John Jr.   63

Harmanson
  John   68

Harmon
  Richard   12

Harper
  Leonard   3

Harrald
  Jonathan   54

Harress
  See Harris

Harris(s)
  James   36
  John   12
  John F.   67
  Patsey   55
  Reuben   12
  Syntha   73
  Taylor   73
  William   20,36

Harrison
  Benjamin   33
  Caskie   89
  Edmond   89
  Capt Henry   2,8,9
  Lucy Norvell   89
  Margaret Caskie   89
  Mrs   87
  Samuel J.   90

Harrison (continued)
  Solomon   36
  William   75
  William Jr.   83

Hart
  Elizabeth   75
  John   10

Hartwell
  David   17

Harwood
  John   12,30

Hathaway
  Francis   22
  Miller   70

Hatfield
  James   17

Harvey
  Edward   36

Hawkes
  John   36

Hawkins
  Joseph   80
  William   36

Hay(s)
  John   65
  Vachal   36

Hazan
  William   12

Hazel
  David   24

Heaslup
  Abner   24
  Albert   24
  (See Haeslup)

114

Heath			Higgins	
William	30,31,36		Lawrence	5,17
Hedgman			Hill	
John	20		Edmund	36
			Elijah	49
Henderson			George	5,29
J. F.	92		James	8,55
			Capt James	44
Hendley			John	25,29,36
John	80		Samuel	32B
			Sarah	55
Hendrick				
Stephen	76		Hilton	
William	76,77		George	31
Hendrin			Hinchey	
John	12		Michael	15
Henley			Hind	
Cornelius	6		Ann	50
			Jane	50
Henry			Samuel	50
James	36			
			Hindmars	
Heson			Thomas	83
Samuel	36			
			Hingham	
Hickman			Joseph	10
Burton	13			
Edwen	47		Hite	
James Sr.	47		Jost	64
James Jr.	47			
			Hitchcock	
Hicks			Thomas	27
David	36			
Joseph	10		Hocking	
			John	85
Hickson				
James	36		Hodson	
			John	6
Higgason				
Caty	82		Hogan	
			William	17,24

115

Hogsett
    John   51

Hogshead
    John   50
    Margaret   50

Holcombe
    Col. John   43

Holebrook
    James   36

Holland
    William   10

Holledge
    William   36

Holloway
    James   15
    See Halloway

Holt
    John   58

Homan
    Robert   3

Hood
    Edward   36

Hook
    John   13
    William   31

Hooper
    Innes   3
    James   4
    John   4

Hope
    Thomas   15

Hopkins
    Charles   52

Hornback
    Joel   31

Horton
    Joseph   62

Housley
    See Ousley

Howard
    Elizabeth   41
    Henry   41
    James   41,70
    Laodicia   41
    Patty   41
    Sarah   41
    Shiplet   12
    Thomas   41

Howell
    Thomas   3

Hudson
    Robert   76
    Thomas   6
    Winny   76

Huff
    James   36
    John   32B

Huffman
    Thomas   70

Hugh(e)s
    Henry   17
    Patrick   6
    Capt Robert   43
    Saunder   29
    Thomas   18,36
    William   32B

Jopling			Kennedy	
Thomas	64		Ana	66
			Andrew	66,67
Jordan			Anthony	13,65,66
Thomas	36		Anthony Jr.	66,67
			Elizabeth	66,67
Joye			Esther	63
Robert	72		John	63,65,66,67
William	72,73		John P. Jr.	66,67
			Joseph	63
Juggins			Mary Ann	66,67
John	20		Nancy C.	65,66
			Philip Pendleton	66,67
Kaddock			Thomas	78
James	37		William	37

Keaton			Kenner	
John	20		Judith	51
			Rodham	51

Keen			Kenniss	
Richard	4		Andrew	20

Kegan			Ketcham	
Thomas	10		John	32

Kell(e)y			Ketting	
Daniel	32B		John	32B
James	13,36			
John	8		Key	
Lawrence	10		John	8
Peter	63			
Thomas	36		Kidd	
			Carter	78

Kelsey			Elizabeth	78
John	30,32		Frances	77
			James	76,77
Kelsick			James H.	77,78
Joseph B.	57		Judith	76,77,78
Parthenia	57		Lucy	78
			Malinda	78
Kemp			Mary	78
John	18		Nancy	78
			Webb	78
Kendrick			William	76,77,78
John	76		William Jr.	78
John Jr.	76		Winny	76

King	
George	55
Mathen	72
Sabbert	37
William	20
Kingston	
Francis	12
Kinsor	
Michael	36
Kirkham	
John	58
Kirkland	
Isham	15
Kirwan	
James D.	86
Kitchin	
John	27
Kite	
Robert	65
Kline	
Adam	65
Klotz	
John	36
Knibb	
Elizabeth	52
John	51
Samuel	51
Thomas	51
Knight	-
Bennett	
James	63
John	62
Knorr	
Catherine L.	81

Knotts	
Thomas	91
Knox	
John	36
L.....	
George	37
Thomas	37
Lacey	
John	32
LaFayette	
General	43
Lain	
Thomas	10
See Lane	
Lairy	
William	37
Lamb	
Joshua	15
Thomas	5,18
William	15,75
Land	
Edward	18
Lane	
Abraham	5
William	37
See Lain	
Lang	
John	37
Langworth	
Samuel	29
Lankford	
Mary	91
Nancy	91

119

Lare		
Edward	23	
Larmour		
Levin	10	
Lasley		
Daniel	5	
Latour		
John	37	
Lattin		
Thomas	20	
Lawson		
Ann	58	
Epaphroditus	58	
John	58	
Leak		
John	10	
Lean		
Richard	64	
Legrand		
John	41	
Nancy	41	
Leland		
John	22,27	
Lenox		
Charles	37	
Leonard		
George	54	
Thomas	54	
William	54	
Lessley		
William	37	

Lewis		
Major Andrew	2,9,11	
Aaron	92	
Charles	86	
Capt. Charles	2,5,12,13	
	14,19,21,24,30	
Fretus(?)	37	
Henry	27	
Jacob	22,27	
Capt. Joshua	2,13,14,16	
Librook		
Henry	37	
Ligon		
Blackman	43	
Blackman Jr.	43	
Elizabeth	43	
John	44,45	
John T.	43	
Joseph	42	
Capt. Joseph	42,43	
Martha H.	44	
Nancy T.	43	
William	43,44,45	
Lilley		
John	37	
Lilvy		
John	20	
Linaham		
Jeremiah	37	
Linch		
Mathew	5	
Lindsay		
Caleb	48	
Lingo		
James	37	

Linn			Logwood	
William	32B		Thomas	63
Linsie			Londren	
Daniel Crawley	32		William	15
Lion			Long	
Samuel	37		Ambrose	20
Liptrot			Lour	
James	15		Andrew	37
Little			Love	
John	6		Joseph	61
Thomas	12			
See Lyttle			Lovit	
			John	32
Loakey				
John	15		Low(e)	
			Beverly	10
Lobey (?)			Henry	37
Thomas	85			
			Lowr(e)y	
Lockard			John	30,32
Archibald	20		William	22
Lockart			Loyd	
Andrew	23		John	37
Loffman			Lucaner	
Edward	12		William	10
John	12			
			Ludwick	
Loflan			Edward	27
Morgan	24			
			Lyle	
Loftis			James	23
John	37			
			Lynch	
Logan			James	6
Colloe	6		Mathew	18
Loggins			Lyttle	
Dixon	74		David G.	91
			George	91
			Harrington	91

121

Lyttle (continued)

    James   91

    Mary A.   91

    See Little

McCaul

    John   37

McCarty

    B.   58,68

McClannahan

    Col. Alexander   43

McClanon

    John   37

McCloud

    Mordecai   30,32

    William   18

McCormick

    Adam   32

McCoy

    Elijah   18

    Patrick   37

McDade

    James   37

McDaniel

    Terence   30

    William   53

McDoel

    See McDuell

McDonald

    Angus   20

    John   23

    Patrick   13

    Robert   7

    Terence   32

McDuell

    Samuel   22,27,28

McEntire

    John   10

McEntyre

    Daniel   23

McFarling

    John   15

McGennett

    David   20

McHenery

    William   10

McKamy -McKem(m)y

    James   50,51

    John   51

    Nancy   50,51

McKay

    Phinley   32B

McKenzie

    John   30,32

    Capt. Robert 2,17,19

McKinley

    John   37

McKoon

    John   92

McLane

    Daniel   18

McLean

    Lochland   29

McMasters

    William   30,32

McMath			Malone	
William	7		James	18
McMillon			Mander	
John	29		William	10
McNamar(r)a			Mannen	
Dennis	5,18		Edward	20
McPherson			Manns	
William	8		John	27
McPike			Marchant	
Patrick	10		Willoughby	56
McQuin			Marnick	
John	37		John	74
McWherter			Marr	
Miss Minnie	42		Nathan	3
McWilliams			Marsh	
Brd't	15		James	15
Mackinvale			Marshall	
John	83		Richard	37
			William	22
Macksfield			Martain	
Wilby	32		Richard	10
Maddox			Martial	
Wilson	61		William	32B
Magennett			Martin	
David	22		John	54
			Peter	80
Major			Sarah	80
John	27			
Malcolm			Mason	
Joseph	51		Abel	29
			Thomas	83
Malldry			William	7
Henry H.	80			

Matheny			Meriwether	
Emma R.	81		William	55
Matlock			Merritt	
Joab	92		Samuel	37
Mat(t)hews			Miller	
Barry	5		Frances	65
James	37		Francis	65
John	20		James	65,66
Mattson			Miles	
John	37		James	27
May			Mills	
Elizabeth	81		Charles H.	48
Gabriel	81		Emanuel	27
Jessy	10		James	20,30
John	81			
Martin	15		Mingeese	
Susanna	81		Peter	20
Maynard			Minor	
William	23		John	47
Maxedent			Miskell	
James	18		William	59
Maxom			Mitchell	
Henry	15		James	15
			John	10
Meeke			Thomas	37
John	37		William	12
Meggs			Moncure	
John	12		John	64
Mercer			Moody	
Capt George	2,19,21		William	23
J.	64			
James	21		Moon	
Capt John	21		Abraham	15
John Fenton	21		Henry	85,86
Merchant				
Thomas	37			

Moore	
Elizabeth	67
John	7
John Jr.	52
Nancy T.	43
Sarah	52
Thomas	67
William A.	67
Moorin	
Dominick	32
See Moran	
Morallee	
Michael	84
Moran	
Dominick	30
Moreland	
Francis	8
Morgan	
Col. Daniel	45
Daniel	3
David	18
John	20
Martha A.	44
Richard	27
Morris	
Jacob	18
Joseph	20
Lewis	37
Robert	80
Thomas	23
Morton	
George	18
Mosby	
Capt. Littleberry	44
Moseley	
Jacob	18
Capt. William	43

Moss	
Casper	79
Thomas	22,27,28
Muckelroy	
Robert	23
Mullen	
Peter	4
Munday	
James	18
Munford	
Colonel	78
Munjoy	
Thomas	20
Murden	
William	56
Murphy	
John	27
Michael	37
Patrick	32B
Robert	10
Murray	
Duncan	20
Richard	30
Murrough	
Lewis	37
Nance	
Elizabeth	41
Napp	
Thomas	29
Nash	
John	32
Robert	29

Naughty
  John   32

Neasom(e)
  Nancy   58
  Robert   58
  Samuel B.   57
  Samuel W.   57,58
  See also Newsome

Neal(l)
  James   30,32

Nealy
  Matthew   20

Needum
  Isaac   37

Nekum
  Peter   38

Nequale
  John   37

Nettles
  Gen. J. B.   55
  Lori H.   55

Nevil
  Gabriel   20
  Henry   20
  James   64

Newell
  Ben   38
  William   27
  See also Norwell

Newil
  William   22

Newman
  Thomas   38
  Walter   37

Newsom(e)
  Catharine A.   57
  Einnifred   57
  William I.   57
  See also Neasome

Newton
  William   38

Nichols
  Edward   27

Noblett
  David   53

Nonery
  Griffith   22

Norment
  Dr. Benjamin C.   55
  Lori H.   55

North
  Anthony   75

Norvell
  James   8
  See Norwell

Norwell
  Martha Jane   87
  Reuben   87

Nott
  Walter   23

Nowel(l)
  Batt   37
  Holdcroft   61

Nuckolls
  Robert   53,94

Nugent
  John   29
  Will   24

Nuland	
Thomas	18
O'Brien	
Terrence	65
O'Conner	
William	8
Odum	
Thomas	62
Oldham	
Jesse	3
Olive	
Widow	74
Organ	
John	20
Orme	
Henry	20
Orsborn	
Elisha	38
Osborn	
Thomas	38
Ousley (Owsley)	
Ann	42
Charity	41
Isaac	42
John	41
John Jr.	41
John Lynch	41
Mathew	42
Stephen	42
Tabitha	41
Thomas	45,46
William	42
Outten	
Abraham	71
Mary	71

Overby	
James L.	52
Owens	
James	38
Packet	
William Stuart	29
Palmer	
Ann	41
Daniel	41
Elias	41
Elisha	41
Elizabeth	41
Parmenas	61
Reuben	61
Robert	61
Thomas	38,41
Palmore	
George	12
Pardoe	
John	7
Parker	
Arthur	53
Colonel	43
Elizabeth	53,73
John	53,62
Joseph	53
Joshua	53
Lemuel	54
Richard	62
Robert	56
Samuel	53
Susanna	53
William	38,53,73
Parks	
Daniel	38
Will	8
Parmore	
Thomas	38

Parr			Pedder	
Isaiah	56		John	23
Mary	56			
William	56		Peed	
			Phillip	15
Parrish				
Agnes	71		Pendergrass	
			John	27
Parsley				
Augustine	22		Penmore	
			John	4
Parsons				
Jerry	38		Penn	
			Benjamin	67,78
Pate			Fanny	49
Thomas	15		Joseph	49
Patram			Percival	
Richard	83		James	72
Patterson			Perkins	
William	7,18		George	12
			Valentine	5
Patton				
James	5		Perkisson (sic)	
			Thomas	10
Paul				
Aaron	13		Perrit	
			Edward	27
Paulett				
Elizabeth	82		Perry	
John Christmas	82		Dicey	48
			Elijah	48
Peachy			Harry	48
Capt. William	2,21,22,28		John	24
			Joseph	20
Peake			Molly	48
William	70		William	38
Pearce			Peterken	
Edward	38		Rev.	55
John S.	85			
			Petersonbrough	
Peay			Peter	15
Capt. George W.	60			
Sarah Ann	60			

Petree			Pollard	
Alexander	38		William	82
Peyton			Pompey	
J. Jr.	65		James	27
Pharnhouse			Ponty	
Thomas	38		John	10
Phipps			Poor	
Thomas	24		Jeremiah	23
Picket(t)			Pope	
Charles Burrus	49		Ephraim	13,15,16
Elizabeth	49		John	20
Henry	10		Porcher	
Pidgeon			Julius T.	55
John Leonard	38		Porter	
Pierce			Austin	54
James	68		Daniel	15
			Frances	54
Pike			Susanna	81
Richard	23		Posey	
Pincham			Benjamin	91
Eliza Kennon Randolph	89		Lucy	91
			Richard	7
Pinmore			Potter	
John	18,94		William	38
Piper			Power(s)	
George	38		James	20
John Henry	4		Richard	23
			Thomas	38
Plowman			Powell	
Robert	38		Captain	44
Plummett			George	27
Thomas	68		Jacob	32B
Poe			Pratt	
Samuel	27		Marshall	32
			Nathaniel	30

129

Prewitt			Quisenberry	
Anderson	48		Francis	47
			Humphrey	13,32
Price			James	48
Elinzer	38		Jane	47,48
John	24		Nicholas	12
Joseph	8,20			
			Raby	
Prichard			Moses	10
James	38			
Polidore	83		Rafferty	
			Thomas	10
Pritchard				
Thomas	7		Ragan	
			William	70
Proctor				
George	18		Ragsdale	
			Benjamin	52
Prue			Mildred	52
Humphrey	38		William	18
Pruit			Rainger	
Thadeus	27		Garrett	16,30
Pugh			Ramsay	
Richard	38		Jo.	64
Pulling			Randall	
Robert	8		George	60
			John	60
Purcell			Mary	60
Edward	27			
			Randolph	
Purdue			Col. Beverly	43
Joseph	16			
			Ratcliffe	
Purnell			James	12
Col. John	44			
			Rawden	
Pursell			John	38
George	59,68			
			Rawls	
Quinn			David	13
Thomas	18		James	8

Redman			Right	
Chris.	22		Thomas	38
			See Wright	
Redmayne				
Charles	27,28		Riley - Rilie	
			Barnard	10
Reese			James	18
Henry	7		John	10
Remeshall			Rine	
John	32		Daniel	27
Reynolds			Robb	
John	32		Joseph	60
Thomas	32			
Thomas F.	59		Roberts	
Thomas T.	68		Evan	38
William	72		Edward	30,32
			Francis	29
Rhodes			Henry	83
John	38		James	27
			Joseph	7,10
Rice			Thomas	18
H.	92		William	47
Richard	7			
			Robertson	
Richardson			David	38
Ezekiel	12		Frances	77
James	30			
Samuel	80		Robins	
			George	78
Richinson				
James	32		Robinson	
			Daniel	24
Riddick			Hamblet	32
Abraham	63		James	18
			John	22,24,29,53
Riddle			John Jr.	29
Richard	18		Samuel	23
			Simon	29
Rigby			William	22,27
Lawrence	27			
			Robottom	
Rigg			Matthew	16
Thomas	10			

131

Rodes		Rosser	
Henry John	4	John	8
Roe		Rounday	
James	18	David	27
Rogers		Roundtree	
Benjamin	11	William	12
Cornelius	38		
Francis	11	Rouse	
William	27	John	4
Romine		Routt - Rowt	
Abram	92	Andrew	16
Daniel	92	John	59
David	92		
Eli	93	Rowe	
Elias	92	Thomas	32B
Ella	93	William	38
Elizabeth	92		
James	93	Rowell	
James Jr.	93	Jacob	32
Joanah	92		
Jonah	92	Royalty	
Joseph	92	Daniel	11
Levi	92		
Mary	92	Royer	
Mary J.	93	Bettie E.	81
Nancy	92	W. P.	81
Naomi	92		
Rebecca	92,93	Rucker	
Sarah	92	George	67,78
Sarah J.	93	James	63
William	92	John	67,78
William J.	93		
		Ruddle	
Rose		Elizabeth	62
Robert	63	Isaac	62
Roseman		Rule	
James B.	43	Agnes	71
		James	71
Ross			
Andrew	20	Russel(I)	
William	23,32	Joseph	70

132

Rutherford
    Ad'm.   16

Ryan - Ryon
    James   22,27,28

Ryley
    John   23

Sadler
    Samuel   39

Sale
    John   23

Salmon
    John   20

Salser
    George   32B

Sanders
    George   4
    John   82
    Mary   82
    Nancy   82
    Riella   82

Sandy
    William   30

Sarbuck
    John   32B

Saunders
    Edward   58,68
    Francis   24
    George   58,68
    John   24
    Samuel   7

Savage
    Ann   69
    Ensign Thomas   69
    Major John   69

Savage (continued)
    Joseph   69
    Margaret   69
    Severn Eyre   69
    Thomas Waters   69
    William   69

Sawer
    Joseph   22

Sawyer
    Joseph   27
    Nathaniel   45

Scarbrough
    James   39

Scattergood
    William   30

Scople
    Willis   27

Scott
    Charles   18
    Harriet A.   88,89
    John   30,32,89
    Capt. Joseph   33
    Thomas   57

Scully
    Chris   20
    Michael   11

Seabrooke
    Elizabeth   83

Seal
    Thomas   8

Seaman
    Robert   21

Seaton
    George   21

Sharp(e)			Short	
James F.	91		John	63
John D.	49		William	27
William	39			
			Shriver	
Sharplin			George	32B
James	38			
			Sidwell	
Shaw			Stephen	39
Abraham	32			
			Sigriff	
Shearg (?)			Hugh	18
John	38			
			Sikes	
Shearer			William	38
James	65			
Mary	65		Simmonds	
			Joel	18
Sheets				
Jacob	51		Simmons	
			John	5
Shennon				
William	13,94		Simonons (sic)	
			Urias	56
Shepherd				
Thomas	32B		Simms	
			Elizabeth	82
Shep(p)erson				
Josiah	66		Simpson	
William	32		Solomon	27
			Thomas	16
Shepler			William	11
Conrod	39			
			Sinclair	
Sherman			See Cinclair	
John	5			
			Sinks	
Sherrod			Jacob	32
Henry Francis	4			
			Skelton	
Shields			John	25
George	18		Thomas	73
Shifflet			Slaughter	
Thomas	11		Capt. Charles	45

134

Smale		Sobey	
Simon	84	See Lobey	
Smerver		Socketts	
John	25,94	Phillip	7
Smiler		Soleleather (?)	
James	39	Philip	39
Smith (Smyth)		Solomon(s)	
Augustine	78	George	27
Benjamin	29	Peter	18
Catherine	91		
Charles	12		
Frances	73	Sommervil	
George Washington	84	James	21
Jacob	39		
James	13	Soons	
John	11,38,79	John	39
Levi	11		
Lewis	79	Southcott	
Rebecca F.	91	Capt. Otho	83
Richard	32		
Samuel	39	Spain	
Thomas	18,22,27,28	Rt. Rev.	55
	32B,39		
William	4,5,11,27,39,73	Spann	
Wratt	49	Thomas	13
Smithers		Sparks	
Gabriel	59	Edward	24
		John	22
Snead			
Charles	71	Speake	
Evan	56	George	25
Frances	56		
James	56	Spencer	
		Zekel	24
Snider			
Fred	39	Spivey	
		George	62
Snipes			
Thomas	21	Spotswood	
		Capt. Rovert	2,23,24

135

Spragg
John 38

Sridder (?)
Martin 39

Stacie - Stacy
Catharine 75
Edmond 75
Elizabeth 75
John 73
Mary 75
Nicholas 75
Robert 73
Simon 73,75
Stephen 75
Susan 75
Thomas 72,73,94

Stainback
Peter Sr. 70

Stanley
Daniel 4
Samuel 39

Stark
Benjamin 21
John 63

Stephens
Adam 62
George William 62
Isaac 62
Jacob 62
James 14
Joseph 62
Lt. Col. 2,24,25
Mary 62
Richard 39

Stephenson
George 39
Nathaniel 12

Stevens
Mary 77

Steward
George 39
James 39

Stewart
Alexander 16
Asael 7
Robert 27
Capt. Robert 2,25,26

Still
(Mrs) Elizabeth 81
Elizabeth 81
Izbell 81
John 81
John Alexander 38
Josiah 81

Stilts
Anthony 14,16

Stith
Griffin 68

Stockstill
William 7

Stone
Benamms (?) 49
Thomas 83

Stout
Reubin 39

Stovall
Jonathan B. 67

Straton
Seth 39

Street
Richard 68

Stripling		Sydner		
Samuel	21	Giles	58	
Sullivan		Syms		
Daniel	16	William	38	
Timothy	4			
		Taffe		
Summers		James	39	
William	7			
		Talbot		
Suple		William	7	
Morris	16			
		Tandy		
Sutliff		Henry	48	
John	32	William	48	
Suttles		Tanner		
Reuben	72	John	76,77	
William	72	Paul	39	
Swain		Tannes (?)		
William	21	Peter	39	
Sweeny		Tapman		
Aron	18	Joseph	11	
Swem		Tarres		
Earl G.	1	William	12	
Swepton		Tate		
Capt.	78	David	11	
		Samuel	4	
Swinburn				
John	11	Taylor		
		James	39	
Swiney		Jeremiah	27	
Terence	11	Jerry	24	
		John	23	
Swope				
Brunetta W.	57	Tegan		
Elijah	57,94	John	11	
James	57			
Mary M.	57	Tell		
		Robert	25	

Tent		Timmons	
Joseph	30	John	18
Terrell		Tims	
John	52	Joseph	59,68
William	52	Molly	59,68
Thomas		Tole	
Francis	12	Timothy	7
James	16		
John	4	Tolley	
Michael	64	Dudley	32
Samuel	21		
William	23	Tomlin	
		William	39
Thompson			
Charles	18	Tompkins	
Edward	22,28	R.	53
Henry	11		
James	4,18	Tooth	
J. A.	61	John Christopher	7
John	25		
Capt. John	42	Townsend	
Thomas	25	Thomas	14,16
Will	8		
Yancey	54	Trahern	
		Nemehiah	74
Thorn			
Edmond	23	Treble	
Robert	18	George	74
Thornton		Tribble	
William	39	Andrew	48
		Sarah	47,48
Thorp			
William	23	Trigg	
		John	29
Tiller			
John	18	Trinon	
		James	39
Tillery			
Samuel	18	Triplett	
		Capt.	45
Timberlake			
David	55	Trotman	
Sarah	55	Samuel	39

Trotter			Underwood	
Richard	32		Thomas	18
Troy			Vance	
Simon	30		Jacob	79
			Joseph	65
Truly				
Peter	18		Vanpelf	
			Samuel	39
Tucker				
Dean	78		Vass	
Elizabeth	78		Reuben	22
Laodicia	41			
Samuel W.	41		Vaughn	
			Andrew	14
Tuder			Gist	7
Thomas	7			
			Venable	
Tulley			James	16
Peter	29			
			Vernon	
Turbon			Joseph	39
Abner	56			
			Vicker	
Turley			John	39
James	70			
			Virginia Magazine of	
Turnbull			History	1
Alexander	7			
John	39		Wade	
Peter	39		Mr	90
Turner			Waggoner	
Daniel	51		Capt. Thomas	2,26,28
James	18			
John	39		Walden	
Thomas	4		Samuel	8
			William	52
Turnstile				
Robert	25		Walker	
			Francis	8
Twentyman				
Henry	72		Wallace	
			William	32,40
Umphries				
John	11			

139

Wallens			Waters	
George	57		John	11
			Margaret	69
Walsh			Philemon	25
Thomas	40		William	8
Walston (?)			Watkins	
Jonathan	40		John	45
Walter(s)			Watts	
George	40,94		Thomas	5,19
Robert	16		William	57
Walthall			Wayne	
William	39		General	43
Waples			Wealch	
Samuel	71		Jeremiah	40
Ward			Weaner	
Barnard	19		Christian	39
Charles	74			
Elizabeth	74		Wells	
George	93		Josiah	16
Kenneth R.	93			
John	16		West	
Joseph	40		Absalom	56
Margaret	93		William	40
Samuel	93			
			Wetherly	
Warden			Peter	85
John	56			
Will	8		Whaley	
			Hercules	91
Warner				
James	19		Wheeler	
			Thomas	75
Warrand				
Donald	65		Whipple	
			John	5
Warton				
Anthony	28		White	
			Ann	75
Washington			Caleb	39
Col. George	1,2,5,7,9 ,11		John	21,39,40
	19,22,24,29,30		Richard	75

140

White (continued)
Thomas 7,19
William 16

Whitecotton
George 30

Whitehead
Edward 29
Matthew 28

Whitlock
Charles 82
James 82
Nathaniel 82
Thomas 82

Wickham
Mrs. E. F. 55
Lucy Carter 55
Mary Fannie 55
W. F. 55

Wiggins
Kedar 63

Wildridge
John 11

Wilkins
Thomas 40

Willet
Benjamin 25

Williams
George 28
Henry 16
James 11,21
John 16,22,28,30
Joseph 21
Peter 7
Thaddeus 58
Thomas 40,63
"W" 58

Williams (continued)
Walter 19
Will 8

Willimore
James 28

Willis
Richard 28

Willow
Joseph 11

Wills
Joseph 14,94

Wilmer
Blackstone 67
Mary 68

Wilson
Aquilla 7
Benjamin 16
Edward 40
George 19,76
Joseph 39
Robert 25
Samuel 7
Will 8

Wimbrough
John 19

Wimbrow
Abram 16

Windledurk (?)
George 40

Winn
Charles 16

Winston
William O. Jr. 80

Winterbuttom
  John   25

Wire
  William   16

Wise
  Cassia   71
  Charles (?)   40
  Elizabeth   71,83
  Major John   71
  Margaret   71
  Mary   71

Witcher
  Daniel   79
  Tabitha   79

With
  Edward   11

Wittaker
  Abraham   7
  Isaac   7

Wolfington
  Abraham   54

Wood
  James   5
  Joseph   50

Woodell
  Joseph   50

Woodford
  Thomas   70

Woodward
  Capt Henry (Harry)   1,3
                29,30,31,32

Woody
  Richard   40

Woomple
  Peter   40

Works
  James   39

Worsham
  John   52
  William   52

Wrenn
  H. B.   70

Wright
  Daniel   28
  David   65
  George   65
  George Jr.   62
  Jane   50
  John   23,64
  Johnson   78
  Lucy   59,78,88
  Richard   59,68
  Robert   30
  Sarah   62
  Thomas   9,11
  William   19,50

Wyatt
  Major John   55
  Patsey   55

Wyley
  Alex   9

Young
  Archibald   79
  Ezekiel   28
  George   79
  Marlin   78,79
  Milton   79
  Tabitha   79
  William   79

142